MW00559436

Modeling Derivatives
in C++

JUSTIN LONDON

WILEY

John Wiley & Sons, Inc.

Published by John Wiley & Sons, Inc., Hoboken, New Jersey.
Published simultaneously in Canada.

Computer code in Appendix E on the CD-ROM is from *Numerical Recipes in C* by William H. Press, Brian P. Flannery, Saul Teukolsky, and Wiliam Vetterling. Copyright © 1988–2003 Numerical Recipes Software. Reproduced with permission.

For general information on our other products and services, or technical support, please contact our Customer Care Department within the United States at 800-762-2974, outside the United States at 317-572-3993 or fax 317-572-4002.

Designations used by companies to distinguish their products are often claimed as trademarks. In all instances where John Wiley & Sons, Inc., is aware of a claim, the product names appear in initial capital or all capital letters. Readers, however, should contact the appropriate companies for more complete information regarding trademarks and registration.

Wiley also publishes its books in a variety of electronic formats. Some content that appears in print may not be available in electronic books.

For more information about Wiley products, visit our web site at www.wiley.com.

Library of Congress Cataloging-in-Publication Data
London, Justin, 1973–
 Modeling derivatives in C++ / Justin London.
  p. cm.—(Wiley finance series)
 Includes index.
 ISBN 0-471-65464-7 (cloth)
  1. Derivative securities—Data processing. 2. C++ (Computer program language)
I. Title. II. Series.

HG6024.A3L66 2004
332.64'57'01135262—dc22

                  2004042045

Printed in the United States of America.

10 9 8 7 6 5 4

To the memory of my grandparents
Milton and Evelyn London,
as well as my parents,
Leon and Leslie,
and my sister, Joanna

Contents

Preface

Derivative modeling is at the heart of quantitative research and development on Wall Street. Practitioners (i.e., Wall Street trading desk quants) and academics alike spend much research, money, and time developing efficient models for pricing, hedging, and trading equity and fixed income derivatives. Many of these models involve complicated algorithms and numerical methods that require lots of computational power. For instance, the HJM lattice for pricing fixed income derivatives often requires coding a nonrecombining bushy tree that cannot be easily traversed and grows exponential in time and memory.

C++ is often the programming language of choice for implementing these models due to the language's object-oriented features, speed, and reusability. However, often the implementation "how-to" of these models is quite esoteric to the model creators and developers due to their algorithmic complexity. Most journal articles and white papers that discuss derivative models provide only a theoretical understanding of them as well as their mathematical derivations. While many research papers provide numerical results, few supply the details for how to implement the model, if for no other reason than to allow readers to replicate and validate their results. There are several reasons for this.

It is often the general nature of academics who publish leading research to be pedantic, writing at a level geared for their academic peers, rather than to practitioners. This often leads to papers that spend much time providing mathematical formulas and proofs as opposed to discussions of practical applications and implementations. Few if any of these published papers discuss in detail how these derivative models are to be correctly and efficiently implemented for practical use in the real world. After all, what good is a model if it cannot be used in practice in research and trading environments?

Another reason for the lack of implementation discussions is that many top quant researchers and professors, often with doctorates in mathematics and physics, spend their time developing the mathematical and theoretical underpinnings of the models and leave the actual code implementations to their graduate research students. Graduate research students often are given the task of implementing the models of their advisers as part of collaborative work. Consequently, often only the numerical results, if any, are provided, usually generated from the code implementations of the graduate student.[1]

---

[1]There are instances where code is provided by the graduate research student. In the paper "Fast Greeks in Forward LIBOR Models" by P. Glasserman and Z. Zhao, the code is given at www-1.gsb.columbia.edu/faculty/pglasserman/Other/get_code.html and is discussed in Chapter 13 of this book.

However, as is more often the case, the code developed by quant researchers and programmers working on Wall Street trading desks is highly valuable and proprietary to the Wall Street institutions just as the Windows operating system code is proprietary to Microsoft and not the developers who work on it. The code is the powerful engine that gives trading desks their competitive advantage over other players in the market. If Wall Street trading desks have a proprietary model that allows them to capture arbitrage opportunities based on "mispricings" between derivative market prices and their theoretical model values, then if this code was readily available to all market participants, the model would be exploited by all those using it, quickly eliminating the profit opportunity and removing the competitive edge of the institution where it was developed.

Similarly, professors and researchers who own the code for the models they develop often are unwilling to release it to the public because keeping it in-house can lead to lucrative consulting contracts with Wall Street institutions and companies that want to contract them to implement and license use of their proprietary model. For example, GFI Group, Inc., states on its web site that two top researchers, John Hull and Alan White, have assisted the company in its development of software for credit derivatives pricing using the Hull-White credit model.

When I was a graduate student in the Financial Engineering Program at the University of Michigan, the theory and mathematical derivations of the models were taught and emphasized. An understanding of stochastic calculus, stochastic processes, partial differential equations, and probability theory was emphasized and was a prerequisite for being able to model, price, and hedge complicated derivatives securities. Since students were assumed to know how to program in C and use Excel, little emphasis was made on efficient coding implementation. At the time, our code was written on Sun Sparc workstations. Upon graduating and completing several other graduate degrees in mathematics and computer science, being able to program became more important than actually understanding the theory behind the models because Wall Street positions for developing code and models to support trading desks require excellent programming skills. However, since one cannot usually program efficient models without an understanding of the theoretical and mathematical intricacies behind them, both an understanding of the theory and being able to program well are necessary. In fact, throughout the book, the theory and mathematical derivations of some of the models are based on the work and lectures of Dr. Vadim Linetsky, who taught the financial engineering courses.[2]

Over time the University of Michigan Financial Engineering Program has been modified to include more practical coding exercises through use of real-time Reuters data feeds. Other well-known financial engineering, mathematical finance, and computational finance programs, such as those at the University of California–Berkley,

---

[2]Dr. Vadim Linetsky is now an associate professor at Northwestern University in the Department of Industrial Engineering and Management Sciences. He teaches financial engineering courses similar to the ones he taught at the University of Michigan.

the University of Chicago, and Carnegie-Mellon, respectively, may start to adapt their curricula, if they have not done so already, to place more emphasis on the practical implementation and coding of models as many of their graduates head to Wall Street to work in quantitative research and trading development groups.

I felt that since no book bridged the gap between the two and because such a book would have helped me both in school and afterward on the job as a quantitative developer, I should write such a book so as to help others. Such a book was an enormous undertaking and required contacting many of the model developers of some of the more complicated models to try to understand how they implemented them and in some cases to even obtain their code. In those cases where I was not able to get model details or code from an author, I was able to verify the accuracy and robustness of the code I developed by being able to reproduce numerical results of the models in published papers and books.

Modeling Derivatives in C++ is the first book to provide the source code for most models used for pricing equity and fixed income derivatives. The objective of the book is to fill the large gap that has existed between theory and practice of the quantitative finance field. Readers will learn how to correctly code in C++ many derivatives models used by research and trading desks. The book bridges the gap between theory and practice by providing both the theory and mathematical derivations behind the models as well as the actual working code implementations of these models. While there have been other books that have helped bridge this gap such as Clewlow and Strickland's *Implementing Derivatives Models* (John Wiley & Sons, 1998a), they provide only pseudocode and do not emphasize robust and efficient object-oriented code that is reusable. The assumption that readers can easily or correctly translate pseudocode, which may have complex embedded subroutines of numerical computations that is needed, often is mistaken. Sometimes, readers learn by analyzing and reviewing the complete and working code, which is what this book attempts to accomplish. However, *Implementing Derivatives Models* does contain useful model discussions and pseudocode implementations, some of which are implemented and built upon in this book using C++, such as the hedge control variate method discussed in Chapter 2 and the alternating direction implicit method discussed in Chapter 5.

Modeling Derivatives in C++ goes several steps beyond just providing C++ code; it discusses inefficiencies in some of the implementations and how they can be improved with more robust object-oriented implementations by providing code from the QuantLib, an open source quantitative pricing library, as well as by providing alternative implementations. For instance, three separate implementations are given for the Hull-White model to show readers different coding approaches. The book contains hundreds of classes, and there is a complete pricing engine library on the CD-ROM accompanying this book, which includes the code discussed and given in the book. QuantPro, an MFC Windows application, for pricing many equity and fixed income derivatives using the models discussed in the book, as well as for simulating derivatives trades, is also provided on the CD-ROM.

It is the goal of the book that readers will be able to write their own models in

C++ and then be able to adapt some of the coded models in this book to their own pricing libraries and perhaps even use to trade. Most important, the book is intended to guide readers through the complexities and intricacies of the theory and of applying it in practice. The book is aimed at advanced undergraduate students well as graduate (MBA and Ph.D.) students in financial economics, computer science, financial engineering, computational finance, and business as well as Wall Street practitioners working in a quantitative research or trading group who need a comprehensive reference guide for implementing their models.

Readers should have a basic understanding of stochastic calculus, probability theory, linear algebra, partial differential equation (PDEs), and stochastic processes. For those readers who may be lacking the background in some of this material or need to review, the appendixes provide a review of some of this material. Due to the comprehensiveness of the book, it can be used by professors as either a primary text or a supplementary text in their courses.

The chapters are grouped into two main sections: The first focuses on the pricing of equity derivatives and comprises Chapter 1 to Chapter 9, and the second part focuses on the pricing of interest rate derivatives: Chapter 10 to Chapter 14.

Chapter 1 focuses on the derivation and foundations of the Black-Scholes model for asset pricing in the risk-neutral world. The Black-Scholes partial differential equation describes the evolution of all derivatives whose payoff is a function on a single underlying asset following geometric Brownian motion (GBM) and time.

Chapter 2 discusses Monte Carlo methods for valuation of European as well as path-dependent derivatives. Various random number generators for pseudorandom, quasi-random (deterministic), Sobol, and Faure sequences are discussed. Variance reduction techniques using control variates and antithetics are discussed to overcome the computational inefficiency of the Monte Carlo method in its basic form, which typically requires hundreds of thousands of simulations to achieve good accuracy.

Chapter 3 discusses the binomial tree model for pricing European and American equity options. The binomial tree is shown to be a two-state discrete approximation to continuous GBM: The mean and variance of the binomial model match the mean and variance of the lognormal distribution underlying GBM. Furthermore, the binomial model can be adapted to incorporate time-varying volatility, to pricing path-dependent options, and to pricing derivatives depending on more than one asset with two-variable binomial trees.

Chapter 4 generalizes binomial trees to the more flexible and widely used trinomial trees, which approximate GBM diffusion processes with three states. It also discusses implied trees, which are trees constructed to fit observable market prices. Thus, this method builds trees implied by the market.

Chapter 5 discusses finite-difference methods, numerical methods (actually, extensions of the trinomial method) for discretizing PDEs that (path-dependent) derivatives with complex payoffs must satisfy and then solving them over a state-time lattice. The explicit, implicit, and Crank-Nicolson finite-difference methods are discussed as well as the alternating direction implicit method for pricing options that depend on multiple-state variables.

Chapter 6 discusses pricing exotic options including Asian, lookback, and barrier options.

Chapter 7 discusses stochastic volatility models that are used to capture volatility skews and smiles observed in the options markets. Since the constant volatility assumption of Black-Scholes is not valid in the real world, alternative models such as the constant elasticity of variance (CEV), jump diffusion, and multifactor stochastic volatility models can each be used to fit pricing model parameters to observable option market quotes.

Chapter 8 focuses on statistical models for volatility estimation including GARCH models. Chapter 9 deals with stochastic multifactor models for pricing derivatives like basket options.

Chapter 10 begins the second part of the book and focuses on fixed income models. The chapter discusses single-factor short rate models including the Vasicek, Hull-White (HW), Black-Derman-Toy (BDT), and Cox-Ingersoll-Ross (CIR) models.

Chapter 11 focuses on tree-building procedures for the short rate models discussed in Chapter 10. It shows how to calibrate the BDT and HW models initially to the yield curve and then to both the yield and volatility curves, and explains how to price discount bonds, bond options, and swaptions with the models.

Chapter 12 discusses two-factor models as well as the HJM model for pricing fixed income derivatives.

Chapter 13 provides an in-depth discussion of the LIBOR market model (also known as the Brace-Gatarek-Musiela/Jamshidian (BGM/J) model, showing how to calibrate the model to cap and swaption volatilites for pricing. Correlation structures and stochastic extensions of the model are also discussed. The chapter shows the difference and inconsistencies between the LIBOR forward-rate model (LFM) for pricing caps and the Libor swap model (LSM) for pricing swaptions and swaps.

Chapter 14 discusses exotic interest rate derivatives. Bermudan swaptions, range notes, index-amortizing swaps, trigger swaps, and quantos are discussed along with pricing models and implementations for them. Gaussian quadrature is also discussed as a useful tool for evaluating certain numerical integrals used in derivatives pricing such as those for spread options and quantos.

Appendix A contains a probability review of important probability concepts used throughout the book. Appendix B contains a stochastic calculus review of Brownian motion, stochastic integrals, and Ito's formula. Appendix C contains a discussion of the fast Fourier transform (FFT) method, a powerful numerical technique for valuation of higher-dimensional integrals. Appendix D discusses building models, pricing engines, and calibrating models in practice with a focus on building robust models. Appendix E contains some useful code routines including the random number generator for generating uniform deviates for Monte Carlo simulation from Press et al., *Numerical Recipes in C* (1992). Appendix F shows the mathematical details for solving the Black-Scholes PDE using Green's function.

(Appendixes A and B can be found at the end of the book; Appendixes C through F are available as PDFs on the CD-ROM.)

It is my hope and intention that readers will get a lot of value from this book and that it will help them in both their academic studies as well as at work on their jobs. I hope that readers enjoy it as much as I enjoyed writing it. Finally, while I have attempted to be quite complete in the topics covered, the book does not cover everything. In particular, mortgage-backed securities and credit derivatives are not discussed. They will, however, be included in my next undertaking.

JUSTIN LONDON

Chicago, Illinois
October 2004

Acknowledgments

"If I have seen farther than others, it is because I was standing on the shoulders of giants."

—Isaac Newton

Many of the models discussed and implemented in this book are based on the work of many leading professors and practitioners such as Fischer Black, Robert Merton, Ricardo Rebonato, John Hull, Alan White, David Heath, Paul Glasserman, Mark Rubinstein, Les Clewlow, Chris Strickland, Robert Jarrow, James Bodurtha, Vadim Linetsky, Peter Carr, Damiano Brigo, Fabio Mercurio, and Ferdinand Ametrano and members of the QuantLib team, as well as many others cited in the References.

J. L.

CHAPTER 1

Black-Scholes and Pricing Fundamentals

This chapter discusses the most important concepts in derivatives models, including risk-neutral pricing and no-arbitrage pricing. We derive the renowned Black-Scholes formula using these concepts. We also discuss fundamental formulas and techniques used for pricing derivatives in general, as well as those needed for the remainder of this book. In section 1.1, we discuss forward contracts, the most basic and fundamental derivative contract. In section 1.2, we derive the Black-Scholes partial differential equation (PDE). In section 1.3, we discuss the concept of risk-neutral pricing and derive Black-Scholes equations for European calls and puts using risk-neutral pricing. In section 1.4, we provide a simple implementation for pricing these European calls and puts. In section 1.5, we discuss the pricing of American options. In section 1.6, we discuss fundamental pricing formulas for derivatives in general. In section 1.7, we discuss the important change of numeraire technique—useful for changing asset dynamics and changing drifts. In section 1.8, Girsanov's theorem and the Radon-Nikodym derivative are discussed for changing probability measures to equivalent martingale measures. In section 1.9, we discuss the T-forward measure, a useful measure for pricing many derivatives; and finally, in section 1.10, we discuss considerations for choosing a numeraire in pricing. (A probability review is provided in Appendix A at the back of the book and a stochastic calculus review is provided in Appendix B.)

1.1 FORWARD CONTRACTS

A security whose value is contingent on the value of an underlying security or macroeconomic variable such as an interest rate or commodity like oil is known as a derivative since the security "derives" its value and is contingent on the value of the underlying asset. Derivatives are known as contingent claims. The simplest derivative and most fundamental financial transaction is a *forward contract*, which is an agreement between two parties to buy or sell an asset, such as a foreign currency, at a certain time $T > 0$ for a certain delivery price, K, set at the contract inception t_0.

Forward contracts are traded over-the-counter (OTC). Standardized exchange-traded contracts, such as those on the Chicago Mercantile Exchange, are known as *futures*.

In a forward contract, there are two parties, usually two financial institutions or a financial institution and its customer: One party agrees to buy the asset in the forward contract at maturity, time T, and is said to be long, and the counterparty agrees to sell the asset to the buyer at T and is said to be short. The contract is settled at maturity T: The short delivers the asset to the long in return for a cash amount K.

If the price of the asset in the spot market at T is S_T, then the payoff, f_T, from the long position at T is:

$$f_T = S_T - K \tag{1.1}$$

since the long receives an asset worth S_T and pays the delivery price K. Conversely, the payoff from the short position is:

$$f_T = K - S_T \tag{1.2}$$

since the short receives the amount K and delivers an asset worth S_T in exchange.

Let's use some notation to help in the pricing analysis over time. Let S_t, $0 \leq t \leq T$ be the current underlying price at time t, let $f_{t,T}$ be the present value of a forward contract at time t maturing at time T, let $F_{t,T}$ be the forward price at time t, and let r be the risk-free rate per annum (with continuous compounding). The forward price is such a delivery price K that makes the present value of a forward contract equal to zero, $f_{0,T} = 0$:

$$K = F_{0,T} = S_0 e^{r(T-t_0)} \tag{1.3}$$

We can show that this must be the forward price using an absence of arbitrage argument: If $F_{0,T} > S_0 e^{r(T-t_0)}$, we can create a synthetic forward position and arbitrage an actual forward contract against this synthetic forward. At time t_0, we can borrow S_0 dollars for a period of $T - t_0$ at the risk-free rate r; we can then use these dollars to buy the asset at the spot price S_0; and finally, we take a short position in the forward contract with delivery price $F_{0,T}$. At time T, we (1) sell the asset for the forward price $F_{0,T}$ and (2) use an amount $e^{r(T-t_0)}S_0$ of the proceeds to repay the loan with accrued interest. This yields an arbitrage profit of $F_{0,T} - S_0 e^{r(T-t_0)}$. Similarly, assuming $F_{0,T} < S_0 e^{r(T-t_0)}$, we do the reverse transaction: At time t, we go long the forward contract and short the synthetic forward position—we invest the proceeds S_0 at rate r, and at time T buy the spot asset at $F_{0,T}$, earning an arbitrage profit of $S_0 e^{r(T-t_0)} - F_{0,T}$. Thus, in the absence of arbitrage we have shown that equation (1.3) must hold. The absence of arbitrage is equivalent to the impossibility of investing zero dollars today and receiving a nonnegative amount tomorrow that is positive with positive probability. Thus, two portfolios having the same payoff at a given future date T must have the same price today. Moreover, by constructing a portfolio of securities having the same instantaneous return as that of a riskless investment—that is, a money market account (MMA)—the portfolio instantaneous return must be the risk-free rate. Investors are then said to be risk-neutral: They expect that all investments with no risk (i.e., uncertainty) should earn the risk-free rate. Investors can always remove systematic (market) risk from the portfolio by holding securities that can be hedged against one another.

We can also show that $F_{0,T} = S_0 e^{r(T-t_0)}$ by using risk-neutral pricing and calculating the present value (PV) directly:

$$f_{0,T} = e^{-r(T-t_0)}E_{t_0}[S_T - K] = e^{-r(T-t_0)}(e^{r(T-t_0)}S_0 - K) = 0 \qquad (1.4)$$

where E_{t_0} is the expectation operator at time t_0. Thus, $K = F_{0,T} = e^{r(T-t_0)}S_0$. The risk-free rate is used as both an expected growth rate of the asset $E_{t_0}[S_T] = e^{r(T-t_0)}S_0$ and the discount rate.

We can also calculate the present value of a seasoned forward position at some time t after inception, known as marking to market. At some time t after inception, $0 < t < T$, the PV is generally different from zero:

$$f_{t,T} = e^{-r(T-t)}E_t[S_T - K] = S_t - e^{-r(T-t)}K = S_t - e^{r(T-t_0)}S_0 \qquad (1.5)$$

$$= S_t - F_{0,t} = e^{-r(T-t)}[F_{t,T} - F_{0,T}] \qquad (1.6)$$

Thus, the present value of a seasoned forward contract can be valued by taking the difference between the forward price at time t and the forward price at time 0 and discounting back to get the PV. If $t = 0$ (i.e., today), then the present value of the forward contract is 0, which is what we would expect. It is important to note that the arbitrage-free and risk-neutral arguments are valid only for traded assets. Forwards on commodities that are held for consumption purposes cannot be valued by these arguments.

These arguments can be used to value a forward on an asset providing a known cash income such as coupon bonds or stocks with discrete dividend payments. Let I_0 be the PV at time t_0 of all income to be received from the asset between times t_0 and T (discounting at the risk-free rate). It is left as an exercise for the reader to show that $K = F_{0,T} = e^{r(T-t_0)}(S_0 - I_0)$ and that at $0 < t < T$ the present value is $f_{t,T} = e^{-r(T-t)}E_t[(S_T - I_T) - K] = S_t - I_t - e^{-r(T-t)}K$. If the asset pays a continuous known dividend yield q, then the growth and discount rates are $e^{(r-q)(T-t)}$ and $e^{-(r-q)(T-t)}$, respectively. If the underlying asset is a foreign currency, then we can view the yield q as the foreign risk-free rate r_f so that the growth and discount rates of the underlying currency S_0 are $e^{(r-rf)(T-t)}$ and $e^{-(r-rf)(T-t)}$, respectively, and the price of a forward contract on S_0 (i.e., British pounds) at time 0 is $F_{0,T} = S_0 e^{(r-rf)(T-t)}$.

Forward contracts and futures contracts are relatively straightforward to value given that the underlying is a traded asset and all variables are known at time t_0: the price of the underlying, the risk-free rate, the time to contract expiration, T, and any cash flows that will occur between t_0 and T. Most derivatives are not easy to value because of the stochastic nature of the underlying variables. In most cases, the underlying factors of a derivative contract are not even traded assets (i.e., volatility and interest rates). Interest rates in a simple model are assumed constant. In actuality, rates fluctuate and one must estimate and consider the evolution of the term structure of rates. Moreover, underlying assets such as stocks, bonds, and foreign currencies follow stochastic (diffusion) processes that must be considered in any realistic financial model.

Throughout this book, we incorporate the stochastic nature of financial variables into all of our models, and our implementations incorporate time evolution. Initially, we assume time-homogenous variables (i.e., constant interest rates), but eventually we relax this assumption and assume variables are a function not only of time, but also of other underlying factors. We begin our examination of derivative models by examining and deriving the most fundamental and ubiquitous pricing model, Black-Scholes.

1.2   BLACK-SCHOLES PARTIAL DIFFERENTIAL EQUATION

Consider a riskless asset (a money market account or bank account), A_t, started at time 0 that grows with the constant continuously compounded risk-free rate of return r. The value of our money market account (MMA) at time t is:

$$A_t = e^{r(T-t)} \tag{1.7}$$

and it is a solution to a stochastic differential equation (SDE) with zero diffusion coefficient:

$$dA_t = rA_t dt \tag{1.8}$$

subject to $A_0 = \$1$. Equation (1.8) states that an infinitesimal change in our MMA value, dA_t, must be equal to the risk-free rate earned over the change in time, dt. If we know that value of our MMA at $t > 0$, then at time $T > t$, the value is:

$$A_t = A_0 e^{r(T-t)} \tag{1.9}$$

As will be shown, the MMA serves as a good *numeraire*, any positive non-dividend-paying asset, when we need to change measures to get an equivalent martingale measure for risk-neutral pricing of many derivatives (as we discuss in section 1.10).

Now suppose that S_t is the price at time t of a risky stock that pays no dividends (we extend to the case with dividends later). We model its time evolution by some diffusion process with Brownian motion (see Appendix B for a discussion of Brownian motion). But which one to select? The price process we select must satisfy three requirements:

1. The price should always be greater than or equal to zero. That is, our diffusion must have a natural boundary at zero. This immediately rules out arithmetic Brownian motion as a candidate for the realistic stock price process since arithmetic Brownian motion can have negative values.
2. If the stock price hits zero, corporate bankruptcy takes place. Once bankruptcy occurs, $S = 0$; the price can never rise above zero again. So zero should be an *absorbing* (cemetery) boundary.
3. The expected percentage return required by investors from a stock should be independent of the stock's price. Indeed, risk-averse investors will require some rate of return $m = r + r_e$ on the stock, where r_e is the required excess return over and above the risk-free rate r that investors require to compensate for taking the risk of holding the stock (risk premium). We will assume initially that this excess return is constant over time.

These restrictions limit the choice of our stochastic model to:

$$dS_t = mS_t dt + b(S_t, t)dz_t \qquad (1.10)$$

where m is the drift coefficient, which in this case is the constant expected rate of return on the stock (in the real world) and $b(S_t, t)$ is some diffusion coefficient, and z_t is a Wiener process—that is, $z_t \sim N(0,1)$. If $b = 0$, then it is the SDE for the risk-free asset. For any risky asset, b cannot be zero. Since we require that zero is an absorbing boundary for the stock price process, we impose an extra restriction on b: $b(0, t) = 0$. Thus, if the stock ever hits zero, it will never rise above zero again (both the drift and diffusion terms are equal to zero in this state, and there is nothing to lift it out of zero). Thus, we can parameterize our diffusion coefficient as follows:

$$b(S, t) = \sigma(S, t)S \qquad (1.11)$$

where σ is any positive function of S and t, or possibly some other stochastic variables influencing the stock. It is referred to as the *volatility* of the stock price and is a measure of variability or uncertainty in stock price movements. Clearly, the simplest choice is a constant volatility process:

$$dS_t = mS_t dt + \sigma S_t dz_t$$

or:

$$dS = mSdt + \sigma Sdz \qquad (1.12)$$

where we have dropped the time subscript for ease of notation. Here, m and σ are the constant instantaneous expected rate of return on the stock (drift rate) and volatility of the stock price, respectively.

It turns out that this choice of constant volatility, although not entirely realistic, as we will see, is very robust and leads to a tractable model. The process is called *geometric Brownian motion* (geometric refers to the multiplicative nature of fluctuations). The assumption of constant volatility is reasonable as a first approximation. It means that the variance of the percentage return in a short period of time, dt, is the same regardless of the stock price. Then $\sigma^2 dt$ is the variance of the proportional change in the stock price in time dt, and $\sigma^2 S^2 dt$ is the variance of the actual change in the stock price, S, during dt.

The SDE in equation (1.12) can be integrated in closed form. Indeed, suppose we know the stock price S at time t, S_t, and we are interested in the price S_T at time T. We will solve the SDE subject to this initial condition by first introducing a new variable, x:

$$x = f(S) = \ln S \qquad (1.13)$$

Ito's lemma (see Appendix B) tells us that any function f of S follows a diffusion process:

$$df = \left(\frac{df}{dt} + mS\frac{df}{dS} + \frac{1}{2}\sigma^2 S^2 \frac{d^2 f}{dS^2} \right)dt + \sigma S \frac{df}{dS}dz \qquad (1.14)$$

In the case of the logarithmic function we have:

$$dx = \left(m - \frac{\sigma^2}{2} \right)dt + \sigma dz \qquad (1.15)$$

or

$$dx = \mu dt + \sigma dz$$

where $\mu = m - \sigma^2/2$.

Hence, a logarithm of the stock price follows an arithmetic Brownian motion with the drift rate $\mu = m - \sigma^2/2$ and diffusion coefficient σ. This SDE can be immediately integrated to yield:

$$x_T = x + \left(m - \frac{\sigma^2}{2} \right)\tau + \sigma\sqrt{\tau}\varepsilon_T \qquad (1.16)$$

where we have made use of the fact that

$$dz = \varepsilon\sqrt{dt}, \ \tau = T - t$$

and ε is a standard normal deviate. Thus, since $x = \ln S$, then:

$$\ln\frac{S_T}{S} = \left(m - \frac{\sigma^2}{2}\right)\tau + \sigma\sqrt{\tau}\varepsilon_T \qquad (1.17)$$

or

$$S_T = S\left\{\left(m - \frac{\sigma^2}{2}\right)\tau + \sigma\sqrt{\tau}\varepsilon_T\right\} \qquad (1.18)$$

This is a closed-form solution to the Brownian motion SDE. We can now find the transition probability density (the probability distribution function of S_T at T given S at t). Given x at t, x_T is normally distributed:

$$x_T \sim N\left(x + \left(m - \frac{\sigma^2}{2}\right)(T-t), \sigma\sqrt{T-t}\right) \qquad (1.19)$$

or:

$$p(x_T, T \mid x, t)dx_T = \frac{1}{\sqrt{2\pi\sigma^2\tau}}\exp\left\{-\frac{(x_T - x - \mu\tau)^2}{2\sigma^2\tau}\right\}dx_T \qquad (1.20)$$

where $\mu = m - \sigma^2/2$. Then $\ln S_T$ is also normally distributed:

$$\ln S_T \sim N\left(\ln S + \mu(T-t), \sigma\sqrt{T-t}\right)$$

or:

$$p(x_T, T \mid x, t)dx_T = \frac{1}{\sqrt{2\pi\sigma^2\tau}}\exp\left\{-\frac{\left(\ln\left(\frac{S_T}{S}\right) - \mu\tau\right)^2}{2\sigma^2\tau}\right\}\frac{dS_T}{dS} \qquad (1.21)$$

(Note that $dx_T = dS_T/dS$.) This is the *lognormal distribution.*

We can now calculate the moments of the lognormal distribution around zero. We need to calculate the mean and variance by taking expectations:

$$M_n(0) = E_{t,S}\left[S_T^n\right] = \int_0^\infty S_T^n p(S_T,\ T\,|\,S,\ t)dS_T \qquad (1.22)$$

where $E_{t,S}$ is the expectation operator taken over S at time t. However, we can actually calculate the moments without calculating the integral. Since $S_T = \exp(x_T)$, we need to calculate the expectation:

$$M_n(0) = E_{t,x}[e^{nx_T}] \qquad (1.23)$$

Since x_T is normally distributed, we can use the characteristic function of the normal distribution to help calculate expectations:

$$\phi(\lambda) = E[e^{i\lambda x_T}] = \exp\left(i\lambda(x+\mu\tau) - \frac{\sigma^2\tau\lambda^2}{2}\right) \qquad (1.24)$$

Substituting $i\lambda \to n$ and recalling that $x = \ln S$ and $\mu = m - \sigma^2/2$, we have:

$$M_n(0) = E_{t,S}[e^{nx_T}] = S^n \exp\left(n\mu\tau + \frac{n^2\sigma^2\tau}{2}\right) \qquad (1.25)$$

$$= S^n \exp\left(nm\tau + \frac{n(n-1)}{2}\sigma^2\tau\right) \qquad (1.26)$$

In particular, the mean:

$$E_{t,S}[S_T] = e^{m\tau}S \qquad (1.27)$$

and the variance is:

$$\text{Var}_{t,S} = S^2\,[e^{2mr+\sigma^2\tau} - e^{2mr}] = S^2 e^{2mr}[e^{\sigma^2\tau} - 1]$$

We will use these moments when we need to match moments to the binomial distribution when we value options using binomial and trinomial trees (lattices). We already made use of equation (1.27) when we calculated the present value of forward contracts in equation (1.5).

We now have the framework to price options on stocks. Consider a derivative security $f_T = F(S_T)$ at time T. Suppose that the underlying asset follows a geometric Brownian motion with drift as in equation (1.12). Suppose we construct a portfolio Π containing a short position in one option f and a certain number of shares Δ:

$$\Pi = \Delta S - f \tag{1.28}$$

Note that we fix the number of shares at the beginning of the interval dt and hold it fixed through dt. From Ito's lemma, a change in the portfolio value is given by:

$$d\Pi = \Delta dS - df \tag{1.29}$$

$$= \Delta(mSdt + \sigma Sdz) - \left(\frac{df}{dt} + mS\frac{df}{dS} + \frac{1}{2}\sigma^2 S^2 \frac{d^2 f}{dS^2}\right)dt - \sigma S\frac{df}{dS}dz \tag{1.30}$$

$$= \sigma S\left(\Delta - \frac{df}{dS}\right)dz + \left(ms\left(\Delta - \frac{df}{dS}\right) - \frac{df}{dt} - \frac{1}{2}\sigma^2 S^2 \frac{d^2 f}{dS^2}\right)dt \tag{1.31}$$

where we have made use of equation (1.14) for df. Note that we do not have to differentiate Δ since this is just the number of shares we keep fixed through this infinitesimal time interval dt. Let's select the number of shares to hold (the hedge ratio) Δ so that:

$$\Delta = \frac{df}{dS} \tag{1.32}$$

This selection makes our portfolio instantaneously riskless—the term with the Wiener process dz (risk) falls out of equation (1.31). However, the portfolio is riskless only instantaneously for an infinitesimal time period dt since we have fixed our hedge ratio Δ. To keep the portfolio riskless through the next time period dt, we will need to rebalance—to change the delta to reflect the changing stock price.

Since our portfolio is now instantaneously riskless (over an infinitesimal time period dt), its rate of return must be equal to the risk-free rate r (otherwise, there is a clear arbitrage opportunity). The interest that accrues on our portfolio during an infinitesimal time period dt is:

$$d\Pi = r\Pi dt \tag{1.33}$$

The drift of the process for the portfolio must be equal to r:

$$\frac{\partial f}{\partial t} + \frac{1}{2}\sigma^2 S^2 \frac{\partial^2 f}{\partial S^2} + r\Pi = 0 \tag{1.34}$$

or:

$$\frac{1}{2}\sigma^2 S^2 \frac{\partial^2 f}{\partial S^2} + rS \frac{\partial f}{\partial S} - rf = -\frac{\partial f}{\partial t} \qquad (1.35)$$

Consequently, the option price f must satisfy the partial differential equations (PDEs) as a consequence of the no-arbitrage assumption. This is the Black-Scholes equation. Mathematically, this is a diffusion or heat equation.

1.3   RISK-NEUTRAL PRICING

We can also analyze equation (1.35) in the context of a risk-neutral world. We can rewrite (1.35) as

$$D_{s,t}f - rf = -\frac{\partial f}{\partial t} \qquad (1.36)$$

where $D_{s,t}$ is the generator of the *risk-neutral price process*:

$$D_{s,t} = \frac{1}{2}\sigma^2 S^2 \frac{\partial^2}{\partial S^2} + rS \frac{\partial}{\partial S} \qquad (1.37)$$

Note that the true drift rate m (the drift of the real-world price process) falls out of the equation, and the risk-neutral drift rate equal to the risk-free rate r takes its place. The risk-neutral price process (the stock price process in a risk-neutral world—a world where all investors are risk-neutral) is:

$$dS = rSdt + \sigma Sdz \qquad (1.38)$$

At the same time, the discount rate is also risk-neutral. Note also that the delta, or hedge ratio, depends on both time and the underlying price:

$$\Delta(S,t) = \frac{\partial f(S,t)}{\partial t} \qquad (1.39)$$

As t and S change, we need to rebalance our portfolio at each (infinitely small) time step. Thus, we must use a dynamic trading strategy where we adjust our delta over a given Δt. Otherwise, the hedge will leak and we will not replicate the derivative exactly. Moreover, the portfolio is not risk-free so that in fact we need to differentiate the delta when calculating the change in our portfolio. Thus, we need to adjust Δ as soon as S changes to be fully hedged.

We will show that the option price must also satisfy equation (1.35) via an entire dynamic trading strategy replicating the option from time 0 to maturity T. Suppose there are only three securities traded in our world: a stock; a European option on the stock expiring at time T and paying off an amount at maturity equal to $F(S_T)$, where F is a given payoff function and S_T is the stock price at T; and a risk-free money market account A. We start at time 0. The stock price is S_0, and the quoted option price is f_0. We also set up a money market account at time 0 with one share priced at $A_0 = \$1$. At time 0, we set up our portfolio as follows: We (1) sell one option (short) for f_0; (2) buy Δ_0 shares of stock; and (3) sell short N_0 shares of the money market account (this is equivalent to borrowing N_0 dollars at the risk-free money market rate r, since the MMA shares are worth \$1 at time 0). The value of our portfolio at time 0 is:

$$\Pi_0 = \Delta_0 S_0 - N_0 - f_0 \tag{1.40}$$

We will actively trade in shares of stock and the MMA by rebalancing our portfolio every infinitesimal time increment dt by changing both Δ_t and N_t at every instant in time. We will keep our short option position unchanged all the way to maturity T. At some intermediate time t (t is our running time parameter), our portfolio is worth:

$$\Pi_t = \Delta_t S_t - N_t A_t - f_t \tag{1.41}$$

where Δ_t is the number of shares of stock held at time t in our portfolio, S_t is the stock price at t, N_t is the number of shares of the money market account we are short at t, A_t is the money market share price at t, f_t is the quoted (market) option price at t, $A_t = e^{rt}$. $N_t A_t$ is the total dollar value of our debt at time t (our short position in the MMA).

A pair of stochastic processes $\{(\Delta_t, N_t), 0 \le t \le T\}$ that is a sequence of trading decisions is a *dynamic trading strategy*: The Δ_t and N_t, viewed as functions of time, are stochastic processes since we do not know their values at the beginning of our future trading decisions. We will make our trading decisions based on our observations of the stock price process in equation (1.12). Thus, our decisions $\Delta_t = \Delta(S_t, t)$ and $N_t = N(S_t, t)$ are functions of the stock price and time.

After a small time increment dt, the value of our portfolio changes according to:

$$d\Pi_t = \Delta_t dS - N_t dA_t - df_t + d\Delta_t (S_t + dS_t) - dN_t (A_t + dA_t) \tag{1.42}$$

where dA_t is the change in the value of one share of the money market account over dt—see equation (1.8); $d\Delta_t$ is the change in the number of (long) shares of stock made during dt; dS_t is the change in the stock price given by the SDE in equation

(1.12); and dN_t is the change in the number of (short) shares of the money market account we made during dt. More generally, we can define the portfolio as a linear combination of the assets in the portfolio,

$$\Pi_t = a(t)S_t + b(t)A_t + c(t)f \qquad (1.43)$$

weighted by the position held in each security where $a(t) = \Delta_t$, $b(t) = -N_t$, and $c(t) = -1$. Thus, taking the differentials on both sides of equation (1.43) will yield equation (1.42).

DEFINITION. A dynamic trading strategy $\phi \equiv \{(\Delta_t, N_t), 0 \leq t \leq T\}$ is said to be *self-financing* if no capital is added to or withdrawn from the portfolio Π_t after the initial setup at time 0. That is, we are only reallocating the capital between our long position in the stock and the short position in the money market account (borrowing). If we buy more stock, we short more shares of the MMA to borrow the money to fund the stock purchase. If we sell some shares of the stock, then we use the proceeds to reduce our debt (buy back some shares in the MMA we sold short). The self-financing condition is equivalent to the following:

$$\Pi_t = \Pi_0 + \int_0^t a(s)dS + \int_0^t b(s)dA + \int_0^t c(s)df \qquad (1.44)$$

which can occur if and only if

$$d\Delta_t(S_t + dS_t) - dN_t(A_t + dA_t) = 0 \qquad (1.45)$$

Indeed, the first term in equation (1.45), known as the *balance equation*, is the change in the total dollar capital invested in the stock. The second term is the change in our debt (short position in the MMA). The equality means that we reallocate the capital between the stock and the MMA without adding to or withdrawing from the portfolio. Hence, the portfolio is self-financing. That is, for any self-financing strategy, the terms coming from differentiating the weights Δ_t and N_t cancel out.

The total profit/loss (P/L) from the trading strategy at time T (maturity of the option) is given by the sum of all individual P/Ls over each time increment dt.

$$\Pi_T - \Pi_0 = \lim_{\Delta t \to 0} \left[\sum_{t=0}^{N-1} \Delta(S_i, t_i)(S_{i+1} - S_i) - \sum_{i=0}^{N-1} N(S_i, t_i)(A(t_{i+1}) - A(t_i)) \right]$$
$$- (f(S_T, T) - f(S_0, 0)) \qquad (1.46)$$

$$= \int_0^T \Delta_t dS_t - \int_0^T N_t dA_t - (F(S_T) - f(S_0,\ 0)) \qquad (1.47)$$

where $f(S_t, T) = F(S_T)$ is the payoff from the option—that is, $F(S_T) = \max(S_T - K, 0)$ for a standard European call option; $f(S_0, 0)$ is the initial option price at $t = 0$;

$$\int_0^T \Delta_t dS_t$$

is the P/L from all stock trades. In the limit of infinitesimal time changes it is given by the stochastic Ito integral[1] (limit of the sum; see Appendix B for a derivation);

$$\int_0^T N_t dA_t$$

is the P/L from all money market account trades (this is a standard integral over time since the price of one share of the money market account is not stochastic).

We now want to find such a self-financing dynamic trading strategy $\phi \equiv \{(\Delta_t, N_t), 0 \le t \le T\}$ such that it exactly replicates an option with the given payoff $F(S_T)$. If such a strategy does exist, we call it a *replicating strategy*.

DEFINITION. If such a self-financing strategy exists using a finite number of securities then the contingent claim (i.e., option) is said to be *attainable*. We wish to find such a trading strategy ϕ that its P/L at time T always exactly matches the option payoff $F(S_T)$ for every possible terminal stock price $S_T \in (0, \infty)$. If such a trading strategy does exist that matches the option payoff in all possible states of the world, the no-arbitrage principle requires that the fair value of the option f_t at any time t, $0 \le t \le T$, should equal the value of the replicating portfolio $(\Delta_t S_t - N_t A_t)$ at time t:

$$\Delta_t S_t - N_t A_t - f_t = 0 \qquad (1.48)$$

From Ito's lemma we can express the process for the option's price:

$$df = m_f f dt + \sigma_f f dz \qquad (1.49)$$

---

[1]We need Ito's stochastic integrals in finance to express P/Ls of continuous-time dynamic trading strategies.

where m_f and σ_f are, respectively, the instantaneous expected rate of return on the option and the instantaneous volatility of the option. From equation (1.14), we know:

$$m_f = \frac{\frac{\partial f}{\partial t} + mS\frac{\partial f}{\partial S} + \frac{1}{2}\sigma^2 S^2 \frac{\partial f}{\partial S^2}}{f} \tag{1.50}$$

and

$$\sigma_f = \frac{\sigma S \frac{\partial f}{\partial S}}{f} \tag{1.51}$$

Equation (1.50) states that the drift rate is equal to the rate of return on the option, that is, the drift coefficient divided by the option price. From equation (1.48), we have for an infinitesimal time increment dt,

$$\Delta_t dS - N_t dA - df_t = 0$$

and

$$m_f f dt + \sigma_f f dz - \Delta m S dt - \Delta \sigma S dz + rNA dt = 0 \tag{1.52}$$

Recall that $NA = \Delta S - f$. Substituting this into equation (1.52), we get

$$((m_f - r)f - \Delta S(m - r))dt + (\sigma_f f - \Delta \sigma S)dz = 0 \tag{1.53}$$

This can be true if and only if:

$$\Delta = \frac{\sigma_f f}{\sigma S} = \frac{\partial f}{\partial S} \tag{1.54}$$

and

$$m_f = r + \frac{\sigma_f}{\sigma}(m - r)$$

or

$$\frac{m_f - r}{\sigma_f} = \frac{m - r}{\sigma} \equiv \lambda \tag{1.55}$$

Equation (1.54) expresses the delta (the hedge ratio) as the ratio of the actual price volatility of the option to the actual price volatility of the stock. Equation (1.55) is the central relation of arbitrage pricing theory. It is known as the *market price of risk* and is fundamental to general derivatives pricing since it is used to change probability measures in one stochastic process to an equivalent martingale measure in another process according to Girsanov's theorem discussed in section 1.8. Note, however, we have already made use of Girsanov's theorem when we moved from the real-world asset price dynamics in equation (1.12) to the risk-neutral one in equation (1.38). Changing measures allowed us to use the risk-free rate r for the drift instead of m, which is unobservable. The market price of risk relates the risk premium required by investors in the option to the option's volatility, the stock's volatility, and the risk premium on the stock. What does it tell us about the fair (arbitrage-free) price of the option? Substitute the expression for m_f and σ_f from Ito's lemma into equation (1.50):

$$\frac{\partial f}{\partial t} + mS\frac{\partial f}{\partial S} + \frac{1}{2}\sigma^2 S^2 \frac{\partial^2 f}{\partial S^2} = rf + (m-r)S\frac{\partial f}{\partial S}$$

The two terms with m cancel out and we arrive at the Black-Scholes PDE:

$$\frac{\partial f}{\partial t} + rS\frac{\partial f}{\partial S} + \frac{1}{2}\sigma^2 S^2 \frac{\partial^2 f}{\partial S^2} = rf \qquad (1.56)$$

To summarize: (1) To prevent arbitrage, the fair price of the option $f = f(S, t)$ must satisfy the Black-Scholes PDE subject to the payoff condition. (2) There exists a unique dynamic replicating strategy $\{(\Delta_t, N_t), 0 \le t \le T\}$ with the P/L matching the option's payoff in all states of the world. The weights in the replicating portfolio are:

$$\Delta_t = \frac{\partial f}{\partial S}(S_t, t) \text{ and } N_t = \frac{\Delta_t S_t - f_t}{A_t}$$

where $f = f(S, t)$ is the fair (arbitrage-free) price of the option—a unique solution to the Black-Scholes PDE subject to the payoff condition. In practice, the option cannot be replicated exactly due to transaction costs, which we are assuming to be 0.

The solution to the PDE in equation (1.56) if $C = f(S, t)$ is a call option such that the payoff at T is $\max(S_T - X)$ is (see Appendix E in the CD-ROM for a detailed derivation of the solution to the Black-Scholes PDE):

$$C(S, t) = SN(d_1) - Xe^{-r\tau}N(d_2) \qquad (1.57)$$

where $N(\cdot)$ is the cumulative normal distribution,

$$d_1 = \frac{\ln(S/X) + (r+\sigma^2/2)\tau}{\sigma\sqrt{\tau}}$$

and

$$d_2 = d_1 - \sigma\sqrt{\tau}$$

where $\tau = T - t$. If $P = f(S, t)$ is a put option with a payoff at T of $\max(X - S_T)$ then

$$P(S, t) = Xe^{-r\tau}N(-d_2) - SN(-d_1) \qquad (1.58)$$

Note that $\Delta = N(d_1)$ for a call and $N(-d_1)$ for a put. If the stock pays a continuous dividend yield q, then the formula for a call option becomes:

$$C(S, t) = Se^{-q\tau}N(d_1) - Xe^{-r\tau}N(d_2) \qquad (1.59)$$

where

$$d_1 = \frac{\ln(S/X) + (r - q + \sigma^2/2)\tau}{\sigma\sqrt{\tau}}$$

and

$$d_2 = d_1 - \sigma\sqrt{\tau}$$

A put option on a stock paying a continuous dividend yield is priced analogously:

$$P(S, t) = Xe^{-r\tau}N(-d_2) - Se^{-q\tau}N(-d_1) \qquad (1.60)$$

There is an important relationship between European calls and puts, known as *put-call parity*:

$$C(S, t) + Xe^{-r\tau} = P(S, t) + Se^{-q\tau} \qquad (1.61)$$

If this relationship does not hold, then arbitrage opportunities may exist depending on transaction costs. As an example, if we assume there are zero transaction costs and $C(S, t) + Xe^{-r\tau} > P(S, t) + Se^{-q\tau}$, then we can sell the call short (receiving the call premium C), borrow an amount $Xe^{-r\tau}$, go long one put option, and purchase $Se^{-q\tau}$ shares of the underlying security with the amount borrowed. If the call option expires in-the-money, $S > X$, the put expires worthless, but we give the stock to the call buyer (who exercises the call against us) and receive X, which is used to pay of the loan. We make a profit of $C - P$. If the call expires out-of-the-money, then we exercise the put option, selling the stock we are long for X, which is used to pay off the loan. We get to keep the premium we received for selling the call short, and make a profit of $C - P$. Thus, in the absence of arbitrage, put-call parity must hold.

There is an intuitive meaning behind the Black-Scholes formula. The first term in equation (1.57), $SN(d_1)$, is the stock price multiplied times the probability the stock price will finish in-the-money—thus, it is the expected value of receiving the stock if and only if $S_T > X$, while the second term, $Xe^{-rT}N(d_2)$, is the discounted strike price multiplied by the probability that the stock finishes in-the-money—it is the present value of paying the strike price if and only if $S_T > X$. There is another useful interpretation of the formula based on portfolio replication. As we have shown, a call option, C, is equivalent to a portfolio that is long delta shares of the stock, ΔS, and short the money market account (or equivalently, risk-free bonds) so that $C = \Delta S - B$. Consequently, the first term in the Black-Scholes formula, $SN(d_1)$, is the amount invested in the stock, and the second term, $Xe^{-rT}N(d_2)$, is the amount borrowed.

It is important to note that the asset price process that led to the Black-Scholes formula has an important property: Possible percentage changes in the asset price over any period do not depend on the level of the initial asset price. In fact, changes in the asset price over any time interval are independent and identically distributed (i.i.d.) to the changes in any other time interval. Thus, the Black-Scholes world assumes a stationary process of the asset price dynamics—it is independent of time. Since the drift term under geometric Brownian motion (GBM) is deterministic (i.e., all variables are known at time t) and has a zero expectation if the asset is valued in a risk-neutral world under an equivalent martingale measure, then the only uncertain component is from the diffusion term with the Wiener process $z(t)$. But the Wiener term is normally distributed with mean zero and variance dt, and changes in Wiener processes—that is, $z(t + \Delta t) - z(t)$—have i.i.d. increments so that the price process has i.i.d. percentage change increments.[2]

The price process that generates the Black-Scholes model also has the important property that the sizes of asset price changes are small over a very small time interval so that there are no large jumps over this time interval. This assumption is relaxed in alternative models to the Black-Scholes such as the jump diffusion volatility model.

1.4 BLACK-SCHOLES AND DIFFUSION PROCESS IMPLEMENTATION

Since we are interested in implementing an option pricing model, we can now define an *Option* class since we know what attributes compose an option—underlying security price, strike, maturity, volatility, risk-free rate, and dividend yield. We will use this class throughout the book and build on it by adding functionality and

---

[2]This assumption is no longer true with other alternative models presented in this book such the constant elasticity of variance (CEV) volatility model, in which volatility is dependent on the level of the stock price so that changes (and the distribution of changes) in the stock price are then dependent on its level.

implementing more methods. First, we want to define new diffusion process classes including a *BlackScholesProcess* and an *OrnsteinUhlenbeckProcess* that will be useful as well when we start to approximate them with trees and lattices later in the book. These classes contain methods to compute means (expectations) and variances of the process.

```
typedef double Time;
typedef double Rate;

/******************************************************************************
General diffusion process classes
This class describes a stochastic process governed by dx(t) = mu(t, x(t))dt +
sigma(t, x(t))dz(t).
******************************************************************************/
class DiffusionProcess
{
  public:
    DiffusionProcess(double x0) : x0_(x0) {}
    virtual ~DiffusionProcess() {}

    double x0() const { return x0_; }

    // returns the drift part of the equation, i.e. mu(t, x_t)
    virtual double drift(Time t, double x) const = 0;

    // returns the diffusion part of the equation, i.e. sigma(t,x_t)
    virtual double diffusion(Time t, double x) const = 0;

    // returns the expectation of the process after a time interval
    // returns E(x_{t_0 + delta t} | x_{t_0} = x_0) since it is Markov.
    // By default, it returns the Euler approximation defined by
    // x_0 + mu(t_0, x_0) delta t.
    virtual double expectation(Time t0, double x0, Time dt) const {
      return x0 + drift(t0, x0)*dt;
    }

    // returns the variance of the process after a time interval
    // returns Var(x_{t_0 + Delta t} | x_{t_0} = x_0).
    // By default, it returns the Euler approximation defined by
    // sigma(t_0, x_0)^2 \Delta t .
    virtual double variance(Time t0, double x0, Time dt) const {
      double sigma = diffusion(t0, x0);
      return sigma*sigma*dt;
    }
  private:
    double x0_;
};


/******************************************************************************
Black-Scholes diffusion process class
```

```
This class describes the stochastic process governed by dS = (r - 0.5{sigma^2}) dt
+ sigmadz(t).
*****************************************************************************/
class BlackScholesProcess : public DiffusionProcess
{
  public:
    BlackScholesProcess(Rate rate, double volatility, double s0 = 0.0)
      : DiffusionProcess(s0), r_(rate), sigma_(volatility) {}

    double drift(Time t, double x) const {
      return r_ - 0.5*sigma_*sigma_;
    }
    double diffusion(Time t, double x) const {
      return sigma_;
    }
  private:
    double r_, sigma_;
};


/*****************************************************************************
Ornstein-Uhlenbeck process class
This class describes the Ornstein-Uhlenbeck process governed by dx = -a x(t) dt +
sigma dz(t).
*****************************************************************************/
class OrnsteinUhlenbeckProcess : public DiffusionProcess
{
  public:
    OrnsteinUhlenbeckProcess(double speed, double vol, double x0 = 0.0)
      : DiffusionProcess(x0), speed_(speed), volatility_(vol) {}

    double drift(Time t, double x) const {
      return - speed_*x;
    }
    double diffusion(Time t, double x) const {
      return volatility_;
    }
    double expectation(Time t0, double x0, Time dt) const {
      return x0*exp(-speed_*dt);
    }
    double variance(Time t0, double x0, Time dt) const {
      return 0.5*volatility_*volatility_/speed_* (1.0 - exp(-2.0*speed_*dt));
    }
  private:
    double speed_, volatility_;
};


/*****************************************************************************
Square-root process class
This class describes a square-root process governed by dx = a (b - x_t) dt + \sigma
sqrt{x_t} dW_t.
*****************************************************************************/
class SquareRootProcess : public DiffusionProcess
```

```
{
  public:
    SquareRootProcess(double b, double a, double sigma, double x0 = 0)
      : DiffusionProcess(x0), mean_(b), speed_(a), volatility_(sigma) {}
    double drift(Time t, double x) const {
      return speed_*(mean_ - x);
    }
    double diffusion(Time t, double x) const {
      return volatility_*sqrt(x);
    }
  private:
    double mean_, speed_, volatility_;
};
```

Next we define an *Instrument* class that will serve as the abstract parent for all derivative securities:

```
/************************************************************************
Abstract Instrument class
This class is purely abstract and defines the interface of concrete instruments
which will be derived from this one. It implements the Observable interface
************************************************************************/
class Instrument : public Patterns::Observer, public Patterns::Observable
{
  public:
    Instrument(const std::string& isinCode, const std::string& description)
      : NPV_(0.0), isExpired_(false), isinCode_(isinCode),
        description_(description), calculated(false) {}
    virtual ~Instrument() {}

    // inline definitions
    // returns the ISIN code of the instrument, when given.
    inline std::string isinCode() const {
      return isinCode_;
    }
    // returns a brief textual description of the instrument.
    inline std::string description() const {
      return description_;
    }
    // returns the net present value of the instrument.
    inline double NPV() const {
      calculate();
      return (isExpired_ ? 0.0 : NPV_);
    }
    // returns whether the instrument is still tradable.
    inline bool isExpired() const {
      calculate();
      return isExpired_;
    }
    // updates dependent instrument classes
```

```
  inline void update() {
    calculated = false;
    notifyObservers();
  }
  /*
```

This method forces the recalculation of the instrument value and other results which would otherwise be cached. It is not declared as const since it needs to call the non-const *notifyObservers* method. Explicit invocation of this method is not necessary if the instrument registered itself as observer with the structures on which such results depend.

```
  */
  inline void recalculate() {
    performCalculations();
    calculated = true;
    notifyObservers();
  }
  /*
```

This method performs all needed calculations by calling the *performCalculations* method.

Instruments cache the results of the previous calculation. Such results will be returned upon later invocations of *calculate*. The results depend on arguments such as term structures which could change between invocations; the instrument must register itself as observer of such objects for the calculations to be performed again when they change.

This method should not be redefined in derived classes. The method does not modify the structure of the instrument and is therefore declared as constant. Temporary variables are declared as mutable.

```
  */
  inline double calculate() const {
    if (!calculated)
      performCalculations();
    calculated = true;
    return 0.0;
  }
protected:
  // This method must implement any calculations which must be
  // (re)done in order to calculate the NPV of the instrument.
  virtual void performCalculations() const = 0;

  // The value of these attributes must be set in the body of the
  // performCalculations method.
  mutable double NPV_;
  mutable bool isExpired_;
private:
  std::string isinCode_, description_; // description of instrument
  mutable bool calculated; // tracks if instrument was calculated
};
```

The *Instrument* class implements the *Observable* interface that allows all (dependent) subclasses to be notified and updated if observed changes are made to their parent class. (See Appendix D in the CD-ROM for interface definition.)

We now define a generic *Option* class that subclasses *Instrument* (i.e., *Option* is a subclass of *Instrument*). Other classes that *Option* uses can be seen in the source code on the CD-ROM that comes with the book.

```
class Option : public Instrument
{
  public:
    enum Exercise { European = 'E', American = 'A' };
    enum Type { Call = 'C', Put = 'P' };
    Option();
    Option(double price, double strike, double vol, double rate, double div, double
      T, char type, char exercise);
    Option(const Handle<PricingEngine>& engine);
    virtual ~Option() {}
    friend class OptionGreeks;
    void setPricingEngine(const Handle<PricingEngine>& engine);
    virtual void performCalculations() const;
    virtual void setupEngine() const = 0; // set up pricing engine
    virtual double calculate() const = 0; // compute price

    // option greeks
    class OptionGreeks
    {
      public:
        StatUtility util; // statistical utility class
        OptionGreeks() {}
        double calcVega(double price, double strike, double rate, double div,
          double vol, double T);
        double calcDelta(double price, double strike, double rate, double div,
          double vol, double T, char type);
        double calcGamma(double price, double strike, double rate, double div,
          double vol, double T);
        double calcRho(double price, double strike, double rate, double div,
          double vol, double T, char type);
        double calcTheta(double price, double strike, double rate, double div,
          double vol, double T, char type);
      private:
        // Greek sensitivities
        double delta;                      // delta
        double gamma;                      // gamma
        double theta;                      // theta
        double vega;                       // vega
        double rho;                        // rho
    };
  protected:
    double strike_;                        // strike price
```

```
        double rate_;                        // interest rate
        double T_;                           // maturity
        double price_;                       // underlying asset
        double vol_;                         // volatility
        double dividend_;                    // dividend yield
        char type_;                          // option type 'C'all or 'P'ut
        char exercise_;                      // exercise type 'E'uropean and 'A'merican
        Handle<PricingEngine> engine_;       // pricing engine
        OptionGreeks og;                     // option greeks
        StatUtility util;                    // statistical utility class
        MatrixUtil mu;                       // matrix utility class
};
```

The class has the following method definitions:

```
// default constructor
Option::Option()
  : price_(50.0), strike_(50.0), rate_(0.06), dividend_(0.0), T_(1), type_('C'),
    exercise_('E')
{}

// overloaded constructor
Option::Option(double price, double strike, double vol, double rate, double div,
  double T, char type, char exercise)
  : price_(price), strike_(strike), vol_(vol), rate_(rate), dividend_(div), T_(T),
    type_(type), exercise_(exercise)
{}

/**********************************************************************************/
calcDelta              : calculates delta (sensitivity to the underlying stock price)
[in] : double price   : stock price
       double strike  : strike price
       double rate    : interest rate
       double div     : dividend yield
       double vol     : volatility
       double T       : time to maturity
       char type      : 'C'all or 'P'ut
[out]: double         : delta
**********************************************************************************/
double Option::OptionGreeks::calcDelta(double price, double strike, double rate,
  double div, double vol, double T, char type)
{
  double d1, delta;

  d1 = (log(price/strike) + (rate - div + (vol*vol/2))*T)/(vol*sqrt(T));
  if (type == 'C')
    delta = exp(-div*T)*util.normalCalcPrime(d1);
  else
```

```
    delta = exp(-div*T)*(util.normalCalc(d1) - 1);

  return delta;
}


/*****************************************************************************
calcVega            : calculates vega (sensitivity to volatility)
[in] :  double price   : stock price
        double strike  : strike price
        double rate    : interest rate
        double div     : dividend yield
        double vol     : volatility
        double T       : time to maturity
[out]:  double         : vega
*****************************************************************************/
double Option::OptionGreeks::calcVega(double price, double strike, double rate,
  double div, double vol, double T, double t)
{
  double d1, vega, normalPrime;

  d1 = (log(price/strike) + (rate - div + (vol*vol/2))*T)/(vol*sqrt(T));
  normalPrime = util.normalCalcPrime(d1);
  vega = (normalPrime*exp(-div*T))*price*sqrt(T);

  return vega;
}


/*****************************************************************************
calcGamma           : calculates gamma (sensitivity to the change in delta)
[in] :  double price   : stock price
        double strike  : strike price
        double rate    : interest rate
        double div     : dividend yield
        double vol     : volatility
        double T       : time to maturity
[out]:  double         : gamma
*****************************************************************************/
double Option::OptionGreeks::calcGamma(double price, double strike, double rate,
  double div, double vol, double T)
{
  double d1, gamma, normalPrime;

  d1 = (log(price/strike) + (rate - div + (vol*vol)/2)*T)/(vol*sqrt(T));
  normalPrime = util.normalCalcPrime(d1);
  gamma = (normalPrime*exp(-div*T))/(price*vol*sqrt(T));

  return gamma;
}


/*****************************************************************************
calcDelta           : calculates rho (sensitivity to the risk-free rate)
[in] :  double price   : stock price
        double strike  : strike price
```

```
               double rate     : interest rate
               double div      : dividend yield
               double vol      : volatility
               double T        : time to maturity
               char type       : 'C'all or 'P'ut
[out]:  double           : rho
**********************************************************************************/
double Option::OptionGreeks::calcRho(double price, double strike, double rate,
  double div, double vol, double T, char type)
{
  double d1 = (log(price/strike) + (rate - div + (vol*vol)/2)*T)/(vol*sqrt(T));
  double d2 = d1 - vol*sqrt(T);
  double rho = 0.0;

  if (type == 'C')
    rho = strike*T*exp(-rate*T)*util.normalCalc(d2);
  else
    rho = -strike*T*exp(-rate*T)*util.normalCalc(-d2);

  return rho;
}


/**********************************************************************************/
calcTheta                  : calculates theta (sensitivity to time to maturity)
[in] :  double price     : stock price
        double strike    : strike price
        double rate      : interest rate
        double div       : dividend yield
        double vol       : volatility
        double T         : time to maturity
        char type        : 'C'all or 'P'ut
[out]:  double           : theta
**********************************************************************************/
double Option::OptionGreeks::calcTheta(double price, double strike, double rate,
  double div, double vol, double T, char type)
{
  double d1 = (log(price/strike) + (rate - div + (vol*vol)/2)*T)/(vol*sqrt(T));
  double d2 = d1 - vol*sqrt(T);
  double theta = 0.0;
  if (type == 'C')
    theta = (-price*util.normalCalc(d1)*vol*exp(-div*T))/(2*sqrt(T)) +
      div*price*util.normalCalc(d1)*exp(-div*T) -
      rate*strike*exp(-rate*T)*util.normalCalc(d2);
  else
    theta = (-price*util.normalCalc(d1)*vol*exp(-div*T))/(2*sqrt(T)) -
      div*price*util.normalCalc(-d1)*exp(-div*T) +
      rate*strike*exp(-rate*T)*util.normalCalc(-d2);

  return theta;
}

// overloaded constructor
Option::Option(const Handle<PricingEngine>& engine)
```

```
    : engine_(engine) {
      QL_REQUIRE(!engine_.isNull(), "Option::Option : null pricing engine not
        allowed");
}


/***************************************************************************
setPricingEngine                          : initializes pricing engine
[in] : Handle<PricingEngine>& engine      : pricing engine
[out]: void
***************************************************************************/
void Option::setPricingEngine(const Handle<PricingEngine>& engine)
{
  QL_REQUIRE(!engine.isNull(), "Option::setPricingEngine : null pricing engine not
    allowed");
  engine_ = engine;
  // this will trigger recalculation and notify observers
  update();
  setupEngine();
}


/***************************************************************************
performCalculations : calculates and stores price of security
[in] : none
[out]: void
***************************************************************************/
void Option::performCalculations() const
{
  setupEngine();
  engine_->calculate();
  const OptionValue* results = dynamic_cast<const OptionValue*>(engine_-
    >results());
  QL_ENSURE(results != 0, "Option::performCalculations : no results returned from
    option pricer");
  NPV_ = results->value;
}
```

We can now define a plain-vanilla option class for computing Black-Scholes option prices:

```
// Vanilla option (no discrete dividends, no barriers) on a single asset
class VanillaOption : public Option
{
  public:
    VanillaOption() { }
    VanillaOption(double price, double strike, double rate, double div, double vol,
      double T,
```

```
      Option::Type type, Option::Exercise exercise, const Handle<PricingEngine>&
        engine);
    double impliedVolatility(double targetValue, double accuracy = 1.0e-4,
      Size maxEvaluations = 100, double minVol = 1.0e-4, double maxVol = 4.0)
        const;
    double delta() const;   // get delta
    double gamma() const;   // get gamma
    double theta() const;   // get theta
    double vega() const;    // get vega
    double rho() const;     // get rho
protected:
    void setupEngine() const;
    void performCalculations() const;
    virtual double calculate() const { return NPV_; }
    Date exerciseDate_; // exercise Date
    RelinkableHandle<TermStructure> riskFreeRate; // spot rate term structure
    // results
    mutable double delta_, gamma_, theta_, vega_, rho_, dividendRho_;
    // arguments
    Option::Type type_;
    Option::Exercise exercise_;
    double underlying_;     // underlying price
    double strike_;         // strike price
    double dividendYield_;  // dividend yield
    double riskFreeRate_;   // spot risk-free rate
    double maturity_;       // time to maturity (years)
    double volatility_;     // volatility
private:
    // helper class for implied volatility calculation
    class ImpliedVolHelper : public ObjectiveFunction
    {
      public:
        StatUtility util;

        ImpliedVolHelper(const Handle<PricingEngine>& engine, double targetValue);
        std::map<int,double> calcImpliedVols(double price, std::vector<double>
          opPrices,
        std::vector<int>strikes, double rate, double dividend, double T,
          Option::Type type);

        std::map<std::pair<double,int>,double> calcImpliedSurface(double price,
          std::vector<double> opPrices, std::vector<int>strikes,
            std::vector<double> T, std::map<double,double> rates, double dividend,
             Option::Type type);
        double operator()(double x) const;
      private:
        Handle<PricingEngine> engine_;
        double targetValue_;
        const OptionValue* results_;
    };
};
```

We can now define a *BlackScholesOption* class that inherits from the Vanilla Option, which can provide the methods to compute European option values:

```
// Black-Scholes-Merton option
class BlackScholesOption : public VanillaOption {
  public:
    BlackScholesOption() { }
    BlackScholesOption(Option::Type type, double underlying, double strike, double
      dividendYield, double riskFreeRate, double residualTime, double volatility);
    virtual ~BlackScholesOption() {}
    // modifiers
    virtual void setVolatility(double newVolatility);
    virtual void setRiskFreeRate(double newRate);
    virtual void setDividendYield(double newDividendYield);
    double calcBSCallPrice(double price, double strike, double vol, double rate,
      double div, double T);
    double calcBSPutPrice(double vol, double rate, double div, double strike,
      double price, double T);
  protected:
    Option::Type type_;
    Option::Exercise exercise_;
    double underlying_;
    double strike_;
    double dividendYield_;
    double riskFreeRate_;
    double residualTime_;
    double volatility_;
    double value_;
};
```

Since we know the values of a European call and a European put using Black-Scholes we can write the code to implement *calcBSCallPrice*() and *calcBSPut-Price*(). We will make use of Hull's approximation of the cumulative normal distribution.[3]

```
/*****************************************************************************
normalCalc      : computes cumulative normal distribution probabilities
[in] double d   : critical value argument
[out]: double   : probability
*****************************************************************************/
double StatUtility::normalCalc(double d)
{
```

_____
[3]Hull (1996), 234–244.

```
const double a1 = 0.319381530;
const double a2 = -0.356563782;
const double a3 = 1.781477937;
const double a4 = -1.821255978;
const double a5 = 1.330274429;
const double gamma = 0.2316419;
const double k1 = 1/(1 + gamma*d);
const double k2 = 1/(1 - gamma*d);
const double normalprime = (1/(sqrt(2*PI)))*exp(-d*d/2);
double value = 0.0;
double h = 0.0;

if (d >= 0)
  value = 1- normalprime*(a1*k1 + a2*pow(k1,2) + a3*pow(k1,3) + a4*pow(k1,4) +
    a5*pow(k1,5));
else
  value = normalprime*(a1*k2 + a2*pow(k2,2) + a3*pow(k2,3) + a4*pow(k2,4) +
    a5*pow(k2,5));

return value;
}


/******************************************************************************
calcBSCall Price       : calculates Black Scholes call price
[in]  :  double vol    : volatility
         double rate   : interest rate
         double div    : dividend yield
         double strike : strike price
         double price  : stock price
         double T      : time to maturity
[out]:   double        : call price
******************************************************************************/
double BlackScholesModel::calcBSCallPrice(double vol, double rate, double div,
  double strike, double price, double T)
{
  double prob1;
  double prob2;
  double d1, d2;
  double callprice;
  d1 = (log(price/strike) + (rate - dividend + (vol)*(vol)/2)*T)/(vol*sqrt(T));
  d2 = d1 - vol*sqrt(T);

  prob1 = normalCalc(d1);
  prob2 = normalCalc(d2);
  callprice = price*exp(-div*T)*prob1 - strike*exp(-rate*T)*prob2;

  return callprice;
}


/******************************************************************************
calcBSPutPrice         : calculates Black Scholes put price
[in] : double vol      : volatility
```

```
          double rate    : interest rate
          double div     : dividend yield
          double strike  : strike price
          double price   : stock price
          double T       : time to maturity
[out]:    double         : put price
*************************************************************************/
double BlackScholesModel::calcBSPutPrice(double vol, double rate, double div,
   double strike, double price, double T)
{
   double prob1;
   double prob2;
   double putprice;
   double d1, d2;

   d1 = (log(price/strike) + (rate - div + (vol)*(vol)/2)*T)/(vol*sqrt(T));
   d2 = d1 - vol*sqrt(T);

   prob1 = normalCalc(-d1);
   prob2 = normalCalc(-d2);
   putprice = strike*exp(-rate*T)*prob2 - price*exp(-div*T)*prob1;

   return putprice;
}
```

1.5   AMERICAN OPTIONS

While the Black-Scholes option pricing model can be used to price European options, it cannot be used to price American options since it cannot account for the early exercise feature. With the valuation problem of European options, we know which boundary conditions to use and where to apply them. However, with the valuation problem of American options, we do not know a priori where to apply boundary conditions and so have a *free boundary* S_f. The valuation of American options is more complicated since we have to determine not only the option value, but also, for each value of S, whether to exercise early. In general, at each time t, there is a particular value of S that delineates the boundary S_f between the early exercise region and the holding region. Consequently, lattice methods and finite difference schemes must be used to price American options. The Black-Scholes PDE was derived through arbitrage arguments. This argument is only partially valid for American options.

As before, we can set up a delta-hedged portfolio between the underlying asset and the money market account to synthetically replicate the option. However, because the option is American, it is not necessarily possible for positions in the replicated option to be both long and short since there are times when it is optimal to exercise the option so that the writer of an option may be exercised against early.[4] Consequently, the arbitrage arguments used for the European option no longer lead to a unique value for the return on the portfolio. It turns out that the price of an American put option P satisfies only the Black-Scholes PDE inequality:

$$\frac{\partial P}{\partial t} + \frac{1}{2}\sigma^2 S^2 \frac{\partial^2 P}{\partial S^2} + rS\frac{\partial P}{\partial S} - rP \leq 0$$

When it is optimal to hold the option (not exercise), the equality holds, and when it is optimal to exercise early, strict inequality holds. To see why this is true, suppose we have an American put option. If we plug the put payoff $P = X - S$ into the preceding equation we get $-rX < 0$. It turns out the price of an American call option on a non-dividend-paying asset satisfies the Black-Scholes PDE with equality, but satisfies an inequality if the option is on a dividend-paying asset.

The American put problem can be written as a free boundary problem. For each time t, we divide the asset price axis into two distinct regions. The first, $0 \leq S < S_f$, is the early exercise region so that for $P = X - S$,

$$\frac{\partial P}{\partial t} + \frac{1}{2}\sigma^2 S^2 \frac{\partial^2 P}{\partial S^2} + rS\frac{\partial P}{\partial S} - rP < 0$$

The other region, $S_f < S < \infty$, is where early exercise is not optimal so that for $P > X - S$,

$$\frac{\partial P}{\partial t} + \frac{1}{2}\sigma^2 S^2 \frac{\partial^2 P}{\partial S^2} + rS\frac{\partial P}{\partial S} - rP = 0$$

The boundary conditions at $S = S_f(t)$ are that P and its slope (delta) are continuous:

$$P(S_f(t),\ t) = \max(X - S_f(t),\ 0), \quad \frac{\partial P}{\partial S}(S_f(t),\ t) = -1$$

The payoff boundary condition determines the option value on the free boundary, and the slope determines the location of the free boundary. Since we do not know a priori where S_f is, an additional condition is required to determine it. Arbitrage arguments show that the gradient of f should be continuous. Thus, the condition

---

[4]Wilmott, Howison, and Dewynne (1995), 112.

$(\partial P/\partial S)(S_f(t), t) = -1$ helps us determine it. Arbitrage arguments show why the slope cannot be greater or less than -1.[5]

Since an American option gives us the right to exercise early then it should be worth more than a European option that does not gives us that right. Consider that we can exercise an American put early and invest the proceeds in a money market account earning the risk-free rate, which we cannot do with a European put. We know then that an American option should be worth at least as much as a European option. For an American call value $C^{American}$, we know that

$$C^{American} \geq C^{European} \geq \max(S - X, 0)$$

and for an American put value $P^{American}$,

$$P^{American} \geq P^{European} \geq \max(X - S, 0)$$

In fact, equation (1.57) gives the value of an American call option on a non-dividend-paying stock since an American option on a non-dividend-paying stock satisfies the Black-Scholes PDE. There are no exact analytic formulas for the value of an American put option on a non-dividend-paying stock, so numerical procedures have to be used.

For an American call option on dividends, the price must satisfy the Black-Scholes PDE inequality:

$$\frac{\partial P}{\partial t} + \frac{1}{2}\sigma^2 S^2 \frac{\partial^2 P}{\partial S^2} + (r - q)S \frac{\partial P}{\partial S} - rP \leq 0$$

where q is the dividend yield and we assume $r > q > 0$. At the optimal exercise boundary $S = S_f$, we have the free boundary conditions:

$$C(S_f(t), t) = \max(S_f(t) - X, 0), \quad \frac{\partial C}{\partial S}(S_f(t), t) = 1$$

Only if $C > S - X$ does the American call price satisfy the PDE with equality at the boundary $S = S_f$. Note that $C = S - X$ is not a solution and therefore does not satisfy the equality; that is, plugging the payoff in the PDE results in $rX - qS < 0$. Local analysis of the free boundary shows that as $t \to T$,

$$S_f(t) \sim \frac{rX}{q}\left(1 + \xi_0 \sqrt{\frac{1}{2}\sigma^2(T - t)} + \ldots\right)$$

---

[5]Ibid., 113.

where $\xi_0 = 0.9034\ldots$ is a "universal constant" of call option pricing and is the solution of a transcendental equation; see Wilmott, Howison, and Dewynne (1995) for the derivation details. Moreover, an exact numerical procedure for calculating values of American calls on dividend-paying stocks is given by Roll, Geske, and Whaley.[6]

1.6   FUNDAMENTAL PRICING FORMULAS

Any attainable contingent claim with a payoff H_T at time $T > t$ can be priced in a risk-neutral world by assuming the existence of a risk-neutral measure Q. Denote by π_t the price of a derivative at time t. Then the value of π_t can be given by the risk-neutral expectation:

$$\pi_t = E\left(e^{-\int_t^T r(s)\,ds} H_T \bigg| \mathfrak{I}_t \right) \qquad (1.62)$$

where the expectation is conditional on $\mathfrak{I}_t$, the sigma field (information set) generated up to time t.

There is a fundamental relationship between the absence of arbitrage and the mathematical property of the existence of a probability measure known as the equivalent martingale measure (or risk-neutral measure or risk-adjusted measure).

DEFINITION. An *equivalent martingale measure Q* is a probability measure on the probability space $(\Omega, \mathfrak{I})$ where Ω is the event set and $\mathfrak{I}$ is a filtration, that is, an increasing sequence of sigma algebras included in $\mathfrak{I} : \mathfrak{I}_0, \mathfrak{I}_1, \ldots, \mathfrak{I}_n$,[7] such that:

- Q_0 and Q are equivalent measures where $Q_0(A) = 0$ if and only if $Q(A) = 0$, for every $A \in \mathfrak{I}$.
- The Radon-Nikodym derivative dQ/dQ_0 belongs to $L^2(\Omega, \mathfrak{I}, Q_0)$; that is, it is square integrable with respect to Q_0.
- The discounted asset process $S/B(0,\cdot)$ is a Q-martingale, that is, E^Q $(S(t)/B(0, t)|$ $\mathfrak{I}_u) = S(u)/B(0, u)$, for $0 \leq u \leq t \leq T$, with E^Q denoting expectation under Q and

$$B(0,T) = e^{\int_0^T r(s)\,ds}$$

---

[6]Hull (1996), 219–220.

[7]$\mathfrak{I}_n$ can be interpreted as the information available at time n and is sometimes called the sigma algebra of events up to time n.

The following proposition, proved by Harrison and Pliska (1981), provides the mathematical relationship of the unique no-arbitrage price associated with any attainable contingent claim:

PROPOSITION. Assume there exists an equivalent martingale measure Q and let H be an attainable contingent claim. Then, for each time t, $0 \leq t \leq T$, there exists a unique price π_t associated with H, that is,

$$\pi_t = E^Q \left(D(t, T)H | \Im_t \right) \tag{1.63}$$

This result generalizes that of Black and Scholes (1973) to the pricing of any claim, which may be path-dependent.

DEFINITION. A financial market is *complete* if and only if every contingent claim is attainable.

Harrison and Pliska (1983) proved that a financial market is (arbitrage-free and) complete if and only if there exists a unique equivalent martingale measure. Thus, the existence of a unique equivalent martingale measure both makes markets arbitrage-free and allows for the derivation of a unique price associated with any contingent claim.[8] Consequently, the following three results characterize no-arbitrage pricing by martingales:

1. The market is arbitrage-free if (and only if) there exists a martingale measure.
2. The market is complete if and only if the martingale measure is unique.
3. In an arbitrage-free market, not necessarily complete, the price of any attainable claim is uniquely given either by the value of the associated replicating strategy or by the risk-neutral expectation of the discounted claim payoff under any of the equivalent (risk-neutral) martingale measures.[9]

We see that a self-replicating strategy must yield the same price as the discounted claim payoff under a risk-neutral measure if and only if there is to be an absence of arbitrage. Equation (1.63) gives the unique no-arbitrage price of an attainable contingent claim H under a given equivalent martingale measure Q. However, Geman et al. (1995) noted that an equivalent martingale measure is "not necessarily the most natural and convenient measure for pricing the claim H."[10] For example, under stochastic interest rates, the presence of the stochastic discount factor $D(t, T)$ can considerably complicate the calculation of the expectation. In such cases, a change of numeraire can help simplify the calculation. Jamshidian (1989) uses the change of numeraire approach to compute bond-option prices under the Vasicek (1977) model.

---

[8]Brigo and Mercurio (2001a), 26.
[9]Ibid., 26.
[10]Ibid., 26.

1.7   CHANGE OF NUMERAIRE

Geman et al. (1995) introduced the concept of a numeraire, which is defined as any positive non-dividend-paying asset. A numeraire N is identifiable with a self-financing strategy $\phi \equiv \{(\Delta_T, N_t), 0 \leq t \leq T\}$ in that $N_t = V_t(\phi)$, where V is the market value of the portfolio ϕ, for each t. Thus, a numeraire is a reference asset chosen so as to normalize all other asset prices S_k, $k = 0, \ldots, n$, with respect to it so that relative prices S_k/N are considered rather than the asset prices themselves.

PROPOSITION. Let ϕ be a trading strategy and let N be a numeraire. Then, ϕ is self-financing if and only if

$$\frac{V_t(\phi)}{N} = \tilde{V}_t(\phi) = V_0(\phi) + \sum_{i=1}^{n} \phi_i \Delta \tilde{S}_i \qquad (1.64)$$

where $\tilde{S}_i = S_i/N$. This proposition can be extended to any numeraire, so that any self-financing strategy remains self-financing after a change of numeraire. The self-financing condition

$$dV_t(\phi) = \sum_{k=0}^{n} \phi_t^k dS_t^k$$

implies that:[11]

$$d\left(\frac{V_t(\phi)}{N_t}\right) = \sum_{k=0}^{n} \phi_t^k d\left(\frac{S_t^k}{N_t}\right)$$

so that an attainable claim is also attainable under any numeraire.

PROPOSITION. Assume there exists a numeraire N and a probability measure Q^N, equivalent to the initial measure Q_0, such that the price of any traded asset X (without intermediate payments) relative to N is a martingale under Q^N; that is,[12]

$$\frac{X_t}{N_t} = E^N\left[\frac{X_T}{N_T}\Big| \Im_t\right]$$

Let U be an arbitrary numeraire. Then there exists a probability measure Q^U, equivalent to the initial Q_0, so that the price of any attainable claim X normalized by U is a martingale under Q^U; that is,

$$\frac{X_t}{U_t} = E^U\left[\frac{X_T}{U_T}\Big| \Im_t\right]$$

---

[11]Ibid., 27.
[12]Ibid.

DEFINITION. The *Radon-Nikodym* derivative defining the measure Q^U is given by[13]

$$\frac{dQ^U}{dQ^N} = \frac{\left(\dfrac{U_T}{U_0}\right)}{\left(\dfrac{N_T}{N_0}\right)} = \frac{U_T N_0}{U_0 N_T} \tag{1.65}$$

By definition of Q^N, we know that for any tradable asset Z,

$$E^N\left[\frac{Z_T}{N_T}\right] = E^U\left[\frac{U_0}{N_0}\frac{Z_T}{U_T}\right] \tag{1.66}$$

By definition of the Radon-Nikodym derivative, we know also that for all Z,

$$E^N\left[\frac{Z_T}{N_T}\right] = E^U\left[\frac{Z_T}{N_T}\frac{dQ^N}{dQ^U}\right] \tag{1.67}$$

By comparing the right-hand sides of equations (1.66) and (1.67) (both equal Z_0/N_0), we get equation (1.65). To see this, note:

$$E^U\left[\frac{Z_T}{N_T}\frac{dQ^N}{dQ^U}\right] = E^U\left[\frac{Z_T}{U_T}\frac{U_0}{N_0}\right] = \frac{U_0}{N_0}E^U\left[\frac{Z_T}{U_T}\right] = \frac{Z_0}{N_0}$$

When it is necessary to compute the expected value of an integrable random variable X, it may be useful to switch from one measure $\tilde{Q}$ to another equivalent measure Q:

$$\tilde{E}[X] = \int_\Omega X d\tilde{Q} = \int_\Omega X \frac{d\tilde{Q}}{dQ}dQ = E\left[X\frac{d\tilde{Q}}{dQ}\right]$$

where the tilde on the expectation denotes the expectation under the measure $\tilde{Q}$. Thus, the expectation under the new measure is the expectation of the random variable X multiplied by the Radon-Nikodym derivative. When dealing with conditional expectations, it can be shown that:

$$\tilde{E}\left[X|\Im_t\right] = \frac{E\left[X\dfrac{d\tilde{Q}}{dQ}|\Im_t\right]}{\dfrac{d\tilde{Q}}{dQ}|\Im_t}$$

---

[13]Ibid.

When changing from a first numeraire N (associated with a measure Q^N) to a second numeraire U (associated with a measure Q^U), we also change the drift in the dynamics of the asset. Following Brigo and Mercurio,[14] we can make use of the following proposition to characterize the change in drift:

PROPOSITION. Assume that the two numeraires S and U evolve under Q^U according to

$$dS(t) = (\,\ldots\,)dt + \sigma^S(t)Cdz^U(t)$$
$$dU(t) = (\,\ldots\,)dt + \sigma^U(t)Cdz^U(t)$$

where both $\sigma^S(t)$ and $\sigma^U(t)$ are $1 \times$ vectors, z^U is an n-dimensional standard Brownian motion, and C is a variance-covariance matrix of the Brownian motions such that $CC' = \rho$. Then, the drift of the process X under the numeraire U is:

$$\mu^U(X_t,\ t)=\mu^N(X_t,\ t)-\sigma(X_t,\ t)\rho\left(\frac{\sigma_N}{S(t)}-\frac{\sigma_U}{U(t)}\right)' \qquad (1.68)$$

We can also make use of the following proposition provided by Brigo and Mercurio (2001a):

PROPOSITION. If we assume "level-proportional" functional forms for volatilities, that is,

$$\sigma^S(t) = v^S(t)S(t)$$
$$\sigma^U(t) = v^U(t)U(t)$$
$$\sigma(X_t,\ t) = \mathrm{diag}(X_t)\mathrm{diag}(v^X(t))$$

where the v's are deterministic $1 \times n$-vector functions of time, and $\mathrm{diag}(X_t)$ denotes the diagonal matrix whose diagonal elements are the entries of vectors X. Then we get

$$\mu^U(X_t,\ t)=\mu^S(X_t,\ t)-\mathrm{diag}(X_t)\mathrm{diag}(v^X(t))\rho(v^S(t)-v^U(t))'$$
$$=\mu^S(X_t,\ t)-\mathrm{diag}(X_t)\frac{d<\ln X,\ \ln(S/U)'>_t}{dt}$$

where the quadratic covariation and the logarithms, when applied to vectors, are meant to act componentwise. In the "fully lognormal" case, where the drift of X under Q^S is deterministically level proportional, that is,

$$\mu^S(X_t) = \mathrm{diag}(X_t)m^S(t)$$

---

[14]Ibid., 30.

with m^S a deterministic $n \times 1$ vector, it turns out that the drift under the new measure Q^U is of the same type; that is,

$$\mu^U(X_t) = \text{diag}(X_t)m^U(t)$$

where

$$m^U(t) = m^S(t) - \text{diag}(v^X(t))\rho(v^S(t) - v^U(t))' = m^S(t) - \frac{d < \ln X, \ln(S/U)' >_t}{dt}$$

which is often written as:

$$m^U(t) = m^S(t) - (d\ln X_t)(d\ln(S_t/U_t)) \tag{1.69}$$

1.8 GIRSANOV'S THEOREM

We now give Girsanov's theorem, a fundamental theorem when we need to change the drift of a stochastic differential equation. Consider an SDE,

$$dx(t) = \mu(x(t), t)dt + \sigma(x(t), t)dz(t)$$

under the measure Q. Let there be a new drift $\tilde{\mu}(x(t),t)$, and assume

$$\frac{\tilde{\mu}(x(t),\ t) - \mu(x(t),\ t)}{\sigma(x)}$$

is bounded. Define the measure $\tilde{Q}$ by

$$\frac{d\tilde{Q}}{dQ} = \exp\left\{ -\frac{1}{2}\int_0^t \left(\frac{\tilde{\mu}(x,\ s) - \mu(x,\ s)}{\sigma(x,\ s)}\right)^2 ds + \int_0^t \frac{\tilde{\mu}(x,\ s) - \mu(x,\ s)}{\sigma(x,\ s)} dz(s) \right\} \tag{1.70}$$

Then $\tilde{Q}$ is equivalent to Q. Moreover, the process $\tilde{z}$ defined by

$$d\tilde{z}(t) = -\left[\frac{\tilde{\mu}(x,\ t) - \mu(x,\ t)}{\sigma(x,\ t)}\right]dt + dz(t)$$

is a Brownian motion under $\tilde{Q}$, and

$$dx(t) = \tilde{\mu}(x(t),\ t)dt + \sigma(x(t),\ t)d\tilde{z}(t)$$

As we have seen, by defining a new probability measure $\tilde{Q}$ via a suitable Radon-Nikodym derivative, we can change the drift of the SDE in terms of the difference of the new drift minus the given drift. A classic example of the application of Girsanov's theorem is when one moves from the real-world asset price dynamics of:

$$dx(t) = \mu x(t)dt + \sigma x(t)dz(t)$$

to the risk-neutral dynamics of:

$$dx(t) = rx(t)dt + \sigma x(t)d\tilde{z}(t)$$

Using Girsanov's theorem, we get:

$$\tilde{E}[X] = E\left[X \frac{d\tilde{Q}}{dQ} \right] = E\left[X \exp\left\{ -\frac{1}{2}\left(\frac{\mu - r}{\sigma} \right)^2 t - \left(\frac{\mu - r}{\sigma} \right) z(t) \right\} \right]$$

The expectation term contains geometric Brownian motion if we define the process $Y(t) = e^{z(t)}$. Since $z(t)$ is normal with mean 0 and variance t, its moment-generating function is given by:

$$E\left[e^{sz(t)} \right] = e^{ts^2/2}$$

so that:

$$E\left[e^{-\left(\frac{\mu - r}{\sigma} \right) z(t)} \right] = e^{\frac{1}{2}\left(\frac{\mu - r}{\sigma} \right)^2 t}$$

We can now evaluate the expectation:

$$E\left[Xe^{-\frac{1}{2}\left(\frac{\mu - r}{\sigma} \right)^2 t} e^{\frac{1}{2}\left(\frac{\mu - r}{\sigma} \right)^2 t} \right] = E[X]$$

which shows the equivalence between $\tilde{Q}$ and Q; that is, $\tilde{Q} \sim Q$.
   The quantity

$$\frac{\mu - r}{\sigma} = \lambda$$

as noted from (1.55) is known as the market price of risk. Girsanov's theorem allows for a change in measure via the Radon-Nikodym derivative, which can be expressed in terms of the market price of risk:

$$\frac{d\tilde{Q}}{dQ} = \exp\left(-\frac{1}{2}\lambda^2 t + \lambda z(t)\right)$$

We can also write the Brownian process $\tilde{z}$:

$$\tilde{z}(t) = z(t) - \int_0^t \lambda(s)ds$$

If the market price of risk is not time-homogenous, that is,

$$\lambda(t) = \frac{\mu(r(t),\ t) - r(t)}{\sigma(r(t),\ t)}$$

then we use

$$\frac{d\tilde{Q}}{dQ} = \exp\left(-\frac{1}{2}\int_0^t \lambda^2(s)ds + \int_0^t \lambda(s)dz(s)\right)$$

In interest rate derivative pricing, Girsanov's theorem plays an important role when changing measures. In the Vasicek model (discussed in Chapter 10), for example, the market price of risk can have the functional form

$$\lambda(t) = \lambda r(t)$$

so that the Girsanov change of measure is:

$$\frac{dQ}{d\tilde{Q}} = \exp\left(-\frac{1}{2}\int_0^t \lambda^2 r(s)^2\, ds + \int_0^t \lambda r(s)d\tilde{z}(s)\right)$$

Under this formulation, the short rate process is tractable under both risk-neutral and objective measures. Tractability under the risk-neutral measure Q allows computations of the expected payoff so that claims can be priced in a simplified manner in the risk-neutral world. Tractability under the objective measure is useful for estimation of the objective parameters a, $\bar{r}$, λ, and σ, since historical observations of interest rate data in the real world are made under the objective measure $\tilde{Q}$. Historical (daily) series of interest rate data are collected for estimation purposes. The statistical properties of the data also characterize the distribution of the interest rate process under the objective measure. However, the market price of risk can also be chosen to be constant—that is, $\lambda(t) = \lambda$—as well, while still retaining tractability. Similarly, in the Cox-Ingersoll-Ross (CIR) model (see Chapter 10), the market price of risk is assumed to have the following functional form:

$$\lambda(t) = \lambda \sqrt{r(t)}$$

so that the change of measure is:

$$\frac{dQ}{d\tilde{Q}} = \exp\left(-\frac{1}{2} \int_0^t \lambda^2 r(s)ds + \int_0^t \lambda \sqrt{r(s)}d\tilde{z}(s) \right)$$

1.9   THE FORWARD MEASURE

A useful numeraire to use is the zero-coupon bond whose maturity T coincides with that of the derivative to price. The T-maturity zero-coupon bond simplifies derivatives pricing since $S_T = P(T, T) = 1$. Thus, pricing the derivative involves computing the expectation of the payoff, which in turn involves dividing by 1. We denote by Q^T the T-forward risk-adjusted measure (or just T-forward measure), the measure associated with the bond maturing at time T. The related expectation is denoted E^T.

The T-forward measure is useful because a forward rate spanning a time interval up to T is a martingale under the measure; that is,[15]

$$E^T\left[F(t; S, T)\big|\Im_u\right] = F(u; S, T) \tag{1.71}$$

for each $0 \leq t \leq S \leq T$. In particular, the forward rate spanning the interval $[S, T]$ is the Q_T—the expectation of the future simply compounded spot rate, $R(S, T)$, at time S for the maturity T; that is,

$$E^T\left[R(S, T)\big|\Im_t\right] = F(t; S, T) \tag{1.72}$$

for each $0 \leq t \leq S \leq T$.

PROOF. To see this, note that from the definition of a simply compounded forward rate[16]

$$F(t; S, T) = \frac{1}{\tau(S, T)}\left[\frac{P(t, S)}{P(t, T)} - 1 \right]$$

---

[15]Ibid., 34.
[16]Ibid.

where $\tau(S, T)$ is the year fraction from S to T, so that

$$F(t; S, T)P(t, T) = \frac{1}{\tau(S, T)}\left[P(t, S) - P(t, T)\right]$$

is the price of a traded asset since it is a multiple of the difference of two bonds. Thus, by definition of the T-forward measure,

$$\frac{F(t; S, T)P(t, T)}{P(t, T)} = F(t; S, T)$$

is a martingale under the measure. The relation indicated in equation (1.70) then follows since $F(S; S, T) = R(S, T)$.

Equation (1.70) can be extended to instantaneous rates as well. The expected value of any future instantaneous spot interest rate is related to the instantaneous forward rate, under the T-forward measure:

$$E^T\left[r(T)|\Im_t\right] = f(t, T)$$

for each $0 \le t \le T$.

PROOF. Let $h_T = r(T)$ and using the risk-neutral valuation formula shown in equation (1.63) we get[17]

$$E^T\left[r(T)|\Im_t\right] = \frac{1}{P(t, T)}E\left[r(T)e^{-\int_t^T r(s)ds}\middle|\Im_t\right]$$

$$= -\frac{1}{P(t, T)}E\left[\frac{\partial}{\partial T}e^{-\int_t^T r(s)ds}\middle|\Im_t\right]$$

$$= -\frac{1}{P(t, T)}\frac{\partial P(t, T)}{\partial T}$$

$$= f(t, T)$$

1.10   THE CHOICE OF NUMERAIRE

In pricing derivatives, a payoff $h(S_T)$ is given that depends on an underlying variable S, such as a stock price, an interest rate, an exchange rate, or a commodity

---

[17]Ibid., 35.

price, at time T. Typically, pricing such a payoff amounts to computing the risk-neutral expectation

$$E^Q\left[\frac{h(S_T)}{B(T)}\right]$$

The risk-neutral numeraire is the money market (bank) account:

$$B(t) = D(0,\,t)^{-1} = \exp\left(\int_0^t r(s)ds\right)$$

By using equation (1.66) for pricing under a new numeraire N, we obtain[18]

$$E^Q\left[\frac{h(S_T)}{B(0,\,T)}\right] = N_0 E^{Q^N}\left[\frac{h(S_T)}{N_T}\right]$$

As an example, suppose the payoff $h(S_T)$ is that of a European call option with maturity T and strike X, and written on a unit-principal zero-coupon bond $P(T, S)$ with maturity $S > T$. Under the risk-neutral measure (using the bank-account numeraire):

$$E^Q\left[\frac{\max(0,\,P(T,\,S)-X)}{B(0,\,T)}\Big|\Im_t\right] = E^Q\left[e^{-\int_0^t r(s)ds}\max(0,\,P(T,\,S)-X)\Big|\Im_t\right]$$

Suppose we change the measure from the bank-account numeraire $B(t)$ to the zero-coupon bond $P(t, T)$ (the T-bond numeraire) such that:

$$P(t,\,T) = E\left[\exp\left(-\int_t^T r(t)dt\right)\right]$$

Then we need to change the underlying probability measure to the T-forward measure Q^T defined by the Radon-Nikodym derivative:[19]

$$\frac{dQ^T}{dQ} = \frac{\left(\dfrac{P(T,\,T)}{P(0,\,T)}\right)}{\left(\dfrac{B(T)}{B(0)}\right)} = \frac{P(T,\,T)B(0)}{P(0,\,T)B(T)} = \frac{e^{-\int_0^T r(s)ds}}{P(0,\,T)} = \frac{D(0,\,T)}{P(0,\,T)} \qquad (1.73)$$

---

[18]Ibid., 33.
[19]Ibid., 36.

Note $P(T, T) = B(0) = E[dQ^T/dQ] = 1$, so that the price of at time t of the derivative is:

$$\pi_t = P(t, T)E^T\left[h(T)|\Im_t\right]$$

Thus, the value of the bond call option on the zero-coupon bond is:

$$C(t, T, S, X) = P(t, T)E^T\left[\max(0, P(t, S) - X)|\Im_t\right]$$

The preceding expectation reduces to a Black-like formula if $P(T, S)$ has a lognormal distribution conditional on $\Im_t$ under the T-forward measure. Note that we can go back to the original bank-account (i.e., MMA) measure by evaluating

$$\pi_t = P(t, T)E^Q\left[h(T)\frac{dQ}{dQ^T}|\Im_t\right]$$

In general, a numeraire should be chosen so that $S(t)N_t$ is a *tradable* asset. If so, then $(S(t)N_t)/N_t = S(t)$ is a martingale under the measure Q^N. This eliminates the drift for the dynamics of S:

$$dS(t) = \sigma(t)S(t)dz(t)$$

and simplifies computing expected values of functions of S. Moreover, under a martingale measure, one can use lognormal dynamics:

$$\ln S(t) \sim N\left(\ln S_0 - \frac{1}{2}\int_0^t \sigma(s)^2\,ds, \int_0^t \sigma(s)^2\,ds\right)$$

CHAPTER 2

Monte Carlo Simulation

In this chapter we discuss Monte Carlo simulation, a technique for pricing many types of derivatives when closed-form analytical solutions are not available as well as for pricing (complex) path-dependent derivatives and for simulating multifactor stochastic diffusion processes. The technique was first used by Boyle (1977).[1] In its basic form, Monte Carlo simulation is computationally inefficient. A large number of simulations (i.e., 100,000) generally are required to achieve a high degree of pricing accuracy. However, its efficiency can be improved using control variates and quasi-random numbers (deterministic sequences).

In section 2.1, we describe the general Monte Carlo framework. In section 2.2, we discuss simulating sample paths and how to generate normal deviates to simulate Brownian motion. In section 2.3, correlated deviates and how to generate them are discussed. In section 2.4, quasi-random sequences are discussed as an improvement over pseudorandom number generators. In section 2.5, variance reduction and control variate techniques are discussed as means for improving Monte Carlo estimates. In section 2.6, a Monte Carlo implementation is provided. In section 2.7, we discuss hedge control variates—an improved control variate technique that uses the Greek hedge statistics as variates. In section 2.8, we discuss Monte Carlo simulation for valuation of path-dependent securities such as Asian options. In section 2.9, we discuss the Brownian bridge technique for simulating long-term horizon paths. In section 2.10, we discuss simulating jump-diffusion and constant elasticity of variance processes by generating Poisson and gamma deviates. Finally, in section 2.11, we give a more robust object-oriented implementation of the Monte Carlo method.

2.1 MONTE CARLO

We are interested in actually implementing the model in equation (1.18) using a Monte Carlo simulation. Suppose we wish to simulate a sample path of geometric Brownian motion process for the stock price. We divide the time interval $T - t$ into

---

[1]Boyle (1977), 323–338.

N equal time steps $\Delta t = (T - t)/N$ and simulate a path $\{S(t_i), i = 0, 1, \ldots, N\}$ starting at the known state (initial price) S_0 at time t_0. Since we already found an exact solution to the stochastic differential equation (SDE) in equation (1.8), we know that over a time step Δt the stock price changes according to:

$$S_{i+1} = S_i \exp\left\{\left(m - \frac{\sigma^2}{2}\right)\Delta t + \sigma\sqrt{\Delta t}\varepsilon_{i+1}\right\}$$

$$= S_{i+1} = S_i \exp\left\{\mu\Delta t + \sigma\sqrt{\Delta t}\varepsilon_{i+1}\right\} \tag{2.1}$$

where ε_{i+1} is a standard normal deviate and $\mu = m - \sigma^2/2$. Note that the term in the drift coefficient, $\sigma^2\tau/2$, came from the square of the Wiener increment, $(\sigma^2/2)\Delta t\varepsilon_{i+1}^2$. We know that the variance of this random variable is of the second order in Δt and we can assume that it is a deterministic quantity equal to its mean. If the stock pays a dividend, then the discretization becomes

$$S_{i+1} = S_i \exp\left\{\left(m - q - \frac{\sigma^2}{2}\right)\Delta t + \sigma\sqrt{\Delta t}\varepsilon_{i+1}\right\} \tag{2.2}$$

where q is the dividend yield, so that $\mu = m - q - (\sigma^2/2)$.

It is important to note that we cannot use equation (2.2) directly since m is unobservable in the real world as it depends on the risk preferences of investors. Thus, we let $m = r$, the risk-free rate, so that $\mu = r - q - \sigma^2/2$ and we are now pricing in the risk-neutral world. Equation (2.1) holds if we assume the log of the stock price follows an arithmetic Brownian motion as in (1.15). This is an exact approximation to the continuous-time process. This approximation matches the mean and variance of the lognormal distribution exactly. Indeed,

$$E[S_{i+1} \mid S_i] = E[S_i \exp(\mu t + \sigma\sqrt{t}\varepsilon_{i+1})]$$

$$= S_i e^{\mu\Delta t} E[e^{\sigma\varepsilon_{i+1}\sqrt{\Delta t}}]$$

The term inside the expectation operator is the moment-generating function of the standard normal. Thus,

$$E[S_{i+1} \mid S_i] = S_i e^{\mu\Delta t} e^{\frac{\sigma^2\Delta t}{2}} = S_i e^{(r - \frac{\sigma^2}{2})\Delta t + \frac{\sigma^2\Delta t}{2}}$$

$$= S_i e^{r\Delta t} \tag{2.3}$$

which is the same mean as the lognormal distribution in continuous time. The same holds true for the variance (the exercise is left to the reader). The only problem with the exact solution is that there is some computational overhead since one needs to call the exponential function every time. Note that

$$E[e^{\sigma \varepsilon_{i+1} \sqrt{\Delta t}}] = \frac{1}{\sqrt{2\pi}} \int_{-\infty}^{\infty} e^{\sigma x \sqrt{\Delta t} - x^2/2} dx = e^{\frac{\sigma^2 \Delta t}{2}}$$

In many cases, an exact solution to an SDE cannot be found, and a first- or second-order Euler approximation can be used. If we expand equation (2.1) into a Taylor series and keep only the terms of the first order in Δt, we have:

$$S_{i+1} = S_i \left(1 + r\Delta t + \sigma \sqrt{\Delta t} \varepsilon_{i+1}\right) \tag{2.4}$$

The differences between using the exact simulation in equation (2.1) and the first-order approximation in (2.4) is $O(\Delta t^2)$.

One could also use a higher-order approximation scheme for SDEs such as a Milstein approximation. For simplicity, assume that the drift and the diffusion coefficients depend on the state variable only and not on time; that is, $dx_i = \mu(x_i)dt + \sigma(x_i)dz_t$. The Milstein approximation is given by

$$x_{i+1} = x_i + \left[\mu(x_i) - \frac{1}{2}\sigma(x_i)\sigma'(x_i)\right]\Delta t + \sigma(x_i)\sqrt{\Delta t}\varepsilon_{i+1} + \frac{1}{2}\sigma(x_i)\sigma'(x_i)\varepsilon_{i+1}^2 \Delta t$$

$$+ v(x_i)\varepsilon_{i+1}(\Delta t)^{\frac{3}{2}} + \eta(x_i)(\Delta t)^2$$

$$\text{where } v(x_i) = \frac{1}{2}\mu(x)\sigma'(x) + \frac{1}{2}\mu'(x)\sigma(x) + \frac{1}{4}\sigma(x)^2\sigma''(x) \tag{2.5}$$

$$\eta(x) = \frac{1}{2}\mu(x)\mu'(x) + \frac{1}{4}\mu''(x)\sigma(x)^2$$

and prime indicates a derivative with respect to x.

2.2   GENERATING SAMPLE PATHS AND NORMAL DEVIATES

To generate sample paths you need to generate a sequence of standard normal deviates $\{\varepsilon_1, \varepsilon_2, \ldots, \varepsilon_N\}$. First it is necessary to generate uniform random numbers from 0 to 1, $\{\xi_1, \xi_2, \ldots, \xi_N\}$ and then transform them into standard normal deviates. The graph in Figure 2.1 shows a plot of some simulated asset price paths using Monte Carlo simulation. The path are computed by equation (2.1) and are driven by the random standard normal deviates.[2]

---

[2]Note that to compute each simulated path, the initial asset price, asset volatility, time to maturity, number of time steps, and drift term need to be specified.

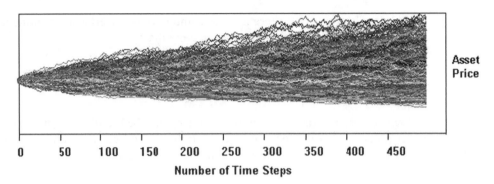

FIGURE 2.1 Simulated Asset Price Paths

No deterministic random number generators built into computer compilers are capable of producing true random numbers. These algorithms produce pseudorandom numbers usually generated from the internal computer clock. The algorithms are based on huge deterministic sequences of numbers though you provide a seed to tell the algorithm where in the sequence to start.

There are two serious problems that can occur with pseudorandom number generators: (1) The number of trials in simulation performed is larger than the size of the sequence or cycle of the random number generator, and (2) serial correlation between the numbers exists. Thus, in practice, pseudorandom number generators are not good enough for simulations for many runs since they have cycles not long enough and/or may produce "random" numbers with serial correlation.

To solve this problem and generate uniform random numbers, we will use the random number generator, *ran1*, found in Press et al., *Numerical Recipes in C* (1992). The function uses a Box-Muller transformation (described later) to ensure that a randomly generated number, using the *ran1* function, will lie in a unit circle. In turn, *gasdev* generates a Gaussian (normal) deviate from the uniform random number generated in *ran1* and takes a pointer to a long integer, which is the address of an arbitrary seed number.[3]

In the early days of simulation, one approach to generating a standard normal, $N(0, 1)$, deviate was to use the central limit theorem. Note that

$$\frac{\sum_{i=1}^{n} U_i - (n/2)}{\sqrt{n/12}} \rightarrow N(0, 1) \text{ as } n \rightarrow \infty$$

provided $U_1, \ldots, U_n$ are independent uniform $(0, 1)$ random variables. Setting $n = 12$ yields

$$\sum_{i=1}^{12} U_i - 6 \xrightarrow{D} N(0, 1)$$

---

[3]While the algorithm is good for research and projects, it is not good enough to use in commercial systems. It has been shown to produce subtle statistical biases if a sequence of "standard normal deviates" is generated with it. For commercial system, a Mersenne Twister generator can be used.

This convolution method is quite fast, but is not exact.

The most commonly used exact algorithms for generating normal random variables is to generate them in pairs. The reason is that the bivariate normal density for two independent normal random variables having mean zero and unit variance:

$$N(a,b) = \int\limits_{-\infty}^{a} \int\limits_{-\infty}^{b} \frac{1}{2\pi} \exp\left(-\frac{1}{2}\left(x^2 + y^2\right)\right) dxdy$$

has a particularly nice structure in polar coordinates. Specifically, suppose (N_1, N_2) is such a pair of normal random variables. Then, (N_1, N_2) can be expressed in polar coordinates as:

$$(N_1, N_2) = R\cos\theta, R\sin\theta$$

where θ $(0 \le \theta \le 2\pi)$ is the angular component (in radians) and R is the radial component. Due to the spherical symmetry of such a bivariate normal density, θ is normally distributed on $[0, 2\pi]$ and independent of R. Furthermore,

$$R = \sqrt{N_1^2 + N_2^2} = \sqrt{\chi^2(2)}$$

where $\chi^2(2)$ is a chi-square random variable with two degrees of freedom. Since a $\chi^2(2)$ random variable has the same distribution as $2X$, where X is exponential with parameter 1—that is, $X \sim e^{-(x-1)}$—we can utilize the following algorithm, known as the Box-Muller algorithm:

1. Generate two independent uniform $(0, 1)$ random variates U_1 and U_2.

2. Set $N_1 = \sqrt{-2\log U_1}\,\cos(2\pi U_2)$ and $N_2 \sqrt{-2\log U_2}\,\sin(2\pi U_1)$.

This can be a bit slow because of the cosine and sine calculation that needs to be performed. A variant (that is typically fast) is the polar rejection (transformation) method. This method also involves an acceptance-rejection procedure. Generate two independent uniform $(0, 1)$ random variates U_1 and U_2.

1. Set $V_1 = 2U_1 - 1$ and $V_2 = 2U_2 - 1$.

2. Compute $W = V_1^2 + V_2^2$.

3. If $W > 1$, return to step 1. Otherwise, set

$$N_1 = \sqrt{\frac{(-2\log W)}{W}}V_1 \quad \text{and} \quad N_2 = \sqrt{\frac{(-2\log W)}{W}}V_2$$

These algorithms generate pairs of independent $N(0, 1)$ random variates. To generate $N(\mu, \sigma^2)$ random variates, use the following relationship:

$$N(\mu, \sigma^2) \sim \mu + \sigma N(0, 1)$$

2.3   GENERATING CORRELATED NORMAL RANDOM VARIABLES

In many Monte Carlo simulations, especially in simulations of multivariate (multifactor) diffusion processes and multidimensional stochastic simulations (i.e., spread option models), correlation between the variates exists and must be considered since the underlying factors themselves are correlated. For example, in a stochastic volatility model, the underlying asset and its stochastic volatility are correlated, and this correlation must be captured in the correlation between variates driving the diffusion process of the underlying asset and the diffusion process of its volatility. In general, any model with multivariate normal random variables has a correlation/covariance matrix that exists. Such correlation/covariance matrix can be used to generate the joint probability distributions between the random variables.

Suppose that we wish to generate a random variable X that is multivariate normal with mean vector μ and covariance Σ. Suppose furthermore that X is a two-dimensional vector, with mean vector and covariance matrix:

$$\mu = \begin{pmatrix} \mu_1 \\ \mu_2 \end{pmatrix} \text{ and } \Sigma = \begin{pmatrix} \sigma_{11} & \sigma_{12} \\ \sigma_{21} & \sigma_{22} \end{pmatrix} = \begin{pmatrix} \sigma_1^2 & \rho\sigma_1\sigma_2 \\ \rho\sigma_1\sigma_2 & \sigma_2^2 \end{pmatrix} \tag{2.6}$$

Here, $\mu = E(X_i)$, $\sigma_i^2 = \text{Var}(X_i)$, and ρ is the correlation between X_1 and X_2. We now describe a means of generating X_1 and X_2 from a pair of independent $N(0, 1)$ random variables N_1 and N_2. Note that we may express X_1 in terms of N_1 as follows:

$$X_1 = \mu_1 + \sigma_1 N_1$$

For X_2, we try to write it in the form:

$$X_2 = \mu_2 + a N_1 + b N_2$$

Recall that since N_1 is independent of N_2,

$$\text{Var}(X_2) = E[(X_2 - \mu_2)^2] = a^2 + b^2 = \sigma_2^2$$

Also,

$$\text{Cov}(X_1, X_2) = E[(X_1 - \mu_1)(X_2 - \mu_2)] = a\sigma_1 - \rho\sigma_1\sigma_2$$

Solving these two equations, we get

$$a = \rho\sigma_2 \quad \text{and} \quad b = \sqrt{(1-\rho^2)}\sigma_2$$

In other words,

$$\begin{pmatrix} X_1 \\ X_2 \end{pmatrix} = \begin{pmatrix} \mu_1 \\ \mu_2 \end{pmatrix} + \begin{pmatrix} \sigma_1 & 0 \\ \rho\sigma_2 & \sqrt{1-\rho^2}\,\sigma_2 \end{pmatrix} \begin{pmatrix} N_1 \\ N_2 \end{pmatrix} \tag{2.7}$$

or in matrix notation, $\mathbf{X} = \mu + \mathbf{LN}$ where $\mathbf{L}$ is lower triangular. Thus, by generating a pair of independent $N(0, 1)$ random variables, we can obtain $\mathbf{X}$ via the preceding affine transformation. That methodology works in general (for $\mathbf{X}$ having more than 2 components). In general, $\mathbf{X}$ can be written in the form

$$\mathbf{X} = \mu + \mathbf{LN} \tag{2.8}$$

where $\mathbf{N}$ has the same number of components as does $\mathbf{X}$ (i.e., same vector size) and consists of $N(0, 1)$ random variables. To connect the matrix $\mathbf{L}$ to Σ, observe that

$$\Sigma = E[(\mathbf{X} - \mu)(\mathbf{X} - \mu)'] = E[(\mathbf{LN})(\mathbf{LN})'] = E[(\mathbf{LN})(\mathbf{N'L'})]$$

Since $\mathbf{N}$ consists of $N(0, 1)$ random variables, $E[\mathbf{NN'}] = \mathbf{I}$, the identity matrix,[4] and we can write Σ as

$$\Sigma = E[(\mathbf{LL'})] = I \tag{2.9}$$

Let $\mathbf{L} = \Sigma^{1/2}$ so that $\mathbf{L}$ is a "square root" of Σ. Furthermore, because Σ is symmetric and positive semidefinite, $\mathbf{L}$ can always be chosen to be a lower triangular matrix with real entries. Writing

$$\Sigma = \mathbf{LL'} \tag{2.10}$$

is called the Cholesky factorization[5] of Σ. Clearly, the key to generating $\mathbf{X}$ is the computation of the Cholesky factor $\mathbf{L}$. Thus, to produce correlated variables from

---

[4]

$$E[\mathbf{NN'}] = E\begin{bmatrix} \chi^2(1) & 0 \\ 0 & \chi^2(1) \end{bmatrix} = \begin{bmatrix} 1 & 0 \\ 0 & 1 \end{bmatrix} = \mathbf{I}$$

Note that the expectation (mean) of chi-squared random variable is its number of degrees of freedom.
[5]See Press et al. (1992), 96–98. See also R. B. Davies' Newmat matrix library (www.robertnz.net).

uncorrelated (independent) ones, we need to find an **L** that solves the matrix equation (2.10).

We can use a Cholesky decomposition for $n = 3$ deviates. Suppose z_1, z_2, and z_3 are random samples from three independent normal distributions with the following correlation structure:

$$\rho = \begin{pmatrix} 1 & \rho_{12} & \rho_{13} \\ \rho_{21} & 1 & \rho_{23} \\ \rho_{31} & \rho_{32} & 1 \end{pmatrix}$$

where $\rho_{ij} = \rho_{ji}$ since ρ is symmetric. Random deviates with this correlation structure are

$$x_1 = z_1$$

$$x_1 = \rho_{12} z_1 + \sqrt{1 - \rho_{12}^2}\, z_2$$

$$x_3 = \alpha_1 z_1 + \alpha_2 z_2 + \alpha_3 z_3 \qquad (2.11)$$

where

$$\alpha_1 = \rho_{13}$$

$$\alpha_2 = \frac{\rho_{23} - \rho_{12}\rho_{13}}{\sqrt{1 - \rho_{12}^2}}$$

$$\alpha_3 = \sqrt{1 - \alpha_1^2 + \alpha_2^2}$$

so that

$$\mathbf{L} = \begin{pmatrix} 1 & 0 & 0 \\ \rho_{12} & \sqrt{1 - \rho_{12}^2} & 0 \\ \rho_{13} & \dfrac{\rho_{23} - \rho_{12}\rho_{13}}{\sqrt{1 - \rho_{12}^2}} & \sqrt{1 - \rho_{13}^2 - \dfrac{(\rho_{23} - \rho_{12}\rho_{13})^2}{1 - \rho_{12}^2}} \end{pmatrix} \qquad (2.12)$$

An alternative approach to generating n correlated deviates, z_i, $i = 1, \ldots, n$, that are jointly normally distributed with mean zero and variance 1 with infinitesimal increments dz_i, is to use principal component analysis[6] to write their correlation/covariance matrix, Σ as

$$\Sigma = \Gamma\Lambda\Gamma'$$

---

[6]Clewlow and Strickland (1998a), 128.

where Γ is the matrix of n eigenvectors $\mathbf{v}_i$'s, $i = 1, \ldots, n$, and Λ is the matrix of n associated eigenvectors λ_i's, Γ:

$$\Gamma = \begin{bmatrix} v_{11} & v_{12} & \cdots & v_{1n} \\ v_{21} & v_{22} & \cdots & v_{2n} \\ \cdots & \cdots & \cdots & \cdots \\ v_{n1} & v_{n2} & \cdots & v_{nn} \end{bmatrix} \quad \text{and} \quad \Lambda = \begin{bmatrix} \lambda_1 & 0 & 0 & 0 \\ 0 & \lambda_2 & 0 & 0 \\ 0 & 0 & \cdots & 0 \\ 0 & 0 & 0 & \lambda_n \end{bmatrix}$$

This is the eigensystem representation of the covariance matrix of the correlated variables. Since the eigenvectors are linear combinations of the correlated variables that give independent variables, we can invert this relationship to obtain the linear combinations of independent variables that reproduce the original covariance matrix. Since the transpose of Γ is equal to its inverse (the eigenvectors of Γ are orthogonal to each other), the rows of Γ represent the proportions of a set of n independent Brownian motions dw_i, $i = 1, \ldots, n$, which when linearly combined reproduce the original correlated Brownian motions. The eigenvalues represent the variances of the independent Brownian motions. Thus, we can reproduce the correlated Brownian motions dz_i from the linear combination of the independent Brownian motions dw_i:

$$dz_1 = v_{11}\sqrt{\lambda_1}dw_1 + v_{12}\sqrt{\lambda_2}dw_2 + \ldots + v_{1n}\sqrt{\lambda_n}dw_n$$
$$dz_2 = v_{21}\sqrt{\lambda_2}dw_1 + v_{22}\sqrt{\lambda_2}dw_2 + \ldots + v_{2n}\sqrt{\lambda_n}dw_n$$
$$\ldots$$
$$dz_n = v_{n1}\sqrt{\lambda_2}dw_1 + v_{n2}\sqrt{\lambda_2}dw_2 + \ldots + v_{nn}\sqrt{\lambda_n}dw_n$$

This method is used extensively when pricing multivariate diffusion processes such as a stochastic volatility spread option (see section 7.10 and Chapter 9) where correlated deviates must be generated.

The following is the code that will generate the preceding procedure for four correlated deviates.

```
class MatrixUtil
{
  public:
    /*******************************************************************************
    genCorrelatedDeviates : computes 4 correlated deviates for Monte Carlo
       simulation
    [in]:   const SymmetricMatrix& R   : (symmetric) correlation matrix
            double dt                  : time step size
            double z[]                 : array to store correlated deviates
    [out]:  double z[]                 : array of correlated deviates
    *******************************************************************************/
```

```cpp
double* genCorrelatedDeviates(const SymmetricMatrix& R, double dt, double z[])
{
  int i, j;
  double sum[4] = {0.0};
  double deviate = 0.0;                       // standard normal deviate
  int m = R.Nrows();                          // number of rows in correlation
                                              // matrix

  std::vector<double> dz;                     // vector of correlated deviates
  std::vector<double> eigenValue;             // vector of eigenvalues
  std::vector<double> eigenVector[4];         // array of vector of
                                              // eigenvectors
  std::vector<double>::iterator eigenVecIter; // vector iterator
  double lambda[4] = {0.0};                   // stores eigenvalues of
                                              // correlation matrix R

  double dw[4] = {0.0};                       // stores correlated deviates
  DiagonalMatrix D(m);                        // diagonal matrix
  Matrix V(m,m);                              // m x n matrix
  D = genEigenValues(R);                      // get eigenvalues
  V = genEigenVectors(R);                     // get eigenvectors
  // store eigenvalues
  for (i = 0; i < m; i++)
  {
    eigenValue.push_back(D.element(i,i));
    lambda[i] = D.element(i,i);
  }

  // stores rows of eigenvectors so that we can compute
  // dz[i] = v[i][1]*sqrt(eigenvalue[1])*dw1 + v[i][2]*sqrt(eigenvalue[2])*dw2
  // + . . .
  for (i = 0; i < m; i++)
  {
    for (j = 0; j < m; j++)
    {
      eigenVector[i].push_back(V.element(i,j));
    }
  }

  srand(0);                            // initialize random number generator
  long seed = (long) rand() % 100;     // generate seed
  long *idum = &seed;

  // generate uncorrelated deviates
  for (i = 0; i < m; i++)
  {
    deviate = util.NormalDeviate(idum);
    dw[i] = deviate*sqrt(dt);
  }

  // generate correlated deviates
  for (i = 0; i < m; i++)
  {
    eigenVecIter = eigenVector[i].begin();
    for (j = 0; j < m; j++)
    {
```

```
            sum[i] += (*eigenVecIter)*sqrt(lambda[j])*dw[j];
            eigenVecIter++;
        }
        z[i] = sum[i];
    }
    return z;
}

    // other defined methods . . .
};
```

The code for generating correlated deviates from a Cholesky decomposition is:

```
#include "newmatap.h"
#include <vector>
#include <math.h>
#include "Constants.h"
#include "StatUtility.h"
class MatrixUtil
{
  public:
    /**********************************************************************
    genCorrelatedDeviatesCholesky    : computes correlated deviates from a
                                       Cholesky decomposition
    [in]:  SymmetricMatrix& R         : correlation matrix
           double dt                  : step size
           double z[]                 : correlated deviates array to be returned
    [out]: double z[]                 : array of correlated deviates
    **********************************************************************/
    double* genCorrelatedDeviatesCholesky(const SymmetricMatrix& R, double dt,
      double z[])
    {
      int m = R.Nrows();               // number of rows
      int n = R.Ncols();               // number of columns
      Matrix lb(m,n);                  // lower-banded (lb) matrix
      StatUtil util;                   // Statistical utility class
      double deviate = 0.0;            // standard normal deviate
      double dw[4] = {0.0};            // stores deviate*sqrt(dt)
      double sum = 0.0;
      long seed = 0;                   // seed for RNG
      long* idum = 0;                  // stores address of seed
      int i, j;

      lb = Cholesky(R);                // calls Cholesky routine in NEWMAT library

      srand(time(0));                  // initialize RNG
      seed = (long) rand() % 100;      // generate seed
      idum = &seed;                    // store address of seed
      // generate uncorrelated deviates
```

```
    for (i = 0; i < m; i++)
    {
      deviate = util.gasdev(idum); // generate normal (gaussian) deviate
      dw[i] = deviate*sqrt(dt);
    }

    // generate correlated deviates
    for (i = 0; i < m; i++)
    {
      sum = 0;
      for (j = 0; j < m; j++)
      {
        sum += lb.element(i,j)*dw[j];
      }
      z[i] = sum;
    }
    return z;
  }
  . . .
};
```

The code makes use of a good matrix library, Newmat, written by R. B. Davies.[7] The matrix library contains many matrix manipulation and computational routines such as the computation of the eigenvectors and eigenvalues from a given (symmetric) matrix like the covariance/correlation matrix Σ. However, such a covariance/correlation matrix that is passed into the method *genCorrelatedDeviates* needs to be known a priori. One can make assumptions about what these will be or try to estimate them from historical data. For example, if one wants to estimate the correlation between the deviates of a stock and its volatility, one could use the estimated historical correlation. However, because correlation estimates are time-varying and unstable, one must use caution when inputting a specified correlation matrix at different times.

2.4   QUASI-RANDOM SEQUENCES

A quasi-random sequence, also called a low-discrepancy sequence, is a deterministic sequence of representative samples from a probability distribution. Quasi-random number generators (RNGs) differ from pseudo-RNGs in that pseudo-RNGs try to generate realistic random numbers, while quasi-generators create numbers that are evenly spaced in an interval—they have a more uniform discrepancy than pseudo-

---

[7]It can be downloaded at www.robertnz.net/download.html.

RNGs.[8] For M simulations, quasi-random sequences have a standard error proportional to $1/M$, which is much smaller for large M than the standard error of pseudo-RNGs, which is proportional to

$$1/\sqrt{M}$$

Moreover, for a discrepancy of n points, D_n, low-discrepancy sequences have a discrepancy in the order of $O((\log n)^d/n)$ while a uniform random number sequence has a discrepancy in the order of

$$O\left(1/\sqrt{n}\right)$$

Thus, quasi-RNGs are more efficient than pseudorandom numbers. Figure 2.2 shows how 2,000 quasi-random values are uniformly distributed while the 2,000 pseudorandom values are not.

As can be seen, the problem with pseudorandom numbers is that clumpiness occurs, which biases the results. A very large number of samples is needed to make the bias negligible. On the other hand, quasi-random numbers or low-discrepancy sequences are designed to appear random, but not clumpy. In fact, a quasi-random sample is not independent from previous samples. It "remembers" the previous samples and tries to position itself away from all previous samples so that points are more uniformly distributed, and thus have a low discrepancy. This characteristic of low-discrepancy sequences yields fast convergence in Monte Carlo simulation and is why they are preferred to pseudorandom numbers.

Two well-known low-discrepancy sequences are Sobol (1967) and Faure (1982).[9] The Sobol method generates numbers between 0 and 1 from a set of binary fractions of length w bits called direction numbers V_i, $i = 1, \ldots, w$. The jth number X_j is generated by doing a bitwise exclusive-or (XOR) of all the direction

---

[8] The mathematical definition of discrepancy of n sample points is

$$D_n = \sup_{J} \left| \frac{A(J; n)}{n} - V(J) \right|$$

where

$$J = \prod_{j=1}^{d} [0, u_i) = [0, u_i)^d, \; u_i \le 1$$

d is the dimension, $A(J; n)$ are the number of points landed in region J, and $V(J)$ is the volume of J.

[9] There are other low-discrepancy sequences, including Halton (1960), Niederreiter (1992), and Niederreiter and Shiue (1995).

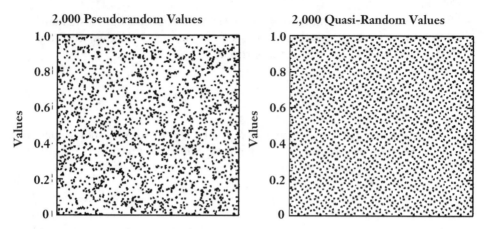

FIGURE 2.2   Pseudorandom and Quasi-Random Values

numbers so that the ith bit of the number is nonzero. The effect is such that the
bits toggle on and off at different rates. The kth bit switches once in 2^{k-1} steps so
that the least significant bit switches the fastest, and the most significant bit
switches the slowest.

Each different "Sobol sequence (or component of an n-dimensional sequence)
is based on a different primitive polynomial over the integers modulo 2, that is, a
polynomial whose coefficients are either 0 or 1, and which generates a maximal
length shift register sequence."[10] Following Press et al. (1992), suppose P is such a
polynomial, of degree q,

$$P = x^q + a_1 x^{q-1} + a_2 x^{q-2} + \ldots + a_{q-1} x + 1$$

Define a sequence of integers M_i by the q-term recurrence relation,

$$M_i = 2a_1 M_{i-1} \oplus 2^2 a_2 M_{i-2} \oplus \Lambda \oplus 2^{q-1} M_{i-q+1} a_{q-1} \oplus (2^q M_{i-q} \pm M_{i-q})$$

The bitwise XOR operator is denoted $\oplus$. The starting values for this recurrence are
that $M_1, \ldots, M_q$ can be arbitrary odd integers less than $2, \ldots, 2^q$, respectively.
Then, the direction numbers V_i are given by[11]

$$V_i = M_i / 2^i \qquad i = 1, \ldots, w$$

---

[10]Press et al. (1992), 311.
[11]Ibid., 312.

The following is code to compute a Sobol sequence.[12] The methods are an inline part of the *StatUtility* class that contains methods for aiding in numerical and statistical computations.

```cpp
#include <time.h>

#define GRAY(n) (n ^ ( n >> 1 )) // for Sobol sequence
#define MAXDIM 5
#define VMAX 30

struct sobolp
{
  double sequence[MAXDIM];
  int x[MAXDIM];
  int v[MAXDIM][VMAX];
  double RECIPD;
  int _dim;     // dimension of the sample space
  int _skip;
  unsigned long _nextn;
  unsigned long cur_seed;
};

class StatUtility
{
  public:
    /***********************************************************************
    sobolp_generateSamples             : generates a Sobol sequence
    [in]:  struct sobolp* config       : pointer to Sobol structure
           double* samples             : pointer to sample values
    [out]: void
    ***********************************************************************/
    inline void sobolp_generateSamples(struct sobolp* config, double* samples)
    {
      int i;
      nextSobol(config, config->cur_seed);
      config->cur_seed++;
      for(i = 0; i < config->_dim; i++ )
        samples[i] = config->sequence[i];
    }

    /***********************************************************************
    nextSobolNoSeed                    : generates the next Sobol seed number to
                                         generate the next Sobol value
    [in]: struct sobolp* config        : pointer to Sobol structure
    [out]: void
    ***********************************************************************/
    inline static void nextSobolNoSeed(struct sobolp* config)
```

---

[12]The code was adapted from Austen McDonald (www.austenmcdonald.com/montecarlo), who massaged the original Sobol version into a parallel version. A version from Press et al., *Numerical Recipes in C*, is given in Appendix E.

```
{
  int c = 1;
  int i;
  int save = config->_nextn;
  while((save %2) == 1)
  {
    c += 1;
    save = save /2;
  }
  for(i=0;i<config->_dim;i++)
  {
    config->x[i] = config->x[i]^(config->v[i][c-1]<< (VMAX-c));
    config->sequence[i] = config->x[i]*config->RECIPD;
  }
  config->_nextn += 1;
}
/*****************************************************************************
sobolp_init                  : initializes the Sobol algorithm
[in]:   sobolp* config       : pointer to Sobol
        int dim              : dimension of the sample spaces
        unsigned long seed   : seed for Sobol number generator
[out] : void
*****************************************************************************/
inline void sobolp_init(struct sobolp* config, int dim, unsigned long seed)
{
  int d[MAXDIM], POLY[MAXDIM];
  int save;
  int m,i,j,k;

  config->_dim = dim;
  config->_nextn = 0;
  config->RECIPD = 1.0 / pow( 2.0, VMAX );
  config->cur_seed = seed;

  POLY[0] = 3; d[0] = 1;    // x + 1
  POLY[1] = 7; d[1] = 2;    // x^2 + x + 1
  POLY[2] = 11; d[2] = 3;   // x^3 + x + 1
  POLY[3] = 19; d[3] = 4;   // x^4 + x + 1
  POLY[4] = 37; d[4] = 5;   // x^5 + x^2 + 1

  for(i = 0; i < config->_dim; i++ )
    for(j = 0; j < d[i]; j++ )
      config->v[i][j] = 1;

  for( i = 0; i < config->_dim; i++ )
  {
    for( j = d[i]; j < VMAX; j++ )
    {
      config->v[i][j] = config->v[i][j-d[i]];
      save = POLY[i];
      m = pow( 2, d[i] );
      for( k = d[i]; k > 0; k-- )
      {
        config->v[i][j] = config->v[i][j] ^ m*(save%2)*config->v[i][j-k];
```

```
            save = save/2;
            m = m/2;
         }
      }
   }

   for( i = 0; i < config->_dim; i++ )
      config->x[i]=0;

   config->_skip = pow( 2, 6 );

   for( i = 1; i <= config->_skip; i++ )
      nextSobolNoSeed(config);
   }
};
```

Another Sobol implementation is given in Appendix E from *Numerical Recipes in C* by Press et al. (1992), which is actually faster since there are fewer method calls. Here is a Monte Carlo implementation using the Sobol sequence:

```
/**************************************************************************/
MonteCarloSobol       : values a European call option using Faure sequence for
                        variance reduction
[in]:   double price  : asset price
        double strike : strike price
        double vol    : volatility
        double rate   : risk-free rate
        double div    : dividend yield
        double T      : option maturity
        char type     : type of option
        long N        : number of time steps
        long M        : number of simulations
[out] : double        : call price
**************************************************************************/
double MonteCarloMethod::MonteCarloSobol(double price, double strike, double vol,
   double rate, double div, double T, char type, long N, long M)
{
   int i, j;
   double sum1 = 0.0;              // sum of payoffs
   double sum2 = 0.0;              // sum of squared payoffs
   double value = 0.0;            // stores value of option for each simulation
   double S1 = price;             // stock price for +deviate
   double S2 = price;             // stock price for -deviate
   double lnS1 = log(price);      // log of the initial stock price for +deviate
   double lnS2 = log(price);      // log of the initial stock price for -deviate
   double SD;                     // standard deviation
   double SE;                     // standard error
   long dim = N;                  // dimension of Sobol sequence
```

```
double dt = T/N;                        // time step
double mu = rate - div - 0.5*vol*vol;   // drift
double rands[5];                        // stores random variables
cout.precision(4);                      // output decimal format precision
int cnt = 0;                            // counter
struct sobolp sp;                       // Sobol sequence structure
srand(time(0));                         // initialize RNG
long seed = (long) rand() % 100;        // generate seed

// initialize Sobol sequnce
util.sobolp_init(&sp,dim,seed);

for (i = 0; i < M; i++)
{
  // initalize stock price for the next simulation
  lnS1 = log(price);
  lnS2 = log(price);

  for (j = 0; j < N; j++)
  {
    // generate Sobol samples
    util.sobolp_generateSamples(&sp,rands);

    // generate path and antithetic path
    lnS1 = lnS1 + mu*dt + vol*sqrt(dt)*rands[cnt];
    lnS2 = lnS2 = mu*dt + vol*sqrt(dt)*(-rands[cnt]);

    // keep track of Sobol number to use
    if ((cnt + 1) % N == 0)
      cnt = 0;
    else
      cnt++;
  }

  // convert back to lognormal random variables
  S1 = exp(lnS1);
  S2 = exp(lnS2);

  if (type == 'C')
    value = 0.5*(max(0, S1 - strike) + max(0, S2 - strike));
  else
    value = 0.5*(max(0, strike - S1) + max(0,strike - S2));

  sum1 = sum1 + value;
  sum2 = sum2 + value*value;
}

// compute standard deviation
SD = sqrt((exp(-2*rate*T)/(M-1))*(sum2 - (sum1*sum1)/M));
cout << "stddev " << " " < SD < endl;

// compute standard error
SE = SD/sqrt(M_);
cout << "stderr " << " " << SE << endl;

return exp(-rate*T)*sum1/M;
}
```

The number of time steps to be used along each path should equal the dimension of the Sobol sequence.

In a Monte Carlo simulation, the number of time steps N is the dimension of a low-discrepancy sequence, that is, the number of independent quasi-random numbers to be generated simultaneously. The quasi-random numbers are generated simultaneously so that the samples and increments along the path are independent and identically distributed. Let x_k, $k = 1, \ldots, N$, be N quasi-random numbers. Then the Faure sequence of length M (the number of simulations) is defined by

$$x_k = \sum_{l=0}^{m} \frac{a_{k,l}}{p^{l+1}}$$

(2.13)

where m is the number of digits in the p representation of M, that is,

$$m = \text{int}\left[\frac{\log(M)}{\log(p)}\right]$$

$$a_{0,l} = \text{int}\left[\frac{M\%p^{l+1}}{p}\right]$$

(2.14)

$$a_{k,l} = \sum_{q-l}^{m} \frac{q!}{l!(q-l)!}a_{k-1,q}\%p$$

and p is the smallest prime number greater than or equal to N.[13] The "int" operator denotes the integer part of the expression in brackets and % denotes the modulo operator that is the remainder after division.

The following is code to implement a Faure sequence. The function *generateFaure* is an inline function in the StatUtility class. Other helper inline utility functions are also provided.

```
class StatUtility
{
  public:
    /***********************************************************************/
    generateFaure M              : generates a Faure sequence of length M
    [in] long N                  : number of time steps
      long M                     : number of simulations
    [out]: vector<double> X      : the Faure sequence
    ***********************************************************************/
    inline vector<double> generateFaure(long N, long M)
```

---

[13]Clewlow and Strickland (1998a), 131.

```
{
  int p = generatePrime(N);
  int l, q, k;
  long v1, v2, v3;
  long value = 0;
  long a[250][250] = {0};
  int m = (int) (log(M)/log(p));
  if (m == 0)
    m = 1;
  long x[] = {0};
  unsigned long fact = 0;

  for (k = 1; k <= N; k++)              // number of time steps
  {
    for (l = 0; l <= m; l++)
    {
      value = pow(p,l+1);
      a[0][l] = (int)((M % value)/p);

      for (q = 1; q <= m; q++)
      {
        v1 = factorial(q);
        v2 = factorial(q-1);
        v3 = factorial(l);
        fact = v1/(v2*v3);

        value = fact*a[k-1][q] % p;
        a[k][l] = a[k][l] + value;
      }
      x[k] = x[k] + a[k][l]/pow(p,l+1);
    }
    X.push_back((double)x[k]);
  }
  return X;
}

/******************************************************************************
factorial : computes the factorial of a number
[in]: N : number to factorialize
[out]: N!
******************************************************************************/
inline long factorial(long N)
{
if ((N == 1) || (N == 0))
  return 1;
else
  return N*factorial(N-1);
}

/******************************************************************************/
generatePrime: This function computes the smallest prime greater than or equal
               to N
[in]: long N : find prime >= N
```

```
[out]: prime >= N
/**************************************************************************/
inline long generatePrime(long N)
{
  long i = N;
  bool flag = false;

  do
  {
    // check if number is prime
    if ((i % 2 != 0) && (i % 3 != 0) && (i % 4 != 0) && (i % 5 != 0)
      && (i % 7 != 0) && (i % 8 != 0) && (i % 9 != 0))
      flag = true;
    else
      i++;

  }
  while (flag != true);

  return i;
}

/**************************************************************************/
polarRejection
This function computes two standard deviates using polar rejection
  (transformation) method Returns the first deviate and stores the second
  deviates in a vector Y so that is can be used for another call rather than
  throwing it away.

[in]:  double y       : seed value
       int i          : ith standard deviate
[out]: Y[i]           : ith standard normal deviate in Y
/**************************************************************************/
inline double polarRejection(double y, int i)
{
  double w = 0.0;
  double x1, x2, z1, z2, c;
  double temp = 0.0;
  double *idum = &y;

  do
  {
    x1 = gasdev((long*)idum);
    x2 = gasdev((long*)idum);
    w = x1*x1 + x2*x2;
  }
  while (w >= 1);

  c = sqrt(-2*(log(w)/w));
  z1 = c*x1;
  Y.push_back(z1);
  z2 = c*x2;
  Y.push_back(z2);

  return Y[i];
```

```
    }
    . . . // other methods
    . . .
};
```

The following is a Monte Carlo implementation using the Faure sequence to value a European call option with maturity *T*.

```
/**************************************************************************/
MonteCarloFaureQuasiRandom : values a European call option using Faure sequence for
                             variance reduction
[in]:     double S         : asset price
          double X         : strike price
          double vol       : volatility
          double rate      : risk-free rate
          double div       : dividend yield
          double T         : option maturity
          long N           : number of time steps
          long M:          : number of simulations
[out] : double             : callValue
/**************************************************************************/
double MonteCarloMethod::MonteCarloFaureQuasiRandom (double S, double X, double
  vol, double rate, double div, double T, long N, long M)
{
  int i, j, k;
  double dt = T/N;                            // step step
  double mudt = (rate - div - 0.5*vol*vol)*dt; // drift
  double voldt = vol*sqrt(dt);                // diffusion term
  double sum = 0.0;
  double sum1 = 0.0;
  double lnSt, lnSt1, St, St1;
  double lnS = log(S);
  double deviate = 0.0;
  double callValue = 0.0;I
  double SD = 0.0;                            // standard deviation
  double SE = 0.0;                            // standard error
  vector<double> x;                           // stores Faure sequence
  cout.setf(ios::showpoint);
  cout.precision(3);

  k = 0;
  for (i = 1; i <= M; i++)
  {
    // generate Faure sequence
    x = util.generateFaure(N,M);

    // initialize log asset prices for next simulation path
    lnSt = lnS;
    lnSt1 = lnS;
```

```
for (j = 0; j < N; j++)
{
  // get standard normal deviate using polar rejection method
  deviate = util.polarRejection(x[j],k);

  nSt = lnSt + mudt + voldt*deviate;

  // compute antithetic
  lnSt1 = lnSt1 + mudt + voldt*(-deviate);
  // increment index to retrieve deviate stored in vector Y in polar rejection
     method
  k++;
}
St = exp(lnSt);
St1 = exp(lnSt1);

  callValue = 0.5*(max(0, St - X) + max(0,St1-X));
  sum = sum + callValue;
  sum1 = sum1 + callValue*callValue;
}

callValue = exp(-rate*T)*(sum/M)
SD = sqrt(exp(-2*rate*T)*(sum1/M) - callValue*callValue);
cout << "stdev = " << SD << endl;

SE = SD/sqrt(M-1);
cout << "stderr = " << SE << endl;

return callValue;
}
```

2.5   VARIANCE REDUCTION AND CONTROL VARIATE TECHNIQUES

Suppose we can simulate an independent and identically distributed (i.i.d.) sequence $\{f_i^*, i = 1, \ldots, M$, where each f_i^* has expectation f and variance σ^2. An estimator of f based on M simulations is then the sample mean:

$$\frac{1}{M} \sum_{i=1}^{M} f_i^* \tag{2.15}$$

By the central limit theorem, for large M this sample mean is approximately normally distributed with mean f and standard deviation

$$\sigma/\sqrt{M}$$

The estimate of the option's price converges to the true option's price f with the standard error

$$\sigma/\sqrt{M}$$

The 95 percent confidence interval is

$$f - 1.96\left(\sigma/\sqrt{M}\right) < f^* < f + 1.96\left(\sigma/\sqrt{M}\right)$$

Convergence of the crude Monte Carlo is slow to the order of

$$1/\sqrt{M}$$

To increase the accuracy 10 times, we need to run 100 times more simulations of sample paths. On the other hand, decreasing the variance σ^2 by a factor of 10 does as much for error reduction as increasing the number of simulations by a factor of 100.

The simplest variance reduction procedure is use of *antithetic variates*. For each path simulated with ε_i^k (denoted as the ith deviate, $i = 1 \ldots N$ on the kth path, $k = 1 \ldots M$) an identical path is simulated with $-\varepsilon_i^k$. The payoff F_k for the path is calculated with ε_i^k, and also the payoff $\hat{F}_k$ for the path with $-\varepsilon_i^k$. Then the average is taken:

$$\frac{1}{2}(F_k + \hat{F}_k)$$

Although ε_i^k's are samples from a standard normal distribution with mean 0, in a sample you will get some nonzero mean. The antithetic variates procedure corrects this bias by averaging out the deviations and centers the mean at 0.

Another variance reduction technique is to use *control variates*. Control variates are random variables, whose expected value (mean) that we know is correlated with the variable we are trying to estimate (i.e., the derivative security we want to value).[14] The principle underlying this technique is to "use what you know." Suppose you are trying to simulate an estimate for the price of a complex security. Suppose also that you know a closed-form analytical formula for the price of a similar, but simpler, security. The price of the complex security can be represented as:

$$f_{complex} = f_{simple} + (f_{complex} - f_{simple}) \tag{2.16}$$

---

[14]Ibid., 95.

Since you know the price f_{simple} from the closed-form formula, you need only estimate the difference $\varepsilon^* = (f_{complex} - f_{simple})$ via simulation:

$$f^*_{complex} = f_{simple} + \varepsilon^* \tag{2.17}$$

Since the securities are similar, the difference ε^* is small relative to the value f_{simple}, we can find the bulk of the value of our complex security exactly without errors, and our errors are in the relatively smaller estimate of the difference in ε^*.

As an example for practical use of control variates, we use arithmetic and geometric Asian options. We know the analytical formula for the price of a geometric Asian option (see Chapter 5), but in practice we are most interested in the price of an arithmetic Asian option. There is no simple analytical formula for arithmetic Asian options. We note that the price of otherwise identical arithmetic and geometric Asian options are rather close. Thus, we can represent the price of an arithmetic Asian option as:

$$f^*_{arithmetic} = f^*_{geometric} + \varepsilon^*$$

We evaluate this technique in section 2.8.

2.6   MONTE CARLO IMPLEMENTATION

The best way to simulate geometric Brownian motion (GBM) of the underlying asset (random variable) is to use the process for the natural logarithm of the variable, which follows arithmetic Brownian motion (ABM) and is normally distributed. Let $x(t) = \ln(S(t))$. Then we have

$$dx(t) = (r - q - \frac{1}{2}\sigma^2)dt + \sigma dz(t) \tag{2.18}$$

Equation (2.18) can be discretized by changing the infinitesimal changes dx, dt, and dz into small discrete changes Δx, Δt, and Δz:

$$\Delta x = (r - q - \frac{1}{2}\sigma^2)\Delta t + \sigma \Delta z \tag{2.19}$$

This representation involves no approximation since it is actually the solution of the SDE in equation (2.8), which can be be written as

$$x(t + \Delta t) = x(t) + (r - q - \frac{1}{2}\sigma^2)\Delta t + \sigma(z(t + \Delta t) - z(t)) \tag{2.20}$$

We can write equation (2.20) in terms of the underlying asset price S:

$$S(t + \Delta t) = S(t) \exp\left((r - q - \frac{1}{2}\sigma^2)\Delta t + \sigma\left(z(t + \Delta t) - z(t)\right) \right) \qquad (2.21)$$

where $z(t)$ is standard Brownian motion. The random increment $z(t + \Delta t) - z(t)$ has mean zero and variance Δt. It can be simulated by random samples of

$$\varepsilon\sqrt{\Delta t}$$

where ε is a standard deviate drawn from a standard normal distribution. Dividing up the time to maturity (the time period over which we want to simulate), T, into N time steps, each time step is of size $\Delta t = T/N$. Consequently, we can generate values of $S(t)$ at the end of these intervals, $t_i = i\Delta t$, $i = 1, \ldots, N$ using equation (2.20) by computing:

$$x(t_i) = x(t_{i-1}) + (r - q - \frac{1}{2}\sigma^2)\Delta t + \sigma\varepsilon_i\sqrt{\Delta t} \quad i = 1, \ldots, N \qquad (2.22)$$

then computing:

$$S(t_i) = \exp(x(t_i)) \qquad\qquad i = 1, \ldots, N \qquad (2.23)$$

for each time step of each of the M simulations, and then finally computing the payoff $\max(0, S(T) - X)$ at maturity (i.e., the final time step on a given path). To obtain an estimate $\hat{C}$ of the call price, C we take the discounted average of all the simulated payoffs.

$$\hat{C} = e^{-rT} \frac{1}{M} \sum_{j=1}^{M} \max(0, S_j(T) - X) \qquad (2.24)$$

Note that to compute a European call estimate under GBM we can let $N = 1$. Moreover, since we have a closed-form solution—equation (2.21)—to the underlying SDE, samples of $S(T)$ can be found directly without simulating the entire path. In general, however, $N > 1$, since there are many types of derivatives (i.e., path-dependent options), where only an approximate discretization of the SDE to the continuous SDE can be used by taking small time steps.

The following code implements the Monte Carlo simulation under the risk-neutral process in equation (2.23). It uses the antithetic variates to reduce the variance.

```
/****************************************************************************/
MonteCarloAntithetic      : values a European call option using antithetic variates
[in]:    double price     : asset price
         double strike    : strike price
         double vol       : volatility
         double rate      : risk-free rate
         double div       : dividend yield
         double T         : option maturity
         long N           : number of time steps
         long M           : number of simulations
[out]    double value       call value
/****************************************************************************/
double MonteCarloMethod::MonteCarloAntithetic (double price, double strike, double
  vol, double rate, double div, double T, long M, long N, char type)
{

  int i, j;
  double deviate;                          // standard normal deviate
  double sum1 = 0.0;                       // sum of payoffs
  double sum2 = 0.0;                       // sum of squared payoffs
  double value = 0.0;                      // value of option
  double S1 = price;                       // stock price for +deviate
  double S2 = price;                       // stock price for -deviate
  double lnS1 = log(price);                // log of the initial stock price for
                                           // +deviate
  double lnS2 = log(price);                // log of the initial stock price for
                                           // -deviate
  double SD;                               // standard deviation
  double SE;                               // standard error
  double deltat = (double) T/N;            // time step
  double mu = rate - div - 0.5*vol*vol;    // drift

  srand(time(0));                          // initialize RNG
  long seed = (long) rand() % 100;         // generate seed
  long* idum = &seed;                      // store seed address

  cout.setf(ios::showpoint);
  cout.precision(4);

  for (i = 0; i < M; i++)
  {
    // initalize stock price for the next simulation
    lnS1 = log(price);
    lnS2 = log(price);

    for (j = 0; j < N; j++)
    {
      deviate = util.gasdev(idum);

      // simulate paths
```

```
    lnS1 = lnS1 + mu*deltat + vol*sqrt(deltat)*deviate;
    lnS2 = lnS2 + mu*deltat + vol*sqrt(deltat)*(-deviate);
}

// convert back to lognormal random variables

S1 = exp(lnS1);
S2 = exp(lnS2);

if (type == 'C')
   value = 0.5*(max(0, S1 - strike) + max(0,S2 - strike));
else // if put
   value = 0.5*(max(0, strike - S1) + max(0, strike - S2));

sum1 = sum1 + value;
sum2 = sum2 + value*value;
}

value = exp(-rate*T)*sum1/M
cout << "value = " << value << endl;

// compute standard deviation
SD = sqrt((exp(-2*rate*T)/(M-1))*(sum2 - (sum1*sum1)/M));
cout << " stdev = " << SD << endl;
// compute standard error
SE = SD/sqrt(M);
cout << " stderr = " << SE << endl;

return value;
}
```

Suppose we want to calculate the price of European call option in a Black-Scholes world with antithetic variance reduction where $S = 50$, $X = 50$, $r = 5.5$ percent, $q = 2$ percent, $T = 0.75$ (9 months), and $\sigma = 0.20$. We make the following method call to *MonteCarloAntithetic* with $M = 100$, 1,000, 10,000, and 100,000 (changing M in the method call) simulations, and $N = 10$ time steps.

Table 2.1 summarizes the results. Notice that as the number of simulations increases, both the standard deviation and standard error decrease. Moreover, as the number of simulations increases by a factor of 10, the standard error decreases by approximately a factor of 3. The Black-Scholes price is $4.03. Thus, increasing the number of simulations narrows the confidence interval of the estimate since the standard error decreases.

Monte Carlo is used extensively for simulating outcomes—that is, profit and losses (P/L)—of dynamic trading strategies. A single sample diffusion path is simulated, and the dynamic trading strategy is executed over this path. The P/L is then calculated. Then, the process is repeated M times for M sample paths. The mean is an estimate of the expected P/L from the trading strategy. A standard deviation of

TABLE 2.1   Simulation Results

Number of Simulations	Monte Carlo Call Price	Standard Deviation	Standard Error
100	3.935	3.458	0.360
1,000	4.013	3.200	0.101
10,000	4.057	3.153	0.032
100,000	4.037	3.093	0.010

P/Ls around this mean tells you how stable the trading strategy is. Monte Carlo is used extensively in risk and portfolio management to compute value at risk (VaR) of a portfolio. A confidence level is chosen—for example, 95 percent or 99 percent; the underlying factors of each security are simulated, and the P/L of each position in each security is calculated based on the realization of the simulated factor values. The process is repeated for each security M times and then, based on the simulated P/L probability distribution generated by the aggregated P/L of all securities in the portfolio, the VaR can be computed by looking at the P/L value that lies to the left of confidence level of the P/L probability distribution. Figure 2.3 shows a simulated stock return distribution generated from Monte Carlo.

As a practical application, suppose we want to implement a dynamic replication strategy $\{(\Delta_t, N_t), 0 \le t \le T\}$ of going long a stock and going short a call option on the stock. We know from equation (1.48) that the option price at time t is $f_t = \Delta_t S_t - N_t A_t$. The following code implements a dynamic replication strategy on a call

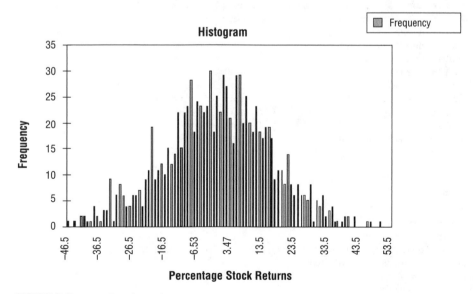

FIGURE 2.3   Simulated Stock Return

option. We are always rebalancing between our long equity position and short position in the money market account (to finance our stock purchases) so that the strategy is self-financing.

```
/*********************************************************************************
dynamicReplication       : synthetically replicates option using stock and money
                           market account
[in]:   double price    : stock price
        double strike   : strike price
        double vol      : volatility
        double rate     : interest rate
        double div      : dividend yield
        double T        : option maturity
        char type       : 'C'all or 'P'ut
        long M          : number of simulations
        long N          : number of time steps
[out]   double          : synthetic option price
*********************************************************************************/
double MonteCarloMethod::dynamicReplication(double price, double strike, double
  vol, double rate, double div, double T, char type, long M, long N)
{
  // initialize variables
  int i, j;
  double S = 0.0;                     // stock price
  double lnS;                         // log of S
  double delta;                       // delta of option
  double totalStockShares = 0;        // total shares of stock
  double totalMMAShares = 0.0;        // total number of MMA shares
  double numShares = 1.0;             // number of shares bought or sold at time t
  double numMMA = 0.0;                // number of MMA shares bought at time t
  double MMAValue = 0.0;              // value of money market account at time t
  double totalMMAValue;               // = MMAValue*totalMMAShares
  double d1 = 0.0;                    // used to calculate delta
  double portValue = 0.0;             // portfolio value
  double deviate = 0.0;               // normal deviates used for Monte Carlo
  double temp = 0.0;                  // temp variable to hold delta value
  double totalStockValue = 0.0;       // total stock value
  long seed = -1;                     // initial seed value
  long* idum = 0;                     // used for gasdev function
  double dt = T/M;                    // step size
  double mu = 0.0;                    // drift

  StatUtility util;
  // initial states
  d1 = (log(price/strike) + (rate - div + (vol)*(vol)/2)*(T))/(vol*sqrt(T));
  delta = util.normalCalc(d1);
  numShares = delta;                  // number of shares
  totalStockValue = numShares*price;
  MMAValue = numShares*price;         // initialize value of money market account
```

```
numMMA = numShares;
totalMMAValue = numMMA*price;
totalMMAShares = numMMA;
totalStockShares = numShares;
temp = delta;
portValue = totalStockValue - totalMMAValue;

srand(unsigned(0));
seed = (long) rand() % 100;
idum = &seed;

for (i = 0; i < M; i++)
{
  // initialize starting price
  lnS = log(price);

  // do simulations on each path
  for (j = 0; j < N; j++)
  {
    deviate = util.gasdev(idum);
    lnS  = lnS + (rate - div - 0.5*vol*vol)*dt + vol*sqrt(dt)*deviate;
  }

  S = exp(lnS);
  MMAValue = MMAValue*exp(rate*dt);

  // compute current delta
  if (i != M-1)
  {
    d1 = (log(price/strike) + (rate - div + (vol)*(vol)/2)*(T-i*dt))/(vol*sqrt(T-
      i*dt));
    delta = util.normalCalc(d1);
  }
  else
    delta = 1.0;

  // adjust total delta
  delta = delta - temp;

  if (S >= price)
  {
    // buy shares
    temp = delta;
    numShares = delta;
    totalStockShares = totalStockShares + numShares;
    totalStockValue = totalStockShares*price;

    // finance purchase of stock by selling shares (borrowing) from MMA
    numMMA = numShares;
    totalMMAShares = totalMMAShares + numMMA;

    MMAValue = MMAValue + numMMA*price;
```

```
    totalMMAValue = MMAValue*totalMMAShares;
    portValue = totalStockValue - totalMMAValue;
  }
  else
  {
    // sell shares
    temp = delta;
    numShares = delta;
    totalStockShares = totalStockShares - numShares;
    totalStockValue = totalStockShares*price;

    // buy back the money market shares shorted
    numMMA = -numShares;
    totalMMAShares = totalMMAShares + numMMA;
    MMAValue = MMAValue + numMMA*price;
    totalMMAValue = MMAValue*totalMMAShares;
    portValue = totalStockValue - totalMMAValue;
  }
}
std::cout << "final cost: " << totalMMAValue - totalStockValue << endl;

return totalMMAValue - totalStockValue;
}
```

2.7   HEDGE CONTROL VARIATES

Clewlow and Carverhill (1994) developed the general approach of using hedges (Greeks) as control variates. Because the payoff of a hedged portfolio has a lower standard deviation than the payoff of an unhedged one, using delta and gamma hedges can reduce the volatility of the value of the portfolio. Consider the case of writing a European call option with maturity T. We can replicate the payoff by selling the option, investing the premium in a savings account, and rebalancing the holding in the asset at discrete interval times $t_i = 1, \ldots, N$, with resultant cash flows placed into and out of the savings account (when selling and buying shares, respectively) so as to maintain a self-financing portfolio.[15] A delta hedge consists of holding $\Delta = \partial C/\partial S$ shares in the underlying asset, which is rebalanced at the discrete time intervals. While the hedge is not perfect due to discrete rebalancing, it is quite good with frequent rebalancing.

At time T, the hedge consists of the savings account and the asset, which closely replicates the payoff of the option. This can be expressed as

$$C_{t_0} e^{r(T-t_0)} - \left[\sum_{i=0}^{N} \left(\frac{\partial C_{t_i}}{\partial S} - \frac{\partial C_{t_{i-1}}}{\partial S} \right) S_{t_i} e^{r(T-t_i)} \right] = C_T + \eta \qquad (2.25)$$

[15]Ibid., 92.

where $\partial C_{t_{-1}}/\partial S = \partial C_{t_N}/\partial S = 0$ (the hedge does not exist before t_0 and the asset is assumed to be liquidated from the previous rebalancing date into cash at maturity). Following Clewlow and Strickland (1998a), the first term is the premium received for writing the option, inflated at the risk-free rate up to the maturity time T, the second term represents the cash flows from rebalancing the hedge at each date t_i, and the third term on the right-hand side is the payoff of the option C_T and the hedging error η. The expression in square brackets is the delta hedge. Equation (2.25) can be rewritten (expand the terms in the brackets and group like delta terms $\partial C_{t_i}/\partial S$) as

$$C_{t_0} e^{r(T-t_0)} + \left[\sum_{i=0}^{N-1} \frac{\partial C_{t_i}}{\partial S} \left(S_{t_{i+1}} - S_{t_i} \right) e^{r(T-t_{i+1})} \right] = C_T + \eta \qquad (2.26)$$

The delta hedge (term in brackets) is called a delta-based martingale control variate cv_1 and can be expressed as

$$cv_1 = \sum_{i=0}^{N-1} \frac{\partial C_{t_i}}{\partial S} (S_{t_{i+1}} - E[S_{t_i}]) e^{r(T-t_{i+1})} \qquad (2.27)$$

Thus, because cv_1 is a martingale, its mean is zero. Rearranging equation (2.26), we get

$$C_{t_0} e^{r(T-t_0)} = C_T - \left[\sum_{i=0}^{N-1} \frac{\partial C_{t_i}}{\partial S} (S_{t_{i+1}} - E[S_{t_i}]) e^{r(T-t_{i+1})} \right] + \eta \qquad (2.28)$$

which, as Clewlow and Strickland suggest, can be interpreted as meaning that the expectation of the payoff plus the hedge is equal to the initial premium inflated to the maturity date at the risk-free rate of interest. As a result, if we simulate the payoff and the hedge and compute the mean of these, we can obtain an estimate of the option value but with a much smaller variance.[16] Since cv_1 is a random variable whose mean we know as zero, then cv_1 is a suitable control variate.

We can also compute the *gamma* hedge control variate:

$$cv_2 = \sum_{i=0}^{N-1} \frac{\partial^2 C_{t_i}}{\partial S^2} \left((\Delta S_{t_i})^2 - E[(\Delta S_{t_i})^2] e^{r(T-t_{i+1})} \right) \qquad (2.29)$$

where $E[(\Delta S_{t_i})^2] = S_{t_i}^2 (e^{(2r+\sigma^2)\Delta t_i} - 2e^{r\Delta t_i} + 1)$ and $\Delta S_{t_i} = S_{t_{i+1}} - S_{t_i}$.

---

[16]Ibid., 93.

Let $t_0 = 0$ and assume there are n control variates. Then, in the general case of a European option with a payoff C_T at time T, equation (2.28) can be written as

$$C_0 e^{rT} = C_T - \sum_{k=1}^{n} \beta_k cv_k + \eta \qquad (2.30)$$

where the β coefficients are included to account for the sign of the hedge, for errors in the hedge due to discrete rebalancing, and for having only approximate hedge sensitivities (i.e., delta, gamma, etc.).[17] We can rewrite equation (2.30) in the form

$$C_T = \beta_0 + \sum_{k=1}^{n} \beta_k cv_k + \eta \qquad (2.31)$$

where $\beta_0 = C_0 e^{rT}$ is the forward price of the option. Equation (2.31) can be interpreted as a linear regression equation where the payoff of the option is regressed against the control variates. The β's can be viewed as the regression coefficients that measure the sensitivity of changes in the control variates to changes in the payoff. The η represents the noise which comes from discrete rebalancing and imperfect sensitivities. If we perform M simulations, then we can view the payoffs and control variates $(C_{T,j}, cv_{1,j}, \ldots, cv_{n,j}; j = 1, \ldots, M)$ as samples from this regression equation. Consequently, we can an obtain an estimate of β by least-squares regression. The least-squares estimate of β is:

$$\hat{\beta} = (X'X)'X'Y$$

where $\hat{\beta} = (\hat{\beta}_0, \hat{\beta}_1, \ldots, \hat{\beta}_n)$, X is $M \times n$ matrix whose rows correspond to each simulation and are $(1, cv_{1,j}, \ldots, cv_{n,j})$ and Y is the $M \times 1$ vector of simulated payoffs. The matrices $X'X$ and $X'Y$ can be computed during the simulation via accumulation

$$(X'X)_{i,j,k+1} = (X'X)_{i,j,k} + cv_{i,j,k+1} cv_{j,k+1}$$
$$(X'X)_{i,k+1} = (X'X)_{i,k} + cv_{i,k+1} C_{T,k+1}$$

where i and j index the rows and columns of the matrix and k is the time step. Clewlow and Strickland note that since the payoffs and control variates are not jointly normally distributed, then $\hat{\beta}$, the estimate of β, will be biased. This is especially important for the forward price of the option, β_0, as we do not want the estimate for option price to be biased. To overcome this problem, Clewlow and Strickland suggest precomputing the β_k's, $k = 1, \ldots, N$, by the least-squares regres-

---

[17]Ibid., 95.

sion or fixing them at some appropriate value for the type of hedge. Thus, by keeping the β_k's fixed, all options can be valued by taking the mean of the hedged portfolio under a different set of simulated paths.[18]

The following is the code for Monte Carlo valuation of a European call option
using antithetic, delta, and gamma-based control variates:

```
/*****************************************************************************
MonteCarloADG : values a European Call option using Monte Carlo with antithetic,
  delta, and gamma control variates. Adapted from Clewlow and Strickland (1998a)
[in]:    double S      : asset price
         double X      : strike price
         double vol    : volatility
         double rate   : risk-free rate
         double div    : dividend yield
         double T      : option maturity
         long N        : number of time steps
         long M        : number of simulations
[out] : double          callValue
*****************************************************************************/
double MonteCarloMethod::MonteCarloADG(double S, double X, double vol, double rate,
  double div, double T, long N, long M)
{
    int i, j;
    double dt = T/N;
    double mudt = (rate - div - 0.5*vol*vol)*dt;
    double voldt = vol*sqrt(dt);
    double erddt = exp((rate - div)*dt); // helps compute E[Si] efficiently
    double egamma = exp((2*(rate - div)  // helps compute gamma control variate
      + vol*vol)*dt)-2*erddt + 1;
    double beta1 = -1;                    // fixed beta coefficient on delta control
                                          // variate
    double beta2 = -0.5;                  // fixed gamma coefficient of gamma control
                                          // variate
    double sum = 0.0;                     // summation of call values
    double sum1 = 0.0;                    // summation of squared call values
    double t;                             // current time
    double St, St1;                       // stock prices at current time
    double Stn, Stn1;                     // stock prices at next time step
    double CT;                            // call value at maturity at end of
                                          // simulation path
    double cv1;                           // delta control variate
    double cv2;                           // gamma control variate
    double delta, gamma;                  // delta and gamma of positive antithetic
    double delta1, gamma1;                // delta and gamma of negative antithetic
    double deviate;                       // standard deviate
    double SD;                            // standard deviation
```

---
[18]Ibid., 96.

```cpp
  double SE;                             // standard error

  srand(time(0));                        // initialize RNG
  long seed = (long) rand() % 100;       // seed for random number generator
  long *idum = &seed;                    // used for generating standard normal
                                         // deviate

  double callValue;                      // call value

  cout.setf(ios::showpoint);             // output format
  cout.precision(4);                     // set output decimal precision

  for (i = 1; i <= M; i++)
  {
    // initialize variables for simulation
    St = S;
    St1 = S;
    cv1 = 0;
    cv2 = 0;

    for (j = 1; j <= N; j++)
    {
      // compute hedge sensitivities
      t = (j-1)*dt;
      delta = og.calcDelta(St,X,rate,div,vol,T,t);
      delta1 = og.calcDelta(St1,X,rate,div,vol,T,t);
      gamma = og.calcGamma(St,X,rate,div,vol,T,t);
      gamma1 = og.calcGamma(St1,X,rate,div,vol,T,t);

    // generate gaussian deviate
      deviate = util.gasdev(idum);

      // evolve asset price
      Stn = St*exp(mudt + voldt*deviate);
      Stn1 = St1*exp(mudt + voldt*(-deviate));

      // accumulate control deviates
      cv1 = cv1 + delta*(Stn - St*erddt) + delta1*(Stn1 - St1*erddt);
      cv2 = cv2 + gamma*((Stn - St)*(Stn - St) - pow(St,2*egamma))
        + gamma1*((Stn1 - St1)*(Stn1 - St1) - pow(St1,2*egamma));
      St = Stn;
      St1 = Stn1;
    }

    // compute value with antithetic and control variates
    CT = 0.5*(max(0,St - X) + max(0, St1 - X) + beta1*cv1 + beta2*cv2);
    sum = sum + CT;
    sum1 = sum1 + CT*CT;
  }

  callValue = exp(-rate*T)*(sum/M);
  cout << "value = " << callValue << endl;

  SD = sqrt((sum1 - sum1*sum1/M)*exp(-2*rate*T)/(M-1));
  cout << "stddev = " << SD << endl;
```

```
    SE = SD/sqrt(M);
    cout << "stderr = " << SE << endl;

    return callValue;
}
```

The functions to calculate delta and gamma control variates in the preceding code are given in the *Option::OptionGreeks* class in Chapter 1.

Monte Carlo is also well suited for valuation of spread options and basket options (options on a portfolio of assets). Consider two stocks, S_1 and S_2, that each follow the risk-neutral price processes:

$$dS_1 = (r - q_1)S_1 dt + \sigma_1 S_1 dz_1$$

and

$$dS_2 = (r - q_2)S_2 dt + \sigma_2 S_2 dz_2$$

where $dz_1 dz_2 = \rho dt$. Price paths follow a two-dimensional discretized geometric Brownian motion that can be simulated according to:

$$S_{1,i+1} = S_{1,i} \exp((r - q_1 - \frac{\sigma_1^2}{2})\Delta t + \sigma_1 \sqrt{\Delta t}\varepsilon_{1,i+1})$$

and

$$S_{2,i+1} = S_{2,i} \exp((r - q_2 - \frac{\sigma_2^2}{2})\Delta t + \sigma_2 \sqrt{\Delta t}(\rho\varepsilon_{1,i+1} + \sqrt{1-\rho^2}\varepsilon_{2,i+1}))$$

for $i = 0, 1, \ldots, N$, where $\varepsilon_{1,i+1}$ and $\varepsilon_{2,i+1}$ are samples from the standard normal. The same seed is used for all simulations. The following code is an implementation to value a European spread call (or put) option with payoff

$$e^{-r(T-t)}E^Q[\max(S_1(T) - S_2(T) - X, 0 \mid \Im_t]$$

for a call and

$$e^{-r(T-t)}E^Q[\max(X - S_1(T) + S_2(T), 0) \mid \Im_t]$$

for a put.

```
/*******************************************************************************/
calcMCEuroSpreadOption : computes the value of a European spread option
[in]    double price1   : price of asset 1
        double price2   : price of asset 2
        double strike   : strike price
        double rate     : risk-free rate
        double vol1     : volatility of asset 1
        double vol2     : volatility of asset 2
        double div1     : dividend yield of asset 1
        double div2     : dividend yield of asset 2
        double rho      : correlation of dz1 and dz2
        double T        : maturity of option
        char type       : option type (C)all or (P)ut
        long M          : number of simulations
        long N          : number of time steps
[out] : double          : price of spread option
*******************************************************************************/
double SpreadOption::calcMCEuroSpreadOption(double price1, double price2, double
  strike, double rate, double vol1, double vol2, double div1, double div2, double
  rho, double T, char type, int M, int N)
{
  int i, j;
  double dt = T/N;                            // size of time step
  double mu1 = (rate - div1 - 0.5*vol1*vol1); // drift for stock price 1
  double mu2 = (rate - div2 - 0.5*vol2*vol2); // drift for stock price 2
  double srho = sqrt(1 - rho*rho);            // square root of 1 - rho*rho
  double sum1 = 0.0;                          // sum of all the call values on
                                              // stock 1 at time T
  double sum2 = 0.0;                          // sum of all the call values on
                                              // stock 2 at time T
  double S1 = 0.0;                            // stock price 1
  double S2 = 0.0;                            // stock price 2
  double deviate1 = 0.0;                      // deviate for stock price 1
  double deviate2 = 0.0                       // deviate for stock price 2
  double z1 = 0.0;                            // correlated deviate for stock
                                              // price 1
  double z2 = 0.0;                            // correlated deviate for stock
                                              // price 2
  double CT = 0.0;                            // option price at maturity
  double SD = 0.0;                            // standard deviate of price
  double SE = 0.0;                            // standard error of price
  double value = 0.0;                         // spread option price

  srand(time(0));                             // initialize RNG
  long seed = (long) rand() % 100;            // generate seed
  long* idum = &seed;
  N = 1;                                      // no path dependency

  for (i = 0; i < M; i++)
  {
    // initialize prices for each simulation
    S1 = price1;
```

```
      S2 = price2;

      for (j = 0; j < N; j++)
      {
         // generate deviates
         deviate1 = util.gasdev(idum);
         deviate2 = util.gasdev(idum);

         // calculate correlated deviates
         z1 = deviate1;
         z2 = rho*deviate1 + srho*deviate2;
         S1 = S1*exp(mu1*dt + vol1*z1*sqrt(dt));
         S2 = S2*exp(mu2*dt + vol2*z2*sqrt(dt));
      }

      if (type == 'C')
         CT = max(S1 - S2 - strike, 0);
      else
         CT = max(strike - S1 + S2,0);

      sum1 = sum1 + CT;
      sum2 = sum2 + CT*CT;
   }

   value = exp(-rate*T)*(sum1/M);
   SD = sqrt((sum2 - sum1*sum1/M)*exp(-2*rate*T)/(M-1));
   SE = SD/sqrt(M);

   return value;
}
```

Suppose $S_1 = 50$, $S_2 = 50$, $X = 1$, $r = 0.06$, $q_1 = 2$ percent, $q_2 = 3$ percent, $\sigma_1 = 30$ percent, $\sigma_2 = 20$ percent, $T = 0.5$. Figure 2.4 shows a plot of call and put spread option prices as a function of correlation $\rho = -1, -0.9, \ldots, 0.9, 1$, for $M = 100,000$ simulations. Note that since the option is European, we can speed the computation by using only $N = 1$ time step.

Notice that as correlation increases, the option price (monotonically) decreases for both call and put spread options. When $\rho = 1$, the second random factor $\varepsilon_{2,i}$ cancels out of the second geometric Brownian equation for S_2. Consequently, both S_1 and S_2 are being driven by only one (the same) source of randomness or uncertainty $\varepsilon_{1,i}$. Thus, $z_{1,i}$ and $z_{2,i}$ move in the same direction so that random movements of both assets occur in the same direction and make the spread $S_1 - S_2$ decrease since the same direction movements are offset. However, when $\rho = -1$ the randomness of $+\varepsilon_{1,i}$ in the equation of the first asset is offset by $-\varepsilon_{1,i}$ in the equation of the second asset, and so movements in one direction of one asset are magnified by movements in the opposite direction of the other asset. Thus, a widening of the spread $S_1 - S_2$ occurs, making the option worth more. Other numerical techniques for valuing spread op-

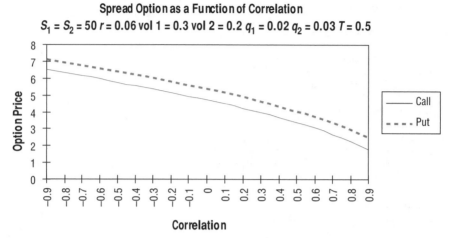

FIGURE 2.4   Call and Put Spread Option Prices

tions include a two-variable binomial method (see section 3.10), fast Fourier transform (FFT) methods (see Appendix C in the CD-ROM), and Gaussian quadrature (see section 14.10).

2.8   PATH-DEPENDENT VALUATION

To price a path-dependent derivative by Monte Carlo, meaning the payoff is dependent on the entire path taken by the underlying security, we need to estimate the conditional expectation. Suppose we want to price a European-style claim of the underlying process; that is, the payoff

$$f_T = F(\{S_t, \, 0 \leq t \leq T\})$$

depends on the entire path from 0 to T. The risk-neutral pricing formula gives the price of the security at time 0 as a discounted expectation:

$$f_0 = e^{-rT} E_{0,S}^Q [F(\{S_t, \, 0 \leq t \leq T\})] \qquad (2.32)$$

The expectation is calculated over all possible paths of the risk-neutral process from 0 to T started at $(S, 0)$. We can estimate this expectation in the following steps:

1. Divide the path into N time steps Δt, and simulate M sample paths of the risk-neutral diffusion process.

2. Calculate the terminal payoff for each path. The payoff on the kth path, $\{S_i^k, i = 0, 1, \ldots, N\}$, $k = 1, 2, \ldots, M$ (i—time counter on a give path; k—counts different paths): $F(S_0^k, S_1^k, \ldots, S_N^k)$.
3. Discount with the risk-free rate r.
4. The crude Monte Carlo estimate f^* of the security price is just an average of all the discounted payoffs over M sample paths generated:

$$f_0^* = e^{-r\tau} \frac{1}{M} \sum_{k=1}^{M} F(S_0^k, S_1^k, \ldots, S_N^k) \tag{2.33}$$

f_0^* is a Monte Carlo estimate of the N-dimensional integral:

$$f_0^* = e^{-r\tau} \int_0^\infty \ldots \int_0^\infty F(S_0, S_1, \ldots, S_N)$$
$$\cdot p^Q(S_N, t_N \mid S_{N-1}, t_{N-1}) \ldots p^Q(S_1, t_1 \mid S, t) dS_1 \ldots dS_N \tag{2.34}$$

where

$$p^Q(S_{i+1}, t_{i+1} \mid S_i, t_i) = \frac{1}{S_{i+1} \sqrt{2\pi\sigma^2\tau}} \exp\left\{ -\frac{\left(\ln\left(\frac{S_{i+1}}{S_i}\right) - \mu\tau \right)^2}{2\sigma^2\tau} \right\}, \quad \mu = r - \frac{\sigma^2}{2}$$

is the risk-neutral probability density (i.e., lognormal distribution density) of S_{i+1} given S_i. Monte Carlo simulation is used to calculate these multidimensional integrals involving integration over multiple points on the path.

Suppose we want to price an Asian option (Chapter 6), an option whose value depends on the average price of the underlying security over the life of the option, by simulation. We generate M sample paths $\{S_i^k, i = 0, 1, \ldots, N\}$, $k = 1, 2, \ldots, M$, index i counts time points on a given path, index k counts paths, $t_i = i\Delta t$,

$$\Delta t = \frac{T}{N}, \text{ and } S_{i+1} = S_i \exp(\mu\Delta t + \varepsilon_{i+1}\sigma\sqrt{\Delta t})$$

Compute the average price A_k for each path:

$$A_k = \frac{1}{N} \sum_{i=1}^{N} S_i^k$$

Estimate the option price:

$$f(S,\,t) = \frac{e^{-r\tau}}{M} \sum_{i=1}^{M} \max(A_k - X,\,0)$$

(2.35)

To reduce variance, always use antithetic variates. Note that it is not necessary to save all the prices on the path and then compute the average price. The average price can be computed efficiently by the recurrent relation:

$$A_{k,j+1} = \frac{1}{j+1}\left(jA_{k,j} + S_{j+1}\right)$$

where A_j is the average price between time t_0 and t_j. One updates the average at each time step. This saves computing time and memory.

We can create an *AsianOption* class the inherits from the *Option* class because an Asian option is an option; that is, it is a subclass (derived) from an *Option*.

```
class AsianOption : public Option
{
  public:
    AsianOption(double price, double strike, double vol, double rate, double div,
      double T);
    AsianOption() : value_(0.0) {}
    ~AsianOption() {}
    // modified Black Scholes pricing formula
    double calcBSAsianPrice(double price, double strike, double vol, double rate,
      double div, double T, char type);

    // calculate arithemic ave. Asian option using Monte Carlo (MCA)
    double calcMCAAsianPrice(double price, double strike, double vol, double rate,
      double div, double T, char type, int M, int N);

    // calculate geometric ave. Asian option using Monte Carlo (MCG)
    double calcMCGAsianPrice(double price, double strike, double vol, double rate,
      double div, double T, char type, int M, int N);
    virtual void setupEngine() const { }
    virtual double calculate() const { return value_ ; }
  private:
    double volA;    // Arithmetic ave. volatility for modified Black-Scholes formula
    double qA;      // Arithmetic ave. dividend yield for modified Black-Scholes
                    // formula
    double value_; // Asian option price
};
```

The following is a Monte Carlo implementation to price an Asian option using geometric averaging on a stock with $S = 45$, $X = 42$, $\sigma = 20$ percent, $r = 5.5$ percent, $q = 1.5$ percent, and $T = 1$ using $M = 1,000$ simulations with $N = 10$ time steps (equally spaced fixing times) so that $t_i - t_{i-1} = T/N = \Delta t$ for all $i = 1, \ldots, N$. We make the following call:

```
void main()
{
  cout.setf(ios::showpoint);
  cout.precision(4);

  AsianOption ao;
  double price = ao.calcMCGAsianPrice(45,42,0.20,0.055,0.015,1,'C');
  cout << "Geometric Asian price = " << price << endl;
}
```

The function implementation is:

```
/***************************************************************************
calcMCGAsianPrice: computes the price of a geometric Asian option using Monte Carlo
  simulation
[in]:   double price    : initial stock price
        double strike   : strike price
        double vol      : volatility
        double rate     : risk-free rate
        double div      : dividend yield
        double T        : time to maturity
        char type       : (C)all or (P)ut
        int M           : number of simulations
        int N           : number of time steps
[out]   double          : price of geometric Asian option
****************************************************************************/
double AsianOption::calcMCGAsianPrice(double price, double strike, double vol,
  double rate, double div, double T, char type, long M, long N)
{
  // initialize variables
  int i, j;
  double G = 0.0;          // price of geometric average Asian option
  double mu = 0.0;         // drift
  double deviate;          // normal deviate
  double S = 0.0;          // stock price
  double sum = 0.0;        // sum of payoffs
  double sum2 = 0.0;       // sum of squared payoffs
  double product = 0.0;    // product of stock prices
  double payoff = 0.0;     // option payoff
  double deltat = 0.0;     // step size
```

```
double stddev = 0.0;                // standard deviation
double stderror = 0.0;              // standard error
deltat = T/N;                       // compute change in step size
mu = rate - div - 0.5*vol*vol;      // compute drift
cout.precision(4);                  // set output decimal format

srand(time(0));                     // initialize RNG
long seed = (long) rand() % 100;    // generate random number generator
long *idum = &seed;                 // store address of seed

// for each simulation
for (i = 0; i <= M; i++)
{
  S = price;
  product = 1;

  for (j = 0; j < N; j++)
    {
    deviate = util.gasdev(idum);
    S = S*exp(mu*deltat + vol*sqrt(deltat)*deviate);
    product *= S;
  }

  // compute geometric average
  G = pow(product,(double)1/N);
  if (type == 'C')
    payoff = max(G - strike,0);
  else
    payoff = max(strike - G,0);

  sum += payoff;

  sum2 += payoff*payoff;
}
value_ = exp(-rate*T)*(sum/M);
stddev = sqrt((sum2 - sum*sum/M)*exp(-2*rate*T)/(M-1));
stderror = stddev/sqrt(M);

return value_;
}
```

The price of the geometric average Asian call is $5.76 with a standard deviation of 5.00 and a standard error of 0.50. We now price an arithmetic Asian price option using the same values for the geometric average Asian call.

```
/*********************************************************************/
calcMCAsianPrice : computes the price of an arithmetic Asian option using Monte
                   Carlo simulation
```

```
[in]:   double price   : initial stock price
        double strike  : strike price
        double vol     : stock volatility
        double rate    : risk-free rate
        double div     : dividend yield
        double T       : time to maturity
        char type      : (C)all or (P)ut
        int M          : number of simulations
        int N          : number of time steps
[out]:  double         : price of arithmetic Asian option
*******************************************************************************/
double AsianOption::calcMCAAsianPrice(double price, double strike, double vol,
  double rate, double div, double T, char type, int M, int N)
{
  // initialize variables
  double A = 0.0;                    // arithmetic average
  double mu = 0.0;                   // drift
  int i, j;
  double deviate;                    // normal deviate
  double stddev = 0.0;               // standard deviation
  double stderror = 0.0;             // standard error
  double S = 0.0;                    // stock price
  double sum = 0.0;                  // sum of payoffs
  double sum1 = 0.0;                 // sum of stock prices
  double sum2 = 0.0;                 // sum of squared payoffs
  double payoff = 0.0;               // payoff of option
  deltat = T/N;                      // step size
  mu = rate - div - 0.5*vol*vol;     // compute drift
  cout.precision(4);                 // set output decimal format

  srand(time(0));                    // initializer RNG
  long seed = (long) rand() % 100;   // generate seed
  long *idum = &seed;

  // for each simulation
    for (i = 0; i <= M; i++)
  {
    // reinitialize for each simulation
    S = price;
    sum1 = 0;

    for (j = 0; j <N; j++)
    {
      deviate = util.gasdev(idum);
      S = S*exp(mu*deltat + vol*sqrt(deltat)*deviate);
      sum1 += S;
    }
    A = sum1/N;

    if (type == 'C')
      payoff = max(A - strike, 0);
    else
```

```
    payoff = max(strike - A,0);

  sum += payoff;
  sum2 += payoff*payoff;
}

value_= exp(-rate*T)*(sum/M);
cout << value = " << value_ <<endl;

stddev = sqrt((sum2 - sum*sum/M)*exp(-2*rate*T)/(M-1));
stderror = stddev/sqrt(M);
cout << " stddev = " << stddev << " " << "stderror " << stderror << endl;

return value_;
}
```

The price of the arithmetic average is approximately \$5.90 with a standard deviation of 5.134 and a standard error of 0.514. It is not surprising that the arithmetic average is higher than the geometric average price since arithmetic average of a series of values is always greater than or equal to the geometric average of a series of values.

As discussed, the geometric average option makes a good control variate for the arithmetic average option. It lowers the standard deviation, and thus standard error, of the estimate. The following is an implementation for pricing an arithmetic average option using a geometric average control variate:

```
/**************************************************************************/
  calcMCGAsianPrice      : computes the price of an geometric Asian option with a
                           control variate using Monte Carlo simulation
[in]:    double price    : initial stock price
         double strike   : strike price
         double vol      : stock volatility
         double rate     : risk-free rate
         double div      : dividend yield
         double T        : time to maturity
         char type       : (C)all or (P)ut
         int M           : number of simulations
         int N           : number of time steps
[out]:   double          : price of geometric Asian option with a control variate
***************************************************************************/
double AsianOption::calcMCAAsianGCV(double price, double strike, double vol, double
  rate, double div, double T, char type, int M, int N)
{
  // initialize variables
  int i, j;
  double geo = 0.0;      // geometric average
  double ave = 0.0;      // arithmetic average
```

```
double mu = 0.0;                      // drift
double stddev = 0.0;                  // standard deviation
double stderror = 0.0;                // standard error
double deviate;                       // standard deviate
double S = 0.0;                       // stock price
double sum = 0.0;                     // sum of payoffs
double sum1 = 0.0;                    // sum of squared payoffs
double product = 0.0;                 // product of stock prices
double payoff = 0.0;                  // option payoff
double dt = T/N;                      // step size

cout.precision(4);                    // set output decimal format

srand(time(0));                       // initialize RNG
long seed = (long) rand() % 100;      // generate seed
long* idum = &seed;                   // store address of seed

mu = rate - div - 0.5*vol*vol;        // drift

// simulation
for (i = 0; i <= M; i++)
{
  // initialize for each simulation
  S = price;
  product = 1;
  sum = 0;
  sum1 = 0;

  for (j = 0; j < N; j++)
  {
    deviate = util.gasdev(idum);
    S = S*exp(mu*deltat + vol*sqrt(dt)*deviate);
    sum = sum + S;
    product *= S;
  }

  ave = sum/N;                        // calculate arithmetic average
  geo = pow(product,(double)1/N);     // calculate geometric average

  if (type == 'C')
    payoff = max(0, (ave - strike) - (geo - strike));
  else
    payoff = max(0, (strike - ave) - (strike - geo));

  sum += payoff;
  sum1 += payoff*payoff;
}

value_ = exp(-rate*T)*(sum/M) +
  calcMCGAsianPrice(price,strike,vol,rate,div,T,'C');
cout << value = " << value_ <<endl;

stddev = sqrt((sum1 - sum*sum/M)*exp(-2*rate*T)/(M-1));
```

```
stderror = stddev/sqrt(M);
cout << " stddev = " << stddev << " " << "stderror " << stderror << endl;

return value_;
}
```

The arithmetic price is approximately $5.90 with a standard deviation of 0.185 and a standard error of 0.019. Table 2.2 summarizes the Monte Carlo results of the Asian option using different methods using $M = 1,000$ simulations and $N = 10$ time steps per path. Note how much smaller the standard error is using the control variate technique than using the arithmetic average Monte Carlo.

2.9 BROWNIAN BRIDGE TECHNIQUE

In order to capture path-dependencies, it may be necessary to simulate the values that a stochastic factor (i.e., an interest rate) can take at many points over a time horizon. While (unconditional) Monte Carlo can be used to estimate values over short time horizons, a more robust method needs to be used to simulate values over longer time horizons that may be conditional on a final state being reached. A Brownian bridge is a stochastic process that evolves over time conditional on reaching a given final state at a given final time. The Brownian bridge, suggested by Caflisch and Moskowitz (1995), can be used to generate Brownian motion at a specified number of time points between a given initial and a final state. Intuitively, a Brownian bridge is a stochastic interpolation between the initial state and the final state so that simulated paths are consistent with the initial and final states. Brownian bridges are useful for stress testing because they can be used to generate paths that lead to extreme and unlikely final states (stress scenarios).

Suppose the final condition of the stochastic factor, say a stock price, is $S(t) = S_T$ at time T. Suppose that $S(t)$ follows the SDE:

$$dS(t) = \mu S(t)dt + \sigma S(t)dZ(t) \tag{2.36}$$

TABLE 2.2 Monte Carlo Results of the Asian Option

Monte Carlo	Estimate	Standard Deviation	Standard Error
Arithmetic average	$5.898	5.134	0.514
Geometric average	$5.760	5.000	0.500
Geometric control variate	$5.898	0.185	0.019

where $Z(t)$ is Brownian motion (a Wiener process). The solution to equation (2.36) is given by

$$S(t) = S(0) \exp\left((\mu - \frac{\sigma^2}{2})t + \sigma Z(t) \right) \qquad (2.37)$$

so that $S(t)$ is lognormally distributed. The drift μ and volatility σ can be estimated from historical data. For generating price paths, one could use Monte Carlo simulation using equation (2.1). In the case of long-term simulations, the model itself poses a problem. Over a long period of time the drift dominates the volatility such that small errors in the drift lead to large differences in the future price distribution, whereas for short-term simulations the volatility dominates the drift so that the effects of the drift are negligible. Moreover, other assumptions of price behavior over short-term horizons—like successive one-day returns that have the same volatility and are independent of one another, which implies that the variance of returns is a linear function of time or that stock price returns follow a random walk—do not hold over long-term horizons. However, a Brownian bridge can be used to overcome these problems.

The final condition at time T leads to a final condition for the Brownian motion at time T, which can be deduced from equation (2.37):

$$Z(T) = \underbrace{\frac{1}{\sigma}\left(\log\left(\frac{S(T)}{S(0)} \right) - \left(u - \frac{\sigma^2}{2} \right)T \right)}_{z(T)}$$

Mathematically, the paths of the Wiener process that end up at the same value $z(T)$ are defined by a (one-dimensional) Brownian bridge $B(t)$, $t \in [0, T]$ defined by

$$B(T) = z(0) + \left(z(T) - z(0) \right)\frac{t}{T} + Z^*(t) - \frac{t}{T}Z^*(T) \qquad (2.38)$$

where $z(0) = 0$ and $Z^*(t)$ is a Wiener process that is independent of $Z(t)$. We can write (2.38) as

$$B(T) = \left(z(T) - Z^*(T) \right)\frac{t}{T} + Z^*(t) \qquad (2.39)$$

When simulating the Brownian bridge, we have to construct this independent Wiener process along some appropriate time steps within the time interval of interest, $0 = t_0 < t_1 < \ldots < t_n = T$, by setting

$$i) \; Z^*(0) = 0$$

$$ii)\ Z^*(t_{i+1}) = Z^*(t_i) + \varepsilon\sqrt{t_{i+1} - t_i}\,,\ i = 0,\ \ldots,\ n-1$$

where $\varepsilon \sim N(0,1)$ are standard normally distributed deviates and where we assume the intervals $t_{i+1} - t_i,\ i = 0,\ \ldots,\ n-1$ are the same length.

The Brownian bridge now replaces the Wiener process $Z(t)$ for $0 < t < T$ in (2.37),

$$
\begin{aligned}
S(t) &= S(0)\exp\left((\mu - \frac{\sigma^2}{2})t + \sigma B(t) \right) \\
&= S(0)\exp\left((\mu - \frac{\sigma^2}{2})t + \left[\log\left(\frac{S(T)}{S(0)} \right) - (\mu - \frac{\sigma^2}{2})T \right]\frac{t}{T} + \sigma\left(Z^*(t) - \frac{t}{T}Z^*(T) \right) \right) \\
&= S(0)\exp\left(\log\left(\frac{S(T)}{S(0)} \right)\frac{t}{T} + \sigma\left(Z^*(t) - \frac{t}{T}Z^*(T) \right) \right)
\end{aligned}
\tag{2.40}
$$

As can be seen from equation (2.40), the drift term μ drops out (the drift of the Brownian bridge is determined by the given initial and final states), which solves the problem of having to estimate the drift. Thus, only the volatility needs to be estimated. This advantage comes at the cost of having to estimate the final probability distribution of the price at time T. The probability distribution implicitly incorporates the drift of the price evolution. However, since the drift is unknown (the drift could be any more or less complicated term) there is no need for the standard deviation of the estimated probability distribution to be consistent with the volatility of the Brownian bridge.

The Brownian bridge construction first generates $Z(T)$, and then using this value and $Z(0) = 0$, generates $Z(T/2)$. It generates $Z(T/4)$ using $Z(0)$ and $Z(T/2)$, and it generates $Z(3T/4)$ using $Z(T/2)$ and $Z(T)$. The construction proceeds recursively filling in the midpoints of the subintervals.[19] Consequently, the sampled Brownian path is generated by determining its values at $T, T/2, T/4, 3T/4, \ldots,$ $(n-1)T/n$, using a vector of generated standard normal deviates $\varepsilon = \{\varepsilon_1, \varepsilon_2, \ldots, \varepsilon_n\}$ according to:

$$Z(T) = \sqrt{T}\varepsilon_1$$

$$Z(T/2) = \frac{1}{2}Z(T) + \frac{\sqrt{T}}{2}\varepsilon_2$$

---

[19]Papageorgiou (2001), 4.

$$Z(T/4) = \frac{1}{2} Z(T/2) + \frac{\sqrt{2T}}{4} \varepsilon_3$$

$$Z(3T/4) = \frac{1}{2} (Z(T/2) + Z(T)) + \frac{\sqrt{2T}}{4} \varepsilon_4$$

$$\vdots$$

$$Z((n-1)T/n) = \frac{1}{2} (Z((n-2)T/n) + Z(T)) + \sqrt{\frac{T}{2n}} \varepsilon_n$$

The Brownian bridge can be generalized to include time intervals of unequal lengths. For $t_{j+1} = t_j + \Delta t$, $j = 0, \ldots, n-1$, $\Delta t = T/n$, we can simulate a future value $Z(t_k)$, $k > j$, given the value $Z(t_j)$, according to

$$Z(t_k) = Z(t_j) + \varepsilon \sqrt{(k-j)\Delta t} \tag{2.41}$$

where $\varepsilon \sim N(0,1)$ are standard normally distributed deviates.[20] We can simulate $Z(t_i)$ at any intermediate point $t_j < t_i < t_k$, given the values $Z(t_j)$ and $Z(t_k)$, according to the Brownian bridge formula:

$$Z(t_i) = (1-\gamma)Z(t_j) + \gamma Z(t_k) + \varepsilon \sqrt{\gamma(1-\gamma)(k-j)\Delta t} \tag{2.42}$$

where $\varepsilon \sim N(0,1)$ and $\gamma = (i-j)/(k-j)$.

We give the following *BrownianBridge* implementation adapted from Jäckel (2002):

```
class BrownianBridge
{
  public:
    BrownianBridge(unsigned long numberOfSteps);
    virtual ~BrownianBridge() {};
    void buildPath(vector<double>& theWienerProcessPath, const vector<double>&
      gaussianVariates);
    void generateDeviates(unsigned long numberOfSteps);
  private:
    unsigned long numberOfSteps;
    vector<unsigned long> leftIndex;
    vector<unsigned long> rightIndex;
```

---

[20]Ibid., 5.

```
    vector<unsigned long> bridgeIndex;
    vector<double> leftWeight;
    vector<double> rightWeight;
    vector<double> stddev;
    vector<double> normalVariates;
    StatUtility util;
};
```

The class has the following method definitions:

```
/*****************************************************************************
 BrownianBridge    : Constructor , initializes Brownian bridge
 [in] numberOfSteps: number of steps on path
 [out] none
 *****************************************************************************/
BrownianBridge::BrownianBridge(unsigned long numberOfSteps):
  numberOfSteps(numberOfSteps), leftIndex(numberOfSteps),
  rightIndex(numberOfSteps), bridgeIndex(numberOfSteps),
  leftWeight(numberOfSteps), rightWeight(numberOfSteps), stddev(numberOfSteps)
{

  vector<unsigned long> map(numberOfSteps);
  unsigned long i, j, k, l;


  // map is used to indicated which points are already constructed. If map[i] is
  // zero, path point i is yet unconstructed. map[i] - 1 is the index of the
  // variate that constructs the path point i.
  map[numberOfSteps-1] = 1;              // the first point in the construction is
                                         // the global step
  bridgeIndex[0] = numberOfSteps - 1;    // bridge index
  stddev[0] = sqrt(numberOfSteps);       // the standard deviation of the global
                                         // step
  leftWeight[0] = rightWeight[0] = 0;    // global step to the last point in time

  for (j = 0, i = 0; i < numberOfSteps; ++i)
  {
    while (map[j])
      ++j;                               // find the next unpopulated entry in the
                                         // map
    k = j;
    while ((!map[k]))
      ++k;                               // find the next unpopulated entry in the
                                         // map from there

    l = j + ((k - 1 - j) >> 1);          // l is now the index of the point to
                                         // be constructed next
```

```
        map[l] = i;
        bridgeIndex[i] = l;      // the ith gaussian variate to be used to set point l
        leftIndex[i] = j;        // point j-1 is the left strut of the bridge for
                                 // point l
        rightIndex[i] = k;       // point k is the right strut of the bridge
        leftWeight[i] = (k - l)/(k + 1- j);
        rightWeight[i] = (l + 1 - j)/(k+ 1- j);
        stddev[i] = sqrt(((l + 1 - j)*(k-1))/(k+1-j));
        j = k + 1;

        if (j >= numberOfSteps)
            j = 0;  // wrap around
    }
}


/******************************************************************************
buildPath: builds a path using a Brownian bridge
[in] path                : simulated Brownian path
[in] normalVariates      : vector of normal deviates
[out] none
******************************************************************************/
void BrownianBridge::buildPath(vector<double>& path, const vector<double>&
  normalVariates)
{
    assert(normalVariates.size() == numberOfSteps && path.size() == numberOfSteps);
    unsigned long i, j, k, l;

    path[numberOfSteps - 1] = stddev[0]*normalVariates[0];

    for (i = 1; i < numberOfSteps; i++)
    {
        j = leftIndex[i];
        k = rightIndex[i];
        l = bridgeIndex[i];
        if (j)
            path[l] = leftWeight[i]*path[j-1] + rightWeight[i]*path[k] +
                stddev[i]*normalVariates[i];
        else
            path[l] = rightWeight[i]*path[k] + stddev[i]*normalVariates[i];
    }
}


/******************************************************************************
generateDeviates: generates a sequences of normal random deviates
[in] numberOfSteps: number of steps per path (= number of deviates needed per path)
[out] none
******************************************************************************/
void BrownianBridge::generateDeviates(unsigned long numberOfSteps)
{
    double deviate = 0.0;
    srand(time(0));                 // initialize RNG
    long seed = (long) rand();      // generate random seed
    long* idum = &seed;
```

```
for (int i=0; i < numberOfSteps; i++)
{
  deviate = util.gasdev(idum);
  normalVariates.push_back(deviate);
}
}
```

It has been thought by many researchers that the Brownian bridge speeds up the convergence of quasi–Monte Carlo by reducing the deterministic error bound more than the standard discretization approach, which uses a Cholesky decomposition of the covariance matrix C into AA' to generate uncorrelated deviates. The choice of the matrix A in the Cholesky decomposition affects quasi–Monte Carlo convergence since the decomposition can be thought of as a change in the integrand or as a change in sample points.[21] Thus, the deterministic error bound of quasi–Monte Carlo depends on the integrand and on the discrepancy of the sample points and one should consider both factors when choosing A.[22] The Brownian bridge results in a matrix B such that $C = BB'$, where B is different from that of A in the Cholesky decomposition and is thought to reduce the deterministic error bound more than A.

Some researchers believe that in high-dimension (i.e., greater than 50) finance problems where it is necessary to evaluate integrals with Gaussian weights, the first coordinates of low-discrepancy points will be more uniformly distributed than the rest. It is believed that points sampled from the multidimensional Gaussian distribution used to evolve the Brownian bridge will result in an integrand that depends more on the presumably more uniform coordinates of these samples, and thus lead to faster convergence. Moreover, the Brownian bridge is thought to reduce the dimensionality of the problem. However, Papageorgiou (2001) shows that the Brownian bridge, which uses points from the same low-discrepancy sequence (i.e., Faure or Sobol) as a standard discretization but uses a different matrix covariance decomposition, can actually lead to worse convergence errors for both high- and low-dimension quasi–Monte Carlo integrals. Consequently, it is not clear that the Brownian bridge consistently outperforms the standard discretization method in quasi–Monte Carlo.

2.10 JUMP-DIFFUSION PROCESS AND CONSTANT ELASTICITY OF VARIANCE DIFFUSION MODEL

Certain types of stochastic processes are best modeled using random "jumps" drawn from a Poisson process such as the default time of a bond issuer or even a

---

[21]Ibid.
[22]Ibid.

stock price that jumps from unexpected market news. Such a jump-diffusion process, proposed by Merton (1973),[23] can be modeled as:

$$\frac{dS}{S} = (\mu - \lambda\kappa)dt + \sigma dz + dq \qquad (2.43)$$

where μ is the expected return from the asset, λ is the rate (intensity) at which jumps occur, κ is the average jump size measured as a proportional increase in the asset price, and $\lambda\kappa$ is the average growth rate from the jumps. Thus, the expected growth rate from the geometric Brownian motion of the asset is $\mu - \lambda\kappa$. Also, Δ is the volatility of the asset that follows geometric Brownian motion, dz is a Brownian motion process, and dq is the Poisson process generating the jumps (dz and dq are assumed to be independent processes).

Jump-diffusion processes yield fatter tails, and thus capture more realistic asset return distribution dynamics than continuous lognormal diffusion processes, since jumps can be either positive or negative. Merton made the important assumption that the jump factor of the asset's return represents nonsystematic risk that can be hedged away. Consequently, a Black-Scholes type of portfolio must earn the risk-free rate since the uncertainty arising from geometric Brownian motion can be eliminated.[24]

We can implement a jump-diffusion process using Monte Carlo to value a European call option:

```
/**********************************************************************/
JumpModel              : values a European call option using a jump-diffusion
                         process
[in]:   double price:  : asset price
        double strike  : strike price
        double vol     : volatility
        double rate    : risk-free rate
        double div     : dividend yield
        double T       : option maturity
        int N          : number of time steps
        int M          : number of simulations
        double lambda  : rate (intensity) of jumps
        double kappa   : average jump sized measured as a proportional increase in
                         the stock price
[out] : double         callValue
**********************************************************************/
double MonteCarlo::JumpDiffusion(double price, double strike, double vol, double
  rate, double div, double T, int M, int N, double lambda, double kappa)
{
```

----

[23]Merton (1973), 125–144.
[24]Hull (1996), 499.

```
int i, j;
double dt;                                 // time increment, (yrs)
double deviate = 0.0;                      // standard normal deviate
double deviate1 = 0.0;                     // Poisson deviate
double payoff = 0.0;                       // option payoff
double sum = 0.0;                          // sum payoffs
double S = price;                          // store stock price
double mu = rate - div - lambda*kappa;     // expected return
long seed;                                 // seed for random number generator
long* idum = 0;                            // identifies address of seed
StatUtility util;                          // statistic utility class

srand(time(0));                            // initialize random number generator
seed = (long) rand() % 100;                // generate seed
idum = &seed;
dt = T/N;                                  // time step

for (i = 0; i < M; i++)
{
  // initialize stock price for each simulation
  S = price;

  for(j = 0; j < N; j++)
  {
    deviate = util.gasdev(idum);           // generate gaussian deviate
    deviate1 = util.poisson(lambda);       // generate Poisson deviate

    S = S*exp(mu*dt+ vol*sqrt(dt)*deviate + sqrt(dt)*deviate1);
  }
  payoff = max(S - strike, 0);
  sum += payoff;
}
return exp(-rate*T)*(sum/M);
}
```

To generate a Poisson random variable from a Poisson process with rate λ, we need to simulate the number of events or arrivals that have occurred over a given time interval $[0, t]$. Let $N(t)$ be the number of arrivals over this time period. If the interarrival times are independent random variables and exponentially distributed with rate λ, then $N(t)$ has a Poisson distribution with mean λt. To simulate a Poisson process, we perform the following steps:

1. Set $n = 0$, $T_n = 0$.
2. Generate the random deviate ξ from an exponential (λ) distribution.
3. Set $n = n + 1$, $T_n = T_{n-1} + \xi$.
4. Return to step 2.

Then, T_n is the time at which the nth "jump" arrives. To generate a Poisson random variable, we let

$$T_n = -\frac{1}{\lambda} \sum_{i=1}^{n} \log U_i$$

Then

$$N(1) = \max\{n = 0 : T_n = 1\} = \max\left\{n \geq 0 : -\frac{1}{\lambda} \sum_{i=1}^{n} \log U_i\right\}$$

where U_i is the ith uniform $(0, 1)$ deviate. Thus, by generating successive i.i.d. uniform $(0, 1)$ random variables until such times as their product is less than $e^{-\lambda}$, we can generate a Poisson (λ) random variable. The Poisson random variable is one less than the number of uniform factors required to make the product less than $e^{-\lambda}$. The code to generate the Poisson random variable is given as an in-line function of a statistical *Utility* class:

```
class Utility
{
  . . .
  inline int poisson(double lambda)
  {
    assert (lambda > 0. );

    double a = exp( -lambda );
    double b = 1;

    // initialize random number generator
    srand(0);
    long seed = (long) rand() % 100;
    long* idum = &seed;

    for (int i = 0; b >= a; i++ )
      b *= gasdev(idum);

    return i - 1;
  }
  . . .
};
```

In the simplest case of Merton's jump-diffusion model, the logarithm of the size of the proportional jump has a normal distribution with a mean of $-0.5\delta^2$ and a standard deviation of δ. In this case, a closed-form solution for European call option C exists:

$$C = \sum_{n=0}^{\infty} \frac{e^{-\bar{\lambda}}(\bar{\lambda}t)^n}{n!} C_n(S,\, K,\, t,\, \bar{r},\, \sqrt{\sigma^2 + \delta^2\,(n/t)}\,)$$

where $\bar{\lambda} = \lambda(1 + \kappa)$ and C_n is the nth Black-Scholes option price with the instantaneous variance rate

$$\sqrt{\sigma^2 + \delta^2\,(n/t)}$$

and risk-free rate $\bar{r} = r - \lambda\kappa + \ln(1 + \kappa)(n/t)$.

Another popular alternative model used in simulation is the constant elasticity of variance (CEV) diffusion model proposed by Cox and Ross.[25] In the CEV model, the instantaneous volatility of the stock price $\sigma(t, S)$ has the form $\sigma S^{-\alpha}$ for some α where $0 \leq \alpha \leq 1$. If $\alpha = 1$, the CEV model simplifies to the absolute diffusion model where the volatility is inversely proportional to the stock price. The CEV model captures the financial leverage effect that occurs as firms have fixed costs to pay regardless of their firm's operating performance.[26] Volatility increases as the stock price decreases since the firm's fixed costs do not change but operating performance may have declined, leading to more uncertainty about the firm's ability to pay these obligations. The CEV process, which can be simulated by Monte Carlo, is given by

$$dS = \mu S dt + \sigma S^{1-\alpha}\, dz \tag{2.44}$$

This family of processes has the property that the elasticity of variance is constant, that is, $(\partial\sigma/\partial S)(S/\sigma) = -\alpha$. While the model is easy to apply, it has the weakness that stock prices can become negative. A closed-form solution for an American call under a CEV process is given by Cox and Rubinstein (1985), which utilizes the gamma density function and the gamma distribution function into computation.[27]

2.11   OBJECT-ORIENTED MONTE CARLO APPROACH

We conclude this chapter by providing a Monte Carlo object-oriented implementation[28] that is more robust since the functionality of generating the price paths

---

[25]Cox and Ross (1976), 145–166.
[26]Hull (1996), 497.
[27]Cox and Rubinstein (1985), 363.
[28]See QuantLib Library on the CD-ROM.

through a path generator class is separate from the path pricer that computes the
values, and thus prices, of the derivative along each path. Finally, we use an aggre-
gator (statistics) class that provides the statistics, discounted average (expected
value), and standard deviation from the sum of all prices of all the paths. We first
define a new Monte Carlo method class:

```
#include "handle.h"
typdef size_t Size;
typdef double Time;

namespace QuantLib
{
  namespace MonteCarlo
  {
    // General purpose Monte Carlo model for path samples
    /* Any Monte Carlo which uses path samples has three main components,
    namely,
    - S, a sample accumulator,
    - PG, a path generator,
    - PP, a path pricer.
    MonteCarloModel<S, PG, PP> puts together these three elements.
    The constructor accepts two safe references, i.e. two smart
    pointers, one to a path generator and the other to a path pricer.
    In case of control variate technique the user should provide the
    additional control option, namely the option path pricer and the
    option value.

    The minimal interfaces for the classes S, PG, and PP are:
    class S
    {
      void add(VALUE_TYPE sample, double weight) const;
    };
    class PG
    {
      Sample<PATH_TYPE> next() const;
    };
    class PP :: unary_function<PATH_TYPE, VALUE_TYPE>
    {
      VALUE_TYPE operator()(PATH_TYPE &) const;
    };

    */
    template<class S, class PG, class PP>
    class MonteCarloModel
    {
      public:
        typedef typename PG::sample_type sample_type;
        typedef typename PP::result_type result_type;
        MonteCarloModel(const Handle<PG>& pathGenerator,
        const Handle<PP>& pathPricer,
```

```cpp
        const S& sampleAccumulator,
        const Handle<PP>& cvPathPricer = Handle<PP>(),
        result_type cvOptionValue = result_type());
      void addSamples(Size samples);
      const S& sampleAccumulator(void) const;
    private:
      Handle<PG> pathGenerator_;          // path generator
      Handle<PP> pathPricer_;             // path pricer
      S sampleAccumulator_;               // sample accumulator
      Handle<PP> cvPathPricer_;           // control variate path price
      result_type cvOptionValue_;         // control variate option value
      bool isControlVariate_;
  };


  // inline definitions
  template<class S, class PG, class PP>
  inline MonteCarloModel<S, PG, PP>::MonteCarloModel(
    const Handle<PG>& pathGenerator,
    const Handle<PP>& pathPricer, const S& sampleAccumulator,
    const Handle<PP>& cvPathPricer,
    MonteCarloModel<S, PG, PP>::result_type cvOptionValue
      : pathGenerator_(pathGenerator), pathPricer_(pathPricer),
      sampleAccumulator_(sampleAccumulator), cvPathPricer_(cvPathPricer),
      cvOptionValue_(cvOptionValue)
  {
    if (cvPathPricer_.isNull())
      isControlVariate_= false;          // no control variates
    else
      isControlVariate_= true;           // use control variates
  }


  template<class S, class PG, class PP>
  inline void MonteCarloModel<S, PG, PP>::addSamples(Size samples)
  {
    for(Size j = 1; j <= samples; j++)
    {
      sample_type path = pathGenerator_->next();
      result_type price = (*pathPricer_)(path.value);
      if (isControlVariate_)
        price += cvOptionValue_-(*cvPathPricer_)(path.value);
      sampleAccumulator_.add(price, path.weight);
    }
  }


  template<class S, class PG, class PP>
  inline const S& MonteCarloModel<S, PG, PP>::sampleAccumulator() const {
    return sampleAccumulator_;
  }
 }
}
```

We next define a *PathGenerator* class that generates all the paths:

```
#include "ql/MonteCarlo/path.h"
#include "ql/RandomNumbers/randomarraygenerator.h"
#include "ql/diffusionprocess.h"

namespace QuantLib {

  namespace MonteCarlo {

    /***************************************************************************
    Generates random paths from a random number generator
    ***************************************************************************/
    template <class RNG>
    class PathGenerator {
      public:
        typedef Sample<Path> sample_type;
        // constructors
        PathGenerator(double drift,
          double variance,
          Time length,
          Size timeSteps,
          long seed = 0);
        // warning the initial time is assumed to be zero
        // and must not be included in the passed vector
        PathGenerator(double drift,
          double variance,
          const std::vector<Time>& times,
          long seed = 0);
        PathGenerator(const std::vector<double>& drift,
          const std::vector<double>& variance,
          const std::vector<Time>& times,
          long seed = 0)
      private:
        mutable Sample<Path> next_;
        Handle<RandomNumbers::RandomArrayGenerator<RNG> > generator_;
    };

    template <class RNG>
    PathGenerator<RNG>::PathGenerator(double drift, double variance,
      Time length, Size timeSteps, long seed): next_(Path(timeSteps),1.0)
    {

      QL_REQUIRE(timeSteps > 0, "PathGenerator: Time steps(" +
      IntegerFormatter::toString(timeSteps) + ") must be greater than zero");
      QL_REQUIRE(length > 0, "PathGenerator: length must be > 0");

      Time dt = length/timeSteps;

      for (Size i=0; i<timeSteps; i++)
```

```
    {
        next_.value.times()[i] = (i+1)*dt;
    }

    next_.value.drift() = Array(timeSteps, drift*dt);

    QL_REQUIRE(variance >= 0.0, "PathGenerator: negative variance");

    generator_ = Handle<RandomNumbers::RandomArrayGenerator<RNG> >(
        new RandomNumbers::RandomArrayGenerator<RNG>(
        Array(timeSteps, variance*dt), seed));
}


template <class RNG>
PathGenerator<RNG>::PathGenerator(double drift, double variance,
    const std::vector<Time>& times, long seed)
    : next_(Path(times.size()),1.0)
{
    QL_REQUIRE(variance >= 0.0, "PathGenerator: negative variance");
    QL_REQUIRE(times.size() > 0, "PathGenerator: no times given");
    QL_REQUIRE(times[0] >= 0.0, "PathGenerator: first time(" +
        DoubleFormatter::toString(times[0]) + ") must be non negative");

    Array variancePerTime(times.size());
    Time dt = times[0];
    next_.value.drift()[0] = drift*dt;
    variancePerTime[0] = variance*dt;
    for(Size i = 1; i < times.size(); i++)
    {
        // check current time is greater than previous time
        QL_REQUIRE(times[i] >= times[i-1],
            "MultiPathGenerator: time(" + IntegerFormatter::toString(i-1)+")="
            " + DoubleFormatter::toString(times[i1])
            " is later than time(" + IntegerFormatter::toString(i) + ")=" +
            DoubleFormatter::toString(times[i]));

        dt = times[i] - times[i-1];
        next_.value.drift()[i] = drift*dt;
        variancePerTime[i] = variance*dt;
    }
    next_.value.times() = times;

    generator_ = Handle<RandomNumbers::RandomArrayGenerator<RNG> >(
        new RandomNumbers::RandomArrayGenerator<RNG>(variancePerTime,
        seed));
}


template <class RNG> PathGenerator<RNG>::PathGenerator(
    const std::vector<double>& drift,
    const std::vector<double>& variance,
```

```
    const std::vector<Time>& times, long seed) : next_(Path(times.size()),1.0)
  {

    // data validity check
    QL_REQUIRE(times.size() > 0, "PathGenerator: no times given");
    QL_REQUIRE(times[0] >= 0.0, "PathGenerator: first time(" +
      DoubleFormatter::toString(times[0]) + ") must be non negative");
    QL_REQUIRE(variance.size()==times.size(),
      "PathGenerator: mismatch between variance and time arrays");
    QL_REQUIRE(drift.size()==times.size(),
      "PathGenerator: mismatch between drift and time arrays");

    Array variancePerTime(times.size());
    double dt = times[0];
    next_.value.drift()[0] = drift[0]*dt;

    QL_REQUIRE(variance[0] >= 0.0, "PathGenerator: negative variance");
    variancePerTime[0] = variance[0]*dt;

    for(Size i = 1; i < times.size(); i++)
    {
      QL_REQUIRE(times[i] >= times[i-1], "MultiPathGenerator: time(" +
        IntegerFormatter::toString(i-1)+")=" +
        DoubleFormatter::toString(times[i-1]) + " is later than time(" +
          IntegerFormatter::toString(i) + ")=" +
        DoubleFormatter::toString(times[i]));

      dt = times[i] - times[i-1];
      next_.value.drift()[i] = drift[i]*dt;

      QL_REQUIRE(variance[i] >= 0.0, "PathGenerator: negative variance");
      variancePerTime[i] = variance[i]*dt;
    }
    next_.value.times() = times;

    generator_ = Handle<RandomNumbers::RandomArrayGenerator<RNG> >(
      new RandomNumbers::RandomArrayGenerator<RNG>(variancePerTime,
      seed));
  }
  template <class RNG> inline const typename PathGenerator<RNG>::sample_type&
  PathGenerator<RNG>::next() const
  {
    const Sample<Array>& sample = generator_->next();
    next_.weight = sample.weight;
    next_.value.diffusion() = sample.value;
    return next_;
  }

 }
}
```

We next define a *Path* class that contains methods for handling computations of the drift and diffusion terms along each path:

```cpp
namespace QuantLib
{
  namespace MonteCarlo
  {
    /**************************************************************************
    Path class for handling computations of drift and diffusion terms along a path
    single factor random walk.
    **************************************************************************/
    class Path
    {
      public:
        Path(Size size);
        Path(const std::vector<Time>& times, const Array& drift, const Array&
          diffusion);
        // inspectors
        double operator[](int i) const;
        Size size() const;
        // read/write access to components
        const std::vector<Time>& times() const;
        std::vector<Time>& times();
        const Array& drift() const;
        Array& drift();
        const Array& diffusion() const;
        Array& diffusion();
        private:
        std::vector<Time> times_; // vector of time instances
        Array drift_;
        Array diffusion_;
    };

    // inline definitions

    inline Path::Path(Size size)
      : times_(size), drift_(size), diffusion_(size) {}

    inline Path::Path(const std::vector<Time>& times, const Array& drift, const
      Array& diffusion)
      : times_(times), drift_(drift), diffusion_(diffusion)
    {

      QL_REQUIRE(drift_.size() == diffusion_.size(),
        "Path: drift and diffusion have different size");
      QL_REQUIRE(times_.size() == drift_.size(),
        "Path: times and drift have different size");
    }
```

```
// overloaded [] operator
inline double Path::operator[](int i) const
{
  return drift_[i] + diffusion_[i];
}
inline Size Path::size() const {
  return drift_.size();
}
inline const std::vector<Time>& Path::times() const
{
  return times_;
}
inline std::vector<Time>& Path::times()
{
  return times_;
}
inline const Array& Path::drift() const
{
  return drift_;
}
inline Array& Path::drift()
{
  return drift_;
}
inline const Array& Path::diffusion() const
{
  return diffusion_;
}
inline Array& Path::diffusion()
{
  return diffusion_;
}
}
}
```

Next we define the Monte Carlo pricer class *McPricer* for pricing derivatives along each path:

```
namespace QuantLib
{
  namespace Pricers
  {

    /***********************************************************************/
    Base class for Monte Carlo pricers
    Deriving a class from McPricer gives an easy way to write
    a Monte Carlo Pricer.
```

```
See McEuropean as example of one factor pricer,
Basket as example of multi factor pricer.
****************************************************************************/
template<class S, class PG, class PP>
class McPricer
{
  public:
    virtual ~McPricer() {}
    // add samples until the required tolerance is reached
    double value(double tolerance, Size maxSample = QL_MAX_INT) const;
    // simulate a fixed number of samples
    double valueWithSamples(Size samples) const;
    // error Estimated of the samples simulated so far
    double errorEstimate() const;
    // access to the sample accumulator for more statistics
    const S& sampleAccumulator(void) const;
  protected:
    McPricer() {}
    mutable Handle<MonteCarlo::MonteCarloModel<S, PG, PP>> mcModel_;
    static const Size minSample_;
};


template<class S, class PG, class PP>
const Size McPricer<S, PG, PP>::minSample_ = 100;


    // inline definitions
/****************************************************************************
value : add samples until the required tolerance is reached
[in] : none
[out]: double mean : mean of sample
****************************************************************************/
template<class S, class PG, class PP>
inline double McPricer<S, PG, PP>::value(double tolerance, Size maxSamples)
  const
{
  Size sampleNumber = mcModel_->sampleAccumulator().samples();
  if (sampleNumber<minSample_)
  {
    mcModel_->addSamples(minSample_-sampleNumber);
    sampleNumber = mcModel_->sampleAccumulator().samples();
  }


  Size nextBatch;
  double order;
  double result = mcModel_->sampleAccumulator().mean();
  double accuracy = mcModel_->sampleAccumulator().errorEstimate()/result;
  while (accuracy > tolerance)
  {
    // conservative estimate of how many samples are needed
    order = accuracy*accuracy/tolerance/tolerance;
```

```
      nextBatch = Size(max(sampleNumber*order*0.8-sampleNumber,
        double(minSample_)));

      // do not exceed maxSamples
      nextBatch = min(nextBatch, maxSamples-sampleNumber);

      QL_REQUIRE(nextBatch>0, "max number of samples exceeded");

      sampleNumber += nextBatch;
      mcModel_->addSamples(nextBatch);
      result = mcModel_->sampleAccumulator().mean();
      accuracy = mcModel_->sampleAccumulator().errorEstimate()/result;
    }
    return result;
}

/********************************************************************
valueWithSamples    : simulate a fixed number of samples
[in] : Size samples : number of data points
[out]: double mean
********************************************************************/
template<class S, class PG, class PP>
inline double McPricer<S, PG, PP>::valueWithSamples(Size samples) const
{
    QL_REQUIRE(samples>=minSample_,
    "number of requested samples (" + IntegerFormatter::toString(samples) + ")
    lower than minSample_ ("+ IntegerFormatter::toString(minSample_) + ")");

    Size sampleNumber = mcModel_->sampleAccumulator().samples();

    QL_REQUIRE(samples>=sampleNumber,
    "number of already simulated samples (" +
      IntegerFormatter::toString(sampleNumber) + ")
    greater than requested samples (" + IntegerFormatter::toString(samples) +
      ")");

    mcModel_->addSamples(samples-sampleNumber);

    return mcModel_->sampleAccumulator().mean();
}

/********************************************************************
errorEstimate : error Estimated of the samples simulated so far
[in] : none
[out]: double error
********************************************************************/
template<class S, class PG, class PP>
inline double McPricer<S, PG, PP>::errorEstimate() const
{
    Size sampleNumber = mcModel_->sampleAccumulator().samples();

    QL_REQUIRE(sampleNumber>=minSample_, "number of simulated samples lower than
      minSample_");
```

```
      return mcModel_->sampleAccumulator().errorEstimate();
   }

   /***********************************************************************
   sampleAccumulator: simulate a fixed number of samples
   [in] : none
   [out]: Math::Statistics object
   ***********************************************************************/
   template<class S, class PG, class PP>
   inline const S& McPricer<S, PG, PP>::sampleAccumulator() const
   {
      return mcModel_->sampleAccumulator();
   }
  }
}
```

The sample size is taken from a *Sample* structure:

```
namespace QuantLib
{
  namespace MonteCarlo
  {
    // weighted sample
    template <class T>
    struct Sample
    {
      public:
        Sample(const T& value, double weight) : value(value), weight(weight) {}
        T value;
        double weight;
    };
  }
}
```

We define the following Monte Carlo typedefs:

```
namespace QuantLib
{
  namespace MonteCarlo
  {
    // default choice for Gaussian path generator.
    typedef PathGenerator<RandomNumbers::GaussianRandomGenerator>
      GaussianPathGenerator;

    // default choice for Gaussian multi-path generator.
```

```
    Typedef MultiPathGenerator<RandomNumbers::RandomArrayGenerator<
      RandomNumbers::GaussianRandomGenerator> > GaussianMultiPathGenerator;

    // default choice for one-factor Monte Carlo model.
    typedef MonteCarloModel<Math::Statistics, GaussianPathGenerator,
      PathPricer<Path> >
      OneFactorMonteCarloOption;

    // default choice for multi-factor Monte Carlo model.
    typedef MonteCarloModel<Math::Statistics, GaussianMultiPathGenerator,
      PathPricer<MultiPath> >
      MultiFactorMonteCarloOption;
  }
}
```

As an example for pricing options using Monte Carlo, we define the *European-PathPricer* class, which prices European options along each path:

```
#include "PathPricer.h"
#include "Path.h"

namespace QuantLib
{
  namespace MonteCarlo
  {
    // path pricer for European options
    class EuropeanPathPricer : public PathPricer<Path>
    {
    public:
      EuropeanPathPricer(Option::Type type, double underlying, double strike,
        DiscountFactor discount, bool useAntitheticVariance);
      double operator()(const Path& path) const;
    private:
      Option::Type type_;
      double underlying_, strike_;
    };
  }
}
```

The class has the following method definitions:

```
#include "EuropeanPathPricer.h"
#include "SingleAssetOption.h"
```

```cpp
using QuantLib::Pricers::ExercisePayoff;

namespace QuantLib
{
  namespace MonteCarlo
  {
  /************************************************************************
  EuropeanPathPricer constructor
  [in]: Option:Type          : option type
  double underlying          : underlying asset
  double strike              : strike price
  DiscountFactor discount    : discount factor
  bool useAntitheticVariance : flag for using
  *************************************************************************/
  EuropeanPathPricer::EuropeanPathPricer(Option::Type type,
    double underlying, double strike, DiscountFactor discount,
    bool useAntitheticVariance)
    : PathPricer<Path>(discount, useAntitheticVariance), type_(type),
    underlying_(underlying), strike_(strike)
  {
      QL_REQUIRE(underlying>0.0, "EuropeanPathPricer:" "underlying less/equal zero
        not allowed");
      QL_REQUIRE(strike>0.0,
        "EuropeanPathPricer: "
        "strike less/equal zero not allowed");
  }


  /************************************************************************
  operator() : operator for pricing option on a path
  [in]: Path& path: path instance
  [out]: double : discounted value (price of option)
  *************************************************************************/
  double EuropeanPathPricer::operator()(const Path& path) const
  {
    Size n = path.size();
    QL_REQUIRE(n>0, "EuropeanPathPricer: the path cannot be empty");

    double log_drift = 0.0, log_random = 0.0;
    for (Size i = 0; i < n; i++)
    {
      log_drift += path.drift()[i];
      log_random += path.diffusion()[i];
    }

    if (useAntitheticVariance_)
      return (
        ExercisePayoff(type_, underlying_ *exp(log_drift+log_random), strike_) +
        ExercisePayoff(type_, underlying_ *exp(log_drift-log_random), strike_))
          *discount_/2.0;
    else
```

```
        return ExercisePayoff(type_, underlying_ *exp(log_drift+log_random), strike_)
          *discount_;


    }
  }
}
```

Each *Pricer* has an abstract *PathPricer* base class that prices using the path given:

```
#include "ql/option.h"
#include "ql/types.h"
#include <functional>


namespace QuantLib
{
  namespace MonteCarlo
  {
    // base class for path pricers
    // Given a path the value of an option is returned on that path.
    template<class PathType, class ValueType=double>
    class PathPricer : public std::unary_function<PathType, ValueType>
    {
      public:
        PathPricer(DiscountFactor discount, bool useAntitheticVariance);
        virtual ~PathPricer() {}
        virtual ValueType operator()(const PathType& path) const=0;
      protected:
        DiscountFactor discount_;
        bool useAntitheticVariance_;
    };


    template<class P,class V>
    PathPricer<P,V>::PathPricer(DiscountFactor discount, bool
      useAntitheticVariance)
      : discount_(discount), useAntitheticVariance_(useAntitheticVariance)
    {

      QL_REQUIRE(discount_ <= 1.0 && discount_ > 0.0, "PathPricer: discount must be
        positive");
    }
  }
}
```

The *EuropeanPathPricer* is used in the *McEuropean* class that does the actual pricing:

```
#include "ql/option.h"
#include "ql/types.h"
#include "ql/Pricers/mcpricer.h"
#include "ql/MonteCarlo/mctypedefs.h"

namespace QuantLib
{
  namespace Pricers
  {
    // European Monte Carlo pricer
    class McEuropean : public McPricer<Math::Statistics,
      MonteCarlo::GaussianPathGenerator, MonteCarlo::PathPricer<MonteCarlo::Path> >
    {
      public:
        McEuropean(Option::Type type,
          double underlying,
          double strike,
          Spread dividendYield,
          Rate riskFreeRate,
          double residualTime,
          double volatility,
          bool antitheticVariance,
          long seed=0);
    };
  }
}
```

The class has the following method definitions:

```
#include "ql/Pricers/mceuropean.h"
#include "ql/MonteCarlo/europeanpathpricer.h"

namespace QuantLib
{
  namespace Pricers
  {
    using Math::Statistics;
    using MonteCarlo::Path;
    using MonteCarlo::GaussianPathGenerator;
    using MonteCarlo::PathPricer;
```

```
using MonteCarlo::MonteCarloModel;
using MonteCarlo::EuropeanPathPricer;

McEuropean::McEuropean(Option::Type type,
  double underlying, double strike, Spread dividendYield,
  Rate riskFreeRate, double residualTime, double volatility,
  bool antitheticVariance, long seed)
{

  // Initialize the path generator
  double mu = riskFreeRate - dividendYield - 0.5 * volatility * volatility;

  Handle<GaussianPathGenerator> pathGenerator(
    new GaussianPathGenerator(mu, volatility*volatility, residualTime, 1,
      seed));

  // Initialize the pricer on the single Path
  Handle<PathPricer<Path> > euroPathPricer(
    new EuropeanPathPricer(type, underlying, strike, exp(-
      riskFreeRate*residualTime), antitheticVariance));

  // Initialize the one-factor Monte Carlo
  mcModel_ = Handle<MonteCarloModel<Statistics, GaussianPathGenerator,
    PathPricer<Path> > > (
    new MonteCarloModel<Statistics, GaussianPathGenerator, PathPricer<Path> >
      (pathGenerator, euroPathPricer, Statistics()));
    }
  }
}
```

Finally, we can use the *Statistics* class that aggregates the results of the Monte
Carlo and provides the statistics:

```
namespace QuantLib
{
  namespace Math
  {
    /*******************************************************************************/
    Statistic tool
    It can accumulate a set of data and return statistic quantities
    as mean, variance, std. deviation, skewness, and kurtosis.
    *******************************************************************************/
    class Statistics
    {
      public:
```

```cpp
Statistics();
// inspectors

// number of samples collected
Size samples() const;

// sum of data weights
double weightSum() const;

// returns the mean, defined as
// x_mean = {sum w_i x_i}/{sum w_i}.
double mean() const;

// returns the variance, defined as
// N/N-1*x- x_mean^2.
double variance() const;

// returns the standard deviation sigma, defined as the
// square root of the variance.
double standardDeviation() const;

// returns the downside variance, defined as
// N/N-1 *sum_{i=1}^{N}
// theta*x_i^{2}}{sum_{i=1}^{N} w_i},
// where theta = 0 if x > 0 and theta =1 if x <0
double downsideVariance() const;

// returns the downside deviation, defined as the
// square root of the downside variance.
double downsideDeviation() const;

// returns the error estimate epsilon, defined as the
// square root of the ratio of the variance to the number of
// samples.
double errorEstimate() const;

// returns the skewness, defined as
// [ \frac{N^2}{(N-1)(N-2)} \frac{\left\langle \left(
// x-\langle x \rangle \right)^3 \right\rangle}{\sigma^3}. ]
// The above evaluates to 0 for a Gaussian distribution.
double skewness() const;

// returns the excess kurtosis, defined as
// N(N+1)/(N-1)(N-2)(N-3)
// \frac{\left\langle \left( x-\langle x \rangle \right)^4
// \right\rangle}{\sigma^4} - \frac{3(N-1)^2}{(N-2)(N-3)}.
// The above evaluates to 0 for a Gaussian distribution.
double kurtosis() const;

/* returns the minimum sample value */
double min() const;

/* returns the maximum sample value */
double max() const;
```

```
      // name Modifiers
      // adds a datum to the set, possibly with a weight
      void add(double value, double weight = 1.0);

      // adds a sequence of data to the set
      template <class DataIterator>
      void addSequence(DataIterator begin, DataIterator end)
      {
        for (; begin!=end;++begin)
          add(*begin);
      }

      // adds a sequence of data to the set, each with its weight
      template <class DataIterator, class WeightIterator>
      void addSequence(DataIterator begin, DataIterator end, WeightIterator
        wbegin)
      {
        for (;begin!=end;++begin,++wbegin)
        add(*begin, *wbegin);
      }
      // resets the data to a null set
      void reset();
   private:
      Size sampleNumber_;
      double sampleWeight_;
      double sum_, quadraticSum_, downsideQuadraticSum_, cubicSum_,
        fourthPowerSum_;
      double min_, max_;
};

// inline definitions
/* pre weights must be positive or null */
inline void Statistics::add(double value, double weight)
{
  QL_REQUIRE(weight>=0.0,
    "Statistics::add : negative weight (" +
    DoubleFormatter::toString(weight) + ") not allowed");

  Size oldSamples = sampleNumber_;
  sampleNumber_++;
  QL_ENSURE(sampleNumber_ > oldSamples, "Statistics::add : maximum number of
    samples reached");

  sampleWeight_ += weight;

  double temp = weight*value;
  sum_ += temp;
  temp *= value;
  quadraticSum_ += temp;
  downsideQuadraticSum_ += value < 0.0 ? temp : 0.0;
  temp *= value;
  cubicSum_ += temp;
```

```
    temp *= value;
    fourthPowerSum_ += temp;
    min_ = min(value, min_);
    max_ = max(value, max_);
}

inline Size Statistics::samples() const
{
    return sampleNumber_;
}

inline double Statistics::weightSum() const
{
    return sampleWeight_;
}

inline double Statistics::mean() const
{
    QL_REQUIRE(sampleWeight_>0.0, "Stat::mean() : sampleWeight_=0, insufficient");
    return sum_/sampleWeight_;
}

inline double Statistics::variance() const
{
    QL_REQUIRE(sampleWeight_>0.0, "Stat::variance() : sampleWeight_=0,
        insufficient");

    QL_REQUIRE(sampleNumber_>1, "Stat::variance() : sample number <=1,
        insufficient");

    double v = (sampleNumber_/(sampleNumber_-1.0)) *(quadraticSum_ -
        sum_*sum_/sampleWeight_)/sampleWeight_;

    if (fabs(v) <= 1.0e-6)
        v = 0.0;

    QL_ENSURE(v >= 0.0, "Statistics: negative variance (" +
        DoubleFormatter::toString(v,20) + ")");

    return v;
}

inline double Statistics::standardDeviation() const
{
    return QL_SQRT(variance());
}

inline double Statistics::downsideVariance() const
{
    QL_REQUIRE(sampleWeight_>0.0, "Stat::variance() : sampleWeight_=0,
        insufficient");
```

```
      QL_REQUIRE(sampleNumber_>1, "Stat::variance() : sample number <=1,
        insufficient");

    return sampleNumber_/(sampleNumber_-1.0)*
      downsideQuadraticSum_ /sampleWeight_;
}


inline double Statistics::downsideDeviation() const
{
  return sqrt(downsideVariance());
}


inline double Statistics::errorEstimate() const
{
  double var = variance();
  QL_REQUIRE(samples() > 0, "Statistics: zero samples are not sufficient");
  return QL_SQRT(var/samples());
}


inline double Statistics::skewness() const
{
  QL_REQUIRE(sampleNumber_>2, "Stat::skewness() : sample number <=2,
    insufficient");
  double s = standardDeviation();
  if (s==0.0)
    return 0.0;

  double m = mean();

  return sampleNumber_*sampleNumber_/ ((sampleNumber_-1.0)*(sampleNumber_-
    2.0)*s*s*s)*(cubicSum_-3.0*m*quadraticSum_+2.0*m*m*sum_)/sampleWeight_;
}


inline double Statistics::kurtosis() const
{
  QL_REQUIRE(sampleNumber_>3, "Stat::kurtosis() : sample number <=3,
    insufficient");

  double m = mean();
  double v = variance();

  if (v==0)
    return - 3.0*(sampleNumber_-1.0)*(sampleNumber_-1.0) / ((sampleNumber_-
      2.0)*(sampleNumber_-3.0));

  double kurt = sampleNumber_*sampleNumber_*(sampleNumber_+1.0) /
    ((sampleNumber_-1.0)*(sampleNumber_-2.0) * (sampleNumber_-3.0)*v*v) *
    (fourthPowerSum_ - 4.0*m*cubicSum_ + 6.0*m*m*quadraticSum_
    -3.0*m*m*m*sum_)/sampleWeight_ -3.0*(sampleNumber_-1.0)*
    (sampleNumber_-1.0) / ((sampleNumber_-2.0)*(sampleNumber_-3.0));
```

```
        return kurt;
    }

    inline double Statistics::min() const
    {
        QL_REQUIRE(sampleNumber_>0, "Stat::min_() : empty sample");
        return min_;
    }

    inline double Statistics::max() const
    {
        QL_REQUIRE(sampleNumber_>0, "Stat::max_() : empty sample");
        return max_;
    }
  }
}
```

To actually price a European option, we can use the following code segment:

```
    . . .
method ="MC (crude)";
bool antitheticVariance = false;
McEuropean mcEur(Option::Call, underlying, strike, dividendYield, riskFreeRate,
   maturity, volatility, antitheticVariance);
// use an error tolerance of 0.002%
value = mcEur.value(0.02);
estimatedError = mcEur.errorEstimate();
discrepancy = QL_FABS(value-rightValue);
relativeDiscrepancy = discrepancy/rightValue;
// print out results
std::cout << method << "\t"
   << DoubleFormatter::toString(value, 4) << "\t"
   << DoubleFormatter::toString(estimatedError, 4) << "\t\t"
   << DoubleFormatter::toString(discrepancy, 6) << "\t"
   << DoubleFormatter::toString(relativeDiscrepancy, 6)
   << std::endl;
```

where we pass the option type, underlying price, strike price, dividend yield, risk-free rate, option maturity, volatility, and "antitheticVariance" Boolean flag into the *McEuropean* class constructor.

CHAPTER 3

Binomial Trees

In this chapter, we discuss approximating diffusion processes by two-state lattices known as binomial trees. Binomial trees are useful for pricing a variety of European-style and American-style derivatives. In section 3.1, we discuss the general binomial tree framework. In section 3.2, we discuss the Cox-Ross-Rubinstein (CRR) binomial tree. In section 3.3, we discuss the Jarrow-Rudd (JR) binomial tree while in section 3.4 we discuss general binomial trees. In section 3.5, we discuss binomial diffusion processes that incorporate dividend payments. In section 3.6, we discuss using binomial trees to price derivatives with American exercise features. In section 3.7, CRR and JR binomial tree implementations are provided. In section 3.8, we discuss computing hedge sensitivities from binomial trees. In section 3.9, we discuss binomial models with time-varying volatility. In section 3.10, we discuss two-state binomial processes that are constructed using quadrinomial trees (binomial trees with four branches at each node). Finally, in section 3.11, we show how convertible bonds can be priced using a binomial tree.

3.1 USE OF BINOMIAL TREES

We can model diffusion processes using binomial trees. Suppose we have a stock price at time $t = 0$ with initial value S_0. The stock price can move up with probability p and down with probability $1 - p$. Over one time period, Δt, if the stock price moves up, the value is Su where $u = e^{\sigma \Delta t}$; and if it moves down, the value is Sd where $d = 1/u = e^{-\sigma \Delta t}$. We know that in a risk-neutral world, investors expect to earn the risk-free rate on riskless portfolios. Thus,

$$pSu + (1 - p)Sd = Se^{r\Delta t} \tag{3.1}$$

Solving for p, we find

$$p = \frac{e^{r\Delta t} - d}{u - d} \text{ and } 1 - p = \frac{u - e^{r\Delta t}}{u - d}$$

We can extend this analysis to a multiperiod binomial model. Let $\tau = T - t = N\Delta t$ where N is the number of time periods (there are $N + 1$ nodes at time step N and $N + 1$ different terminal prices and payoffs). Thus, there are 2^N possible price paths from (t, S) to (T, S_T). Node (i, j) denotes the jth node at the ith time step. The price S_{ij} at the node (i, j) is given by:

$$S_{i,j} = S_0 u^j d^{i-j} \qquad i = 0, \ldots, N, \qquad j = 0, \ldots, i \qquad (3.2)$$

where i is the number of time steps to the node (i, j) and j is the number of up moves to the node (i, j). The payoff after N periods, denoted $f_{N,j}$, is

$$f_{N,j} = F(S_0 u^j d^{i-j}) \qquad (3.3)$$

We can use backward induction to price European options. The price of an option at node (i, j) over one period, Δt, is given by:

$$f_{i,j} = e^{-r\Delta t}\left(p f_{i+1,j+1} + (1-p)f_{i+1,j}\right) \qquad (3.4)$$

The value of the option at node (i, j) is found by taking the expected value of the option at time $i + 1$. The option will be worth either $f_{i+1,j+1}$ with probability p or $f_{i+1,j}$ with probability $1 - p$. We discount this value back by the risk-free rate since we want the present value of this future expected payoff. The multiperiod binomial valuation formula for European options is:

$$f = e^{-r\tau}\sum_{j=1}^{N} p_{N,j} f_{N,j} \qquad (3.5)$$

where $f_{N,j} = F(S_{N,j}) = F(S_0 u^j d^{N-j})$ is the payoff in state j at expiration N and $p_{N,j}$ is the risk-neutral binomial probability to end up in state (N, j):

$$p_{N,j} = \binom{N}{j} p^j (1-p)^{N-j} \qquad (3.6)$$

We now need to link the binomial price process with the Black-Scholes geometric Brownian motion process so that the binomial model is consistent with it. We have two models to describe the asset price dynamics, a discrete-time multiplicative binomial model with parameters (u, d, p, r) and the continuous-time Black-Scholes-Merton model with parameters (σ, r). In the limit of infinitesimally small time steps, $N \to \infty$ and $\Delta t \to 0$, the binomial option pricing formula must converge to the Black-Scholes option pricing formula:

$$f = e^{-r\tau}\int_0^{\infty} F(S_T) p^Q (S_T, T \mid S, t) dS_T \qquad (3.7)$$

for the two formulations to be consistent. This requires that the distribution of the terminal stock price in the binomial model converge to the lognormal distribution as $\Delta t \to 0$.

PROPOSITION. The distribution of the terminal stock price in the binomial model with parameters (u, d, p, r) converges to the Black-Scholes lognormal distribution with parameters (σ, r) as $\Delta t \to 0$ if and only if:

$$p \ln\left(\frac{u}{d}\right) + \ln d = \mu \Delta t + o(\Delta t) \tag{3.8}$$

and

$$p(1 - p)\left(\ln\left(\frac{u}{d}\right)\right)^2 = \sigma^2 \Delta t + o(\Delta t) \tag{3.9}$$

PROOF. The proof is based on the central limit theorem. In the Black-Scholes model (BSM), the terminal stock price is a random variable

$$S_T = S^{\mu\tau + \sigma\sqrt{\tau}\varepsilon}$$

where ε is a standard normal random variable. The continuously compounded return over the time period τ is a normal random variable:

$$\eta = \ln\left(\frac{S_T}{S}\right) = \mu\tau + \sigma\sqrt{\tau}\varepsilon \tag{3.10}$$

On the other hand, consider a binomial model where $\tau = T - t$ is divided into a large number N of time steps. The return over the entire time period τ is a sum of individual returns over each time step Δt,

$$\eta = \sum_{i=1}^{M} \eta_i$$

where the η_i's are i.i.d. random variables that can take two values: either $\ln u$ with probability p or $\ln d$ with probability $1 - p$. The mean m and variance s^2 of η_i are:

$$m = p \ln u + (1 - p)\ln d$$

and

$$
\begin{aligned}
s^2 &= p(\ln u)^2 + (1-p)(\ln d)^2 - (p\ln u + (1-p)\ln d)^2 \\
&= p(\ln u)^2 + (1-p)(\ln d)^2 - p^2(\ln u)^2 - (1-p)^2(\ln d)^2 - 2p(1-p)\ln u \ln d \\
&= p(1-p)(\ln u - \ln d)^2 \\
&= p(1-p)\left(\ln\left(\frac{u}{d}\right)\right)^2
\end{aligned}
\tag{3.11}
$$

Now, the central limit theorem states that for a large N, the distribution of the sum η of N i.i.d. random variables η_i is approximately normal with mean mN and variance s^2N. Further, the binomial model converges to the Black-Scholes model if and only if:

$$
\sum_{i=1}^{N}\eta_i \xrightarrow{\ N\to\infty\ } \mu\tau + \sigma\sqrt{\tau}\varepsilon
\tag{3.12}
$$

and we have

$$
mN \xrightarrow{\ N\to\infty\ } \mu\tau \text{ and } s^2N \xrightarrow{\ N\to\infty\ } \sigma^2\tau
$$

Noting that $\Delta t = \tau/N$ we can rewrite the above two limits as: $m = p\ln(u/d) + \ln d = \mu\Delta t + o(\Delta t)$ and $s^2 = p(1-p)(\ln(u/d))^2 = \sigma^2\Delta t + o(\Delta t)$.

We can prove this more formally. By starting at the expiration date and working backward, we can find the valuation of a call option at any period n. Since we assume the stock price follows a multiplicative binomial probability distribution, we have

$$
C_{binomial} = r^{-n}\left\{\sum_{j=0}^{n}\left(\frac{n!}{j!(n-j)!}\right)p^j(1-p)^{n-j}\max\left[0,\ Su^j d^{n-j} - X\right]\right\}
\tag{3.13}
$$

Let a denote the minimum number of upward moves that the stock must make over the next n periods for the call to finish in-the-money. Thus, a is the smallest non-negative integer such that $Su^a d^{n-a} > K$. Taking the natural logarithms of both sides of the inequality, we get:

$$
a = \left\lceil \frac{\log\left(\dfrac{X}{Sd^n}\right)}{\log\left(\dfrac{u}{d}\right)} \right\rceil
\tag{3.14}
$$

Thus, a is the smallest nonnegative integer greater than $(X/Sd^n)/\log(u/d)$. For all $j < a$, $\max[0, Su^j d^{n-j} - X] = 0$ and for all $j \geq a$, $\max[0, Su^j d^{n-j} - X] = Su^j d^{n-j} - X$. Therefore,

$$C_{binomial} = \frac{1}{r^n} \left\{ \sum_{j=a}^{n} \left(\frac{n!}{j!(n-j)!} \right) p^j (1-p)^{n-j} [Su^j d^{n-j} - X] \right\} \quad (3.15)$$

Note that if $a > n$, the call will finish out-of-the-money even if the stock moves upward every period, so its current value must be zero.

We can rewrite equation (3.15) as:

$$\begin{aligned} C_{binomial} = S &\left(\sum_{j=a}^{n} \left(\frac{n!}{j!(n-j)!} \right) p^j (1-p)^{n-j} \left(\frac{u^j d^{n-j}}{r^n} \right) \right) \\ &- Xr^{-n} \left(\sum_{j=a}^{n} \left(\frac{n!}{j!(n-j)!} \right) p^j (1-p)^{n-j} \right) \end{aligned} \quad (3.16)$$

The second parenthesized term is the complementary binomial distribution function $\Phi[a; n, p]$. The first parenthesized term is also a complementary binomial distribution function $\Phi[a; n, p']$, where

$$p' \equiv (u/r)p \text{ and } 1 - p' = (d/r)(1 - p) \quad (3.17)$$

The term p' is a probability since $0 < p' < 1$. Note that $p < (r/u)$ and

$$p^j (1-p)^{n-j} \left(\frac{u^j d^{n-j}}{r^n} \right) = \left[(u/r)p \right]^j \left[(d/r)(1-p) \right]^{n-j} = p'^j (1-p')^{n-j} \quad (3.18)$$

Consequently, from equation (3.16), we can define the binomial option pricing formula for a call option:

$$C = S\Phi[a; n, p'] - Xr^{-n}\Phi[a; n, p] \quad (3.19)$$

where $p = (r - d)/(u - d)$, $p' = (u/r)p$, and a is the smallest nonnegative integer greater than $\log(X/Sd^n)/\log(u/d)$. If $a > n$, $C = 0$.

Following Cox and Rubinstein (1985), we can now show that the binomial formula in equation (3.19) converges to the Black-Scholes formula, equation (1.57), and that the multiplicative binomial probability distribution of the stock price converges to the lognormal distribution. To show convergence of the distributions, we need to show that as

$$n \to \infty, \ \Phi[a; n, p'] \to N(d) \text{ and } \Phi[a; n, p] \to N(d - \sigma\sqrt{\tau})$$

The complementary binomial distribution function $\Phi[a; n, p]$ is the probability that the sum of n random variables, each of which can take on the value 1 with probability p and 0 with probability $1 - p$, will be greater than or equal to a. We know that the random value of this sum, j, has mean np and standard deviation

$$\sqrt{np(1-p)}$$

Thus,

$$1 - \Phi[a;\, n,\, p] = \text{Prob}[j \le a - 1] = \text{Prob}\left[\frac{j - np}{\sqrt{np(1-p)}} < \frac{(a-1) - np}{\sqrt{np(1-p)}}\right] \quad (3.20)$$

If we consider our binomial model of the stock price that in each period moves up with probability p to Su and down with probability $1 - p$ to Sd, then over n periods, we have $\tilde{S} = Su^j d^{n-j}$ so that

$$\log(\tilde{S}/S) = j \log(u/d) + n \log d \quad (3.21)$$

The mean and variance of the continuously compounded rate of return of this stock are:

$$\tilde{\mu}_p = p \log(u/d) + \log d \quad \text{and} \quad \tilde{\sigma}_p^2 = p(1 - p)(\log(u/d))^2 \quad (3.22)$$

Using the equalities in equations (3.21) and (3.22) we can derive the following relationship:

$$\frac{j - np}{\sqrt{np(1-p)}} = \frac{\log(\tilde{S}/S) - \tilde{\mu}_p n}{\tilde{\sigma}_p^2 \sqrt{n}} \quad (3.23)$$

It is known from the binomial formula that

$$a - 1 = \log(K/Sd^n)/\log(u/d) - \varepsilon = (\log(X/S) - n \log d)/\log(u/d) - \varepsilon$$

where $\varepsilon \in (0, 1)$. Using this and the equations in (3.22), with some algebra, we can show:

$$\frac{a - 1 - np}{\sqrt{np(1-p)}} = \frac{\log(X/S) - \tilde{\mu}_p n - \varepsilon \log(u/d)}{\tilde{\sigma}_p \sqrt{n}} \quad (3.24)$$

Consequently, we get the following result:

$$1 - \Phi[a; \, n, \, p] = \text{Prob} \left[\frac{\log(\tilde{S}/S) - \mu_p n}{\tilde{\sigma}_p \sqrt{n}} \leq \frac{\log(X/S) - \tilde{\mu}_p n - \varepsilon \log(u/d)}{\tilde{\sigma}_p \sqrt{n}} \right] \quad (3.25)$$

We can use the central limit theorem. However, we must first check that the third moment, an initial condition of the central limit theorem,[1] tends to 0 as $n \to \infty$. We must show

$$\frac{p\left|\log u - \tilde{\mu}_p\right|^3 + (1-p)\left|\log d - \tilde{\mu}_p\right|^3}{\tilde{\sigma}_p \sqrt{n}} = \frac{(1-p)^2 + p^2}{\sqrt{np(1-p)}} \to 0$$

is satisfied as $n \to \infty$. Recall that $p = (\tilde{r} - d) / (u - d)$, and that

$$\tilde{r} = r^{t/n}, \; u = e^{\sigma \sqrt{t/n}}$$

and

$$d = e^{-\sigma \sqrt{t/n}}$$

Making the appropriate substitutions, it can be shown that

$$p \to \frac{1}{2} + \frac{1}{2} \frac{(\log r - \frac{1}{2}\sigma^2)}{\sigma} \sqrt{\frac{t}{n}}$$

so that the third moment goes to 0 as $n \to \infty$. Thus, we are justified in using the central limit theorem. In equation (3.25), we need to evaluate $\tilde{\mu}_p n$, $\sigma_p^2 n$, and $\log(u/d)$ as $n \to \infty$. In the limiting case where $n \to \infty$, we have

$$\tilde{\mu}_p n \to (\log r - \frac{1}{2}\sigma^2)t \text{ and } \tilde{\sigma}_p \sqrt{n} \to \sigma\sqrt{t}$$

Moreover,

$$\log(u/d) = 2\sigma\sqrt{t/n} \to 0 \text{ as } n \to \infty$$

---

[1]The initial condition of the central limit theorem states roughly that higher-order moments of the distributions, such as how it is skewed, become less and less important relative to the standard deviation as $n \to \infty$.

Using the central limit theorem, we can write:

$$\frac{\log(X/S) - \tilde{\mu}_p n - \varepsilon\log(u/d)}{\tilde{\sigma}_p\sqrt{n}} \to z = \frac{\log(X/S) - (\log r - \frac{1}{2}\sigma^2)t}{\sigma\sqrt{t}}$$

We have:

$$1 - \Phi[a;\, n,\, p] \to N(z) = N\left[\frac{\log(Xr^{-t}/S)}{\sigma\sqrt{t}} + \frac{1}{2}\sigma\sqrt{t}\right] \tag{3.26}$$

From the symmetry of the standard normal distribution, $1 - N(z) = N(-z)$. Therefore, as $n \to \infty$,

$$\Phi[a:\, p,\, n] \to N(-z) = N\left[\frac{\log(S/Xr^{-t})}{\sigma\sqrt{t}} - \frac{1}{2}\sigma\sqrt{t}\right] = N(d - \sigma\sqrt{t})$$

A similar argument holds for $\Phi[a;\, n,\, p]$, which completes the proof of convergence of the binomial option pricing formula to the Black-Scholes as the number of time steps tends to infinity, that is, as we divide the time to maturity into more and more subintervals.

We call a given binomial model (u, d, p, r) consistent with the Black-Scholes model (σ, r) if the two relations just given are satisfied. Clearly, an infinite number of binomial models are consistent with any given continuous-time Black-Scholes model. First, we have two relations for three unknowns (u, d, p) relating them to (σ, r). Second, the two relations are required to hold only in the first order in Δt; higher-order terms $o(\Delta t)$ become irrelevant in the limit $\Delta t \to 0$.

The convergence of the binomial model to the Black-Scholes model requires mean and variance of the return distributions for a single period Δt to match up to the higher-order terms. To speed up the convergence, we can strengthen this, and require that the mean and variance of the stock price distribution at the end of the period Δt match exactly the mean and variance of the lognormal distribution.

Consider a time period Δt in the Black-Scholes model. The price at the end of the period is a lognormal random variable (in the risk-neutral world)

$$S_{t+\Delta t} = S_t \exp(\mu\Delta t + \sigma\sqrt{\Delta t})$$

where $\mu = r - \sigma^2/2$ with mean

$$E^Q_{t,S}[S_{t+\Delta t}] = e^{r\Delta t}S \tag{3.27}$$

and variance

$$V^Q_{t,S}[S_{t+\Delta t}] = e^{2r\Delta t}(e^{\sigma^2\Delta t} - 1)S^2 \tag{3.28}$$

where the expectation and variance of the future price is taken at time t over the stock price process with risk-neutral probability measure Q. At the same time, in the binomial model the price at the end of a single period Δt is a random variable with two possible states Su and Sd with probability p and $1 - p$.

$$E^{binomial}_{t,S}[S_{t+\Delta t}] = (pu + (1 - p)d)S \tag{3.29}$$

$$E^{binomial}_{t,S}[S^2_{t+\Delta t}] = pu^2 + (1 - p)d^2)S^2 \tag{3.30}$$

For the underlying price at the end of the period to have the same mean and variance in both the multiplicative binomial and the Black-Scholes models, the following two identities must hold where the moments are matched.

$$pu + (1 - p)d = e^{r\Delta t} \tag{3.31}$$

$$pu^2 + (1 - p)d^2 = e^{(2r+\sigma^2)\Delta t} \tag{3.32}$$

Equation (3.31) can be solved for

$$p = \frac{e^{r\Delta t} - d}{u - d}$$

the same probability we derived from equation (3.1). Equation (3.32) provides the link between u and d in the binomial model and the volatility σ in the Black-Scholes model. Substitution of p into equation (3.32) yields:

$$e^{r\Delta t}(u + d) - du = e^{(2r+\sigma^2)\Delta t} \tag{3.33}$$

To solve for u and d in terms of r and σ we need an additional equation since we have one equation in two unknowns. There are several choices for a second equation: (1) Cox-Ross-Rubinstein (CRR) approach, (2) Jarrow-Rudd approach, and (3) a general approach.

3.2 COX-ROSS-RUBINSTEIN BINOMIAL TREE

Cox, Ross, and Rubinstein, in their original model, assume the identity $ud = 1$ so that $u = 1/d$. Substituting this identity for u and d into equation (3.33), we get $d^2 - 2Ad + 1 = 0$ where

$$A = \frac{1}{2}(e^{-r\Delta t} + e^{(r+\sigma^2)\Delta t})$$

The solutions for u and d are

$$u = A + \sqrt{A^2 - 1} \qquad (3.34)$$

and

$$d = A - \sqrt{A^2 - 1} \qquad (3.35)$$

Thus, we have specified all of the parameters u, d, and p in terms of the risk-free rate r and volatility σ. If we linearize the preceding solution for u and d and keep only the terms of the first order in Δt we have:

$$u = 1 + \sigma\sqrt{\Delta t} + \frac{1}{2}\sigma^2 \Delta t, \; d = 1 - \sigma\sqrt{\Delta t} + \frac{1}{2}\sigma^2 \Delta t$$

$$p = \frac{1}{2} + \frac{1}{2}\left(\frac{\mu}{\sigma}\right)\sqrt{\Delta t}, \text{ and } 1 - p = \frac{1}{2} - \frac{1}{2}\left(\frac{\mu}{\sigma}\right)\sqrt{\Delta t}$$

One easily sees that $ud = 1$. Terms of higher orders in Δt can be added without violating the relations since they become infinitesimally small as $\Delta t \to 0$. Thus, we can use the more common form of

$$u = e^{\sigma\sqrt{\Delta t}}$$

and

$$d = e^{-\sigma\sqrt{\Delta t}}$$

The CRR has traditionally been the most widely used version of the binomial model. This is an approximation to the exact solution with u in equation (3.34) and d in equation (3.35). In the limit $\Delta t \to 0$, both the binomial and Black-Scholes converge to the same limit. But the exact version of the binomial tree converges faster since the mean and variance are matched exactly as in equations (3.31) and (3.32).

3.3   JARROW-RUDD BINOMIAL TREE

Jarrow and Rudd choose equal probabilities for up and down price movements; that is, $p = 1 - p = 1/2$. Substituting this into the two moment-matching equations in (3.31) and (3.32) we get

$$u + d = 2e^{r\Delta t} \qquad (3.36)$$

$$u^2 + d^2 = 2e^{(2r+\sigma^2)\Delta t} \qquad (3.37)$$

The exact solution to these equations yields:

$$u = e^{r\Delta t}(1 + \sqrt{e^{\sigma^2 \Delta t} - 1}) \qquad (3.38)$$

$$d = e^{r\Delta t}(1 - \sqrt{e^{\sigma^2 \Delta t} - 1}) \qquad (3.39)$$

An approximate solution keeping only the lower-order terms is:

$$u = 1 + r\Delta t + \sigma\sqrt{\Delta t}$$

and

$$d = 1 + r\Delta t - \sigma\sqrt{\Delta t}$$

The higher-order terms can be added since they tend to zero as $\Delta t \to 0$ and maintain the convergence to the BSM. The most popular choice for the Jarrow-Rudd (JR) binomial tree is:

$$u = e^{\mu\Delta t + \sigma\sqrt{\Delta t}} \qquad (3.40)$$

and

$$d = e^{\mu\Delta t - \sigma\sqrt{\Delta t}} \qquad (3.41)$$

where

$$\mu = r - \frac{1}{2}\sigma^2$$

The difference between the CRR and JR trees is that the CRR tree is symmetric since $ud = 1$ (a down movement following an up movement brings us back to the original price S), but the up and down probabilities are not equal. In the JR tree, the probabilities are equal, but the tree is skewed since $ud = e^{2\mu\Delta t}$.

3.4   GENERAL TREE

Assume $ud = e^{2v\Delta t}$ where v is some scalar. Then the following is a possible solution:

$$u = e^{v\Delta t + \sigma\sqrt{\Delta t}} \qquad (3.42)$$

and

$$d = e^{v\Delta t - \sigma\sqrt{\Delta t}} \qquad (3.43)$$

where the probabilities of an up and down movement are

$$p = \frac{1}{2} + \frac{1}{2}\left(\frac{\mu - v}{\sigma}\right)\sqrt{\Delta t} \text{ and } 1 - p = \frac{1}{2} - \frac{1}{2}\left(\frac{\mu - v}{\sigma}\right)\sqrt{\Delta t}$$

respectively. The CRR and JR choices are $v = 0$ and $v = \mu$, respectively. It is important to note that the CRR and JR formulations are good only over small time intervals: Arbitrarily large time steps cannot be used. We can solve this problem by reformulating the problem in terms of the natural logarithm of the asset price.[2] We know that the continuous-time risk-neutral process of geometric Brownian motion is:

$$dx = \mu dt + \sigma dz$$

where $x = \ln S$ and

$$\mu = r - \frac{1}{2}\sigma^2$$

The variable x can go up to $\Delta x_u = x + \Delta x$ with probability p_u or down to $\Delta x_d = x - \Delta x$ with probability $p_d = 1 - p_u$. This is described as the additive binomial process as opposed to the multiplicative binomial process.[3] We must equate the mean and variance of the additive binomial process for x to the mean and variance of the continuous-time process over the time interval Δt. Thus, we get the following equations:[4]

$$E[\Delta x] = p_u\Delta x_u + p_d\Delta x_d = \mu\Delta t$$

$$E[\Delta x^2] = p_u\Delta x_u^2 + p_d\Delta x_d^2 = \sigma^2\Delta t + \mu^2\Delta t^2 \qquad (3.44)$$

Equations (3.44) with equal probabilities yield

$$\frac{1}{2}\Delta x_u + \frac{1}{2}\Delta x_d = \mu\Delta t$$

$$\frac{1}{2}\Delta x_u^2 + \frac{1}{2}\Delta x_d^2 = \sigma^2\Delta t + \mu^2\Delta t^2 \qquad (3.45)$$

---

[2]Clewlow and Strickland (1998a), 19.
[3]Ibid.
[4]Ibid.

Solving (3.45) gives

$$\Delta x_u = \frac{1}{2}\mu\Delta t + \frac{1}{2}\sqrt{4\sigma^2\Delta t - 3\mu^2\Delta t^2}$$
$$\Delta x_d = \frac{3}{2}\mu\Delta t - \frac{1}{2}\sqrt{4\sigma^2\Delta t - 3\mu^2\Delta t^2} \tag{3.46}$$

Assuming equal jump sizes in (3.44) gives

$$p_u(\Delta x) + p_d(\Delta x) = \mu\Delta t$$
$$p_u\Delta x^2 + p_d\Delta x^2 = \sigma^2\Delta t + \mu^2\Delta t^2 \tag{3.47}$$

Solving (3.47) we get

$$\Delta x = \sqrt{\sigma^2\Delta t + \mu^2\Delta t^2}$$
$$p_u = \frac{1}{2} + \frac{1}{2}\frac{\mu\Delta t}{\Delta x} \tag{3.48}$$

This last solution was proposed by Trigeorgis (1991). It has on average slightly better accuracy than the CRR and JR models.

3.5   DIVIDEND PAYMENTS

The CRR, JR, and general binomial trees can be extended to the case where the underlying security pays continuous dividends with a constant dividend yield q. The growth rate of the asset price becomes $r - q$, and it is necessary to substitute $r \rightarrow r - q$ into the formulas. Thus, in the CRR model, the probability of an up movement becomes

$$p = \frac{e^{(r-q)\Delta t} - d}{u - d} \quad \text{and } 1 - p = \frac{u - e^{(r-q)\Delta t}}{u - d}$$

In the JR model, the up and down movements are as in equations (3.40) and (3.41) except $\mu = r - q - \sigma^2/2$. If the time $i\Delta t$ is after the stock goes ex-dividend, the nodes correspond to the stock prices

$$S_0(1 - q)u^j d^{i-j} \qquad j = 0, 1, \ldots, i \tag{3.49}$$

If there are several known dividend yields during the life of the option, then the nodes at time $i\Delta t$ correspond to

$$S_0(1 - q_i)u^j d^{i-j}$$

where q_i is the total dividend yield associated with all ex-dividend dates between time zero and time $i\Delta t$.

If the stock pays a known dollar dividend, a more realistic assumption, then the tree does not recombine, assuming the volatility, σ, is constant. This means that the number of nodes that have to be evaluated can become quite large, especially if there are several dividend dates. Hull (1997) describes an approach that will allow the tree to recombine so that there are $i + 1$ nodes at time i rather than $2i$.

Hull supposes that a stock price has two components: an uncertain part and a part that is the present value of all future dividends during the life of the option. Assume there is only one ex-dividend date, τ, during the life of the option where $i\Delta t \leq \tau \leq (i + 1)\Delta t$. Let $\tilde{S}$ be the uncertain component at time $i\Delta t$ such that $\tilde{S} = S$ when $i\Delta t > \tau$ and $\tilde{S} = S - De^{-r(\tau - i\Delta t)}$ when $i\Delta t \leq \tau$, where D is the dividend payment in dollars. Define $\tilde{\sigma}$ as the volatility of $\tilde{S}$ and assume $\tilde{\sigma}$ is constant. The parameters p, u, and d can be calculated as before using CRR, JR, or the general approach. With σ replaced by $\tilde{\sigma}$, we can build the tree and have it recombine for $\tilde{S}$. We can use a linear transformation and convert the tree into another tree that models S by adding the present value of future dividends (if any) to the stock price at each node. Thus, at time $i\Delta t$, the nodes on the tree correspond to the stock prices

$$S^* u^j d^{i-j} + De^{-r(\tau - i\Delta t)} \qquad j = 0, 1, \ldots i \qquad (3.50)$$

when $i\Delta t < t$ and

$$S^* u^j d^{i-j} \qquad j = 0, 1, \ldots i \qquad (3.51)$$

when $i\Delta t \geq \tau$.

If we have dividends, then we must ensure that the risk-neutral probabilities must be positive:

$$p = \frac{e^{(r-q)\Delta t} d}{u - d} > 0 \text{ or } e^{(r-q)\Delta t} > d \qquad (3.52)$$

and

$$1 - p = \frac{u - e^{(r-q)\Delta t}}{u - d} > 0 \text{ or } u > e^{(r-q)\Delta t} \qquad (3.53)$$

It is necessary to check that the choices for u and d are consistent with these restrictions. To prevent negative or zero probabilities, the CRR tree must satisfy

$$(r - q)\Delta t > -\sigma\sqrt{\Delta t} \text{ and } (r - q)\Delta t < \sigma\sqrt{\Delta t}$$

or equivalently,

$$| (r - q)\sqrt{\Delta t} \, | < \sigma \tag{3.54}$$

The JR model has the advantage that the probabilities are always 0.5 > 0 and thus positive for all values of the parameters.

3.6 AMERICAN EXERCISE

Binomial trees can be extended to the case of American-style options with early exercise in the presence of dividends. Suppose $F(S_T)$ is the terminal payoff. If the option is exercised at time t before the final maturity date T, the option holder receives the payoff $F(S_T)$. To value an American option, we need to evaluate whether early exercise is optimal at each node. Thus, we need to run the dynamic programming algorithm on the tree starting at the final (maturity) nodes:

$$f_{i,j} = \max(F(Su^j d^{i-j}), e^{-r\Delta t}[pf_{i+1,j+1} + (1 - p)f_{i+1,j}]) \tag{3.55}$$

In the case of a call option, at each node we evaluate

$$f_{i,j} = \max(Su^j d^{i-j} - X, e^{-r\Delta t}[pf_{i+1,j+1} + (1 - p)f_{i+1,j}]) \tag{3.56}$$

where X is the strike price. In the case of a put, we evaluate

$$f_{i,j} = \max(X - Su^j d^{i-j}, e^{-r\Delta t}[pf_{i+1,j+1} + (1 - p)f_{i+1,j}]) \tag{3.57}$$

We can extend the model to price American-style options on foreign currencies (FX options), stock indexes, and options on futures by letting $r \to r - r_f$ where r_f is the foreign risk-free rate, $r \to r - q$ where q is the dividend yield on the index, and $r \to q$ ($r = q$), respectively. Thus, for an FX option, the up probability is

$$\frac{e^{(r-r_f)\Delta t} - d}{u - d}$$

3.7   BINOMIAL TREE IMPLEMENTATION

The following is an implementation of the CRR model on an American option.

```
/*********************************************************************************
buildBinomialTreeCRRAmerican : computes the value of an American option using
  backwards induction in a CRR binomial tree
[in]:   double price    :   asset price
        double strike   :   strike price
        double rate     :   risk-free interest rate
        double div      :   dividend yield
        double vol      :   volatility
        double T        :   time to maturity
        int N           :   number of time steps
        char exercise   :   'E'uropean or 'A'merican
        char type       :   'C'all or 'P'ut
[out]:  double          :   value of American option
*********************************************************************************/
double CRRBinomialTree::buildBinomialTreeCRRAmerican(double price, double strike,
  double rate, double div, double vol, double T, int N, char type)
{
  int i,j;
  double prob;                 // probability of up movement
  double S[200][200] = {0.0};  // stock price at node i,j
  double c[200][200] = {0.0};  // call price at node i, j
  double a;
  double num = 0.0;
  double up = 0.0;
  double down = 0.0;
  double dt = 0.0;

  dt = T/N;                    // time step size
  up = exp(vol*sqrt(dt));      // up movement
  down = 1/up;                 // down movement
  a = exp((rate-div)*dt);      // growth rate in prob
  prob = (a - down)/(up - down);

  // compute stock price at each node
  // initialize call prices
  for (i = 0; i <= N; i++)
  {
    for (j = 0; j <= i; j++)
    {
      S[i][j] = price*(pow(up,j))*(pow(down,i-j));
      c[i][j] = 0;
    }
  }
```

```
// compute terminal payoffs
for (j = N; j >= 0; j--)
{
  if (type == 'C')
    c[N][j] = max(S[N][j]-strike,0);
  else
    c[N][j] = max(strike-S[N][j],0);
}

// work backwards
for (i = N-1; i >= 0; i--)
{
  for (j = i; j >= 0; j--)
  {
    c[i][j] = exp(-rate*dt)*(prob*(c[i+1][j+1]) + (1- prob)*(c[i+1][j]));
    if (type == 'C')
      c[i][j] = max(S[i][j] - strike,c[i][j]);
    else
      c[i][j] = max(strike - S[i][j],c[i][j]);
  }
}

return c[0][0];
}
```

Suppose we let the initial stock price $S_0 = 33.75$, $X = 35$, $\sigma = 15$ percent, $r = 5.5$ percent, $q = 0$ percent, and $T = 9$ months (0.75 years). The code will generate the prices and option prices of the tree shown in Figure 3.1 (we assume $N = 4$ time steps so that $\Delta t = T/N = 0.75/4 \cong 0.188$ years. The stock price is the top value in each node, and the option price is the bottom value.

The price of the call option is \$1.87. This is close to the BSM price of \$1.83, which shows that the two models price consistently (as $N \to \infty$ and $\Delta t \to 0$, the binomial price will converge to the BSM price). This shows that an American call option on a non-dividend-paying stock is worth the same as the corresponding European call option. It is never optimal to exercise an American call option early due to the insurance it provides: Once the option has been exercised and the exercise price has been exchanged for the stock price, the insurance vanishes.

The tree for a put with the same parameters is shown in Figure 3.2.

The price of the American put is \$1.71. As the number of time steps increases and thus $\Delta t \to 0$, the American put price approaches the (European) BSM price, as Table 3.1 shows.[5]

---

[5]The Black-Scholes formula cannot be used to value American-style options. However, the Roll, Geske, and Whaley closed-form analytical solution for American-style options can be used. See Hull (1996), page 259.

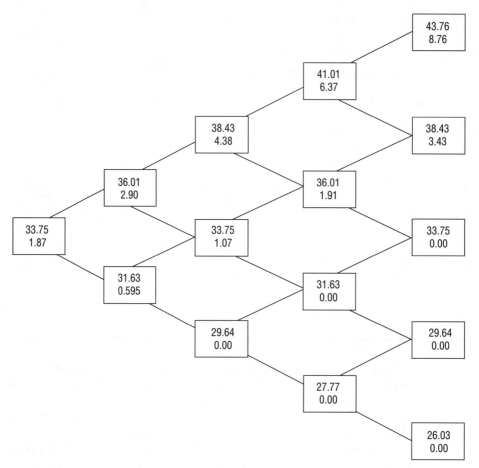

FIGURE 3.1   Tree for a Call Option

Figure 3.3 shows the put price as a function of only up to 25 time steps. As can be seen, while the price converges slowly, Figure 3.4 shows that at about 75 time steps (large N), the binomial price converges to the European Black-Scholes price of $1.633.

3.8   COMPUTING HEDGE STATISTICS

It is often necessary to compute hedge statistics of an option: delta, gamma, vega, theta, and rho. Their computations can be approximated by finite difference ratios

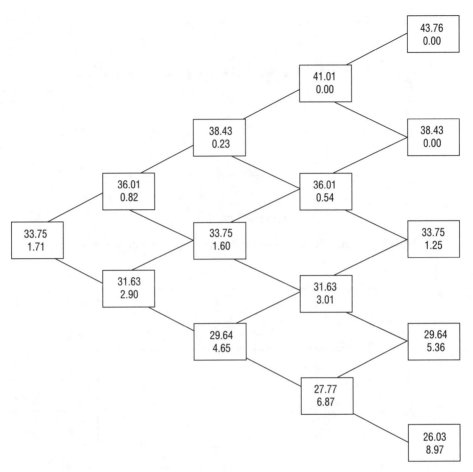

FIGURE 3.2 Tree for a Put Option

TABLE 3.1 American/European Put Prices

N (Number of Time Steps)	American Put Price	(European) Black-Scholes Model
4	$1.712	$1.663
10	$1.697	$1.663
20	$1.678	$1.663
80	$1.664	$1.663
100	$1.663	$1.663

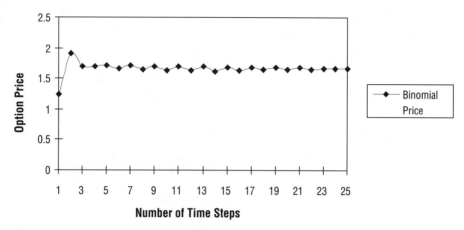

FIGURE 3.3   American Put Option Prices Computed with Binomial Tree

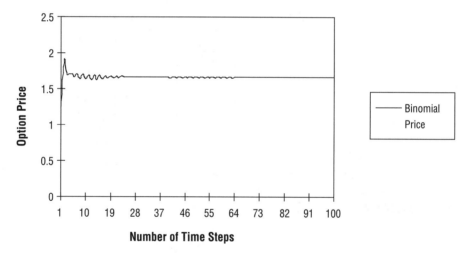

FIGURE 3.4   American Put Option Prices Computed with Binomial Tree (Larger Number of Steps)

in a binomial tree. Delta, the change in the option price as the price of the underlying asset changes, can be estimated as

$$\Delta = \frac{\partial C}{\partial S} \approx \frac{\Delta C}{\Delta S} = \frac{C_{1,1} - C_{1,0}}{S_{1,1} - S_{1,0}} \tag{3.58}$$

Using the American put example in the preceding section, we can compute delta:

$$\Delta = \frac{0.82 - 2.90}{36.01 - 31.63} = -0.475$$

Gamma can be computed as

$$\gamma = \frac{\partial^2 C}{\partial S^2} \approx \frac{[(C_{2,2} - C_{2,1})/(S_{2,2} - S_{2,1})] - [(C_{2,1} - C_{2,0})/(S_{2,1} - S_{2,0})]}{0.5 \cdot (S_{2,2} - S_{2,0})}$$

$$\approx \frac{[(0.23 - 1.60)/(38.43 - 33.75)] - [(1.60 - 4.65)/(33.75 - 29.64)]}{0.5 \cdot (38.43 - 29.64)} \quad (3.59)$$

$$\approx 0.1022$$

Vega, rho, and theta can be computed by recomputation of the option price for small changes in the volatility, risk-free rate, and time to maturity, respectively:

$$\upsilon = \frac{\partial C}{\partial \sigma} \approx \frac{C(\sigma + \Delta\sigma) - C(\sigma + \Delta\sigma)}{2\Delta\sigma} \quad (3.60)$$

$$\rho = \frac{\partial C}{\partial r} \approx \frac{C(r + \Delta r) - C(r - \Delta r)}{2\Delta r} \quad (3.61)$$

$$\theta = \frac{\partial C}{\partial T} \approx \frac{C(T + \Delta T) - C(T - \Delta T)}{2\Delta T} \quad (3.62)$$

where, for example, $C(\sigma + \Delta\sigma)$ is the value computed with $\Delta\sigma$, a small fraction of σ (i.e., $\Delta\sigma = 0.001\sigma$). Thus, we can compute vega, rho, and theta as:

$$\upsilon \approx \frac{1.664 - 1.661}{2 \cdot (0.00015)} = 10$$

$$\rho \approx \frac{1.662 - 1.663}{2 \cdot (0.000055)} = -9.09$$

$$\theta \approx \frac{1.663 - 1.662}{2 \cdot (0.00075)} = 0.667$$

Thus, a 1 percent or 0.01 increase in volatility (from 15 percent to 16 percent) increases the value of the option by approximately 0.10. A 1 percent or 0.01 increase in the risk-free rate (from 5.5 percent to 6.5 percent) decreases the value of the option by approximately 0.091. A 1 percent increase in the time to maturity increases the option price by 0.667.

3.9   BINOMIAL MODEL WITH TIME-VARYING VOLATILITY

In practice, models with time-varying volatility are used since the assumption of constant volatility is not realistic. Option pricing models must be consistent with observed implied volatilities from market prices of options. The binomial model can be adapted to time-varying volatility by fixing the space step Δx and varying the probabilities p_i, time steps Δt_i, interest rate r_i, and volatilities σ_i where subscript i is the time step. We can rewrite equation (3.30) as

$$p_i \Delta x - (1 - p_i)\Delta x = \mu_i \Delta t_i$$

$$p_i \Delta x^2 + (1 - p_i)\Delta x^2 = \sigma_i^2 \Delta t_i + \mu_i^2 \Delta t_i^2 \tag{3.63}$$

which yields

$$\Delta t_i = \frac{1}{2\mu_i^2}(-\sigma_i^2 +/- \sqrt{\sigma_i^4 + 4\sigma_i^2 \Delta x^2})$$

$$p_i = \frac{1}{2} + \frac{\mu_i \Delta t_i}{2\Delta x} \tag{3.64}$$

Set Δx to

$$\Delta x = \sqrt{\overline{\sigma}^2 \overline{\Delta t} + \overline{\mu}^2 \overline{\Delta t}^2}$$

where

$$\overline{\sigma} = \frac{1}{N}\sum_{i=1}^{N}\sigma_i \text{ and } \overline{\mu} = \frac{1}{N}\sum_{i=1}^{N}\sigma_i \tag{3.65}$$

Then $\overline{\Delta t}$ will be approximately the average time step that is obtained when the tree is built.[6] When implementing this approach with just constant volatility, but variable time steps, the time steps can be stored in an array or vector t so that the time step between two times, Δt_i, can be calculated as $t[i + 1] - t[i]$.

---

[6]Clewlow and Strickland (1998a), 38.

3.10 TWO-VARIABLE BINOMIAL PROCESS

The binomial model can be extended to price options whose payoffs depend on more than one asset such as a spread option. A multidimensional binomial tree can be built to model the joint evolution of more than one asset. Derivatives that depend on more than one asset have to factor in correlation between the assets. In a simple two-variable model such as a spread option between two stocks S_1 and S_2, we assume that both stocks follow correlated GBMs:

$$dS_1 = (r - q_1)S_1 dt + \sigma_1 S_1 dz_1$$

$$dS_2 = (r - q_2)S_1 dt + \sigma_2 S_2 dz_2$$

where S_1 and S_1 have correlated Brownian motions ρ; that is, $dz_1 dz_2 = \rho dt$. Instead of two branches at each node, we now have four based on the four different possible price movements. If we assume a multiplicative two-variable binomial process, we get the branches at each node shown in Figure 3.5.

If we work in terms of the logarithms of the asset prices, the model is simplified as with the single-asset binomial tree, and we get the additive two-variable binomial process shown in Figure 3.6, where the $x_1 = \ln S_1$ and $x_2 = \ln S_2$ follow the following processes:

$$dx_1 = \mu_1 dt + \sigma_1 dz_1$$

$$dx_2 = \mu_2 dt + \sigma_2 dz_2$$

with drifts $\mu_1 = r - q_1 - 0.5\sigma_1^2$ and $\mu_2 = r - q_2 - 0.5\sigma_2^2$. If we allow equal up and down jump sizes, we can compute their expectations and the probabilities so that

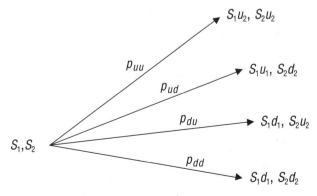

FIGURE 3.5 Multiplicative Two-Variable Binomial Process

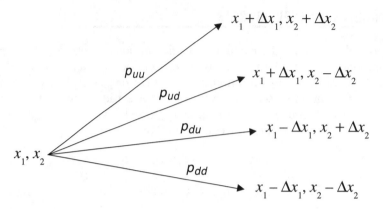

FIGURE 3.6   Additive Two-Variable Binomial Process

the means and variances of the risk-neutral process are matched. Following Clewlow and Strickland, we get[7]

$$E[\Delta x_1] = (p_{uu} + p_{ud})\Delta x_1 - (p_{du} + p_{dd})\Delta x_1 = \mu_1 \Delta t$$
$$E[\Delta x_1^2] = (p_{uu} + p_{ud})\Delta x_1^2 - (p_{du} + p_{dd})\Delta x_1^2 = \sigma_1^2 \Delta t$$
$$E[\Delta x_2] = (p_{uu} + p_{du})\Delta x_2 - (p_{ud} + p_{dd})\Delta x_2 = \mu_1 \Delta t \qquad (3.66)$$
$$E[\Delta x_2^2] = (p_{uu} + p_{du})\Delta x_2^2 - (p_{ud} + p_{dd})\Delta x_2^2 = \sigma_2^2 \Delta t$$
$$E[\Delta x_1 x_2] = (p_{uu} - p_{ud} - p_{du} - p_{dd})\Delta x_1 \Delta x_2 = \rho\sigma_1\sigma_2 \Delta t$$

and the sum of the probabilities is 1:

$$p_{uu} + p_{ud} + p_{du} + p_{dd} = 1$$

The solution to the system of equations is

$$\Delta x_1 = \sigma_1\sqrt{\Delta t}$$
$$\Delta x_2 = \sigma_2\sqrt{\Delta t}$$

---

[7]Ibid., 47.

$$p_{uu} = \frac{1}{4} \frac{(\Delta x_1 \Delta x_2 + (\Delta x_2 \mu_1 + \Delta x_1 \mu_2 + \rho \sigma_1 \sigma_2)\Delta t)}{\Delta x_1 \Delta x_2}$$

$$p_{ud} = \frac{1}{4} \frac{(\Delta x_1 \Delta x_2 + (\Delta x_2 \mu_1 + \Delta x_1 \mu_2 - \rho \sigma_1 \sigma_2)\Delta t)}{\Delta x_1 \Delta x_2}$$

$$p_{du} = \frac{1}{4} \frac{(\Delta x_1 \Delta x_2 - (\Delta x_2 \mu_1 - \Delta x_1 \mu_2 + \rho \sigma_1 \sigma_2)\Delta t)}{\Delta x_1 \Delta x_2}$$

$$p_{dd} = \frac{1}{4} \frac{(\Delta x_1 \Delta x_2 - (\Delta x_2 \mu_1 + \Delta x_1 \mu_2 - \rho \sigma_1 \sigma_2)\Delta t)}{\Delta x_1 \Delta x_2}$$

(3.67)

Nodes in the binomial tree are referenced by (i, j, k), which references the node at time step i, level j of asset 1, and level k of asset 2 so that

$$S_{1,i,j,k} = S_1 \exp(j\Delta x_1) \text{ and } S_{2,i,j,k} = S_2 \exp(k\Delta x_2)$$

Since the tree has two asset prices at each time step, nodes are separated by two space steps and the space indexes step by two. The following is an implementation of a spread option using the additive binomial tree.

```
/********************************************************************************
buildTwoVarBinomialTree : computes the value of an American spread option using a 2
                          variable binomial tree
[in]:   double S1        : asset price 1
        double S2        : asset price 2
        double strike    : strike price of spread option
        double rate      : risk-free interest rate
        double div1      : dividend yield of asset 1
        double div2      : dividend yield of asset 2
        double rho       : correlation of asset 1 and asset 2
        double vol1      : volatility of asset 1
        double vol2      : volatility of asset 2
        double T         : time to maturity
        int N            : number of time steps
        char exercise    : 'E'uropean or 'A'merican
        char type        : 'C'all or 'P'ut
[out]:  double           : value of spread option
********************************************************************************/
double TwoDimBinomialTree::buildTwoVarBinomialTree (double S1, double S2, double
  strike, double rate, double div1, double div2, double rho, double vol1, double
  vol2, double T, int N, char exercise, char type)
{
  double dt = T/N;                              // time step
  double mu1 = rate - div1 - 0.5*vol1*vol1;     // drift for stock 1
  double mu2 = rate - div2 - 0.5*vol2*vol2;     // drift for stock 2
  double dx1 = vol1*sqrt(dt);                   // state step for stock 1
  double dx2 = vol2*sqrt(dt);                   // state step for stock 2
```

```
double puu, pud, pdu, pdd, dx;              // probabilities
double S1t[100] = { 0.0 };                  // array of stock price 1
double S2t[100] = { 0.0 };                  // array of stock price 2
double c[100][100] = { 0.0 };               // call price at time step i and node j
int i,j,k;

// compute probabilities
puu = ((dx1*dx2 + (dx2*mu1 + dx1*mu2 + rho*vol1*vol2)*dt)/(4*dx1*dx2));
pud = ((dx1*dx2 + (dx2*mu1 - dx1*mu2 - rho*vol1*vol2)*dt)/(4*dx1*dx2));
pdu = ((dx1*dx2 + (-dx2*mu1 + dx1*mu2 - rho*vol1*vol2)*dt)/(4*dx1*dx2));
pdd = ((dx1*dx2 + (-dx2*mu1 - dx1*mu2 + rho*vol1*vol2)*dt)/(4*dx1*dx2));

// initialize asset prices at maturity
S1t[-N] = S1*exp(-N*dx1);
S2t[-N] = S2*exp(-N*dx2);

// compute stock prices at each node
for (j = -N+1; j <= N; j++)
{
  S1t[j] = S1t[j-1]*exp(dx1);
  S2t[j] = S2t[j-1]*exp(dx2);
}

// compute early exercise payoff at each node
for (j = -N; j <= N; j += 2)
{
  for (k = -N; k <= N; k += 2)
  {
    if (type == 'C')
      C[j][k] = max(0.0, S1t[j] - S2t[k] - strike);
    else
      C[j][k] = max(0.0, strike - St1[j] + St2[k]);
  }
}

// step back through the tree applying early exercise
for (i = N-1; i >= 0; i--)
{
  for (j = -i; j <= i; j +=2 )
  {
    for (k = -i; k <= i; k += 2)
    {
      // compute risk-neutral price
      C[j][k] = exp(-rate*T)*(pdd*C[j-1][k-1] + pud*C[j+1][k-1] + pdu*C[j-
        1][k+1] + puu*C[j+1][k+1]);

      if (exercise == 'A')
      {
        if (type == 'C')
          C[j][k] = max(C[j][k], S1t[j] - S2t[k] - strike);
        else
          C[j][k] = max(C[j][k], strike - St1[j] + St2[k]);
```

```
            }
         }
      }
   }
   return C[0][0];
}
```

An example, the value of an American spread call option with $S_1 = 50$, $S_2 = 50$, $X = 1$, $T = 1$, $r = 0.055$, $q_1 = 0.015$, $q_2 = 0.0$, $\rho = 0.60$, $\sigma_1 = 0.25$, $\sigma_2 = 0.35$, with $N = 3$ time steps is \$4.54. Figure 3.7 shows a plot of the two-variable binomial method as the number of time steps increases. You can see that the two-variable binomial method is much less efficient than in the one-variable case and does not converge to the true theoretical price that can be computed using numerical methods. In practice, to achieve efficient pricing for more than one variable, implicit difference methods must be used,[8] though other numerical methods exist. In Chapter 7, a two-factor stochastic volatility model for valuing a spread option is shown. A spread option can be valued using the fast Fourier transform method discussed in Appendix C on the CD-ROM. Gaussian quadrature, a numerical integration method discussed in section 14.10, can also be an efficient method for valuing spread options and other derivatives.

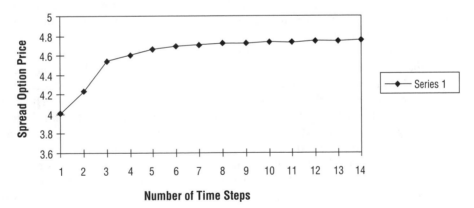

FIGURE 3.7   Two-Variable Binomial Spread Option

---

[8]Ibid., 51.

3.11   VALUATION OF CONVERTIBLE BONDS

A convertible bond is a corporate debt security that can be converted into—that is, exchanged for—a predetermined number of shares of the issuer's common stock at any time prior to the maturity of the bond. It is a hybrid derivative security, part debt and part equity, whose value is derived from the debt and equity underlying it. Most convertible bonds are subordinated debt of the issuer that may have callable and putable provisions that complicate their valuation.

From an investor's viewpoint, one can think of a convertible bond as a straight corporate bond (with periodic coupon payments made by the issuer) plus an equity call option that allows the convertible bondholder to exchange the bond for equity. From an issuer's viewpoint, a convertible bond can be seen as equity and a put option to exchange the equity for a straight bond with a swap to maturity that pays bond coupons to the investor in exchange for the equity's dividends. Convertible bonds can be European or American style. Various features of convertibles make them attractive to both issuers and investors. Issuers can lower their cost of debt funding by issuing convertibles compared to issuing straight debt, and an issuer may not even be able to issue straight debt due to its low credit rating. Convertible bonds often provide a higher yield than the dividend yield of common stock as well as offer greater stability of income than common stock.[9]

Various debt and equity factors as well as specific terms detailed in the bond indenture affect the theoretical value of the convertible bond. In addition to factors that affect all bond prices such as principal amount, coupon amount, and coupon frequency, convertible bonds are also affected by the conversion ratio, conversion price, parity, first conversion date, call provisions, put provisions, and stock performance call provisions.

The *conversion ratio* is the number of shares of the underlying stock for which the convertible bond can be exchanged. This ratio is usually established at issue, and changed only to account for stock dividends or splits of the underlying shares, so as to preserve the total equity value that can be exchanged.[10] The *conversion price* is the principal amount divided by the conversion ratio, which effectively is the price paid for each underlying share on conversion, assuming the bond principal is used to pay for the shares received. *Parity* is the market value of the underlying shares, namely, the conversion ratio multiplied by the current stock price. The *first conversion date* is the first date after issue at which the bond can be converted into equity. Sometimes there is a lockout period after issue during which conversion is not allowed.

A *call provision* gives the issuer the right to purchase back the bond at the call price and is specified in a call schedule, which gives the call price at each future call date. Usually, convertible bonds are call-protected for a certain amount of time and

---

[9]Derman, Ergener, and Kani (1994), 2.
[10]Ibid., 8.

become callable only after a certain date. A call provision can be viewed as a call option sold by the investor to the issuer that reduces the value of the bond compared to an otherwise similar noncallable convertible bond. *Stock performance call provisions* are call provisions subject to the constraint that the issuer can exercise the call only if the underlying stock rises above a certain level, the provisional call level. These provisions reduce the value of the bond by forcing the investor to convert to equity and give up the remaining value of the option.

Put provisions allow the bondholder to put the bond to the issuer for a specific cash price on specific dates of the put schedule. A put provision provides extra downside protection for the convertible bondholder and thus adds value to the bond. It can be regarded as a put option that has been sold to the investor by the issuer, and so increases the value when compared with similar nonputable convertible bonds.

In addition to security-specific features, the value of the convertible bond also depends on market variables including the common stock price, stock price volatility, dividend yield, risk-free rate, stock loan rate, and the issuer's credit spread. The stock loan rate is the interest rate earned on funds received from shorting the stock, a rate typically less than the cost of funds since a rebate fee may have to be paid to the lender.[11] The issuer's credit spread provides information about the likelihood of default of payments of a convertible bond's coupons and principal, and how this possibility of default affects the value of the convertible.[12] Such credit spread is accounted for in the credit-adjusted discount rate that is used for discounting cash flows when conversion will not occur and the bond is held.

Convertible bonds can be valued using an n-period binomial tree similar to equity options. Assume the underlying stock price satisfies the following SDE:

$$dS = (r(t) - q(t))Sdt + \sigma(t)Sdz \tag{3.68}$$

where $r(t)$ is the instantaneous risk-free rate at time t, $q(t)$ is the instantaneous dividend yield, $\sigma(t)$ is the instantaneous volatility, and dz is a standard Brownian motion that represents the uncertainty in stock returns over an infinitesimal time dt. We can approximate this diffusion process with a discrete-time binomial tree with time steps Δt.

The formulas for up and down movements from a given stock price S are:

$$S_u = S \exp\left((r(t) - q(t) - \frac{1}{2}\sigma^2(t))\Delta t + \sigma(t)\sqrt{\Delta t} \right) \tag{3.69}$$

---

[11]Ibid., 9.
[12]Ibid., 10.

and

$$S_d = S \exp\left((r(t) - q(t) - \frac{1}{2}\sigma^2(t))\Delta t - \sigma(t)\sqrt{\Delta t}\right) \qquad (3.70)$$

The value of the convertible bond at any node on the convertible tree is given by

$$V = \max(NS, P + I, (\min(H, C + I))) \qquad (3.71)$$

where V is the convertible bond value, N is the conversion ratio, S is the stock price at the node, P is the put value, C is the call value, I is the accrued interest, and H is the holding value at the node. The holding value is computed from the convertible bond values V_u and V_d one period later as

$$H = 0.5\left(\frac{V_u + I}{1 + y_u \Delta t} + \frac{V_d + I}{1 + y_d \Delta t}\right)$$

where y is the credit-adjusted discount rate. Thus, the holding value of the convertible at a node in the tree is the sum of the present value of the coupons paid over the next period, plus the expected present value of the convertible at the two nodes at the end of the period. The probability of conversion p at the node is determined as follows. If the convertible is put or redeemed, $p = 0$. If conversion occurs, $p = 1$. If the convertible bond is neither put nor converted, $p = 0.5(p_u + p_d)$, where p_u and p_d are the risk-neutral up and down probabilities, respectively. The credit-adjusted discount rate at the node is defined by:

$$y = pr + (1 - p)d$$

where r is the risk-free rate d is the risky rate that includes the credit spread. It is noted that a convertible with parity much greater than its face value is certain to convert at some time in the future and so has a credit-adjusted rate equal to the riskless rate so that coupons are discounted as though they have no default risk.[13] The model can be varied, however, to always discount coupons at the risky rate.

The following steps summarize how to construct a binomial tree for valuing convertible bonds:[14]

1. Build a Cox-Ross-Rubinstein stock price tree that extends from the valuation date to the maturity date of the convertible.
2. At maturity, compute the payoff of the convertible bond as the greater of its fixed-income redemption value and its conversion value. Set the probability of conversion to one at nodes where it pays to convert, and zero otherwise.

---

[13]Ibid., 22.
[14]Ibid., 31.

3. Using backward induction, move backward in time down the tree, one level at a time. At each node within each level, define the conversion probability as the average of the probabilities at the two connected future nodes. Calculate the credit-adjusted discount rate at each node using this conversion probability. Then compute the holding value at each node as the sum of the cash flows occurring over the next period as the expected bond values of the two nodes one period in the future, discounted at the credit-adjusted discount rate.

4. Compute the actual convertible value by comparing the holding value at the node to the values of the call, put, and conversion provisions (if applicable).

5. If the value of the convertible at any node results from the bond being put, set the conversion probability at that node to zero, because its value is completely subject to default. If the value at the node results from conversion, set the node's conversion probability to one.

On November 11, 2003, suppose we want to value a callable convertible bond of Charter Communications that matures on June 6, 2006. We can use Bloomberg to see all listed Charter bond quotes as shown in Figure 3.8.

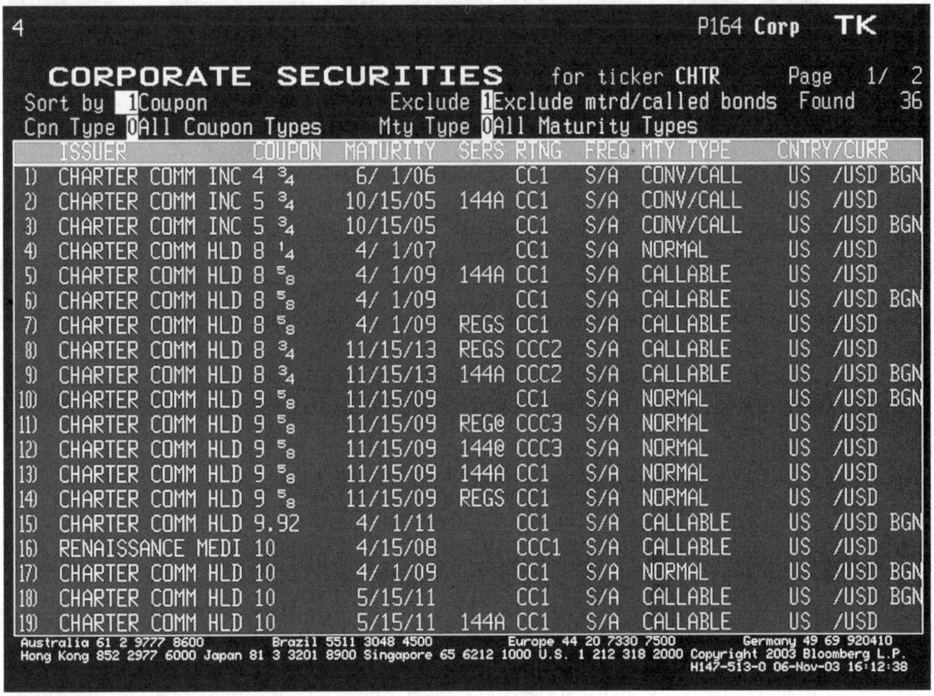

```
4                                               P164 Corp   TK

   CORPORATE SECURITIES        for ticker CHTR     Page   1/ 2
   Sort by  1Coupon              Exclude  1Exclude mtrd/called bonds  Found    36
   Cpn Type 0All Coupon Types    Mty Type 0All Maturity Types
       ISSUER          COUPON  MATURITY  SERS RTNG  FREQ MTY TYPE   CNTRY/CURR
    1)  CHARTER COMM INC 4 3/4   6/ 1/06       CC1   S/A  CONV/CALL   US  /USD BGN
    2)  CHARTER COMM INC 5 3/4  10/15/05  144A CC1   S/A  CONV/CALL   US  /USD
    3)  CHARTER COMM INC 5 3/4  10/15/05       CC1   S/A  CONV/CALL   US  /USD BGN
    4)  CHARTER COMM HLD 8 1/4   4/ 1/07       CC1   S/A  NORMAL      US  /USD
    5)  CHARTER COMM HLD 8 5/8   4/ 1/09  144A CC1   S/A  CALLABLE    US  /USD
    6)  CHARTER COMM HLD 8 5/8   4/ 1/09       CC1   S/A  CALLABLE    US  /USD BGN
    7)  CHARTER COMM HLD 8 5/8   4/ 1/09  REGS CC1   S/A  CALLABLE    US  /USD
    8)  CHARTER COMM HLD 8 3/4  11/15/13  REGS CCC2  S/A  CALLABLE    US  /USD
    9)  CHARTER COMM HLD 8 3/4  11/15/13  144A CCC2  S/A  CALLABLE    US  /USD BGN
   10)  CHARTER COMM HLD 9 5/8  11/15/09       CC1   S/A  NORMAL      US  /USD BGN
   11)  CHARTER COMM HLD 9 5/8  11/15/09  REG@ CCC3  S/A  NORMAL      US  /USD
   12)  CHARTER COMM HLD 9 5/8  11/15/09  144@ CCC3  S/A  NORMAL      US  /USD
   13)  CHARTER COMM HLD 9 5/8  11/15/09  144A CC1   S/A  NORMAL      US  /USD
   14)  CHARTER COMM HLD 9 5/8  11/15/09  REGS CC1   S/A  NORMAL      US  /USD
   15)  CHARTER COMM HLD 9.92    4/ 1/11       CC1   S/A  CALLABLE    US  /USD BGN
   16)  RENAISSANCE MEDI 10      4/15/08       CCC1  S/A  CALLABLE    US  /USD
   17)  CHARTER COMM HLD 10      4/ 1/09       CC1   S/A  NORMAL      US  /USD BGN
   18)  CHARTER COMM HLD 10      5/15/11       CC1   S/A  CALLABLE    US  /USD BGN
   19)  CHARTER COMM HLD 10      5/15/11  144A CC1   S/A  CALLABLE    US  /USD
Australia 61 2 9777 8600    Brazil 5511 3048 4500    Europe 44 20 7330 7500    Germany 49 69 920410
Hong Kong 852 2977 6000 Japan 81 3 3201 8900 Singapore 65 6212 1000 U.S. 1 212 318 2000 Copyright 2003 Bloomberg L.P.
                                                                 H147-513-0 06-Nov-03 16:12:38
```

FIGURE 3.8 Bond Quotes for Charter Communications
Source: Used with permission from Bloomberg L.P.

The initial Charter Communications stock price on November 11, 2003, is $4.06, the dividend yield is 0.0, the stock volatility (computed from historical volatility[15]) is 0.746, and the time to maturity is 2.57 years. For simplicity, we will use 2.5 years. The convertible bond has a semiannual coupon of 4.75 percent. It is also callable. Figure 3.9 shows the call schedule.

As we see, the next call date is June 4, 2004, when it is callable at $101.9 until June 4, 2005, when it is callable at $100.85. The convertible bond price was issued on June 30, 2001, at par value of $100. We find the conversion ratio, parity values, and assume the (interpolated) stock loan rate is equal is to 2.347 percent, which is also the interpolated 2.5-year risk-free rate obtained from the yield and spread analysis screen shown in Figure 3.10.

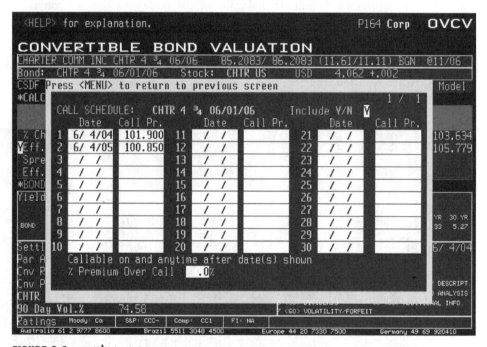

FIGURE 3.9 Call Schedule
Source: Used with permission from Bloomberg L.P.

---

[15]Typically, one uses the 90-day historical volatility as an estimate. However, we could also try to estimate the (implied) volatility from option prices. We would want to use an option that has the same maturity as the convertible bond, but if one cannot be found, we should use the closest available maturity. In this case, Jan 05 calls were listed though for this example the 90-day historical volatility on Bloomberg was used.

```
2                                                      P164 Corp   YAS
Enter #<GO> for Detailed Analysis. Enter 99<GO> for Menu of Related Functions.
YIELD & SPREAD ANALYSIS                       CUSIP16117MAC  PCS BGN
CHARTER COMM INC CHTR 4 ³₄ 06/06   85.2083/ 86.2083 (11.61/11.11) BGN @11/06
   SETTLE 11/13/03   FACE AMT      1000 M or PROCEEDS          883,458.36
1) YA        YIELDS        2) YASD  RISK &  CHTR 4 ³₄ 06/06
PRICE  86.208336              N     HEDGE     workout        HEDGE BOND
YIELD   11.106 Wst                  RATIOS  6/ 1/06  OAS        OAS
 SPRD   908.30 bp  yld-decimals3/3  Mod Dur  2.24              1.94
          versus                    Risk     1.977             1.923
2yr  T 1 ⁵₈ 10/31/05      BENCHMARK  Convexity 0.06            0.05
    PRICE 99-7+     Save  Delete    Workout HEDGE Amount:1,032 M
    YIELD  2.023 %   sd: 11/10/03     OAS HEDGE Amount:
   Yields are: Semi-Annual
3) OAS      SPREADS      4) ASW  5) FPA      FINANCING
OAS:      CRV#     VOL    Opt     Repo% 0.960 (360/365)360  Days  1
OAS:      CRV#          TED: -835.6  Int Income   131.94  Carry P&L
ASSET SWAP: (A/A) 746.1 Z-Sprd: 837.2  Fin Cost  -23.56      108.39
ISPRD  835.8 CRV# I52 US $ SWAP 30/360  Amortiz  133.33<->   241.72
  Yield Curve:I25  US TREASURY ACTIVES  Forwrd Prc  86.197497
+ 876   v 2.5yr ( 2.347 %) INTERPOLATED  Prc Drop   0.010839
+ 863   v 3yr  ( 2.47) T 2 ³₈ 08/15/06  Drop (bp)     1.22
+ 766   v 5yr  ( 3.45) T 3 ¹₈ 10/15/08  Accrued Interest /100  2.137500
+ 666   v 10yr ( 4.45) T 4 ¹₄ 08/15/13  Number Of Days Accrued  162
+ 584   v 30yr ( 5.26) T 5 ³₈ 02/15/31
Australia 61 2 9777 8600   Brazil 5511 3048 4500  Europe 44 20 7330 7500  Germany 49 69 920410
Hong Kong 852 2977 6000 Japan 81 3 3201 8900 Singapore 65 6212 1000 U.S. 1 212 318 2000 Copyright 2003 Bloomberg L.P.
                                                              H147-513-0 07-Nov-03 13:52:14
```

FIGURE 3.10 Yield and Spread Analysis
Source: Used with permission from Bloomberg L.P.

The 4¾ 6/06 Charter Communications convertible bond, which is CC1 rated, has a credit spread of 908.30 basis points. The convertible bond valuation screen, shown in Figure 3.11, can be used to obtain the conversion ratio, conversion price, parity, yield to maturity, yield to call, and other information pertaining to the convertible bond.

We find the conversion ratio is 38.095 and the conversion price is \$26.25, as shown in Figure 3.12.[16]

Since there are no put provisions, the payoff at each node becomes:

$$V = \max(NS, \min(H, C + I))$$

We will construct a binomial tree with five time steps so that our time steps are $\Delta t = 2.5/5 = 0.5$.

---

[16]The investor will not convert unless the stock price exceeds the conversion price.

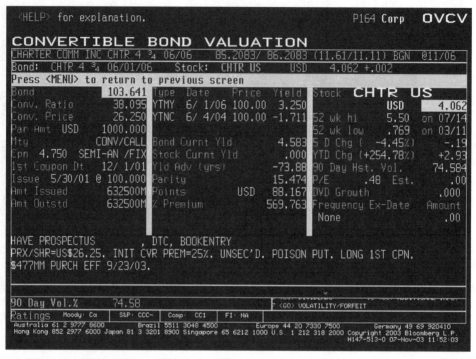

FIGURE 3.11   Convertible Bond Valuation I
Source: Used with permission from Bloomberg L.P.

To compute the theoretical value we define a *ConvertibleBond* class:

```
class ConvertibleBond
{
  public:
    ConvertibleBond();
    virtual ~ConvertibleBond();
    double calcConvertibleBond(double price, double vol, double rate, double
       dividend, double T, double principal, double coupon, double frequency, int N,
       double conversionRatio, double conversionPrice, double creditSpread);
  private:
    double S[20][20];                  // value of stock price at node i,j
    double V[20][20];                  // value of convertible bond at node i,j
    double cp[20][20];                 // conversion probability at node i,j
    double creditAdjustedRate;         // credit spread at each node i,j
    double call[20][20];               // callable value
};
```

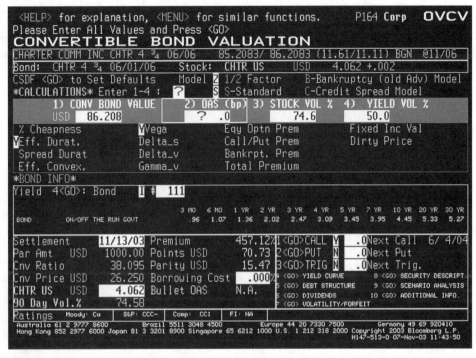

FIGURE 3.12   Convertible Bond Valuation II
Source: Used with permission from Bloomberg L.P.

We define the *calcConvertibleBond* method:

```
/***************************************************************************/
calcConvertibleBond
computes the value of convertible bond with callable provisions
[in]:   double price               : stock price
        double vol                 : stock volatility
        vector<double> rates       : contains zero-curve rates
        double dividend            : stock dividend yield
        double T                   : time to maturity of convertible bond
        double principal           : par value of bond
        double couponRate          : coupon rate of bond
        double frequency           : frequency of coupon payments
        int N                      : number of time steps
        double conversionRatio     : conversion ratio
        double conversionPrice     : conversion price
        double creditSpread        : credit spread of issuer
        map<int,double> callSchedule : call schedule map of times to call prices
[out]   double
```

```
/*****************************************************************************/
double ConvertibleBond::calcConvertibleBond(double price, double vol,
  vector<double> rates, double dividend, double T, double principal, double
  couponRate, double frequency, int N, double conversionRatio, double
  conversionPrice, double creditSpread, map<int,double> callSchedule)
{
  int i,j;
  double up = 0.0;                          // up movement
  double down = 0.0;                        // down movement
  double interest = 0.0;                    // interest
  double H = 0.0;                           // holding value
  double rate = rates[rates.size()-1];      // initial short rate
  double dt = T/N;                          // compute time step
  up = exp(vol*sqrt(dt));                   // up movement
  down = 1/up;                              // down movement


  // build CRR stock tree
  for (i = 0; i <= N; i++)
  {
    for (j = 0; j <= i; j++)
    {
      S[i][j] = price*(pow(up,j))*(pow(down,i-j));
    }
  }
  interest = principal*coupon*dt;           // interest payment


  for (j = N; j >= 0; j--)
  {
    double payment = principal + principal*coupon*dt;
    if (S[N][j] >= conversionPrice)
      V[N][j] = max(conversionRatio*S[N][j],payment);
    else
      V[N][j] = payment;

    if (V[N][j] == conversionRatio*S[N][j])
      cp[N][j] = 1.0;
    else
      cp[N][j] = 0.0;
  }


  // work backwards
  for (i = N-1; i >= 0; i--)
  {
    for (j = i; j >= 0; j--)
    {
      // compute call schedule price at current node
      // in practice, we would want to check that the call date coincides exactly
      // with the time step on the tree. However, we are not using enough time
      // steps for them to coincide (N would have to be substantially increased)
      // and just assume that the bond is callable at each time step
```

```
    call[i][j] = callSchedule[i];

    // compute conversion probability
    cp[i][j] = 0.5*(cp[i+1][j+1] + cp[i+1][j]);

    // compute credit adjusted discount rate
    creditAdjustedRate = cp[i][j]*rates[i] + (1- cp[i][j])*creditSpread;

    // compute holding value
       H = 0.5*((V[i+1][j+1] + interest)/(1 + creditAdjustedRate*dt) + (V[i+1][j]
       + interest)/(1 + creditAdjustedRate*dt));

    // check that stock price exceeds conversion price
    if (S[i][j] >= conversionPrice)
      V[i][j] = max(conversionRatio*S[i][j],min(H,call[i][j] + interest));
    else
      V[i][j] = min(H,call[i][j] + interest);
    }
  }
  return V[0][0];
}
```

We can compute the theoretical value of the 4¾ 6/06 Charter Communications convertible bond now:

```
void main()
{
  double price = 4.06;                 // initial price
  double coupon = 0.0475;              // coupon
  double frequency = 2;                // frequency of payment
  double rate = 0.02347;               // 2.5 yr risk-free rate
  double conversionRatio = 38.095;     // conversion ratio
  double conversionPrice = 26.25;      // conversion price
  double vol = 0.746;                  // stock price volatility
  double bondPrice = 100;              // maturity redemption value
  double divYield = 0.0;               // dividend yield
  double T = 2.5;                      // maturity of convertible bond
  double creditSpread = 0.9083         // credit spread of Charter
  map<int,double> callSchedule;        // call schedule
  vector<double> rates;                // term structure
  double value = 0.0;                  // convertible bond value
  int N = 5;                           // number of time steps

  ConvertibleBond cb;

  // we could also use a date class to map the call date to call price, i.e.
     map<date,double> callSchedule
  callSchedule[0] = 103.00;   // today November 11, 2003 call value
  callSchedule[1] = 101.90;   // June 11, 2004
```

```
callSchedule[2] = 101.90;     // November 11, 2004
callSchedule[3] = 100.85;     // June 11, 2005
callSchedule[4] = 100.85;     // November 11, 2005
callSchedule[5] = 100.00;     // bond is assumed to be redeemed at maturity for
                              // par on June 11, 2006

                              // instead June 6, 2006 for simplicity
// yield curve
rates.push_back(0.0107);      // 6 month
rates.push_back(0.0136);      // 1 year
rates.push_back(0.0145);      // 1.5 year
rates.push_back(0.0202);      // 2 year
rates.push_back(0.02347);     // 2.5 year

value = calcConvertibleBond(price,vol,rates,divYield,T,bondPrice,coupon,
    frequency,N,conversionRatio, conversionPrice, creditSpread,callSchedule));

cout << "Convertible bond price: " << value << endl;
}
```

We find that the theoretical value of $103.678 is in close agreement with the Bloomberg computed value of $103.641 (see Figure 3.11).[17] Note that $103.678 is the holding value while $105.589 is the call value, which is closer to the investment value of $105.589 seen in the Bloomberg convertible price behavior screen (Figure 3.13).

Figure 3.14 shows the convertible tree built to compute the *theoretical* price. Currently, the Charter Communications convertible bond is trading at $86.20, 16.9 percent below its theoretical value. As time continues to approach maturity, the bond should trade closer to its theoretical value, as Figure 3.13 shows. Note that unless the stock price exceeds the conversion price, the convertible bond value will be the smaller of either the holding value or the callable price at each node.

As the tree in Figure 3.14 shows, most likely the bond will be held until maturity where it will be redeemed for its face value (plus accrued interest) by the issuer. The convertible bond computations could also be modified to handle putable provisions.

A formal mathematical valuation of convertible bonds has been described by Tsiveriotis and Fernandes (1998) that treats the total convertible value as a decomposition of an equity component and a bond component, E and B, respectively.[18]

---

[17]Differences could be due to number of time steps used, compounding frequency of interest, and perhaps a different pricing model used by Bloomberg such as use of a trinomial tree.
[18]Tsiveriotis and Fernandes (1998), 95–102.

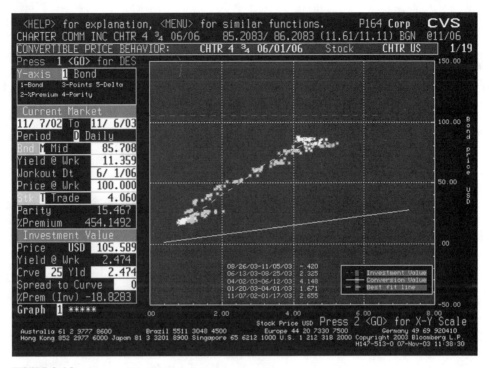

FIGURE 3.13   Convertible Price Behavior
Source: Used with permission from Bloomberg L.P.

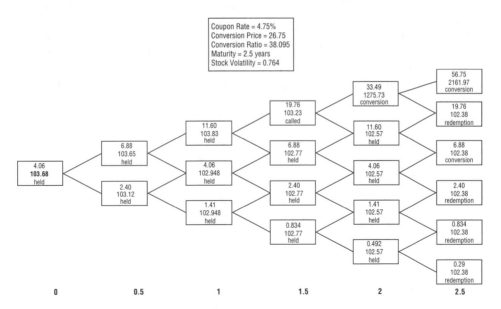

FIGURE 3.14   Convertible Bond Tree for Charter Communications

They derive the convertible value $V(S, t)$ as a solution of a partial differential equation where the equity component is discounted at the constant risk-free rate r while the bond component is discounted at a risky rate—the risk-free rate plus a credit spread, $r + s$, due to credit and interest rate risk:

$$\frac{\partial V}{\partial t} + \frac{1}{2}\sigma^2 S^2 \frac{\partial^2 V}{\partial S^2} + (r - q)S\frac{\partial V}{\partial S} - r(V - B) - (r + s)B \leq 0 \qquad (3.72)$$

which can be reduced to

$$\frac{\partial V}{\partial t} + \frac{1}{2}\sigma^2 S^2 \frac{\partial^2 V}{\partial S^2} + (r - q)S\frac{\partial V}{\partial S} - rV - sB \leq 0 \qquad (3.73)$$

subject to the constraints

$$V \geq \max(B_p, NS)$$
$$V \leq \max(B_c, NS) \qquad (3.74)$$

and boundary conditions

$$V(S, T) = Z$$
$$V(0, t) = Ze^{-r(T-t)} \qquad (3.75)$$

where Z is the face value of the bond, B is the bond price, B_p is the putable bond price, and B_c is the callable bond price. To incorporate default risk into the model, one can set the spread $s = p(1 - R)$ where R is the recovery rate on the bond upon default and p is the hazard rate (probability of default). If coupon payments, $C(S, t)$, on the bond are included as well as discrete dividend payments, $D(S, t)$, we can modify (3.73) by

$$\frac{\partial V}{\partial t} + \frac{1}{2}\sigma^2 S^2 \frac{\partial^2 V}{\partial S^2} + (rS - D(S, t))\frac{\partial V}{\partial S} - rV - sB + C(S, t) \leq 0 \qquad (3.76)$$

The problem can be solved numerically as an American option problem using finite difference methods (see Chapter 5). It can be shown that an increase in the dividend amount D makes early exercise more likely, while an increase in the coupon payment makes early exercise less likely.[19]

---

[19]Wilmott, Howison, and Dewynne (1995), 288.

If the decomposition of the total convertible bond price is specified as $V = B + E$, the decomposition can be written as a coupled set of equations:[20]

$$\left.\begin{array}{l} \mathcal{L}E = 0; \;\; \mathcal{L}B + p(1-R)B = 0 \;\; \text{if } V \neq B_p \text{ and } V \neq B_c \\[4pt] B = B_p; \;\; E = 0 \;\; \text{if } V = B_p \\[4pt] B = 0; \;\; E = B_c \;\; \text{if } V = B_c \end{array}\right\} \text{if } B_p > NS \quad (3.77)$$

$$\left.\begin{array}{ll} \mathcal{L}E = 0; \;\; \mathcal{L}B + p(1-R)B = 0 & \text{if } V \neq \max(NS,\, B_c) \\[4pt] E = \max(NS,\, B_c); \;\; B = 0 & \text{if } V = \max(NS,\, B_c) \end{array}\right\} \text{if } B_p \leq NS \quad (3.78)$$

where $\mathcal{L}$ is the linear operator such that

$$\mathcal{L}V \equiv -\frac{\partial V}{\partial t} - \left(\frac{1}{2}\sigma^2 S^2 \frac{\partial^2 V}{\partial S^2} + (r(t) - q)S \frac{\partial V}{\partial S} - r(t)V \right)$$

If interest rates are stochastic so that there are two factors (two sources of risk) where the stock price follows the standard diffusion process in equation (3.68) and interest rates follow the process

$$dr = u(r, t)dt + w(r, t)dx$$

where $u(r, t)$ is the drift term, w is the volatility of the short rate, and the Wiener processes of the stock and interest rates are correlated by $E[dzdx] = \rho dt$, then using no-arbitrage arguments and Ito's lemma, it can be shown that the convertible bond pricing equation becomes a two-dimensional PDE:

$$\begin{aligned} \frac{\partial V}{\partial t} + \frac{1}{2} &\left(\sigma^2 S^2 \frac{\partial^2 V}{\partial S^2} + 2\rho\sigma Sw \frac{\partial^2 V}{\partial S \partial r} + w^2 \frac{\partial^2 V}{\partial r^2} \right) \\[4pt] &+ (rS - D)\frac{\partial V}{\partial S} + (u - w\lambda)\frac{\partial V}{\partial r} - rV - sB + C \leq 0 \end{aligned} \quad (3.79)$$

with the same constraints and boundary conditions as in (3.74) and (3.75), where $\lambda = \lambda(r, S, t)$ is the market price of interest rate risk.[21] Equation (3.79) can be solved using numerical methods such as the alternating direction implicit (ADI) difference method (see section 5.9). The Black-Scholes PDE is a special case when $(u = w = s = 0)$.

---

[20] Ayache, Forsyth, and Vetzal (2003), 17.
[21] Wilmott, Howison, and Dewynne (1995), 291–292.

It should finally be noted that Ayache, Forsyth, and Vetzal (2003) have pointed out inconsistencies in the Tsiveriotis-Fernandes (TF) model that they address and correct using a linear complementary approach.[22] In particular, they show that in the TF model, if the bond is called the instant before maturity, say T^- the bond price is required to be 0 as part of the boundary condition in equation (3.78), which means that the solution for B is $B = 0$ for all $t < T^-$ so that the equation for the convertible bond price reduces to

$$\mathcal{L}V = 0$$

$$V(S, T^-) = \max(S, Z - \varepsilon)$$

for very small $\varepsilon > 0$. Consequently, the hazard rate has no effect on the price, making the convertible bond value independent of the credit risk of the issuer, which is clearly inappropriate.[23]

---

[22]Ayache, Forsyth, and Vetzal (2003), 9–30.
[23]Ibid., 18.

CHAPTER 4

Trinomial Trees

In this chapter, we examine diffusion processes that are approximated by three-state lattices known as trinomial trees. In section 4.1, we discuss the general movement of assets in a Cox-Ross-Rubinstein (CRR) framework, as well as in a Jarrow-Rudd (JR) framework. In section 4.2, we examine the JR trinomial tree in more detail. In section 4.3, we examine the CRR trinomial tree in more detail. In section 4.4, we discuss the optimal parameter λ for changing branching probabilities. In section 4.5, we provide trinomial tree implementations for the CRR and JR trees. In section 4.6, we give an implementation for building generic trinomial trees that approximate various diffusion processes. In section 4.7, we discuss implied trees that are based on constructing trinomial trees based on Arrow-Debreu state prices.

4.1   USE OF TRINOMIAL TREES

Trinomial trees are used in practice more than binomial trees since they allow for three states: up, down, and middle moves. We can approximate diffusions using trinomial random walks with both the CRR and JR trees. We can price both European and American options with trinomial trees. Let $f_{N,j} = F(S_{N,j})$ be the payoff at time t. Then the stock price at node (i, j) in the CRR tree is

$$S_{i,j} = Su^j \qquad j = -i, -i + 1, \ldots, 0, \ldots, i + 1 \qquad (4.1)$$

and in the JR tree:

$$S_{i,j} = Su^j e^{i\mu\Delta t} \qquad j = -i, -i + 1, \ldots, 0, \ldots, i + 1 \qquad (4.2)$$

where

$$u = e^{\lambda\sigma\sqrt{\Delta t}}$$

and $S = S_{0,0}$.

4.2   JARROW-RUDD TRINOMIAL TREE

Consider the Monte Carlo simulation:

$$S_{i+1} = S_i e^{\mu \Delta t + \sigma \sqrt{\Delta t} \varepsilon_{i+1}}$$

where ε_{i+1} is a standard normal variable. We can approximate this standard normal variable by a discrete random variable ξ_{i+1} with three possible outcomes, $+\lambda$, 0, and $-\lambda$, with some probabilities p_u, p_m, and p_d for up, middle, and down price movements, respectively, where λ is some scalar. It approximates the standard normal distribution by a three-state random variable. In this approximation, we can write the stock price distribution as

$$S_{i+1} = S_i e^{\mu \Delta t + \sigma \sqrt{\Delta t} \varepsilon_{i+1}} = \begin{cases} S_i U = S_i e^{\mu \Delta t + \lambda \sigma \sqrt{\Delta t}} \\ S_i M = S_i e^{\mu \Delta t} \\ S_i D = S_i e^{\mu \Delta t - \lambda \sigma \sqrt{\Delta t}} \end{cases} \qquad (4.3)$$

where the up move is

$$U = e^{\mu \Delta t + \lambda \sigma \sqrt{\Delta t}}$$

with probability p_u, the middle move is $M = e^{\mu \Delta t}$ with probability p_m, and the down move is

$$D = e^{\mu \Delta t - \lambda \sigma \sqrt{\Delta t}}$$

The elementary tree structure is shown in Figure 4.1.

We need to determine the probabilities. Clearly, $p_m = 1 - p_u - p_d$. We need to

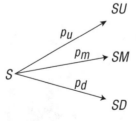

FIGURE 4.1   Elementary Tree Structure

determine the remaining two probabilities. The necessary and sufficient condition for the tree to recombine is: $UD = M^2$. That is, an up move followed by a down move gets us to the same node as two consecutive middle moves. This tree is not symmetric. The model has a built-in deterministic drift $M = e^{\mu \Delta t}$ and is a counterpart of the JR binomial tree. We need to find p_u and p_d so that the three-state distribution correctly approximates the normal distribution. We will match mean and variance of the two distributions and solve these two equations for the probabilities. Let $U = u e^{\mu \Delta t}$, $D = d e^{\mu \Delta t}$, and $k = e^{(\sigma 2 \Delta t)/2}$. The moment-matching conditions are:

$$E_{t,S}^{trinomial}[S_{t+\Delta t}] = E_{t,S}^{Q}[S_{t+\Delta t}] = Se^{r\Delta t}$$

and

$$p_u u + (1 - p_u - p_d) + p_d d = k \tag{4.4}$$

for the mean and

$$E_{t,S}^{trinomial}[(S_{t+\Delta t})^2] = E_{t,S}^{Q}[S_{t\Delta t})^2] = S^2 e^{(2\,r + \sigma 2)}\Delta t$$

and

$$p_u u^2 + (1 - p_u - p_d) + p_d d^2 = k^4 \tag{4.5}$$

for the variance. We can now solve for the probabilities:

$$p_u = \frac{k^4 - (d+1)k + d}{(u-d)(u-1)} \tag{4.6}$$

and

$$p_d = \frac{k^4 - (u+1)k + u}{(u-d)(1-d)} \tag{4.7}$$

where

$$u = e^{\lambda \sigma \sqrt{\Delta t}}, \quad d = e^{-\lambda \sigma \sqrt{\Delta t}}, \quad \text{and } k = e^{(\sigma^2 \Delta t)/2}$$

Thus, we express all the probabilities in terms of u and d. The stretch parameter λ is still ambiguous in the definition of u and d. However, any choice of λ will produce a trinomial tree that converges to the Black-Scholes lognormal process (as long as the probabilities are positive for this particular choice).

4.3 COX-ROSS-RUBINSTEIN TRINOMIAL TREE

The CRR trinomial tree is obtained by setting $M = 1$. Thus, as shown in Figure 4.2, we have a symmetric elementary tree structure where

$$u = e^{\lambda\sigma\sqrt{\Delta t}} \text{ and } d = e^{-\lambda\sigma\sqrt{\Delta t}}$$

and $p_m = 1 - p_u - p_d$. We now have three parameters to determine: λ, p_u, and p_d. We can determine the two probabilities by matching the first two moments of the trinomial and lognormal distributions. The first-order approximation results are:

$$p_u = \frac{1}{2\lambda^2} + \frac{1}{2}\left(\frac{\mu}{\lambda\sigma}\right)\sqrt{\Delta t} \tag{4.8}$$

$$p_d = \frac{1}{2\lambda^2} - \frac{1}{2}\left(\frac{\mu}{\lambda\sigma}\right)\sqrt{\Delta t} \tag{4.9}$$

$$p_m = 1 - \frac{1}{\lambda^2} \tag{4.10}$$

Note that λ should be chosen so that the probabilities are positive. We can compute the option value in a trinomial tree as the discounted expectation in a risk-neutral world by computing:

$$f_{i,j} = e^{-r\Delta t}(p_u f_{i+1,j+1} + p_m f_{i+1,j} + p_d f_{i+1,j-1}) \tag{4.11}$$

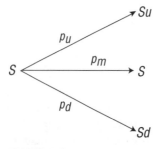

FIGURE 4.2 Symmetric Elementary Tree Structure

4.4   OPTIMAL CHOICE OF λ

Kamrad and Ritchken (1991) have shown that the value of λ that produces the best convergence rate is

$$\lambda = \sqrt{3/2}$$

With this choice of λ we get the CRR trinomial tree with probabilities:

$$p_u = \frac{1}{3} + \left(\frac{\mu}{\sigma}\right)\sqrt{\frac{\Delta t}{6}}$$

$$p_d = \frac{1}{3} + \left(\frac{\mu}{\sigma}\right)\sqrt{\frac{\Delta t}{6}} \tag{4.12}$$

$$p_m = \frac{1}{3}$$

where the up and down movements are

$$u = e^{\sigma\sqrt{3\Delta t/2}} \text{ and } d = e^{-\sigma\sqrt{3\Delta t/2}}$$

respectively. In the limit $\Delta t \rightarrow 0$, the probabilities of up, down, and unchanged are equal to 1/3. If we choose λ = 1, we get the probabilities:

$$p_u = \frac{1}{2} + \frac{1}{2}\left(\frac{\mu}{\sigma}\right)\sqrt{\Delta t}$$

$$p_d = \frac{1}{2} - \frac{1}{2}\left(\frac{\mu}{\sigma}\right)\sqrt{\Delta t} \tag{4.13}$$

$$p_m = 0$$

where the up and down movements are

$$u = e^{\sigma\sqrt{\Delta t}} \text{ and } d = e^{-\sigma\sqrt{\Delta t}}$$

respectively. Notice that this is just the CRR binomial model. If λ < 1, then the middle probability is negative since $1 - 1/\lambda^2 < 0$, and the numerical procedure is unstable. Thus, the stretch parameter λ should always be greater than 1 to ensure positive probabilities and numerical stability. The binomial model is right on the edge of numerical stability with λ = 1.

4.5   TRINOMIAL TREE IMPLEMENTATIONS

The following code implements an American CRR trinomial tree with $\lambda = \sqrt{3/2}$. Suppose we use the trinomial tree to price an at-the-money (ATM) European put option on a stock priced at \$50, strike price of 50, volatility of 20 percent, risk-free rate of 6 percent, dividend yield of 2.5 percent, and time to maturity of 1 year. Thus, $S = 50$, $X = 50$, $\sigma = 0.20$, $r = 0.06$, $q = 0.03$, and $T = 1$. Assume there are $N = 4$ time steps. The type parameter is either 'C' (call) or 'P' (put).

```
/************************************************************************
buildTrinomialTreeCRRAmerican : builds a CRR trinomial tree to price American
   options
[in]     double price:        : initial price of asset
         double strike        : strike price
         double vol           : volatility
         double div           : dividend yield
         double rate          : risk-free rate
         double T             : time to maturity
         int N                : number of time steps
         char type            : type of option
[out]    double               : price of option
************************************************************************/
double CRRTrinomialTree::buildTrinomialTreeCRRAmerican(double price, double strike,
   double vol, double rate, double div, double T, long N, char type)
{
  int i, j;
  double pd;                             // down probability
  double pm;                             // middle probability
  double pu;                             // up probability
  double S[250][250];                    // stock price at node i, j
  double c[250][250];                    // call price at node i,j
  double up = 0.0;                       // up movement
  double down =0.0;                      // down movement
  double dt = T/N;                       // time step
  double drift = rate - div - 0.5*vol*vol;  // drift

  pu = 0.33333 + (drift/vol)*sqrt(dt/6);
  pd = 0.33333 - (drift/vol)*sqrt(dt/6);
  pm = 0.33333;
  up = exp(vol*sqrt(3*dt/2));
  down = 1/up;

  // compute stock prices at each node
  for (i = N; i >= 0; i--)
  {
    for (j = -i; j <= i; j++)
    {
```

```
      S[i][j] = price*pow(up,j);
   }
}

// compute payoffs at the final time step
  for (j = N; j >= -N; j--)
{
  if (type == 'C')
    c[N][j] = max(S[N][j] - strike,0);
  else
    c[N][j] = max(strike - S[N][j],0);
}
// backwards induction
for (i=N-1; i >= 0; i--)
{
  for (j=i; j >= -i; j--)
  {
    if (type == 'C')
      c[i][j] = max(exp(-rate*dt)*(pu*c[i+1][j+1] + pm*c[i+1][j] + pd*c[i+1][j-
        1]), S[i][j] - strike);
    else
      c[i][j] = max(exp(-rate*dt)*(pu*c[i+1][j+1] + pm*c[i+1][j] + pd*c[i+1][j-
        1]), strike - S[i][j]);
  }
}
  return c[0][0];
}
```

The trinomial tree that is generated is shown in Figure 4.3. The value of the call option is \$4.51. The price of the call using Black-Scholes is \$4.57. The value of the call will converge closer to the Black-Scholes price as $\Delta t \rightarrow 0$.

The trinomial trees for each value of λ approach the Black-Scholes price closely at around $N = 100$ steps, as shown in Table 4.1. As we will see, the trinomial tree proves to be equivalent to the explicit finite-difference scheme (see Chapter 5) and has the same convergence properties.

The scheme becomes unstable if certain stability conditions are not met. For an explicit finite-difference scheme, it is important to ensure positive probabilities and that the following stability and convergence condition be satisfied:

$$\Delta x \geq \sigma\sqrt{3\Delta t} \qquad (4.14)$$

Clewlow and Strickland (1998a) suggest that a reasonable range of asset price values at the maturity of the option is three standard deviations either side of the

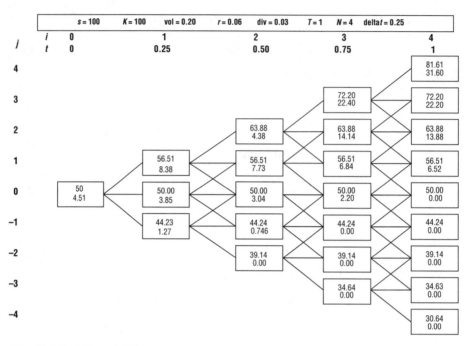

| | s = 100 | K = 100 | vol = 0.20 | r = 0.06 | div = 0.03 | T = 1 | N = 4 | deltat = 0.25 |

FIGURE 4.3 Trinomial Tree

TABLE 4.1 Comparison of Trinomial Trees with Different Lambdas

N	$\lambda = \sqrt{3/2}$	$\lambda = \sqrt{3}$	$\lambda = 1$	Black-Scholes
4	4.506	4.309	4.334	4.568
10	4.542	4.471	4.472	4.568
30	4.558	4.537	4.535	4.568
50	4.560	4.550	4.548	4.568
70	4.561	4.556	4.556	4.568
100	4.560	4.563	4.558	4.568
200	4.563	4.569	4.563	4.568

mean, and a reasonable number of asset price values is 100 ($2N_j + 1 = 100$).[1] Under these assumptions, the space step required is then

$$\Delta x = 6\sigma\sqrt{T}/100 \qquad (4.15)$$

---

[1]Clewlow and Strickland (1998a), 65.

Substituting Δx in equation (4.14) into (4.15), we get the upper bound on the size of the time step

$$\Delta t \leq \frac{1}{3} \left(\frac{\Delta x}{\sigma} \right)^2 \tag{4.16}$$

Finally, using n_{SD} (for the number of standard deviations) instead of 6 in equation (4.15) and rearranging, we find that the number of steps required for suitable convergence is:

$$N = \frac{T}{\Delta t} \geq 3 \left(\frac{2N_j + 1}{n_{SD}} \right)^2 \tag{4.17}$$

If we require the ratio of the number of asset values to the number of standard deviations

$$\left(\frac{2N_j + 1}{n_{SD}} \right)$$

to be at least 15 in order to have a good approximation to the asset price distribution, then we require that $N \geq 675$.

Figure 4.4 shows the convergence rate of trinomial trees for $N = 1, \ldots, 50$ time

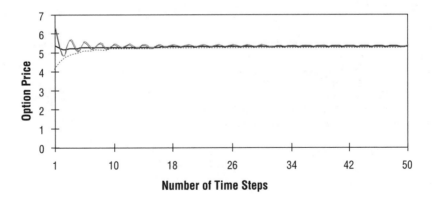

FIGURE 4.4 Convergence Comparison of Trinomial and Binomial Trees

steps for an ATM European call option with $S = 50$, $X = 50$, $r = 0.055$, $q = 0.0$, $\sigma = 0.25$, $T = 0.75$. Note the convergence rate and stability are very good at about 50 time steps.

4.6 APPROXIMATING DIFFUSION PROCESSES WITH TRINOMIAL TREES

In practice, we would want to provide a trinomial tree framework that can approximate different diffusion processes. This can be accomplished by using the drifts and variances of the diffusion process (see Chapter 1 for *DiffusionProcess* classes) in the construction of the tree while containing methods to compute the branching via a *TrinomialBranching* helper class that is member of the *TrinomialTree* class.

```cpp
#include "qldiffusionprocess.h"
#include "ql/Lattices/tree.h"

namespace QuantLib
{
  namespace Lattices
  {
  /************************************************************************
  class TrinomialBranching : Recombining trinomial tree class
     This class defines a recombining trinomial tree approximating a diffusion. The
     diffusion term of the SDE must be independent of the underlying process.
     ************************************************************************/
  class TrinomialBranching
  {
    public:
      TrinomialBranching() : probs_(3) {}
      virtual ~TrinomialBranching() {}
      inline Size descendant(Size index, Size branch) const {
        return (k_[index] - jMin()) - 1 + branch;
      }
      inline double probability(Size index, Size branch) const {
        return probs_[branch][index];
      }
      inline int jMin() const {
        return *std::min_element(k_.begin(), k_.end()) - 1;
      }
    private:
      friend class TrinomialTree;
      std::vector<int> k_;    // branch k
      std::vector<std::vector<double> > probs_;    // branching probabilities
  };

class TrinomialTree : public Tree
{
```

```
public:
  TrinomialTree() { }
  TrinomialTree(const Handle<DiffusionProcess>& process,
    const TimeGrid& timeGrid,
    bool isPositive = false);

  double dx(Size i) const { return dx_[i]; }
  double underlying(Size i, Size index) const;
  const TimeGrid& timeGrid() const { return timeGrid_; }

  inline int descendant(int i, int index, int branch) const {
    return branchings_[i]->descendant(index, branch);
  }

  inline double probability(int i, int j, int b) const {
    return branchings_[i]->probability(j, b);
  }
  inline int size(int i) const {
    if (i==0)
      return 1;

    const std::vector<int>& k = branchings_[i-1]->k_;
    int jMin = *std::min_element(k.begin(), k.end()) - 1;
    int jMax = *std::max_element(k.begin(), k.end()) + 1;

    return jMax - jMin + 1;
  }
  double underlying(int i, int index) const {
    if (i==0) return x0_;
    const std::vector<int>& k = branchings_[i-1]->k_;
    int jMin = *std::min_element(k.begin(), k.end()) - 1;
    return x0_ + (jMin*1.0 + index*1.0)*dx(i);
  }
protected:
  std::vector<Handle<TrinomialBranching> > branchings_;
  double x0_;
  std::vector<double> dx_; // vector of step sizes
  TimeGrid timeGrid_;
};
```

The class has the following definition of the *TrinomialTree* constructor:

```
TrinomialTree::TrinomialTree(const Handle<DiffusionProcess>& process, const
  TimeGrid& timeGrid, bool isPositive) : Tree(timeGrid.size()), dx_(1, 0.0),
  timeGrid_(timeGrid)
{
  x0_ = process->x0();
  int nTimeSteps = timeGrid.size() - 1;
  int jMin = 0;
```

```
int jMax = 0;

for (int i = 0; i < nTimeSteps; i++)
{
  Time t = timeGrid[i];
  Time dt = timeGrid.dt(i);

  // variance must be independent of x
  double v2 = process->variance(t, 0.0, dt);
  double v = sqrt(v2);
  dx_.push_back(v*sqrt (3.0));

  Handle<TrinomialBranching> branching(new TrinomialBranching());
  for (int j = jMin; j <= jMax; j++)
  {
    double x = x0_ + j*dx_[i];
    double m = process->expectation(t, x, dt);
    int temp = (int)floor ((m-x0_)/dx_[i+1] + 0.5);

    if (isPositive)
    {
      while (x0_+(temp-1)*dx_[i+1] <= 0)
        temp++;
    }

    branching->k_.push_back(temp);
    double e = m - (x0_ + temp*dx_[i+1]);
    double e2 = e*e;
    double e3 = e*sqrt (3.0);

    branching->probs_[0].push_back((1.0 + e2/v2 - e3/v)/6.0);
    branching->probs_[1].push_back((2.0 - e2/v2)/3.0);
    branching->probs_[2].push_back((1.0 + e2/v2 + e3/v)/6.0);
  }
  branchings_.push_back(branching);

  const std::vector<int>& k = branching->k_;
  jMin = *std::min_element(k.begin(), k.end()) - 1;
  jMax = *std::max_element(k.begin(), k.end()) + 1;
  }
}
```

Notice that inside the constructor, the branching probabilities and state values are determined by the expected mean (drift) and variance (diffusion term) of the diffusion process. Thus, this generic constructor builds a trinomial tree that approximates various diffusion processes such as an Ornstein-Uhlenbeck process, Black-Scholes geometric Brownian motion process, and square-root process.

We can build a trinomial tree by using the following code:

```cpp
#include "quantlib.h"
using namespace QuantLib;
using namespace QuantLib::Instruments;
using DayCounters::Actual360;
using TermStructures::PiecewiseFlatForward;
using TermStructures::RateHelper;

void main()
{
  try
  {
    Date todaysDate(20, October, 2003);
    Calendar calendar = Calendars::TARGET();
    Date settlementDate(19, July, 2004);

    // Deposit rates
    DayCounter depositDayCounter = Thirty360();

    // Instruments used to bootstrap the yield curve:
    std::vector<Handle<RateHelper> > instruments;

    // Black Scholes diffusion parameters
    double rate = 0.06;
    double vol = 0.20;
    double price = 50;

    // List of times that have to be included in the timegrid
    std::list<Time> times;

    // bootstrapping the yield curve - class definition in Quantlib
    Handle<PiecewiseFlatForward> myTermStructure(new
      PiecewiseFlatForward(todaysDate, settlementDate, instruments,
        depositDayCounter));

    const std::vector<Time> termTimes = myTermStructure->times();
    for (int i = 0; i < termTimes.size(); i++)
      times.push_back(termTimes[i]);

    times.sort();
    times.unique();

    // Building time-grid
    TimeGrid grid(times, 30);

    // define Black Scholes diffusion process
    Handle<DiffusionProcess> bsd (new BlackScholesProcess(rate, vol,price));

    // build trinomial tree to approximate Black Scholes diffusion process
    Handle<TrinomialTree> trinomialTree (new TrinomialTree(bsd,grid,true));
```

```
    }
    catch (const char* s)
    {
        std::cout << s << std::endl;
    }
}
```

4.7   IMPLIED TREES

The implied trees approach is a way that practitioners have tried to build trees that price options consistent with actual market prices of European options. Implied trees can be considered a generalization of binomial and trinomial trees. Implied trees are based on the work of Derman and Kani (1994); Derman, Kani, and Ergener (1995); and Dupire (1994). Such trees try to incorporate the volatility smiles and maturity effects of options that can be implied from such market prices. Exchange-traded European option market prices contain important information about market expectations of the future. Practitioners incorporate market information into the tree by making constant parameters such as probabilities time-dependent and to "imply these time-dependent parameters such that the tree returns the market prices of the standard options."[2]

Implied trees are constructed using forward induction. Each node in the tree has the calculated price today of an instrument that pays off a dollar in the future if node (i, j) is reached at time step i and zero otherwise. Such prices are called state prices or Arrow-Debreu securities, denoted at node (i, j) by $Q_{i,j}$. As before, we denote i as the time step and j as the level of the asset price relative to the initial asset price so that at node (i, j) we have $t = i\Delta t$ and $S_{i,j} = \exp(j\Delta x)$. The price of a European call with strike price X and maturity date $N\Delta t$ in the tree is:

$$C(S, X, \Delta t) = \sum_{j=-N}^{N} \max(S_{N,j} - X, 0)Q_{N,j} \qquad (4.18)$$

We would like to compute the state prices for the nodes at time step N in the tree so that they are consistent with the prices of standard European call and put options. Following Clewlow and Strickland, if we start at the highest node in the tree (N, N) at time step N, then the price of a European call with a strike equal to the level of the asset price at the next node below, $S_{N,N-1}$, and with a maturity date at time step N, is:

$$C(S_{N,N-1}, N\Delta t) = (S_{N,N} - S_{N,N-1})Q_{N,N} \qquad (4.19)$$

---

[2]Ibid., 134.

because for all the nodes below (N, N) the payoff of the call option is zero. We can solve for $Q_{N,N}$ at node (N, N) in terms of the known call price, asset price, and strike price. For a European option with a strike price equal to the asset price $S_{N,N-2}$ at node $(N, N-2)$, its price is given by:

$$C(S_{N,N-2}, N\Delta t) = (S_{N,N-1} - S_{N,N-2})Q_{N,N-1} + (S_{N,N} - S_{N,N-2})Q_{N,N}$$

The only unknown quantity is $Q_{N,N-1}$ since $Q_{N,N}$ has already been computed using equation (4.19). We can continue to work down the nodes at time step N to the middle of the tree computing the state prices. In general, for node (N, j), the option price is given by

$$C(S_{N,j-1}, N\Delta t) = (S_{N,j} - S_{N,j-1})Q_{N,j} + \sum_{k=j+1}^{N} (S_{N,k} - S_{N,j-1})Q_{N,k}$$

where all quantities are known except $Q_{N,j}$. When the central node is reached, namely $Q_{N,0}$, the same process can be used for the bottom nodes in the tree; that is $-N \le j < 0$, using put option prices due to numerical errors that accumulate from the iterative process with call options. In general, for node (i, j), the state price is given by:

$$Q_{i,j} = \frac{C(N_{i,j-1}, i\Delta t) - \sum_{k=j+1}^{i} (S_{i,k} - S_{i,j-1})Q_{i,k}}{(S_{i,j} - S_{i,j-1})} \qquad (4.20)$$

We want to compute the transitional probabilities given the state prices at every node in the tree. We can use no-arbitrage relationships that must hold at each node. Following Clewlow and Strickland, the first no-arbitrage relationship is that the discounted expected value of a one-period pure discount bond must be equal to the discount factor over the next time step:

$$e^{-r\Delta t}(p_{d,i,j} + p_{m,i,j} + p_{u,i,j}) = e^{-r\Delta t} \qquad (4.21)$$

which is equivalent to the requirement that the transitional probabilities sum to 1:

$$p_{d,i,j} + p_{m,i,j} + p_{u,i,j} = 1 \qquad (4.22)$$

The second condition is that the asset price at node (i, j) must be equal to its local discounted expected value over the next time step:

$$S_{i,j} = e^{-r\Delta t}(p_{d,i,j}S_{i+1,j-1} + p_{m,i,j}S_{i+1,j} + p_{u,i,j}S_{i+1,j+1}) \qquad (4.23)$$

Third, we get the forward evolution equation for the Arrow-Debreu state prices at node $(i + 1, j + 1)$:

$$Q_{i+1,j+1} = e^{-r\Delta t}(p_{d,i,j+2}Q_{i,j+2} + p_{m,i,j+1}Q_{i,j+1} + p_{u,i,j}Q_{i,j}) \qquad (4.24)$$

We can rearrange equation (4.24) to find $p_{u,i,j}$ directly:

$$p_{u,i,j} = \frac{e^{r\Delta t}Q_{i+1,j+1} - p_{d,i,j+2}Q_{i,j+2} - p_{m,i,j+1}Q_{i,j+1}}{Q_{i,j}} \qquad (4.25)$$

Equations (4.22) and (4.23) can be solved simultaneously for $p_{m,i,j}$ and $p_{d,i,j}$:

$$p_{m,i,j} = \frac{e^{r\Delta t}S_{i,j} - S_{i+1,j-1} - p_{u,i,j}(S_{i+1,j+1} - S_{i+1,j-1})}{(S_{i+1,j} - S_{i+1,j-1})} \qquad (4.26)$$

$$p_{d,i,j} = 1 - p_{m,i,j} - p_{u,i,j} \qquad (4.27)$$

At the highest node (i, i) at time step i, equation (4.25) reduces to

$$p_{u,i,j} = \frac{e^{r\Delta t}Q_{i+1,i+1}}{Q_{i,i}} \qquad (4.28)$$

and we can determine $p_{m,i,j}$ and $p_{d,i,j}$. At node $(i, i - 1)$ equation (4.26) reduces to

$$p_{u,i,j-1} = \frac{e^{r\Delta t}Q_{i+1,i} - p_{m,i,i}Q_{i,i}}{Q_{i,i-1}} \qquad (4.29)$$

Equations (4.26) and (4.27) can be used to obtain $p_{m,i,j-1}$ and $p_{d,i-1}$. We can solve for the transitional probabilities by starting at the top of the tree and iteratively working downward until the lowest node of the tree. However, due to numerical errors that build up from the iterative calculations (the transitional probabilities we obtain depend on previously computed transitional probabilities), we stop at the central node and determine the probabilities for the lower nodes in the tree by working up from the bottom node to the central node. Thus, for the lower half of the tree, one obtains $p_{d,i,j}$ directly from the evolution of the state prices in equation (4.24). Then $p_{m,i,j}$ and $p_{u,i,j}$ are determined by solving the remaining two equations simultaneously. Thus, equations (4.25) to (4.29) become

$$p_{d,i,j} = \frac{e^{r\Delta t}Q_{i+1,j-1} - p_{u,i,j-2}Q_{i,j-2} - p_{m,i,j-1}Q_{i,j-1}}{Q_{i,j}} \qquad (4.30)$$

$$p_{m,i,j} = \frac{e^{r\Delta t}S_{i,j} - S_{i+1,j+1} - p_{d,i,j}(S_{i+1,j-1} - S_{i+1,j+1})}{(S_{i+1,j} - S_{i+1,j+1})} \qquad (4.31)$$

$$p_{u,i,j} = 1 - p_{m,i,j} - p_{d,i,j} \qquad (4.32)$$

$$p_{d,i,-i} = \frac{e^{r\Delta t}Q_{i+1,-i-1}}{Q_{i,-i}} \qquad (4.33)$$

$$p_{d,i,-i+1} = \frac{e^{r\Delta t}Q_{i+1,-i} - p_{m,i,-i}Q_{i,-i}}{Q_{i,-i+1}} \qquad (4.34)$$

Since the implied tree method is an explicit difference scheme, it is necessary to ensure that the transitional probabilities remain in position and that the stability condition

$$\Delta x \geq \sigma\sqrt{3\Delta t}$$

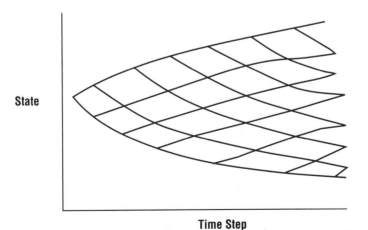

State

Time Step

FIGURE 4.5   Schematic Representation of an Implied Binomial Tree

be satisfied at every node. A robust way to ensure that the transitional probabilities remain positive and that the stability condition is satisfied is to set the space step as

$$\Delta x = \sigma_{max} \sqrt{3\Delta t}$$

where σ_{max} is the maximum implied volatility obtained from the standard options to which the tree is being calibrated. Clewlow and Strickland (1998a) show how implied trees can be used to price American puts as well as exotic path-dependent options like barrier and lookback options.

Figure 4.5 shows a schematic representation of an implied binomial tree. Notice that in the implied binomial tree the node spacing varies with market level and time, as specified by the local volatility function $\sigma(S, t)$ implied from implied volatilities of quoted option prices.

CHAPTER 5

Finite-Difference Methods

We discuss numerical methods known as finite-difference methods for pricing derivatives by approximating the diffusion process that the derivative must follow. Finite-difference methods are a means for generating numerical solutions to partial differential equations and linear complementary (free boundary) problems such as those used to price American options. Finite-difference schemes are useful for valuation of derivatives when closed-form analytical solutions do not exist or for solutions to complicated multifactor (multidimensional) models. By discretizing the continuous-time partial differential equation that the derivative security must follow, it is possible to approximate the evolution of the derivative and therefore the present value of the security.

In section 5.1, we discuss explicit finite-difference methods where the value at any time instant can be explicitly determined from its previous values in different states (up, down, middle) at the previous time instant. In section 5.2, an explicit difference method implementation is given. In section 5.3, the implicit difference method is discussed where the derivative value at any time instant is determined implicitly from its values in different states (up, down, middle) at the next time instant. In section 5.4, the LU decomposition is discussed for use in solving linear systems of implicit difference equations. In section 5.5, an implicit difference method implementation is given. In section 5.6, more robust object-oriented implementations of finite-difference methods are provided. In section 5.7, iterative methods, another technique for solving implicit difference schemes, is discussed. In section 5.8, the Crank-Nicolson scheme, a scheme that combines both explicit and implicit scheme features, is discussed. In section 5.9, we discuss the alternating direction implicit (ADI) method, an extended finite-difference method used for handling multifactor models.

5.1 EXPLICIT DIFFERENCE METHODS

Binomial and trinomial trees work well for pricing European and American options. However, there are alternative numerical methods that can be used to value these standard options as well as more complex derivatives with nonlinear payoffs such as exotic options. Finite-difference methods are used to price derivatives by solving the differential equation in conjunction with the initial asset price condition and boundary value condition(s) (i.e., payoffs) that the derivative must also satisfy. The differential equation is converted into a system of difference equations that are solved iteratively. Consider the Black-Scholes PDE:

$$\frac{\partial f}{\partial t} + (r - q)S\frac{\partial f}{\partial S} + \frac{1}{2}\sigma^2 S^2 \frac{\partial^2 f}{\partial S^2} = rf \tag{5.1}$$

subject to the payoff condition $f(S_T, T) = (S_T - X)^+$. We can extend the trinomial tree approach by creating a rectangular grid or lattice by adding extra nodes above and below the tree so that we have $2N_j + 1$, $N_j \geq N$, nodes at every time step i rather than $2i + 1$. In a similar manner to trinomial trees, when implementing finite-difference methods, we divide space and time into discrete intervals, Δt and Δx, which generates the lattice. We add boundary conditions to the grid, which determines option prices as a function of the asset price for high and low values so that $\partial f/\partial S = 1$ for S large and $\partial f/\partial S = 0$ for S small. We can simplify the Black-Scholes PDE by replacing the PDE with finite differences. Thus, we can discretize the PDE to develop a numerical finite-difference scheme. First, we simplify the PDE; let $x = \ln(S)$ so that

$$\frac{\partial f}{\partial t} + \mu\frac{\partial f}{\partial x} + \frac{1}{2}\sigma^2 \frac{\partial^2 f}{\partial x^2} = rf$$

where $\mu = r - q$. To get rid of the rf term on the left-hand side, let $u(x, t)$ be a new function: $u(x, t) = e^{r(T-t)}f(e^x, t)$. The term u is a forward price of the option f and satisfies the PDE:

$$\frac{1}{2}\sigma^2 \frac{\partial^2 u}{\partial x^2} + \mu\frac{\partial u}{\partial x} = -\frac{\partial \mu}{\partial t} \tag{5.2}$$

We will discretize this PDE by taking the central difference of the state variable, x, and the forward difference of the time variable t. Denote $u_{i,j} = u(x_j, t_i)$, $t_i = i\Delta t$, and $x_j = j\Delta x$. Substituting the finite differences into the PDE:

$$\frac{1}{2}\sigma^2\left(\frac{u_{i+1,j+1} - 2u_{i+1,j} + u_{i+1,j-1}}{\Delta x^2}\right) + \mu\left(\frac{u_{i+1,j+1} - u_{i+1,j-1}}{2\Delta x}\right) = -\left(\frac{u_{i+1,j} - u_{i,j}}{\Delta t}\right) \tag{5.3}$$

Rearranging terms, we have the recurrent relation for the forward option price:

$$u_{i,j} = \tilde{p}_u u_{i+1,j+1} + \tilde{p}_m u_{i+1,j} + \tilde{p}_d u_{i+1,j-1} \qquad (5.4)$$

where

$$\tilde{p}_u = \frac{\sigma^2 \Delta t}{2\Delta x^2} + \frac{\mu \Delta t}{2\Delta x}$$

$$\tilde{p}_m = 1 - \frac{\sigma^2 \Delta t}{\Delta x^2} \qquad (5.5)$$

$$\tilde{p}_d = \frac{\sigma^2 \Delta t}{2\Delta x^2} - \frac{\mu \Delta t}{2\Delta x}$$

Note that $\tilde{p}_u + \tilde{p}_m + \tilde{p}_d = 1$. Denote $\alpha = \Delta t/(\Delta x)^2$ and $\beta = \mu \Delta t/\Delta x$. We can rewrite equations (5.5)

$$\tilde{p}_u = \frac{1}{2}(\sigma^2 \alpha + \beta)$$

$$\tilde{p}_m = 1 - \sigma^2 \alpha$$

$$\tilde{p}_d = \frac{1}{2}(\sigma^2 \alpha - \beta)$$

The relationship of trinomial trees to finite-difference discretizations of the Black-Scholes PDE can be seen as follows. Substitute the present value of the option $f_{i,j} = e^{-r(T-t_i)} u_{i,j}$ into equation (5.4). We arrive at the backward induction relationship:

$$f_{i,j} = e^{-r\Delta t} \left(\tilde{p}_u f_{i+1,j+1} + \tilde{p}_m f_{i+1,j} + \tilde{p}_d f_{i+1,j-1} \right) \qquad (5.6)$$

This is similar to the backward induction to the trinomial tree in equation (4.11). This is equivalent to the discounted expectation of the forward option price (under a risk-neutral measure). Thus, we have shown that the explicit finite-difference scheme is equivalent to approximating the diffusion process by a discrete trinomial process.

Figure 5.1 shows a schematic view of the explicit finite-difference discretization.

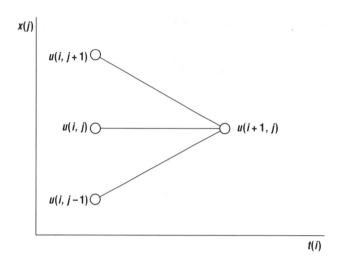

FIGURE 5.1   Explicit Finite-Difference Scheme

5.2   EXPLICIT FINITE-DIFFERENCE IMPLEMENTATION

Consider the following explicit difference class:

```
class ExplicitDiffMethod : public FiniteDifferenceMethod
{
  public:
    ExplicitDiffMethod() {}
    ExplicitDiffMethod(long N, long M);
    ~ExplicitDiffMethod() {}
    virtual void solve() {}
    double explicitDiffEuropean(double price, double strike, double rate, double
      div, double volatility, double T, int N, int M, char type, char bc);
    double explicitDiffAmerican(double price, double strike, double rate, double
      div, double volatility, double T, int N, int M, char type, char bc);
  private:
    long N_;            // number of time steps
    long M_;            // number of space steps
};
```

where:

```
// Generic finite difference model
class FiniteDifferenceMethod
```

```
{
public:
  enum MethodType { ExplicitDifference, ImplicitDifference,
    AlternatingDirectImplicit, SOR, ProjectedSOR, CrankNicolson };
  enum BoundaryConditions { Dirichlet, Neumann };
  virtual void solve() const { }
  // constructor
  FiniteDifferenceMethod() { }
  virtual ~FiniteDifferenceMethod() { }
};
```

The following is an implementation of an explicit finite-difference scheme. N is the total number of time steps where each time step is $\Delta t = T/N$ and $|M|$ is the total number of state movements (in either direction from the initial state at time 0) where the state variable is S_j, $j = -M \ldots -1, 0, 1, \ldots M$.

```
/*****************************************************************************
explicitDiffAmerican : values an American option using the explicit difference
                       method
[in]: double price   : asset price
      double strike  : strike price
      double vol     : volatility
      double rate    : risk-free rate
      double div     : dividend yield
      double T       : time to maturity
      int N          : number of time steps
      int M          : number of space steps
      char type      : (C)all or (P)ut
      char bc        : boundary conditions (D)irichlet or (N)eumann
[out] double         : option price

*****************************************************************************/
double ExplicitDiffMethod::explicitDiffAmerican(double price, double strike, double
  vol, double rate, double div, double T, int N, int M, char type, char bc)
{
  int i, j;
  double dt = T/N;
  double drift = rate - div - 0.5*(vol*vol);
  double dx = vol*sqrt(3*dt/2);
  double pu, pm, pd;
  double C[150][150] = {0.0};   // stores option prices
  double S[150][150] = {0.0};   // stores asset prices
```

```
pu = (vol*vol*dt)/(2*dx*dx) + (drift*dt)/(2*dx);
pm = 1.0 - (vol*vol*dt)/(dx*dx);
pd = (vol*vol*dt)/(2*dx*dx) - (drift*dt)/(2*dx);

// initialize asset prices at maturity
for (j = -M; j <= M; j++)
{
  S[N][j] = price*exp(j*dx);
}

if (type == 'C')
{
  // compute payoff at maturity
  for (j = -M; j <= M; j++)
    C[N][j] = max(S[N][j] - strike,0);

  // boundary conditions for high and low asset prices
  for (i = 0; i < N; i++)
  {
    if (bc == 'D')
    {
      C[i][-M] = 0.0;
      C[i][M]  = max(S[N][M] - strike,0);
    }
    else
    {
      C[i][M]  = C[i][M-1] + (S[i][M] - S[i][M-1]);
      C[i][-M] = C[i][-M+1];
    }
  }

  for (i = N-1; i >= 0; i--)
  {
    for (j = M-1; j >= -(M-1); j--)
    {
      C[i][j] = pu*C[i+1][j+1] + pm*C[i+1][j] + pd*C[i+1][j-1];
      C[i][j] = max(S[N][j] - strike, C[i][j]);
    }
  }
}
else //if (type == 'P')
{
  // boundary conditions for high and low asset prices
  for (i = 0; i < N; i++)
  {
    C[i][0] = strike;
    C[i][M] = 0;
  }
  for (j = -M; j <= M; j++)
  {
    C[N][j] = max(strike - S[N][j],0);
  }
```

```
    }

    for (j = -M; j <= M; j++)
    {
       C[N][j] = max(strike - S[N][j],0);
    }
    // boundary conditions for high and low asset prices
    for (i = 0; i < N; i++)
    {
       if (bc == 'D')
       {
          C[i][-M] = strike;
          C[i][M] = max(0,strike - S[N][j]);
       }
       else // Neumann bc
       {
          C[i][M]  = C[i][M-1];
          C[i][-M] = C[i][-M+1] + (S[i][-M] - S[i][-M+1]);
       }
    }

    for (i = N-1; i >= 0; i--)
    {
       for (j = M-1; j >= -M; j--)
       {
          C[i][j] = pu*C[i+1][j+1] + pm*C[i+1][j] + pd*C[i+1][j-1];
          C[i][j] = max(strike - S[N][j], C[i][j]);
       }
    }
  }
  return C[0][0];
}
```

Suppose we want to price the same ATM American-style call option we priced earlier in the trinomial tree: $S = 50$, $X = 50$, $\sigma = 0.20$, $r = 0.06$, $q = 0.03$, $N = 4$, $M = 5$, and $T = 1$. Figure 5.2 shows the lattice that is generated. The value of the call option marching backward from the maturity date $T = 1$ is \$4.76.

Figure 5.3 shows a convergence comparison of the explicit difference method with the trinomial method using the parameters as before.

As shown, the explicit difference method provides a rough approximation to the trinomial prices though differences exist due to errors from convergence conditions that need to be satisfied in order to have a good approximation to the trinomial diffusion process (see section 4.5). Note that all trinomial tree methods (different lambdas) quickly converge to one another while the explicit difference schemes (different lambdas) converge to each another. As $N \to \infty$, however, the explicit difference schemes will converge to the trinomial diffusion process.

S	j	i	t 1.0 0	0.75 1	0.50 2	0.25 3	0.0 4
72.20	3		22.20	22.20	22.20	22.20	22.20
63.88	2		15.47	15.09	14.65	14.36	13.88
56.51	1		9.39	8.70	7.97	6.94	6.51
50.00	0		4.76	4.03	3.13	2.24	0.00
44.24	−1		1.91	1.33	0.77	0.00	0.00
39.14	−2		0.55	0.26	0.00	0.00	0.00
34.63	−3		0.00	0.00	0.00	0.00	0.00

FIGURE 5.2   Lattice for ATM American-Style Call Option

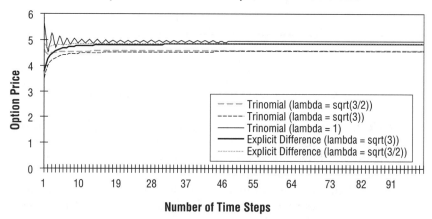

FIGURE 5.3   Convergence Comparison

5.3 IMPLICIT DIFFERENCE METHOD

If the backward difference,

$$\frac{u_{i,j} - u_{i-1,j}}{\Delta t}$$

is used instead of the forward difference for the time derivative, $\partial f/\partial t$, in equation (5.3), we will get an implicit difference scheme in which $u_{i+1,j}$ is implicitly dependent on $u_{i,j+1}$, $u_{i,j}$, and $u_{i,j-1}$.

$$u_{i+1,j} = \tilde{p}_u u_{i,j+1} + \tilde{p}_m u_{i,j} + \tilde{p}_d u_{i,j-1} \qquad (5.7)$$

where the probabilities $\tilde{p}_u$, $\tilde{p}_m$, and $\tilde{p}_d$ are defined in equation (5.5). If we substitute the present value of the option $f_{i,j} = e^{-r(T-t_i)} u_{i,j}$ into equation (5.7), we get the risk-neutral expected value:

$$f_{i+1,j} = e^{-r\Delta t}(\tilde{p}_u f_{i,j+1} + \tilde{p}_m f_{i,j} + \tilde{p}_d f_{i,j-1}) \qquad (5.8)$$

If $f_{i,j}$ is a put option, then when the stock price is zero, we get the boundary condition:

$$f_{i,-M} = X \qquad i = 0, 1, \dots, N \qquad (5.9)$$

The value of the option tends to zero as the stock price tends to infinity. We may use the boundary condition:

$$f_{i,M} = 0 \qquad i = 0, 1, \dots, N \qquad (5.10)$$

The value of the put at maturity (time T) is:

$$f_{N,j} = \max(X - S_j, 0) \qquad j = -M, \dots, -1, 0, 1, \dots, M \qquad (5.11)$$

Figure 5.4 is a schematic view of an implicit finite-difference discretization.

Equations (5.9), (5.10), and (5.11) define the value of the put option along the boundaries of the grid. To solve for the value of f at all other points we use equation (5.8). First, the points corresponding to $T - \Delta t$ are solved. Equation (5.8) with $i = N - 1$ yields $2M - 1$ linear simultaneous equations:

$$f_{N,j} = e^{-r\Delta t}\left(\tilde{p}_u {}_{N-1,j+1} + \tilde{p}_m f_{N-1,j} + \tilde{p}_d f_{N-1,j-1}\right) \quad j = -M+1, \dots, M+1 \quad (5.12)$$

Unlike the explicit finite-difference method, each equation cannot be solved individually for the option values at time step i. These equations must be considered

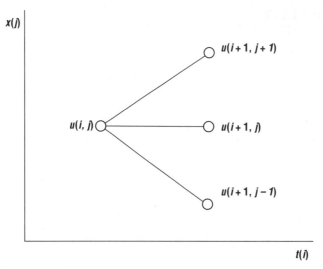

FIGURE 5.4 Implicit Finite-Difference Scheme

with the boundary conditions. The system of equations can be rewritten as a tridi-agonal matrix form. We can rewrite equation (5.7) as:

$$
\begin{bmatrix}
\tilde{p}_m & \tilde{p}_d & 0 & \cdots & \cdots & \cdots & 0 \\
\tilde{p}_u & \tilde{p}_m & \tilde{p}_d & 0 & \cdots & \cdots & 0 \\
0 & \tilde{p}_u & \tilde{p}_m & \tilde{p}_d & 0 & \cdots & 0 \\
\cdots & \cdots & \cdots & \cdots & \cdots & \cdots & \cdots \\
0 & \cdots & 0 & \tilde{p}_u & \tilde{p}_m & \tilde{p}_d & 0 \\
0 & \cdots & \cdots & 0 & \tilde{p}_u & \tilde{p}_m & \tilde{p}_d \\
0 & \cdots & \cdots & \cdots & 0 & \tilde{p}_u & \tilde{p}_d
\end{bmatrix}
\begin{bmatrix}
u_{i,-M} \\
u_{i,-M+1} \\
u_{i,-M+2} \\
\cdots \\
u_{i,M-2} \\
u_{i,M-1} \\
u_{i,M}
\end{bmatrix}
=
\begin{bmatrix}
u_{i+1,-M} \\
u_{i+1,-M+1} \\
u_{i+1,-M+2} \\
\cdots \\
u_{i+1,M-2} \\
u_{i+1,M-1} \\
u_{i+1,M}
\end{bmatrix}
\quad (5.13)
$$

where the (probability) elements of the matrix in (5.13) are given in equation (5.5).

Let β_U be the upper boundary (for a put $\beta_U = 0$ if S is much larger than X) and β_L be a lower boundary (for a put $\beta_L = X$ if $S = 0$) when the asset price reaches the high and low points, respectively. Then $u_{i+1,-M} = \beta_L$ and $u_{i+1,M} = \beta_U$. However, we will be using the partial derivatives (Neumann boundary conditions) of the option price at the boundaries when we use finite-difference schemes. Note that $u_{N,j} = f(S) = \max(S - X, 0)$ for a call and $\max(X - S, 0)$ for a put option $j = -M, \ldots, M$. We can rewrite equations (5.13) as:

$$
\mathbf{M}\mathbf{u}^i = \mathbf{b}^{i+1} \qquad i = 0, 1, \ldots, N-1 \qquad (5.14)
$$

which can be solved for $\mathbf{u}^i$ since $\mathbf{M}$ is nonsingular; that is, it can be inverted:

$$\mathbf{u}^i = \mathbf{M}^{-1}\mathbf{b}^{i+1} \qquad (5.15)$$

where $\mathbf{M}^{-1}$ is the inverse of M. Making use of the boundary conditions, we can solve (5.15) iteratively starting at time $i = N - 1$ and solving for $\mathbf{u}^{N-1}$ (we know $\mathbf{b}^N$ since they are given by the boundary conditions in (5.9), (5.10), and (5.11). Once we solve for $\mathbf{u}^{N-1}$ at time $i = N - 1$, we can use it to solve for $\mathbf{u}^{N-2}$ at time $i = N - 2$ since $\mathbf{b}^{N-1} = \mathbf{u}^{N-1}$. Thus, we can solve for each $\mathbf{u}^i$, $i = N - 1, \ldots, 0$, sequentially working backward starting from time $i = N - 1$ until we solve for $\mathbf{u}^0$, which gives us a vector solution of option prices.

Since $\mathbf{M}$ is tridiagonal (i.e., only the diagonal, superdiagonal, and subdiagonal entries are nonzero), we do not have to store all the zeros, but just the nonzero elements. The inverse of $\mathbf{M}$, $\mathbf{M}^{-1}$, is not tridiagonal and requires a lot more storage than M.

We can rewrite the system of equations in (5.13) as:

$$\begin{bmatrix} 1 & p^*_{-M,d} & 0 & \ldots & & \ldots & \ldots & 0 \\ 0 & 1 & p^*_{-M+1,d} & 0 & & \ldots & \ldots & 0 \\ 0 & 0 & 1 & p^*_{-M+2,d} & 0 & & \ldots & 0 \\ \ldots & \ldots & \ldots & \ldots & & \ldots & \ldots & \ldots \\ 0 & \ldots & 0 & 0 & 1 & p^*_{M-2,d} & 0 \\ 0 & \ldots & & 0 & & 0 & 1 & p^*_{M-1,d} \\ 0 & \ldots & & \ldots & & & 0 & 0 & 1 \end{bmatrix} \begin{bmatrix} u_{i,-M} \\ u_{i,-M+1} \\ u_{i,-M+2} \\ \ldots \\ u_{i,M-2} \\ u_{i,M-1} \\ u_{i,M} \end{bmatrix} = \begin{bmatrix} u^*_{i+1,-M} \\ u^*_{i+1,-M+1} \\ u^*_{i+1,-M+2} \\ \ldots \\ u^*_{i+1,M-2} \\ u^*_{i+1,M-1} \\ u^*_{i+1,M} \end{bmatrix} \qquad (5.16)$$

where

$$p^*_{-M,d} = \frac{\tilde{p}_d}{\tilde{p}_m}, \qquad \tilde{p}^*_{j+1,d} = \frac{\tilde{p}_d}{\tilde{p}_m - \tilde{p}_u p^*_{j,d}} \qquad j = -M+1, \ldots, M-2 \qquad (5.17)$$

and

$$u^*_{i+1,-M} = \frac{u_{i+1,-M}}{\tilde{p}_m}, \qquad u^*_{i+1,j+1} = \frac{u_{i+1,j+1} - \tilde{p}_u u^*_{i+1,j}}{\tilde{p}_m - \tilde{p}_u p^*_{j,d}} \qquad j = -M+1, \ldots, M-1 \quad (5.18)$$

Solving (5.17) and (5.18) from bottom to top, we get:

$$u_{i,M} = u^*_{i+1,M}, \ u_{i,j} = u^*_{i+1,j} - p^*_{j,d} u_{i,j+1} \qquad i = 0 \ldots N-1, j = -M+1, \ldots, M-1 \qquad (5.19)$$

We could also use an LU decomposition to solve for $\mathbf{u}^i$ in (5.14) without having to invert $\mathbf{M}$.

5.4 LU DECOMPOSITION METHOD

In an LU decomposition, we decompose the matrix $\mathbf{M}$ into a product of a lower triangular matrix $\mathbf{L}$ and an upper triangular matrix $\mathbf{U}$, namely $\mathbf{M} = \mathbf{LU}$, of the form:

$$
\begin{bmatrix}
p_m & p_d & 0 & \cdots & \cdots & & \cdots & 0 \\
p_u & p_m & p_d & 0 & & & & 0 \\
0 & p_u & p_m & p_d & 0 & & & 0 \\
& \ddots & \ddots & \ddots & & & & \vdots \\
\vdots & & 0 & p_u & p_m & p_d & & \vdots \\
& & & 0 & p_u & p_m & p_d & \\
0 & \cdots & \cdots & \cdots & 0 & p_u & p_d &
\end{bmatrix}
=
\begin{bmatrix}
1 & 0 & \cdots & & \cdots & 0 & 0 \\
v_M & 1 & 0 & & & & \vdots \\
0 & v_{M-1} & 1 & 0 & & & \\
\vdots & & v_{M-2} & 1 & & \ddots & \vdots \\
& & & \ddots & \ddots & & 0 \\
\vdots & & & & \ddots & \ddots & \vdots \\
0 & \cdots & \cdots & \cdots & & v_{-M+1} & 1
\end{bmatrix}
\begin{bmatrix}
y_M & z_M & 0 & \cdots & & 0 \\
0 & y_{M-1} & z_{M-1} & 0 & & \vdots \\
0 & 0 & y_{M-2} & z_{M-2} & & \vdots \\
0 & & \ddots & \ddots & \ddots & 0 \\
\vdots & & & & & z_{-M+1} \\
0 & \cdots & \cdots & 0 & 0 & y_{-M}
\end{bmatrix}
\tag{5.20}
$$

In order to determine the quantities v_j, y_j, and z_j, $j = -M + 1, \ldots, M - 1$, we multiply the two matrices on the right-hand side of equation (5.20) and set the result to the left-hand side. After some simple calculations:

$$
y_M = p_m
$$

$$
y_j = p_m - \frac{p_u p_d}{y_{j-1}} \qquad j = -M+1, \ldots, M-1 \tag{5.21}
$$

$$
z_j = p_d, \; v_j = \frac{p_u}{y_j} \qquad j = -M+1, \ldots, M
$$

The only quantities we need to calculate and store are the y_j, $j = -M + 2, \ldots, M - 1$. We can rewrite the original problem in $\mathbf{M}\mathbf{u}^i = \mathbf{b}^{i+1}$ as $\mathbf{L}(\mathbf{U}\mathbf{u}^i) = \mathbf{b}^{i+1}$, $i = 0, \ldots, N - 1$, which may be broken down into two simpler subproblems:

$$
\mathbf{L}\mathbf{q}^i = \mathbf{b}^i, \; \mathbf{U}\mathbf{u}^{i+1} = \mathbf{q}^i \tag{5.22}
$$

Where $\mathbf{q}^i$ is an intermediate vector. We eliminate the v_j from $\mathbf{L}$ and the z_j from $\mathbf{U}$ using (5.21), the solution procedure is to solve two subproblems:

$$
\begin{bmatrix}
1 & 0 & \cdots & \cdots & 0 & 0 \\
-\dfrac{p_u}{y_M} & 1 & 0 & & & \vdots \\
0 & -\dfrac{p_u}{y_{M-1}} & 1 & 0 & & \vdots \\
\vdots & & \ddots & \ddots & & \vdots \\
0 & \cdots & & -\dfrac{p_u}{y_{-M+1}} & 1 &
\end{bmatrix}
\begin{bmatrix}
q_{i,M} \\
q_{i,M-1} \\
\vdots \\
\vdots \\
q_{i,-M+1} \\
q_{i,-M}
\end{bmatrix}
=
\begin{bmatrix}
b_{i,M} \\
b_{i,M-1} \\
\vdots \\
\vdots \\
b_{i,-M+1} \\
b_{i,-M}
\end{bmatrix}
\tag{5.23}
$$

and

$$
\begin{bmatrix}
y_M & p_d & \cdots & & 0 \\
0 & y_{M-1} & p_d & & 0 \\
 & & & & \\
\vdots & \vdots & \vdots & \vdots & \vdots \\
 & & & p_d & \\
0 & \cdots & & y_{-M} &
\end{bmatrix}
\begin{bmatrix}
u_{i+1,M} \\
u_{i+1,M-1} \\
\vdots \\
u_{i+1,-M+1} \\
u_{i+1,-M}
\end{bmatrix}
=
\begin{bmatrix}
q_{i,M} \\
q_{i,M-1} \\
\vdots \\
q_{i,-M+1} \\
q_{i,-M}
\end{bmatrix}
\tag{5.24}
$$

The intermediate quantities $q_{i,j}$ are found by forward substitution. We can read off the value of $q_{i,M}$ directly, while any other equation in the system relates only $q_{i,j}$ and $q_{i,j-1}$. If we solve the system in decreasing i-incidental order, we have $q_{i,j}$ available at the time available we have to solve for $q_{i,j+1}$. Consequently, we can find $q_{i,j}$:

$$
q_{i,M} = b_{i,M}, \qquad q_{i,j} = b_{i,j} + \frac{p_u q_{i,j+1}}{y_{j+1}} \qquad j = -M+1, \ldots, M-1 \tag{5.25}
$$

Solving (5.24) for the $u_{i,j}$ (once we find the intermediate $q_{i,j}$) is achieved through backward substitution. We can read $u_{i+1,-M}$ directly (it is the value of the boundary), and if we solve in increasing i-incidental order we can find all of the $u_{i,j}$ in the same manner:

$$
u_{i+1,-M} = \frac{q_{i,-M}}{y_{-M}} \qquad u_{i+1,j} = \frac{q_{i,j} + p_d u_{i+1,j+1}}{y_j} \qquad j = -M+1, \ldots, M-1 \tag{5.26}
$$

At the boundary, we get conditions

$$u_{i,M} - u_{i,M-1} = \beta_U \tag{5.27}$$

$$u_{i,-M+1} - u_{i,-M} = \beta_L \tag{5.28}$$

β_U and β_L are the derivatives at the boundary so that

$$\beta_U = S_{i,M} - S_{i,M-1}, \beta_L = 0$$

for a call and

$$\beta_U = 0, \beta_L = -1 \cdot (S_{i,-M+1} - S_{i,-M})$$

for a put.

5.5   IMPLICIT DIFFERENCE METHOD IMPLEMENTATION

Consider an implicit difference class that inherits from a finite-difference class:

```
class ImplicitDiffMethod : public FiniteDifferenceMethod
{
  public:
    ImplicitDiffMethod();
    ImplicitDiffMethod(long N, long M);
    ~ImplicitDiffMethod() {}
    double implicitDiffEuropean(double price, double strike, double vol,
      double rate, double div, double T, long N, long M, char type, char bc);
    double implicitDiffAmerican(double price, double strike, double vol,
      double rate, double div, double T, long N, long M, char type, char bc);
    void solveTridiagonalAmer(double strike, long N, long M, double pu, double pm,
      double pd, double *d, double *c1, double *d1, char type);
    void solveTridiagonalEuro(double strike, long N, long M, double pu, double pm,
      double pd, double *d, double *c1, double *d1, char type);
  private:
    long N_;                 // number of time steps
    long M_;                 // number of state steps
    double C[200][200];      // stores option prices
    double S[200][200];      // stores asset prices
};
```

The following is an implementation of the implicit finite-difference method of the same put option we valued with the explicit finite-difference method.

```
/****************************************************************************
implicitDiffAmerican: values an American option using the implicit difference
                  method
[in]:    double price  : asset price
         double strike : strike price
         double vol     : volatility
         double rate    : risk-free rate
         double div     : dividend yield
         double T       : maturity
         int N          : number of time steps
         int M          : number of space steps
         char type: (C)all or (P)ut
         char bc: boundary conditions (D)irichlet or (N)eumann
[out]:   option price
****************************************************************************/
double ImplicitDiffMethod::implicitDiffAmerican(double price, double strike, double
  vol, double rate, double div, double T, long N, long M, char type, char bc)
{
  double c1[350] = {0.0};              // array to store values in
                                       // tridiagonal system
  double d[350] = {0.0};
  double d1[350] = {0.0};
  double x[350] = {0.0};
  double dx = 0.0;                     // space size
  double drift = rate - div - vol*vol/2;  // drift
  double pu, pm, pd;                   // risk neutral probabilities
  int i, j;

  double dt = T/N;
  dx = vol*sqrt(3*dt/2);

  pu = -0.5*dt*((vol*vol)/(dx*dx) + drift/dx);
  pm = 1 + dt*((vol*vol)/(dx*dx)) + rate*dt;
  pd = -0.5*dt*((vol*vol)/(dx*dx) - drift/dx);

  for (j = -M; j <= M; j++)
  {
    S[N][j] = price*exp(j*dx);
    S[0][j] = price;
  }

  for (i = 1; i < N; i++)
  {
    for (j = -M; j <= M; j++)
    {
      S[i][j] = S[i-1][j]*exp(j*dx);
    }
```

```
    }

    // calculate payoffs
    if (type == 'P')
    {
      for (j = -M; j <= M; j++)
      {
        C[N][j] = max(strike - S[N][j],0);
      }

      // calculate boundary conditions
      for (i = 0; i < N; i++)
      {
        if (bc == 'D')                        // Dirichlet boundary conditions
        {
          C[i][-M] = strike;
          C[i][M]  = max(strike - S[i][M],0);
        }
        else                                  // Neumann boundary conditions
        {
          C[i][-M] = C[i][-M+1] + (S[i][-M] - S[i][-M+1]);
          C[i][M]  = C[i][M-1];
        }
      }
    }
    else // if type == 'C'
    {
      // calculate boundary condition at maturity
      for (j = -M; j <= M; j++)
      {
        C[N][j] = max(S[N][j] - strike,0);
      }

      // calculate boundary conditions on grid
      for (i = 0; i < N; i++)
      {
        if (bc == 'D')                        // Dirichlet boundary conditions
        {
          C[i][-M] = 0;
          C[i][M]  = max(S[i][M] - strike,0);
        }
        else                                  // Neumann boundary condition
        {
          C[i][-M] = C[i][-M+1];
          C[i][M]  = C[i][M-1] + (S[i][M] - S[i][M-1]);
        }
      }
    }
    solveTridiagonalAmer(strike,N,M,pu,pm,pd,d,c1,d1,type);

    return C[0][1];
}
```

The following is the implementation of the method to solve the system of equations in the tridiagonal matrix in (5.16) using a LU decomposition.

```
/**************************************************************************/
solveTridiagonalAmer: solves a tridiagonal system with American exercise conditions
[in]:   double strike      : strike price
        long N              : number of time steps
        long M              : number of space steps
        double pu           : up probability
        double pm           : middle probability
        double pd           : down probability
        double *d, *c1, *d1: stores elements of tridiagonal matrix
        char type           : (C)all or (P)ut
[out]: option price
**************************************************************************/
void ImplicitDiffMethod::solveTridiagonalAmer(double strike, long N, long M, double
  pu, double pm, double pd, double *d, double *c1, double *d1, char type)
{

  int i,j;

  for (j = -M; j <= M; j++)
    d[j] = C[N][j];

  d1[-M]  = d[-M]/pm;
  c1[-M]  = pd/pm;

  c1[-M+1] = pd/pm;
  d1[-M+1] = d[-M+1]/pm;

  for (j = -M+1; j <= M-2; j++)
    c1[j+1] = pd/(pm - pu*c1[j]);

  for (j = -M+1; j <= M-1; j++)
    d1[j+1] = (d[j+1] - pu*d1[j])/(pm - pu*c1[j]);

  for (i = N-1; i >= 0; i--)
  {
    for (j = -M+1; j <= M-1; j++)
    {
      if (i != N-1)
        d[j] = C[i+1][-j];
      if (j == -M+1)
      {
        d1[-M+1] = d[-M+1]/pm;
      }
      d1[j+1] = (d[j+1] - pu*d1[j])/(pm - pu*c1[j]);
      C[i][-j] = d1[-j] - c1[-j]*C[i][-j+1];
```

```
// check early exercise condition
if (type =='P')
{
  if (C[i][-j] < strike - S[N][-j])
    C[i][-j] = strike - S[N][-j];
}
else
{
  if (C[i][-j] < S[N][-j] - strike)
    C[i][-j] = S[N][-j] - strike;
}
}
}
}
```

Suppose we price an ATM American-style put with $S = 50$, $X = 50$, $\sigma = 0.20$, $r = 0.06$, $q = 0.03$, $N = 4$, $M = 5$, and $T = 1$. Then, we generate the lattice shown in Figure 5.5. The option price is \$3.77. If we increase N and M, the price estimate gets better since $\Delta t \to 0$. Suppose $N = 5$ and $M = 5$. Then, we generate the lattice shown in Figure 5.6.

Figure 5.7 shows a plot of the implicit difference scheme as a function of time

$S = 50$	$x = 50$	vol = 0.20	$r = 0.06$	$q = 0.03$	$T = 1$	$N = 4$	$M = 4$	deltat = 0.25	$dx = 0.12$

S	j	t i	1.0 0	0.75 1	0.50 2	0.25 3	0.0 4
30.63	4		0.00	0.00	0.00	0.00	0.00
34.63	3		0.58	0.25	0.00	0.25	0.00
39.14	2		1.11	0.47	0.47	0.47	0.00
44.24	1		2.21	1.27	1.27	2.24	0.00
50.00	0		3.77	3.58	2.21	2.21	0.00
56.51	-1		6.40	6.36	5.96	5.96	5.76
63.88	-2		10.86	10.86	10.86	10.86	10.86
72.20	-3		15.37	15.37	15.37	15.37	15.37
81.61	-4		19.37	19.37	19.37	19.37	19.37

FIGURE 5.5 Lattice for ATM American-Style Put Option ($N = 4$)

			S = 50	x = 50	vol = 0.20	r = 0.06	q = 0.03	T = 1	N = 5	M = 5	deltat = 0.20	dx = 0.11

		t	1.0	0.80	0.60	0.45	0.20	0.00
S	j	i	0	1	2	3	4	5
28.91	−5		0.00	0.00	0.00	0.00	0.00	0.00
32.26	−4		0.25	0.25	0.08	0.08	0.08	0.00
36.00	−3		0.67	0.67	0.27	0.27	0.27	0.00
40.16	−2		1.05	1.05	0.43	0.43	0.43	0.00
44.81	−1		2.32	2.32	1.29	1.29	1.29	0.00
50.00	0		4.30	3.51	3.30	2.04	2.04	0.00
55.79	1		7.53	6.88	6.84	6.05	6.05	5.19
62.25	2		9.88	9.84	9.84	9.84	9.84	9.84
69.45	3		14.00	14.00	14.00	14.00	14.00	14.00
77.49	4		17.74	17.74	17.74	17.74	17.74	17.74
86.47	5		21.09	21.09	21.09	21.09	21.09	21.09

FIGURE 5.6   Lattice for Put Option (n = 5)

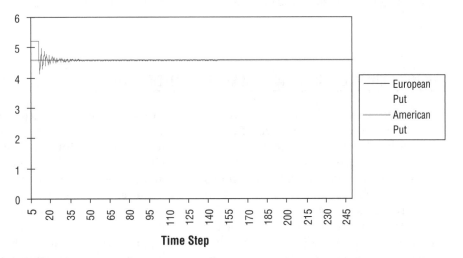

FIGURE 5.7   Implicit Difference Method Valuation of European and American Puts

S	j	t 1.0 / i 0	0.75 / 1	0.50 / 2	0.25 / 3	0.0 / 4
81.61	4	31.61	31.61	31.61	31.61	31.61
72.20	3	22.20	22.20	22.20	22.20	22.20
63.88	2	13.88	13.88	13.88	13.88	13.88
44.24	1	7.05	6.82	6.82	6.82	6.51
50.00	0	2.27	2.22	1.37	1.37	0.00
44.24	-1	0.63	0.62	0.28	0.27	0.00
39.14	-2	0.16	0.16	0.06	0.05	0.00
34.63	-3	0.05	0.04	0.00	0.00	0.00
30.63	-4	0.00	0.00	0.00	0.00	0.00

FIGURE 5.8   Lattice for American Call Option

steps (equal to the number of space steps, i.e., $N = M$) for the European and American put with the same parameters as used earlier.

Figure 5.8 is the lattice for an American call option with the same parameters as the put.

5.6   OBJECT-ORIENTED FINITE-DIFFERENCE IMPLEMENTATION

In order to provide more robustness and flexibility to the implementation, we need to make several important changes. First, the previous implementation can only handle small grid sizes. Memory needs to be allocated for both the option price and the asset price at each node. It is limited by the use of predefined array dimensions, which in turn are limited by system memory. In fact, the previous implementation cannot handle the memory requirements for larger-dimension grids (i.e., a 200×800 grid) often used in practice. Moreover, it is not efficient to statically allocate arrays of large dimensions as it uses too much memory from the heap, as opposed to dynamically allocating memory from the stack. Even if we could statically allocate memory for very large (double) array sizes, we would have to change the dimension sizes in the array declarations each time we wanted to change them, which is not practical. While dynamically allocated double arrays could be used to create an $N \times M$ grid (array) to hold option and asset values, for example,

```
double** C = (double **) new double[N*sizeof(double*)]; // for option price
double** S = (double **) new double[(N*sizeof(double*)] // for asset price
for(i= 0; i < N;i++)
{
  C[i]= (double *) new double[(M * sizeof(double)];
  S[i] = (double *) new double[(M * sizeof(double)];
}
```

or even a *struct* could be used to hold the values, that is,

```
struct
{
  double price;
  double optionPrice;
} nodeValues;
```

and then memory could be dynamically allocated,

```
nodeValues** nodePtr = (nodeValues**) malloc(N*sizeof(nodeValues*));
for(i= 0; i < N;i++)
{
  nodePtr[i]= (nodeValues) malloc(M*sizeof(nodeValues));
}
```

there are still serious memory management issues with such an approach, especially for more than two dimensions. A more efficient and practical solution is to use an *Array* class that contains methods and operations to manipulate arrays (see source code for implementation details) and which can manage the memory. For example,

```
typedef size_t Size;

class Array
{
  public:
    // creates the array with the given dimension
```

```
explicit Array(Size size = 0);
// creates the array and fills it with values
Array(Size size, double value);
// brief creates the array and fills it according to
// a_{0} = value, a_{i}=a_{i-1}+increment


Array(Size size, double value, double increment);
Array(const Array& from);
template <class Iter> Array(const VectorialExpression<Iter>& e)
  : pointer_(0), n_(0), bufferSize_(0) { allocate_(e.size()); copy_(e); }
~Array();
Array& operator=(const Array& from);
template <class Iter> Array& operator=(
  const VectorialExpression<Iter>& e) {
    resize_(e.size()); copy_(e); return *this;
}


Array& operator+=(const Array&);
Array& operator+=(double);
Array& operator-=(const Array&);
Array& operator-=(double);
Array& operator*=(const Array&);
Array& operator*=(double);
Array& operator/=(const Array&);
Array& operator/=(double);
template <class Iter> Array& operator+=(
  const VectorialExpression<Iter>& e) {
    QL_REQUIRE(size() == e.size(), "adding arrays with different sizes");
    iterator i = begin(), j = end();
    while (i != j) { *i += *e; ++i; ++e; }
    return *this;
}
template <class Iter> Array& operator-=( const VectorialExpression<Iter>& e) {
    QL_REQUIRE(size() == e.size(), "subtracting arrays with different sizes");
    iterator i = begin(), j = end();
    while (i != j) { *i -= *e; ++i; ++e; }
    return *this;
}
template <class Iter> Array& operator*=( const VectorialExpression<Iter>& e) {
    QL_REQUIRE(size() == e.size(), "multiplying arrays with different sizes");
    iterator i = begin(), j = end();
    while (i != j) { *i *= *e; ++i; ++e; }
    return *this;
}
template <class Iter> Array& operator/=( const VectorialExpression<Iter>& e) {
    QL_REQUIRE(size() == e.size(), "dividing arrays with different sizes");
    iterator i = begin(), j = end();
    while (i != j) { *i /= *e; ++i; ++e; }
    return *this;
}
```

```
    // name Element access
    double operator[](Size) const;
    // read-write
    double& operator[](Size);
    // dimension of the array
    Size size() const


    typedef double* iterator;
    typedef const double* const_iterator;
    typedef QL_REVERSE_ITERATOR(double*,double) reverse_iterator;
    typedef QL_REVERSE_ITERATOR(double*,double) const_reverse_iterator;
    // name Iterator access
    const_iterator begin() const;
    iterator begin();
    const_iterator end() const;
    iterator end();
    const_reverse_iterator rbegin() const;
    reverse_iterator rbegin();
    const_reverse_iterator rend() const;
    reverse_iterator rend();

  private:
    void allocate_(Size size);
    void resize_(Size size);
    void copy_(const Array& from) {
      std::copy(from.begin(),from.end(),begin());
    }
    template <class Iter> void copy_( const VectorialExpression<Iter>& e) {
      iterator i = begin(), j = end();
      while (i != j) {
        *i = *e;
        ++i; ++e;
      }
    }
    double* pointer_;
    Size n_, bufferSize_;
};
```

The class has the following method definitions:

```
// inline definitions
/****************************************************************************
Array: Constructor
[in] Size size: size of array
****************************************************************************/
```

```
inline Array::Array(Size size) : pointer_(0), n_(0), bufferSize_(0)
{
  if (size > 0)
    allocate_(size);
}


/***************************************************************************
Array: Constructor
[in] Size size: size of array
***************************************************************************/
inline Array::Array(Size size, double value) : pointer_(0), n_(0),
  bufferSize_(0)
{
  if (size > 0)
    allocate_(size);
  std::fill(begin(),end(),value);
}


/***************************************************************************
Array: Constructor
[in] Size size          : size of array
     double value       : value to initialize array
     double increment   : increments value
***************************************************************************/
inline Array::Array(Size size, double value, double increment)
  : pointer_(0), n_(0), bufferSize_(0)
{
  if (size > 0)
    allocate_(size);
  for (iterator i=begin(); i!=end(); i++,value+=increment)
    *i = value;
}


/***************************************************************************
Array: Constructor
[in] Size size          : size of array
     double value       : value to initialize array
     double increment   : increments value
***************************************************************************/
inline Array::Array(const Array& from)
  : pointer_(0), n_(0), bufferSize_(0)
{
  allocate_(from.size());
  copy_(from);
}


/***************************************************************************
Array: Destructor
Delete allocated memory and clean up
***************************************************************************/
inline Array::~Array()
{
  if (pointer_ != 0 && bufferSize_ != 0)
```

```
      delete[] pointer_;
   pointer_ = 0;
   n_ = bufferSize_ = 0;
}



/*****************************************************************************
operator= : overloaded assignment operator
Copies the elements of one array to another
[in] Array from : array to copy from
[out] Array&: copy of array
*****************************************************************************/
inline Array& Array::operator=(const Array& from)
{
   if (this != &from)
   {
      resize_(from.size());
      copy_(from);
   }
   return *this;
}



/*****************************************************************************
operator+ : overloaded assignment operator
Copies the elements of one array to another
[in] Array from : array to add to
[out] Array&: sum of arrays
*****************************************************************************/
inline Array& Array::operator+=(const Array& v)
{
   QL_REQUIRE(n_ == v.n_, "arrays with different sizes cannot be added");
   std::transform(begin(),end(),v.begin(),begin(),std::plus<double>());
   return *this;
}


inline Array& Array::operator+=(double x)
{
   std::transform(begin(),end(),begin(), std::bind2nd(std::plus<double>(),x));
   return *this;
}


inline Array& Array::operator-=(const Array& v) {
   QL_REQUIRE(n_ == v.n_,"arrays with different sizes cannot be subtracted");
   std::transform(begin(),end(),v.begin(),begin(),std::minus<double>());
   return *this;
}


inline Array& Array::operator-=(double x)
{
   std::transform(begin(),end(),begin(),std::bind2nd(std::minus<double>(),
      x));
   return *this;
```

```cpp
}

inline Array& Array::operator*=(const Array& v)
{
  QL_REQUIRE(n_ == v.n_, "arrays with different sizes cannot be multiplied");
  std::transform(begin(),end(),v.begin(),begin(), std::multiplies<double>());
  return *this;
}

inline Array& Array::operator*=(double x)
{
  std::transform(begin(),end(),begin(),
    std::bind2nd(std::multiplies<double>(),x));
  return *this;
}

inline Array& Array::operator/=(const Array& v)
{
  QL_REQUIRE(n_ == v.n_, "arrays with different sizes cannot be divided");
  std::transform(begin(),end(),v.begin(),begin(), std::divides<double>());
  return *this;
}

inline Array& Array::operator/=(double x)
{
  std::transform(begin(),end(),begin(),
    std::bind2nd(std::divides<double>(),x));
  return *this;
}

inline double Array::operator[](Size i) const {
  QL_REQUIRE(i<n_, "array cannot be accessed out of range");
  return pointer_[i];
}

inline double& Array::operator[](Size i) {
  QL_REQUIRE(i<n_, "array cannot be accessed out of range");
  return pointer_[i];
}

inline Size Array::size() const {
    return n_;
}
inline void Array::resize_(Size size) {
  if (size != n_)
  {
    if (size <= bufferSize_)
    {
      n_ = size;
    } else {
      Array temp(size);
```

```
          std::copy(begin(),end(),temp.begin());
          allocate_(size);
          copy_(temp);
      }
  }
}
inline Array::const_iterator Array::begin() const {
  return pointer_;
}
inline Array::iterator Array::begin() {
  return pointer_;
}
inline Array::const_iterator Array::end() const {
  return pointer_+n_;
}
inline Array::iterator Array::end() {
  return pointer_+n_;
}
inline Array::reverse_iterator Array::rbegin() {
  return reverse_iterator(end());
}
inline Array::reverse_iterator Array::rend() {
  return reverse_iterator(begin());
}
inline void Array::allocate_(Size size)
{
  if (pointer_ != 0 && bufferSize_ != 0)
    delete[] pointer_;
  if (size <= 0)
  {
    pointer_ = 0;
  }
  else
  {
    n_ = size;
    bufferSize_ = size+size/10+10;
    try
    {
      pointer_ = new double[bufferSize_];
    }
    catch ( . . . ) {
      pointer_ = 0;
    }
    if (pointer_ == 0)
    {
      n_ = bufferSize_ = size;
      try
      {
        pointer_ = new double[bufferSize_];
      }
      catch ( . . . )
      {
```

```
            pointer_ = 0;
          }
        if (pointer_ == 0)
        {
          n_ = bufferSize_ = 0;
          throw "Out Of Memory Error Array";
        }
      }
    }
  }
```

We can then create a *Grid* class for handling the spacial steps and a *TimeGrid* class for handling the time steps. The *TimeGrid* will give us a finer granularity over the spacing and number of time steps.

```cpp
// spatial grid class
class Grid : public Array
{
public:
  Grid(double center, double dx, int steps);
};

// time grid class
class TimeGrid : public std::vector<double>
{
  public:
    TimeGrid() {}
    // Regularly spaced time-grid
    TimeGrid(double end, int steps);
    // double grid with mandatory time-points (regularly spaced between them)
    TimeGrid(const std::list<double>& times, int steps);
    int findIndex(double t) const;
    double dt(int i) const;
};

// inline definitions
inline Grid::Grid(double center, double dx, int steps) : Array(steps)
{
  for (int i=0; i<steps; i++)
    (*this)[i] = center + (i - steps/2.0)*dx;
}

inline TimeGrid::TimeGrid(double end, int steps)
{
  double dt = end/steps;
  for (int i=0; i<=steps; i++)
    push_back(dt*i);
```

```cpp
}

inline TimeGrid::TimeGrid(const std::list<double>& times, int steps) :
  std::vector<double>(0)
{
  double last = times.back();
  double dtMax;
  // The resulting timegrid have points at times listed in the input
  // list. Between these points, there are inner-points which are
  // regularly spaced.
  if (steps == 0)
  {
    std::vector<double> diff;
    std::back_insert_iterator<std::vector<double> > ii(diff);
    std::adjacent_difference(times.begin(), times.end(), ii);
    if (diff.front()==0.0)
      diff.erase(diff.begin());
    dtMax = *(std::min_element(diff.begin(), diff.end()));
  }
  else
  {
    dtMax = last/steps;
  }

  double periodBegin = 0.0;
  std::list<double>::const_iterator t;
  for (t = times.begin(); t != times.end(); t++)
  {
    double periodEnd = *t;
    if (periodBegin >= periodEnd)
      continue;
    int nSteps = (int)((periodEnd - periodBegin)/dtMax + 1.0);
    double dt = (periodEnd - periodBegin)/nSteps;
    for (int n=0; n<nSteps; n++)
      push_back(periodBegin + n*dt);
    periodBegin = periodEnd;
  }
  push_back(periodBegin); // Note periodBegin = periodEnd
}

inline int TimeGrid::findIndex(double t) const
{
  const_iterator result = std::find(begin(), end(), t);
  QL_REQUIRE(result!=end(), "Using inadequate tree");
  return result - begin();
}

inline double TimeGrid::dt(int i) const
{
  return (*this)[i+1] - (*this)[i];
}
```

Second, it would be useful to create a generic *Tridiagonal Operator* class for manipulating and solving tridiagonal linear systems for many types of finite difference schemes—explicit methods, implicit methods, Crank-Nicolson scheme, and so on. Consider the following *TridiagonalOperator* class:

```
class TridiagonalOperator
{
    // unary operators
    friend TridiagonalOperator operator+(const TridiagonalOperator&);
    friend TridiagonalOperator operator-(const TridiagonalOperator&);
    // binary operators
    friend TridiagonalOperator operator+(const TridiagonalOperator&, const
      TridiagonalOperator&);
    friend TridiagonalOperator operator-(const TridiagonalOperator&, const
      TridiagonalOperator&);
    friend TridiagonalOperator operator*(double, const TridiagonalOperator&);
    friend TridiagonalOperator operator*(const TridiagonalOperator&, double);
    friend TridiagonalOperator operator/(const TridiagonalOperator&, double);
  public:
    typedef Array arrayType;
    // constructors
    TridiagonalOperator(Size size = 0);
    TridiagonalOperator(const Array& low, const Array& mid, const Array& high);
    TridiagonalOperator(const TridiagonalOperator& L);
    TridiagonalOperator& operator=(const TridiagonalOperator& L);
    // apply operator to a given array
    Array applyTo(const Array& v) const;
    // solve linear system for a given right-hand side
    Array solveFor(const Array& rhs) const;
    // solve linear system with SOR approach.,m
    Array SOR(const Array& rhs, double tol) const;
    // identity instance
    static TridiagonalOperator identity(Size size);
    Size size() const;
    bool isdoubleDependent();
    void setFirstRow(double, double);
    void setMidRow(Size, double, double, double);
    void setMidRows(double, double, double);
    void setLastRow(double, double);
    void setdouble(double t);
    void setTime(double t) { time_ = t; }
    bool isTimeDependent() { return isTimeDependent_; }
    // encapsulation of double-setting logic
    class doubleSetter {
      public:
        virtual ~doubleSetter() {}
        virtual void setdouble(double t, TridiagonalOperator& L) const = 0;
    };
  protected:
    Array diagonal_, belowDiagonal_, aboveDiagonal_;
```

```
      Handle<doubleSetter> doubleSetter_;
      double time_;
      bool isTimeDependent_;
};
inline TridiagonalOperator::TridiagonalOperator(const TridiagonalOperator& L)
{
  belowDiagonal_ = L.belowDiagonal_;
  diagonal_  = L.diagonal_;
  aboveDiagonal_ = L.aboveDiagonal_;
  doubleSetter_ = L.doubleSetter_;
}
/*******************************************************************************
operator=                 : overloaded assignment operator
Copies the elements of one Tridiagonal operator to another
[in] Array from           : array to copy from
[out] TridiagonalOperator&: copy of tridiagonal operator
*******************************************************************************/
inline TridiagonalOperator& TridiagonalOperator::operator=( const
  TridiagonalOperator& L)
{
  belowDiagonal_ = L.belowDiagonal_;
  diagonal_  = L.diagonal_;
  aboveDiagonal_ = L.aboveDiagonal_;
  doubleSetter_ = L.doubleSetter_;
  return *this;
}

inline Size TridiagonalOperator::size() const
{
  return diagonal_.size();
}

inline bool TridiagonalOperator::isdoubleDependent()
{
  return !doubleSetter_.isNull();
}

// set values of first row of matrix
inline void TridiagonalOperator::setFirstRow(double valB, double valC)
{
  diagonal_[0] = valB;
  aboveDiagonal_[0] = valC;
}

// set values of middle row of matrix
inline void TridiagonalOperator::setMidRow(Size i, double valA, double valB, double
  valC) {
  QL_REQUIRE(i>=1 && i<=size()-2, "out of range in TridiagonalSystem::setMidRow");
  belowDiagonal_[i-1] = valA;
  diagonal_[i] = valB;
  aboveDiagonal_[i] = valC;
}

// set values of middle rows of matrix
inline void TridiagonalOperator::setMidRows(double valA, double valB, double valC)
```

```
{
  for (int i=1; i<=size()-2; i++)
  {
    belowDiagonal_[i-1] = valA;
    diagonal_[i] = valB;
    aboveDiagonal_[i] = valC;
  }
}


inline void TridiagonalOperator::setLastRow(double valA, double valB)
{
  belowDiagonal_[size()-2] = valA;
  diagonal_[size()-1] = valB;
}


inline void TridiagonalOperator::setdouble(double t)
{
  if (!doubleSetter_.isNull())
    doubleSetter_->setdouble(t,*this);
}


inline TridiagonalOperator operator+(const TridiagonalOperator& D)
{
  return D;
}


inline TridiagonalOperator operator-(const TridiagonalOperator& D)
{
  Array low = -D.belowDiagonal_, mid = -D.diagonal_,
  high = -D.aboveDiagonal_;
  TridiagonalOperator result(low,mid,high);
  return result;
}


inline TridiagonalOperator operator+(const TridiagonalOperator& D1,
  const TridiagonalOperator& D2)
{
  Array low = D1.belowDiagonal_+D2.belowDiagonal_,
  mid = D1.diagonal_+D2.diagonal_,
  high = D1.aboveDiagonal_+D2.aboveDiagonal_;
  TridiagonalOperator result(low,mid,high);
  return result;
}


inline TridiagonalOperator operator-(const TridiagonalOperator& D1,
  const TridiagonalOperator& D2)
{
  Array low = D1.belowDiagonal_-D2.belowDiagonal_,
  mid = D1.diagonal_-D2.diagonal_,
  high = D1.aboveDiagonal_-D2.aboveDiagonal_;
  TridiagonalOperator result(low,mid,high);
```

```
    return result;
}

inline TridiagonalOperator operator*(double a,
  const TridiagonalOperator& D)
{
  Array low = D.belowDiagonal_*a, mid = D.diagonal_*a,
  high = D.aboveDiagonal_*a;
  TridiagonalOperator result(low,mid,high);
  return result;
}

inline TridiagonalOperator operator*(const TridiagonalOperator& D, double a)
{
  Array low = D.belowDiagonal_*a, mid = D.diagonal_*a,
  high = D.aboveDiagonal_*a;
  TridiagonalOperator result(low,mid,high);
  return result;
}

inline TridiagonalOperator operator/(const TridiagonalOperator& D, double a)
{
  Array low = D.belowDiagonal_/a, mid = D.diagonal_/a,
  high = D.aboveDiagonal_/a;
  TridiagonalOperator result(low,mid,high);
  return result;
}
```

The other method definitions are:

```
TridiagonalOperator::TridiagonalOperator(Size size)
{
  if (size>=3) {
    diagonal_     = Array(size);
    lowerDiagonal_ = Array(size-1);
    upperDiagonal_ = Array(size-1);
  } else if (size==0) {
    diagonal_     = Array(0);
    lowerDiagonal_ = Array(0);
    upperDiagonal_ = Array(0);
  } else {
    throw Error("invalid size for tridiagonal operator" "(must be null or >= 3)");
  }
}

/*******************************************************************************
TridiagonalOperator: constructor
```

```
**********************************************************************/
TridiagonalOperator::TridiagonalOperator(
  const Array& low, const Array& mid, const Array& high)
  : diagonal_(mid), lowerDiagonal_(low), upperDiagonal_(high) {
  QL_ENSURE(low.size() == mid.size()-1, "wrong size for lower diagonal vector");
  QL_ENSURE(high.size() == mid.size()-1, "wrong size for upper diagonal vector");
}


/**********************************************************************
applyTo           : applies tridiagonal operator to grid points
[in]: Array& v:   : grid points
[out]: Array      : results of operation
**********************************************************************/
Array TridiagonalOperator::applyTo(const Array& v) const {
  QL_REQUIRE(v.size()==size(),
    "TridiagonalOperator::applyTo: vector of the wrong size (" +
    IntegerFormatter::toString(v.size()) + "instead of " +
    IntegerFormatter::toString(size()) + ")" );
  Array result(size());

  // matricial product
  result[0] = diagonal_[0]*v[0] + upperDiagonal_[0]*v[1];
  for (Size j=1;j<=size()-2;j++)
    result[j] = lowerDiagonal_[j-1]*v[j-1]+ diagonal_[j]*v[j] +
      upperDiagonal_[j]*v[j+1];
    result[size()-1] = lowerDiagonal_[size()-2]*v[size()-2] + diagonal_[size()-1]*
      v[size()-1];

  return result;
}


/**********************************************************************
solve for         : solves the tridiagonal system
[in]: Array& rhs: : rhs of system
[out]: Array      : solution of rhs of tridiagonal system
**********************************************************************/
Array TridiagonalOperator::solveFor(const Array& rhs) const {
  QL_REQUIRE(rhs.size()==size(),
    "TridiagonalOperator::solveFor: rhs has the wrong size");

  Array result(size()), tmp(size());

  double bet=diagonal_[0];
  QL_REQUIRE(bet != 0.0, "TridiagonalOperator::solveFor: division by zero");

  result[0] = rhs[0]/bet;
  Size j;
  for (j=1;j<=size()-1;j++)
  {
    tmp[j]=upperDiagonal_[j-1]/bet;
    bet=diagonal_[j]-lowerDiagonal_[j-1]*tmp[j];
    QL_ENSURE(bet != 0.0, "TridiagonalOperator::solveFor: division by zero");
    result[j] = (rhs[j]-lowerDiagonal_[j-1]*result[j-1])/bet;
```

```
    }

    // cannot be j>=0 with Size j
    for (j=size()-2;j>0;j--)
      result[j] -= tmp[j+1]*result[j+1];
    result[0] -= tmp[1]*result[1];

    return result;
}
```

The class contains overloaded operators to manipulate elements along the diagonals of any tridiagonal matrix.

We can also improve the finite-difference scheme by creating a generic abstract template class for boundary conditions that can in turn be used for subclassing into, say, Dirichlet or Neumann boundary classes.

```
// Abstract boundary condition class for finite difference problems
template <class Operator>
class BoundaryCondition
{
  public:
    // types and enumerations
    typedef Operator operatorType;
    typedef typename Operator::arrayType arrayType;
    enum Side { None, Upper, Lower };
    // destructor
    virtual ~BoundaryCondition() {}
    // interface
    // This method modifies an operator L before it is
    // applied to an array u so that v = Lu will
    // satisfy the given condition.
    virtual void applyBeforeApplying(operatorType&) const = 0;
    // This method modifies an array u so that it satisfies
    // the given condition.
    virtual void applyAfterApplying(arrayType&) const = 0;
    // This method modifies an operator L before the linear
    // system Lu' = u is solved so that u' will
    // satisfy the given condition.
    virtual void applyBeforeSolving(operatorType&, arrayType& rhs) const = 0;
    // This method modifies an array so that it satisfies the given condition.
    virtual void applyAfterSolving(arrayType&) const = 0;
    // This method sets the current time for time-dependent boundary conditions.
    virtual void setTime(Time t) = 0;
};

// Neumann boundary condition (i.e., constant derivative)
class NeumannBC : public BoundaryCondition<TridiagonalOperator>
```

```
{
  public:
    NeumannBC(double value, Side side);
    // interface
    void applyBeforeApplying(TridiagonalOperator&) const;
    void applyAfterApplying(Array&) const;
    void applyBeforeSolving(TridiagonalOperator&, Array& rhs) const;
    void applyAfterSolving(Array&) const;
    void setTime(Time t) {}
  private:
    double value_;
    Side side_;
};

// DirichletBC boundary condition (i.e., constant value)
class DirichletBC : public BoundaryCondition<TridiagonalOperator>
{
  public:
    DirichletBC(double value, Side side);
    // interface
    void applyBeforeApplying(TridiagonalOperator&) const;
    void applyAfterApplying(Array&) const;
    void applyBeforeSolving(TridiagonalOperator&, Array& rhs) const;
    void applyAfterSolving(Array&) const;
    void setTime(Time t) {}
  private:
    double value_;
    Side side_;
  };
```

The class has the following method definitions:

```
NeumannBC::NeumannBC(double value, NeumannBC::Side side)
  : value_(value), side_(side) {}

  /**********************************************************************************
  applyBeforeApplying : apply Neumann boundary conditions before applying
  Tridiag Operator
  [in] : TridiagonalOperator& L : tridiag operator
  [out]: none
  **********************************************************************************/
void NeumannBC::applyBeforeApplying(TridiagonalOperator& L) const {
  switch (side_) {
    case Lower:
      L.setFirstRow(-1.0,1.0);
      break;
    case Upper:
      L.setLastRow(-1.0,1.0);
```

```
      break;
    default:
      throw Error("Unknown side for Neumann boundary condition");
  }
}

/*****************************************************************************
applyAfterApplying : apply Neumann boundary conditions after applying Triadiagonal
                     Operator
[in] : Array& L     : array of values
[out]: none
*****************************************************************************/
void NeumannBC::applyAfterApplying(Array& u) const {
  switch (side_) {
    case Lower:
      u[0] = u[1] - value_;
      break;
    case Upper:
      u[u.size()-1] = u[u.size()-2] + value_;
      break;
    default:
      throw Error("Unknown side for Neumann boundary condition");
  }
}

/*****************************************************************************
applyAfterApplying : apply Neumann boundary conditions before solving system
[in] : TridiagonalOperator& L   : tridiagonal operator
       Array& L                 : array of values
[out]: none
*****************************************************************************/
void NeumannBC::applyBeforeSolving(TridiagonalOperator& L, Array& rhs) const
{
  switch (side_)
  {
    case Lower:
      L.setFirstRow(-1.0,1.0);
      rhs[0] = value_;
      break;
    case Upper:
      L.setLastRow(-1.0,1.0);
      rhs[rhs.size()-1] = value_;
      break;
    default:
      throw Error("Unknown side for Neumann boundary condition");
  }
}

void NeumannBC::applyAfterSolving(Array&) const {}

// Dirichlet conditions

DirichletBC::DirichletBC(double value, DirichletBC::Side side)
```

```
    : value_(value), side_(side) {}

/*****************************************************************************
applyBeforeApplying : apply Dirichlet boundary conditions before solving system
[in] : TridiagonalOperator& L : tridiagonal operator
[out]: none
*****************************************************************************/
void DirichletBC::applyBeforeApplying(TridiagonalOperator& L) const
{
  switch (side_)
  {
    case Lower:
      L.setFirstRow(1.0,0.0);
      break;
    case Upper:
      L.setLastRow(0.0,1.0);
      break;
    default:
      throw Error("Unknown side for Neumann boundary condition");
  }
}

/*****************************************************************************
applyAfterApplying : apply Dirichlet boundary conditions after applying
                     Triadiagonal Operator
[in] : Array& L     : array of values
[out]: none
*****************************************************************************/
void DirichletBC::applyAfterApplying(Array& u) const
{
  switch (side_)
  {
    case Lower:
      u[0] = value_;
      break;
    case Upper:
      u[u.size()-1] = value_;
      break;
    default:
      throw Error("Unknown side for Neumann boundary condition");
  }
}

/*****************************************************************************
applyAfterApplying : apply Dirichlet boundary conditions before solving system
[in] : TridiagonalOperator& L : tridiagonal operator
         Array& L             : array of values
[out]: none
*****************************************************************************/
void DirichletBC::applyBeforeSolving(TridiagonalOperator& L,
  Array& rhs) const
{
  switch (side_)
```

```
  {
    case Lower:
      L.setFirstRow(1.0,0.0);
      rhs[0] = value_;
      break;
    case Upper:
      L.setLastRow(0.0,1.0);
      rhs[rhs.size()-1] = value_;
      break;
    default:
      throw Error("Unknown side for Neumann boundary condition");
  }
}
void DirichletBC::applyAfterSolving(Array&) const {}
```

Moreover, we can create a generic finite-difference model template that can be used for all types of finite-difference schemes. Consider the *FiniteDifference Model* class.

```
// Generic finite difference model
template<class Evolver>
class FiniteDifferenceModel
{
  public:
    typedef typename Evolver::arrayType arrayType;
    typedef typename Evolver::operatorType operatorType;
    typedef BoundaryCondition<operatorType> bcType;
    // constructor
    FiniteDifferenceModel(const operatorType& L, const std::vector<Handle<bcType>
      >& bcs, const std::vector<Time>& stoppingTimes=std::vector<Time>())
      : evolver_(L,bcs), stoppingTimes_(stoppingTimes) {}

    // solves the problem between the given times, possibly
    // applying a condition at every step.
    // being a rollback, from time must be a later time than to time.
    void rollback(arrayType& a, Time from, Time to, Size steps,
      Handle<StepCondition<arrayType> > condition = Handle<StepCondition<arrayType>
        >());
  private:
    Evolver evolver_;
    std::vector<Time> stoppingTimes_;
};

// template definitions
template<class Evolver>
void FiniteDifferenceModel<Evolver>::rollback(
  FiniteDifferenceModel::arrayType& a,
```

```
  Time from, Time to, Size steps,
  Handle<StepCondition<arrayType> > condition)
{
  Time dt = (from-to)/steps, t = from;
  evolver_.setStep(dt);

  for (in i=0; i<steps; i++, t -= dt)
  {
    int j;
    for(j=0; j < stoppingTimes_.size(); j++)
      if(t-dt <= stoppingTimes_[j] && stoppingTimes_[j] < t)
        break;
    if(j == stoppingTimes_.size())
    {
      // No stopping time was hit
      evolver_.step(a,t);
      if (!condition.isNull())
        condition->applyTo(a,t-dt);
    }
    else
    {
      // A stopping time was hit
      // First baby step from t to stoppingTimes_[j]
      evolver_.setStep(t-stoppingTimes_[j]);
      evolver_.step(a,t);
      if (!condition.isNull())
        condition->applyTo(a,stoppingTimes_[j]);

      // Second baby step from stoppingTimes_[j] to t-dt
      evolver_.setStep(stoppingTimes_[j] - (t-dt));
      evolver_.step(a,stoppingTimes_[j]);
      if (!condition.isNull())
        condition->applyTo(a,t-dt);

      evolver_.setStep(dt);
    }
  }
}
```

This class makes use of an abstract *StepCondition* class that aids in the valuation process by applying step conditions along the grid at every step:

```
// condition to be applied at every time step
template <class arrayType>
class StepCondition
{
  public:
    virtual ~StepCondition() {}
    virtual void applyTo(arrayType& a, Time t) const = 0;
};
```

We can then create a *FiniteDifferenceOption* class that contains the properties and methods to value a plain-vanilla Black-Scholes-type option numerically:

```
class FiniteDifferenceOption : public SingleAssetOption
{
  public:
    FiniteDifferenceOption(Option::Type type, double underlying,
       double strike, Spread dividendYield, Rate riskFreeRate,
       Time residualTime, double volatility, Size gridPoints);
    // accessors
    virtual void calculate() const = 0;
    double value() const;
    double delta() const;
    double gamma() const;
    Array getGrid() const{return grid_;}

  protected:
    // methods
    virtual void setGridLimits(double center, double timeDelay) const;
    virtual void initializeGrid() const;
    virtual void initializeInitialCondition() const;
    virtual void initializeOperator() const;
    // input data
    Size gridPoints_;
    // results
    mutable double value_, delta_, gamma_;

    mutable Array grid_;
    mutable FiniteDifferences::BlackScholesOperator finiteDifferenceOperator_;
    mutable Array initialPrices_;
    typedef FiniteDifferences::BoundaryCondition<
      FiniteDifferences::TridiagonalOperator>
      BoundaryCondition;
    mutable std::vector<Handle<BoundaryCondition> > BCs_;
    // temporaries
    mutable double sMin_, center_, sMax_;
  private:
    // temporaries
    mutable double gridLogSpacing_;
    Size safeGridPoints(Size gridPoints, Time residualTime);

};

// This is a safety check to be sure we have enough grid points.
#define QL_NUM_OPT_MIN_GRID_POINTS      10
// This is a safety check to be sure we have enough grid points.
#define QL_NUM_OPT_GRID_POINTS_PER_YEAR      2

// The following is a safety check to be sure we have enough grid
// points.
```

```
inline Size FiniteDifferenceOption::safeGridPoints( Size gridPoints, Time
  residualTime) {
  return QL_MAX(gridPoints, residualTime>1.0 ?
    static_cast<Size>(
      (QL_NUM_OPT_MIN_GRID_POINTS + (residualTime-1.0) *
        QL_NUM_OPT_GRID_POINTS_PER_YEAR)): QL_NUM_OPT_MIN_GRID_POINTS);
}
```

This class has the following method definitions:

```
FiniteDifferenceOption::FiniteDifferenceOption(Option::Type type,
  double underlying, double strike, Spread dividendYield,
  Rate riskFreeRate, Time residualTime, double volatility, Size gridPoints)
    : SingleAssetOption(type, underlying, strike, dividendYield, riskFreeRate,
      residualTime, volatility),
    gridPoints_(safeGridPoints(gridPoints, residualTime)),
    grid_(gridPoints_), initialPrices_(gridPoints_),
    BCs_(2)
{
  hasBeenCalculated_ = false;
}


/******************************************************************************
value : returns price of option using finite differences
[in] :   none
[out]:   double    : value
******************************************************************************/
double FiniteDifferenceOption::value() const
{
  if (!hasBeenCalculated_)
    calculate();
  return value_;
}


/******************************************************************************
delta : returns delta of option using finite differences
[in] :   none
[out]:   double    : delta
******************************************************************************/
double FiniteDifferenceOption::delta() const
{
  if (!hasBeenCalculated_)
    calculate();
  return delta_;
}
```

```
/*****************************************************************************
gamma : returns gamma of option using finite differences
[in] :  none
[out]:  double    : gamma
*****************************************************************************/
double FiniteDifferenceOption::gamma() const
{
  if(!hasBeenCalculated_)
    calculate();
  return gamma_;
}


/*****************************************************************************
setGridLimits : sets grid limits of minimum and maximum sizes
[in] : double center  : value of center
[out]: void
*****************************************************************************/
void FiniteDifferenceOption::setGridLimits(double center, double timeDelay) const
{
  center_ = center;
  double volSqrtTime = volatility_*sqrt(timeDelay);
  // the prefactor fine tunes performance at small volatilities
  double prefactor = 1.0 + 0.02/volSqrtTime;
  double minMaxFactor = exp(4.0 * prefactor * volSqrtTime);
  sMin_ = center_/minMaxFactor; // underlying grid min value
  sMax_ = center_*minMaxFactor; // underlying grid max value
  // insure strike is included in the grid
  double safetyZoneFactor = 1.1;
  if(sMin_ > strike_/safetyZoneFactor)
  {
    sMin_ = strike_/safetyZoneFactor;
    // enforce central placement of the underlying
    sMax_ = center_/(sMin_/center_);
  }
  if(sMax_ < strike_*safetyZoneFactor){
    sMax_ = strike_*safetyZoneFactor;
    // enforce central placement of the underlying
    sMin_ = center_/(sMax_/center_);
  }
}

/*****************************************************************************
initializeGrid : initializes grid and grid spacing
[in] : none
[out]: void
*****************************************************************************/
void FiniteDifferenceOption::initializeGrid() const
{
  gridLogSpacing_ = (log(sMax_)-log(sMin_))/(gridPoints_-1);
  double edx = exp(gridLogSpacing_);
  grid_[0] = sMin_;
  Size j;
  for (j=1; j<gridPoints_; j++)
```

```
      grid_[j] = grid_[j-1]*edx;
}

/*****************************************************************************
initializeGridCondition : sets grid initial conditions
[in] : none
[out]: void
*****************************************************************************/
void FiniteDifferenceOption::initializeInitialCondition() const
{
  Size j;
  switch (type_)
  {
    case Option::Call:
      for(j = 0; j < gridPoints_; j++)
        initialPrices_[j] = max(grid_[j]-strike_,0.0);
      break;
    case Option::Put:
      for(j = 0; j < gridPoints_; j++)
        initialPrices_[j] = max(strike_-grid_[j],0.0);
      break;
    default:
      throw Error("FiniteDifferenceOption: invalid option type");
  }
}


/*****************************************************************************
initializeOperator : initializes boundary condition operator
[in] : none
[out]: void
*****************************************************************************/
void FiniteDifferenceOption::initializeOperator() const
{
  finiteDifferenceOperator_ = BlackScholesOperator(gridPoints_,
    gridLogSpacing_, riskFreeRate_, dividendYield_, volatility_);

  BCs_[0] = Handle<BoundaryCondition>(
    new NeumannBC(initialPrices_[1]-initialPrices_[0], BoundaryCondition::Lower));
  BCs_[1] = Handle<BoundaryCondition>(
    new NeumannBC(initialPrices_[gridPoints_-1] - initialPrices_[gridPoints_-2],
      BoundaryCondition::Upper));
}
```

Additionally, we can create a more specific *FiniteDifferenceEuropean* class to value European options:

```
// Example of European option calculated using finite differences
```

```
class FiniteDifferenceEuropean : public FiniteDifferenceOption
{
  public:
    FiniteDifferenceEuropean(Option::Type type,
      double underlying,
      double strike,
      double dividendYield,
      double riskFreeRate,
      double residualTime,
      double volatility,
      long timeSteps = 200,
      long gridPoints = 800);
    Array getPrices() const;
    Handle<SingleAssetOption> clone() const{
      return Handle<SingleAssetOption>( new FiniteDifferenceEuropean(*this));
    }
    inline Array getPrices() const{
      value();
      return euroPrices_;
    }
  protected:
    void calculate() const;
  private:
    Size timeSteps_;
    mutable Array euroPrices_;
};
```

The class has the following method definitions:

```
using FiniteDifferences::valueAtCenter;
using FiniteDifferences::firstDerivativeAtCenter;
using FiniteDifferences::secondDerivativeAtCenter;

FiniteDifferenceEuropean::FiniteDifferenceEuropean(Option::Type type,
  double underlying, double strike, double dividendYield,
  double riskFreeRate, double residualTime, double volatility,
  Size timeSteps, Size gridPoints)
    : FiniteDifferenceOption(type, underlying, strike, dividendYield,
      riskFreeRate, residualTime, volatility, gridPoints),
      timeSteps_(timeSteps), euroPrices_(gridPoints_) {}

/******************************************************************************
calculate : compute European prices using finite difference
[in]   : none
[out] : void
******************************************************************************/
void FiniteDifferenceEuropean::calculate() const
{
  setGridLimits(underlying_, residualTime_);
```

```
initializeGrid();
initializeInitialCondition();
initializeOperator();

FiniteDifferences::StandardFiniteDifferenceModel
  model(finiteDifferenceOperator_,BCs_);

euroPrices_ = initialPrices_;

// solve
model.rollback(euroPrices_, residualTime_, 0, timeSteps_);

value_ = valueAtCenter(euroPrices_);
delta_ = firstDerivativeAtCenter(euroPrices_, grid_);
gamma_ = secondDerivativeAtCenter(euroPrices_, grid_);

hasBeenCalculated_ = true;
}
```

where the computation methods are:

```
namespace FiniteDifferences
{
  /*****************************************************************************
  valueAtCenter:   : returns the middle or average option value
  [in] Array& a    : array of option grid prices
  [out] double     : value of center price
  *****************************************************************************/
  double valueAtCenter(const Array& a)
  {
    Size jmid = a.size()/2;
    if (a.size() % 2 == 1)
      return a[jmid];
    else
      return (a[jmid]+a[jmid-1])/2.0;
  }

  /*****************************************************************************
  firstDerivativeAtCenter : returns the first derivative (delta)
  ] Array& a              : array of option prices
  Arrary& g               : array of stock prices
  [out] double            : first derivative at center value
  *****************************************************************************/
  double firstDerivativeAtCenter(const Array& a, const Array& g)
  {
    QL_REQUIRE(a.size()==g.size(), "firstDerivativeAtCenter:" "a and g must be of
      the same size");
    QL_REQUIRE(a.size()>=3, "firstDerivativeAtCenter:"  "the size of the two vectors
      must be at least 3");
```

```
   Size jmid = a.size()/2;
   if(a.size() % 2 == 1)
     return (a[jmid+1]-a[jmid-1])/(g[jmid+1]-g[jmid-1]);
   else
     return (a[jmid]-a[jmid-1])/(g[jmid]-g[jmid-1]);
}

/*************************************************************************
secondDerivativeAtCenter : returns the second derivative (gamma)
[in]   Array& a           : array of option prices
       Array& g           : array of stock prices
[out]  double             : second derivative at center value
*************************************************************************/
double secondDerivativeAtCenter(const Array& a, const Array& g)
{
   QL_REQUIRE(a.size()==g.size(), "secondDerivativeAtCenter:" "a and g must be of
     the same size");
   QL_REQUIRE(a.size()>=4, "secondDerivativeAtCenter:" "the size of the two
     vectors must be at least 4");
   Size jmid = a.size()/2;
   if(a.size() % 2 == 1)
   {
     double deltaPlus = (a[jmid+1]-a[jmid])/(g[jmid+1]-g[jmid]);
     double deltaMinus = (a[jmid]-a[jmid-1])/(g[jmid]-g[jmid-1]);
     double dS = (g[jmid+1]-g[jmid-1])/2.0;
     return (deltaPlus-deltaMinus)/dS;
   }
   else{
     double deltaPlus = (a[jmid+1]-a[jmid-1])/(g[jmid+1]-g[jmid-1]);
     double deltaMinus = (a[jmid]-a[jmid-2])/(g[jmid]-g[jmid-2]);
     return (deltaPlus-deltaMinus)/(g[jmid]-g[jmid-1]);
   }
}

// default choice for finite-difference model
typedef FiniteDifferenceModel<CrankNicolson<TridiagonalOperator>
  StandardFiniteDifferenceModel;

// default choice for step condition
typedef StepCondition<Array> StandardStepCondition;
}
```

Finally, we can create a *FiniteDifferenceStepCondition* class that evaluates the option price at each time step it rolls back through the lattice:

```
// option executing additional code at each time step
class FiniteDifferenceStepCondition : public FiniteDifferenceOption
{
  protected:
```

```
    // constructor
    FiniteDifferenceStepConditionOption(Option::Type type, double underlying,
      double strike,
      double dividendYield, Rate riskFreeRate,
      Time residualTime, double volatility,
      int timeSteps, int gridPoints);
    void calculate() const;
    virtual void initializeStepCondition() const = 0;
    mutable Handle<FiniteDifferences::StandardStepCondition > stepCondition_;
    int timeSteps_;
};
```

The class has the following method definitions:

```
using FiniteDifferences::StandardStepCondition;
using FiniteDifferences::StandardFiniteDifferenceModel;
using FiniteDifferences::valueAtCenter;
using FiniteDifferences::firstDerivativeAtCenter;
using FiniteDifferences::secondDerivativeAtCenter;

FiniteDifferenceStepConditionOption::FiniteDifferenceStepConditionOption(Option::
  Type type, double underlying, double strike, double dividendYield, Rate
  riskFreeRate, Time residualTime, double volatility, int timeSteps, int
  gridPoints)
    : FiniteDifferenceOption(type, underlying, strike, dividendYield, riskFreeRate,
      residualTime, volatility, gridPoints),
      timeSteps_(timeSteps) {}

/*******************************************************************************
calculate : computes the option value using control variates and greeks
[in] : none
[out]: void
*******************************************************************************/
void FiniteDifferenceStepConditionOption::calculate() const
{
  setGridLimits(underlying_, residualTime_);
  initializeGrid();
  initializeInitialCondition();
  initializeOperator();
  initializeStepCondition();
  // StandardFiniteDifferenceModel is Crank-Nicolson.
  // Alternatively, ImplicitEuler or ExplicitEuler
  // could have been used instead
  StandardFiniteDifferenceModel model(finiteDifferenceOperator_, BCs_);

  // Control-variate variance reduction:
  // (1) calculate value/greeks of the European option analytically
  EuropeanOption analyticEuro(type_, underlying_, strike_,
```

```
        dividendYield_, riskFreeRate_, residualTime_, volatility_);

   // (2) Initialize prices on the grid
   Array europeanPrices = initialPrices_;
   Array americanPrices = initialPrices_;

   // (3) Rollback
   model.rollback(europeanPrices, residualTime_, 0.0, timeSteps_);
   model.rollback(americanPrices, residualTime_, 0.0, timeSteps_, stepCondition_);

   // (4) Numerically calculate option value and greeks using
   // the european option as control variate

   value_ = valueAtCenter(americanPrices) - valueAtCenter(europeanPrices) +
     analyticEuro.value();

   delta_ = firstDerivativeAtCenter(americanPrices, grid_) -
     firstDerivativeAtCenter(europeanPrices, grid_)
   + analyticEuro.delta();

   gamma_ = secondDerivativeAtCenter(americanPrices, grid_)
   - secondDerivativeAtCenter(europeanPrices, grid_)
   + analyticEuro.gamma();

   hasBeenCalculated_ = true;
}
```

We can price a European option with this implicit difference implementation using the following code segment:

```
// define parameters
double price = 50;
double strike = 50;
double vol = 0.20;
double rate = 0.06;
double div = 0.03;
double T = 0.05;
int M = 200;
int N = 800;

Instruments::VanillaOption option(
   price,strike,vol,rate,div,T,Option::Call,Option::Exercise::European,
   Handle<QuantLib::PricingEngine>(new PricingEngines::EuropeanBinomialEngine()));

// run implicit difference method
option.setPricingEngine(Handle<PricingEngine>(
   new PricingEngines::FiniteDifferenceEngine(price,strike,vol,rate,
   div,T, Option::Call, Option::Exercise::European,
   PricingEngines::FiniteDifferenceEngine::MethodType::ImplicitDifference, M, N,
```

```
    FiniteDifferenceMethod::BoundaryConditions::Dirichlet)));

std::cout << "value" << " " << option.engine_->calculate() << endl;

// run explicit difference method
option.setPricingEngine(Handle<PricingEngine>(
    new PricingEngines::FiniteDifferenceEngine(price,strike,vol,rate,
    div,T, Option::Call, Option::Exercise::American,
    PricingEngines::FiniteDifferenceEngine::MethodType::ExplicitDifference, N, M,
    FiniteDifferenceMethod::BoundaryConditions::Dirichlet)));

std::cout << "value" << " " << option.engine_->calculate() << endl;
```

Running this code, we find the implicit difference price is \$4.5677 and the explicit difference price is \$4.5676, which shows that both methods convergence to the trinomial diffusion process discussed in section 5.2 since the convergence properties in section 4.5 are satisfied.

5.7   ITERATIVE METHODS

The LU method is a direct method for solving a linear system as in equation (5.16) if the objective is to find the unknowns exactly and in one pass. An alternative approach is to employ an iterative method. Iterative methods differ from direct methods in that one starts with an initial guess for the solution and successively improves it until it converges to the exact solution (or close enough to the exact solution). A direct method obtains a solution without any iterations. While iterative methods are slower than direct methods, they do have the advantage that they are easier to program and that they generalize in a straightforward way to American option problems and nonlinear models.[1]

The successive overrelaxation (SOR) method is a type of iterative method. The SOR is a refinement of the Gauss-Seidel method, another iterative method, which in turn is a development of the Jacobi method. All three iterative methods rely on the fact that equation (5.14) (for a simple diffusion process) can be written in the form

$$u_{i+1,j} = \frac{1}{1+2\alpha}(b_{i,j} + \alpha(u_{i+1,j-1} + u_{i+1,j+1})) \qquad (5.29)$$

The idea behind the Jacobi method is to take some initial guess for $u_{i+1,j}$ for $N^- + 1 \leq j \leq N^+ - 1$ (a good initial guess is the values of u from the previous step, i.e., $u_{i,j}$).

---

[1]Wilmott, Howison, and Dewynne (1995), 150.

Then one substitutes this value into equation (5.29) to generate a new guess for $u_{i+1,j}$ (on the left-hand side). The process is repeated until the approximations cease to change (the error is less than a specified value). Once this happens, a solution is found.

More formally, the Jacobi method works as follows. Let $u_{i+1,j}^k$ denote the kth iterate for $u_{i+1,j}$. This initial guess given by $u_{i+1,j}^0$ and as $k \to \infty$, we expect $u_{i+1,j}^k \to u_{i+1,j}$. Thus, given $u_{i+1,j}^k$, we calculate $u_{i+1,j}^{k+1}$ using a modified version of equation (5.29):

$$u_{i+1,j}^{k+1} = \frac{1}{1+2\alpha}(b_{i,j} + \alpha(u_{i+1,j-1}^k + u_{i+1,j+1}^k)) \quad N^- < j < N^+ \tag{5.30}$$

The entire process is repeated until the error measured by the norm

$$\left\| u_{i+1}^{k+1} - u_{i+1}^k \right\|^2 = \sum_{j=N^-+1}^{N^+-1} \left(u_{i+1,j}^{k+1} - u_{i+1,j}^k \right)^2$$

becomes sufficiently small so that we then take the $u_{i+1,j}^{k+1}$ as the value for $u_{i+1,j}$. The method converges for any $\alpha > 0$.

The Gauss-Seidel method improves on the Jacobi method by using the fact that when we compute $u_{i+1,j}^{k+1}$ in equation (5.30) we already know $u_{i+1,j-1}^{k+1}$. Thus, we use $u_{i+1,j-1}^{k+1}$ instead of $u_{i+1,j-1}^k$ so that we use an updated guess immediately when it becomes available (the Jacobi method uses updated guesses only when they are all available).[2] The Gauss-Seidel method given by

$$u_{i+1,j}^{k+1} = \frac{1}{1+2\alpha}\left(b_{i,j} + \alpha\left(u_{i+1,j-1}^{k+1} + u_{i+1,j+1}^k\right) \right) \quad N^- < j < N^+ \tag{5.31}$$

where $\alpha = \Delta t/(\Delta x)^2$.

Since the Gauss-Seidel method uses the most recent information when it becomes available, it converges more rapidly than the Jacobi method and is therefore more computationally efficient.

The SOR method is a refinement of the Gauss-Seidel algorithm and converges to the correct solution if $\alpha > 0$. First, notice the (seemingly trivial) observation that

$$u_{i+1,j}^{k+1} = u_{i+1,j}^k + (u_{i+1,j}^{k+1} - u_{i+1,j}^k)$$

As the sequence converges as $k \to \infty$ one can think of $(u_{i+1,j}^{k+1} - u_{i+1,j}^k)$ as a correction term to be added to $u_{i+1,j}^k$ to bring it closer to the exact value of $u_{i+1,j}$. The possibility exists that the sequence will converge more rapidly if we overcorrect, which holds

---

[2]Ibid., 151.

true if the sequence of iterates $u_{i+1,j}^k \rightarrow u_{i+1,j}$ monotonically as k increases, rather than oscillating.[3] Thus, if set

$$z_{i+1,j}^{k+1} = \frac{1}{1+2\alpha}\left(b_{i,j} + \alpha\left(u_{i+1,j-1}^{k+1} + u_{i+1,j+1}^k\right)\right)$$

$$(5.32)$$

$$u_{i+1,j}^{k+1} = u_{i+1,j}^k + \omega\left(z_{i+1,j}^{k+1} - u_{i+1,j}^k\right)$$

where $\omega >$ is the overcorrection or overrelaxation parameter. (Note that $z_{i+1,j}^{k+1}$ is the value that the Gauss-Seidel method would give for $u_{i+1,j}^{k+1}$, whereas in the SOR we view the term $z_{i+1,j}^{k+1} - u_{i+1,j}^k$ as a correction to be made to $u_{i+1,j}^k$ in order to obtain $u_{i+1,j}^{k+1}$.) It can be shown that the SOR method converges to the correct solution in equation (5.14) if $\alpha > 0$ and provided $0 < \omega < 2$. When $0 < \omega < 1$, the method is referred to as underrelaxation in contrast to overrelaxation, which is used for $1 < \omega < 2$. It can be shown that there is an optimal value of ω in the interval $1 < \omega < 2$, which leads to a much more rapid convergence than other values of ω.[4] The optimal value of ω depends on the dimension of the matrix involved and, more generally, on the details of the matrix (i.e., rank, sparseness, etc.). It is often much quicker to change ω each time step until a value is found (that minimizes the number of iterations of the SOR loop) than to estimate the optimal value of ω.[5]

The following is an implementation of the SOR technique:

```
/*********************************************************************
SOR :   solve tridiagonal system with SOR technique
[in]    Array& rhs  : initial guess for solution
        double tol  : error tolerance
[out]   Array       : solution of tridiagonal system
**********************************************************************/
Array TridiagonalOperator::SOR(const Array& rhs, double tol) const
{
  QL_REQUIRE(rhs.size()==size(), "TridiagonalOperator::solveFor: rhs has the wrong
    size");

  // initial guess
  Array result = rhs;

  // solve tridiagonal system with SOR technique
  Size sorIteration, i;
  double omega = 1.5;        // omega
  double err=2.0*tol;        // error
  double temp;               // temporarily stores SOR values

  for (sorIteration=0; err>tol ; sorIteration++)
```

[3]Ibid., 152.
[4]Ibid., 153.
[5]Ibid., 153.

```
{
   QL_REQUIRE(sorIteration<100000,
      "TridiagonalOperator::SOR: tolerance [" + DoubleFormatter::toString(tol) +
         "] not
      reached in " + IntegerFormatter::toString(sorIteration) + " iterations.
         The error still is "
      + DoubleFormatter::toString(err));

   err=0.0;
   for (i = 1; i < size()-2 ; i++)
   {
      temp = omega * (rhs[i] - upperDiagonal_[i] * result[i+1]-
         diagonal_[i] * result[i] - lowerDiagonal_[i-1] * result[i-1]) /
            diagonal_[i];
      err += temp * temp;
      result[i] += temp;
   }
}
return result;
}
```

5.8   CRANK-NICOLSON SCHEME

The Crank-Nicolson is a type of finite-difference scheme that is used to overcome the stability limitations imposed by the stability and convergence restrictions of the explicit finite-difference scheme. The Crank-Nicolson converges faster than the implicit and explicit finite-difference schemes. The rate of convergence of the Crank-Nicolson scheme is $O((\Delta t)^2)$ whereas it is $O((\Delta t))$ for the implicit and explicit finite-difference methods.

Essentially, the Crank-Nicolson method is an average of the implicit and explicit methods. Consider a simple diffusion equation. If we use a forward-difference approximation for the time partial derivative, we obtain the explicit scheme:

$$\frac{u_{i+1,j} - u_{i,j}}{\Delta t} + O(\Delta t) = \frac{u_{i,j+1} - 2u_{i,j} + u_{i,j-1}}{(\Delta x)^2} + O((\Delta t)^2)$$

and if we take the backward difference we get the implicit scheme:

$$\frac{u_{i+1,j} - u_{i,j}}{\Delta t} + O(\Delta t) = \frac{u_{i+1,j} - 2u_{i+1,j} + u_{i+1,j-1}}{(\Delta x)^2} + O((\Delta t)^2)$$

Taking the average of these two equations, we get:[6]

$$\frac{u_{i+1,j} - u_{i,j}}{\Delta t} + O(\Delta t) = \frac{1}{2}\left(\frac{u_{i,j+1} - 2u_{i,j} + u_{i,j-1}}{(\Delta x)^2} + \frac{u_{i+1,j+1} - 2u_{i+1,j} + u_{i+1,j-1}}{(\Delta x)^2}\right) + O((\Delta x)^2) \qquad (5.33)$$

Ignoring the error terms, we get the Crank-Nicolson scheme:

$$u_{i+1,j} - \frac{1}{2}\alpha\left(u_{i+1,j+1} - 2u_{i+1,j} + u_{i+1,j-1}\right) = u_{i,j} + \frac{1}{2}\alpha\left(u_{i,j+1} - 2u_{i,j} + u_{i,j-1}\right) \qquad (5.34)$$

where $\alpha = \Delta t/(\Delta x)^2$. Notice that $u_{i+1,\,j-1}$, $u_{i+1,\,j}$, and $u_{i+1,\,j+1}$ are now determined implicitly in terms of $u_{i,\,j}$, $u_{i,\,j+1}$, and $u_{i,\,j-1}$. Equation (5.34) can be solved in the same manner as the implicit scheme in equation (5.7) since everything on the right-hand side can be evaluated explicitly if the $u_{i,\,j}$'s are known. Denote the left-hand side of (5.34) by $Z_{i,\,j}$. The problem of solving (5.28) reduces to first computing

$$Z_{i,j} = (1 - \alpha)u_{i,j} + \frac{1}{2}\alpha\left(u_{i,j-1} + u_{i,j+1}\right) \qquad (5.35)$$

which is an explicit formula for $Z_{i,\,j}$, and then solving

$$(1 + \alpha)u_{i+1,j} - \frac{1}{2}\alpha\left(u_{i+1,j-1} + u_{i+1,j+1}\right) = Z_{i,j} \qquad (5.36)$$

We can write (5.36) as a linear system:

$$\mathbf{A}\mathbf{u}^{i+1} = \mathbf{b}^i \qquad (5.37)$$

where the matrix $\mathbf{A}$ is given by

$$\mathbf{A} = \begin{bmatrix} 1+\alpha & -\frac{1}{2}\alpha & 0 & \cdots & & 0 \\ -\frac{1}{2}\alpha & 1+\alpha & -\frac{1}{2}\alpha & & & \vdots \\ 0 & -\frac{1}{2}\alpha & & \ddots & & 0 \\ \vdots & \vdots & & \ddots & & -\frac{1}{2}\alpha \\ 0 & 0 & \cdots & & -\frac{1}{2}\alpha & 1+\alpha \end{bmatrix} \qquad (5.38)$$

---

[6]It can be shown that the error terms in equation (5.33) are accurate to $O((\Delta t)^2)$ rather than $O(\Delta t)$.

and the vectors $\mathbf{u}^{i+1}$ and $\mathbf{b}^i$ are given by

$$
\mathbf{u}^{i+1} = \begin{bmatrix} u_{i+1,N^-+1} \\ \cdots \\ u_{i+1,0} \\ \cdots \\ u_{i+1,N^+-1} \end{bmatrix}, \quad \mathbf{b}^i = \begin{bmatrix} Z_{i,N^-+1} \\ \cdots \\ Z_{i,0} \\ \cdots \\ Z_{i,N^+-1} \end{bmatrix} + \frac{1}{2}\alpha \begin{bmatrix} u_{i+1,N^-} \\ 0 \\ \cdots \\ 0 \\ u_{i+1,N^+} \end{bmatrix} \tag{5.39}
$$

The vector on the far right-hand side of (5.39), in $\mathbf{b}^i$, comes from the boundary conditions applied at the end points of a finite mesh where $x = N^-\Delta x$ and $x = N^+\Delta x$. N^- and N^+ are integers, chosen to be sufficiently large that no significant errors are introduced.

To implement the Crank-Nicolson scheme, we first generate the vector $\mathbf{b}^i$ using known quantities. Then we use either an LU decomposition solver or an SOR solver to solve the system (5.37). The scheme is both stable and convergent for all values of $\alpha > 0$.

We can apply the Crank-Nicolson scheme to the Black-Scholes diffusion equation by replacing time and space derivatives with finite differences centered at the time step $i + 1/2$.

$$
\frac{1}{2}\sigma^2\left(\frac{(u_{i+1,j+1}-2u_{i+1,j}+u_{i+1,j-1})+(u_{i,j+1}-2u_{i,j}+u_{i,j-1})}{2\Delta x^2}\right)+
$$
$$
\mu\left(\frac{(u_{i+1,j+1}-u_{i+1,j-1})+(u_{i,j+1}-u_{i,j-1})}{4\Delta x}\right)+\frac{u_{i+1,j}-u_{i,j}}{\Delta t}-r\left(\frac{u_{i+1,j}+u_{i,j}}{2}\right)=0
$$

which can be written as:

$$
p_u u_{i,j+1} + p_m u_{i,j} + p_d u_{i,j-1} = -p_u u_{i+1,j+1} - (p_m - 2)u_{i+1,j} - p_d u_{i+1,j-1} \tag{5.40}
$$

where

$$
p_u = -\frac{1}{4}\Delta t\left(\frac{\sigma^2}{\Delta x^2}+\frac{\mu}{\Delta x}\right)
$$

$$
p_m = 1 + \Delta t\,\frac{\sigma^2}{2\Delta x^2}+\frac{r\Delta t}{2} \tag{5.41}
$$

$$
p_d = -\frac{1}{4}\Delta t\left(\frac{\sigma^2}{\Delta x^2}-\frac{\mu}{\Delta x}\right)
$$

We can write (5.40) in the form in (5.35). First, set

$$Z_{i,j} = p_u u_{i,j+1} + p_m u_{i,j} + p_d u_{i,j-1}$$

and then solve

$$-p_u u_{i+1,j+1} - (p_m - 2)u_{i+1,j} - p_d u_{i+1,j-1} = Z_{i,j}$$

using an LU decomposition.

The following is an implementation for the Crank-Nicolson scheme:

```
/***********************************************************************************
solveCrankNicolson: values an option using the Crank Nicolson scheme in (5.39)
[in]:    double price     : asset price
         double strike    : strike price
         double vol       : volatility
         double rate      : risk-free rate
         double div       : dividend yield
         double T         : maturity
         int N            : number of time steps
         int M            : number of space steps
         char type        : (C)all or (P)ut
[out] :  double option price

************************************************************************************/
   double CrankNicolson::solveCrankNicolson(double price, double strike, double T,
     double vol, double rate, double div, long M, long N, char type)
{
   double b[50]   = {0.0};                     // vector of Z(i,j)'s
   double c1[50]  = {0.0};
   double d[50]   = {0.0};
   double x[100]  = {0.0};
   double dx = 0.0;                            // state step size
   double drift = rate - div - vol*vol/2;      // drift rate
   double pu, pm, pd;                          // risk neutral probabilities
   int i, j;
   double a = 0.0;
   double deltat = T/N;                        // time step size
   cout.setf(ios::showpoint);
   cout.precision(2);

   dx = vol*sqrt(3*deltat/2);
   // we multiply by 0.5 because we are using Crank-Nicolson
   a = 0.5*(deltat/(dx*dx));

   // compute probabilities
   pu = -0.5*deltat*((vol*vol)/(dx*dx) + drift/dx);
   pm = 1 + deltat*(vol*vol/(dx*dx)) + rate*deltat;
```

```
pd = -0.5*deltat*((vol*vol)/(dx*dx) - drift/dx);

// calculate coefficients
for (j = -M; j <= M; j++)
{
  S[N][j] = price*exp(j*dx);
  S[0][j] = price;
}

// compute stock prices
for (i = 1; i < N; i++)
{
  for (j = -M; j <= M; j++)
    S[i][j] = S[i-1][j]*exp(j*dx);
}

// calculate payoffs
if (type == 'P')
{
  for (j = -M; j <= M; j++)
  {
    P[N][j] = max(strike - S[N][j],0);
  }
  // calculate boundary conditions
  for (i = 0; i < N; i++)
  {
    P[i][-M] = P[i][-M+1] + 1*(S[i][-M+1]-S[i][-M]); // derivative boundary
                                                     // condition
    P[i][M] = 0;
  }
}
else // if type == 'C'
{
  // calculate boundary conditions
  for (j = -M; j <= M; j++)
  {
    P[N][j] = max(S[N][j] - strike,0);
  }

  // calculate boundary conditions
  for (i = 0; i < N; i++)
  {
    P[i][-M] = 0;
    P[i][M] = P[i][M-1] + (S[i][M] - S[i][M-1]); // derivative boundary condition
  }
}

for (j = -M+1; j < M; j++)
  b[j] = (1-a)*P[N][j] + a*(P[N][j+1] + P[N][j-1]);

b[-M+1]= b[-M+1] + a*P[N][-M];
b[M-1] = b[M-1] + a*P[N][M];
```

```
    solveCNTridiagonal(N,M,pu,pm,pd,d,c1,b,type,strike);

    // print out mesh
    for (i = 0; i <= N; i++)
      cout << " " << T - deltat*i ;
    cout << "\n\n" << endl;

    for (j = M; j >= -M; j--)
    {
      cout << " " << S[N][j];
      for (i = 0; i <= N; i++)
      {
        cout << " " << endl;
        if (j != -M)
          cout << " " <<P[i][j];
        else
        cout << " " << P[N][-M];
        cout << "\n";
      }
    }
    cout << "\n" << endl;

    return P[0][0];
}


/***************************************************************************************
solveCNTridiagonal       : solves the Crank Nicolson tridiagonal system of equations
[in]:    int N           : number of time steps
         int M           : number of state steps
         double pu       : up probability
         double pm       : middle probability
         double pd       : down probability
         double* d:      : array used in solving tridiagonal system
         double* c1:     : array used in solving tridiagonal system
         double* d1:     : array of Z(i,j)'s
         char type       : (C)all or (P)ut
         double strike   : strike price
[out] : double           : option price
***************************************************************************************/
void CrankNicolson::solveCNTridiagonal(int N, int M, double pu, double pm, double
  pd, double *d, double *c1, double *d1, char type, double strike)
{
  int i,j;

  for (j = -M; j <= M; j++)
    d[j] = P[N][j];

  // set values at boundary points
    d1[-M]   = d[-M]/pm;
    d1[-M+1] = d[-M+1]/pm;
    c1[-M]   = pd/pm;
    c1[-M+1] = pd/pm;
```

```
for (j = -M+1; j <= M-2; j++)
  c1[j+1] = pd/(pm - pu*c1[j]);


for (j = -M+1; j <= M-1; j++)
  d1[j+1] = (d[j+1] - pu*d1[j-1])/(pm - pu*c1[j]);


// solve tridiagonal system
for (i = N-1; i >= 0; i--)
{
  for (j = -M+1; j <= M-1; j++)
  {
    if (i != N-1)
      d[j] = P[i+1][j];

    if (j == -M+1)
      d1[-M+1] = d[-M+1]/pm;

    d1[j+1] = (d[j+1] - pu*d1[j-1])/(pm - pu*c1[j]);

    P[i][-j] = d1[-j] - c1[-j]*P[i][-j+1];

    // check early exercise
    if (type == 'P')
    {
      if (P[i][-j] < strike - S[N][-j])
        P[i][-j] = strike - S[N][-j];
    }
    else
    {
      if (P[i][-j] < S[N][-j] - strike)
        P[i][-j] = S[N][-j] - strike;
    }
  }
}
}
```

5.9 ALTERNATING DIRECTION IMPLICIT METHOD

Finite difference methods, in general, can be extended to handle multiple state variables. However, if we have 100 grid points in one space dimension, then with two space dimensions we will have 100×100 grid points and thus 100 times as much computation. Consequently, in order to obtain reasonable computation times, much smaller grid sizes must be used.

Consider the case of an option that has a payoff that depends on the values of two assets, S_1 and S_2, which both follow geometric Brownian motions:

$$dS_1 = (r - q_1)S_1 dt + \sigma_1 S_1 dz_1$$
$$dS_2 = (r - q_2)S_2 dt + \sigma_2 S_2 dz_2$$

where the assets have a correlation of ρ (i.e., $dz_1 \cdot dz_2 = \rho dt$).

The PDE that the option on the two assets follows is:

$$
rf = \frac{\partial f}{\partial t} + (r - q)S_1 \frac{\partial f}{\partial S_1} + (r - q)S_2 \frac{\partial f}{\partial S_2}
$$
$$
+ \frac{1}{2}\sigma_1^2 S_1^2 \frac{\partial^2 f}{\partial S_1^2} + \frac{1}{2}\sigma_2^2 S_2^2 \frac{\partial^2 f}{\partial S_2^2} + \rho\sigma_1\sigma_2 S_1 S_2 \frac{\partial^2 f}{\partial S_1 \partial S_2} \tag{5.42}
$$

If we try to apply the Crank-Nicolson scheme to equation (5.42), we obtain a system of $(2N_j - 1)(2N_k - 1)$ linear equations where N_j and N_k are the number of nodes on either side of the current level of S_1 and S_2, respectively. Together with the $2(2N_j - 1) + 2(2N_k + 1)$ boundary conditions we have a system of $(2N_j - 1)(2N_k - 1)$ linear equations for the $(2N_j - 1)(2N_k - 1)$ unknown option values.[7] The result matrix no longer has a simple tridiagonal structure and must be solved using sparse matrix methods; see Press et al. (1992). The alternating direction implicit (ADI) method allows one to overcome this problem. It is an adaptation of the Crank-Nicolson scheme that allows one to obtain simple tridiagonal matrices.

We follow Clewlow and Strickland (1998a) in the following discussion. To use the ADI, we first transform equation (5.42) into a standard diffusion equation with constant coefficients. We transform by setting $x_1 = \ln(S_1)$ and $x_2 = \ln(S_2)$, which gives the following PDE:

$$
rf = \frac{\partial f}{\partial t} + \mu_1 \frac{\partial f}{\partial x_1} + \mu_2 \frac{\partial f}{\partial x_2} + \frac{1}{2}\sigma_1^2 \frac{\partial^2 f}{\partial x_1^2} + \frac{1}{2}\sigma_2^2 \frac{\partial^2 f}{\partial x_2^2} + \rho\sigma_1\sigma_2 \frac{\partial^2 f}{\partial x_1 \partial x_2} \tag{5.43}
$$

where

$$
\mu_1 = r - q_1 - \frac{1}{2}\sigma_1^2 \text{ and } \mu_2 = r - q_1 - \frac{1}{2}\sigma_2^2
$$

---

[7]Clewlow and Strickland (1998a), 78.

Second, since the ADI cannot handle mixed second-order derivatives, we must transform to uncorrelated space variables. We can achieve this by doing an eigenvector-eigenvalue decomposition on the covariance matrix of x_1 and x_2:

$$\begin{pmatrix} v_{11} & v_{12} \\ v_{21} & v_{22} \end{pmatrix} \begin{pmatrix} \lambda_1 & 0 \\ 0 & \lambda_2 \end{pmatrix} \begin{pmatrix} v_{11} & v_{21} \\ v_{12} & v_{22} \end{pmatrix} = \begin{pmatrix} \sigma_1^2 & \rho\sigma_1\sigma_2 \\ \rho\sigma_1\sigma_2 & \sigma_2^2 \end{pmatrix}$$

The eigenvectors give the linear combination of x_1 and x_2, which are uncorrelated. Under this transformation, we get the PDE

$$rf = \frac{\partial f}{\partial t} + \alpha_1 \frac{\partial f}{\partial y_1} + \alpha_2 \frac{\partial f}{\partial y_2} + \frac{1}{2}\lambda_1 \frac{\partial^2 f}{\partial y_1^2} + \frac{1}{2}\lambda_2 \frac{\partial^2 f}{\partial y_2^2} \tag{5.44}$$

where

$$\begin{aligned}
y_1 &= v_{11}x_1 + v_{12}x_2 \\
y_2 &= v_{21}x_1 + v_{22}x_2 \\
\alpha_1 &= v_{11}\mu_1 + v_{12}\mu_2 \\
\alpha_2 &= v_{21}\mu_1 + v_{22}\mu_2 \\
dy_1 &= \alpha_1 dt + \sqrt{\lambda_1}\,dw_1 \\
dy_2 &= \alpha_2 dt + \sqrt{\lambda_2}\,dw_2
\end{aligned} \tag{5.45}$$

and dw_1 and dw_2 are uncorrelated Brownian motions.

To simplify the problem, we will get rid of the left-hand zero term, rf, in equation (5.44) and first-order terms

$$\alpha_1 \frac{\partial f}{\partial y_1} + \alpha_2 \frac{\partial f}{\partial y_1}$$

through the transformation

$$f(y_1, y_2, t) = \exp(a_1 y_1 + a_2 y_2 + a_3 t)U(y_1, y_2, t) \tag{5.46}$$

to equation (5.39). Setting the coefficients of the zeroth and first-order terms to zero, we get

$$-\frac{\partial U}{\partial t} = \frac{1}{2}\lambda_1 \frac{\partial^2 U}{\partial y_1^2} + \frac{1}{2}\lambda_2 \frac{\partial^2 U}{\partial y_2^2} \tag{5.47}$$

and

$$a_1 = -\frac{\alpha_1}{\lambda_1}, \quad a_2 = -\frac{\alpha_2}{\lambda_2}, \quad a_3 = \frac{\alpha_1^2}{2\lambda_1} + \frac{\alpha_2^2}{2\lambda_2} + r$$

Finally, we transform so that the coefficients on the second-order terms in equation (5.42) are equal by setting:

$$y_2' = \sqrt{\frac{\lambda_1}{\lambda_2}} y_2 \qquad (5.48)$$

which yields:

$$-\frac{\partial U}{\partial t} = \frac{1}{2}\lambda_1\left(\frac{\partial^2 U}{\partial y_1^2} + \frac{\partial^2 U}{\partial y_2'^2}\right) \qquad (5.49)$$

The ADI can be applied to equation (5.44), which is a two-dimensional diffusion equation. The ADI replaces the partial derivatives by their Crank-Nicolson-style finite-difference approximations in two stages. In the first stage, the derivatives with respect to y_1 are replaced by finite-difference approximations at time step $i + 1/2$, while the derivatives with respect to y_2' are approximated by finite differences at time step $i + 1$. Thus, the ADI reduces to the following finite-difference equation:

$$
-\frac{U_{i+1,\,j,\,k} - U_{i+1/2,\,j,\,k}}{\frac{1}{2}\Delta t}
$$

$$
= \frac{1}{2}\lambda_1\left(\frac{\left(U_{i+1/2,\,j+1,\,k} - 2U_{i+1/2,\,j,\,k} + U_{i+1/2,\,j-1,\,k}\right)}{\Delta y_1^2} + \frac{\left(U_{i+1,\,j,\,k+1} - 2U_{i+1,\,j,\,k} + U_{i+1,\,j,\,k-1}\right)}{\Delta y_2'^2}\right)
\qquad (5.50)
$$

which can be rewritten as

$$
p_u U_{i+1/2,j+1,k} + p_m U_{i+1/2,j,k} + p_d U_{i+1/2,j-1,k} = -\frac{2}{\Delta t} U_{i+1,j,k}
$$

$$
-\frac{1}{2}\lambda_1\left(\frac{\left(U_{i+1,j,k+1} - 2U_{i+1,j,k} + U_{i+1,j,k-1}\right)}{\Delta y_2'^2}\right)
\qquad (5.51)
$$

where

$$p_u = \frac{\lambda_1}{2\Delta y_1^2}$$

$$p_m = -\frac{2}{\Delta t} - \frac{\lambda_1}{\Delta y_1^2}$$

$$p_d = \frac{\lambda_1}{2\Delta y_1^2}$$

and i denotes the time step, j denotes the state of asset 1, and k denotes the state of asset 2.

In the second stage, the derivatives with respect to y_2' are replaced by finite-difference approximations at time step i, while the derivatives with respect to y_1 are approximated by finite differences at time step $i + 1/2$. This gives to the following finite-difference equation:

$$-\frac{U_{i+1/2,j,k} - U_{i,j,k}}{\frac{1}{2}\Delta t}$$
$$= \frac{1}{2}\lambda_1 \left(\frac{\left(U_{i+1/2,j+1,k} - 2U_{i+1/2,j,k} + U_{i+1/2,j-1,k}\right)}{\Delta y_1^2} + \frac{\left(U_{i,j,k+1} - 2U_{i,j,k} + U_{i,j,k-1}\right)}{\Delta y_2'^2} \right) \tag{5.52}$$

which can be rewritten as

$$p_u U_{i,j,k+1} + p_m U_{i,j,k} + p_d U_{i,j,k-1} = -\frac{2}{\Delta t} U_{i+1/2,j,k}$$
$$-\frac{1}{2}\lambda_1 \left(\frac{\left(U_{i+1/2,j+1,k} - 2U_{i+1/2,j,k} + U_{i+1/2,j-1,k}\right)}{\Delta y_2'^2} \right) \tag{5.53}$$

where $p_u = \dfrac{\lambda_1}{2\Delta y_2'^2}$

$$p_m = -\frac{2}{\Delta t} - \frac{\lambda_1}{\Delta y_2'^2}$$

$$p_d = \frac{\lambda_1}{2\Delta y_2'^2}$$

CHAPTER 6

Exotic Options

Certain derivatives, such as Asian options, barrier options, and lookback options, have payoffs that are dependent on the entire price path of the underlying security. These derivatives are known as *path-dependent* since they cannot be valued analytically, and hence are dependent on the entire path of the security from (S, t) to (S_T, T). If S_t is the value of the underlying security at time t, then the payoff of a path-dependent derivative at time T is $F(\{S_t, t_0 \le t \le T\})$.

In general, simple analytical formulas do exist for certain classes of exotic options, these options being classified by the property that the path-dependent condition applies to the continuous path. Those exotic options, such as lookback and Asian options where usually the path-dependent condition is observed at discrete fixing or stopping times, either have complicated formulas or cannot be valued analytically. However, we can value these securities using Monte Carlo simulations and trees when such closed-formula solutions are nonexistent. There are European path-dependent options that are contingent on the entire path from (S, t) to (S_T, T) but are paid only at maturity T, American path-dependent options where the option holder can exercise prior to maturity, as well as Bermudan path-dependent options that are exercisable only on specified discrete exercise dates.

In section 6.1, we discuss barrier options and provide analytical solutions. In section 6.2, we provide an implementation for an up-and-out American barrier put option. In section 6.3, we discuss Asian options. In section 6.4, we discuss pricing Asian options with geometric averaging, while in section 6.5, we discuss pricing Asian options with arithmetic averaging. In section 6.6, we discuss pricing seasoned Asian options. We devote section 6.7 to discussing lookback options. In section 6.8, an implementation for pricing a floating-strike lookback put option is given, while section 6.9 gives an implementation for pricing a fixed-strike lookback put option.

6.1 BARRIER OPTIONS

Barrier options are standard call or put options except that they disappear (knock-out) or appear (knock-in) if the asset price crosses a predetermined barrier B at a predetermined set of fixing dates t_i, $i = 1, \ldots, n$. Sometimes a barrier option contains a provision that in the event the barrier is hit a rebate R is paid to the option holder to mitigate the loss of the option. There are actually eight types of barrier options classified by type of option payoff (call or put), whether the barrier is below or above the current asset price ("down" or "up"), and whether the option disappears or appears when the barrier is crossed ("out" or "in"). Table 6.1 summarizes the barrier types, where $\mathbf{1}_A$ is the indicator function for condition A.

Because of the probability of the option disappearing at one of the fixed dates for a knock-out barrier or the probability of an option not appearing on one of the fixed dates for a knock-in barrier, barrier options are cheaper than standard options. The cheaper premium makes barriers attractive to risk managers who want to reduce their hedging costs. However, barrier options have a hedging problem: At the barrier, delta is discontinuous and gamma tends to infinity. Thus, barrier options become almost unhedgeable when the price nears the barrier.

It turns out that we can actually price a down-and-out call analytically. We need to solve the Black-Scholes PDE:

$$\frac{\partial f}{\partial t} + rS \frac{\partial f}{\partial S} + \frac{1}{2}\sigma^2 S^2 \frac{\partial^2 f}{\partial S^2} = rf$$

subject to the payoff condition:

$$f(S_T, T) = \max(S_T - X, 0)$$

and an extra boundary condition:

$$f(B, t^*) = 0 \text{ for } t^* \in [t, T]$$

TABLE 6.1 Barrier Types

Type	Payoff
Down-and-out call	$\max(0, S_T - K)\mathbf{1}_{\min(S_{t_i},\dots,S_{t_n})>B}$
Up-and-out call	$\max(0, S_T - K)\mathbf{1}_{\max(S_{t_i},\dots,S_{t_n})<B}$
Down-and-in call	$\max(0, S_T - K)\mathbf{1}_{\min(S_{t_i},\dots,S_{t_n})\leq B}$
Up-and-in call	$\max(0, S_T - K)\mathbf{1}_{\max(S_{t_i},\dots,S_{t_n})\geq B}$
Down-and-out put	$\max(0, K - S_T)\mathbf{1}_{\min(S_{t_i},\dots,S_{t_n})>B}$
Up-and-out put	$\max(0, K - S_T)\mathbf{1}_{\max(S_{t_i},\dots,S_{t_n})<B}$
Down-and-in put	$\max(0, K - S_T)\mathbf{1}_{\min(S_{t_i},\dots,S_{t_n})\leq B}$
Up-and-in put	$\max(0, K - S_T)\mathbf{1}_{\max(S_{t_i},\dots,S_{t_n})\geq B}$

This boundary condition sets the option price to 0 at the down-and-out barrier $S = B$. Denote a down-and-out call price with the barrier B by $C_B(S, t)$. The solution to the preceding boundary value problem can be written in the form:

$$C_B(S, t) = e^{-r\tau}E_{t,S}^Q\left[1_{\{m_{t,T}>B\}}\max(S_T - X, 0)\right]$$

$$= e^{-r\tau}\int_{-\infty}^{\infty}\max(e^{x_T} - X, 0)p_B(x_T, T|x, t)dx_T \qquad (6.1)$$

$$= e^{-r\tau}\int_{\ln X}^{\infty}(e^{x_T} - X)p_B(x_T, T|x, t)dx_T$$

where $1_{\{m_{t,T}>B\}}$ is an indicator function that is equal to 1 if the minimum underlying price achieved between the option inception at time t and expiration at date T,

$$m_{t,T} = \min_{t^* \in [t,T]} S(t^*)$$

is greater than the barrier B (i.e., the barrier was never hit during the lifetime of the option), zero otherwise; $p_B(x_T, T \mid x, t)$ is the conditional probability density function of the terminal state x_T at time T of the Brownian motion path with drift, $dx = \mu dt + \sigma dz$ where $\mu = r - \sigma^2/2$, conditional on (1) the initial state x at time t and (2) the barrier B not hit during the time interval $[t, T]$; $x = \ln S$; and $x_T = \ln S_T$.

This conditional probability density is also a fundamental solution, Green's function, of the heat equation with drift:

$$\frac{\sigma^2}{2}\frac{\partial^2 p_B}{\partial x^2} + \mu\frac{\partial p_B}{\partial x} = \frac{\partial p_B}{\partial \tau} \qquad (6.2)$$

where $\tau = T - t$, subject to the boundary condition

$$p_B(x_T, T \mid b, t) = 0, b = \ln B$$

The boundary value problem for the heat equation with drift can be reduced to the boundary value problem for the standard heat equation without drift. If we let

$$p_B = \exp\left\{\frac{\mu}{\sigma^2}(x_T - x) - \frac{\mu^2\tau}{2\sigma^2}\right\}p_{0,B} \qquad (6.3)$$

where $p_{0,B}$ is the Green's function, and plug it into (6.2), we get the standard heat equation:

$$\frac{\sigma^2}{2} \frac{\partial^2 p_{0,B}}{\partial x^2} = \frac{\partial p_{0,B}}{\partial \tau}, \ \tau = T - t \tag{6.4}$$

subject to the boundary condition

$$p_B(x_T, T \mid b, t) = 0, \ b = \ln B$$

This boundary value problem for the heat equation can be solved by either of three methods: (1) separation of variables, (2) reflection principle (method of images), and (3) Laplace method.

The result is:

$$p_{0,B}(x_T, T \mid x, t) = \frac{1}{\sqrt{2\pi\sigma^2\tau}} \left(\exp\left\{ -\frac{(x_T - x)^2}{2\sigma^2} \right\} - \exp\left\{ -\frac{(x_T + x - 2b)^2}{2\sigma^2\tau} \right\} \right) \tag{6.5}$$

The solution with the drift is:

$$p_B(x_T, T \mid x, t) = \frac{1}{\sqrt{2\pi\sigma^2\tau}} \left(\exp\left\{ -\frac{(x_T - x - \mu\tau)^2}{2\sigma^2\tau} \right\} - \exp\left\{ \frac{2(b - x)\mu}{\sigma^2} \right\} \exp\left\{ -\frac{(x_T + x - 2b - \mu\tau)^2}{2\sigma^2\tau} \right\} \right)$$

The first term is the standard probability density and the second is the probability density conditional on the barrier being hit. The difference is the density conditional on the barrier not being hit.

Substituting this into the integral for the down-and-out call price we have:

$$\begin{aligned} C_B^{DAO}(S, t) = e^{-r\tau} &\int_{\ln X}^{\infty} (e^{x_T} - X) \frac{1}{\sqrt{2\pi\sigma^2\tau}} \exp\left\{ -\frac{(x_T - x - \mu\tau)^2}{2\sigma^2\tau} \right\} dx_T \\ &- \int_{\ln X}^{\infty} (e^{x_T} - X) \exp\left\{ \frac{2(b - x)\mu}{\sigma^2} \right\} \exp\left\{ -\frac{(x_T + x - 2b - \mu\tau)^2}{2\sigma^2\tau} \right\} dx_T \end{aligned} \tag{6.6}$$

The first term is just the Black-Scholes integral and is equal to the Black-Scholes price:

$$C(S, t) = SN(d_1) - e^{-r\tau}XN(d_2)$$

where

$$d_2 = \frac{\ln\left(\dfrac{S}{X}\right) + \mu\tau}{\sigma\sqrt{\tau}}, \quad d_2 = d_1 + \sigma\sqrt{\tau}, \text{ and } \mu = r - \frac{\sigma^2}{2}$$

The second integral is calculated similarly to the Black-Scholes integral calculation:

$$\exp\left\{\frac{2(b-x)\mu}{\sigma^2}\right\}\int_{\ln X}^{\infty}(e^{x_T}-X)\exp\left\{-\frac{(x_T+x-2b-\mu\tau)^2}{2\sigma^2\tau}\right\}dx_T=\left(\frac{B}{S}\right)^{\gamma}C(Q,\ t)$$

where we recall that $b=\ln B$ and $x=\ln S$ and let $\gamma=2\mu/\sigma^2$ and $Q=\exp(2b-x)=B^2/S$. Putting it all together we arrive at the analytical pricing formula for down-and-out calls:

$$C_B^{DAO}(S,\ t)=C(S,\ t)-\left(\frac{B}{S}\right)^{\gamma}C\left(\frac{B^2}{S},\ t\right) \qquad (6.7)$$

where C is the Black-Scholes call formula as a function of the initial price and time. The first term is a standard vanilla call option and the second term is the discount for including a knockout provision in the option contract. It is equal to the price of a down-and-in call, that is,

$$C_B^{DAI}(S,\ t)=\left(\frac{B}{S}\right)^{\gamma}C\left(\frac{B^2}{S},\ t\right)$$

Closed-form formulas for other barriers are given by Douady (1998) and Hull (1997). Boyle and Lau (1994) discuss how to price barriers with binomial trees.

Barrier options can be valued using binomial trees, but in general the barrier will lie between two horizontal layers of nodes. In fact, there are two types of inaccuracies caused by modeling options on a (binomial) lattice. The first type of inaccuracy, known as *quantization error*, is caused by the unavoidable existence of the lattice itself, which quantizes the asset price so that the asset price is allowed to take only the values of those points on the lattice.[1] Essentially, when one uses a lattice, one values an option on a stock that moves discretely, which leads to theoretically correct prices for a stock that actually displays such quantized behavior. Consequently, one must use a lattice with infinitesimal increments to approximate continuous diffusions and thus display real-world stock price movements. However, Ritchken (1996) notes, "refining the partition size may not necessarily produce more precise results" and suggests use of a trinomial tree as a better solution.[2]

The second type of inaccuracy, known as *specification error*, occurs because of the inability of the lattice to accurately represent the terms of the option. Once a lattice is selected, available stock prices are fixed; so if the exercise price or barrier

---

[1]Derman, Kani, Ergener, and Bardhan (1995), 4.
[2]Ritchken (1995), 19–28.

level of the option does not coincide with one of the available stock prices, one has to effectively move the exercise price or barrier level to the closest stock price available. Then the option valued on the lattice has contractual terms different from the actual option—the option is thus misspecified.

Convergence is slow on lattices since a large number of time steps is required to obtain an accurate value. This can be attributed to the fact that the barrier assumed by the tree is different from the true barrier. The reason for this is because a tree with a certain number of time steps cannot differentiate between barrier levels that lie between two rows of nodes. Consequently, the tree will assign option prices to the nodes nearest to, but not beyond, the barrier that is too high. Typically, the analytical convergence on a binomial lattice displays a sawtooth pattern like Figure 6.1.

There are two ways to overcome these problems: (1) position nodes on the barrier or (2) adjust for nodes not lying on barriers.

In the first case, we suppose there are two barriers, an outer barrier B_1 and an inner barrier B_2, $B_1 > B_2$. In a trinomial tree, there are three possible price movements at each node: up by a proportional amount u, stay the same, and down by an amount $d = 1/u$. We can always choose u so that nodes lie on both barriers. Following Hull (1997), the condition that must be satisfied by u is $B_2 = B_1 u^N$ for some integer N so that $\ln B_2 = \ln B_1 + N \ln u$. Typically, trinomial trees are used where

$$u = e^{\sigma\sqrt{3\Delta t}}$$

so that

$$\ln u = \sigma\sqrt{3\Delta t}$$

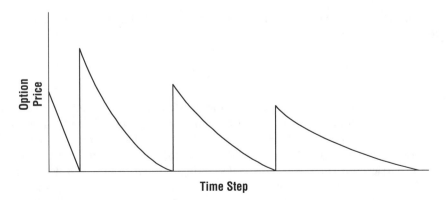

Time Step

FIGURE 6.1 Sawtooth Pattern

Thus, we set

$$\ln u = \frac{\ln B_2 - \ln B_1}{N}$$

where

$$N = \mathrm{int}\left[\frac{\ln B_2 - \ln B_1}{\sigma\sqrt{3\Delta t}} + 0.5\right]$$

The trinomial tree is constructed so that the central node is the initial stock price. Afterward, the central node of tree becomes $B_1 u^M$, where M is the integer that makes this value as close as possible to the initial stock price, which is

$$M = \mathrm{int}\left[\frac{\ln S - \ln B_1}{\ln u} + 0.5\right]$$

The probabilities on all branches are chosen to match the first two moments of the distribution followed by the underlying asset.

Furthermore, following Linetsky (1999), suppose one builds a CRR-type trinomial tree to approximate the diffusion price process. We know from section 4.3 that

$$u = e^{\lambda\sigma\sqrt{\Delta t}}, \ d = e^{-\lambda\sigma\sqrt{\Delta t}}$$

$$p_u = \frac{1}{2\lambda^2} + \frac{1}{2}\left(\frac{\mu}{\lambda\sigma}\right)\sqrt{\Delta t}, \ p_d = \frac{1}{2\lambda^2} - \frac{1}{2}\left(\frac{\mu}{\lambda\sigma}\right)\sqrt{\Delta t}, \text{ and } p_m = 1 - \frac{1}{\lambda^2}$$

The stretch parameter λ is chosen so that the probabilities are positive. For vanilla options, the optimal choice is

$$\lambda = \sqrt{3/2}$$

For barrier options, we choose λ so that one of the layers of nodes lies exactly on the barrier so that problems are avoided from errors registered from the barrier-crossing event. The condition is $d^n S = B$ for some positive integer n, $n = 1, 2, 3, \ldots$. That is, n down jumps from the initial price S put us right on the barrier, and we can register the barrier-hitting event exactly. Substituting in the formula for d, we have

$$e^{-n\lambda\sigma\sqrt{\Delta t}}S = B$$

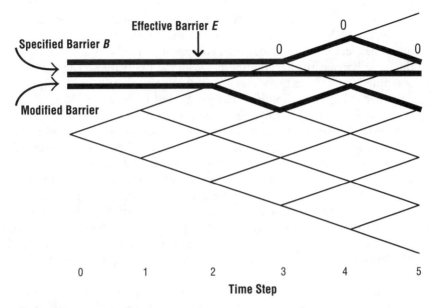

FIGURE 6.2   Modified Barrier

and the stretch parameter is selected as follows:

$$\lambda = \frac{1}{n\sigma\sqrt{\Delta t}}\ln\left(\frac{S}{B}\right)$$

Since there are multiple choices of n that put one of the layers of nodes on the barrier, one selects n such that the resulting λ is as close as possible to the choice

$$\lambda = \sqrt{3/2} \approx 1.2247$$

The second approach, similar to that of Derman, Kani, Ergener, and Bardhan,[3] adjusts for nodes not lying on a horizontal (specified) barrier by (1) calculating the price of the derivative on the assumption that the lower barrier, known as the modified barrier, is the true barrier; (2) calculating the value of the derivative on the assumption that the upper barrier E, known as the effective barrier, is the true barrier; and (3) interpolating between the two prices. The modified barrier is computed as the set of nodes naively computed from a knock-out at the effective barrier, rather than at the specified barrier B. As a result, values on these modified barrier nodes are larger than they should be since the effective barrier is higher than the specified barrier. Figure 6.2 shows the modified barrier used for pricing a knock-out barrier option (the call payoffs on the effective barrier are zero).

---

[3]Derman, Kani, Ergener, and Bardhan (1995).

One can work backward through the tree, calculating two values of the derivative on the nodes that form the modified lower barrier assuming both the lower and upper barriers are correct and then computing a final estimate for the derivative on the inner barrier by interpolating between the two values. The method can also be computed from the fact the derivative of the option price with respect to the stock price occurring at the specified barrier B, that is, $\partial C/\partial S$ (S, B, t) (the sensitivity at which a barrier option value grows away from the barrier) can be expanded as a first-order Taylor series since the barrier is independent of the location of the barrier to first order. As Derman, Kani, Ergener, and Bardhan summarize, "the modified barrier method is a sort of bootstrap method. You first value the (slightly) *wrong* option by backward induction from the *wrong* (effective) barrier to get (almost) *right* numerical values for the derivative of the *true* option at all times on its barrier. You then use these derivatives at each level of the tree in a first-order Taylor series on the barrier to obtain modified barrier values for the true option. Finally, you value the correct option by backward induction from the modified barrier."[4] The following is the algorithm from an interpolation point of view:[5]

1. Value a target option $T(S)$ (i.e., the security the barrier option knocks into—a security with zero value and that pays no rebate) and the barrier option $V(S)$ at each node on the tree with the barrier at the effective (upper) barrier. The computed value of $V(S)$ on this modified barrier is then $V(D)$, the value from an un-enhanced computation.
2. Value $T(S)$ and $V(S)$ with the specified barrier moved down to the modified (lower) barrier. The value of $V(S)$ on the modified barrier is then exactly $T(D)$, the value of the target option it knocks into.
3. Replace $V(D)$ on the lower barrier by the value $\tilde{V}(D)$ obtained by interpolating between $V(D)$ and $T(D)$ according the specified (true) barrier B's distance from the effective barrier and the modified barrier:

$$\tilde{V}(D) = \left(\frac{B-D}{U-D}\right)V(D) + \left(\frac{U-B}{U-D}\right)T(D)$$

4. Use backward induction from the modified barrier with $\tilde{V}(D)$ as the boundary values to find the value of $V(S)$ at all other nodes inside the barrier.

Figure 6.3 shows the modified barrier algorithm interpreted as an interpolation between the upper and lower barriers.

There are many variations of barrier options that are traded in the marketplace, including double-barrier, double-barrier step, and delayed-barrier options.

---

[4]Ibid., 11.
[5]Ibid., 14.

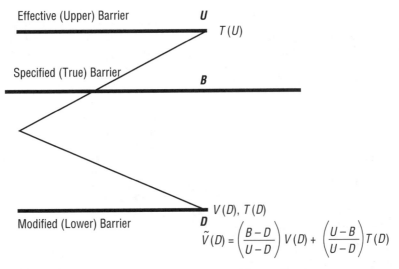

FIGURE 6.3   Interpolation between Upper and Lower Barriers

For a detailed analysis of the pricing (using numerical methods), structuring, and hedging of these barrier types, the interested reader should see Linetsky (1999), Linetsky and Davydov (2002), Schroder (2000), Rubinstein and Reiner (1991), Geman and Yor (1996), Rogers and Zane (1997), Taleb (1997), Hui (1997), and Sidenious (1998).

6.2   BARRIER OPTION IMPLEMENTATION

The following is an implementation for valuing an up-and-out American barrier put option where $S = 50$, $X = 51$, barrier = 56, rebate = 0, $r = 0.06$, $q = 0.01$, $\sigma = 0.20$, $T = 1$, and $N = 4$.

```
/*****************************************************************************
valueUpAndOutPut       : computes the value of an up and out barrier put option
                         with a Derman-Kani adjustment
[in]: double price     : asset price
      double strike    : strike price
      double barrier   : barrier price
      double rate      : risk-free interest rate
      double dividend  : dividend yield
      double vol       : volatility
      double rebate    : rebate if barrier is hit
      double T         : time to maturity
      int N            : number of time steps
      char exercise    : 'A'merican or 'E'uropean
```

```
[out]:   double       : value of up and out put
******************************************************************************/
double BarrierOption::valueUpAndOutPut(double price, double strike, double barrier,
  double rate, double dividend, double vol, double rebate, double T, int N, char
  exercise)
{
  int i, j;                              // for counters
  double pd;                             // down probability
  double pm;                             // middle probability
  double pu;                             // up probability
  double S[120][100];                    // stores stock prices
  double p[120][100];                    // put prices
  double up = 0.0;                       // up movement
  double down = 0.0;                     // down movement
  double dt = T/N;                       // time step
  double drift = rate - dividend - vol*vol/2;   // drift rate
  double dx = vol*sqrt(3*dt);            // state step

  // compute risk neutral probabilities
  pu = sqrt(dt/12)*(drift/vol) + 0.16667;
  pd = -sqrt(dt/12)*(drift/vol) + 0.16667;
  pm = 0.666667;
  up = exp(dx);
  down = 1/up;

  // compute the stock price at each node
  for (i = N; i >= 0; i--)
  {
    for (j = -i; j <= i; j++)
    {
      S[i][j] = price*pow(up,j);
    }
  }
    // compute payoff at maturity
    for (j = N; j >= -N; j--)
    {
      if (S[N][j] < barrier)
        p[N][j] = strike - S[N][j];
      else
        p[N][j] = rebate;
    }

    // compute payoffs at all other time steps
    for (i=N-1; i >= 0; i--)
    {
      for (j=i; j >= -i; j--)
      {
        if (S[i][j] < barrier)
        {
          p[i][j] = exp(-rate*dt)*(pu*p[i+1][j+1] + pm*p[i+1][j] + pd*p[i+1][j-
            1]);
          if (exercise == 'A')
```

```
      p[i][j]= max(p[i][j],strike-S[i][j]);
    else
      p[i][j] = rebate;

    // Derman Kani adjustment
    if ((S[i][j] < barrier) && (S[i][j+1] >= barrier))
    {
      p[i][j] = (rebate-p[i][j])/(S[i][j+1] - S[i][j])*(barrier - S[i][j]);
    }
   }
  }
 }
 return p[0][0];
}
```

The price of the barrier option is approximately $2.91. Figure 6.4 shows the trinomial tree for the up-and-out barrier put.

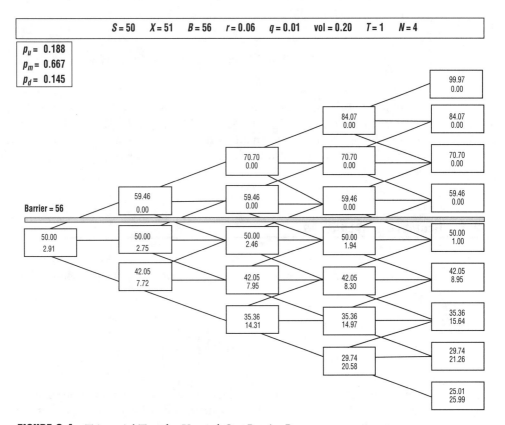

FIGURE 6.4   Trinomial Tree for Up-and-Out Barrier Put

6.3 ASIAN OPTIONS

An Asian option, also called an average price option, is an option that depends on the average price of the underlying security during the life of the option. Suppose the payoff at time T is a function $F(S_T, A_{t,T})$ of both the terminal stock price S_T and the average price between t and T: $A_{t,T}$. Then the risk-neutral price at time t of this path-dependent option can be written as an expectation:

$$f(S, t) = e^{-r\tau} E_{t,S}^Q \big[F(S_T, A_T) \big]$$

$$= e^{-r\tau} \int_0^\infty \int_0^\infty F(S_T, A_{t,T}) p^Q(S_T, A_{t,T}, T \mid S, t) dS_T dA_{t,T}$$

where $p^Q(S_T, A_{t,T}, T \mid S, t)$ is a joint (risk-neutral) probability density of the terminal stock price and the average price over $[t, T]$ conditional on the initial stock price at time t. If the payoff depends only on the average price and not on S_T (as in the average price options), then

$$f(S, t) = e^{-r\tau} \int_0^\infty F(A_{t,T}) p^Q(A_{t,T}, T \mid S, t) dA_{t,T} \qquad (6.8)$$

where $p^Q(A_{t,T}, T \mid S, t)$ is a density of the average price conditional on S at t. Thus, our job is to find $p^Q(S_T, A_{t,T}, T \mid S, t)$ and $p^Q(A_{t,T}, T \mid S, t)$. This can be found by employing the theory of Brownian motion. We will be interested only in pricing average price calls and puts, so we need only the density $p^Q(A_{t,T}, T \mid S, t)$ to derive the pricing formulas.

6.4 GEOMETRIC AVERAGING

Suppose the averaging is continuous and geometric. Define the geometric average as:

$$G_T = \left(\prod_{i=1}^N S_{t_i} \right)^{1/N} \qquad (6.9)$$

The geometric average of the product of lognormal random variables is also lognormal. Thus, $p^Q(A_{t,T}, T \mid S, t)$ is a lognormal density. It is quite easy to find the parameters of the lognormal density based on stochastic processes theory.

PROPOSITION. $p^Q(A_{t,T}, T \mid S)$ is a lognormal density of the Black-Scholes form:

$$p^Q(A_{t,T}, T \mid S, t)dA_{t,T} = \frac{1}{\sqrt{2\pi\sigma_A^2\tau}} \exp\left\{-\frac{\left(\ln\left(\frac{S_T}{S}\right) - \mu_A\tau\right)^2}{2\sigma_A^2\tau}\right\} \frac{dA_{t,T}}{A_{t,T}} \qquad (6.10)$$

where $\mu_A = r - q_A - \sigma_A^2/2$. The volatility of the continuous geometric average is

$$\sigma_A = \sigma/\sqrt{3}$$

and the risk-neutral drift of the continuous geometric average is

$$r - q_A = \frac{1}{2}\left(r - q - \frac{\sigma^2}{6}\right)$$

where q is the dividend yield on the underlying security. We can use the Black-Scholes formulas to price geometric average price calls and puts where we need to substitute

$$\sigma_A = \sigma/\sqrt{3}$$

for the volatility of the average and

$$q_A = \frac{1}{2}(r + q + \frac{\sigma^2}{6})$$

for the effective dividend yield on the geometric average price. This analytic formula is used if the averaging is continuous. If the averaging is taken at certain fixing dates, then the formula becomes:

$$G_{Geo\_Ave} = e^{-rT}\left(e^{(a+\frac{1}{2}b)}N(d_1) - XN(d_1 - \sqrt{b})\right) \qquad (6.11)$$

where

$$a = \ln(G_t) + \frac{N-j}{N}(\ln(S) + \mu(t_{j+1} - t) + \frac{1}{2}\mu(T - t_{j+1}))$$

$$b = \frac{(N-j)^2}{N^2}\sigma^2(t_{j+1} - t) + \frac{\sigma^2(T - t_{j+1})}{6N^2}(N-j)(2(N-j)-1)$$

$$\mu = r - q - \frac{1}{2}\sigma^2$$

$$d_1 = \frac{a + b - \ln(X)}{\sqrt{b}}$$

where G_t is the current geometric average and j is the last known fixed date.[6]

---

[6]Clewlow and Strickland (1998a), 118–119.

6.5   ARITHMETIC AVERAGING

In practice, most average price options are priced using arithmetic averaging, not geometric averaging. This creates a problem: An arithmetic average of a set of lognormal random variables is not itself lognormal. This distribution is quite complicated as it is expressed through Bessel functions (Geman-Yor formulas). However, there exists a rather accurate approximation. We can approximate this complicated distribution by a lognormal distribution, and match the first two moments of the complicated exact distribution and an approximating lognormal distribution. The resulting approximation, known as the Turnbull-Wakeman approximation, is quite accurate.

The first moment of the continuous arithmetic average price distribution between t and T is $M_1 S$ where[7]

$$M_1 = \frac{e^{(r-q)\tau} - 1}{(r-q)\tau}$$

The second moment of the continuous arithmetic average is $M_2 S^2$ where

$$M_2 = \frac{2e^{(2(r-q)+\sigma^2)\tau}}{(r-q+\sigma^2)(2(r-q)+\sigma^2)\tau^2} + \frac{2}{(r-q)\tau^2}\left(\frac{1}{2(r-q)+\sigma^2} - \frac{e^{(r-q)\tau}}{(r-q+\sigma^2)} \right)$$

Equating the first two moments of the lognormal distribution yields:

$$e^{(r-q_A)}S = M_1 S$$

and

$$e^{(2(r-q)+\sigma_A^2)\tau} S = M_2 S^2$$

Solving for the effective volatility σ_A and the dividend yield q_A of the arithmetic average yields:

$$q_A = r - \frac{\ln M_1}{\tau} \tag{6.12}$$

and

$$\sigma_A^2 = \frac{\ln M_2}{\tau} - 2(r - q_A) \tag{6.13}$$

---

[7]Hull, J. (1997), 466.

We can use the Black-Scholes formula to price Asian average price calls and puts, where you use the effective average rate volatility σ_A and dividend yield q_A of the average. We have assumed that the average is taken continuously. In practice, the average is taken discretely based on daily, weekly, or monthly closing prices. For daily averaging, continuous averaging provides a good approximation. For weekly and monthly averaging, one needs to develop formulas for discrete averaging.

6.6 SEASONED ASIAN OPTIONS

We need to price an Asian option at time t^* inside the averaging interval $[t, T]$ (in season). The averaging period is composed of two periods: $\tau_1 = t^* - t$ (the time period where prices have already been observed) and $\tau_2 = T - t^*$ (the time period in the future). The average $A_{t,T}$ can be represented as the sum of two averages:

$$A_{t,T} = \frac{A_{t,t^*}\tau_1 + A_{t^*,T}\tau_2}{\tau_1 + \tau_2}$$

Then the payoff for an Asian option can be represented as follows:

$$\max(A_{t,T} - X,\ 0) = \max\left(\frac{A_{t,t^*}\tau_1 + A_{t^*,T}\tau_2}{\tau_1 + \tau_2} - X,\ 0\right) = \alpha\max(A_{t,t^*} - X^*,\ 0) \quad (6.14)$$

where the multiplier and adjusted strike are

$$\alpha = \frac{\tau_2}{\tau_1 + \tau_2} \text{ and } X^* = \frac{\tau_1 + \tau_2}{\tau_2}X - \frac{\tau_1}{\tau_2}A_{t,t^*}$$

Thus, we can price a seasoned Asian option in the same manner as newly written Asian options using the modified Black-Scholes formula where

$$A_{t,t^*} = \frac{1}{N}\sum_{i=1}^{N}S_i^k,\ k = 1,\ \ldots,\ M$$

for the underlying asset price and X^* for the strike, and then we multiply the value by α.

As shown in section 2.8, we can also value Asian options using Monte Carlo simulation. For a comparison of analytical and Monte Carlo methods for pricing Asian options see Fu, Madan, and Wang (1999). See also Geman and Yor (1992),

Kemma and Vorst (1990), Levy (1990), and Boyle (1991) for a more detailed discussion for pricing Asian options.

6.7   LOOKBACK OPTIONS

Lookback options are standard calls or puts, except that either the final asset price or the strike price is set equal to the minimum or maximum asset price observed on one of a set of predetermined fixing dates t_i, $i = 1, \ldots , N$. Denote

$$m_{t,T} = \min_{t^* \in [t, T]} S(t^*) = S_{\min} : \text{minimum price achieved over } [t, T]$$

and

$$M_{t,T} = \max_{t^* \in [t, T]} S(t^*) = S_{\max} : \text{maximum price achieved over } [t, T]$$

A fixed-strike lookback call option written at time t gives its holder the right, but not the obligation, to buy the underlying asset at time T, $T > t$, at the minimum price reached on one of the fixing dates, t_i, $i = 1, \ldots , N$, between the contract inception t and the option expiration T. The payoff is:

$$\max(m_{t,T} - X, 0) \tag{6.15}$$

A floating-strike lookback call allows the holder to purchase the stock at the minimum price achieved on any of the fixing dates during the lifetime of the option. Thus the payoff is:

$$\max(S_T - m_{t,T}, 0) = S_T - m_{t,T} \geq 0 \tag{6.16}$$

A fixed-strike lookback put option gives the holder the right, but not the obligation, to sell the underlying asset at time T, $T > t$, at the minimum price reached on one of the fixing dates, t_i, $i = 1, \ldots , N$, between the contract inception t and the option expiration T. The payoff is:

$$\max(X - m_{t,T}, 0) \tag{6.17}$$

A floating-strike lookback put option gives the holder the right, but not the obligation, to sell the underlying asset for the maximum price achieved at any of the fixing dates from the contract inception t to contract expiration T. The payoff to the holder is the difference between the maximum price between t and T and the price at expiration:

$$\max(M_{t,T} - S_T, 0) = M_{t,T} - S_T \geq 0 \qquad (6.18)$$

Suppose a lookback expiring at T was written at inception time t_0. We can price (mark to market) at some time t, $t_0 < t < T$. The risk-neutral expectations for seasoned floating-strike lookback calls and puts are:

$$C_{Lookback}(S, S_{min}, t) = S - e^{-r\tau}E_{t,S_{min}}^Q[m_{t_0,T}]$$

and

$$P_{Lookback}(S, S_{max}, t) = e^{-r\tau}E_{t,S_{max}}^Q[M_{t_0,T}] - S$$

We need to calculate the mean of the maximum and minimum prices, both random variables, of the risk-neutral process between t_0 and T. Once the probability densities for these random variables are calculated, the expectations can be taken and analytical formulas for floating-strike lookback calls and puts can be derived. It turns out that the closed-form solution for the call is:

$$C_{Lookback}(S, S_{min}, t) = C(S, t \mid S_{min}, T) + \frac{\sigma^2}{2(r-q)}\left\{e^{-r\tau}S_{min}\left(\frac{S_{min}}{S}\right)^{\gamma}N(d) - e^{-q\tau}SN(-d_1)\right\} (6.19)$$

where $C(S, t \mid S_{min}, T) = e^{-q\tau}SN(d_1) - e^{-r\tau}S_{min}N(d_2)$,

$$d_2 = \frac{\ln\left(\frac{S}{S_{min}}\right) + \mu\tau}{\sigma\sqrt{\tau}}, \quad d_1 = d_2 + \sigma\sqrt{\tau}, \quad d = \frac{\ln\left(\frac{S_{min}}{S}\right) + \mu\tau}{\sigma\sqrt{\tau}}, \quad \mu = r - q - \frac{\sigma^2}{2}, \quad \text{and } \gamma = \frac{2\mu}{\sigma^2}$$

Note that if pricing a newly written lookback call at contract inception, the initial stock price, S_0, is used in place of S_{min}.

We can price a floating-strike lookback put similarly:

$$P_{Lookback}(S, S_{max}, t) = P(S, t \mid S_{min}, T) + \frac{\sigma^2}{2(r-q)}\left\{e^{-q\tau}SN(d_1) - e^{-r\tau}S_{max}\left(\frac{S_{max}}{S}\right)^{\gamma}N(d)\right\} (6.20)$$

where $P(S, t \mid S_{max}, T) = e^{-r\tau}S_{max}N(-d_2) - e^{-q\tau}SN(-d_1)$,

$$d_2 = \frac{\ln\left(\dfrac{S}{S_{max}}\right) + \mu\tau}{\sigma\sqrt{\tau}}, \; d_1 = d_2 + \sigma\sqrt{\tau}, \; d = \frac{\ln\left(\dfrac{S_{max}}{S}\right) + \mu\tau}{\sigma\sqrt{\tau}},$$

$$\mu = r - q - \frac{\sigma^2}{2}, \text{ and } \gamma = \frac{2\mu}{\sigma^2}$$

If pricing a newly written lookback put at contract inception, the initial stock price, S_0, is substituted in place of S_{max}.

Lookbacks can also be priced numerically by two-state variable binomial or trinomial trees. We will illustrate by example of a floating-strike lookback put option. Pricing a lookback in a trinomial tree is similar to pricing a vanilla (plain) option. We use backward induction. However, when we step back through the tree, we have to deal with the possibility of more than one maximum asset price at each node. We store the maximum asset prices achievable on paths leading to the node. At each interior node, we only store two maximum values. For each node (i, j) in the upper half of the tree, the maxima are the current stock price as well as the maximum reached at node $(i - 1, j + 1)$. We don't need to store $(i - 1, j)$ since it is the same as (i, j). For each node in the center or lower half of the tree, we store the value of the initial asset price (since it is greater than or equal to all of the lower asset prices at each of nodes as well as the maximum reached at $(i - 1, j + 1)$). Once we compute the maximum values at each node, we can work backward to compute the option values for each maximum value by taking the discounted expected value of the option (risk-neutral pricing):

$$f_{i,j} = e^{-r\Delta t}(p_u f_{i+1, j+1} + p_m f_{i+1, j} + p_d f_{i+1, j-1})$$

If the lookback is American, early exercise is considered by comparing the discounted expected value to the intrinsic value, then taking the higher of both values. We note that assuming we store the maximum values in ascending order at each node, the first maximum value will be computed by taking the discounted value of the first maximum value stored at nodes $(i + 1, j + 1)$ and $(i + 1, j)$, but we use the second maximum value at $(i, j - 1)$ since it is smaller than this value. The second maximum value is computed by taking the discounted value of the first maximum value at node $(i, j + 1)$ and the second (higher) maximum values stored at nodes (i, j) and $(i, j + 1)$. Working backward in this manner will give us the value at the first node.

6.8   IMPLEMENTATION OF FLOATING LOOKBACK OPTION

The following is an implementation of a floating lookback put option with $S = 50$, $\sigma = 0.40$, $r = 0.10$, $q = 0$, and $T = 0.25$ (3 months), $N = 3$ (time steps), so that $\Delta t = 0.08333$.

```
/********************************************************************************
calcLookBackPutFloatStrike : computes the value of a floating lookback put
[in]   double price    : asset price
       double rate      : risk-free interest rate
       double div       : dividend yield
       double vol       : volatility
       double T         : time to maturity
       int N            : number of time steps
       char exercise    : 'A'merican or 'E'uropean
[out] double           : value of up and out put
********************************************************************************/
double LookBackOption::calcLookBackPutFloatStrike(double price, double vol, double
   rate, double div, double T, int N, char exercise)
{
   int i, j;
   double pd;                       // down probability
   double pm;                       // middle probability
   double pu;                       // up probability
   double S[100][100];              // stock price at node i, j

   struct Node                      // structure at node i, j
   {
   double maxima[2];                // stores current and previous maximum prices
   double optionPrice[2];           // stores current and previous option prices for
                                    // max prices
   double intrinsicValue;           // intrinsic option value at node
   double stockPrice;               // stock price at node
   } node[20][20];

   double up = 0.0;                 // up movement
   double down = 0.0;               // down movement
   double drift = 0.0;              // drift
   double dx = 0.0;                 // state space
   double dt = T/N;                 // time step
   drift = rate - div - vol*vol/2;

   pu = 0.33333 + (drift/vol)*sqrt(dt/6);
   pd = 0.33333 - (drift/vol)*sqrt(dt/6);
   pm = 0.33333;
   up = exp(vol*sqrt(3*dt/2));
   down = 1/up;

   // compute stock price at each node
   for (i = N; i >= 0; i--)
```

```
{
  for (j = -i; j <= i; j++)
  {
    S[i][j] = price*pow(up,j);
  }
}


// initialize first node
node[0][0].stockPrice = price;
node[0][0].maxima[0]  = price;
node[0][0].maxima[1]  = price;


// use forward induction to calculate maxima at each node
for (i = 1; i <= N; i++)
{
  for (j = -i; j <= i; j++)
  {
    node[i][j].stockPrice = S[i][j];
    if (j == i)
    {
      node[i][j].maxima[0] = node[i][j].stockPrice;
    }
    else if (j == -i)
    {
      node[i][j].maxima[0] = node[0][0].stockPrice;
    }
    else if ((j == i-1) || (j == -i+1))
    {
      node[i][j].maxima[0] = node[i-1][j].maxima[0];
      node[i][j].maxima[1] = node[i-1][j].maxima[0];
    }
    else if (j == i-2)
    {
      node[i][j].maxima[0] = node[i-1][j].maxima[0];
      node[i][j].maxima[1] = node[i-1][j+1].maxima[0];
    }
    else if (j == -i+2)
    {
      node[i][j].maxima[0] = node[i-1][j].maxima[0];
      node[i][j].maxima[1] = node[i-1][j+1].maxima[1];
    }
    else
    {
      node[i][j].maxima[0] = node[i-1][j].maxima[0];
      node[i][j].maxima[1] = node[i-1][j+1].maxima[1];
    }
  }
}

for (j = N; j >= -N; j--)
```

```
{
  node[N][j].optionPrice[0] = max(node[N][j].maxima[0] - S[N][j],0);
  node[N][j].optionPrice[1] = max(node[N][j].maxima[1] - S[N][j],0);
}



// use backwards induction to price lookback option
for (i=N-1; i >= 0; i--)
{
  for (j = i; j >= -i; j--)
  {
    if (i == j)
    {
      node[i][j].optionPrice[0]=exp(rate*dt)*(pu*(node[i+1][j+1].optionPrice[0
        ])
        + pm*(node[i+1][j].optionPrice[0]) + pd*(node[i+1] [j-
          1].optionPrice[1]));


      node[i][j].optionPrice[1] = exp(-rate*dt)*(pu*(node[i+1][j+1].option
        Price[0]) + pm*(node[i+1][j].optionPrice[1]) + pd*(node[i+1]
        [j-1].optionPrice[1]));
    }
    else if (i == -j)
    {
      node[i][j].optionPrice[0] = exp(-rate*dt)*
        (pu*(node[i+1][j+1].optionPrice[1])
        + pm*(node[i+1][j].optionPrice[0]) + pd*(node[i+1] [j-
          1].optionPrice[0]));


      node[i][j].optionPrice[1] = exp(-rate*dt)*(pu*(node[i+1][j+1].option
        Price[1]) + pm*(node[i+1][j].optionPrice[0]) + pd*(node[i+1]
        [j-1].optionPrice[0]));
    }
    else if (j == 0)
    {
      node[i][j].optionPrice[0] = exp(-rate*dt)*(pu*(node[i+1][j+1].option
        Price[1]) + pm*(node[i+1][j].optionPrice[0]) + pd*(node[i+1]
        [j-1].optionPrice[0]));


      node[i][j].optionPrice[1] = exp(-rate*dt)* (pu*(node[i+1][j+1].option
        Price[1]) + pm*(node[i+1][j].optionPrice[1]) + pd*(node[i+1]
        [j-1].optionPrice[1]));
    }
    else
    {
      node[i][j].optionPrice[0] = exp(-rate*dt)*(pu*(node[i+1][j+1].option
        Price[1]) + pm*(node[i+1][j].optionPrice[0]) + pd*(node[i+1]
        [j-1].optionPrice[0]));
```

```
        node[i][j].optionPrice[1] = exp(-rate*dt)*(pu*(node[i+1][j+1].option
          Price[1]) + pm*(node[i+1][j].optionPrice[0]) + pd*(node[i+1]
          [j-1].optionPrice[1]));
      }


      // if stock price is the same for first and second stock prices, use higher
      // option price
      if (node[i][j].maxima[0] == node[i][j].maxima[1])
        node[i][j].optionPrice[0] =
          max(node[i][j].optionPrice[0],node[i][j].optionPrice[1]);


      // check for early exercise
      if (exercise == 'A')
      {
        node[i][j].intrinsicValue = node[i][j].maxima[0] - S[i][j];
        node[i][j].optionPrice[0] =
          max(node[i][j].optionPrice[0],node[i][j].intrinsicValue);


        node[i][j].intrinsicValue = node[i][j].maxima[1] - S[i][j];
        node[i][j].optionPrice[1] =
          max(node[i][j].optionPrice[1],node[i][j].intrinsicValue);
      }
    }
  }
  return node[0][0].optionPrice[0];
}
```

The value of the floating lookback put option is \$7.57 using

$$\lambda = \sqrt{3}$$

Figure 6.5 shows the trinomial tree generated.

6.9   IMPLEMENTATION OF FIXED LOOKBACK OPTION

The following is an implementation of an ATM European fixed-strike lookback put with the same parameters as the floating-strike lookback put discussed in the preceding section.

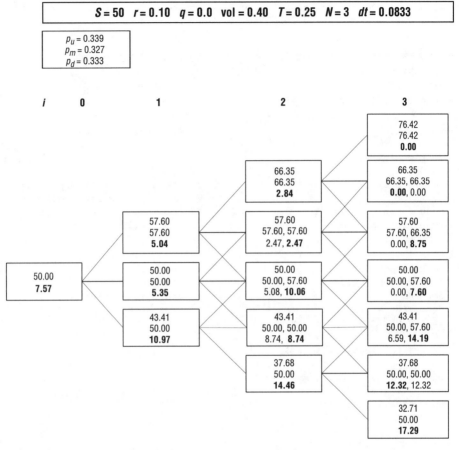

$S = 50$ $r = 0.10$ $q = 0.0$ vol $= 0.40$ $T = 0.25$ $N = 3$ $dt = 0.0833$

FIGURE 6.5   Trinomial Tree for Floating-Strike Lookback Put Option

```
/*************************************************************************************
calcLookBackPutFixedStrike : This function computes the value of a floating lookback
                             put
[in]   double price      : asset price
       double strike     : strike price
       double barrier    : barrier price
       double rate       : risk-free interest rate
       double div        : dividend yield
       double vol        : volatility
       double T          : time to maturity
       int N             : number of time steps
       char exercise     : 'A'merican or 'E'uropean
[out] double             : value of up and out put
*************************************************************************************/
```

```
double LookbackOption::calcLookBackPutFixedStrike(double price, double strike,
  double vol, double rate,double div, double T, int N, char exercise)
{
  int i, j;
  double pd;                             // down probability
  double pm;                             // middle probability
  double pu;                             // up probability
  double S[100][100];                    // stock price at node i,j

  struct Node                            // structure of node i,j
  {
    double minima[2];                    // stores current and previous minimum
                                         // prices
    double optionPrice[2];               // stores current and previous option
                                         // prices for minimum prices
    double intrinsicValue;               // intrinsic value of option
    double stockPrice;                   // stock price at node
    } node[20][20];

    double up = 0.0;                     // up movement
    double down = 0.0;                   // down movement
    double dx = 0.0;                     // state space step
    double dt = T/N;                     // time step
    double drift = rate - div - vol*vol/2; // drift

    // use for lambda = sqrt(3/2)
    pu = 0.33333 + (drift/vol)*sqrt(dt/6);
    pd = 0.33333 - (drift/vol)*sqrt(dt/6);
    pm = 0.33333;
    up = exp(vol*sqrt(3*dt/2));
    down = 1/up;

    // compute stock prices at each node
    for (i = N; i >= 0; i--)
    {
      for (j = -i; j <= i; j++)
      {
        S[i][j] = price*pow(up,j);
      }
    }

    // initialize first node
    node[0][0].stockPrice = price;
    node[0][0].minima[0] = price;

    // use forward induction to calculate maxima at each node
    for (i = 1; i <= N; i++)
    {
      for (j = -i; j <= i; j++)
      {
        node[i][j].stockPrice = S[i][j];
```

```
    if ((i == 1) && (j != -1))                    // nodes at time step 1 only
                                                  // have one minimum
    {
      node[i][j].minima[0] = node[0][0].stockPrice;
      node[i][j].minima[1] = 0;                   // dummy place holder
    }
    else if (j == i) // edge nodes only have one minimum
    {
      node[i][j].minima[0] = node[0][0].stockPrice;
      node[i][j].minima[1] = 0;                   // dummy place holder
    }
    else if ((j == -i) && (i != N))               // edge nodes only have one
                                                  // minimum
    {
      node[i][j].minima[0] = node[i][j].stockPrice;
      node[i][j].minima[1] = 0;
    }
    else if ((j == -i) && (i == N))
    {
      node[i][j].minima[0] = node[i-1][j+1].stockPrice;
      node[i][j].minima[1] = 0;                   // dummy place holder
    }
    else if (j == -i+1)
    {
      node[i][j].minima[0] = node[i-1][j].minima[0];
      node[i][j].minima[1] = node[i][j].stockPrice;
    }
    else
    {
      node[i][j].minima[0] = node[i-1][j-1].minima[0];
      node[i][j].minima[1] = node[i-1][j].minima[0];
    }
  }
}


// compute payoffs at final node
for (j = N; j >= -N; j--)
{
  node[N][j].optionPrice[0] = max(strike - node[N][j].minima[0],0);
  node[N][j].optionPrice[1] = max(strike - node[N][j].minima[1],0);
}


//use backwards induction to price lookback option
for (i=N-1; i >= 0; i--)
{
  for (j = i; j >= -i; j--)
  {
    node[i][j].optionPrice[0] = exp(-rate*dt)*(pu*(node[i+1][j+1].option
      Price[0])+ pm*(node[i+1][j].optionPrice[0]) + pd*(node[i+1]
      [j-1].optionPrice[0]));
```

```
      node[i][j].optionPrice[1] = exp(-rate*dt)*(pu*(node[i+1][j+1].option
        Price[0])+ pm*(node[i+1][j].optionPrice[0]) + pd*(node[i+1]
        [j-1].optionPrice[1]));

      if (exercise == 'A')
      {
        node[i][j].intrinsicValue = strike - node[i][j].minima[0];
        node[i][j].optionPrice[0] =
          max(node[i][j].optionPrice[0],node[i][j].intrinsicValue);

        node[i][j].intrinsicValue = strike - node[i][j].minima[1];
        node[i][j].optionPrice[1] =
          max(node[i][j].optionPrice[1],node[i][j].intrinsicValue);
      }
    }
  }

  return node[0][0].optionPrice[0];
}
```

The value of the fixed-strike lookback put option is \$7.45 using

$$\lambda = \sqrt{3/2}$$

Figure 6.6 shows the trinomial tree generated using

$$\lambda = \sqrt{3/2}$$

For a more detailed discussion of lookback options, see Goldman, Sosin, and Gatto (1979) (who first introduced lookback options), Conze and Viswanathan (1991), and Dewynne and Wilmott (1993). For variations of lookbacks such as double lookbacks, see He, Keirstead, and Rebholz (1998). For a discussion of pricing lookbacks (and barrier options) using a constant elasticity of variance process, see Boyle and Tian (1999).

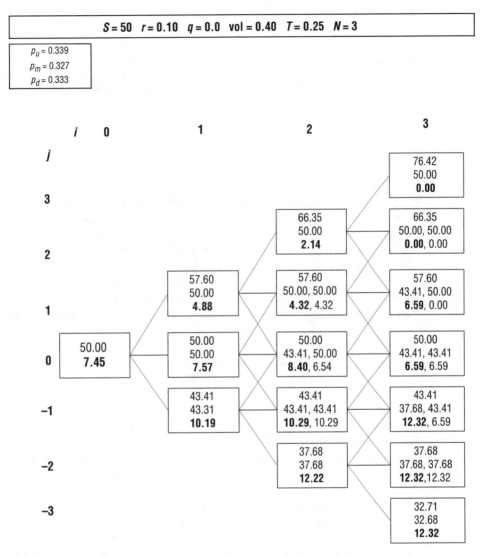

FIGURE 6.6   Trinomial Tree for Fixed-Strike Lookback Put Option

CHAPTER 7

Stochastic Volatility

Volatility is the one unobservable factor affecting option prices. Modeling volatility structures is important for practitioners and traders since it can capture observable skews and smirks where low-strike options are seen to exhibit higher implied volatilities than higher-strike options. Volatility structures in the market seen to exhibit such skews and smirks give traders an indication of the relative liquidity and degree of riskiness placed by the marketplace on various strikes and maturities. There may be "vol" arbitrage opportunities if implied volatilities from observable market prices differ from volatilities implied from calibrated models. The focus of this chapter is to discuss various techniques for measuring and extracting implied volatilities from market option prices. We initially examine deterministic (constant) volatility and then discuss how to model stochastic volatility—nondeterministic parametric forms that can be used in diffusion processes to capture observable market volatility structures.

In section 7.1, we discuss implied volatility and how to compute it using an iterative numerical method like Newton-Raphson. In section 7.2, volatility skews and smiles are discussed. In section 7.3, empirical explanations are given for why such skews are observed. In section 7.4, we discuss constructing and fitting implied volatility surfaces from market data using numerical procedures like nonparametric methods. In section 7.5, one-factor parametric volatility structures are discussed. In section 7.6, constant elasticity variance (CEV) models are discussed for modeling volatility structures. In section 7.7, we discuss recovering implied "vol" surfaces. In section 7.8, we discuss an approach by Brigo and Mercurio for constructing local volatility surfaces. In section 7.9, we discuss jump-diffusion models for modeling volatility. In section 7.10, two-factor parametric volatility structures are examined. In two-factor models, correlation is incorporated to capture co-movements in factors not captured by one-factor models. Finally, in section 7.11, we discuss the important topic of hedging with stochastic volatility.

7.1   IMPLIED VOLATILITY

The Black-Scholes model assumes that volatility, often referred to as "vol" by practitioners, is constant. We have assumed up to this point that asset prices follow a lognormal diffusion process under the risk-neutral measure Q with constant volatility. This is not a realistic assumption as it incorrectly implies (1) historical volatility estimated from time series data is constant over time; (2) all options with different strikes and maturities must trade at the same implied volatilities; and (3) the risk-neutral probability distributions of future asset prices are lognormal. To correct for this serious problem, practitioners model volatility as a stochastic factor of asset prices and often model volatility as following its own diffusion process with drift and diffusion parameters.

Consider a call expiring at time T with strike price X. Suppose C_{market} is a market quote for the call. The Black-Scholes model provides a fair value for this call $C_{BS}(\sigma)$, which depends on the historical volatility estimate. We can estimate the historical volatility as follows. Suppose we have a time series of daily price data for N days: S_i, $i = 1, 2, \ldots, N$. We first calculate the time series of N logarithmic returns:

$$u_i = \ln\left(\frac{S_i}{S_{i-1}}\right) \quad i = 1, 2, \ldots, N \tag{7.1}$$

where u_i is the continuously compounded (not annualized) return in the ith interval. The usual unbiased estimate of volatility $\hat{\sigma}$ is give by

$$\hat{\sigma}^2 \Delta t = \frac{1}{N-1} \sum_{i=1}^{N} (u_i - \bar{u})^2 \tag{7.2}$$

where $\bar{u}$ the mean of the u_i's and Δt is the interval between observations. Implied volatility $\sigma^{implied}$ is such a value of the volatility parameter σ that the Black-Scholes price *matches* the observed price:

$$C_{BS}(\sigma^{implied}) = C_{market} \tag{7.3}$$

Since the Black-Scholes price is a known function of (constant) volatility, this equation can be inverted to find $\sigma^{implied}$. The closed-form solution to this problem does not exist, but it can be solved using the Newton-Raphson numerical procedure: Initially, make an initial guess σ_0 (say, 10 percent) of the volatility. Second, estimate σ_1 by using the Newton-Raphson equation, which is a first-order Taylor approximation of $C_{BS}(\sigma)$:

$$\sigma_1 = \sigma_0 - \frac{C_{BS}(\sigma_1) - C_{market}}{\kappa_{BS}(\sigma_1)}$$

where

$$\kappa_{BS}(\sigma_1) = \frac{\partial C_{BS}(\sigma_1)}{\partial \sigma}$$

is the Greek hedge statistic vega (kappa). We then use σ_1 in the next iteration to find σ_2. We continue the following iteration at step i:

$$\sigma_{i+1} = \sigma_i - \frac{C_{BS}(\sigma_i) - C_{market}}{\kappa_{BS}(\sigma_i)} \tag{7.4}$$

iteratively, until the desired accuracy is reached:

$$|C_{market} - C(\sigma_{i+1})| \le \varepsilon \tag{7.5}$$

where epsilon, ε, is a very small value such as 0.0001.

The Newton-Raphson method can easily be used for European options where the analytical formula for the option price is available. For American or exotic options, one can use the bisection method that does not require knowing vega. The procedure works as follows:

Step 1: Pick two values for the volatility, σ_H and σ_L, so that σ_H is clearly above the true implied vol and σ_L is clearly below (i.e., 1 percent and 100 percent), and calculate two option prices C_H and C_L corresponding to these vols. The market price should be somewhere in between.

Step 2: Suppose σ_H and σ_L and prices C_H and C_L are from the previous step. Then calculate:

$$\sigma_{i+1} = \sigma_L + (C_{market} - C_L)\frac{\sigma_H - \sigma_L}{C_H - C_L} \tag{7.6}$$

Replace σ_L with σ_{i+1} if $C(\sigma_{i+1}) < C_{market}$, or else replace σ_H with σ_{i+1} if $C(\sigma_{i+1}) > C_{market}$. This is continued until the desired accuracy is achieved: $|C_{market} - C(\sigma_{i+1})| \le \varepsilon$.

In practice, traders often use implied vols inferred from quoted option prices in favor of historical volatility estimated from historical time series data. In fact, in the over-the-counter (OTC) options market, option prices are quoted by their implied volatility rather than the option price itself.

7.2   VOLATILITY SKEWS AND SMILES

It is an empirical fact that implied volatility is not constant across different strikes and maturities. Suppose we have a listing of all market option quotes. We can observe traded strikes, X_j, traded maturities, T_j, and the current quoted market price for a call with maturity T_i and strike X_j, $C_{ij}(S, t) = C(S, t; X_j, T_j)$. Suppose we calculate an implied volatility for each of these calls $\sigma_{ij}^{implied}$. If the Black-Scholes model were correct, then implied volatilities for all options with different strikes and maturities would be equal. However, an empirical fact is that implied vols are different

TABLE 7.1   IBM Call Chain on September 20, 2002

Jan 03	35.00	40.50	Jan 03	95.00	0.30
Jan 03	40.00	25.30	Jan 03	100.00	0.20
Jan 03	45.00	29.50	Jan 03	105.00	0.05
Jan 03	50.00	16.80	Jan 03	110.00	0.10
Jan 03	55.00	12.60	Jan 03	115.00	0.15
Jan 03	60.00	9.30	Jan 03	120.00	0.15
Jan 03	65.00	6.40	Jan 03	125.00	0.10
Jan 03	70.00	4.10	Jan 03	130.00	0.10
Jan 03	75.00	2.60	Jan 03	140.00	0.10
Jan 03	80.00	1.50	Jan 03	150.00	0.05
Jan 03	85.00	0.90	Jan 03	155.00	0.00
Jan 03	90.00	0.50	Jan 03	160.00	0.05

for all i and j. Volatility changes with both strike and maturity, known as the *volatility smile* or *smirk* and the *term structure of volatility*, respectively. Consider the option chain in Table 7.1 of IBM stock taken on September 20, 2002.

We can compute the volatility smile for January 2003 contracts on Friday, September 20, 2002, using the stock price of IBM, $S = 63.92$, $T = 4/12 = 0.333$, the three-month Treasury bill rate $r = 1.64$ percent, the dividend yield $q = 0.6$ percent, and the market option prices C_j for different strikes X_j, which are given in the chain.

Figure 7.1 shows the implied volatility curve generated from the option chain whose values are shown in Table 7.1. Notice that the curve is a shaped like a smile. The minimum implied volatility falls roughly around the ATM strike. The curve falls then rises as the strike prices increases beyond the ATM strike.

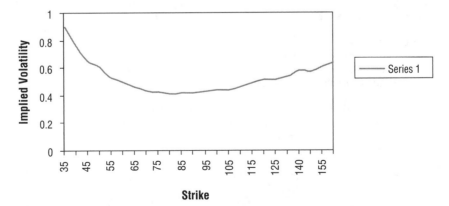

FIGURE 7.1   Implied Volatility Curve of IBM January 2003 Calls Computed on September 20, 2002

The following is an implementation that reads the option chain information from a file, *optionData.txt*, and computes the implied vols. The volatility smile curve is generated in Excel using the strikes and their corresponding implied vols using the Newton-Raphson method.

```
void main()
{
  OptionCalc option;                        // option object
  vector<double> prices;                    // vector of option prices
  vector<int> strikes;                      // vector of strikes
  char buffer[100];                         // buffer for line read
  char dataBuffer[100];                     // stores current data string read
  char *str = NULL;                         // pointer to data string
  const char *file = "optionData.txt";      // file with option chain info
  ifstream fin;                             // input file stream

  fin.clear();
  fin.open(file);

  if (fin.good())
  {
    while (!fin.eof())
    {
      // read in one line at a time
      fin.getline(buffer,sizeof(buffer)/sizeof(buffer[0]));
      istrstream str1(buffer);

      // Get data
      str1 >> dataBuffer;                    // read data from file
      while (!str1.eof())
      {
        // read in contract maturity, strike, and price
        str1 >> dataBuffer;                  // read option maturity month
        str1 >> dataBuffer;                  // read option maturity year

        str1 >> dataBuffer;                  // read option maturity strike
        // convert strike char* data to integers
        // and add to strike vector
        strikes.push_back(atoi(dataBuffer));

        str1 >> dataBuffer;                  // read option  market price
        // convert option price char* data to floats
        // and add to strike vector
        prices.push_back(atof(dataBuffer));
      }
      buffer[strlen(buffer) + 1] = '\0';
    }
  }
  else
  {
```

```
      cout << "File not good!" << "\n";
  }
  // close file
  fin.close();
  // calculate implied vols
  option.calcImpliedVols(63.92,prices,strikes,0.0164,0.006,0.3333,'C');
}
```

The following is the implementation of the *calcImpliedVols* method:

```
/*********************************************************************************
calcImpliedVols:               : calculates implied volatilities
[in]:  double price            : price of the stock
       vector<double> opPrices  : vector of option prices
       vector<double> strikes   : vector of strike prices
       double rate              : risk-free rate
       double dividend          : dividend yield
       double T                 : time to maturity (in years)
       char type                : option type (call or put)
[out]: map of implied volatilities (key is strike price)
**********************************************************************************/
map<int,double> OptionCalc::calcImpliedVols(double price, vector<double> opPrices,
    vector<int> strikes,double rate, double dividend, double T, char type)
{
  int j = 0;
  int cnt = 0;
  const double epsilon = 0.00001;            // error tolerance
  map<int,double> opMap;                     // map of strikes to prices
  vector<double>::iterator priceIter;        // vector iterator
  double vol1 = 0.0;                         // implied volatility
  double error = 0.0;                        // error between market and model
                                             // price
  double vol2 = 0.0;                         // stores updated volatility in
                                             // calibration
  double vega = 0.0;                         // option vega
  double BSPrice = 0.0;                      // black scholes price
  double marketPrice = 0.0;                  // market price
  int* strike = new int[strikes.size()];     // array of strike prices
  double* call  = new double[opPrices.size()]; // array of call prices

  // copy strike prices stored in vectors
  // into array used in Newton-Raphson
  copy(strikes.begin(),strikes.end(),strike);

  // compute implied vols for each option contract
  for (priceIter = opPrices.begin(); priceIter != opPrices.end(); priceIter++)
  {
    marketPrice = *priceIter;
    vol1 = 0.55; // initial guess of implied volatility for Newton-Raphson
```

```
  do
  {
    BSPrice = calcBSCallPrice(vol1,rate,dividend,strike[cnt],price,T);
    vega = calcVega(price,strike[cnt],rate,dividend,vol1,T);
    vol2 = vol1 - (BSPrice - marketPrice)/(vega);
    error = vol2 - vol1;
    vol1 = vol2;
  }
  while (abs(error) > epsilon);

  opMap[cnt] = vol1;
  cnt++;
}

// print implied vols
for (j = 0; j < opMap.size(); j++)
  cout << opMap[j] << endll;

// return a map of strikes and their implied vols
return opMap;
}
```

Each iteration of the Newton-Raphson procedure makes a call to the *calcBSCall-Price* method and the *calcVega* method, which computes vega as follows:

```
/*****************************************************************************
double OptionCalc::calcVega(double price,double strike, double rate, double div,
  double vol, double T)
{
  double d1 = (log(price/strike) + (rate - dividend +(vol)*(vol)/2)*T)/
    (vol*sqrt(T));
  return price*sqrt(T)*normalCalcPrime(d1);
}
*****************************************************************************/
```

Table 7.2 is the option chain for IBM January 2003 puts on Friday, September 20, 2002, and Figure 7.2 shows the implied volatility curve generated from these market prices. Notice that the curve initially has the skew effect—lower strikes have higher implied volatility than higher strikes—but then it oscillates starting at around a strike price of 90[1] due to the very low liquidity and thinly traded con-

---

[1]Typically, implied volatility smiles and volatility surfaces filter moneyness values outside the interval [0.5, 1.5] (i.e., $X/S < 0.5$ or $X/S > 1.5$) since the numerical uncertainty on implied volatility may be too high and the liquidity very low. The irregularity at moneyness at 1.5 and above can be seen in Figure 7.2.

TABLE 7.2   IBM Put Chain on September 20, 2002

Jan 03	35.00	0.50	Jan 03	95.00	31.00
Jan 03	40.00	0.85	Jan 03	100.00	35.90
Jan 03	45.00	1.40	Jan 03	105.00	40.50
Jan 03	50.00	2.10	Jan 03	110.00	45.90
Jan 03	55.00	3.30	Jan 03	115.00	49.90
Jan 03	60.00	5.00	Jan 03	120.00	55.00
Jan 03	65.00	7.15	Jan 03	125.00	47.00
Jan 03	70.00	10.00	Jan 03	130.00	60.70
Jan 03	75.00	13.00	Jan 03	140.00	62.00
Jan 03	80.00	16.90	Jan 03	150.00	85.30
Jan 03	85.00	21.60	Jan 03	155.00	85.00
Jan 03	90.00	24.60	Jan 03	160.00	90.90

tracts of these options. If we focus on just the moneyness around ATM contracts, we get a smoother skew as shown in Figure 7.3.

The smile is skewed: Low-strike implied volatilities are greater than higher-strike implied vols. Since there is finite liquidity by market makers who take the other sides of these trades selling out-of-the-money (OTM) puts and buying OTM calls, market makers demand a liquidity premium, which is reflected in the skew. Consequently, these OTM puts are priced at higher implied vols compared with OTM calls, which are priced at lower implied vols.

Prior to the 1987 market crash, there appeared to be symmetry around the zero moneyness—the degree to which an option is in-the-money (ITM) or out-of-the-

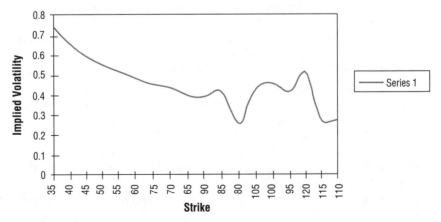

FIGURE 7.2   Implied Volatility Curve of IBM January 2003 Puts on September 20, 2002

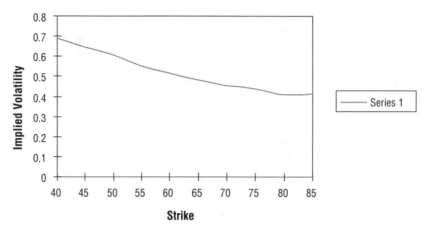

FIGURE 7.3   Implied Volatility Curve of IBM January 2003 Puts on September 20, 2002

money—where OTM and ITM options traded at higher implied volatilities than the implied volatilities of ATM options. However, since the 1987 crash, the "smile" has changed to a "sneer" shape in many markets, particularly for stock indexes. Dumas, Fleming, and Whaley (1998) have shown the volatility structure change from a smile to a sneer for S&P 500 options. Option implied volatilities are observed to decrease monotonically as the option goes deeper out-of-the-money (call) or in-the-money (put).

In general, the smirk in equity markets is very highly skewed with OTM puts priced at significantly higher vols than OTM calls. Rubinstein (1997) provides several fundamental economic reasons for this phenomenon: (1) leverage effect: As stock prices fall, debt-equity ratio rises, which leads to a rise in volatility; (2) correlation effect: Stocks become more highly correlated in down markets, which leads the volatility of the S&P 500 market index to rise since the benefits of diversification are reduced due to increasing correlation; (3) investor wealth effect: As the market falls, investors feel poorer and become more risk averse so that any news leads to greater market reactions and trading, which causes volatility to rise; and (4) risk effect: As volatility rises, risk premiums increase, leading to declines in the market. There is also a technical supply-demand view: There is strong demand for OTM puts created by portfolio hedgers and there is a strong supply of OTM calls by portfolio overwriters.

In the currency markets, this situation is different. There is a strong demand for OTM calls and puts on both sides of the market by hedgers in the two countries, and market makers demand some premium for their services by providing liquidity to the hedgers on both sides of the market. Thus in the currency markets, there is a symmetric smile where the minimum is around the ATM options and the implied volatility increases for both OTM calls and puts.

7.3   EMPIRICAL EXPLANATIONS

If the Black-Scholes model were the correct model in its assumption of constant volatility, then the implied volatilities of all options of the same type should be constant across strike prices. In fact, this is not the case as market prices reflect properties of the price process not assumed in the Black-Scholes model, which is captured in skews of implied volatilites. One empirical explanation for the smile is that return distributions may be "fat-tailed," rather than normally distributed under geometric Brownian motion (GBM). Price movements may not be properly modeled by assuming GBM as large price movements may be observed with a frequency that is greater than that assumed in the Black-Scholes model. As Carol Alexander notes, "if returns distributions are normal but volatility is stochastic, or if volatility is constant but returns are fat-tailed—or indeed, both—then large price changes will be more likely, and consequently an OTM option will have a higher chance of becoming ITM than is assumed in the Black-Scholes model. Therefore, the Black-Scholes model price will be less than the market price for an OTM option."[2] Given that volatility is the only unknown parameter in the model, the only way for Black-Scholes model prices to equal market prices is to increase the implied volatilities of OTM options. Consequently, implied volatilities of OTM options will be greater than ATM implied volatilities.

In many equity markets, there is a clear negative correlation between ATM volatility and the underlying asset, but the strength of the correlation depends on the time period and current market regime. Derman (1999) has formulated a hypothesis that attempts to explain the skew in volatility by changes in market regimes. In a range-bounded regime, volatility is constrained within certain ranges so that volatility is independent of changes in price movements. In a stable or trending market, there is little change in realized volatility over the long run as markets change in a stable manner. In a jumpy market, realized volatility increases as the probability of price jumps increases. Consequently, fixed-strike volatilities decrease when the asset price increases and increases when the asset price falls.

In Derman's models, the skew is approximated as a linear function of the strike price whose form depends on the market regime.[3] In the range-bounded regime, the market skew is

$$\sigma_X(T) = \sigma_0 - \beta(T)(X - S_0)$$

where $\sigma_X(T)$ is the implied volatility of an option with maturity T and strike X, S_0 is the initial asset price, and σ_0 is the initial implied volatility. Thus, a fixed-strike volatility is independent of the asset level; if the asset changes, the fixed-strike volatilities will not change.

---

[2]Alexander (2001a), 30.
[3]Derman (1999), 7.

7.4   IMPLIED VOLATILITY SURFACES

Volatility smiles are generated for a specific maturity. They do not tell us how volatility evolves (changes) over time with different maturities. However, if we plot volatility across time and strikes, an implied volatility surface can be generated. The following is an implementation to generate the implied vol for a given maturity and given strike. It stores the implied vol in a map where the key to the map is a pair structure containing the maturity and strike:

```
/*************************************************************************
calcImpliedSurface                  : computes the volatility surface of an option
                                      chain
[in]:   double price                : price of the stock
        vector<double> strikes      : vector of strike prices
        vector<double> maturities:  : vector of maturities
        map<double, double> rates   : vector of risk-free interest rates
        double  dividend            : dividend yield of stock
[out]: map of implied volatilities  : (key is a pair<strike,maturity>
*************************************************************************/
map<pair<double,int>,double> OptionCalc::calcImpliedSurface(double price,
  vector<double> opPrices, vector<int> strikes, vector<double> maturities,
  map<double, double> rates, double dividend)
{
  map<pair<double,int>,double> surfaceMap;         // map strike and maturity
                                                   // to implied vol

  pair<double,int> TXPair;                          // time (maturity) - strike
                                                    // pair

  vector<pair<double,int> > vecPair;                // vector of TXPairs
  vector<pair<double,int> >::iterator vecPairIter;  // vector map iterator
  vector<double>::iterator priceIter;               // vector price iterator
  int j = 0;
  int cnt = 0;
  const double epsilon = 0.000001;                 // error tolerance
  double error = 0.0;                              // error of between market
                                                   // and model prices

  double vol1 = 0.0;                               // implied vol
  double vol2 = 0.0;                               // temp stores vols
  double vega = 0.0;                               // option vega
  double BSPrice = 0.0;                            // black scholes price
  double marketPrice = 0.0;                        // market price
  int* strike = new int[strikes.size()];           // array of strikes
  double* maturity = new double[maturities.size()]; // array of maturities
  double* call  = new double[opPrices.size()];     // array of call prices
  cout.setf(ios::showpoint);
```

```
cout.precision(3).

copy(strikes.begin(),strikes.end(),strike);
copy(opPrices.begin(),opPrices.end(),call);
copy(maturities.begin(),maturities.end(),maturity);

if (type == 'C')
{
  for (priceIter = opPrices.begin(); priceIter != opPrices.end(); priceIter++)
  {
    marketPrice = *priceIter;
    vol1 = 0.65; // initial volatility guess for Newton-Raphson
    do
    {
      BSPrice =
        calcBSCallPrice(vol1,rates[maturity[cnt]],dividend,strike[cnt],price,T);
      vega = calcVega(price,strike[cnt],rates[maturity[cnt]],dividend,vol1,T);
      vol2 = vol1 - (BSPrice - marketPrice)/(vega);
      error = vol2 - vol1;
      vol1 = vol2;
    }
    while (abs(error) > epsilon);
    TXPair.first = maturity[cnt];
    TXPair.second = strike[cnt];
    vecPair.push_back(TXPair);
    surfaceMap[TXPair] = vol1;
    cnt++;
  }
}
else
{
  for (priceIter = opPrices.begin(); priceIter != opPrices.end(); priceIter++)
  {
    marketPrice = *priceIter;
    vol1 = 0.55; // initial volatility guess for Newton-Raphson
    do
    {
      BSPrice =
        calcBSPutPrice(vol1,rates[maturity[cnt]],dividend,strike[cnt],price,T);
      vega = calcVega(price,strike[cnt],rates[maturity[cnt]],dividend,vol1,T);
      vol2 = vol1 - (BSPrice - marketPrice)/(vega);
      error = vol2 - vol1;
      vol1 = vol2;
    }
    while (abs(error) > epsilon);
    TXPair.first = maturity[cnt];
    TXPair.second = strike[cnt];
    surfaceMap[TXPair] = vol1;
    cnt++;
  }
}
```

```
// print out implied vol
for (vecPairIter = vecPair.begin(); vecPairIter != vecPair.end(); vecPairIter++)
  cout <<surfaceMap[*vecPairIter]) << endl;

return surfaceMap;
}
```

The volatility surface generated from IBM market-traded call options on September 20, 2002, is shown in Figure 7.4 for maturities up to six months. There are only a few market quotes for contracts available beyond six months, which are not included; including them would cause discontinuities. However, implied volatilities for options that are not market traded could be calculated and included using linear interpolation.

The same volatility surface viewed from a different angle is shown in Figure 7.5. Notice the smile curvature of the surface along the strike axis. Also notice that the surface is steeper (i.e., the gradient is higher), as the time to maturity increases, especially for at-the-money contracts.

Consider the volatility surface of the S&P 500 on October 7, 2002, shown in Figure 7.6, for maturities ranging from one month to nine months. The S&P 500 closed at 800.58. The dividend yield was approximately 1.48 percent.

If we include maturities more than nine months, 1 year to 1.75 years, as shown in Figure 7.7, we get much more spiked volatility surface at the longer maturities—to smooth the surface, linear interpolation would be required for all options that are not traded across strike and maturity. The surface, like the surface for IBM, has

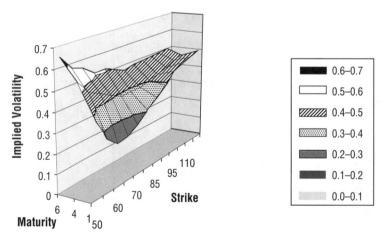

FIGURE 7.4 Volatility Surface of IBM on September 20, 2002

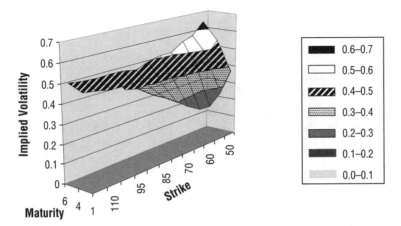

FIGURE 7.5 Volatility Surface of IBM on September 20, 2002—Different Angle

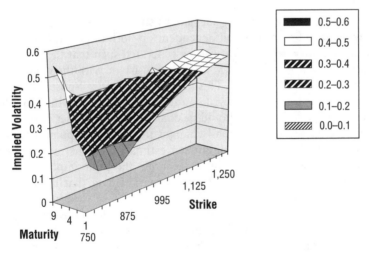

FIGURE 7.6 Implied Volatility of S&P 500 on October 7, 2002

a steep gradient along the maturity axis (the term structure) especially for at-the-money options. With this local volatility surface of the S&P 500 index, one can measure options' market sentiment, to compute the evolution of standard options' implied volatilities, to calculate the index exposure of standard index options, and to value and hedge exotic options.[4]

---

[4]Derman, Kani, and Zou (1995).

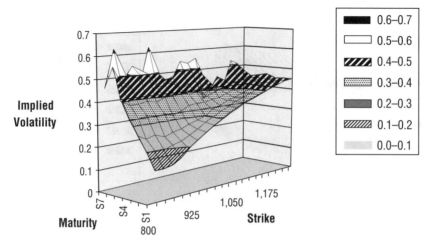

FIGURE 7.7 Volatility Surface of S&P 500 on October 7, 2002

Practitioners generate volatility surfaces to study their evolution, but in pricing theory, they want to find a function dependent on both time and price, $\sigma = \sigma(S, t)$, called a *local volatility surface*, that can be generated such that the risk-neutral diffusion process $dS = (r - q)Sdt = \sigma(S, t)Sdz$ is consistent with the correct set of observable implied volatilities $\sigma_{ij}^{implied}$. This inverse problem is ill-posed, however, since we have only a finite set of traded strikes and maturities from which to infer a continuous function $\sigma = \sigma(S, t)$ that should be consistent with the set of observable implied volatilities. Consequently, small changes in the data inputs into the surface can generate large changes in the parameter estimates. Furthermore, given a local volatility surface, this model will always generate the same implied volatility surface. However, it is known empirically from market data that the actual implied volatility surface is nonstationary.[5]

Cont and da Fonseca (2002) outline a procedure for constructing a smooth volatility surface for arbitrary strikes and maturities. The procedure to interpolate or smooth the discrete data set can be done in a parametric or nonparametric form. The parametric form involves using cubic splines or (piecewise) polynomical functions to fit the implied volatility smile.[6] Cont and da Fonseca focus on a nonparametric approach using a Nadaraya-Watson estimator that filters the data set and constructs for each day a smooth estimator of the implied volatility surface on a fixed grid. The surface estimator is defined as:

$$\hat{\sigma}(m, t) = \frac{\sum_{i=1}^{n} \sigma(m_i, t_i)g(m - m_i, t - t_i)}{\sum_{i=1}^{n} g(m - m_i, t - t_i)} \tag{7.7}$$

---

[5]Cont and da Fonseca (2002).
[6]Dumas, Whaley, and Fleming (1998), 95–106.

where $g(x, y) = (2\pi)^{-1}\exp(-x^2/2h_1)\exp(-y^2/2h_2)$ is a Gaussian kernel, n is the number of options actively traded on the given day, typically around 100, m is the moneyness x/s, and the time to maturity t ranges between a month and a year. The important parameters are the bandwidth parameters in the Gaussian kernel, h_1 and h_2, which determine the degree of smoothing. Values that are too small will lead to a bumpy surface, and values that are too large will smooth away important details. The bandwidth can be determined using a cross-validation criterion or an adaptive bandwidth estimator in order to obtain an optimal bandwidth h.[7]

Large sample properties of these estimators have been studied and are known.[8] After obtaining a daily time series $\{\sigma(m, t), t = 0 \ldots N\}$ of smooth implied volatility surfaces $\sigma : [m_{min}, m_{max}] \times [t_{min}, t_{max}] \to [0, \infty)$, one can apply principal component analysis (PCA), which is used to decompose (random) volatility surfaces into their principal empirically identifiable factors.[9] Alexander (2001a) provides an excellent discussion of how to use PCA to model volatility smiles and skews,[10] and shows how the first three principal components in PCA can explain much of the variation in volatility skews. Alexander (2000), for example, shows that during most of 1998, 80 to 90 percent of the total variation in the fixed-maturity volatility skews of the Financial Times Stock Exchange (FTSE) 100 index can be explained by just three risk factors: parallel shifts, tilts, and curvature changes that are captured by the first three principal components.

The time series of smooth surfaces are then modeled as stationary random surfaces to which one applies a numerical procedure like Karhunen-Loeve decomposition in which each random surface, viewed as a random field, can be expressed as a superposition of uncorrelated random variables, each of which is the product of a scalar random variable (an eigenvector) with a deterministic surface so that the surface has the representation:

$$\sigma_t(m, \tau) = \sigma_0(m, \tau)\exp\left(\sum_{k=1}^{N} x_k(t)f_k\right) \tag{7.8}$$

where

$$x_k(t) = \langle X_t - X_0, f_k \rangle = \int_A X_t(m, \tau)f_k(m, \tau)dmd\tau$$

---

[7]Cont and da Fonseca (2002), 49.
[8]Ibid.
[9]A general discussion of PCA is given in Chapter 9.
[10]One model given by Alexander (2001a) is the PCA of fixed-strike deviations based on the model

$$\Delta(\sigma_X - \sigma_{ATM}) = w_{X_1}P_1 + w_{X_2}P_2 + w_{X_3}P_3$$

where the volatility maturity and the strike of the volatility are both fixed. Time series on the change between the fixed-strike volatility from the at-the-money (ATM) volatility are used to estimate the time series of the principal components P_1, P_2, and P_3 and the constant weight factors w_{X_1}, w_{X_2}, and w_{X_3}.

are (a time series of) principal component processes $\{x_k(t), t = 1, \ldots, N\}$, i.e., Ornstein-Uhlenback processes driven by independent noise sources Z Wiener or jump processes,

$$dx_k(t) = -\lambda_k(x_k(t) - \bar{X}_k)dt + \gamma_k dZ_k(t), k = 1, \ldots, d$$

where λ_k represents the speed of mean reversion along the kth eigenfunction and γ_k is the volatility of implied volatilities along this direction;

$$X_t(m, \tau) = \sum_{k=1}^{d} X_k(t)f_k(m, \tau) = \ln \sigma_t(m, \tau), \sigma_0(m, \tau)$$

is the initial volatility surface, $f_k(m, t)$ are expanded eigenvectors (eigenfunctions) on the basis of a family of smooth functions (surfaces) (h_j), that is, spline functions commonly used for interpolating volatility surfaces and yield curves,

$$f_i(m, \tau) = \sum_{j=1}^{N} a_{ij} h_j(m, \tau) + \varepsilon_N \tag{7.9}$$

and k is the kth principal component. The a_{ij} are the elements of the matrix A found by solving the orthogonality condition

$$CA = DBA \tag{7.10}$$

where C and B are symmetric positive matrices, computed from the data such that

$$C_{ij} = \int_A \int_A \left(h_i(m, \tau) K(m, m', \tau, \tau') h_j(m', \tau') \right) dm d\tau$$

$D = \text{diag}(v_i^2, i = 1, \ldots, N)$ where the v_i^2 are the associated eigenvalues (variances) such that $v_1^2 \geq v_2^2 \geq \ldots \geq 0$, and $B_{ij} = \langle h_i, h_j \rangle$. Numerically solving the generalized eigenvalue problem in (7.10) for D and A and substituting the coefficients of A into (7.9) yields the eigenfunctions f_k. Each eigenfunction is actually a surface: $f_n : A \subset \Re^2 \to \Re$, which is the solution of a Fredholm integral equation defined by the kernel $K(x, y), x, y \in A$, namely,

$$\int K(x, y) f_n(y) dy = v_n^2 f_n(x) \tag{7.11}$$

The kernel is analogous to the covariance matrix of a random vector.[11] Moreover, the kernel K can be decomposed as

$$K(x,\ y) = \sum_{n=1}^{N} v_n^2 f_n(x) f_n(y) \qquad (7.12)$$

which by assuming that the errors in equation (7.9) are orthogonal to the approximating functions $(h_n,\ n = 1,\ \dots,\ N)$ is known as the Galerkin condition. Plugging equation (7.9) into (7.12), we get an error term

$$\varepsilon_N = \sum_{j=1}^{N} a_{ij} \left(\int_A K(m,\ m',\ \tau,\ \tau') h_j(m',\ \tau') dm' d\tau' - v_i^2 h_j(m,\ \tau) \right)$$

Thus, by the Galerkin condition, $< \varepsilon_N,\ h_j > = 0$, we have

$$\sum_{j=1}^{N} a_{ij} \left[\int_A h_i(x) dx \int_A K(x,\ x') h_j(x') dx' - v_j^2 \int_A h_i(x) h_j(x) dx \right] = 0$$

which is just the orthogonality condition in matrix element form of equation (7.10).

Empirical results of the procedure applied to S&P 500 index and FTSE 100 index options are given by Cont and da Fonseca (2002). Cont and da Fonseca also propose a factor model for the implied volatility surface where the (log-) implied volatility surface $\sigma_t(m,\ \tau)$ is represented by the sum of the initial surface and its fluctuations along the principal (component) directions.

Bodurtha and Jermakyan (1999) use a different nonparameteric approach to invert option prices into a state- and time-dependent volatility function. Their approach is a finite-difference-based procedure based on a small-parameter expansion of the option value functions. They consider a family of volatility functions,

$$\sigma_\varepsilon^2 (T,\ Z) = \sigma_0^2 + \sum_{k=1}^{\infty} \varepsilon^k a_k(v,\ Z) \qquad (7.13)$$

where ε, $0 \le \varepsilon \le 1$, is a perturbation parameter used for volatility decomposition purposes. The inverse solution does not depend on ε in any way. Note that $\varepsilon = 0$ corresponds to the Black-Scholes-Merton constant volatility case, while $\varepsilon = 1$ is the solution to their volatility surface estimation problem.

---

[11]Cont and da Fonseca (2002), 50.

Following Bodurtha and Jermakyan, define $F_K = e^{(r-q)\tau}S/K$, the scaled forward price of the spot price (relative to the option exercise price) that follows the forward price diffusion process $dF_k = \alpha(t, S)F_K dt + \sigma(t, S)F_K dz(t)$. A riskless no-arbitrage portfolio for an exercise price-standardized call option is created:

$$\Pi = \lambda F_K + C_K(t, F_K)$$

where

$$C_K(t, F_K) = e^{r\tau}\frac{C(t, S)}{K}$$

Note that underlying F_K and call value C_K are unitless and the strike price is arbitrary. The no-arbitrage condition requires that $d\Pi = 0$ at any time t. By Ito's lemma, we have

$$d\Pi = \left(\frac{\partial C_K}{\partial t} + \frac{1}{2}\sigma^2(t, S)F_K^2\frac{\partial^2 C_K}{\partial F_K^2}\right)dt + \left(\lambda + \frac{\partial C_K}{\partial F_K}\right)dz(t)$$

Thus, the riskless portfolio contains a forward position of $\lambda = -(\partial C_K/\partial F_K)$ and leads to PDE that $C_K(t, F_K)$ satisfies:

$$\left.\begin{array}{l} \dfrac{\partial C_K}{\partial t} + \dfrac{1}{2}\sigma^2(t, S)F_K^2\dfrac{\partial^2 C_K}{\partial F_K^2} = 0, \\[2mm] C_K(0, F_K) = \max(0, F_K - 1), \ C_K(t, 0) = 0 \end{array}\right\}$$

A change in the current time variable t is then made to a scaled time-to-maturity variable so that for an option with maturity T,

$$\left.\begin{array}{l} \dfrac{\partial C_K}{\partial v} + \dfrac{1}{2}\overline{T}\sigma^2(v, S)F_K^2\dfrac{\partial^2 C_K}{\partial F_K^2} = 0, \\[2mm] C_K(0, F_K) = \max(0, F_K - 1), \ C_K(v, 0) = 0 \end{array}\right\} \qquad (7.14)$$

where the new scaled time variable is $v = T/\overline{T}$, $v \in [0, 1]$ where $\overline{T}$ is the maximum option maturity and t is set to 0. An analogous case holds for a put value P_K,

$$\left.\begin{array}{l} \dfrac{\partial P_K}{\partial v} + \dfrac{1}{2}\overline{T}\sigma^2(v, S)F_K^2\dfrac{\partial^2 P_K}{\partial F_K^2} = 0, \\[2mm] P_K(0, F_K) = \max(0, 1 - F_K), \ P_K(v, 0) = 1 \end{array}\right\} \qquad (7.15)$$

The valuation problem requires solving two parabolic PDEs, one for the call PDE (7.14) and one for the put PDE (7.15). Since the strike index K is arbitrary, a new variable Z is introduced such that $Z = \ln(F_K)$ and $U(v, Z) = C_K(v, F_K)$. Thus, F_K defined over the range $(0, \infty)$ is mapped to the variable Z with a range $(-\infty, \infty)$. Plugging in Z and U into equation (7.14) yields

$$
\left.
\begin{aligned}
&\frac{\partial U(v, Z)}{\partial v} + \frac{1}{2}\overline{T}\sigma^2(v, S)\left(\frac{\partial^2 U(v, Z)}{\partial Z^2} - \frac{\partial U(v, Z)}{\partial Z}\right), \\
&U(0, Z) = \max(0, e^Z - 1)
\end{aligned}
\right\}
\tag{7.16}
$$

An analogous equation is given for the put by using $W(0, Z) = P_K(v, F_K)$ in (7.15).[12]

Given a volatility function that is time and spot price dependent, we can numerically solve equation (7.16) for the associated European call option. Recovery of the associated exercise-price-dependent option quotes requires two steps: first, map $U(v, Z)$ into respective forward price and exercise price option prices $C_K(t, F_K)$. Second, compute the actual quotes $C(t, S)$ in the spot price–time space. The mapping is one-to-one with $S(0)$ mapping to $F_K(T)$ and $Z(T)$, $S(T)$ mapping to $F_K(0)$ and $Z(0)$, and the corresponding elements of the spot price and exercise price adjusted forward price sets mapping accordingly.[13]

An ε-analog of equation (7.16) under the volatility specification of (7.13) is formed:

$$
\left.
\begin{aligned}
&\frac{\partial U^\varepsilon(v, Z)}{\partial v} + \frac{1}{2}\overline{T}\sigma_\varepsilon^2(v, S)\left(\frac{\partial^2 U^\varepsilon(v, Z)}{\partial Z^2} - \frac{\partial U^\varepsilon(v, Z)}{\partial Z}\right), \\
&U^\varepsilon(0, Z) = \max(0, e^Z - 1)
\end{aligned}
\right\}
\tag{7.17}
$$

$U^\varepsilon(v, Z)$ is then expanded into a formal power series with respect to ε:

$$
U^\varepsilon(v, Z) = \sum_{n=0}^{\infty} U_n(v, Z)\varepsilon^n
\tag{7.18}
$$

Define

$$
\tilde{a}_0 = \frac{1}{2}\overline{T}\sigma_0^2 \text{ and } \tilde{a}_k = \frac{1}{2}\overline{T}a_k(v, Z)
$$

---

[12]For simplicity, we discuss the volatility estimation problem only in terms of the call option equation, but the process is analogous for the put equation.
[13]Bodurtha and Jermakyan (1999), 33.

Substituting equations (7.13) and (7.18) into equation (7.17) yields

$$
\frac{\partial U_0(v, Z)}{\partial v} + \sum_{n=1}^{\infty} \frac{\partial U_n(v, Z)}{\partial v} \varepsilon^n = \tilde{a}_0 \left(\frac{\partial^2 U_0(v, Z)}{\partial Z^2} - \frac{\partial U_0(v, Z)}{\partial Z} \right)
$$
$$
+ \tilde{a}_0 \sum_{n=1}^{\infty} \left(\frac{\partial^2 U_n(v, Z)}{\partial Z^2} - \frac{\partial U_n(v, Z)}{\partial Z} \right) \varepsilon^n \qquad (7.19)
$$
$$
+ \sum_{n=1}^{\infty} \sum_{k=1}^{n} \tilde{a}_k \left(\frac{\partial^2 U_{n-k}(v, Z)}{\partial Z^2} - \frac{\partial U_{n-k}(v, Z)}{\partial Z} \right) \varepsilon^{n+k-1}
$$

Equating equivalent powers of ε-terms and applying associated initial or boundary conditions yields the following system of equations:

$$
\left. \begin{aligned}
\frac{\partial U_0(v, Z)}{\partial v} &= \tilde{a}_0 \left(\frac{\partial^2 U_0(v, Z)}{\partial Z^2} - \frac{\partial U_0(v, Z)}{\partial Z} \right), \\
U_0(0, Z) &= \max(0, e^Z - 1)
\end{aligned} \right\} \qquad (7.20)
$$

$$
\left. \begin{aligned}
\frac{\partial U_1(v, Z)}{\partial v} &= \tilde{a}_0 \left(\frac{\partial^2 U_1(v, Z)}{\partial Z^2} - \frac{\partial U_1(v, Z)}{\partial Z} \right) + \tilde{a}_1 \left(\frac{\partial^2 U_0(v, Z)}{\partial Z^2} - \frac{\partial U_0(v, Z)}{\partial Z} \right), \\
U_1(0, Z) &= 0
\end{aligned} \right\} \quad (7.21)
$$

...

$$
\left. \begin{aligned}
\frac{\partial U_n(v, Z)}{\partial v} &= \tilde{a}_0 \left(\frac{\partial^2 U_n(v, Z)}{\partial Z^2} - \frac{\partial U_n(v, Z)}{\partial Z} \right) + \sum_{k=1}^{n} \tilde{a}_k \left(\frac{\partial^2 U_{n-k}(v, Z)}{\partial Z^2} - \frac{\partial U_{n-k}(v, Z)}{\partial Z} \right), \\
U_n(0, Z) &= 0
\end{aligned} \right\} \quad (7.22)
$$

In the equation system, all equations, other than (7.20) differ from each other only in the forcing or nonhomogenous term.[14] The forcing term can be determined by iterating over these equations (starting from $n = 1$). At each step of the iterations, the forcing term is obtained from the previous equation calculation. To complete the procedure, one can infer $\tilde{a}_k$ from each equation $k = i, \ldots, n$.

Bodurtha and Jermakyan develop an iterative optimization-based estimation procedure of the parameters. They denote $K_i, i = 1, \ldots, n$ traded strike prices and $T_j, j = 1, \ldots, m$, available option maturities where $T_m = \bar{T}$. Denote $V_j = T_j/\bar{T}$, $Z_{i,j} = \ln(e^{(r-q)\bar{T}v_j} S/K_i)$, and $U^{i,j} = e^{r\bar{T}v_j} C^{i,j}(0, S)/K_i$. $Z_{i,j}$ is the natural logarithm of the time-

---

[14]Ibid., pg. 35.

zero and T_j-maturity forward price weighted by strike price K_i; $C^{i,j}(0, S)$ is the time-zero call option price with strike K_i and maturity T_j; and $U^{i,j}$ is the K_i strike price weighted and T_j-maturity future value of this call.[15]

The input parameter $\tilde{a}_0$ used to solve equation (7.20) is estimated by minimizing the following (least-squares) function:

$$M_0(\tilde{a}_0) = \sum_{j=1}^{m} \sum_{i=1}^{n} \left| U_0(v_j, Z_{i,j}) - U^{i,j} \right|^2 \tag{7.23}$$

Since, for any given $\tilde{a}_0$, there are closed-form expressions for $U_0^{i,j}(v, Z_{i,j})$, one can minimize (7.23) using a Newton-Raphson search for root of the first derivative $M_0(\tilde{a}_0)$. Given this estimate, one can compute both $\partial^2 U_0(v, Z)/\partial Z^2$ and $\partial U_0(v, Z)/\partial Z$ and thus solve equation (7.21).[16] The solution to equation (7.21) has the following form:[17]

$$U_1(v, Z) = \int_0^v \int_{-\infty}^{\infty} \frac{\exp\left(\dfrac{-[(z - \xi) - a_0(v - \kappa)]^2}{4\tilde{a}_0(v - \kappa)} \right)}{\sqrt{4\pi \tilde{a}_0(v - \kappa)}} F_1(\kappa, \xi) d\xi d\kappa \tag{7.24}$$

where

$$F_1(\kappa, \xi) = \tilde{a}_1(\kappa, \xi)\left(\frac{\partial^2 U_0(\kappa, \varepsilon)}{\partial \xi^2} - \frac{\partial U_0(\kappa, \xi)}{\partial \xi} \right)$$

For the $\tilde{a}_1$ volatility perturbation, Bodurtha and Jermakyan define the associated minimizer, known as the minimand, as

$$M_1^{\alpha}(\cdot) = \sum_{j=1}^{m} \sum_{i=1}^{n} \left| U_1(v_j, Z_{i,j}) - [U^{i,j} - U_0(v_j, Z_{i,j})] \right|^2 + \alpha_1 \Omega(\cdot) \tag{7.25}$$

where α_1 is called a regularizing parameters and $\Omega(\cdot)$ is a nonnegative functional, called a stabilizing functional, roughness penalty, or smoother, that satisfies certain

---

[15]Ibid.
[16]Ibid.
[17]Tikhonov and Samarskii (1963).

conditions. While there are different stabilizing functional alternatives to use, the following guarantee good numerical properties such as stability:

$$\Omega(\tilde{a}_1) = \int_0^1 \int_{-\infty}^{\infty} \sum_{k_1+k_2=0}^{p} \left(\frac{\partial^{k_1+k_2}}{\partial v^{k_1} \partial Z^{k_2}} \tilde{a}_1(v, Z) \right)^2 dZ dv \qquad (7.26)$$

$$\Omega(F_1) = \int_0^1 \int_{-\infty}^{\infty} \sum_{k_1+k_2=0}^{p} \left(\frac{\partial^{k_1+k_2}}{\partial v^{k_1} \partial Z^{k_2}} F_1(v, Z) \right)^2 dZ dv \qquad (7.27)$$

These stabilizing functionals are squares of the H^p norm, where p is a suitably chosen nonnegative integer. Once the regularizing parameter α_1 is known, solve for $\tilde{a}_1$ as the minimizer of optimand (7.25). The regularizing parameter can be determined by the discrepancy method of Tikhonov and Arsenin (1977). Define the discrepancy function

$$\rho_1(\alpha_1) = \sum_{j=1}^{m} \sum_{i=1}^{n} \left| U_1(v_j, Z_{i,j}) - (U^{i,j} - U_0(v_j, Z_{i,j})) \right|^2 - \delta^2 \qquad (7.28)$$

where δ is a bound on the least-squares error of the traded option price quotes and is nonnegative. Define $\bar{U}^{i,j}$ as the actual call option value at time zero and spot price $S(0)$. Following the definition of the quoted option prices $U^{i,j}$, the actual values $\bar{U}^{i,j}$ are also scaled by the strike price K_i and maturity time v_j. However, it is not expected that quoted option prices and the actual option values will coincide due to nonsynchronous option and spot quotes, bid-ask costs, and other factors that introduce the error $\bar{U}^{i,j} - U^{i,j}$. The term δ is a chosen as the bound parameter on the size of the least-squares error:

$$\sum_{j=1}^{m} \sum_{i=1}^{n} |\bar{U}^{i,j} - U^{i,j}|^2 \le \delta^2 \qquad (7.29)$$

Given δ, the solution for the unique volatility function, $\tilde{a}_1$, is the minimizer of the optimand in (7.25). The regularizing parameter, α_1, is chosen such that it is a root of the discrepancy function in (7.28) so that $\rho_1(\alpha_1) = 0$. The general theory of Tikhonov and Arsenin (1977) guarantees that a unique solution to the problem exists.

To implement their approach, Bodurtha and Jermakyan use an explicit finite-difference scheme. They solve two separate minimization problems—one to compute the a_k's and one to compute α_1. They first calculate the Black-Scholes-Merton implied volatility for a fixed number of option quotes using a Newton-Raphson search for the roots of the optimand derivative with respect to $\tilde{a}_0$. Given closed-form expressions for $U_1(v_j, Z_{i,j})$ terms and their partial derivatives, numerical integration procedures can be used to discretize them. In particular, they make a change of variables $\xi = Z - \tilde{a}_0 v$ and denote $\tilde{a}_k(v, \xi) = \tilde{a}_k(v, Z)$ for $k = 1, \ldots, n$ and $H_0(v, \xi) = U_0(v, Z)$, $H_1(v, \xi) = U_1(v, Z), \ldots, H_n(v, \xi) = U_n(v, Z)$ which changes the system of equations in (7.20), (7.21), and (7.22) to

$$\left. \begin{aligned} \frac{\partial H_0(v, \xi)}{\partial v} &= \tilde{a}_0 \frac{\partial^2 H_0(v, \xi)}{\partial \xi^2}, \\ H_0(0, \xi) &= \max(0, e^\xi - 1) \end{aligned} \right\} \tag{7.30}$$

$$\left. \begin{aligned} \frac{\partial H_1(v, \xi)}{\partial v} &= \tilde{a}_0 \frac{\partial^2 H_1(v, \xi)}{\partial \xi^2} + \tilde{a}_1(v, \xi)\left(\frac{\partial^2 H_0(v, \xi)}{\partial \xi^2} - \frac{\partial H_0(v, \xi)}{\partial \xi} \right), \\ H_1(0, \xi) &= 0 \end{aligned} \right\} \tag{7.31}$$

$\ldots$

$$\left. \begin{aligned} \frac{\partial H_n(v, Z)}{\partial v} &= \tilde{a}_0 \frac{\partial^2 H_n(v, \xi)}{\partial \xi^2} + \sum_{k=1}^{n} \tilde{a}_k\left(\frac{\partial^2 H_{n-k}(v, \xi)}{\partial \xi^2} - \frac{\partial H_{n-k}(v, \xi)}{\partial \xi} \right), \\ H_n(0, \xi) &= 0 \end{aligned} \right\} \tag{7.32}$$

The system can be discretized using an explicit finite-difference scheme with time steps Δv and state spacing $\Delta \xi$ with $v_0 = 0$, $v_{j+1} = v_j + \Delta v$ for $j = 0, 1, \ldots, M - 1$, where $M = 1/\Delta v$. The state space line can be truncated by a number $L > 0$, that is, $\xi \in [-L, L]$. Boundary conditions are imposed at $\xi \pm L$. For sufficiently large L, it is assumed $H_1(v, \pm L) = 0$ for $0 \le v \le 1$. Moreover, $\xi_0 = L$, $\xi_{i+1} = \xi_i + \Delta \xi$ for $i = 0, 1, \ldots, N$, where $\Delta \xi = 2L/(N + 1)$, $\xi_{N+1} = L$, and $\xi_1, \xi_2, \ldots, \xi_n$ are internal grid points that belong to $(-L, L)$.

Equation (7.31) is discretized with a first-order forward difference formula for $\partial H_1/\partial v$ and a second-order second central difference formula for $\partial^2 H_1/\partial \xi^2$. These discrete approximations lead to the trinomial method. For stability, the risk-neutral probabilities of an up or down movement p satisfy the following inequality:

$$p = \frac{\tilde{a}_0 \Delta v}{(\Delta \xi)^2} \le \frac{1}{2}$$

The discretization of equation (7.31) becomes

$$H_1(i, j+1) = pH_1(i-1, j) + p_m H_1(i, j) + pH_1(i+1, j) + \Delta v \tilde{a}_1(i, j)\frac{\partial^2 H_0(i, j)}{\partial \xi^2} \tag{7.33}$$

for $i = 1, \ldots, N$ and $j = 0, \ldots, M - 1$. The probability of no movement is $p_m = 1 - 2p$. Following Bodurtha and Jermakyan, the updated $(j + 1)$th time step value is computed from p and

$$\frac{\partial^2 H_0(i, j)}{\partial \xi^2} = \frac{\partial^2 H_0(v_j, \xi_i)}{\partial^2 \xi^2}$$

as well as the previous $(j$th$)$ step $H_1(i, j) = H_1(v_j, \xi_i)$, and $\tilde{a}_1(i, j) = \tilde{a}_1(v_j, \xi_i)$. Moreover, at all time steps, the

$$\frac{\partial^2 H_0(i, j)}{\partial \xi^2}$$

terms can be determined from the computation of $H_0(i, j)$. Given boundary conditions $H_1 = 0$ at $\xi \pm L$, equation system (7.33) can be written in matrix form as

$$\mathbf{H}_1[j + 1] = \mathbf{A}\mathbf{H}_1[j] + \mathbf{F}_1[j] \tag{7.34}$$

where

$$\mathbf{H}_1[j] = \begin{bmatrix} H_1(1, j) \\ H_1(2, j) \\ \vdots \\ H_1(N, j) \end{bmatrix}, \quad \mathbf{F}_1[j] = \begin{bmatrix} \Delta v \tilde{a}_1(1, j) \dfrac{\partial^2 H_0(1, j)}{\partial \xi^2} \\ \Delta v \tilde{a}_1(2, j) \dfrac{\partial^2 H_0(2, j)}{\partial \xi^2} \\ \vdots \\ \Delta v \tilde{a}_1(N, j) \dfrac{\partial^2 H_0(N, j)}{\partial \xi^2} \end{bmatrix} \tag{7.35}$$

$$\mathbf{A} = \begin{bmatrix} p_m & p & 0 & 0 & \ldots & 0 & 0 & 0 \\ p & p_m & p & 0 & \ldots & 0 & 0 & 0 \\ 0 & p & p_m & p & \ldots & 0 & 0 & 0 \\ \vdots & \vdots & \vdots & \vdots & \ldots & \vdots & \vdots & \vdots \\ 0 & 0 & 0 & 0 & \ldots & p & p_m & p \\ 0 & 0 & 0 & 0 & \ldots & 0 & p & p_m \end{bmatrix}$$

From the initial condition in equation (7.31), we know $H_1[0] = 0$, and

$$H_1[1] = F_1[0],$$
$$H_1[2] = AH_1[1] + F_1[1] = AF_1[0] + F_1[1],$$
$$H_1[3] = AH_1[2] + F_1[2] = A^2F_1[0] + AF_1[1] + F_1[2],$$
$$\vdots$$
$$H_1[M] = AH_1[M-1] + F_1[M-1]$$
$$= A^{M-1}F_1[0] + A^{M-2}F_1[1] + \ldots + AF_1[M-2] + F_1[M-1]$$

We can write this system as

$$H_1 = \overline{A}F_1 \qquad (7.36)$$

where

$$H_1 = \begin{bmatrix} H_1[1] \\ H_1[2] \\ \vdots \\ H_1[M] \end{bmatrix}, \quad F_1 = \begin{bmatrix} F_1[1] \\ F_1[2] \\ \vdots \\ F_1[M-1] \end{bmatrix} \qquad (7.37)$$

$$\overline{A} = \begin{bmatrix} I & 0 & 0 & 0 & \ldots & 0 & 0 & 0 \\ A & I & 0 & 0 & \ldots & 0 & 0 & 0 \\ A^2 & A & I & 0 & \ldots & 0 & 0 & 0 \\ \vdots & \vdots & \vdots & \vdots & \ldots & \vdots & \vdots & \vdots \\ A^{M-2} & A^{M-3} & A^{M-4} & A^{M-5} & \ldots & A & I & 0 \\ A^{M-1} & A^{M-2} & A^{M-3} & A^{M-4} & \ldots & A^2 & A & I \end{bmatrix}$$

In equation (7.36), H_1 and F_1 are $NM \times 1$ column vectors, $\overline{A}$ is an $NM \times NM$ lower triangular matrix, and I is the $N \times N$ identity matrix. The coordinates of vector H_1 correspond to option quotes that are indexed across maturities and strike prices.[18] Since the option quote set is not complete in the coordinate space of H_1, H_1 is underdetermined, which makes the system in (7.36) underdetermined. To resolve the underdetermination of the system, projection and regularization steps are used. For the projection step, denote m as the number of quoted option maturities and n

---

[18]Bodurtha and Jermakyan (1999), 40.

as the number of quoted option strike prices for each maturity. Then, $\mathbf{P} : \Re^{M \times N} \to \Re^{m \times n}$ is the standard projection of the real $(M \times N)$-dimensional space onto its $(m \times n)$-dimensional subspace. Bodurtha and Jermakyan let $\mathbf{H}_p^1 = \mathbf{P} \cdot \mathbf{H}_1$ and define $\overline{\mathbf{A}}_p$ as the $mn \times MN$ rectangular matrix obtained by eliminating the rows of matrix $\overline{\mathbf{A}}_p$ that correspond to the nonquoted options.[19] Rearranging equation (7.36) yields

$$\mathbf{H}_p^1 = \overline{\mathbf{A}}_p \mathbf{F}_1 \qquad (7.38)$$

However, since system (7.38) has more variables than equations, it is overdetermined and thus has an infinite number of solutions (or no solution at all). To find a unique solution, Tikhonov regularization is used. To define a regularizer, denote $\mathbf{G}$ as a vector on which a set of forward difference operators act (i.e., the function to be regularized),

$$\mathbf{G} = \begin{bmatrix} G[1] \\ G[2] \\ \vdots \\ G[M-1] \end{bmatrix} \text{ and } \mathbf{G}[j] = \begin{bmatrix} G(j,\ 1) \\ G(j,\ 2) \\ \vdots \\ G(j,\ N) \end{bmatrix}$$

which are $MN \times 1$ and $N \times 1$ vectors, respectively. Taking the first-order difference of $\mathbf{G}$ over the state variable yields:

$$\mathbf{D}_\xi(\mathbf{G}) = \frac{1}{\Delta \xi} \begin{bmatrix} G(0,\ 2) - G(0,\ 1) \\ G(0,\ 3) - G(0,\ 2) \\ \vdots \\ G(0,\ N) - G(0,\ N-1) \\ -G(0,\ N) \\ \vdots \\ G(M-1,\ 2) - G(M-1,\ 1) \\ \vdots \\ G(M-1,\ N) - G(M-1,\ N-1) \\ -G(M-1,\ N) \end{bmatrix}$$

---

[19]Ibid., 41.

A good choice for $\mathbf{G} \equiv \bar{\mathbf{a}}_1$ is:

$$
\begin{bmatrix}
\bar{a}_1(1,\,0) \\
\vdots \\
\bar{a}_1(N,\,0) \\
\bar{a}_1(1,\,1) \\
\vdots \\
\bar{a}_1(N,\,M-1)
\end{bmatrix}
\tag{7.39}
$$

which is the vector of values one wants to ultimately solve for as solutions to use in equation (7.13) to determine the volatility surface.

The corresponding first-order difference operator, which corresponds to $\partial/\partial\xi$, is

$$
\overline{\mathbf{D}}_\xi = \frac{1}{\Delta\xi}
\begin{bmatrix}
\mathbf{D}_\xi & 0 & 0 & \dots & 0 \\
0 & \mathbf{D}_\xi & 0 & \dots & 0 \\
0 & 0 & \mathbf{D}_\xi & \dots & \vdots \\
\vdots & \vdots & \vdots & \dots & \vdots \\
0 & 0 & 0 & 0 & \mathbf{D}_\xi
\end{bmatrix}
\text{ with } \mathbf{D}_\xi =
\begin{bmatrix}
-1 & 1 & 0 & \dots & 0 \\
0 & -1 & 1 & \dots & 0 \\
0 & 0 & -1 & \dots & \vdots \\
\vdots & \vdots & \vdots & \dots & 1 \\
0 & 0 & 0 & 0 & -1
\end{bmatrix}
$$

Thus, $\overline{\mathbf{D}}_\xi$ is a bidiagonal $MN \times MN$ matrix with homogenous Dirichlet boundary conditions (from the right). Similarly, we can define the second-order forward difference operator, corresponding to $\partial^2/\partial\xi^2$,

$$
\overline{\mathbf{D}}_{\xi^2} = \frac{1}{\Delta\xi^2}
\begin{bmatrix}
\mathbf{D}_{\xi^2} & 0 & 0 & \dots & 0 \\
0 & \mathbf{D}_{\xi^2} & 0 & \dots & 0 \\
0 & 0 & \mathbf{D}_{\xi^2} & \dots & \vdots \\
\vdots & \vdots & \vdots & \dots & \vdots \\
0 & 0 & 0 & 0 & \mathbf{D}_{\xi^2}
\end{bmatrix}
\text{ where } \mathbf{D}_{\xi^2} =
\begin{bmatrix}
1 & -2 & 0 & \dots & 0 & 0 \\
0 & 1 & -2 & \dots & 0 & 0 \\
0 & 0 & \vdots & \dots & \vdots & \vdots \\
\vdots & \vdots & \vdots & \dots & 1 & -2 \\
0 & 0 & 0 & 0 & 0 & 1
\end{bmatrix}
$$

$\mathbf{D}_{\xi^2}$ is an $(N \times N)$-dimensional matrix, and $\overline{\mathbf{D}}_{\xi^2}$ is an $MN \times MN$ block tridiagonal matrix. The first-order difference operator over time, corresponding to $\partial/\partial v$, is given by

$$
\overline{\mathbf{D}}_v = \frac{1}{\Delta v}
\begin{bmatrix}
-\mathbf{D}_v & \mathbf{D}_v & 0 & \dots & 0 & 0 \\
0 & -\mathbf{D}_v & \mathbf{D}_v & \dots & 0 & 0 \\
0 & 0 & -\mathbf{D}_v & \dots & \vdots & \vdots \\
\vdots & \vdots & \vdots & \dots & -\mathbf{D}_v & \mathbf{D}_v \\
0 & 0 & 0 & \dots & 0 & -\mathbf{D}_v
\end{bmatrix}
\text{ where } \mathbf{D}_v =
\begin{bmatrix}
1 & 0 & 0 & \dots & 0 \\
0 & 1 & 0 & \dots & 0 \\
0 & 0 & 1 & \dots & \vdots \\
\vdots & \vdots & \vdots & \dots & 0 \\
0 & \dots & 0 & 0 & 1
\end{bmatrix}
$$

$\bar{D}_v$ is an $N \times N$ identity matrix, and $\bar{D}_v$ is an $MN \times MN$ matrix. The forward second difference operator over time, corresponding to $\partial^2/\partial v^2$ is given by

$$\bar{D}_{v^2} = \frac{1}{\Delta v^2}\begin{bmatrix} D^1_{v^2} & D^2_{v^2} & D^1_{v^2} & 0 & \ldots & 0 & 0 & 0 \\ 0 & D^1_{v^2} & D^2_{v^2} & D^1_{v^2} & \ldots & 0 & 0 & 0 \\ 0 & 0 & D^1_{v^2} & D^2_{v^2} & \ldots & 0 & 0 & 0 \\ \vdots & \vdots & \vdots & \vdots & \ldots & 0 & 0 & 0 \\ 0 & 0 & 0 & 0 & \ldots & \vdots & D^2_{v^2} & D^1_{v^2} \\ 0 & 0 & 0 & 0 & \ldots & 0 & D^1_{v^2} & D^2_{v^2} \\ 0 & 0 & 0 & 0 & \ldots & 0 & 0 & D^1_{v^2} \end{bmatrix} \text{ with } D^1_{v^2} = \begin{bmatrix} 1 & 0 & 0 & \ldots & 0 \\ 0 & 1 & 0 & \ldots & 0 \\ 0 & 0 & 1 & \ldots & \vdots \\ \vdots & \vdots & \vdots & \ldots & 0 \\ 0 & 0 & 0 & 0 & 1 \end{bmatrix}$$

and

$$D^2_{v^2} = \begin{bmatrix} -2 & 0 & 0 & \ldots & 0 \\ 0 & -2 & 0 & \ldots & 0 \\ \vdots & \vdots & -2 & \ldots & \vdots \\ 0 & 0 & 0 & \ldots & -2 \end{bmatrix}$$

$\bar{D}_{v^2}$ is an $MN \times MN$ block tridiagonal matrix with three $N \times N$ blocks, $D^1_{v^2}$, $D^2_{v^2}$, and again $D^1_{v^2}$. Finally, the mixed forward difference operator, corresponding to $\partial^2/\partial v \partial \xi$, over both time and state is given by

$$\bar{D}_{v\xi} = \frac{1}{\Delta v \Delta \xi}\begin{bmatrix} D_{v\xi} & -D_{v\xi} & 0 & \ldots & 0 & 0 \\ 0 & D_{v\xi} & -D_{v\xi} & \ldots & 0 & 0 \\ \vdots & \vdots & \vdots & \ldots & \vdots & \vdots \\ 0 & 0 & 0 & \ldots & D_{v\xi} & -D_{v\xi} \\ 0 & 0 & 0 & \ldots & 0 & D_{v\xi} \end{bmatrix} \text{ with } D_{v\xi} = \begin{bmatrix} 1 & -1 & 0 & \ldots & 0 & 0 \\ 0 & 1 & -1 & \ldots & 0 & 0 \\ 0 & 0 & 1 & \ldots & \vdots & \vdots \\ \vdots & \vdots & \vdots & \ldots & 1 & -1 \\ 0 & 0 & 0 & \ldots & 0 & 1 \end{bmatrix}$$

$D_{v\xi}$ is an $N \times N$ bidiagonal matrix and $\bar{D}_{v\xi}$ is an $MN \times MN$ block bidiagonal matrix. Denote the operator $(U; V)$ as the L^2 scalar product of the $(MN \times 1)$-dimensional vectors U and V. Then we can write the regularizer as a function of the difference operators and the general column vector G:

$$\Omega(G) = \Delta v \Delta \xi [(G; G) + (\bar{D}_\xi G; \bar{D}_\xi G) + (\bar{D}_{\xi^2}G; \bar{D}_{\xi^2}G) + (\bar{D}_v G; \bar{D}_v G) + (\bar{D}_{v^2}G; \bar{D}_{v^2}G) + (\bar{D}_{v\xi}G; \bar{D}_{v\xi}G)] \quad (7.40)$$

To solve for a unique solution in equation (7.40), we need to solve a discrete analog to the optimand in equation (7.25):

$$M^\alpha_1(F_1) = (\bar{A}_p F_1 - (H_p - H^0_p); \bar{A}_p F_1 - (H_p - H^0_p)) + \alpha_1 \Omega(G) \quad (7.41)$$

The interested reader can find the remaining details for minimizing equation system (7.41), which requires also finding α_1 as a solution to a corresponding discrepancy function, in Bodurtha and Jermakyan's paper, which applies the methodology to Chicago Board Options Exchange (CBOE) S&P 500 option transactions.

7.5   ONE-FACTOR MODELS

If the Black-Scholes assumption of constant volatility is relaxed, we can try to model the evolution of the asset price using a volatility diffusion coefficient that is a deterministic function of time—that is, $\sigma = \sigma(t)$—so that the SDE of the asset price can be written as

$$\frac{dS(t)}{S(t)} = (r - q)dt + \sigma(t)dz(t) \tag{7.42}$$

Define a conditional variance under the risk-neutral measure Q as follows:

$$\text{Var}_t^Q[X(T)] = E_t^Q[X^2(T)] - (E_t^Q[X(T)])^2$$

Then the instantaneous variance of the return on the asset over an infinitesimal time interval dt is

$$\text{Var}_t\left[\frac{dS(t)}{S(t)}\right] = \text{Var}_t\left[\frac{S(t+dt)-S(t)}{S(t)}\right] = E_t\left[\left(rdt + \sigma(t)\sqrt{dt}\varepsilon(t)\right)^2\right] - (rdt)^2 = \sigma^2(t)dt$$

If we consider a random variable

$$\ln\left(\frac{S(T)}{S(t)}\right)$$

the continuously compounded return over the entire finite time horizon, then from Ito's lemma we have:

$$S(T) = S(t)\exp\left\{(r-q)\tau - \frac{1}{2}\int_t^T \sigma^2(u)du + \int_t^T \sigma(u)dz(u)\right\} \tag{7.43}$$

The Ito integral

$$\int_t^T \sigma(u)dz(u)$$

is a normal random variable with mean zero since it is a martingale (i.e., no drift), and with variance

$$
\text{Var}_t \left[\int_t^T \sigma(u) dz(u) \right] = \int_t^T \sigma^2(u) du \tag{7.44}
$$

Therefore, we get

$$
\ln\left(\frac{S(T)}{S(t)} \right) = \mu\tau + \overline{\sigma}\sqrt{\tau}\varepsilon(T) \tag{7.45}
$$

where

$$
\overline{\sigma}^2 = \frac{1}{\tau} \int_t^T \sigma^2(u) du
$$

is defined as the average volatility over the time horizon and

$$
\mu = r - q - \frac{\overline{\sigma}^2}{2}
$$

We can rewrite equation (7.43) as

$$
S(T) = S(t) \exp\left(\mu\tau + \overline{\sigma}\sqrt{\tau}\varepsilon(T) \right) \tag{7.46}
$$

Thus, we see that if we allow the volatility to be a deterministic function of time, the pricing formula is still Black-Scholes, where we need to plug in the average volatility over the lifetime of the option.

The result is also very intuitively simple if we look at it in discrete time. In discrete time:

$$
S(T) = S(t) \exp\left(\mu\tau + \xi\sqrt{\Delta t} \right)
$$

where the random variable

$$
\xi = \sum_{i=1}^N \sigma_i^2 \varepsilon_i
$$

$$
E[\xi] = 0
$$

$$
E[\xi^2] = \sum_{i=1}^N \sigma_i^2 = N\overline{\sigma}^2
$$

where

$$\overline{\sigma}^2 = \frac{1}{N} \sum_{i=1}^{N} \sigma_i^2 = \frac{1}{\tau} \int_t^T \sigma^2(u)du \qquad (7.47)$$

is the average volatility[20] on $[t, T]$. Thus,

$$\xi = \sqrt{N\overline{\sigma}^2}\varepsilon$$

where ε is the standard normal deviate. Then,

$$S(T) = S(t)\exp\left(\mu\tau + \overline{\sigma}\sqrt{\tau}\varepsilon\right)$$

is a lognormal random variable with volatility $\overline{\sigma}$. Notice that this model of time-dependent volatility allows fitting to any term structure of implied volatility and there is no smile effect: Implied volatilities for options of all strikes with the same maturity have the same implied volatility equal to the average volatility.

7.6   CONSTANT ELASTICITY OF VARIANCE MODELS

If we assume that the volatility is a function of the underlying asset, S—that is, $\sigma = \sigma(S)$—then we get the following process:

$$\frac{dS(t)}{S(t)} = (r - q)dt + \sigma(S)dz(t) \qquad (7.48)$$

However, in general, we are no longer able to solve the SDE analytically, and have to do it using numerical methods. The constant elasticity of variance (CEV) model, initially posed by Cox and Ross (1976),[21] assumes such a volatility function:

$$\sigma(S) = \sigma_0 \left(\frac{S}{S(0)}\right)^{\gamma-1} \qquad (7.49)$$

---

[20]Average volatility can be viewed as the volatility implied by ATM options.
[21]Cox and Ross (1976), 145–166. Cox and Ross assume the volatility function is $\sigma S^{-\alpha}$ where $0 \le \alpha \le 1$. Thus, their model for the asset price is $dS = \mu S dt + \sigma S^{1-\alpha}dz$.

where $S(0)$ is the spot level at time 0 (when we calibrate the model). The CEV in (7.20) is characterized by two parameters: the ATM local volatility σ_0 and the skew parameter γ. The estimates of γ that produce the observed implied smile curve in the S&P 500 option market are around –4. The model with $0 < \gamma < 1$ is called restricted CEV since the gamma is not enough to fit the observed smile. The model with $\gamma = 1$ is the standard Black-Scholes lognormal process. Models with $\gamma < 0$ are called unrestricted CEV. They fit the smile rather well. The problem, however, is that for the unrestricted CEV, the volatility goes to infinity as the asset price goes to 0. This is an undesirable feature of the model that can be handled by introducing a cutoff point that prevents the volatility from blowing up. The restricted CEV PDE is actually analytically tractable and can be expressed in terms of hypergeometric (Bessel) functions as shown by Cox and Ross (1976). However, while there are alternative parametric choices that allow the model to fit the observed smile for a given maturity date, such parameterizations do not fit the model to the term structure. Alternative specifications of the volatility are needed.

It is important to note that with the CEV model, the variance of the asset rate of return depends on the price of the underlying asset, and/or time as well. This is a different framework than the Black-Scholes, which assumes constant variance and independence of changes in asset returns on the asset's price level. The Black-Scholes is actually a special case of the CEV model when $\gamma = 1$.

Cox and Rubinstein (1985) provide a closed-form analytic formula for pricing a European call with CEV:

$$C = S \sum_{n=1}^{\infty} g(n, \, x) G(n+\lambda, \, y) - X r^{-t} \sum_{n=1}^{\infty} g(n+\lambda, \, x) G(n, \, y)$$

where

$$\lambda = \frac{1}{2(1-\gamma)}, \ x = \frac{2\lambda \log r}{\tilde{\sigma}^2 (r^{t/\lambda} - 1)} S^{1/\lambda} r^{t/\lambda}, \text{ and } y = \frac{2\lambda \log}{\tilde{\sigma}^2 (r^{t/\lambda} - 1)} X^{1/\lambda}$$

and

$$g(n, \, z) = \frac{e^{-z} z^{n-1}}{(n-1)!}$$

is the gamma probability density function and

$$G(n, \, w) = \int_{w}^{\infty} g(n, \, z) dz$$

is the cumulative gamma distribution function. When using the CEV formula for different values of γ, the values of $\tilde{\sigma}$ are standardized so that the current volatility is the same in each case. Thus, as the skew parameter γ changes, $\tilde{\sigma}$ changes so that $\tilde{\sigma}S^\gamma = \sigma S$. Thus, changes in option prices are due solely to the differences in the way the volatility changes as the asset price changes.[22]

7.7   RECOVERING IMPLIED VOLATILITY SURFACES

In the nonparametric approach, we try to infer the local vol surface from market-traded options using a numerical optimization procedure such as the procedure shown earlier of Bodurtha and Jermakyan (1999). In an ideal world, we would like to find the implied volatility surface $\sigma(S, t)$ that produces the continuum of observable option prices $C(S(0), 0; X, T)$ at time 0. By Dupier's equation, we have

$$\sigma^2(S, t) = \left[\frac{\dfrac{\partial C}{\partial T} + (r - q)X\dfrac{\partial C}{\partial X} - qC}{\dfrac{1}{2}X^2\dfrac{\partial^2 C}{\partial X^2}} \right]_{X \to S, T \to t}$$

Thus, the local volatility is expressed through an infinitesimal calendar spread, an infinitesimal call spread, and an infinitesimal butterfly spread.

The problem with Dupier's equation is that only a finite number of strikes and maturities are actually traded in the market, and the problem of inferring the local volatility surface (and implied probability distribution) from option prices is ill-posed. We can try to overcome this problem by using a nonparametric procedure to handle the case of a finite number of strikes and maturities, known as the inverse problem for the option-pricing PDE. Suppose we have a finite number of market quotes C_{ij} for calls with strikes X_j and maturities T_i. At the same time, these option prices must satisfy the pricing PDE:

$$\frac{1}{2}S^2\frac{\partial^2 C}{\partial S^2} + (r - q)S\frac{\partial C}{\partial S} + \frac{\partial C}{\partial t} = rf$$

subject to the terminal conditions:

$$C(S(T_i), X_j, T_i) = \max(S(T_i) - X_j, 0) \text{ at time } T_i, i = 1, 2, \ldots, N, j = 1, 2, \ldots, M$$

---

[22]Cox and Rubinstein (1985), 364.

The inverse problem for the pricing PDE is to find a local vol surface that produces the observable market quotes for options as solutions to the pricing PDE. Since there are only a finite number of option quotes, the problem is ill-posed. One can try minimizing the least-squares error on the set of option quotes:

$$\sum_{i=1}^{N}\sum_{j=1}^{M}[C(S,\ t;\ X_j,\ T_i)-\overline{C}_{ij}]^2 \tag{7.50}$$

where $C(S,\ t;\ X_j,\ T_i)$ are Black-Scholes vanilla option prices (calculated assuming a functional volatility) and $\overline{C}_{ij}$ are quoted market vanilla option prices (the arithmetic average of recent known bid and offer prices) over a range of strike prices, X_j, $j = 1$, ..., M, and maturities T_i, $i = 1, \ldots, N$.[23]

An additional criterion that we might impose is to find a solution that is also closest to some Black-Scholes (lognormal) prior or which is the smoothest solution. Unfortunately, it is a very complicated numerical optimization problem and gives rise to rather unstable results when a limited number of strikes and expirations is used. In fact, Tikhonov regularization is needed to cope with the ill-posedness of the problem. Such regularization is a self-stabilizing procedure to force "well-posedness" in the problem. Regularization restricts the solution to the smoothest functions that minimize the difference between Black-Scholes prices and quoted market prices. Jackson, Süli, and Howison (1999) use such an approach to generate a deterministic volatility surface represented as a space-time spline by minimizing:

$$\sum_{i=1}^{N}\sum_{j=1}^{M}\left(w_{ij}\left|C(S,\ t;\ X_j,\ T_i)-\overline{C}_{ij}\right|^2\right)^{1/2}+G^2 \tag{7.51}$$

where G is the regularizer:

$$G^2 = \sum_{q=1}^{Q}\sum_{p=1}^{P}\frac{c_1\partial\sigma^2(S_p,\ t_q)/\partial S}{(P+1)(Q+1)}+\sum_{\substack{q=1\\q\neq Q}}^{P}\sum_{p=1}^{P}\frac{c_2\partial\sigma^2(S_p,\ t_q^+)/\partial t}{(P+1)Q}$$

and P is the state-space dimension of the natural cubic spline for $S \in [S_{min}, S_{max}]$, Q is the temporal space dimension of the spline, w is a weighting function that reflects the importance of particular prices; that is, at-the-money prices should be weighted

---

[23]The Black-Scholes prices can be found by solving the Black-Scholes PDE by transforming the problem via a change of variables and then solving the resulting transformed problem by a piecewise quadratic finite-element method in space and Crank-Nicolson finite-difference method in time. See Jackson, Süli, and Howison (1999) for details.

higher than out-of-the-money prices since they are more liquid (it is assumed that $w_{ij} > 0$ and $\Sigma_{ij}\, w_{ij} = 1$), and c_1 and c_2 are positive constants.[24] Their approximation of $\sigma(S, t)$ is specified by the matrix of spline weights $\Sigma_{pq} = \sigma(S_p, t_q)$.

7.8   LOCAL VOLATILITY SURFACES

To fit both the smile and the term structure (the entire implied volatility surface), we need to consider a more general process that allows the volatility to be a function of the asset price and time to maturity, that is, $\sigma = \sigma(t, S)$:

$$dS(t) = \mu S(t)dt + \sigma(t, S)S(t)dz(t) \qquad (7.52)$$

where $\mu = r - q$. We need to solve an inverse problem: find a local volatility surface $\sigma(S, t)$ that produces the given implied volatility surface (matrix). There are two approaches: parametric and nonparametric. In the parametric approach, a parametric form for the local volatility surface is assumed and its parameters are then estimated. After the parameters are estimated, robustness analysis is performed to ensure the model can properly fit the evolution of the surface over time. The model is walked forward on (out of sample) data and the parameters are reestimated at each step. If the parameters are stable (i.e., change slowly over time), the model is said to be robust. Otherwise, if the parameters are unstable (i.e., change sharply over time), the model is not robust. An example of a parametric approach would be to try estimating a CEV process with time-dependent ATM volatilities:

$$dS(t) = \mu S(t)dt + \sigma_0(t)\left(\frac{S(t)}{S(0)}\right)^{\gamma-1} dz(t) \qquad (7.53)$$

---

[24]Jackson, Süli, and Howison (1999), 12.
The natural cubic spline is the smoothest of all piecewise cubic interpolants such that the energy functional

$$\frac{1}{2}\int_{S_{min}}^{S_{max}} \partial^2\sigma(S,\ t)/\partial S^2 dS$$

is minimized. When specifying the spline, $P + 1$ state nodes are used $0 < S_{min} = S_0 < S_1 < \cdots < S_p < \cdots < S_P = S_{max} < \infty$, while $Q + 1$ temporal spline nodes are used $0 = t_0 < t_1 < \cdots < t_q < \cdots t_Q = T_{max}$.

An alternative parametric form is:

$$dS(t) = \mu S(t)dt + \sigma_0(t)\exp\left(-\kappa\left(\frac{S(t) - S(0)}{S(0)}\right)\right)dz(t) \qquad (7.54)$$

The volatility does not blow up as the asset price, $S(t)$, tends to 0, but approaches the finite value $\sigma_0(t)e^\kappa$.

Brigo and Mercurio (2001b, 2001c) have developed a more sophisticated analytic model for finding the local volatility based by allowing the asset marginal (risk-neutral) density to be a mixture of known basic probability densities. They consider an extension of (7.22) to N basic diffusion processes with dynamics[25] given by:

$$dS^i(t) = \mu S^i(t)dt + v_i(S^i(t), t)S^i(t)dz(t), \; i = 1, \ldots, N \qquad (7.55)$$

with an initial value $S^i(0)$ and where, for each t, $p^i(t,\cdot)$ is the density function of $S^i(t)$, that is, $p^i(t, y) = d(Q^T\{S^i(t) \leq y\})/dy$, where $p^i(0)$ is the δ-Dirac function centered in $S_i(0)$, and $v_i(t, y)$'s are real functions satisfying regularity conditions to ensure existence and uniqueness of the solution in (7.24). In particular, for suitable positive constants L and L_i's, the linear-growth conditions hold for the local volatility $\sigma(t, y)$ function and the real-valued volatility functions $v_i(t, y)$:

$$\sigma^2(y, t)y^2 \leq L(1 + y^2) \text{ uniformly in } t \qquad (7.56)$$

and

$$v_i^2(y, t) \leq L_i(1 + y^2) \text{ uniformly in } t, i = 1, \ldots, N \qquad (7.57)$$

We need to find a local volatility such that its T-forward risk-adjusted measure, Q^T-density of S satisfies:

$$p(t, y) = \frac{d}{dy}Q^T\{S(t) \leq y\} = \sum_{i=1}^{N}\lambda_i\frac{d}{dy}Q^T\{S^i(t) \leq y\} = \sum_{i=1}^{N}\lambda_i p^i(t, y) \qquad (7.58)$$

where each $S^i(0)$ is set to $S(0)$, and the λ_i's are strictly positive constants such that

$$\sum_{i=1}^{N}\lambda_i = 1$$

---

[25]S^i can be any asset that follows a diffusion process such as a stock or foreign currency as well as a spot or forward interest rate (simply use F^i instead of S^i).

The λ_i's can be interpreted as weights of each individual marginal density function $p^i(\cdot, t)$. As Brigo and Mercurio show, indeed $p(\cdot, t)$ is a Q^T-density function since, by definition, the T-forward expected asset price is:

$$\int_0^\infty yp(t, y)dy = \sum_{i=1}^N \lambda_i \int_0^\infty yp^i(t, y)dy = \sum_{i=1}^N \lambda_i S(0)e^{\mu t} = S(0)e^{\mu t}$$

Brigo and Mercurio claim that the inverse problem is essentially the reverse of that of finding the marginal density function of the solution of an SDE when the coefficients are known. In particular, $\sigma(t, S(t))$ can be found by solving the Fokker-Planck PDE, which is the equation that must be satisfied for the (random) asset price to be a martingale; that is, the PDE sets the drift of the stochastic process to 0.

$$\frac{\partial}{\partial t} p(t, y) = -\frac{\partial}{\partial y}(\mu y p(t, y)) + \frac{1}{2}\frac{\partial^2}{\partial y^2}(\sigma^2(t, y)y^2 p(t, y)) \qquad (7.59)$$

given that each marginal density $p^i(t, y)$ satisfies the Fokker-Planck equation and assuming the volatility of underlying asset $i = 1, \ldots, N$, is $v_i(t, y) = \sigma(t, y)y$, which is a deterministic function of time and the underlying itself.

$$\frac{\partial}{\partial t} p^i(t, y) = -\frac{\partial}{\partial y}(\mu y p^i(t, y)) + \frac{1}{2}\frac{\partial^2}{\partial y^2}(v_i^2(t, y)p^i(t, y)) \qquad (7.60)$$

Using the linearity of the derivative operator and using definition (7.59),

$$\sum_{i=1}^N \lambda_i \frac{\partial}{\partial t} p^i(t, y) = \sum_{i=1}^N \lambda_i\left[-\frac{\partial}{\partial y}(\mu y p^i(t, y))\right] + \sum_{i=1}^N \lambda_i\left[\frac{1}{2}\frac{\partial^2}{\partial y^2}(\sigma^2(t, y)y^2 p^i(t, y))\right]$$

Then by substituting from (7.60) we get

$$\sum_{i=1}^N \lambda_i\left[\frac{1}{2}\frac{\partial^2}{\partial y^2}(v_i^2(t, y)p^i(t, y))\right] = \sum_{i=1}^N \lambda_i\left[\frac{1}{2}\frac{\partial^2}{\partial y^2}(\sigma^2(t, y)y^2 p^i(t, y))\right] \qquad (7.61)$$

Using the linearity of the second-order derivative operator,

$$\frac{\partial^2}{\partial y^2}\left[\sum_{i=1}^N \lambda_i v_i^2(t, y)p^i(t, y)\right] = \frac{\partial^2}{\partial y^2}\left[\sigma^2(t, y)y^2 \sum_{i=1}^N \lambda_i p^i(t, y)\right]$$

This second-order differential equation for $\sigma(t, \cdot)$ can be solved to yield the general solution:

$$\sigma^2(t, y)y^2 \sum_{i=1}^{N} \lambda_i p^i(t, y) = \sum_{i=1}^{N} \lambda_i v_i^2(t, y)p^i(t, y) + A(t)y + B(t)$$

However, the regularity condition in (7.56) implies that the limit on the left-hand side is zero as $y \to \infty$. In this case, the right-hand side must have a zero limit as well. This occurs if and only if $A(t) = B(t) = 0$ for all t. Therefore, we obtain a function for $\sigma(t, y)$ that is consistent with the marginal density (7.58) and satisfies its regularity condition in (7.56):

$$\sigma(t, y) = \sqrt{\frac{\sum_{i=1}^{N} \lambda_i v_i^2(t, y)p^i(t, y)}{\sum_{i=1}^{N} \lambda_i y^2 p^i(t, y)}} \tag{7.62}$$

Brigo and Mercurio denote

$$\Lambda_i(t, y) = \frac{\lambda_i p^i(t, y)}{\sum_{i=1}^{N} \lambda_i p^i(t, y)} \tag{7.63}$$

for each $i = 1, \ldots, N$ and $(t, y) > (0, 0)$, so that the local volatility can be written as

$$\sigma^2(t, y) = \sum_{i=1}^{N} \Lambda_i(t, y) \frac{v_i^2(t, y)}{y^2}$$

The volatility can be written as a (stochastic) convex combination of the squared volatilities of the basic processes in (7.55). Moreover, for each (t, y), $\Lambda_i(t, y) \geq 0$ for each i and

$$\sum_{i=1}^{N} \Lambda_i(t, y) = 1$$

Moreover, the regularity condition (7.56) is satisfied by setting $L = \max_{i=1, \ldots, N} L_i$ and using the regularity conditions of the basic processes (7.57):

$$\sigma^2(t, y)y^2 = \sum_{i=1}^{N} \Lambda_i(t, y)v_i^2(t, y) \leq \sum_{i=1}^{N} \Lambda_i(t, y)L_i(1 + y^2) \leq L(1 + y^2)$$

While we have shown a strong solution of the local volatility, it is not necessarily unique as verification must done on a case-by-case basis. However, we assume it is and plug (7.62) into the model SDE in (7.50) to yield the asset price dynamics under the forward measure Q^T:

$$dS(t) = \mu S(t)dt + \sqrt{\frac{\sum_{i=1}^{N} \lambda_i v_i^2(t,\ S(t)) p^i(t,\ S(t))}{\sum_{i=1}^{N} \lambda_i S^2(t) p^i(t,\ S)}} S(t) dW(t) \qquad (7.64)$$

Equation (7.64) leads to analytical formulas for European options since using basic densities p^i that are analytically tractable leads to explicit option prices under the model process for the underlying asset which preserves the analytic tractability. In particular, the marginal density as a mixture of lognormals, that is,

$$p^i(t,\ y) = \frac{1}{y V_i(t) \sqrt{2\pi}} \exp\left(-\frac{1}{2V_i^2(t)} \left[\ln \frac{y}{S_0^i} - \mu t + \frac{1}{2} V_i^2(t) \right]^2 \right)$$

where the standard deviation is defined as:

$$V_i(t) = \sqrt{\int_0^t \sigma_i^2(u) du}$$

has been studied often[26] due to its relationship to Black-Scholes and due to its analytical tractability. Moreover, mixtures of lognormal densities work well in practice when used to reproduce market volatility structures. Note that the absence of bounds on the number of basic assets, N, implies that many parameters can be used in the asset-price dynamics to improve consistency with market data. Finally, viewing local volatilities as a mixture of densities can be interpreted by viewing the underlying asset S as a process whose marginal density at time t coincides with the basic density $p^i(t, y)$ with probability λ_i.

7.9 JUMP-DIFFUSION MODELS

The jump-diffusion model allows for large price movements over small time intervals. This is a more realistic model than the Black-Scholes GBM process, which assumes small price movements over small time intervals. In a pure jump process,

---

[26]See Ritchey (1990), Melick and Thomas (1997), and Bhupinder (1998).

each successive price is almost as close to the previous price, but occasionally, there is a low, but nonzero, probability that the price will be significantly different.

Merton proposed a model where in addition to a Brownian motion term, the price process of the underlying asset is allowed to have jumps with frequency λ. The size of the jump is normally distributed. However, the risk of these jumps is assumed to not be priced. It can be shown that the asset price movements converge to a log-Poisson distribution, rather than to a lognormal distribution as $n \to \infty$. The pricing formula of European call option C is

$$C = \sum_{n=0}^{\infty} \frac{e^{-\tilde{\lambda}\tau}(\tilde{\lambda}\tau)^n}{n!} C_{BS}(S, X, r_n, \sigma_n, \tau)$$

where $\tau = T - t$, $\tilde{\lambda} = \lambda(1 + \kappa)$, $C_{BS}(\cdot)$ is the Black-Scholes formula,

$$\sigma_n = \sqrt{\sigma^2 + n\delta^2/\tau}$$

and

$$r_n = r - \lambda\kappa + \frac{n\ln(1+\kappa)}{\tau}$$

In implementing the formula, we need to terminate the infinite sum at some point. But since the factorial function is growing at a much higher rate than any other term, we can terminate at approximately $n = 50$, which should be on the conservative side. To avoid numerical difficulties, use the following expression:

$$\frac{e^{-\tilde{\lambda}\tau}(\tilde{\lambda}\tau)^n}{n!} = \exp\left(\ln\left(\frac{e^{\tilde{\lambda}\tau}(\tilde{\lambda}\tau)^n}{n!}\right)\right) = \exp\left(\tilde{\lambda}\tau + n\ln(\tilde{\lambda}\tau) - \sum_{i=1}^{n}\ln i\right)$$

The following is an implementation for pricing a European call option using Merton's jump-diffusion model:

```
/********************************************************************************
calcJumpDiffusion : calculates the value of a call option with jump diffusion.
[in]:   double price    : price of the stock
        double strike   : strike price
        double rate     : risk-free interest rate
        double div      : dividend yield of stock 1
        double vol      : volatility of stock 1
        double T        : time to maturity (in years)
```

```
           double lambda   : parameter of jump diffusion process
           double kappa    : parameter of jump diffusion process
           double delta    : parameter of jump diffusion process
[out]: double             : call option price
*****************************************************************************/
double JumpDiffusionModel::calcJumpDiffusion(double price, double strike, double
   rate, double vol, double T, double lambda, double kappa, double delta)
{
   const int MAXN = 50;                       // maximum number of iterations
   double lambdatilde = lambda*(1 + kappa);   // lambda tilde
   double logn = 0.0;                         // sum of log(i), i = 1 . . . n
   double r_n = 0.0;                          // adjusted risk-free rate
   double deltasqr = delta*delta;             // delta squared
   double vol_sqr = vol*vol;                  // variance
   double voln = 0.0;                         // sum of volatilities
   double gamma = log(1 + kappa);             // gamma
   double call = exp(lambdatilde*T)*calcBSCallPrice(vol,rate-lambda*kappa,0.0,
      strike,price,T);

   for (int n = 1; n <= MAXN; n++)
   {
      logn += log(n);
      voln = sqrt(vol_sqr + n*deltasqr/T);
      r_n = rate - lambda*kappa + n*gamma/T;
      call += exp(lambdatilde*T + n*log(lambdatilde*T) -
         logn)*calcBSCallPrice(voln,r_n,0.0,strike,price,T);
   }
   return call;
}
```

7.10   TWO-FACTOR MODELS

Since one-factor models cannot capture the evolution of the implied volatility surface, the next stage of generalization is to use a two-factor stochastic model where
both the underlying asset and its volatility, both random variables, evolve simultaneously by SDEs. Such stochastic models are used to model the time evolution of
the implied volatility surface. However, since these two random variables are correlated, it is necessary to impose their correlation into the model:

$$dS / S = \mu(S, t)dt + \sigma(S, t)dW_S$$

$$d\sigma = \alpha(\sigma, t)dt + V(\sigma, t)dW_\sigma$$

where α is the drift of the volatility and V is the volatility of the volatility. Note that
dW's are Wiener processes that are correlated.

$$E[dW_S dW_\sigma] = \rho dt$$

We can translate these correlated deviates into uncorrelated deviates by letting

$$dz_1 = dW_S \quad \text{and} \quad dz_2 = \rho dW_S + \sqrt{1 - \rho^2} \, dW_\sigma$$

so that $E[dz_1 dz_2] = 0$. This two-factor process can be simulated starting from some initial conditions $S(0)$ and $\sigma(0)$.

The correlation is an important part of the model. If the correlation is negative, volatility increases as the underlying asset falls, and volatility decreases as the underlying rises. Empirically, the volatility smirk in the S&P 500 index with a fatter lower tail in the implied probability distribution is observed. If the correlation is zero, the symmetric smile with both slightly fat tails is observed as in the foreign exchange market. If the correlation is greater than zero, volatility decreases as the underlying falls and increases as the underlying rises. Empirically, one gets a skew with a fatter upper tail in the implied probability distribution, which is usually not present in financial markets.

The following is an implementation of a spread option stochastic volatility model. There are two assets (i.e., two stocks), S_1 and S_2, each of which follows a GBM diffusion process, but where the variance of returns, V_1 and V_2, of the assets follows mean reverting square root processes; see Hull and White (1999). S_1 follows

$$dS = (r - q)S dt + \sqrt{V_1} \, S dz_1^S$$

and S_2 follows

$$dS = (r - q)S dt + \sqrt{V_2} \, S dz_2^S$$

where dz_1 and dz_2 are Wiener processes and V_1 and V_2 are the variances of returns of S_1 and S_2, respectively, following this mean-reverting square root process:

$$dV_1 = \alpha(\overline{V}_1 - V_1)dt + \xi_1 \sqrt{V_1} \, dz_1^V$$

and

$$dV_2 = \alpha(\overline{V}_2 - V_2)dt + \xi_2 \sqrt{V_2} \, dz_2^V$$

where α is the rate of mean reversion, $\overline{V}_1$ and $\overline{V}_2$ are the reversion levels, ξ_1 and ξ_2

are the volatilities of the variance of returns, $V_1 = \sigma_1^2$ and $V_2 = \sigma_2^2$, and the dz's are Wiener processes with the following correlation matrix:

$$\boldsymbol{\rho}_z = \begin{bmatrix} 1 & \rho_{12} & \rho_{13} & \rho_{14} \\ \rho_{21} & 1 & \rho_{23} & \rho_{24} \\ \rho_{31} & \rho_{32} & 1 & \rho_{34} \\ \rho_{41} & \rho_{42} & \rho_{43} & 1 \end{bmatrix}$$

We can generate correlated deviates from this matrix, for simulating diffusion paths, by transforming it into an eigensystem:

$$\boldsymbol{\rho}_z = \Gamma \Lambda \Gamma'$$

where Γ is the matrix of eigenvectors and Λ is the matrix with eigenvalues along the diagonal as shown in section 2.3. Correlated deviates can also be generated with a Cholesky decomposition.

The following is an implementation of this stochastic volatility spread option model:

```
/**************************************************************************
calcStochasticVolSpread : calculates the value of a call spread option on two
   stocks.
[in]:   double price1  : price of stock 1
        double price2  : price of stock 2
        double X       : strike price
        double rate    : risk-free interest rate
        double Vbar1   : mean-reversion level for stock 1
        double Vbar2   : mean-reversion level for stock 2
        double div1    : dividend yield of stock 1
        double div2    : dividend yield of stock 2
        double alpha1  : mean reversion rate of the variance for stock 1
        double alpha2  : mean reversion rate of the variance for stock 2
        double T       : time to maturity (in years)
        double eta1    : volatility of the variance of stock 1
        double eta2    : volatility of the variance of stock 2
        double R       : correlation (symmetric) matrix
        int M          : number of simulations
        int N          : number of time steps
[out]: spread call price (double)
**************************************************************************/
double SpreadOption::calcStochasticVolSpread(double price1, double price2,
    double X, double rate, double Vbar1, double Vbar2, double div1, double div2,
    double alpha1, double alpha2, double T, double eta1, double eta2,
    SymmetricMatrix& R, int M, int N)
{
    N = 1;                              // No path dependency
```

```
double dt = T/N;                 // time step size
int i, j;                        // counter
int size = R.Nrows();            // size of correlation matrix (number of rows
                                 // = number of cols)
double sum1 = 0.0;               // sum of all the call values on stock 1 at
                                 // time T
double sum2 = 0.0;               // sum of all the call values on stock 2 at
                                 // time T
double S1 = 0.0;                 // stock price 1
double S2 = 0.0;                 // stock price 2
double lnS1 = 0.0;               // log of stock price 1
double lnS2 = 0.0;               // log of stock price 2
double CT = 0.0;                 // call price at maturity
double SD = 0.0;                 // standard deviate of call price
double SE = 0.0;                 // standard error of call price
double callValue = 0.0;          // call price (return value)
double V1 = Vbar1;               // variance of stock price 1
double V2 = Vbar2;               // variance of stock price 2
double eta1dt = eta1*sqrt(dt);   // volatility of the variance of stock 1
double eta2dt = eta2*sqrt(dt);   // volatility of the variance of stock 2
double z1[4];                    // stores copy of correlated deviates for
                                 // simulation
double* z = new double[4];       // correlated deviates vector returned from
                                 // genCorrelated
MatrixUtil mu;                   // matrix utility class

for (i = 0; i < M; i++) // for each simulation
{
  // for each simulation, reset the initial stock prices
  lnS1 = log(price1);
  lnS2 = log(price2);
  V1 = Vbar1;
  V2 = Vbar2;

  for (j = 0; j < N; j++) // for each time step
  {
    // generate correlated deviates and store them in z
    z = mu.genCorrelatedDeviates(R,dt,z1);

    // simulate variances first
    V1 = V1 +  alpha1*dt*(Vbar1 - V1) + eta1dt*sqrt(V1)*z[2];
    V2 = V2 +  alpha2*dt*(Vbar2 - V2) + eta2dt*sqrt(V2)*z[3];

    // simulate asset prices
    lnS1 = lnS1 + (rate - div1 - 0.5*V1)*dt + sqrt(V1)*sqrt(dt)*z[0];
    lnS2 = lnS2 + (rate - div2 - 0.5*V2)*dt + sqrt(V2)*sqrt(dt)*z[1];
  }

  S1 = exp(lnS1);
  S2 = exp(lnS2);

  CT = max(0, S1 - S2 - X); // calculate payoff
  sum1 = sum1 + CT;
```

```
    sum2 = sum2 + CT*CT;
}
callValue = exp(-rate*T)*sum1/M;
cout << "callValue = " << callVal

SD = sqrt((exp(-2*rate*T)/(M-1))*(sum2 - (sum1*sum1)/M));
cout << "stddev=" << SD <<endl;

SE = SD/sqrt(M);
cout << "stderr = " <<  SE  << endl;

return callValue;
}
```

As an example, suppose $S_1 = 50$, $S_2 = 55$, $X = 1$, $r = 0.06$, $q_1 = 0.02$, $q_2 = 0.03$, $\alpha_1 = 1.0$, $\alpha_2 = 2.0$, $\bar{V}_1 = 0.06$, $\bar{V}_2 = 0.20$, $\xi_1 = 0.09$, $\xi_2 = 0.15$, $T = 1$, $M = 100$, and $N = 1$, and that the correlation matrix is:

$$\rho = \begin{pmatrix} 1.0 & 0.60 & 0.25 & 0.01 \\ 0.60 & 1.0 & 0.01 & 0.32 \\ 0.25 & 0.01 & 1.0 & 0.30 \\ 0.01 & 0.32 & 0.30 & 1.0 \end{pmatrix}$$

The Cholesky decomposition matrix **L** is:

$$L = \begin{pmatrix} 1.0 & 0 & 0 & 0 \\ 0.60 & 0.80 & 0 & 0 \\ 0.25 & -0.175 & 0.952 & 0 \\ 0.01 & 0.392 & 0.385 & 0.835 \end{pmatrix}$$

which can be used to generate correlated deviates. If we use principal component analysis of ρ into an eigenvalue system, we get:

$$\Gamma = \begin{pmatrix} 0.593 & -0.384 & 0.393 & 0.588 \\ -0.622 & 0.337 & 0.346 & 0.616 \\ -0.337 & -0.620 & -0.618 & 0.346 \\ 0.385 & 0.595 & -0.587 & 0.392 \end{pmatrix} \text{ and } \Lambda = \begin{pmatrix} 0.235 & 0 & 0 & 0 \\ 0 & 0.862 & 0 & 0 \\ 0 & 0 & 1.120 & 0 \\ 0 & 0 & 0 & 1.782 \end{pmatrix}$$

The eigenvalues represent the variances of the independent Brownian motions. The rows of Γ represent the proportions of a set of four independent Brownian motions since the transpose of Γ is equal to its inverse. The correlated deviates can be generated from linear combinations of the independent Brownian motions:

$$
\begin{bmatrix} dW_1 \\ dW_2 \\ dW_3 \\ dW_4 \end{bmatrix} = \begin{pmatrix} 0.593 & -0.384 & 0.393 & 0.588 \\ -0.622 & 0.337 & 0.346 & 0.616 \\ -0.337 & -0.620 & -0.618 & 0.346 \\ 0.385 & 0.595 & -0.587 & 0.392 \end{pmatrix} \begin{pmatrix} 0.485 & 0 & 0 & 0 \\ 0 & 0.928 & 0 & 0 \\ 0 & 0 & 1.059 & 0 \\ 0 & 0 & 0 & 1.335 \end{pmatrix} \begin{bmatrix} dz_1 \\ dz_2 \\ dz_2 \\ dz_3 \end{bmatrix}
$$

or

$$
\begin{bmatrix} dW_1 \\ dW_2 \\ dW_3 \\ dW_4 \end{bmatrix} = \begin{pmatrix} 0.288 & -0.357 & 0.416 & 0.785 \\ -0.302 & 0.313 & 0.366 & 0.823 \\ -0.163 & -0.576 & -0.654 & 0.462 \\ 0.187 & 0.522 & -0.621 & 0.524 \end{pmatrix} \begin{bmatrix} dz_1 \\ dz_2 \\ dz_2 \\ dz_3 \end{bmatrix}
$$

Using 10,000 Monte Carlo simulations, the value using an eigenvalue-eigenvector decomposition is \$5.24 with a standard deviation of 7.292 and a standard error of 0.0729, while the price using a Cholesky decomposition is \$5.29 with a standard deviation of 7.093 with a standard error of 0.0709. Note that price estimates can differ between a Cholesky and an eigenvector-eigenvalue decomposition when generating correlated deviates. Note that

$$LL' = \Gamma\Lambda\Gamma' = \Gamma\Lambda^{1/2}\Lambda^{1/2}\Gamma' = \rho$$

and

$$L = \Gamma\Lambda\Gamma'(L')^{-1} = \Gamma\Lambda^{1/2}\Lambda^{1/2}\Gamma'(L')^{-1} = \rho(L')^{-1}$$

holds, but that in general,

$$\Lambda^{1/2}\Gamma'(L')^{-1} \neq I$$

where I is the identity matrix so that

$$Lz \neq \Gamma\Lambda^{1/2}z$$

even though both sides generate correlated deviates. Therefore, both methods decompose the correlation matrix, but they generate different correlated bases, which can lead to different prices. Note L is lower-triangular while $\Gamma\Lambda^{1/2}$ is not.[27] However, as the number of simulations increases the two prices converge.

---

[27]In practice, the Cholesky method is used more often, though one can use either method or take the average of the two methods.

7.11   HEDGING WITH STOCHASTIC VOLATILITY

When volatility is stochastic, it is not possible to maintain a perfect hedge. Errors are introduced by the fact that the actual (process) volatility is unknown. Thus, if the implied (hedging) volatility is not equal to the process volatility, there will be a standard error of the portfolio value. This standard error increases with the volatility error since the variance of the portfolio value is proportional to the variance of the volatility forecast.

Suppose we want to price an option f that pays off $F(S_T)$ at expiration. We will try to hedge it by trading both the underlying asset and another option g that pays off $G(S_T^*)$ at its expiration T^*. We will construct a dynamic self-financing replicating strategy that exactly replicates the option f.

We construct the portfolio

$$\Pi = \Delta S + hg - NA - f$$

That is, we sell one option f and hedge with Δ shares of S and h options g, and finance by selling short N shares of the money market account, effectively borrowing at the risk-free rate.

Assuming our strategy is self-financing so we don't have to differentiate the weights, the change in the portfolio value over dt is

$$
\begin{aligned}
d\Pi &= \Delta dS + hdg - NdA - df \\
&= \Delta(mSdt + \sigma S dz_S^P) + h(m_g gdt + \sigma S \frac{\partial g}{\partial S} dz_\sigma^P + \beta \frac{\partial g}{\partial \sigma} dz_\sigma^P) \\
&\quad - m_f fdt - \sigma S \frac{\partial f}{\partial S} dz_S^P - \beta \frac{\partial f}{\partial \sigma} dz_\sigma^P - r(\Delta S + hg - f)dt
\end{aligned}
$$

where Ito's lemma on two stochastic variables, S and σ, is used (we assume σ follows the general diffusion process $d\sigma = \alpha dt + \beta dz_\sigma^P$ with drift rate α and diffusion rate β, i.e., volatility of the volatility):

$$df = m_f fdt + \sigma S \frac{\partial f}{\partial S} dz_S^P + \beta \frac{\partial f}{\partial \sigma} dz_\sigma^P$$

where

$$m_f f = \frac{\partial f}{\partial t} + mS\frac{\partial f}{\partial S} + \alpha \frac{\partial f}{\partial S} + \frac{1}{2}\sigma^2 S^2 \frac{\partial^2 f}{\partial S^2} + \rho \beta \sigma S \frac{\partial^2 f}{\partial \sigma \partial S} + \frac{1}{2}\beta^2 \frac{\partial^2 f}{\partial \sigma^2}$$

m_f is the drift rate under the real-world measure P, and ρ is the correlation between the underlying asset and its volatility. We can replicate the option f by using the dynamic trading strategy (Δ, h, N), so that $d\Pi(t) = 0$. It can be shown, after some algebra, that this is equivalent to the following relationships:

$$\Delta = \frac{\partial f}{\partial S} - h\frac{\partial g}{\partial S}, \quad h = \frac{\kappa_f}{\kappa_g}, \quad \kappa_f = \frac{\partial f}{\partial \sigma}, \quad \kappa_g = \frac{\partial g}{\partial \sigma}$$

and

$$h\left[(m_g - r)g - (m-r)S\frac{\partial g}{\partial S}\right] = \left[(m_f - r)f - (m-r)S\frac{\partial f}{\partial S}\right]$$

The first relationship states that Δ is the delta of the portfolio of options $f - hg$ where the hedge ratio h is the ratio of two vegas—the vega of option f and the vega of option g. The second relationship can be rewritten as:

$$\frac{(m_g - r)g - (m-r)S\frac{\partial g}{\partial S}}{\beta\kappa_g} = \frac{(m_f - r)f - (m-r)S\frac{\partial f}{\partial S}}{\beta\kappa_f}$$

This is equivalent to the expression that for any claim f the quantity

$$\lambda_\sigma(S,\sigma,t) = \frac{(m_f - r)f - (m-r)S\frac{\partial f}{\partial S}}{\beta\kappa_f}$$

is independent of any features of the claim f and depends on S, σ, and t only. This can be rewritten as:

$$m_f f = rf + \sigma\lambda_S S\frac{\partial f}{\partial S} + \beta\kappa_f\lambda_\sigma$$

That is, the return on the option is equal to the risk-free rate of return plus the risk premium associated with the underlying asset risk (S-risk) and the risk premium associated with the volatility risk (σ-risk). Substituting in the expressions from Ito's lemma, we derive the pricing PDE of a (contingent) claim with stochastic volatility:

$$\frac{1}{2}\sigma^2 S^2 \frac{\partial^2 f}{\partial S^2} + \frac{1}{2}\beta^2\frac{\partial^2 f}{\partial \sigma^2} + \rho\beta\sigma S\frac{\partial^2 f}{\partial S\partial \sigma} + rS\frac{\partial f}{\partial S} + (\alpha - \beta\lambda_\sigma)\frac{\partial f}{\partial \sigma} + \frac{\partial f}{\partial t} = rf$$

where $\alpha - \beta\lambda_\sigma$ is the drift rate of the volatility in the risk-neutral world equal to its drift rate in the real world minus the market price of volatility risk λ multiplied by the volatility of the volatility β. The risk-neutral processes of the underlying asset and volatility are:

$$dS/S = rdt + \sigma dz_S^Q$$

and

$$d\sigma = (\alpha - \beta\lambda_\sigma)dt + \beta dz_\sigma^Q$$

respectively, where Q is the risk-neutral measure and $E[dz_S^Q \, dz_\sigma^Q] = \rho dt$.

The change of measure from the real-world measure P to the risk-neutral measure Q is

$$dz_S^P = dz_S^Q - \lambda_S dt \quad \text{and} \quad dz_\sigma^P = dz_\sigma^Q - \lambda_\sigma dt$$

If volatility were a traded asset, then $\alpha - \beta\lambda = r$. Since volatility itself is not traded, we can only trade derivatives on it.[28]

We need a way to estimate the risk-neutral drift of the volatility. Since volatility itself is not traded, it cannot be directly estimated. If we had liquid futures or forward contracts on volatility, we could estimate the drift from forward prices. However, we have only (liquid) options available, and since they are highly nonlinear in volatility, it is difficult to estimate. We can make assumptions about the risk-neutral volatility drift, and then we can solve the stochastic volatility PDE by Monte Carlo simulation based on the Feynman-Kac formula (see Chapter 1) as an expectation over the two-factor risk-neutral process.

---

[28]This is similar to the case in futures markets with consumption commodities.

CHAPTER 8

Statistical Models

In the previous chapter, we examined various models to describe volatility structures. In this chapter, we examine another way to model volatility—namely using statistical models. Statistical models, such as generalized autoregressive conditional heteroskedasticity (GARCH), provide the advantage over parametric approaches in that they use robust statistical methods to actually estimate volatility structures. We examine several of these models and show how they can be used for volatility estimation and forecasting. In section 8.1, we give an overview of statistical models and why they are needed. In section 8.2, we discuss moving average models and provide an implementation. In section 8.3, we discuss exponential moving average models and provide an implementation. In section 8.4, we discuss GARCH models. In section 8.5, we discuss asymmetric GARCH models. In section 8.6, GARCH models for high-frequency data are examined. In section 8.7, estimation problems of GARCH models are discussed. In section 8.8, we discuss using GARCH in an option pricing model using a lattice. Finally, in section 8.9, we discuss GARCH forecasting and provide a GARCH forecasting example.

8.1   OVERVIEW

Option pricing models such as Black-Scholes, as discussed in Chapter 7, can be used to calculate implied volatilities. In addition, they can be used to forecast the volatility of the underlying asset over the life of the option. Statistical models can also be used to calculate implied and forecasted volatilities and correlations. However, the forecasts and implied volatilities computed from option pricing models and statistical models will differ since the estimates use different data and different models that are based on different assumptions. Moreover, most statistical models use asset returns as data input instead of prices, rates, and yields because the latter are generally nonstationary while the former are not.[1] In contrast, the Black-Scholes model

---

[1]This is especially true in principal component analysis (PCA) where prices, rates, and yields need to be transformed (i.e., normalized) into returns before applying PCA. Otherwise, the first principal component will be dominated by the input variable with the greatest volatility.

uses asset prices since all the parameters are assumed to be constant through the lifetime of the option. Thus, the model assumes stationarity.

Implied methods use current data on market prices of options. Consequently, implied volatilities incorporate the forward expectations of market participants about the likely future movements of the underlying asset. Implied volatility methods are based on Black-Scholes assumptions: complete markets, no arbitrage, constant volatility, and a geometric Brownian motion (GBM) continuous time diffusion process for the underlying asset price. The Black-Scholes pricing model assumes asset price returns are lognormally distributed. But, as discussed in section 8.5, the implied probability distribution of returns has fatter tails and is leptokurtotic.

On the other hand, statistical models used to compute volatility estimates and forecasts use historical data on asset price returns in a discrete time model. Statistical models are based on time series data. The statistical properties of the time series data, such as the mean and variance over a given time interval, are used in turn to make forecasts. Statistical methods do not usually make assumptions about the underlying data distribution a priori especially for stochastic data that is time-varying.[2] However, assumptions about the asymptotic distribution (for very large sample sizes) and statistical properties about the data generating process (i.e., ergodicity, stationarity, or nonstationarity) are often made if such properties are needed to have a robust forecasting model. Certainly, for model parameter estimation, one makes assumptions of the distribution needed to compute maximum likelihood estimates and likelihood ratio test statistics.

In addition, assumptions about the underlying distribution of the sampling errors captured by the noise (error) term in a regression equation, for example, are made. It is common to assume a normally distributed i.i.d. white noise process in many models where it is thought that observations are uncorrelated over time. These assumptions can be tested with confidence and statistical tests such as Durbin-Watson.

It is important to note that when dealing with estimating or forecasting volatility and correlations, the time period horizon can significantly affect the estimates. If a major market event occurs during the observed time period, it can affect and bias future forecasts. *Ghost effects*, for instance, can occur in short-term equally weighted moving average models where there is a large jump in volatility on the day of the market event that remains at elevated levels over the entire moving average period and then drops precipitously the day after the period ends.

As Carol Alexander cites, "the 240-day volatility of the FTSE jumped up to 26 percent the day after Black Monday and stayed at that level for almost a whole year since one large squared return had the same weight in the average for 240 days. But exactly 240 days after the event, the large return fell out of the average and the

---

[2]The actual distribution of the data is often inferred a posteriori only once a large enough (i.e., statistically significant) sample (time series size) has been obtained from the population.

volatility forecast returned based to its long-run level of around 13 percent despite no significant events. This does not reflect actual market conditions so caution must be used in using such a model."[3]

Consequently, the type of statistical model used as well as any adjustments that need to be made to the data needed to be considered. It may be necessary to detrend or make seasonal adjustments with time series data. As an additional note, we take the logarithms of asset returns as in section 7.1 to compute continuously compounded returns, rather than use annualized returns. The reason is simply that we have assumed that the asset follows a continuous time diffusion process. However, in statistical modeling, the frequency of the time series data determines whether continuous, annualized, or n-day returns should be used. Thus, daily or intraday returns, which are high-frequency returns, can be approximated with continuous compounding, while lower-frequency returns such as weekly or monthly returns can be computed on an annualized basis so that the estimate of the variance of returns at time t is:

$$\hat{\sigma}_t^2 = \frac{1}{N-1}\sum_{i=1}^{N}(r_{t-i} - \bar{r})^2 \tag{8.1}$$

where $\bar{r}$ is the mean return over the time period and r_{t-i} is the n-day return at time $t - i, i = 1, \ldots , N$. If we use annualized returns, then:

$$r_{t-i} = \left(\frac{S_t}{S_{t-i}}\right)^{1/A} \tag{8.2}$$

where A is the number of returns (and thus trading days) per year; that is, $A = 252$.[4] The volatility is then annualized by taking the square root of the variance at time t and then multiplying by

$$100/\sqrt{A}$$

so that the annualized volatility at time t is

$$100\hat{\sigma}_t/\sqrt{A}$$

---

[3]Alexander (2001a), 52–53.
[4]If an n-day return is used, then use $1/n$ in the exponent. If $n = 1$, then the one-day return is simply S_t/S_{t-1}.

By annualizing the volatility, returns of different frequencies can be compared on the same scale.[5]

In this section, we provide a *StatModel* class that can expose the methods and functionality we will need for different statistical models such as the moving average, exponential moving average, and GARCH models. We define the *StatModel* class as follows:

```cpp
#ifndef _STATMODEL__
#define _STATMODEL__

#include "newmat.h"      // from Newmat matrix library
#include "Utility.h"     // utility class
#include <vector>        // stl vector
#include <math.h>        // math header
#include <fstream>       // file input output header
#include <numeric>       // numeric library
using namespace std;     // standard template library


class StatModel
{
  protected:
  vector<double> od;              // omega derivatives
  vector<double> ad;              // alpha derivatives
  vector<double> bd;              // beta derivatives
  vector<double> sd;              // second derivatives
  vector<double> returns;         // returns of asset prices
  vector<double> y;               // y = a + bx + e
  vector<double> yhat;            // yhat = a + bx
  vector<double> x;               // independent variable
  vector<double> e2;              // square errors
  vector<double> e;               // regression residual errors
  vector<double> h;               // vector of GARCH volatilities
  vector<double> se;              // standard errors of coefficients
  Matrix X;                       // for multiple regressions
  vector<Matrix> matder;          // vector of Hessian matrices N
  vector<Matrix> matder1;         // vector of matrices of form Z + bN
  vector<Matrix> matder2;         // vector of matrices of form Z' + bN
  ColumnVector LLD;               // column vector of log likelihood derives
  Matrix H;                       // Hessian matrix (holds second order derivatives)
  ColumnVector B;                 // coefficients in multiple regressions
  ColumnVector Y;                 // column vector of dependent variable
  ColumnVector X1;                // column vector of independent variables
```

[5]See Alexander (2001a), 5. The volatility should be annualized regardless of the compounding frequency of the returns.

```
ColumnVector SE;                      // column vector of standard deviations
int T;                                // time series length (number of data points)
public:
  StatModel() {}                      // default constructor
  StatModel(vector<double> y,
    vector<double> x) :
    y(y), x(x), T(y.size()) { }
  StatModel(ColumnVector v,
    Matrix m) :                       // overloaded constructor
    Y(v), X(m) { }
  StatModel(ColumnVector y,
    ColumnVector x) :                 // overloaded constructor
    Y(y), X1(x) { }
  virtual ~StatModel() { }            // destructor
  vector<double> MA(int lag,
    vector<double>& prices);          // computes moving average
  vector<double> MA(int lag);         // overloaded moving average function

  vector<double> EWMA(double          // computes exponential moving average
    lambda, vector<double>& prices);
  ColumnVector GARCH11                // computes GARCH(1,1) parameters
    (vector<double>& prices,
    StatModel &sm);
  double calcConstCoeff();            // computes constant
                                      // regression intercept
  double calcAve(vector<double>       // computes dependent
    & y);                             // variable average
  double calcBeta();                  // computes beta coefficient
                                      // of single var. regression
  double getXAve();                   // return independent
                                      // variable average
  double getYAve();                   // returns dependent
                                      // variable average
  vector<double>& calcErrors();       // computes residual
                                      // regression errors
  vector<double> calcReturns
    (vector<double>& returns);        // compute asset returns
  double calVarEstimator();           // compute variance estimate
  double calcSDEstimator();           // compute standard deviation estimate
  double calcX2Dev();                 // calculates sum of (x - xave)*(x - xave)
  double calcY2Dev();                 // calculates sum of (y - yave)*(y - yave)
  ColumnVector calcLogDerives         // calculates log derivatives w.r.t.
    (ColumnVector theta);             // parameters
  Matrix calcHessian(ColumnVector
    theta);                           // calculates Hessian
  vector<double>& calcSE();           // calculates the standard error
  int getSampleSize();                // returns data sample size
  double calcR2();                    // calculates R2 - correlation coefficient
  ColumnVector calcBetas();           // calculates beta
                                      // regression coefficients
  ColumnVector calcSEs();             // computes a column vector of standard
                                      // errors
  void readData();                    // read data file
```

```
      void printStats();                        // output statistics
      double calcResiduals();                   // compute residual errors
      vector<double> getErrors();               // return vector of errors
      ColumnVector getLogDerives();             // return vector of log derivatives
      ColumnVector getVolDerives(int i,         // return derivative w.r.t. ith data
         double beta);                          // and beta values
      Matrix getVolSecondDerives(int i,         // return second deriv. w.r.t. ith
         double beta);                          // data and beta values
      double calcLambda(ColumnVector theta);    // compute lambda
      double calcBeta1();                       // alternative single var. regression
                                                // coeff. calculation

      void setY(vector<double>& y);             // store dependent regression variables
      void setX(vector<double>& x);             // store independent variables
      void setT(int size);                      // store data time series size
};
#endif _STATMODEL__
```

8.2   MOVING AVERAGE MODELS

Moving average (MA) models of volatility and correlation assume asset returns are independent and identically distributed. There are no time-varying assumptions so that moving averages provide only an estimate of the unconditional volatility, assumed to be a constant, and the current estimate is used as the forecast. Volatility estimates can change over time, but this is due to sampling errors or noise in the MA model since no other model features allow for its variation. Equally weighted MA models are used to make *historic volatility* and correlation estimates and forecasts. An equally weighted average of asset returns is calculated over a fixed time window that is rolled through time, each day adding the new return and taking off the oldest return.

An n-day historic volatility estimate based on an equally weighted average of the logarithms of n mean squared daily returns can be computed using equation (8.1).

The following code is an implementation of a moving average of an arbitrary lag:

```
/****************************************************************************
MA: computes the n-day moving average of the volatility of asset returns
[in]:   int lag : time lag of moving average
        vector<double> prices : vector of asset prices
[out]:  vector<double> of moving average volatilities
****************************************************************************/
vector<double> StatModel::MA(int lag, vector<double>& prices)
```

```cpp
{
  vector<double> returns;               // vector of asset returns
  vector<double> vols;                  // vector of volatilities
  vector<double>::iterator iter;        // vector iterator
  double ret = 0.0;                     // continuously compounded return at time i
  double sum = 0.0;                     // add up total returns
  double var = 0.0;                     // sum of errors squared
  double ave = 0.0;                     // average return
  int N = prices.size();                // cache sizes of time series
  int A = 252;                          // assume 252 trading days per year
  int i, j;

  for (i = 0; i < N-1; i++)
  {
    // calculate continuously compounded return
    ret = log(prices[i+1]/prices[i]);
    returns.push_back(ret);
    sum = sum + ret;
  }
  // calculate mean average return
  ave = sum/N;

  for (i = 0; i < returns.size() - lag; i++)
  {
    var = 0.0;
    for (j = 0; j < lag; j++)
    {
      var += (returns[lag+i-j-1] - ave)*(returns[lag+i-j-1] - ave);
    }
    vols.push_back(100*sqrt(var/((lag-1)*(A))));
  }

  i = 0;
  // print of MA volatilities
  for (iter = vols.begin(); iter != vols.end(); iter++)
  {
    cout << *iter << endl;
    i++;
  }
  return returns;
}
```

Figure 8.1 plots 5-day, 30-day, and 120-day moving averages of the FTSE 100 index using closing index prices from January 3, 1996, to December 16, 1999. These prices are passed into the MA function, along with the time lag, and converted into logarithmic returns that are used in the moving average. As Figure 8.1 shows, the longer the lag, the smoother the time series.

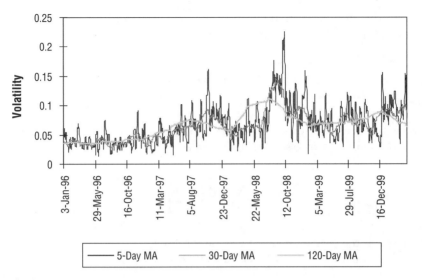

FIGURE 8.1   Moving Averages of FTSE 100

8.3   EXPONENTIAL MOVING AVERAGE MODELS

Another model commonly used to estimate and forecast unconditional variance is the exponential weighted moving average (EWMA) model since if used correctly EWMAs can generate more accurate estimates of short-term volatility or correlation than equally weighted moving averages. EWMA models place more weight on more recent observations. Like the MA model, a large asset return (and thus squared asset return) caused by a market event will cause volatility estimates in the EWMA to react immediately. However, unlike the MA model, the effect of this return in EWMA gradually diminishes over time. The reaction of EWMA volatility estimates to market events persists over time based on the magnitude of the smoothing constant (decay factor) λ, $0 < \lambda < 1$. The larger λ is, the more weight is placed on past observations and the smoother the time series becomes.

The n-period EWMA of a time series $\{y_i\,,\ i = 1, \ldots, N\}$ (i.e., asset returns) is defined as:

$$\frac{\sum_{i=1}^{n} \lambda^{i-1} y_{t-i}}{\sum_{i=1}^{n} \lambda^{i-1}} \tag{8.3}$$

As $n \to \infty$, the exponential weighted moving average places no weight on observations far in the past. An infinite EWMA may be written as:

$$(1-\lambda)\sum_{i=1}^{n}\lambda^{i-1}y_{t-i}$$

since the denominator of equation (8.3) tends to $1/(1 - \lambda)$ as $n \to \infty$. For an EWMA, volatility of asset returns becomes:

$$\hat{\sigma}_t^2 = (1-\lambda)\sum_{i=1}^{n}\lambda^{i-1}r_{t-i}^2 \qquad (8.4)$$

where r_t is the percentage price change for day t.

The equation for EWMA can also be stated as:

$$\hat{\sigma}_t^2 = \lambda\sigma_{t-1}^2 + (1 - \lambda)r_t^2$$

In the EWMA model that is implemented as follows, λ and the vector of asset prices are passed as parameters into the method. The prices are converted into logarithmic returns, which are then used in the EWMA model:

```
/*********************************************************************************
EWMA : computes the exponential weighted moving average of the volatility of asset
       returns
[in]    double lambda            : weight of past observations : decay factor
        vector<double> prices    : vector of asset prices
[out] : vector<double>           : EWMA volatilities
*********************************************************************************/
vector<double> StatModel::EWMA(double lambda, vector<double>& prices)
{
   vector<double> returns;           // vector of returns
   vector<double> vols;              // vector of volatilities
   vector<double>::iterator iter;    // vector iterator
   double ret = 0.0;                 // continuously compounded return at time i
   double sum = 0.0;                 // add up total returns
   double var = 0.0;                 // sum of squared errors
   double ave = 0.0;                 // average return
   int N = prices.size();            // cache sizes of time series
   const int lag = 100;              // moving average time lag
   const int A = 252;                // number of trading days
```

```
int i, j;

for (i = 0; i < N-1; i++)
{
  // calculate continuously compounded return
  ret = log(prices[i+1]/prices[i]);
  returns.push_back(ret);
  sum = sum + ret;
}
// calculate mean average return
ave = sum/N;

for (i = 0; i < returns.size() - lag; i++)
{
  var = 0.0;
  for (j = 1; j < lag; j++)
  {
    var += pow(lambda,j-1)*(returns[lag+i-j-1] - ave)*(returns[lag+i-j-1] - ave);
  }
  var = (1 - lambda)*var;

  // annualize volatility
  vols.push_back(100*sqrt(var/A));
}

// print out of EWMA volatilities
for (iter = vols.begin(); iter != vols.end(); iter++)
{
  cout << *iter << endl;
  i++;
}
return returns;
}
```

Figure 8.2 shows the EWMA of the DAX index from January 1996 to May 2000 for $\lambda = 0.75$, $\lambda = 0.85$, and $\lambda = 0.95$. As expected, as λ gets larger, the moving average series becomes smoother since past observations have more weight.

While the MA and EWMA models work well for modeling i.i.d. returns, in reality returns are not i.i.d., especially for high-frequency returns that exhibit autocorrelation. Lower-frequency returns may not exhibit autocorrelation, but squared returns do, so that returns are not independent. MA and EWMA models do not capture the volatility "clustering" that occurs with positive autocorrelation whereby large returns, of either positive or negative sign, follow large returns of the same sign. In actual financial markets, volatile periods of large returns are interspersed in less volatile (tranquil) periods of small returns.

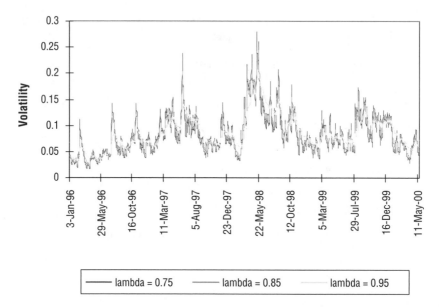

—— lambda = 0.75	—— lambda = 0.85	—— lambda = 0.95

FIGURE 8.2   Exponential Weighted Moving Averages of DAX Index

8.4   GARCH MODELS

The variance of an asset return or a portfolio return is a measure of the risk level of those returns. Empirical data has shown autocorrelation of this riskiness across time. Some time periods are riskier and thus more volatile than others. The expected value of the error term in autoregressive models of asset or portfolio returns is not constant across time so that heteroskedasticity may exist. In other words, the assumption of white noise, $\varepsilon_t \sim N(0, \sigma^2)$, with constant unconditional variance made in regression models for ordinary least squares (OLS) estimation does not hold in financial time series data. In fact, errors are time-varying and the expected value of the error during certain time periods is higher than in others, in which case heteroskedasticity exists.

Risk levels, as measured by the variance of asset or portfolio returns, are not dispersed randomly across quarterly or annual data. In fact, there is a degree of autocorrelation in the variance of financial returns. In order to adequately deal with heteroskedasticity in time series data, a class of econometric models known as autoregressive conditional heteroskedasticity (ARCH) was introduced by Engle (1982) and generalized by Bollerslev (1986) with generalized autoregressive conditional heteroskedasticity (GARCH) models. The main idea of GARCH is to add a conditional variance equation to the standard regression equation or conditional mean equation. The conditional variance equation models a time-varying variance of the unexpected return process: $V_t(\varepsilon_t) = \sigma_t^2$. With time-varying variance, GARCH models can capture the volatility clustering that cannot be captured with MA and EWMA models. GARCH models have important applications in risk management, especially in the calculation of value at risk (VaR). In particular, the use of a GARCH model with a non-Gaussian distribution for the standardized returns can give a more accurate VaR value.

ARCH assumes today's conditional variance is a weighted average of past p squared unexpected returns where the errors are calculated from the regression equation

$$y_t = \beta' x_t + \varepsilon_t$$

where

$$\varepsilon_t \mid I_t \sim N(0, \sigma_t^2)$$

I_t is the information set at time t, and the conditional variance is:

$$\sigma_t^2 = \alpha_0 + \sum_{i=1}^{p} \alpha_i \varepsilon_{t-i}^2$$
$$= \alpha_0 + \alpha_1 \varepsilon_{t-1}^2 + \alpha_2 \varepsilon_{t-2}^2 + \ldots + \alpha_p \varepsilon_{t-p}^2$$
$$\alpha_0 > 0, \ \alpha_1, \ldots, \alpha_p \geq 0$$

ARCH models are not used often since they do not have the volatility dynamics of GARCH models and because of the fact that GARCH models perform better. However, an ARCH model with exponentially declining lag coefficients is equivalent to the GARCH(1, 1) model. So, in fact, a GARCH process is actually an infinite ARCH process, and the two models converge with reasonable constraints on the GARCH coefficients and use of only very few parameters. As the lag increases in an ARCH model, the parameters become more difficult to estimate since the likelihood function becomes flatter and more difficult to maximize.

Forecasting the mean and variance of returns conditioned on past information has been a major application of these models. Suppose r_t is the asset or portfolio return at time t. In this case, r_t can be specified to be equal to the mean value of r_t (that is, the expected value of r_t based on past information) plus the error term, which is the unexpected return or mean deviation return, for the present period:

$$r_t = \mu + \varepsilon_t \tag{8.5}$$

If significant autocorrelation in returns exists, then an AR(1) (autoregressive order 1) model should be used:

$$r_t = \mu + \beta r_{t-1} + \varepsilon_t \qquad (8.6)$$

The conditional variance can be specified with a GARCH(1, 1) model,[6]

$$\sigma_t^2 = \omega + \alpha \varepsilon_{t-1}^2 + \beta \sigma_{t-1}^2$$
$$\omega > 0, \ \alpha > 0, \ \beta \geq 0 \qquad (8.7)$$

This model forecasts the variance of the return at time t as a weighted average of a constant, yesterday's forecast, and yesterday's squared error. The magnitude of the parameters α and β determine the short-term dynamics of the generated volatility time series. β, the lag coefficient, measures the degree of volatility persistence from previous shocks to the conditional variance. The error coefficient, α measures the degree of volatility reactivity to unexpected news. Large β values indicate that previous volatility shocks take a long time to die out. Large α values indicate that volatility reacts intensely to market movements. If α is relatively high and β is relatively low, then volatilities tend to become more spiked.

If $\sigma_t^2 = \sigma^2$ for all t, then the long-term steady-state variance in the GARCH(1, 1) model becomes:

$$\sigma^2 = \frac{\omega}{(1 - \alpha - \beta)} \qquad (8.8)$$

If $\alpha + \beta < 1$, then the returns process is stationary and the GARCH volatility term structure will converge to the long-term steady-state volatility in equation (8.8).

The GARCH(p, q) model can be expressed as:

$$\sigma_t^2 = \omega + \sum_{i=1}^{q} \alpha_i \varepsilon_{t-i}^2 + \sum_{j=1}^{p} \beta_j \sigma_{t-j}^2 \qquad (8.9)$$

Using the lag or backshift operator L, the GARCH(p, q) model is:

$$\sigma_t^2 = \omega + \alpha(L)\varepsilon_t^2 + \beta(L)\sigma_t^2 \qquad (8.10)$$

where $\alpha(L) = \alpha_1 L + \alpha_2 L^2 + \ldots + \alpha_q L^q$ and $\beta(L) = \beta_1 L + \beta_2 L^2 + \ldots + \beta_p L^p$.

---

[6]The (1, 1) in parentheses is a standard notation in which the first number refers to how many autoregressive lags appear in the equation, while the second number refers to how many lags are included in the moving average component of a variable.

If all the roots of the polynomial $| 1 - \beta(L) | = 0$ lie outside the unit circle, we have:

$$\sigma_t^2 = \omega(1 - \beta(L))^{-1} + \alpha(L)(1 - \beta(L))^{-1}\,\varepsilon_t^2 \qquad (8.11)$$

which can be viewed as an ARCH(∞) process since the conditional variance linearly depends on all previous squared residuals. In this case, the conditional variance of y_t can become larger than the unconditional (long-run) variance given by:

$$\sigma^2 = E\left[\varepsilon_t^2\right] = \frac{\omega}{1 - \displaystyle\sum_{i=1}^{q}\alpha_i - \sum_{j=1}^{p}\beta_j} \qquad (8.12)$$

if past realizations of ε_t^2 are larger than σ^2 (Palm 1996).

GARCH models are conditionally heteroskedastic but have a constant unconditional variance since underlying every GARCH model is an unconditional returns distribution. This distribution is stationary if the parameter conditions of equation (8.7) are met. There are many types of GARCH models. Each has a different specified model form. Equation (8.5) or (8.6) with (8.7) comprise what is known as symmetric or vanilla GARCH since responses are symmetric to market news; that is, the same response occurs whether the news is positive or negative. The unexpected return, ε_t, always enters the conditional variance equation squared, so that the sign of the news is irrelevant. Moreover, both the conditional mean return and conditional variance equation can be estimated separately.

8.5 ASYMMETRIC GARCH

In contrast, the asymmetric GARCH (A-GARCH) model of Engle and Ng (1993) allows for asymmetric volatility responses and has the following conditional variance equation:

$$\sigma_t^2 = \omega + \alpha(\varepsilon_{t-1} - \lambda)^2 + \beta\sigma_{t-1}^2$$
$$\omega > 0,\ \alpha,\ \beta,\ \lambda \geq 0 \qquad (8.13)$$

Here λ is a leverage coefficient and is of a similar order of magnitude as daily returns, but is much less significant than other GARCH coefficients.[7] The leverage coefficient allows for a more realistic modeling of the observed asymmetric behavior of returns according to which positive news surprises increase price and lower

---

[7]Alexander (2001a), 81.

subsequent volatility, while negative news surprises decrease price and increase subsequent volatility. As Hamilton (1994) notes, many researchers have found evidence of asymmetry of stock price behavior where negative surprises seem to increase volatility more than positive surprises.[8] This could be attributed to the fact that as stock prices fall, debt ratios increase; a sharp decline in stock prices increases corporate leverage and could thus increase the volatility in the market as the risk of holding stocks increases.

Another asymmetric model that is widely used in practice due to its flexibility of avoiding nonnegativity constraints[9] is the exponential GARCH (E-GARCH) model developed by Nelson (1991), which expresses the conditional variance in terms of logarithms. Moreover, the E-GARCH model captures the dynamics of the leverage effect observed in financial markets. The conditional variance in the E-GARCH model is defined in terms of a standard normal variate z_t which is the standardized unexpected return $\varepsilon_t^2 / \sigma^2$.

$$\ln \sigma_t^2 = \omega + g(z_{t-1}) + \beta \ln \sigma_{t-1}^2 \qquad (8.14)$$

where $g(\cdot)$ is an asymmetric response function defined by:

$$g(z_t) = \lambda z_t + \delta(\mid z_t \mid - \sqrt{2/\pi}) \qquad (8.15)$$

where the term multiplied by the coefficient δ is the mean deviation of z_t since

$$E[\mid z_t \mid] = \sqrt{2/\pi}$$

The structural form of $g(z_t)$ is based on capturing the asymmetry of returns in the market. As Nelson (1991) notes, "to accommodate the asymmetric relation between stock returns and volatility changes . . . the value of $g(z_t)$ must be a function of both the magnitude and the sign of z_t." In equation (8.15), the first term on the left side, λz_t, captures sign effect and the second term,

$$\delta(\mid z_t \mid - \sqrt{2/\pi})$$

captures the magnitude effect. The leverage effect is incorporated by the sign and magnitude of the parameters. If $\delta > 0$ and $\lambda < 0$, then negative shocks to returns will

---

[8]See Pagan and Schwert (1990), Engle and Ng (1991), and the studies cited in Bollerslev, Chou, and Kroner (1992), page 24.
[9]Nelson and Cao (1992) argue that imposing all coefficients to be nonnegative is too restrictive and that some of the coefficients are negative in practice while the conditional variance remains positive (by checking on a case-by-case basis). Consequently, in practice, GARCH parameters are often estimated without nonnegativity restrictions.

cause larger unconditional variance responses than positive shocks.[10] Bollerslev and Mikkelsen (1996) proposed to reexpress E-GARCH as:

$$\ln \sigma_t^2 = \omega + ((1 - \beta(L))^{-1}((1 - \alpha(L))g(z_{t-1}) \tag{8.16}$$

$E[|z_t|]$ depends on the unconditional density of z_t.

Many GARCH models used in practice to model the volatility of daily returns assume that the errors are conditionally normally distributed in the conditional mean equation. However, due to time-varying conditional volatility, the unconditional returns distribution generated by a normal GARCH model will have fat tails and thus be leptokurtic. Moreover, in many financial markets, there is empirical evidence that return distributions have fatter tails and are more skewed than returns assumed by a normal distribution.[11] Consequently, it may be necessary to assume a different type of distribution to capture the full effect of excess kurtosis observed especially with high-frequency data. One possibility is to assume the skewed Student t error distribution for the error process of the conditional mean equation[12] so that:

$$E[|z_t|] = \frac{4\xi^2 \Gamma\left(\frac{1+v}{2}\right)\sqrt{v-2}}{\xi + \frac{1}{\xi}\sqrt{\pi}(v-1)\Gamma\left(\frac{v}{2}\right)} \tag{8.17}$$

where $\Gamma(\cdot)$ is the gamma function and $\xi = 1$ for the symmetric Student.

Nelson (1991) proposed the *generalized error distribution*, normalized to have zero mean and unit variance:

$$f(v_t) = \frac{v \exp\left(-(1/2)|v_t/\lambda|^v\right)}{\lambda 2^{((v+1)/v)} \Gamma(1/v)} \tag{8.18}$$

The term λ is a constant given by:

$$\lambda = \left\{\frac{2^{(-2/v)}\Gamma\left(1/v\right)}{\Gamma\left(3/v\right)}\right\}^{1/2} \tag{8.19}$$

---

[10]Nelson and Cao (1992), 80.
[11]See Palm (1996); Pagan (1996); Bollerslev, Chou, and Kroner (1992).
[12]See Bollerslev (1986); Baillie and Bollerslev (1989); Engle and Gonzalez-Riviera (1991).

and v is a positive parameter that effects the thickness of the tails. For $v = 2$, the constant $\lambda = 1$ and (8.14) becomes the standard normal density. If $v < 2$ the density has thicker tails than the normal, while for $v > 2$ it has thinner tails. The expected value of z_t is:

$$E(|z_t|) = \frac{\lambda \cdot 2^{1/v} \Gamma(2/v)}{\Gamma(1/v)}$$

Note that for the standard normal case ($v = 2$), we get the original mean in equation (8.15),

$$E[|z_t|] = \sqrt{2/\pi}$$

The E-GARCH as with symmetric GARCH can be estimated by maximum likelihood once the probability density for z_t is specified.

8.6   GARCH MODELS FOR HIGH-FREQUENCY DATA

High-frequency data can affect the ability to forecast volatility due to problems of time aggregation.[13] Intra-data data is useful for modeling short-term volatility, but it may not be useful for modeling long-term volatility. Drost and Nijman (1993), along with Müller et al. (1997) have studied and compared GARCH volatilities estimated at different frequencies. They have concluded that a GARCH model estimated with high-frequency data does not predict lower-frequency volatility well, and that it is better to predict high-frequency volatility with a low-frequency model.[14]

In many high-frequency time-series applications, the conditional variance estimated using a GARCH(p, q) process exhibits strong persistence, that is:

$$\sum_{j=1}^{p} \beta_j + \sum_{i=1}^{q} \alpha_i \approx 1$$

If

$$\sum_{j=1}^{p} \beta_j + \sum_{i=1}^{q} \alpha_i < 1$$

---

[13]Alexander (2001a), 82–83.
[14]Ibid., 83.

then the error process is stationary. When forecasting, a shock to the conditional variance σ_t^2 has a decaying impact on the σ_{t+s}^2 when s increases, and is asymptotically negligible. However, if

$$\sum_{j=1}^{p} \beta_j + \sum_{i=1}^{q} \alpha_i \geq 1$$

the effect on σ_{t+s}^2 does not die out asymptotically—the effect is persistent across horizons. If the sum is equal to 1, then current information remains important when forecasting the volatility for all time horizons and the correct model specification is integrated GARCH (I-GARCH), introduced by Engle and Bollerslev (1986). If ε_t follows an I-GARCH process, the unconditional variance of ε_t will be infinite (notice the denominator of n, in which case ε_t and ε_t^2 are not covariance-stationary processes. Note that we can rewrite equation (8.9) as an autoregressive conditional heteroskedasticity (ARCH) process using the lag operator L:

$$(1 - \alpha(L) - \beta(L))\varepsilon_t^2 = \omega + (1 - \beta(L))(\varepsilon_t^2 - \sigma_t^2) \qquad (8.20)$$

When the $(1 - \alpha(L - \beta(L))$ polynomial contains a unit root (i.e., the sum of the α_i's and β_i's is 1), we get the I-GARCH:

$$\phi(L)(1 - L)\varepsilon_t^2 = \omega + (1 - \beta(L))(\varepsilon_t^2 - \sigma_t^2) \qquad (8.21)$$

where $\phi(L) = (1 - \alpha(L) - \beta(L))(1 - L)^{-1}$ is of order $\max(p, q) - 1$.

We can rearrange equation (8.17) to express the conditional variance as a function of the squared residuals. After some manipulations, we get:

$$\sigma_t^2 = \frac{\omega}{1 - \beta(L)} + (1 - \phi(L)(1 - L)(1 - \beta(L))^{-1})\varepsilon_t^2$$

Figures 8.3 and 8.4 show the GARCH(1, 1) volatility and the corresponding logarithmic returns of the asset price with GARCH(1, 1). The GARCH(1, 1) captures volatility clustering and time-varying volatility that the MA and EWMA do not.

What is important to note about the GARCH term structure is the mean reversion to the long-term level of $\sigma^2 = \omega/(1 - \alpha - \beta) = 0.0002/(1 - 0.045 - 0.94) = 0.013$ or a volatility of 11.5 percent.

In practice, statistical packages like RATS[15] (Regression Analysis of Time Series) or S-PLUS can be used to estimate the parameters of a GARCH(p, q) model. GARCH(p, q) parameter estimation is often done using the maximum likelihood

---

[15]See www.estima.com.

Omega = 2E-4, Alpha = 0.045, Beta = 0.94

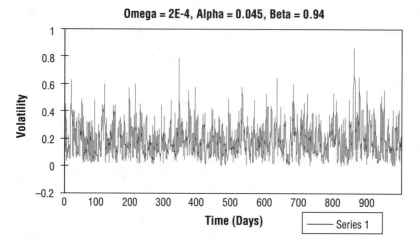

FIGURE 8.3   GARCH(1, 1) Volatility

method where the parameters are chosen to maximize the likelihood of the data under its assumed probability density function. Thus, the objective is to choose parameters 0 that maximize the value of the underlying data generating process distribution that is assumed. Maximum likelihood estimation procedures are widely used because they usually produce consistent, asymptotically normal, and efficient parameter estimates.

Numerical optimization routines such as the Berndt-Hall-Hall-Hausmann (BHHH) or Davidson-Fletcher-Powell (DFP) must be used to determine these pa-

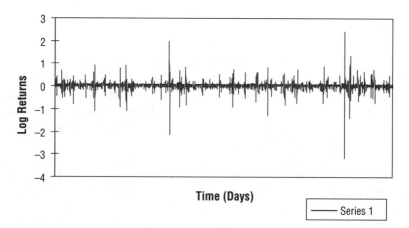

FIGURE 8.4   Log Returns with GARCH(1, 1) Volatility

rameters since there is no closed-form analytical solution. Various quasi-Newton, steepest gradient-descent, and simplex methods exist for nonlinear parameter estimation.[16]

If $f(r_t; \theta)$ is the probability density function of the asset return r_t and if L is the maximum likelihood function, then θ's are chosen to solve:

$$\max_{\theta} \ L(\theta \,|\, r_1, r_2, \ldots, r_T) = \prod_{t=1}^{T} f(r_t; \theta) \tag{8.22}$$

Often, it is easier to work with the log-likelihood function since it is easier to compute the sum of log-likelihoods than the product of (complex) likelihoods. Thus, we can rewrite the problem as:

$$\max_{\theta} \ \ln L(\theta \,|\, r_1, r_2, \ldots, r_T) = \sum_{t=1}^{T} \ln f(r_t; \theta) \tag{8.23}$$

For a normal symmetric GARCH model, the likelihood density function of a single observation r_t is:

$$f(r_t; \theta) = \frac{1}{\sqrt{2\pi\sigma_t^2}} \exp\left(-\frac{\varepsilon_t^2}{2\sigma_t^2}\right) \tag{8.24}$$

where $\varepsilon_t = r_t - \bar{r}$, $\bar{r}$ is the expected return, and σ_t^2 is the GARCH volatility. For a normal symmetric GARCH model the log-likelihood ℓ_t of a single return observation r_t is:

$$\ell_t = -\frac{1}{2}\left(\ln\sigma_t^2 + \frac{\varepsilon_t^2}{\sigma_t^2}\right) \tag{8.25}$$

so that

$$\sum_{t=1}^{T} \ell_t$$

is maximized with respect to the GARCH variance parameters θ; we ignore the term $\ln(2\pi)$ since it does not affect the estimates. Note that this is equivalent to

---

[16]See Hamilton (1994).

minimizing $-2\ln L$. In the GARCH(1, 1) model, $\theta = [\omega, \alpha, \beta]'$. The first derivatives may be written:

$$\frac{\partial \ell_t}{\partial \theta} = \frac{1}{2\sigma_t^2}\left[\left(\frac{\varepsilon_t^2}{\sigma_t^2}\right) - 1\right]\mathbf{g_t} \tag{8.26}$$

where the gradient vector

$$\mathbf{g_t} = \frac{\partial \sigma_t^2}{\partial \theta} = \begin{bmatrix} \partial\sigma_t^2 \big/ \partial\omega \\ \partial\sigma_t^2 \big/ \partial\alpha \\ \partial\sigma_t^2 \big/ \partial\beta \end{bmatrix} \tag{8.27}$$

The derivatives may be calculated recursively,

$$\mathbf{g_t} = \mathbf{z_t} + \beta \mathbf{g_{t-1}} \tag{8.28}$$

$$= \begin{bmatrix} 1 \\ \varepsilon_{t-1}^2 \\ \sigma_{t-1}^2 \end{bmatrix} + \beta \begin{bmatrix} \partial\sigma_{t-1}^2 \big/ \partial\omega \\ \partial\sigma_{t-1}^2 \big/ \partial\alpha \\ \partial\sigma_{t-1}^2 \big/ \partial\beta \end{bmatrix} \tag{8.29}$$

for $t = 1, \ldots, T$. To start the recursion, we need presamples for σ_t^2 and ε_t^2 for $t \leq 0$, so a good choice is the OLS unconditional variance estimate,

$$\frac{1}{T}\sum_{t=1}^{T}\varepsilon_t^2$$

Solving the first-order condition $\partial\sigma_t^2 / \partial\theta = 0$ will yield a set of nonlinear equations that must be solved using quasi-Newton methods like the BHHH. The BHHH iteration is:

$$\theta_{i+1} = \theta_i + \lambda_i H_i^{-1} \mathbf{g}_i \tag{8.30}$$

where λ_i is a variable step length chosen to maximize the likelihood in the appropriate direction (this direction vector can be computed from an OLS regression of a $T \times 1$ vector of 1's on

$$\mathbf{g}_i = \sum_{t=1}^{T} \mathbf{g_t}$$

and $\mathbf{H}_i$ is the Hessian matrix

$$\mathbf{H}_i = \sum_{t=1}^{T} \frac{\partial^2 \ell_t}{\partial \boldsymbol{\theta} \partial \boldsymbol{\theta}'} \tag{8.31}$$

For a GARCH(1, 1), the Hessian is:

$$\mathbf{H}_i = \sum_{t=1}^{T} \begin{bmatrix} \dfrac{\partial^2 \ell_t}{\partial \omega_t^2} & \dfrac{\partial^2 \ell_t}{\partial \alpha_t \partial \omega_t} & \dfrac{\partial^2 \ell_t}{\partial \alpha_t \partial \beta_t} \\[2ex] \dfrac{\partial^2 \ell_t}{\partial \alpha_t \partial \omega_t} & \dfrac{\partial^2 \ell_t}{\partial \alpha_t^2} & \dfrac{\partial^2 \ell_t}{\partial \alpha_t \partial \beta_t} \\[2ex] \dfrac{\partial^2 \ell_t}{\partial \beta_t \partial \omega_t} & \dfrac{\partial^2 \ell_t}{\partial \beta_t \partial \alpha_t} & \dfrac{\partial^2 \ell_t}{\partial \beta_t^2} \end{bmatrix} \Bigg|_{\boldsymbol{\theta} = \boldsymbol{\theta}_i}$$

$$= \begin{bmatrix} \displaystyle\sum_{t=1}^{T} \dfrac{\partial^2 \ell_t}{\partial \omega_t^2} & \displaystyle\sum_{t=1}^{T} \dfrac{\partial^2 \ell_t}{\partial \alpha_t \partial \omega_t} & \displaystyle\sum_{t=1}^{T} \dfrac{\partial^2 \ell_t}{\partial \alpha_t \partial \beta_t} \\[3ex] \displaystyle\sum_{t=1}^{T} \dfrac{\partial^2 \ell_t}{\partial \alpha_t \partial \omega_t} & \displaystyle\sum_{t=1}^{T} \dfrac{\partial^2 \ell_t}{\partial \alpha_t^2} & \displaystyle\sum_{t=1}^{T} \dfrac{\partial^2 \ell_t}{\partial \alpha_t \partial \beta_t} \\[3ex] \displaystyle\sum_{t=1}^{T} \dfrac{\partial^2 \ell_t}{\partial \beta_t \partial \omega_t} & \displaystyle\sum_{t=1}^{T} \dfrac{\partial^2 \ell_t}{\partial \beta_t \partial \alpha_t} & \displaystyle\sum_{t=1}^{T} \dfrac{\partial^2 \ell_t}{\partial \beta_t^2} \end{bmatrix} \Bigg|_{\boldsymbol{\theta} = \boldsymbol{\theta}_i}$$

where the linear sum operator is applied to each of the elements of the Hessian. Note that:

$$\mathbf{H}_i = \sum_{t=1}^{T} (\mathbf{g_t} \mathbf{g_t'}) \text{ and } \mathbf{g}_i = \sum_{t=1}^{T} \frac{\partial \ell_t}{\partial \boldsymbol{\theta}}$$

where $\partial \ell_t / \partial \boldsymbol{\theta}$ is evaluated at $\boldsymbol{\theta}_i$.

The second derivatives in (8.19) may be written:

$$\frac{\partial^2 \ell_t}{\partial\boldsymbol{\theta}\partial\boldsymbol{\theta}'} = \left(\frac{\varepsilon_t^2}{\sigma_t^2} - 1\right)\frac{\partial}{\partial\boldsymbol{\theta}'}\left[\frac{1}{2\sigma_t^2}\frac{\partial\sigma_t^2}{\partial\boldsymbol{\theta}}\right] - \frac{1}{2\sigma_t^2}\frac{\partial\sigma_t^2}{\partial\boldsymbol{\theta}}\frac{\partial\sigma_t^2}{\partial\boldsymbol{\theta}'}\frac{\varepsilon_t^2}{\sigma_t^2} \qquad (8.32)$$

We can thus rewrite equation (8.30):

$$\boldsymbol{\theta}_{i+1} = \boldsymbol{\theta}_i + \lambda_i \left(\sum_{t=1}^{T}\frac{\partial^2 \ell_t}{\partial\boldsymbol{\theta}\partial\boldsymbol{\theta}'}\right)^{-1}\sum_{t=1}^{T}\frac{\partial\ell_{t^-}}{\partial\boldsymbol{\theta}} \qquad (8.33)$$

The iteration converges when $|\boldsymbol{\theta}_{i+1} - \boldsymbol{\theta}_i| < \xi$ where ξ is the error criterion vector that is arbitrarily close to the 0 vector; that is, each element in ξ is very small, such as 0.0001. Viewed another way, convergence occurs when the gradient vector $\mathbf{g}$ is 0. These estimated parameters maximize the likelihood function.

An implementation for estimating the parameters of a GARCH(1, 1) model using the BHHH routine is now given. It makes use of R. B. Davies's Newmat matrix library.[17]

```
/*******************************************************************************
GARCH11 : estimates the parameters of a GARCH(1,1) model
[in]: vector<double>& prices  : vector of asset prices
[out]: vector<double> theta   : vector of GARCH parameters
*******************************************************************************/
ColumnVector StatModel::GARCH11(vector<double>& prices)
{
  vector<double> v2;
  vector<double> ret, ret1;
  double r = 0.0;
  double r1 = 0.0;
  double error1 = 0.0;
  double error2 = 0.0;
  double error3 = 0.0;

  int n = prices.size();
  vector<double> e = getErrors();
  LLD = ColumnVector(3);          // log likelihood derivatives
  ColumnVector theta(3);          // GARCH parameters
  ColumnVector theta1(3);         // stores updated GARCH params
  Matrix H(3,3);                  // Hessian matrix

  // calculate r(t)
```

---

[17]Available at www.robertnz.net.

```
for (int i = 0; i < n-3; i++)
{
  r = prices[i];
  ret.push_back(r);
}

// calculate r(t-1)
for (i = 1; i <= n-3; i++)
{
  r1 = prices[i];
  ret1.push_back(r1);
}

// store returns
setY(ret1);
setX(ret);
setT(n-3);

vector<double> ee = calcErrors();
double sum = accumulate(ee.begin(),ee.end(),0.0);
double ave = sum/T;
double lambda = 5;                    // assume constant direction step

// initialize parameters
od.push_back(1.0);
ad.push_back(ave);
bd.push_back(ave);
sd.push_back(ave);

// initial estimates
theta << 0.0001 << 0.10 << 0.6;
i = 1;
lambda = 2;

try
{
  do
  {
    // normally regress columns of 1's of dl(t)/d(theta)
    lambda = lambda + calcLambda(theta,i);

    ColumnVector LD = calcLogDerives(theta);
    Matrix H = calcHessian(theta);
    ColumnVector r = -lambda*H.i()*LD;

    theta1 = theta + r;
    error1 = theta1(1) - theta(1);
    error2 = theta1(2) - theta(2);
    error3 = theta1(3) - theta(3);
    theta = theta1;
    i++;
  }
```

```
      while ((abs(error1) > 0.0001) || (abs(error2) > 0.0001) || (abs(error3) >
        0.0001));
    }
    catch (char* s)
    {
      throw s;
    }
    cout << "theta(1) = " << theta(1) << " theta(2) = " << theta(2) << " theta(3) =
                        " << theta(3);
    return theta;
}

/***************************************************************************
calcErrors : computes errors/residuals and squared errors/residuals
[in]: none
[out]: vector<double> : vector of squared residuals
***************************************************************************/
vector<double>& StatModel::calcErrors()
{
  double err = 0.0;                     // residual error
  double yh = 0.0;                      // y estimate
  double a = calcConstCoeff();          // compute constant coefficient
  double b = calcBeta();                // compute regression coefficient
  int i;
  e2.clear();

  for (i = 0; i < y.size(); i++)
  {
    yh = a + b*x[i];
    yhat.push_back(yh);
    err = y[i] - yhat[i];
    e.push_back(err);
    e2.push_back(err*err);
  }
  return e2;
}

/***************************************************************************
calcLambda : computes lambda—the step length that maximizes the likelihood function
             in the right direction
[in]:   ColumnVector theta : matrix column (3x1) of parameters
        int i              : current time (ith iteration of BHHH)
[out]: double              : lambda
***************************************************************************/
ColumnVector StatModel::calcLambda(ColumnVector theta, int i)
{
  ColumnVector lambda(T-1);
  Matrix v = calcLogDerives(theta,i);

  for (int j = 1; j < T; j++)
    lambda(j) = 1.0;

  StatModel sm(lambda,v);
```

```
    ColumnVector b = sm.calcBetas(); // compute coefficients

    return b;
}


/*****************************************************************************
calcLogDerives : computes derivative of the log likelihood function
[in]:    ColumnVector theta : matrix column (3x1) of parameters
[out]:   ColumnVector LLD: matrix column with log derivatives with respect to
                 parameters
*****************************************************************************/
ColumnVector StatModel::calcLogDerives(ColumnVector theta)
{
    int i;
    h.clear();                            // initial h[0]

    double sum = accumulate(e2.begin(),   // compute sum of squared residuals
      e2.end(),0.0);
    double ave = sum/T;                   // get average of sum of squared residuals

    // initialize h[0] and e2[0] to 1/T*sum(e^2)
    h.push_back(ave);
    e2[0] = ave;

    // initialize LLD
    LLD << 0 << 0 << 0;
    for (i = 1; i < T; i++)
    {
      h.push_back(theta(1) + theta(2)*e2[i-1] + theta(3)*h[i-1]);
      LLD = LLD + (0.5/h[i])*(e2[i]/h[i] - 1)*(getVolDerives(i,theta(3)));
    }

    for (i = 1; i <=3; i++)
      cout << i: << LLD(i) << endl;

    return LLD;
}


/*****************************************************************************
calcLogDerives : computes derivative of the log likelihood function for the ith
  iteration     : helps compute lambda
[in]:    ColumnVector theta: matrix column (3x1) of parametersint i : current time
         (ith iteration of BHHH)
[out]:   ColumnVector LLD: matrix column with log derivatives with respect to
         parameters
*****************************************************************************/
Matrix StatModel::calcLogDerives(ColumnVector theta, int i)
{
    // initial h[0]
    h.clear();
    Matrix J(T-1,3);
    double sum = accumulate(e2.begin(),e2.end(),0.0);
```

```
    double ave = sum/T;
    // initialize h[0] and e2[0] to 1/T*sum(e^2)
    h.push_back(ave);
    e2[0] = ave;

    ColumnVector C(3);
    for (i = 1; i < T; i++)
    {
      h.push_back(theta(1) + theta(2)*e2[i-1] + theta(3)*h[i-1]);
      C = getVolDerives(i,theta(3));
      for (int k = 1; k <= 3; k++)
        J(i,k) = (0.5/h[i])*(e2[i]/h[i] - 1)*C(k);
    }
    return J;
}


/******************************************************************************
getVolDerivatives : returns the gradient (first derivatives) of the GARCH model
                    volatility function with respect to the parameters
[in]:  ColumnVector theta : matrix column (3x1) of parameters
[out]: ColumnVector V      : a matrix column of GARCH model derivatives with respect
                             to par
******************************************************************************/
ColumnVector StatModel::getVolDerives(int i, double beta)
{
    ColumnVector V(3);
    od.push_back(1 + beta*od[i-1]);        // derivative of volatility w.r.t. omega
    ad.push_back(e2[i-1] + beta*ad[i-1]); // derivative of volatility w.r.t. alpha
    bd.push_back(h[i-1] + beta*bd[i-1]);  // derivative of volatility w.r.t. beta

    V << od[i] << ad[i] << bd[i];
    cout << V(1) << V(2) << V(3) << endl;
    return V;
}


/******************************************************************************
getVolSecondDerives : computes the Hessian matrix of second derivatives of the
  GARCH model with respect to the model parameters. Used for calcHessian function
[in]:  int i             : ith data observation
       double beta        : coefficient on h(i-1) in GARCH model
[out]: vector<Matrix>    : vector of matrices
******************************************************************************/
Matrix StatModel::getVolSecondDerives(int i, double beta)
{
    Matrix M(3,3);
    Matrix Z(3,3);
    Matrix N(3,3);
    vector<double> err = calcErrors();
    double sum = accumulate(err.begin(),err.end(),0.0);
    double ave = sum/T;

    if (i == 1)
    {
```

```
     Z << 0 << 0 << 0
       << 0 << 0 << 0
       << 1 << ave << ave;

     N << 0 << 0 << od[i-1]
       << 0 << 0 << ad[i-1]
       << 0 << 0 << bd[i-1];

     matder.push_back(N);
     matder1.push_back(Z + beta*matder[i-1]);
   }
   else
   {
     Z << 0 << 0 << 0
       << 0 << 0 << 0
       << 1 << e2[i-2] << h[i-2];

     N << 0 << 0 << od[i-1]
       << 0 << 0 << ad[i-1]
       << 0 << 0 << bd[i-1];
     matder.push_back(N);
     matder1.push_back(Z + beta*matder[i-1]);
   }
   matder2.push_back(Z + beta*matder1[i-1]);

   if (i == 1)
     return matder1[i-1];
     else
     return matder2[i-1];
}


/**********************************************************************************
calcHessian : computes the Hessian matrix of second derivatives of the GARCH
              log likelihood function with respect to the model parameters
[in]:  ColumnVector theta : matrix column (3x1) of parameters
[out]: ColumnVector H:     : Hessian matrix of second derivatives
**********************************************************************************/
Matrix StatModel::calcHessian(ColumnVector theta)
{
   int i;
   Matrix H(3,3);
   vector<double> e2 = calcErrors();
   double sum = accumulate(e2.begin(),e2.end(),0.0);
   vector<double> h;
   double ave = sum/T;
   h.clear();
   // initialize h[0] and e2[0] to 1/T*sum(e^2)
   h.push_back(ave);
   e2[0] = ave;

   // initialize Hessian
   H << 0 << 0 << 0
     << 0 << 0 << 0
```

```
<< 0 << 0 << 0;

// compute Hessian
for (i = 1; i < T; i++)
{
  h.push_back(theta(1) + theta(2)*e2[i-1] + theta(3)*h[i-1]);
  ColumnVector CV = getVolDerives(i,theta(3));
  Matrix CV2 = getVolSecondDerives(i,theta(3));
  H = H + (e2[i]/h[i] - 1)*(0.5*((-1/(h[i]*h[i]))*(CV*CV.t()) + (1/h[i])*(CV2)))
    -(0.5/(h[i]*h[i]))*(CV*CV.t())*(e2[i]/h[i]);
}
return H;
}

/************************************************************************************
getLogDerives : returns the column vector of log derivatives
[in]:  none
[out]: ColumnVector LLD: matrix column with log derivatives with respect to
  parameters
*************************************************************************************/
ColumnVector StatModel::getLogDerives()
{
  return LLD;
}
```

As an example of how we can estimate parameters (without using a statistical package), suppose we estimate a GARCH(1, 1) equation from S&P 500 closing prices from January 3, 1996, to July 29, 1998, in a text file "SP.txt." We can call the following function to read the data from the file:

```
/************************************************************************************
readData : read the data file and stores the data in a vector
[in]:   none — could also pass in file name rather than hard code file name in function
[out]: none
*************************************************************************************/
void StatModel::readData()
{
  char buffer[100];               // line buffer
  char dataBuffer[100];           // data character buffer
  char *str = NULL;               // character string
  vector<double> y;               // dependent variables
  vector<double> x;               // independent variables
  const char *file = "c:\\sp.txt"; // data file - could also pass in as a parameter
  ifstream fin;                   // input file stream

  fin.clear();
  fin.open(file);
```

```
if (fin.good())
{
  while (!fin.eof())
  {
    fin.getline(buffer,sizeof(buffer)/sizeof(buffer[0]));
    istrstream str(buffer);
    //Get data
    str >> dataBuffer;
    y.push_back(sqrt(atof(dataBuffer)));
  }
}
else
{
  cout << "File not good!" << "\n";
}
fin.close();

GARCH11(y);
}
```

The estimated GARCH(1, 1) parameters are (ω, α, β), though these values can vary depending on the initial values used, as discussed in the next section.

8.7 ESTIMATION PROBLEMS

Numerical optimization routines such as the BHHH are very sensitive to initial starting values since they affect the initial gradient. Different estimates can be obtained with different starting values. As more parameters are added to the GARCH model, the likelihood function becomes flatter and more difficult to maximize so that a local maximum may be achieved rather than the global maximum. Thus, it may be necessary to run the model with different starting values, recording the likelihood of the optima, to ensure a global optimum has been achieved rather than a local maximum. If many estimates are generated with different starting values, then a model with fewer parameters should be used. A well-specified model should converge to the same estimates with different initial values.

If the initial starting values are not good, then convergence problems may occur if the gradient algorithm used to maximize the likelihood function hits a boundary in which 0 or 1 is returned for the alpha and/or beta estimates. A boundary could also be caused by outliers in the data (i.e., extremely high or low observation values). Thus, different starting values should be tried to change the initial gradient as well as to remove the outliers if a boundary is hit. One might also use a different data period.

If convergence cannot be reached at all, after changing the initial values, removing any outliers, and even modifying the data period, then the GARCH model is misspecified. A different GARCH model should then be used. However, univariate GARCH models usually do not encounter convergence problems if the model is well specified and the data is well behaved.[18] If the model is well specified, then changes in the data will induce some changes in the coefficient estimates, but they should not vary considerably, except when there are "structural breaks in the data generation process."[19]

8.8   GARCH OPTION PRICING MODEL

Using discrete-time generalized GARCH process as well as stochastic volatility bivariate diffusions (which can be represented as limits of a family of GARCH models), Ritchken and Trevor (1999) developed an efficient numerical procedure via a lattice for pricing European and American options.[20] The GARCH model of Ritchken and Trevor (RT) assumes the underlying security satisfies the following diffusion process:

$$\ln\left(\frac{S_{t+1}}{S_t}\right) = r_t + \lambda\sqrt{h_t} - \frac{1}{2}h_t + \sqrt{h_t}\,\varepsilon_{t+1}$$

$$h_{t+1} = \beta_0 + \beta_1 h_t + \beta_2 h_t(\varepsilon_{t+1} - c)^2 \tag{8.34}$$

where S_t is the asset price at time t; h_t is the conditional variance, given information at time t, of the logarithmic return over the period $[t, t + 1]$; ε_{t+1} is a standard normal random variable conditional on time t information; r_t is the riskless rate of return over the period; λ is the unit risk premium for the asset; and c is a nonnegative parameter that captures the negative correlation between return and volatility innovations in the equity markets. β_0, β_1, and β_2 are nonnegative to ensure positive conditional volatility. Let N be the maturity of a tree (in days) and that option to be priced by the tree.

Duan (1995) established that if the price of the underlying security follows the process in equation (8.34), then option price can be computed as simple discounted expected values under a local risk-neutral probability measure:

$$\ln\left(\frac{S_{t+1}}{S_t}\right) = \left(r_t - \frac{1}{2}h_t\right) + \sqrt{h_t}\,\varepsilon_{t+1}$$

$$h_{t+1} = \beta_0 + \beta_1 h_t + \beta_2 h_t(\varepsilon_{t+1} - c^*)^2 \tag{8.35}$$

---

[18]Alexander (2001a), 96.
[19]Ibid.
[20]Ritchken and Trevor (1999), 377–402.

where ε_{t+1} is a standard normal random variable with respect to a risk-neutral measure, conditional on time t information, and $c^* = c + \lambda$. The model has five unknown parameters β_0, β_1, β_2, c^*, and h_0.

The Ritchken and Trevor algorithm first generates a grid of logarithmic prices. Adjacent logarithmic prices have a space of γ_n chosen such that:

$$\gamma_n = \frac{\gamma}{\sqrt{n}}$$

where

$$\gamma = \sqrt{h_0}$$

and n represents a multinomial random variable such that next period's logarithmic price is approximated by a discrete random variable that takes on $2n + 1$ values. For example, when $n = 1$, we have a trinomial random variable such that the price can jump up (to a value larger than the current price), down (to a value smaller than the current price), or stay the same (the value remains unchanged). The size of these $2n + 1$ jumps is restricted to integer multiples of γ_n. To ensure valid probability values over the grid of $2n + 1$ values, it may be necessary to adjust the probabilities by a jump parameter η so that the first two moments of the approximating distribution match when the variance is sufficiently large.[21] The integer η depends on the level of the variance and is computed for each level in the tree (up, middle, and down) for a given time step:

$$\eta - 1 < \frac{\sqrt{h_t}}{\gamma} \leq \eta \tag{8.36}$$

The jump parameter measures how much the two outer branches fan out around the middle branch. The resulting GARCH model, known as the nonlinear asymmetric GARCH (N-GARCH) model,[22] is given by:

$$y_{t+1} = y_t + j\eta\gamma_n$$

$$h_{t+1} = \beta_0 + \beta_1 h_t + \beta_2 h_t (\varepsilon_{t+1} - c^*)^2 \tag{8.37}$$

where the innovations are given by:

$$\varepsilon_{t+1} = \frac{j\eta\gamma_n - (r - \frac{1}{2}h_t)}{\sqrt{h_t}} \tag{8.38}$$

---

[21]Cakici and Topyan (2000).
[22]Engle and Ng (1993).

and $j = 0, \pm 1, \pm 2, \ldots, \pm n$, r is the risk-free rate, and $y_t = \ln S_t$. The model is a bivariate diffusion specified by (y_t, h_t^2) at each node.

The probability distribution for y_{t+1}, conditional on y_t and h_t, is given by:

$$\text{Prob}(y_{t+1} = y_t + j\eta\lambda_n) = P(j) \quad j = 0, \pm 1, \pm 2, \ldots, \pm n$$

where

$$P(j) = \sum_{j_u, j_m, j_d} \binom{n}{j_u j_m j_d} p_u^{j_u} p_m^{j_m} p_d^{j_d} \tag{8.39}$$

with $j_u, j_m, j_d \geq 0$ such that $n = j_u + j_m + j_d$ and $j = j_u - j_d$. The trinomial probabilities for the dynamics of the approximating process are:

$$p_u = \frac{h_t^2}{2\eta^2\gamma_n^2} + \frac{(r - \frac{1}{2}h_t^2)}{2\eta\gamma_n\sqrt{n}} \tag{8.40}$$

$$p_m = 1 - \frac{h_t^2}{\eta^2\gamma_n^2} \tag{8.41}$$

$$p_d = \frac{h_t^2}{2\eta^2\gamma_n^2} - \frac{(r - \frac{1}{2}h_t^2)}{2\eta\gamma_n\sqrt{n}} \tag{8.42}$$

which match the conditional mean and variance of y_{t+1} given (y_t, h_t^2) in the limit. Thus, the tree converges to the continuous-state model (8.37). From equations (8.39) to (8.41), the branching probabilities exist, that is, $0 \leq p_u, p_m, p_d \leq 1$ if and only if:

$$\frac{|r - (h_t^2/2)|}{2\eta\gamma_n\sqrt{n}} \leq \frac{h_t^2}{2\eta^2\gamma_n^2} \leq \min\left(1 - \frac{|r - (h_t^2/2)|}{2\eta\gamma_n\sqrt{n}}, \frac{1}{2}\right) \tag{8.43}$$

Constructing a trinomial tree to price options involves both a forward-building stage and a standard backward recursion process to value the option at time $t = 0$. However, jumps are not necessarily symmetric, and multiple references can be made to several nodes, which allows for multiple variances at each node.[23] For example, at a given node, η_u can be 2, while $\eta_m = \eta_d = 1$. The model goes through:

$$\eta = [h_t/\gamma], [h_t/\gamma] + 1, [h_t/\gamma] + 2, \ldots$$

---

[23]Cakici and Topyan (2000), 74.

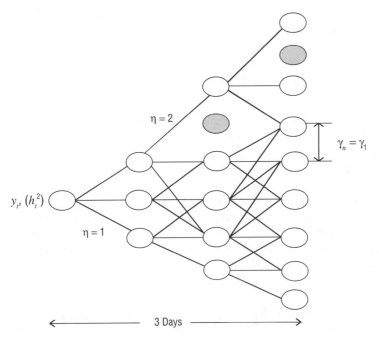

FIGURE 8.5 Possible Geometry of a Ritchken-Trevor Tree

until valid probabilities are obtain or until their nonexistence is confirmed by violations of inequalities in (8.43). Figure 8.5 shows a possible geometry of a three-day Ritchken and Trevor tree.

A day is partitioned into $n = 1$ period. Each node will have as many variances as the number of paths to the node, creating as many distinct option prices. However, some nodes may never be reached and are left empty (shown in gray). To handle this problem, given that typically the number of variances grows exponentially as the number of time steps increases, only the maximum variance, the minimum variance, and an interpolated middle variance value are stored at each node.[24] In particular, the model creates K volatilities between the

---

[24]More than three variance values can be stored at each node. A total of $N > 3$ variances can be stored that are equidistant variances between the minimum and maximum variances at each node with $N - 2$ interpolated variances. However, one will have $N - 2$ additional next-variance calculations in each node during the forward-building stage alone. Thus, $N = 3$ is chosen to keep the model simple and to keep consistent with the approach taken by Ritchken and Trevor (1999).

maximum and minimum h_t (inclusive) per model so that the squared volatilities are equally spaced, given by:

$$h_{min}^2 + j \frac{h_{max}^2 - h_{min}^2}{K-1} \qquad j = 0, 1, 2, \ldots, K-1 \tag{8.44}$$

where h_{min} and h_{max} denote the minimum and maximum volatilities at the node.

Once the terminal time step is reached, the option is valued by computing the option payoff using the security's price alone and then working backward taking the discounted risk-neutral expectation at each node at the prior time step until the first node is reached. However, for a given node prior to maturity, a total of 9 (3×3) option prices need to be computed by taking the first (maximum) variance value in the node, computing a jump parameter value η, referencing it to three nodes in the next period (up, middle, and down), and repeating for the middle and down variances as well. Note that we can compute the next three variances in the tree by combining equations (8.37) and (8.38).

$$h_{next}(j) = \beta_0 + \beta_1 h_t(i, k) + \beta_2 h_t(i, k) \left(\frac{1}{2}(j\eta\gamma_n - r + h_t + \frac{1}{2}h_t(i, k))\sqrt{h_t(i, k)} - c^* \right)^2 \tag{8.45}$$

Cakici and Topyan (2000) modified the Ritchken and Trevor methodology by producing a forward-building procedure that is independent of the number of variances stored, leading to greater accuracy and a more reliable volatility measure. The modified approach uses only real node minimum and maximum variances, not the interpolated ones in between. Under the Ritchken and Trevor (RT) model, minimum and maximum variances originating from the prior day's interpolated variance values can occur at many nodes. Under the Cakici and Topyan (CT) model, this cannot occur since the $K - 2$ interpolated variances per node are computed after the tree is built, but before the backward-induction (recursion) stage starts. With this modification, there may be some out-of-range referencing of the interpolated variances, which can be handled in one of two ways. First, if the next variance is below the minimum (or above the maximum) variance, then the option price corresponding to the minimum (or maximum) variance can be used during the backward induction.[25] Second, an extrapolation can be used to value the option when out-of-range referencing is observed.

For the CT tree, the minimum and maximum volatilities are in fact true volatilities generated by following the updating rule (8.37) of the discrete-state tree model, starting from the initial state (y_0, h_0^2). In the RT tree, the minimum or maximum volatilities may be the result applying the updating rule to an interpolated

---

[25]Cakici and Topyan (2000), 80.

volatility of the previous date so that they may be artifacts in the sense they are not generated as true volatilities.

After the tree is built, backward induction occurs. For a given volatility h_{t+1} following state (y_t, h_t^2) via updating rule (8.37), the algorithm locates the two volatilities that bracket h_{t+1}. However, h_t may be interpolated volatility so that the option price corresponding to h_{t+1} is also interpolated linearly from the option prices corresponding to the bracketing volatilities. After all option prices at all $2n + 1$ nodes are determined, the option price at state (y_t, h_t^2) is calculated as the (risk-neutral) discounted expected value based on the branching probabilities.

However, Wu (2003) shows that there are serious problems from a practical use viewpoint with both the RT and CT models. As Wu points out, both models create exponentially sized trees that can explode if the number of partitions per day, n, exceeds a typically small number. Thus, the trees are not efficient unless n is small, but a small n can result in inaccurate option prices and short-dated options. But, in fact, even the small choice of $n = 1$ can result in explosion. One cannot trade off efficiency for accuracy by using a suitably large n because when explosion occurs, the trees cannot grow beyond a certain maturity, making the trees useless for pricing derivatives with long maturities.[26] In the CT model, an interpolated volatility's successor volatility may branch to an unreachable node that has no option prices at all. Consequently, backward induction cannot continue, which, while rare, can occur when n and N are both large. As Wu shows numerically, the RT model does not converge with increasing n. There is a downward trend in calculated option prices so that option prices may fail to converge as n increases.

Wu develops a mean tracking (MT) option price tree that uses a log-linear interpolation scheme. Such a scheme avoids the convergence problems of the RT model. The rationale for the log-linear scheme, in which logarithmic volatilities are equally spaced as:

$$\exp\left[\ln h_{\min}^2 + j \, \frac{\ln h_{\max}^2 - \ln h_{\min}^2}{K-1} \right] \quad j = 0, 1, 2, \ldots, K-1 \qquad (8.46)$$

is to address problems with the RT and CT models, which both implicitly assume the volatility distribution is uniform since interpolated squared volatilities are equally spaced between the minimum and maximum ones. However, as Wu shows, the actual distribution more closely approximates a lognormal distribution than a uniform one, which suggests that there should be more interpolated volatilities at the lower end of the distribution than at the higher end. The log-linear approach samples smaller volatilities more finely than larger volatilities. The incorporation of mean tracking allows the middle branch of the multinomial tree to track the mean

---

[26]Wu (2003), 2.

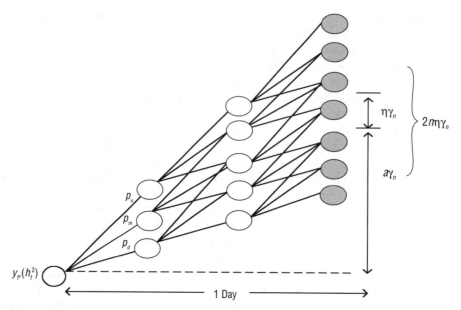

FIGURE 8.6 Mean Tracking Trinomial Tree

of y_{t+1}. Thus, explosion problems and their consequences of shortened maturities cannot occur.

The MT tree is built as follows. At date t, the node is chosen to be that closest to the mean of y_{t+1} given (y_t, h_t^2), that is, $y_t + r - (h_t^2/2)$, where the mean $\mu = r - (h_t^2 / 2)$. By the geometry of the tree, the node's logarithmic price equals $y_t + a\gamma_n$ for some integer a. The criterion by which a node is chosen ensures that:

$$|a\gamma_n - \mu| \leq \gamma_n/2 \qquad (8.47)$$

The multinomial tree is created by making the middle branch of the $(2n + 1)$-nomial tree line up with the node closest to the mean. Though only $2n + 1$ nodes are reached after one day, the top and bottom nodes span over $2n\eta + 1$ nodes.[27] Figure 8.6 shows the MT trinomial tree.

The probabilities for upward, middle, and downward branches processes are given by:

$$p_u = \frac{nh_t^2 + (a\gamma_n - \mu)^2}{2n^2\eta^2\gamma_n^2} - \frac{a\gamma_n - \mu}{2n\eta\gamma_n} \qquad (8.48)$$

---

[27]Ibid., 17.

$$p_m = 1 - \frac{nh_t^2 + (a\gamma_n - \mu)^2}{n^2\eta^2\gamma_n^2} \tag{8.49}$$

$$p_d = \frac{nh_t^2 + (a\gamma_n - \mu)^2}{2n^2\eta^2\gamma_n^2} + \frac{a\gamma_n - \mu}{2n\eta\gamma_n} \tag{8.50}$$

Since the conditional mean and variance of the GARCH process at time $t + 1$ is matched exactly, convergence is guaranteed. State (y_t, h_t^2) at time t is followed by state $(y_t + j\eta\gamma_n, h_{t+1}^2)$ at time $t + 1$, where

$$h_{t+1}^2 = \beta_0 + \beta_1 h_t^2 + \beta_2 h_t^2 (\varepsilon'_{t+1} - c)^2$$

$$\varepsilon'_{t+1} = \frac{j\eta\gamma_n + a\gamma_n - (r - h_t^2/2)}{h_t} \qquad j = 0, \pm 1, \pm 2, \ldots, \pm n \tag{8.51}$$

The underlying trinomial model has transitions that occur with probability given in equation (8.39). It can be shown that the condition for the probabilities to lie within 0 and 1 is:

$$\frac{\sqrt{nh_t^2 + (a\gamma_n - \mu)^2}}{n\gamma_n} \le \eta \le \frac{nh_t^2 + (a\gamma_n - \mu)^2}{n\gamma_n \mid a\gamma_n - \mu \mid} \tag{8.52}$$

The existence of a valid jump parameter η is guaranteed, that is, a positive integer so that the MT tree never stops growing beyond a given maturity. This corrects the problem with the RT and CT trees. Rather than search for value of η, the MT tree simply uses the ceiling of the lower bound of inequality (8.52),

$$\eta = \left\lceil \frac{\sqrt{nh_t^2 + (a\gamma_n - \mu)^2}}{n\gamma_n} \right\rceil \tag{8.53}$$

Moreover, let $H_{min}^2 = \min(h_0^2, \beta_0 / (1 - \beta_1))$ so that $H_{min}^2 \le h_t^2$ for $t \ge 0$. If $\gamma \le H_{min}$, then

$$\gamma_n = \gamma / \sqrt{n}$$

satisfies $\gamma_n \le H_{min}^2$ for all n so that interval (8.52) will contain a positive η value. A smaller γ generally leads to larger trees and longer running times, but results in greater accuracy. Wu shows that the choice $\gamma = H_{min}/2$ leads to option prices that fall within the 95 percent confidence interval of Monte Carlo simulation of the continuous-state model in (8.34) for all $n > 1$.[28] Thus, with the choice of:

$$\gamma_n = \frac{H_{min}}{2\sqrt{n}} \tag{8.54}$$

all the parameters of the MT tree have been chosen. Moreover, the MT tree does not explode if:

$$n \leq \left(\sqrt{\frac{1-\beta_1}{\beta_2}} - c \right)^2 \tag{8.55}$$

If this relation holds, then the tree size is only quadratic in maturity, which is the same as a Cox-Ross-Rubinstein (1979) tree. It turns out that if $c = 0$, the sufficient condition for nonexplosion reduces to $n \leq (1 - \beta_1)/\beta_2$, which is in fact the threshold of explosion for the RT and CT trees. Thus, the threshold of the MT model is in some sense tight and its tree size is asymptotically optimal since relationship (8.55) holds for any n. In fact, a trinomial tree for the Black-Scholes model is obtained in the limit by letting $\beta_1 = 0$ and $\beta_2 \rightarrow 0$. Consequently, Wu has shown that the MT model is the first tree-based GARCH model that is provably efficient.

8.9   GARCH FORECASTING

GARCH models are useful for forecasting volatilities and correlations. GARCH has practical use in risk management. A risk manager can use GARCH to better forecast future volatility and risk of the market and thus manage this risk through use of derivative securities to hedge a portfolio's market risk exposure. In particular, GARCH can be used in value at risk (VaR) estimates of an entire portfolio to movements in underlying market factors like interest rates and exchange rates. GARCH forecasting can be used to generate 95 percent confidence bands on future volatility of asset returns such as the S&P 500 index.

GARCH forecasts perform better than ARCH forecasts and OLS unconditional variance forecasts due to GARCH's long-term memory of past volatility and dynamics of capturing volatility clustering. Suppose we have an AR(1) model for the log return process. Let $y_t = \log(S_t/S_{t-1})$. Then we have the return equation:

$$y_t = \mu + \phi y_{t-1} + \varepsilon_t \tag{8.56}$$

---

[28]Ibid., 19.

where the error's variance follows a conditional variance GARCH(1, 1) process. The errors are used in the forecasts.

The GARCH(1, 1) forecast of the one-day forward at time t is:

$$\hat{\sigma}^2_{t+1|t} = \omega + \alpha\varepsilon_t^2 + \beta\sigma_t^2 \tag{8.57}$$

where the forecasted volatility is conditional on the information at time t and the s-step-ahead forecast is computed iteratively:

$$\hat{\sigma}^2_{t+s} = \omega + (\alpha + \beta)\hat{\sigma}^2_{t+s-1} \tag{8.58}$$

It can be shown[29] that the forecast of ε^2_{t+1} based on ε_t^2, denoted $\varepsilon^2_{t+1|t}$, can be calculated iterating on:

$$\varepsilon^2_{t+1|t} - \tilde{\sigma}^2 = (\alpha + \beta)(\varepsilon_t^2 - \tilde{\sigma}^2) - \beta w_t \tag{8.59}$$

where $w_t = \varepsilon_t^2 - \sigma_t^2$ and $\tilde{\sigma}^2$ is the unconditional mean of ε_t^2, that is, $E[\varepsilon_t^2] = \tilde{\sigma}^2$. More generally, for a GARCH(p, q) model,

$$\varepsilon^2_{t+s|t} - \tilde{\sigma}^2 = \sum_{i=1}^{q}(\alpha_i + \beta_i)(\varepsilon^2_{t+s-i|t} - \tilde{\sigma}^2) - \sum_{i=s}^{p}\beta_i w_{t+s-i} \qquad \text{for } s = 1, 2, \ldots, p$$

and

$$\varepsilon^2_{t+s|t} - \tilde{\sigma}^2 = \sum_{i=1}^{q}(\alpha_i + \beta_i)(\varepsilon^2_{t+s-i|t} - \tilde{\sigma}^2) \qquad \text{for } s = p+1, p+2, \ldots$$

$$\varepsilon^2_{\tau|t} = \varepsilon_\tau^2 \text{ for } \tau < t \text{ and } w_\tau = \varepsilon_\tau^2 - \varepsilon^2_{\tau|\tau-1} \text{ for } \tau = t, t-1, \ldots, t-p+1$$

The linear projection of the s-step-ahead squared error ($s > 1$) forecast of $y_{t+s|t}$ using the GARCH(1, 1) model is

$$\varepsilon^2_{t+s|t} - \tilde{\sigma}^2 = (\alpha + \beta)^s(\varepsilon_t^2 - \tilde{\sigma}^2)$$

or

$$\varepsilon^2_{t+s|t} = \tilde{\sigma}^2(1 - (\alpha + \beta)^s) + (\alpha + \beta)^s\varepsilon_t^2$$

---

[29]Hamilton (1994), 666.

We now provide an example of using a GARCH forecasting application. Using monthly S&P 500 index prices, taken from the Research Seminar in Quantitative Economics (RSQE) database at the University of Michigan[30] from the beginning of January 1948 to January 1997 ($T = 589$ observations), GARCH(1, 1) forecasts were made for in-sample data. The estimated one-step-ahead mean return equation in (8.22) is:

$$y_{t+1|t} = \underset{(0.001897)}{0.005911} + \underset{(0.048627)}{0.22296} y_t + \varepsilon_t \qquad (8.60)$$

where standard errors are in parentheses. The coefficient on the lagged value has a significance level greater than 99 percent (a t-statistic of 6.109), suggesting autocorrelation in returns.[31] However, lagged orders greater than 1 are statistically insignificant as measured by computed autocorrelations and partial autocorrelations. The errors were assumed to follow a GARCH(1, 1) process that was estimated to be:

$$\sigma^2_{t+1|t} = \underset{(0.000063)}{0.000163} + \underset{(0.03049)}{0.1314} \varepsilon^2_t + \underset{(0.07494)}{0.7187} \sigma^2_t \qquad (8.61)$$

for the one-step-ahead forecast. The 95 percent confidence interval for the one-step-ahead forecast is then computed:

$$0.005911 + 0.2229 y_t \pm 1.96 \times (1 - \text{step-ahead GARCH forecast})$$

$$0.005911 + 0.2229 y_t \pm 1.96 \times (0.000163 + 0.1314 \varepsilon^2_t + 0.7187 \sigma^2_t)$$

It was found that a sample proportion of 93.7 percent of the one-step-ahead volatility forecasts fell inside the 95 percent confidence bands. The confidence bands widen when volatility increases and narrows when volatility decreases. Moreover, the sample proportion of volatility forecasts that fall inside the confidence bands increases as the step-ahead size increases. This is because there is more variability over a longer forecast horizon than over a one-period horizon so that the GARCH model has more information (conditional variances) on which to base forecasts. GARCH has a long-term memory of these past conditional variances. For a $s = $ six-step-ahead forecast, the 95 percent confidence interval is:

$$\mu(1 + \phi + \phi^2 + \phi^3 + \phi^4 + \phi^5) + \phi^6 y_t \pm 1.645 \sqrt{\varepsilon^2_{t+6|t}}$$

$$= \mu(1 + \phi + \phi^2 + \phi^3 + \phi^4 + \phi^5) + \phi^6 y_t \pm 1.645 \sqrt{\sigma^2 (1 - (\alpha + \beta)^6) + (\alpha + \beta)^6 \varepsilon^2_t}$$

$$= 0.00761 \pm 1.645 \sqrt{0.000677 + 0.37742 \varepsilon^2_t}$$

---

[30]See http://rsqe.econ.lsa.umich.edu.

[31]Daily returns to equity indexes often exhibit some autocorrelation. Carol Alexander suggests that a possible cause of this autocorrelation in equity indexes is the new arrival process, where information affects trading in some stocks before others. See Alexander, (2001a), 385.

where $\mu = 0.05911$ and $\phi = 0.22296$ from (8.60) and $\alpha = 0.1314$ and $\beta = 0.7187$ from (8.61).

The sample proportion of (in-sample) six-step-ahead forecasts that fell inside the 95 percent band was 99.9 percent with a standard error of approximately zero. The model was not tested out-of-sample after January 1997 so the stability of the parameters is not known. Overall, however, the GARCH(1, 1) does an excellent job of tracking the future variability of the S&P 500 index though the robustness should be tested out-of-sample to ensure stability of the estimated parameters. In general, the GARCH(1, 1) model performs better than ARCH(1) and OLS unconditional variance, especially for longer-term forecasts, due to its long-term memory.

GARCH can also be used to compute the value at risk (VaR) of an asset or portfolio via historical or Monte Carlo simulation using GARCH to forecast the rolling volatility. VaR is computed by multiplying the computed (GARCH) volatility by the multiplication factor of the desired confidence level. For example, the 95 percent confidence multiplier is 1.645 and the 99 percent multiplier is 2.33. Figure 8.7, from Philip Best (1999), shows the price history of gold from November 12, 1991, to November 11, 1996.

Best then computed the 95 percent VaR on a rolling basis (using a one-day horizon) based on a GARCH(1, 1) forecasted rolling volatility. The estimated GARCH(1, 1) equation was:

$$\sigma^2_{t+1|t} = 0.001865 + 0.4789\varepsilon^2_t + 0.9457\sigma^2_t$$

It was then compared to the actual percentage price changes the following day to determine how well the next-day percentage price changes could be captured inside the 95 percent VaR confidence bands using GARCH(1, 1) volatility estimates.

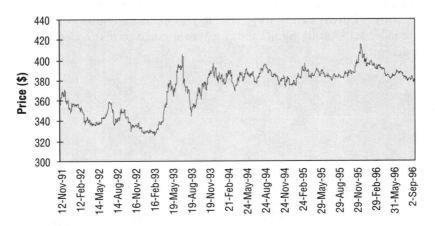

FIGURE 8.7 Gold Price History
Source: Philip W. Best, *Implementing Value at Risk* (Chichester, UK: John Wiley & Sons, 1998). Reprinted with permission.

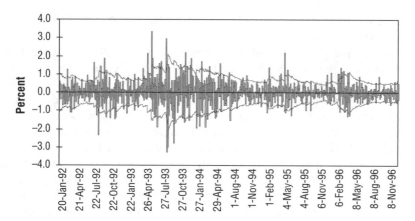

FIGURE 8.8 Gold—VaR versus Price Change, GARCH(1, 1)
Source: Philip W. Best, *Implementing Value at Risk* (Chichester, UK: John Wiley & Sons, 1998). Reprinted with permission.

The comparison of VaR and price changes did not start until the volatility measures covered the observation period of 50 days, which was assumed to be a decay factor of roughly 0.94 (though different asset classes have decay factors that differ significantly from 0.94 for 50 days of observations). Figure 8.8 shows the 95 percent VaR estimates with GARCH(1, 1) to actual price changes.

Actual price changes greater than the 95 percent VaR confidence level were counted as "exceptions" and totaled. It was found that 3.7 percent of the actual percentage price was made up of exceptions. A standard z-score of -2.164 was computed allowing for a rejection of a two-sided 95 percent confidence test, but also allowing an acceptance of a one-sided test. However, if an extreme value of the GARCH decay factor was used, the resultant exception count was found to be a more statistically significant acceptance range so that a two-tailed test could be accepted.

CHAPTER 9

Stochastic Multifactor Models

Many derivative pricing models, such as stochastic interest rate models, hybrid securities pricing models (i.e., convertible bonds), multiasset pricing models (i.e., basket options, quanto options), credit models, and stochastic volatility models, have several underlying assets and several underlying sources of uncertainty. These models are based on multifactor diffusion processes. They require the use of multivariate stochastic calculus to derive pricing formulas.

In the single variable diffusion process, it is assumed that there is only one source of uncertainty dz. We have assumed that in the risk-neutral world, the single underlying asset follows the risk-neutral process in equation (1.38). However, this process can be extended to the case of n sources of uncertainty or risk factors. Instead of working with scalar values stochastic processes, we will work with vector-valued stochastic processes and variance-covariance matrices for n-dimensional vectors of normal variables and n-dimensional Brownian motions.

This chapter provides the mathematical underpinning for n-dimensional diffusion processes, with n sources of uncertainty (factors), which are important for n-dimensional Monte Carlo simulations. Often Monte Carlo simulation is the only method available for pricing path-dependent derivatives dependent on n underlying factors. Thus, we will discuss the tools and techniques needed to model multifactor models.

We will discuss changes of measure for independent and correlated random variables, n-dimensional random walks and Brownian motion, n-dimensional generalized Wiener processes, Ito's lemma for multifactor diffusion processes, Monte Carlo simulation of multivariate diffusion processes, as well as principal component analysis (PCA), a standard method for extracting the most important uncorrelated sources of variation (uncertainty) in multivariate systems. PCA is quite applicable to (multiple) term structures, which are usually highly correlated, as well as a useful tool for risk management in large portfolios. It is also applied to implied volatilities of different options on the same underlying factors. Moreover, we discuss correlation and covariance structures and the role they play in multifactor models.

In section 9.1, we discuss change of measure for independent normal random variables. In section 9.2, we discuss change of measure for correlated normal random variables. In section 9.3, we discuss n-dimensional random walks and

Brownian motions, while in section 9.4 we examine an n-dimensional generalized Wiener process. In section 9.5, we discuss multivariate diffusion processes. In section 9.6, we discuss Monte Carlo simulation of multivariate diffusion processes. In section 9.7, we discuss the n-dimensional lognormal diffusion process. In section 9.8, Ito's lemma for functions of vector-valued diffusion processes is given. In section 9.9, we discuss using principal component analysis (PCA) for multifactor models.

9.1   CHANGE OF MEASURE FOR INDEPENDENT RANDOM VARIABLES

Consider a column vector $\mathbf{Z}$ of n independent normal random variables:

$$\mathbf{Z} = \begin{bmatrix} Z_1 \\ Z_2 \\ \dots \\ Z_n \end{bmatrix}$$

where $E[Z_i] = \mu_i$ and $E[(Z_i - \mu_i)(Z_j - \mu_j)] = 1_{(i=j)}$ is the indicator function equal to 1 if $i = j$ and 0 if not so that $\mathbf{Z}$ has mean vector and the identity covariance matrix:

$$\mu = \begin{bmatrix} \mu_1 \\ \mu_2 \\ \dots \\ \mu_n \end{bmatrix} \text{ and } \mathbf{1} = \begin{bmatrix} 1 & 0 & 0 & \dots & 0 \\ 0 & 1 & 0 & \dots & 0 \\ \dots & \dots & \dots & \dots & 0 \\ 0 & 0 & 0 & \dots & 1 \end{bmatrix} \tag{9.1}$$

The probability measure is:

$$P_\mu\{Z_1 \in dz_1, \dots, Z_n \in dz_n\} = \frac{1}{\sqrt{(2\pi)^n}} \exp\left(-\frac{1}{2}\left|\mathbf{z} - \mu\right|^2\right) dz_1 \dots dz_n \tag{9.2}$$

and

$$P_\mu\{Z_1 \in [a_1, b_1], \dots, Z_n \in [a_n, b_n]\} = \int_{a_1}^{b_1} \dots \int_{a_n}^{b_n} \frac{1}{\sqrt{(2\pi)^n}} \exp\left(-\frac{1}{2}\left|\mathbf{z} - \mu\right|^2\right) dz_1 \dots dz_n \tag{9.3}$$

Thus, if $f(\mathbf{Z})$ is a real-valued function, its expected value with respect to the probability measure P_μ is:

$$E_\mu[f(\mathbf{Z})] = \int_{\Re^n} f(\mathbf{z}) \frac{1}{\sqrt{(2\pi)^n}} \exp\left\{-\frac{1}{2}\left|\mathbf{z}-\boldsymbol{\mu}\right|^2\right\} d^n z \tag{9.4}$$

where the index μ in the notation represents the fact that the underlying random variables we are averaging over have the mean vector $\boldsymbol{\mu}$ and the | | represent the length of the vector the L^2-norm, that is,

$$\sqrt{\sum_{i=1}^n (z_i - \mu_i)^2}$$

We can express the probability measure in equation (9.2) through the probability measure P_0, or simply P, with the zero mean vector as:

$$\xi_\mu(\mathbf{Z}) P\{Z_1 \in dz_1, \ldots, Z_n \in dz_n\} \tag{9.5}$$

where

$$P\{Z_1 \in dz_1, \ldots, Z_n \in dz_n\} = \frac{1}{\sqrt{(2\pi)^n}} \exp\left(-\frac{1}{2}\left|\mathbf{z}\right|^2\right) dz_1 \ldots dz_n \tag{9.6}$$

and $\xi_\mu(\mathbf{Z})$ is a scalar random variable under the measure P given by:

$$\xi_\mu(\mathbf{Z}) = \exp\left(\boldsymbol{\mu}'\mathbf{Z} - \frac{1}{2}\left|\boldsymbol{\mu}\right|^2\right) \tag{9.7}$$

The random variable $\xi_\mu(\mathbf{Z})$ is the Radon-Nikodym derivative of the measure P_μ with respect to the zero-mean measure P, and can be formally written as:

$$\xi_\mu(\mathbf{Z}) = \frac{dP_\mu}{dP} \tag{9.8}$$

It is easy to see that $E[\xi_\mu(\mathbf{Z})] = 1$. Thus, we can write the expectation of a function $f(Z)$ with respect to the probability measure P_μ as:

$$E_\mu[f(\mathbf{Z})] = E[\xi_\mu(\mathbf{Z})f(\mathbf{Z})] \tag{9.9}$$

This states that the expectation of a random variable f under the probability measure P_μ with mean vector $\boldsymbol{\mu}$ is equal to the expectation under the zero-mean measure P of the product of this random variable and the Radon-Nikodym derivative.

Under P, the random variables Z_i are independent standard normal with $E[Z_i] = 0$ and $E[Z_i Z_j] = \mathbf{1}_{(i=j)}$. However, $Z_i - \mu_i$ are independent standard normal random variables under P_μ. Therefore, the change of probability measure $P_\mu \to P$ is equivalent to the change of variables $\mathbf{Z} - \boldsymbol{\mu} \to \mathbf{Z}$, and for the expectations, $E_\mu[f(\mathbf{Z} - \boldsymbol{\mu})] = E[f(\mathbf{Z})]$ and $E_\mu[f(\mathbf{Z})] = E[\xi_\mu(\mathbf{Z})f(\mathbf{Z})]$.

9.2   CHANGE OF MEASURE FOR CORRELATED RANDOM VARIABLES

The change of measure/change of variable result for independent random variables can be extended to the case of correlated normal variables. Consider a column vector of n random variables $Z_1, Z_2, \ldots, Z_n$ where $E[Z_i] = \mu_i$ and $E[(Z_i - \mu_i)(Z_j - \mu_j)] = \sigma_{ij}$ so that $\mathbf{Z}$ has the mean vector $\boldsymbol{\mu}$ and covariance matrix $\boldsymbol{\Sigma}$:

$$
\boldsymbol{\mu} = \begin{bmatrix} \mu_1 \\ \mu_2 \\ \cdots \\ \mu_n \end{bmatrix} \text{ and } \boldsymbol{\Sigma} = \begin{bmatrix} \sigma_{11} & \sigma_{12} & \cdots & \sigma_{1n} \\ \sigma_{21} & \sigma_{22} & \cdots & \sigma_{2n} \\ \cdots & \cdots & \cdots & \cdots \\ \sigma_{n1} & \sigma_{n2} & \cdots & \sigma_{nn} \end{bmatrix}
$$

Note that the diagonal terms along $\boldsymbol{\Sigma}$ are the variances of the standard normal random variables $Z_i - \mu_i$ and the off-diagonal terms are their covariances.

The probability measure is then:

$$
P_\mu\{Z_1 \in dz_1, \ldots, Z_n \in dz_n\} = \frac{1}{\sqrt{(2\pi)^n \det \boldsymbol{\Sigma}}} \exp\left(-\frac{1}{2}(\mathbf{z} - \boldsymbol{\mu})'\boldsymbol{\Sigma}^{-1}(\mathbf{z} - \boldsymbol{\mu})\right) dz_1 \ldots dz_n \quad (9.10)
$$

If $f(\mathbf{Z})$ is a real-valued function, its expected value with respect to the probability measure

$$
E_\mu[f(\mathbf{Z})] = \int_{\mathfrak{R}^n} f(z) \frac{1}{\sqrt{(2\pi)^n \det \boldsymbol{\Sigma}}} \exp\left(-\frac{1}{2}(\mathbf{z} - \boldsymbol{\mu})'\boldsymbol{\Sigma}^{-1}(\mathbf{z} - \boldsymbol{\mu})\right) d^n z \quad (9.11)
$$

As in the standard normal case, we can express the probably measure P_μ through the probability measure P_0, or simple P, with the zero-mean vector as:

$$
\xi_\mu(\mathbf{Z})P\{Z_1 \in dz_1, \ldots, Z_n \in dz_n\} \quad (9.12)
$$

where

$$P\{Z_1 \in dz_1, \ldots, Z_n \in dz_n\} = \frac{1}{\sqrt{(2\pi)^n \det \Sigma}} \exp\left(-\frac{1}{2} \mathbf{z}' \Sigma^{-1} \mathbf{z}\right) dz_1 \ldots dz_n \quad (9.13)$$

and $\xi_\mu(\mathbf{Z})$ is a scalar random variable under the measure P:

$$\xi_\mu(\mathbf{Z}) = \exp\left\{\boldsymbol{\mu}' \Sigma^{-1} \mathbf{Z} - \frac{1}{2} \boldsymbol{\mu}' \Sigma^{-1} \boldsymbol{\mu}\right\} \quad (9.14)$$

Moreover, $E[\xi_\mu(\mathbf{Z})] = 1$. Thus, the expectation of a real-valued function $f(\mathbf{Z})$ with respect to the probability measure P_μ is:

$$E_\mu[f(\mathbf{Z})] = E[\xi_\mu(\mathbf{Z})f(\mathbf{Z})] \quad (9.15)$$

Under P, the random variables Z_i are normal with zero mean and covariance $E[Z_i Z_j] = \sigma_{ij}$. However, $Z_i - \mu_i$ are normal random variables with zero mean and covariance Σ under P_μ. Therefore, the change of probability measure $P_\mu \rightarrow P$ is equivalent to the change of variables $\mathbf{Z} - \boldsymbol{\mu} \rightarrow \mathbf{Z}$ and for expectations, we get $E_\mu[f(\mathbf{Z} - \boldsymbol{\mu})]$ $= E[f(\mathbf{Z})]$ and $E_\mu[f(\mathbf{Z})] = E[\xi_\mu(\mathbf{Z})f(\mathbf{Z})]$.

9.3 *N*-DIMENSIONAL RANDOM WALKS AND BROWNIAN MOTION

Suppose $\mathbf{z}(t)$ is vector-valued process with continuous sample paths:

$$\mathbf{z}(t) = \begin{bmatrix} z_1(t) \\ z_2(t) \\ \ldots \\ z_n(t) \end{bmatrix} \quad (9.16)$$

In the limit of infinitesimal time changes dt, we get:

$$\mathbf{dz}(t) = \boldsymbol{\varepsilon}(t)\sqrt{dt}$$

or written in matrices:

$$
\begin{bmatrix} dz_1(t) \\ dz_2(t) \\ \dots \\ dz_n(t) \end{bmatrix} = \begin{bmatrix} \varepsilon_1(t) \\ \varepsilon_2(t) \\ \dots \\ \varepsilon_n(t) \end{bmatrix} \sqrt{dt} \tag{9.17}
$$

where $E[dz_i(t)] = 0$, $i = 1, \dots, n$ and $\text{Cov}[dz_i(t)dz_j(t)] = 1_{\{i=j\}}dt$ where 1 is the indicator function. $\varepsilon(t)$ for all t are i.i.d. vector random variables so that each vector-valued realization can be considered a drawing from the multivariate standard normal distribution in equation (9.6).

The term $z(t)$ is then an n-dimensional Wiener process (or alternatively, Brownian motion in $\Re^n$)—n sources of uncertainty or stochastic factors if it satisfies three properties:

1. For any $t < T$, the finite increment difference $\Delta z = z(T) - z(t)$ is a vector-valued normal random variable with zero mean $\mathbf{0}$ and covariance matrix $(T - t)\mathbf{I}_{n \times n}$ where I is the $n \times n$ identity matrix with elements $1_{\{a=b\}}$. In other words,

$$
E[z(T) - z(t)] = \begin{bmatrix} 0 \\ 0 \\ \dots \\ 0 \end{bmatrix} \text{ and } E[(z(T) - z(t))(z(T) - z(t))'] = \begin{bmatrix} (T-t) & 0 & \dots & 0 \\ 0 & (T-t) & \dots & 0 \\ 0 & \dots & \dots & 0 \\ 0 & 0 & & (T-t) \end{bmatrix}
$$

   The zero mean expectation implies that the Brownian motion is a martingale and in conjunction with the variance-covariance matrix implies that the Brownian motion processes have identically distributed increments since the variance depends only on the length of the increment. The increments are not correlated since all the nondiagonal elements are 0.

2. For any $0 \le t_1 \le t_2 \le \dots < t_n$, the increments of the vector-valued random variables $z(t_2) - z(t_1)$, $z(t_4) - z(t_3)$, $\dots$, $z(t_n) - z(t_{n-1})$ are independent. In other words, the Brownian motions possess independent increments.

3. $z(t_0) = 0$ with probability 1. Thus, the Brownian motion is started at the origin.

Note that, in addition, Brownian motion is not differentiable with respect to time[1] and that $dz_i(t)dz_j(t) = 1_{\{i=j\}}dt + O(dt^2)$ for a Brownian motion defined in

---

[1]Note that

$$
E\left[\left|\frac{z(s) - z(t)}{s - t}\right|^2\right] = \frac{s - t}{(s - t)^2} = \frac{1}{s - t}
$$

The limit as $s \to t$ does not exist. The property of divergence of this limit is known as unbounded quadratic variation.

equation (9.17). We also assume that the time difference $T - t$ is finite (i.e., the variance of $\mathbf{z}(T) - \mathbf{z}(t) < \infty$), so that the increments will be stationary.

9.4 *N*-Dimensional Generalized Wiener Process

We can generalize the n-dimensional Wiener process to an n-dimensional diffusion process. Consider the process

$$\mathbf{dx}(t) = \boldsymbol{\mu}dt + \boldsymbol{\Sigma}\mathbf{dz}(t) \tag{9.18}$$

where $\boldsymbol{\mu}$ is an $n \times 1$ constant drift vector and $\boldsymbol{\Sigma}$ is an $n \times n$ constant diffusion matrix. In matrix form,

$$\begin{bmatrix} dx_1(t) \\ dx_2(t) \\ \cdots \\ dx_n(t) \end{bmatrix} = \begin{bmatrix} \mu_1(t) \\ \mu_2(t) \\ \cdots \\ \mu_n(t) \end{bmatrix} dt + \begin{bmatrix} \sigma_{11} & \sigma_{12} & \cdots & \sigma_{1n} \\ \sigma_{21} & \sigma_{22} & \cdots & \sigma_{2n} \\ \cdots & \cdots & \cdots & \cdots \\ \sigma_{n1} & \sigma_{n2} & \cdots & \sigma_{nn} \end{bmatrix} \begin{bmatrix} dz_1(t) \\ dz_2(t) \\ \cdots \\ dz_n(t) \end{bmatrix} \tag{9.19}$$

Suppose $\boldsymbol{\Sigma} = 0$, where 0 is an $n \times n$ matrix of 0's. Then we get:

$$\mathbf{dx}(t) = \boldsymbol{\mu}dt \tag{9.20}$$

Adding the diffusion term $\boldsymbol{\Sigma}\mathbf{dz}(t)$ to (9.20) adds random noise to the deterministic motion of a particle in $\Re^n$. We can rewrite (9.19) as:

$$\mathbf{dx}(t) = \boldsymbol{\mu}dt + \boldsymbol{\Sigma}\boldsymbol{\varepsilon}(t)\sqrt{dt}$$

or

$$\begin{bmatrix} dx_1(t) \\ dx_2(t) \\ \cdots \\ dx_n(t) \end{bmatrix} = \begin{bmatrix} \mu_1(t) \\ \mu_2(t) \\ \cdots \\ \mu_n(t) \end{bmatrix} dt + \begin{bmatrix} \sigma_{11} & \sigma_{12} & \cdots & \sigma_{1n} \\ \sigma_{21} & \sigma_{22} & \cdots & \sigma_{2n} \\ \cdots & \cdots & \cdots & \cdots \\ \sigma_{n1} & \sigma_{n2} & \cdots & \sigma_{nn} \end{bmatrix} \begin{bmatrix} dz_1(t) \\ dz_2(t) \\ \cdots \\ dz_n(t) \end{bmatrix} \tag{9.21}$$

The following properties of the continuous generalized Wiener process then hold:

$$E[dx_i(t)] = \mu_i dt \quad \text{and} \quad \text{Cov}[dz_i(t)dz_j(t)] = \sigma_{ij}dt \quad \text{for } i, j = 1, \ldots, n$$

For finite increments of a generalized Wiener process, we get:

$$E[x_i(T) - x_i(t)] = \mu_i(T - t) \quad \text{and} \quad \text{Cov}[(x_i(T) - x_i(t)), (x_j(T) - x_j(t))] = \sigma_{ij}(T - t) \quad \text{for } i, j = 1, \ldots, n$$

9.5 MULTIVARIATE DIFFUSION PROCESSES

Consider a stochastic differential equation (SDE) for the ith state variable of an m-dimensional diffusion process:

$$dx_i = \mu_i(\mathbf{x}(t),\, t)dt + \sum_{j=1}^{n} \sigma_{i,j}(\mathbf{x}(t),\, t)dz_j(t) \quad i = 1,\, \ldots,\, m \qquad (9.22)$$

This SDE can be written in matrix form as:

$$\mathbf{dx}(t) = \boldsymbol{\mu}(\mathbf{x}(t),\, t)dt + \boldsymbol{\Sigma}(\mathbf{x}(t),\, t)\mathbf{dz}(t) \qquad (9.23)$$

or

$$\begin{bmatrix} dx_1(t) \\ dx_2(t) \\ \ldots \\ dx_m(t) \end{bmatrix} = \begin{bmatrix} \mu_1(\mathbf{x}(t),\, t) \\ \mu_2(\mathbf{x}(t),\, t) \\ \ldots \\ \mu_m(\mathbf{x}(t),\, t) \end{bmatrix} dt + \begin{bmatrix} \sigma_{11}(\mathbf{x}(t),\, t) & \sigma_{12}(\mathbf{x}(t),\, t) & \ldots & \sigma_{1n}(\mathbf{x}(t),\, t) \\ \sigma_{21}(\mathbf{x}(t),\, t) & \sigma_{22}(\mathbf{x}(t),\, t) & \ldots & \sigma_{2n}(\mathbf{x}(t),\, t) \\ \ldots & \ldots & \ldots & \ldots \\ \sigma_{m1}(\mathbf{x}(t),\, t) & \sigma_{m2}(\mathbf{x}(t),\, t) & \ldots & \sigma_{mn}(\mathbf{x}(t),\, t) \end{bmatrix} \begin{bmatrix} \varepsilon_1(t) \\ \varepsilon_2(t) \\ \ldots \\ \varepsilon_n(t) \end{bmatrix} \sqrt{dt}$$

where both the drift μ, an $m \times 1$ vector, and diffusion coefficient Σ, an $m \times n$ matrix, are functions of the underlying state vector and time. The term $\varepsilon(t)$ is an $n \times 1$ vector of normal random variables drawn from a multivariate standard normal distribution. A diffusion process $\mathbf{x}(t)$ is defined as a solution of equation (9.23) subject to the initial condition $\mathbf{x}(t_0) = \mathbf{x}_0$ where $\mathbf{x}_0$ is the initial state vector.

If x_i are security prices in the market, then there are three cases to consider:

- Case 1: $n = m$
  The number of securities $x_i, i = 1, \ldots, m$ is equal to the number of independent sources of uncertainty $z_j, j = 1, \ldots, n$. Thus the diffusion coefficient has full rank, the system of diffusion equation is *complete*, and all securities are considered *primary*.

- Case 2: $n < m$
  The number of securities m is more than the number of independent sources of uncertainty n. Some securities are derivatives of other primary securities. For example, x_1 is a stock and x_2 is a traded option on the stock. This a two-dimensional process, but the source of uncertainty is common to both the stock and its option. In this case, the system of diffusion equations is *overdetermined*.

- Case 3: $n > m$
  The number of traded securities m is less than the number of independent sources of uncertainty n in the market. The market is *incomplete*, the system of

diffusion equations is *underdetermined*, and some sources of uncertainty are *external*.

The following are some properties of infinitesimal increments of an *m*-dimensional diffusion processes driven by an *n*-dimensional Brownian motion. The expectation is:

$$E[dx_i(t)] = \mu_i(\mathbf{x}(t), t) \quad i = 1, \ldots, m$$

and the covariance of Brownian motions is:

$$\text{Cov}[dx_i(t), dx_j(t)] = E[dx_i(t)dx_j(t)] - E[dx_i(t)]E[dx_j(t)] = \sigma_{ij}(\mathbf{x}(t), t)dt$$

We can write the state-and-time-dependent covariance matrix as $\Sigma = \sigma\sigma'$ where σ is $m \times n$ matrix (we assume $m = n$ so that markets are complete) found from a Cholesky decomposition of Σ since Σ is positive-definite and symmetric. The diffusion coefficient of the *i*th diffusion process, $i = 1, \ldots, m$, with j stochastic factors, $j = 1, \ldots, n$, can be written as:

$$\sigma_{ij}(\mathbf{x}(t), t) = \sum_{j=1}^{n} \sigma_{i,j}(\mathbf{x}(t), t)\sigma_{j,i}(\mathbf{x}(t), t) \tag{9.24}$$

In general, since μ and Σ are functions of both the state vector and time, it is not possible to find closed-form solutions for the mean and variance of finite increments of an *m*-dimensional diffusion process. Thus, it is usually necessary to integrate the stochastic differential equation numerically via Monte Carlo simulation.

9.6 MONTE CARLO SIMULATION OF MULTIVARIATE DIFFUSION PROCESSES

We can discretize the SDE in equation (9.22) to get the approximation:

$$x_{i,k+1} = x_{i,k} + \mu_i(x_k, t_k)\Delta t + \sum_{j=1}^{n} \sigma_{i,j}(x_k, t_k)\varepsilon_{j,k+1}\sqrt{\Delta t} \tag{9.25}$$

which represents the discrete diffusion process for the *i*th state variable, $i = 1, \ldots,$ *m* at time step $k + 1$, $k = 0, 1, \ldots, N - 1$, with $j = 1, \ldots, n$ stochastic factors and N time steps. $\varepsilon_{j,k}$'s are independent drawings from a standard normal distribution, and $x_{i,0}$'s are the initial values (conditions) of the process. Δt is the time step and

$$N = \frac{T - t}{\Delta t}$$

We simulate a discrete-time approximation to the diffusion process defined by equation (9.22). Each simulation run produces an approximation to a continuous sample path of the diffusion process in $\Re^n$: $x_0 \to x_1 \to x_2 \to \ldots \to x_N$

9.7   *N*-DIMENSIONAL LOGNORMAL PROCESS

We can extend the case of one-dimensional geometric Brownian motion (GBM) to an n-dimensional GBM as a specific type of multivariate diffusion where $n = m$. We can generalize the basic Black-Scholes process for n correlated stocks, currencies, or commodity prices. Let S_i, $i = 1, \ldots, n$ be the ith stock that follows the GBM with n-dimensional Brownian motion, that is, n stochastic factors:

$$\frac{dS_i(t)}{S_i(t)} = m_i dt + \sum_{j=1}^{n} \sigma_{i,j} dz_j(t) \tag{9.26}$$

The correlation matrix of the stocks is:

$$\rho_{ij} = \frac{\sigma_{ij}}{\sigma_i \sigma_j} \tag{9.27}$$

where

$$\sigma_{ij} = \sum_{k=1}^{n} \sigma_{ik} \sigma_{jk}$$

is the covariance matrix, and

$$\sigma_i = \sqrt{\sigma_{ii}}$$

is the volatility of the ith factor. We can use a different basis for the Wiener processes driving the diffusion:

$$dW_i(t) = \frac{1}{\sigma_i} \sum_{j=1}^{n} \sigma_{i,j} dz_j(t) \tag{9.28}$$

It is easy to check that dW_i has the properties:

$$E[dW_i(t)] = 0 \tag{9.29}$$

and

$$E[dW_i(t)dW_j(t)] = \frac{1}{\sigma_i\sigma_j}\sum_{k=1}^{n}\sum_{l=1}^{n}\sigma_{i,k}\sigma_{j,l}1_{\{k=1\}}dt = \rho_{ij}dt \qquad (9.30)$$

where $1_{\{k=1\}}$ is the indicator function. Thus, W_i are correlated Wiener processes with the correlation matrix ρ. We can rewrite equation (9.26) as:

$$\frac{dS_i(t)}{S_i(t)} = m_i dt + \sigma_i dW_i(t) \qquad (9.31)$$

Moreover, equation (9.30) can be made stronger:

$$dW_i(t)dW_j(t) = \rho_{ij}dt + O(dt^2) \qquad (9.32)$$

Thus, we have two bases: $z_j(t)$, an orthogonal basis, and $W_i(t)$, a correlated basis. Either basis can be used depending on the particular need for either. In particular, for Monte Carlo simulation, it is more convenient to first-generate independent deviates ε_j, and then transform them into correlated deviates ξ_i using either a Cholesky decomposition or from principal component analysis with an eigenvector-eigenvalue decomposition (see section 2.3).

As an example, consider a three-dimensional diffusion process with three stocks, S_1, S_2, and S_3, with the following GBM diffusions:

$$\frac{dS_1(t)}{S_1(t)} = m_1 dt + \sigma_1 dW_1(t)$$
$$\frac{dS_2(t)}{S_2(t)} = m_2 dt + \sigma_2 dW_2(t) \qquad (9.33)$$
$$\frac{dS_3(t)}{S_3(t)} = m_3 dt + \sigma_3 dW_3(t)$$

The Cholesky decomposition (see section 2.3) gives the decomposition of W_i onto the orthogonal basis dz_j:

$$dW_1 = dz_1$$
$$dW_2 = \rho_{12}dz_1 + \sqrt{1-\rho_{12}^2}\,dz_2$$
$$dW_3 = \rho_{13}dz_1 + \left(\frac{\rho_{23}-\rho_{12}\rho_{13}}{\sqrt{1-\rho_{12}^2}}\right)dz_2 + \left(\sqrt{1-\rho_{13}^2 - \left(\frac{\rho_{23}-\rho_{12}\rho_{13}}{\sqrt{1-\rho_{12}^2}}\right)^2}\right)dz_3$$

Note that $E[dW_1 dW_2] = \rho_{12}$, $E[dW_1 dW_3] = \rho_{13}$, and $E[dW_2 dW_3] = \rho_{23}$. Moreover, since the dz_i are orthogonal: $E[dz_1 dz_2] = E[dz_1 dz_3] = E[dz_2 dz_3] = 0$, $E[dz_1^2] = E[dz_2^2] = E[dz_3^2] = dt$. We can write the three-dimensional process in the orthogonal basis as:

$$\frac{dS_1(t)}{S_1(t)} = m_1 dt + \sigma_1 dz_1(t)$$

$$\frac{dS_2(t)}{S_2(t)} = m_2 dt + \sigma_2 \left(\rho_{12} dz_1 + \sqrt{1-\rho_{12}^2}\, dz_2 \right)$$

$$\frac{dS_3(t)}{S_3(t)} = m_3 dt + \sigma_3 \left(\rho_{13} dz_1 + \left(\frac{\rho_{23} - \rho_{12}\rho_{13}}{\sqrt{1-\rho_{12}^2}} \right) dz_2 + \left(\sqrt{1-\rho_{13}^2 - \left(\frac{\rho_{23} - \rho_{12}\rho_{13}}{\sqrt{1-\rho_{12}^2}} \right)^2} \right) dz_3 \right)$$

The solution to this three-dimensional SDE is:

$$S_1(t) = S_1(t_0) \exp\left(\mu_1(t-t_0) + \sigma_1 \varepsilon_1 \sqrt{(t-t_0)} \right)$$

$$S_2(t) = S_2(t_0) \exp\left(\mu_2(t-t_0) + \sigma_2 \left(\rho_{12}\varepsilon_1 + \sqrt{1-\rho_{12}^2}\, \varepsilon_2 \right) \left(\sqrt{(t-t_0)} \right) \right)$$

$$S_3(t) = S_3(t_0) \exp\left\{ \mu_3(t-t_0) + \sigma_3 \left[\rho_{13}\varepsilon_1 + \left(\frac{\rho_{23} - \rho_{12}\rho_{13}}{\sqrt{1-\rho_{12}^2}} \right) \varepsilon_2 + \sqrt{1-\rho_{13}^2 - \left(\frac{\rho_{23} - \rho_{12}\rho_{13}}{\sqrt{1-\rho_{12}^2}} \right)^2}\, \varepsilon_3 \right] \left(\sqrt{t-t_0} \right) \right\}$$

where

$$\mu_i = m_i - \frac{\sigma_i^2}{2}$$

and ε_i are standard normal deviates. We can simulate an *exact* sample path of this process as follows:

$$S_1(t) = S_1(t_0) \exp\left(\mu_1 \Delta t + \sigma_1 \varepsilon_1 \sqrt{\Delta t} \right)$$

$$S_2(t) = S_2(t_0) \exp\left(\mu_2 \Delta t + \sigma_2 \left(\rho_{12}\varepsilon_1 + \sqrt{1-\rho_{12}^2}\, \varepsilon_2 \right) \sqrt{\Delta t} \right)$$

$$S_3(t) = S_3(t_0) \exp\left(\mu_3 \Delta t + \sigma_3 \left(\rho_{13}\varepsilon_1 + \left(\frac{\rho_{23} - \rho_{12}\rho_{13}}{\sqrt{1-\rho_{12}^2}} \right) \varepsilon_2 + \sqrt{1-\rho_{13}^2 - \left(\frac{\rho_{23} - \rho_{12}\rho_{13}}{\sqrt{1-\rho_{12}^2}} \right)^2}\, \varepsilon_3 \right) \left(\sqrt{\Delta t} \right) \right)$$

We can also use a first-order approximation:[2]

$$S_1(t) = S_1(t_0)\left(1 + m_1\Delta t + \sigma_1\varepsilon_1\sqrt{\Delta t}\right)$$

$$S_2(t) = S_2(t_0)\left(1 + m_2\Delta t + \sigma_2\left(\rho_{12}\varepsilon_1 + \sqrt{1 - \rho_{12}^2}\,\varepsilon_2\right)\sqrt{\Delta t}\right)$$

$$S_3(t) = S_3(t_0)\left(1 + m_3\Delta t + \sigma_3\left(\rho_{13}\varepsilon_1 + \left(\frac{\rho_{23} - \rho_{12}\rho_{13}}{\sqrt{1 - \rho_{12}^2}}\right)\varepsilon_2 + \sqrt{1 - \rho_{13}^2 - \left(\frac{\rho_{23} - \rho_{12}\rho_{13}}{\sqrt{1 - \rho_{12}^2}}\right)}\varepsilon_3\right)\left(\sqrt{\Delta t}\right)\right)$$

We could build a trinomial tree for this three-dimensional process by approximating the three standard normal deviates with three-state random variables.

As an example, suppose we want to value a basket option on three stocks that follow the preceding processes. We can value the option using Monte Carlo simulation:

```
/******************************************************************************
MonteCarloBasket      : values a basket option on three stocks
[in]    double price1 : initial price of stock1
        double price2 : initial price of stock2
        double price3 : initial price of stock3
        double strike : strike price
        double vol1   : volatility of stock 1
        double vol2   : volatility of stock 2
        double vol3   : volatility of stock 3
        double rate   : risk-free rate
        double div1   : dividend yield on stock1
        double div2   : dividend yield on stock2
        double div3   : dividend yield on stock3
        double T      : maturity of option
        double rho12  : correlation between stock 1 and 2
        double rho13  : correlation between stock 1 and 3
        double rho23  : correlation between stock 2 and 3
        char type     : type of basket option: (C)all or (P)ut
        long M        : number of simulations
        long N        : number of time steps
[out]   double        : price of basket option
******************************************************************************/
double BasketOption::calcMonteCarloBasket(double price1, double price2, double
  price3, double strike, double vol1,double vol2, double vol3, double rate, double
```

---

[2]Sometimes a first-order approximation can be more efficient to calculate than the exact process since the first-order approximation does not have to call the exponential operator, which has a computational cost. Note that the first-order approximation is $O(dt^{3/2})$.

```
      div1, double div2, double div3, double T, double rho12, doublerho13, double
      rho23, char type, int M, int N)
{
    int i, j;
    double value = 0.0;                   // basket option price
    double St1, St2, St3 = 0.0;           // stock prices at time t
    double e1 = 0.0;                      // random deviate for stock 1
    double e2 = 0.0;                      // random deviate for stock 2
    double e3 = 0.0;                      // random deviate for stock 3
    double sum = 0.0;                     // sum of option payoffs
    double sum2 = 0.0;                    // sum of squared option payoffs
    double SD = 0.0;                      // standard deviation
    double SE = 0.0;                      // standard error
    double dt = T/N;                      // time step
    StatUtility util;                     // statistical utility class

    srand(time(0));                       // initialize RNG
    long seed = (long) rand() % 100;      // generate seed
    long *idum = &seed;                   // store address of seed
    std::cout.precision(4);               // set output format

    for(i=0; i < M; i++) // i is the path number
    {
        // reinitialize to initial stock prices
        St1 = price1;
        St2 = price2;
        St3 = price3;

        for(j = 0; j < N; j++) // j is the step along the path
        {
            e1 = util.gasdev(idum);
            e2 = util.gasdev(idum);
            e3 = util.gasdev(idum);

            St1 = St1*(1+(rate-div1)*dt+ vol1*sqrt(dt)*e1);

            St2 = St2*(1+(rate-div2)*dt+ vol2*sqrt(dt)*(rho12*e1 +
                  sqrt(1-rho12*rho12)*e2));

            St3 = St3*(1 + (rate - div3)*dt + vol3*sqrt(dt)*(rho13*e1
                  + ((rho23 - rho12*rho13)/sqrt(1-rho12*rho12))*e2
                  + sqrt(1 - rho13*rho13 - ((rho23 - rho12*rho13)/sqrt
                  (1-rho12*rho12)))*e3));
        }
        if (type == 'C')
            value = max(St1 + St2 + St3 - strike,0);
        else
            value = max(strike - St1 - St2 - St3,0);

        sum = sum + value;
        sum2 = sum2 + value*value;
    }
```

```
// compute basket price
value = exp(-rate*T)*(sum/M));

// compute standard deviation
SD = sqrt((exp(-2*rate*T)/(M-1))*(sum2 - (sum*sum)/M));

// compute standard error
SE = SD/sqrt(M);

// output results
std::cout << "basket price = " << value << endl;
std::cout << "stddev = " << SD << endl;
std::cout << "stderr = " << SE << endl;

return value;
}
```

Suppose we price a basket call option with $S_1 = 50$, $S_2 = 40$, $S_3 = 55$, $X = 150$, $\sigma_1 = 0.20$, $\sigma_2 = 0.30$, $\sigma_3 = 0.25$, $r = 0.10$, $q_1 = 0$, $q_2 = 0.01$, $q_3 = 0.015$, $T = 75$, $\rho_{12} = 0.6$, $\rho_{13} = 0.20$, $\rho_{23} = -0.30$, $M = 100,000$, and $N = 1,000$. We make the function call:

```
void main()
{
  BasketOption bo;
  bo.calcMonteCarloBasket(50,40,55,150,0.2,0.3,0.25,0.1,0.0,0.01,0.015,0.75,0.6,
    0.2,-0.3,'C',100000,1000);
}
```

We find the price is $11.70, with a standard deviation of 16.20 and a standard error of 0.051.

For a more robust object-oriented implementation for multifactor diffusions, we can use Monte Carlo classes defined in section 2.10 to derive a *BasketPath-Pricer* class (from the QuantLib library at www.quantlib.org). First, we define a *MultiPath* class that implements multiple factors evolving at the same time.

```
#include "ql/MonteCarlo/Path.h"

namespace QuantLib
{
  namespace MonteCarlo
  {
    // single random walk
```

```
/*********************************************************************************
MultiPath implements multiple factors evolving at the same time. MultiPath
  contains the list of variations for each asset,
  log {Y^j_{i+1}/{Y^j_i} for} i = 0, . . . , n-1

where Y^j_i is the value of the underlying j at discretized time t_i . The first
  index refers to the underlying, the second to the time position MultiPath[j,i]

*********************************************************************************/
  class MultiPath
  {
    public:
      MultiPath(Size nAsset, Size pathSize);
      MultiPath(const std::vector<Path>& multiPath);
      // name inspectors
      Size assetNumber() const { return multiPath_.size(); }
      Size pathSize() const { return multiPath_[0].size(); }
      // name read/write access to components
      const Path& operator[](Size j) const { return multiPath_[j]; }
      Path& operator[](Size j) { return multiPath_[j]; }
    private:
      std::vector<Path> multiPath_;
  };

  // inline definitions
  // overloaded constructor
  inline MultiPath::MultiPath(Size nAsset, Size pathSize) :
    multiPath_(nAsset,Path(pathSize)) {

    // data validity tests
    QL_REQUIRE(nAsset > 0, "MultiPath: number of asset must be > zero");
    QL_REQUIRE(pathSize > 0, "MultiPath: pathSize must be > zero");
  }

  // overloaded constructor
  inline MultiPath::MultiPath(const std::vector<Path>& multiPath)
    : multiPath_(multiPath) {}
  }
}
```

Each multipath is generated by a *MultiPathGenerator* class that generates the
diffusion paths and computes drifts and diffusion terms for each diffusion process.

```
#include "Multipath.h"
#include "Sample.h"

namespace QuantLib
{
```

```
namespace MonteCarlo
{

// Generates a multipath from a random number generator
/**************************************************************************
MultiPathGenerator<RAG> is a class that returns a random multipath. RAG is a
  sample generator which returns a random array. It must have the minimal
  interface:

RAG {
RAG();
RAG(Matrix& covariance, long seed);
Sample<Array> next();
};
**************************************************************************/
template <class RAG>
class MultiPathGenerator
{
  public:
    typedef Sample<MultiPath> sample_type;
    MultiPathGenerator(const Array& drifts,
      const Math::Matrix& covariance,
      Time length,
      Size timeSteps,
      long seed);
    MultiPathGenerator(const Array& drifts,
      const Math::Matrix& covariance,
      const std::vector<Time>& times,
      long seed=0);
    const sample_type& next() const;
  private:
    Size numAssets_;
    RAG rndArrayGen_;
    mutable sample_type next_;
    std::vector<Time> timeDelays_;
};

    template <class RAG>
  inline MultiPathGenerator<RAG >::MultiPathGenerator(
    const Array& drifts,
    const Math::Matrix& covariance,
    Time length,
    Size timeSteps,
    long seed)
      : numAssets_(covariance.rows()), rndArrayGen_(covariance, seed),
        next_(MultiPath(covariance.rows(),timeSteps),1.0)
  {
    QL_REQUIRE(drifts.size() == numAssets_,
      "MultiPathGenerator covariance and average do not have the same size");
    QL_REQUIRE(timeSteps > 0, "MultiPathGenerator: Time steps(" +
      IntegerFormatter::toString(timeSteps) + ") must be greater than zero");
    QL_REQUIRE(length > 0, "MultiPathGenerator: length must be > 0");

    Time dt = length/timeSteps;
```

```
      timeDelays_ = std::vector<Time>(timeSteps, dt);
      Array variances = covariance.diagonal();
      for (Size j=0; j<numAssets_; j++)
      {
        QL_REQUIRE(variances[j]>=0, "MultiPathGenerator: negative variance");
        for (Size i=0; i<timeSteps; i++)
        {
          next_.value[j].times()[i] = (i+1)*dt;
          next_.value[j].drift()[i]=drifts[j]*timeDelays_[i];
        }
      }
    }


    /*****************************************************************************
    MultiPathGenerator constructor
    [in]: Array& drifts:        : array of drifts
            Math::Matrix& covariance  : covariance matrix
            std::vector<Time>& times  : vector of path times
            long seed  : seed number for RNG
    *****************************************************************************/
    template <class RAG>
    inline MultiPathGenerator<RAG >::MultiPathGenerator(
      const Array& drifts,
      const Math::Matrix& covariance,
      const std::vector<Time>& times,
      long seed)
        : numAssets_(covariance.rows()),
        rndArrayGen_(covariance, seed),
        next_(MultiPath(covariance.rows(),times.size()),1.0),
        timeDelays_(times.size())
    {

      QL_REQUIRE(drifts.size() == numAssets_,
        "MultiPathGenerator covariance and average do not have the same size");
      QL_REQUIRE(times.size() > 0, "MultiPathGenerator: no times given");
      QL_REQUIRE(times[0] >= 0, "MultiPathGenerator: first time("
        + DoubleFormatter::toString(times[0]) + ") must be non negative");

      Array variances = covariance.diagonal();
      timeDelays_[0] = times[0];
       for (Size i = 1; i < times.size(); i++)
      {
        QL_REQUIRE(times[i] >= times[i-1], "MultiPathGenerator: time("
        + IntegerFormatter::toString(i-1)+ ")=" +
        DoubleFormatter::toString(times[i-1]) + "
        is later than time(" + IntegerFormatter::toString(i) + ")=" +
        DoubleFormatter::toString(times[i]));

        timeDelays_[i] = times[i] - times[i-1];
      }

      for (Size j=0; j<numAssets_; j++)
      {
```

```
        next_.value[j].times() = times;

        QL_REQUIRE(variances[j]>=0, "MultiPathGenerator: negative variance");

        for (Size i = 0; i< times.size(); i++)
        {
          next_.value[j].drift()[i] = drifts[j] * timeDelays_[i];
        }
      }
    }
  }

  /*****************************************************************************
  next : generates next diffusion random Brownian motion
  [in] : none
  [out]: MultiPathGenerator<RAG>::sample_type& : sample type
  *****************************************************************************/
  template <class RAG>
  inline const typename MultiPathGenerator<RAG >::sample_type&
  MultiPathGenerator<RAG >::next() const
  {
    Array randomExtraction(numAssets_);
    next_.weight = 1.0;
    for (Size i = 0; i < next_.value[0].times().size(); i++)
    {
      const Sample<Array>& randomExtraction = rndArrayGen_.next();
      next_.weight *= randomExtraction.weight;
      for (Size j=0; j<numAssets_; j++)
      {
        next_.value[j].diffusion()[i] = randomExtraction.value[j] *
          sqrt(timeDelays_[i]);
      }
    }
    return next_;
  }
}
}
```

Now, we can use a *BasketPathPricer* class, which inherits from a *PathPricer* of *MultiPath*.

```
#include "PathPricer.h"
#include "MultiPath.h"

namespace QuantLib
{
  namespace MonteCarlo
  {
  /*****************************************************************************
  Multipath pricer for European-type basket option
```

The value of the option at expiration is given by the value of the underlying which has best performed.
```
*****************************************************************************/
class BasketPathPricer : public PathPricer<MultiPath>
{
  public:
    BasketPathPricer(Option::Type type,
      const Array& underlying,
      double strike,
      DiscountFactor discount,
      bool useAntitheticVariance);
    double operator()(const MultiPath& multiPath) const;
  private:
    Option::Type type_;
    Array underlying_;
    double strike_;
  };
}
}
```

The class has the following method definitions:

```
#include "BasketPathPricer.h"
#include "SingleAssetOption.h"
using QuantLib::Pricers::ExercisePayoff;

namespace QuantLib
{
  namespace MonteCarlo
  {
  /*****************************************************************************
  BasketPathPricer constructor
  [in]: Option:Type    : option type
        Array& underlying    : array of underlying assets
        double strike        : strike price
        DiscountFactor discount    : discount factor
        bool useAntitheticVariance : flag for using
  *****************************************************************************/
  BasketPathPricer::BasketPathPricer(Option::Type type,
    const Array& underlying,
    double strike,
    DiscountFactor discount,
    bool useAntitheticVariance)
      : PathPricer<MultiPath>(discount, useAntitheticVariance), type_(type),
      underlying_(underlying), strike_(strike)
      {
        for (Size j=0; j<underlying_.size(); j++)
        {
```

```
              QL_REQUIRE(underlying_[j]>0.0, "BasketPathPricer: " "underlying
                 less/equal zero not allowed");
              QL_REQUIRE(strike>0.0, "BasketPathPricer: " "strike less/equal zero not
                 allowed");
          }
    }


    /****************************************************************************
    operator()    : operator for pricing option on a path
    [in]: MultiPath& multiPath    : multiPath instance
    [out]: double  : discounted value of price of basket option
    *****************************************************************************/
    double BasketPathPricer::operator()(const MultiPath& multiPath)const
    {
      Size numAssets = multiPath.assetNumber();
      Size numSteps = multiPath.pathSize();
      QL_REQUIRE(underlying_.size() == numAssets,
         "BasketPathPricer: the multi-path must contain "
         + IntegerFormatter::toString(underlying_.size()) +" assets");

      std::vector<double> log_drift(numAssets, 0.0);
      std::vector<double> log_diffusion(numAssets, 0.0);
      Size i,j;
      double basketPrice = 0.0;
      for(j = 0; j < numAssets; j++)
      {
        log_drift[j] = log_diffusion[j] = 0.0;              // initialize drift and
                                                            // diffusion

        for(i = 0; i < numSteps; i++)
        {
          log_drift[j] += multiPath[j].drift()[i];          // compute drift of jth
                                                            // asset
          log_diffusion[j] += multiPath[j].diffusion()[i]; // compute diffusion of jth
                                                            // asset
        }
        basketPrice += underlying_[j]*exp(log_drift[j]+log_diffusion[j]);
      }
      if (useAntitheticVariance_)                           // test if antithetics are
                                                            // used
      {
        double basketPrice2 = 0.0;
        for(j = 0; j < numAssets; j++)
        {
          basketPrice2 += underlying_[j]*exp(log_drift[j]-log_diffusion[j]);
        }
        return discount_*0.5*
          (ExercisePayoff(type_, basketPrice, strike_) + ExercisePayoff(type_,
            basketPrice2, strike_));
      }
      else
      {
        return discount_*ExercisePayoff(type_, basketPrice, strike_);
```

```
         }

     }
   }
 }
}
```

9.8   ITO'S LEMMA FOR FUNCTIONS OF VECTOR-VALUED DIFFUSION PROCESSES

We can find the process that a function, $f(\mathbf{x}, t)$ of the vector-valued $\mathbf{x}(t)$ solution to the m-dimensional SDE in equation (9.22) will follow. We can use a multivariate Taylor expansion to derive the SDE for $f(\mathbf{x}, t)$:

$$df = \frac{\partial f}{\partial t}dt + \sum_{i=1}^{n}\frac{\partial f}{\partial x_i}dx_i + \frac{1}{2}\sum_{i=1}^{n}\sum_{j=1}^{n}\frac{\partial^2 f}{\partial x_i \partial x_j}dx_i dx_j + \sum_{i=1}^{n}\frac{\partial^2 f}{\partial t \partial x_i}dt dx_i + \ \ldots \quad (9.34)$$

We recall the property of an n-dimensional Wiener process: $dz_i dz_j = 1_{\{i=j\}}dt + O(dt^2)$. Thus, $dx_i dx_j = \sigma_{ij}dt + O(dt^2)$. Substituting this into (9.34), we get:

$$df = \left[\frac{\partial f}{\partial t}dt + \sum_{i=1}^{n}\frac{\partial f}{\partial x_i}\mu_i(\mathbf{x},\ t) + \frac{1}{2}\sum_{i=1}^{n}\sum_{j=1}^{n}\frac{\partial^2 f}{\partial x_i \partial x_j}\sigma_{ij}(\mathbf{x},\ t)\right]dt + \sum_{i=1}^{n}\sum_{j=1}^{n}\sigma_{ij}(\mathbf{x},\ t)\frac{\partial f}{\partial x_i}dz_j \quad (9.35)$$

which can be written in matrix form as:

$$df = \left[\frac{\partial f}{\partial t} + \left[\frac{\partial f}{\partial x_1}\ \frac{\partial f}{\partial x_2}\ \cdots\ \frac{\partial f}{\partial x_m}\right]\begin{bmatrix}\mu_1 \\ \mu_2 \\ \cdots \\ \mu_m\end{bmatrix} + \frac{1}{2}tr\begin{pmatrix}\dfrac{\partial^2 f}{\partial x_1^2} & \dfrac{\partial^2 f}{\partial x_1 \partial x_2} & \cdots & \dfrac{\partial^2 f}{\partial x_1 \partial x_m} \\ \dfrac{\partial^2 f}{\partial x_1 \partial x_2} & \dfrac{\partial^2 f}{\partial x_2^2} & \cdots & \dfrac{\partial^2 f}{\partial x_2 \partial x_m} \\ \cdots & \cdots & \cdots & \cdots \\ \dfrac{\partial^2 f}{\partial x_m \partial x_1} & \cdots & \cdots & \dfrac{\partial^2 f}{\partial x_m^2}\end{pmatrix}\right]dt$$

$$+ \left[\frac{\partial f}{\partial x_1}\ \frac{\partial f}{\partial x_2}\ \cdots\ \frac{\partial f}{\partial x_m}\right]\begin{bmatrix}\sigma_{11} & \sigma_{12} & \cdots & \sigma_{1n} \\ \sigma_{21} & \sigma_{22} & \cdots & \sigma_{2n} \\ \cdots & \cdots & \cdots & \cdots \\ \sigma_{m1} & \sigma_{2m} & \cdots & \sigma_{mn}\end{bmatrix}\begin{bmatrix}dz_1 \\ dz_2 \\ \cdots \\ dz_n\end{bmatrix}$$

where *tr* denote the matrix trace. We have suppressed the state vector and time dependence of μ_i and σ_{ij} to ease notation. We can simulate this process by:

$$
df = \left[\frac{\partial f}{\partial t} + \left[\frac{\partial f}{\partial x_1} \; \frac{\partial f}{\partial x_2} \; \cdots \; \frac{\partial f}{\partial x_m} \right] \begin{bmatrix} \mu_1 \\ \mu_2 \\ \cdots \\ \mu_m \end{bmatrix} + \frac{1}{2} tr \begin{pmatrix} \frac{\partial^2 f}{\partial x_1^2} & \frac{\partial^2 f}{\partial x_1 \partial x_2} & \cdots & \frac{\partial^2 f}{\partial x_1 \partial x_m} \\ \frac{\partial^2 f}{\partial x_1 \partial x_2} & \frac{\partial^2 f}{\partial x_2^2} & \cdots & \frac{\partial^2 f}{\partial x_2 \partial x_m} \\ \cdots & \cdots & \cdots & \cdots \\ \frac{\partial^2 f}{\partial x_m \partial x_1} & \cdots & \cdots & \frac{\partial^2 f}{\partial x_m^2} \end{pmatrix} \right] \Delta t
$$

$$
+ \left[\frac{\partial f}{\partial x_1} \; \frac{\partial f}{\partial x_2} \; \cdots \; \frac{\partial f}{\partial x_m} \right] \begin{bmatrix} \sigma_{11} & \sigma_{12} & \cdots & \sigma_{1n} \\ \sigma_{21} & \sigma_{22} & \cdots & \sigma_{2n} \\ \cdots & \cdots & \cdots & \cdots \\ \sigma_{m1} & \sigma_{2m} & \cdots & \sigma_{mn} \end{bmatrix} \begin{bmatrix} \varepsilon_1 \\ \varepsilon_2 \\ \cdots \\ \varepsilon_n \end{bmatrix} \sqrt{\Delta t}
$$

We have shown that $f(\mathbf{x}, t)$ of the diffusion process $\mathbf{x}$ also follows a (scalar) diffusion Ito process that solves the SDE:

$$
df = \mu_f \, dt + \sigma_f \, dz(t)
$$

9.9 PRINCIPAL COMPONENT ANALYSIS

Many financial markets exhibit a high degree of correlation, and thus high collinearity, between market risk factors such as yields on similar bonds of different maturities. Market factors (variables) are highly collinear when there are only a few important sources of information in the data that are common to many factors.[3] Large risk management systems that price and hedge portfolios with many financial assets might use hundreds of different underlying risk factors. However, many of these risk factors are often highly collinear. With principal component analysis (PCA), a method of (symmetric) matrix decomposition into eigenvector and eigenvalues matrices, it is possible to model these correlated systems based on only a few key market risk factors, thereby reducing the dimensionality of the system. Consequently, only the most important independent sources of information (variation) are extracted from the data by a few principal components. Moreover, the lack of correlation and dimensionality reduction advantages of PCA results in computational efficiency. PCA also provides a robust and efficient

---

[3]Alexander (2001a), 143.

method for estimating parameters in multifactor models that have multicollinearity between the explanatory variables.

The data input to PCA must be stationary. Since prices, yields, and interest rates are generally nonstationary, they have to be transformed into returns, which in turn need to be normalized, before PCA is applied. Otherwise, the first principal component will be dominated by the input factor with the greatest volatility.

PCA is based on an eigenvalue and eigenvector analysis of $V = X'X$, the $k \times k$ symmetric matrix of correlations between the variables in X. Each principal component is a linear combination of these columns, where the weights are chosen in such a way that the first principal component explains the largest amount of the total variation of X, the second component explains the greatest amount of the remaining variation, and so forth.

Consider a $T \times k$ stationary data matrix $X \equiv [X_1 \ldots X_k]$ where each element X_i denotes the ith ($T \times 1$) column of X. Thus, X_i is the standardized historical input data on the ith factor in the system. PCA finds the $k \times k$ orthogonal (weight factor) matrix W, the set of eigenvectors of the correlation matrix V, such that

$$V = W\Lambda W' \tag{9.36}$$

where Λ is the $k \times k$ diagonal matrix of eigenvalues of V. The columns of W, $(w_{i,j})$ for $i, j = 1, \ldots, k$, are ordered according to the size of the corresponding eigenvalue so that the mth column of W, denoted $w_m = (w_{1m}, \ldots, w_{km})'$, is the $k \times 1$ eigenvector corresponding to the eigenvalue λ_m where the columns of Λ are ordered so that $\lambda_1 > \lambda_2 > \ldots > \lambda_k$.

Define the mth principal component by:

$$P_m = w_{1m}X_1 + w_{2m}X_2 + \ldots + w_{km}X_k$$

or in matrix notation,

$$P_m = Xw_m$$

Each principal component is a time series of the transformed X factors. The full $T \times k$ matrix of principal components is:

$$P = XW \tag{9.37}$$

To see that the components are uncorrelated, we note that:

$$P'P = W'X'XW = W'VW = W'W\Lambda$$

However, since W is orthogonal, then $W'W = WW' = I$. Thus,

$$P'P = \Lambda \tag{9.38}$$

Since Λ is a diagonal matrix, then the columns of $\mathbf{P}$ are uncorrelated, then the variance of the mth principal component is λ_m. Thus, the proportion of the total variation in $\mathbf{X}$ that is explained by the mth principal component is λ_m/k where k is the sum of the eignvalues, the number of variables in the system. To see this, note that the sum of the eigenvalues is the trace of Λ, the diagonal matrix of eigenvalues of $\mathbf{V}$. However, the trace of Λ equals the trace of $\mathbf{V}$ (since trace is invariant under similarity transforms), and because $\mathbf{V}$ has 1's along its diagonal, the trace of $\mathbf{V}$ is the number of variables in the system,[4] k. Thus, the proportion of variation explained by the first n principal components is:

$$\sum_{i=1}^{n} \lambda_i/k \qquad (9.39)$$

Given the column order labeling in $\mathbf{W}$, the largest eigenvalue λ_1 that corresponds to the first principal component, P_1, explains the largest total proportion of the total variation in $\mathbf{X}$. λ_2 corresponds to P_2 and explains the second largest total proportion, and so on. Since $\mathbf{W}' = \mathbf{W}^{-1}$, equation (9.37) can be written as:

$$\mathbf{X} = \mathbf{PW}' \qquad (9.40)$$

that is,

$$X_i = w_{i1}P_1 + w_{i2}P_2 + \ldots + w_{ik}P_k \qquad (9.41)$$

Equation (9.41) is the *principal components representation* of the original factors. Thus, each vector of input data can be written as a linear combination of the principal components, which reduces the dimension of the system. As we've seen, once the data input $\mathbf{X}$ has been transformed into the principal component system in (9.37), the original system can be transformed back via equation (9.41). Equation (9.41) is also helpful for calculation of the covariance of the original variables. Since the principal components are orthogonal, their unconditional covariance matrix is diagonal so that the covariance structure of $\mathbf{X}$ will also be diagonal.

We consider an application of PCA to Treasury bond yield data. Figure 9.1 is a graph of daily Treasury yield data from January 2, 1990, to December 31, 1999, for 3-month, 6-month, 1-year, 2-year, 3-year, 5-year, 7-year, 10-year, 20-year, and 30-year bond maturities.

As the graph shows, the yields of Treasury bonds of different maturities move in tandem and appear to be highly correlated. Using PCA, we can determine the few important and independent sources of variation in the system. The data input matrix $\mathbf{X}$ is a $2,503 \times 10$ matrix since there is a total of 2,503 days of data for each

---

[4]Ibid., 146.

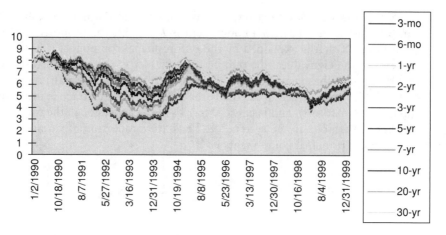

FIGURE 9.1   Treasury Bond Yield Curves (1/2/90–12/31/99)

of the 10 different maturity bonds. Before PCA is used, the data set must be made stationary so that the unconditional correlation matrix $V = X'X$ can be calculated. X is normalized by transforming the data into standardized "returns" by subtracting means and dividing by standard deviations.[5] Once this is done, we find that $X'X$ is as shown in Table 9.1.

If we decompose this correlation matrix into its eigenvectors and eigenvalues, as follows, we find:

$$\Lambda = (8.48, 1.43, 0.065, 0.0078, 0.0068, 0.0013, 0.0011, 0.0009, 0.0003, 0.0001)$$

TABLE 9.1   Correlation Matrix

	3-mo	6-mo	1-yr	2-yr	3-yr	5-yr	7-yr	10-yr	20-yr	30-yr
3-mo	1									
6-mo	0.994	1								
1-yr	0.975	0.992	1							
2-yr	0.931	0.957	0.980	1						
3-yr	0.883	0.913	0.944	0.990	1					
5-yr	0.756	0.789	0.829	0.918	0.964	1				
7-yr	0.693	0.723	0.764	0.868	0.928	0.992	1			
10-yr	0.599	0.629	0.671	0.790	0.867	0.966	0.988	1		
20-yr	0.564	0.597	0.643	0.767	0.848	0.953	0.980	0.995	1	
30-yr	0.453	0.479	0.520	0.655	0.751	0.895	0.937	0.978	0.978	1

[5]One can also make the data stationary by taking the first differences of the yields as a proxy for "returns."

TABLE 9.2   Principal Component Eigenvectors

	P1	P2	P3
1-month	0.043	−0.012	−0.268
3-month	−0.136	0.143	0.056
1-year	−0.161	−0.177	0.689
2-year	−0.164	−0.137	0.108
3-year	−0.331	0.021	0.457
5-year	0.563	−0.244	−0.006
7-year	−0.177	0.807	−0.122
10-year	0.427	0.022	0.107
20-year	−0.453	−0.349	−0.320
30-year	−0.286	−0.311	−0.317

with each element λ_i, $i = 1, \ldots, 10$, in the ith diagonal position in the matrix and with 0's elsewhere. As we see, the first eigenvalue, $\lambda_1 = 8.43$, is much larger than the others which is an indication the system is highly correlated. The weight matrix **W** contains the eigenvectors of **V**. The first three eigenvectors off the correlation matrix are listed in Table 9.2.

Figure 9.2 is a plot of the first three principal component eigenvectors.

The first principal component is called the trend component of the yield curve. As we see, there is a general decline in the factor weights, up to the five-year maturity, which indicates that the trend is roughly decreasing during this time period. In fact, the first principal component eigenvector follows the general shape (movements) of the Treasury yield curve over the entire period. We see that the first eigenvalue explains 8.48/10 = 84.8 percent of the variation over the period and is attributable to (roughly) parallel shifts in the yield curve. The second principal component is neither monotonically increasing nor decreasing.

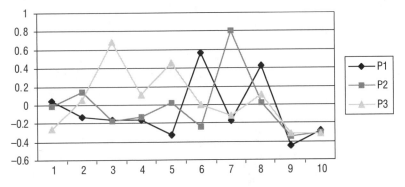

FIGURE 9.2   Plot of Principal Component Eigenvectors

This suggests a fluctuation in changes in the slope of the yield curve over time. The second component is called the "tilt" component and 1.43 percent of the total variation is attributed to it. The factor weights of the third principal component are almost all positive for the short-term rates and negative for the longer-term rates. This component influences the convexity of the yield curve, and 0.65 percent of the variation during the data period is attributable to changes in convexity.

CHAPTER 10

Single-Factor Interest Rate Models

In this chapter, we review interest rate models used to price various interest rate products including bonds, bond options, caps, and swaps. The models are single-factor Markovian models—there is only one source of uncertainty—and the underlying interest rate and the evolution of the short rate do not depend on previous interest rate movements. We analyze in detail the short rate diffusion processes and derive analytical solutions for the Vasicek and Hull-White models. We discuss their properties including mean reversion, analytical tractability, bond pricing PDEs, and calibration to initial term structures. Interest rate tree building procedures are discussed in Chapter 11 for pricing various interest derivatives. In Chapter 12, two-factor models—with two sources of uncertainty, the short rate and short rate volatility—are discussed for the Black-Derman Toy (BDT) and Hull-White models.

In section 10.1, we discuss the general short rate process. In section 10.2, we derive the bond pricing partial differential equation, and in section 10.3, we discuss the risk-neutral drift of the short rate process. In section 10.4, we discuss single-factor models. In section 10.5, we derive Vasicek's (1977) model in detail; in section 10.6, we price discount bonds using the Vasicek model; in section 10.7, we price European bond options on zero-coupon bonds using the Vasicek model. In section 10.8, we introduce the Hull-White (extended Vasicek) model that incorporates time-dependent parameters. In section 10.9, we discuss Jamshidian's decomposition technique to price European options on coupon-bearing bonds. In section 10.10, we introduce the Cox-Ingersoll-Ross (CIR) model that incorporates a square-root volatility in the short rate process, while in section 10.11, we discuss the extended CIR model that incorporates a deterministic shift function of the short rate to better fit the observable market yield curve. In section 10.12, we discuss the popular Black-Derman-Toy (BDT) short rate model. In section 10.13, we discuss Black's (1976) model for pricing caps, and in section 10.14, we discuss Black's model for pricing European swaptions. In section 10.15, we discuss pricing caps, caplets, and swaptions using single-factor short rate models such as the Hull-White (extended Vasicek) model and provide an implementation. In section 10.16, we discuss the valuation of swaps. Finally, in section 10.17, we discuss and provide implementations for calibrating models in practice.

Before discussing the models, it is important to understand notation and the relationships of key quantities in continuous time. We denote the short rate $r(t)$ and the price of the discount bond at time t maturing at time T as $P(t, T)$, where $P(T, T) = 1$. The yield to maturity of $P(t, T)$ is denoted $R(t, T)$. $R(t, T)$, for $t \leq T$, is referred to as the *yield curve*, *term structure*, or *term structure of interest rates*. The forward rate for the period $[T_1, T_2]$ in the future is denoted $f(t; T_1, T_2)$. The instantaneous forward rate at T is denoted $f(t, T)$ and for real values over $t \leq T$ is known as the forward yield curve.

Discount bonds and short rates are related:

$$P(t, T) = E_t^Q \left[\exp\left(-\int_t^T r(u)du \right) \right] \qquad (10.1)$$

where E is the expectation at time t over the risk-neutral measure Q. We will derive this in the next section from no-arbitrage arguments. Discount bonds and the yield to maturity are related:

$$P(t, T) = e^{-R(t,T)\tau} \quad \Leftrightarrow \quad R(t, T) = -\frac{1}{\tau} \ln P(t, T) \qquad (10.2)$$

where $\tau = T - t$. Note that (10.2) implies that the relationship between the yield to maturity and the short rate is:

$$R(t, T) = -\frac{1}{\tau} \ln E_t^Q \left[e^{-\int_t^T r(u)du} \right] \qquad (10.3)$$

The relationship between forward rates and discount bonds and yield to maturities is:

$$f(t; T_1, T_2) = \frac{\ln P(t, T_1) - \ln P(t, T_2)}{T_2 - T_1} \qquad (10.4)$$

$$= \frac{R(t, T_2)(T_2 - t) - R(t, T_1)(T_1 - t)}{T_2 - T_1} \qquad (10.5)$$

where (10.5) is derived from (10.2). The relationships between the forward rate and instantaneous forward rate and discount bond are:

$$f(t, T) = \lim_{T^* \to T} f(t; T, T^*) \tag{10.6}$$

and

$$f(t, T) = -\frac{\partial \ln P(t, T)}{\partial T} \tag{10.7}$$

respectively. The relationship between the forward rate and yield to maturity is:

$$f(t, T) = \frac{\partial[(T-t)R(t, T)]}{\partial T} = R(t, T) + (T-t)\frac{\partial R(t, T)}{\partial T} \tag{10.8}$$

Note that we can express the yield to maturity in terms of the forward rate:

$$R(t, T) = \frac{1}{T-t}\int_t^T f(t, u)du \tag{10.9}$$

This states that the yield on $P(t, T)$ can be viewed as an *average forward rate* over $[t, T]$. The relationship between discount bonds and forward rates is:

$$P(t, T) = \exp\left(-\int_t^T f(t, u)du\right) \tag{10.10}$$

by substituting (10.9) into (10.2). Finally, the relationship between the forward rate and the short rate is:

$$f(t, t) = r(t) \tag{10.11}$$

It should be noted that the term structure can be described in terms of either $P(t, T)$, $R(t, T)$, or $f(t, T)$.

We note that there are various day-counting conventions for computing the time to maturity. Typically, the current time t and the maturity date T are expressed as day/month/year, say $D_1 = (d_1, m_1, y_1)$ and $D_2 = (d_2, m_2, y_2)$, and the amount of time between them, $T - t$, is expressed in terms of the number of days (in years) between them. One day-count convention used for Treasury bonds is actual/365 where a year is 365 days long and the year fraction between the two dates is the actual number of days between them divided by 365, that is, $(D_2 - D_1)/365$ where D_1 is included and D_2 is excluded.

A second convention typically used for corporate and municipal bonds is actual/360 where a year is assumed to be 360 days long and the year fraction is $(D_2 - D_1)/360$.

Another convention used for Treasury bills and other money market instruments is to assume 30/360 where months are assumed 30 days long and years are assumed 360 days long. The year fraction is given by

$$\frac{\max(30 - d_1,\ 0) + \min(d_2,\ 30) + 360(y_2 - y_1) + 30(m_2 - m_1 - 1)}{360}$$

The year fractions can be adjusted for holidays, by leaving out holidays and including the first working days that follow them.

Finally, we assume quoted market prices for Treasury bonds (quoted in dollars and 32nds of a dollar) and coupon-bearing bonds are the *clean price*, while the cash price is the *dirty price* where the two prices are related by

Cash price = Quoted price + Accrued interest since last coupon date

10.1   SHORT RATE PROCESS

We assume that the short rate follows a general diffusion process in the real world (under the physical measure P) that solves the SDE:

$$dr = m(r, t)dt + \sigma(r, t)dz \tag{10.12}$$

subject to some initial condition:

$$r(0) = r_0$$

m and σ are drift and volatility of the short rate (generally both time- and state-dependent). For notational ease, we suppress the explicit dependence of the short rate on time; that is, $r = r(t)$.

The bond price is a function of r and follows a process under P:

$$\frac{dP(r, t, T)}{P(r, t, T)} = m_P(r, t, T)dt + \sigma_P(r, t, T)dz(t) \tag{10.13}$$

The drift and volatility coefficients are given by Ito's lemma:

$$m_P P = \frac{\partial P}{\partial t} + m\frac{\partial P}{\partial r} + \frac{1}{2}\sigma^2\frac{\partial^2 P}{\partial r^2} \tag{10.14}$$

and

$$\sigma_P P = \sigma \frac{\partial P}{\partial r}$$

Using Ito's lemma, we can also find the process for the yield:

$$dR(t,\ T) = d\left(-\frac{1}{T-t}\ln P(t,\ T)\right)$$

and for the instantaneous forward rate:

$$f(t,\ T) = -\frac{\partial \ln P(t,\ T)}{\partial T}$$

10.2 DERIVING THE BOND PRICING PARTIAL DIFFERENTIAL EQUATION

To derive the bond pricing PDE similar to the Black-Scholes PDE, we will dynamically replicate a zero-coupon bond $P(t,\ T_1)$ with a bond with a different maturity $P(t,\ T_2)$; that is, we will consider a replicating portfolio:

$$\Pi(t) = P(t,\ T_1) - hP(t,\ T_2) \tag{10.15}$$

where h is the hedge ratio. Over an infinitesimal time period dt we have:

$$d\Pi = dP_1 - hdP_2 = m_{P_1}P_1 dt + \sigma_{P_1}P_1 dz - h(m_{P_2}P_2 dt + \sigma_{P_2}P_2 dz)$$

The hedge ratio that makes the portfolio riskless is:

$$h = \frac{\partial P_1 / \partial r}{\partial P_2 / \partial r} \tag{10.16}$$

With this h, we can perfectly hedge P_1 with the position in the second bond, h of P_2, instantaneously.

Now the portfolio, Π, is riskless and thus must earn the risk-free rate $r(t)$ by the assumption of no-arbitrage:

$$d\Pi(t) = r(t)\Pi(t)dt = r(P_1 - hP_2)dt \tag{10.17}$$

Substituting the result for h, we get

$$\frac{\frac{\partial P_1}{\partial t} + \frac{1}{2}\sigma^2 \frac{\partial^2 P_1}{\partial r^2} - rP_1}{\partial P_1 / \partial r} = \frac{\frac{\partial P_2}{\partial t} + \frac{1}{2}\sigma^2 \frac{\partial^2 P_2}{\partial r^2} - rP_2}{\partial P_2 / \partial r} \tag{10.18}$$

The right-hand side can only depend on T_2 and is independent of T_1. The left-hand side can only depend on T_1 and is independent of T_2. This equality can only hold if and only if for any zero-coupon bond

$$\frac{\frac{\partial P}{\partial t} + \frac{1}{2}\sigma^2 \frac{\partial^2 P_1}{\partial r^2} - rP}{\partial P / \partial r} = -\mu(r, t) \tag{10.19}$$

is independent of the maturity T. Then the zero-coupon bond price must satisfy a bond pricing PDE ($P = P(r, t, T)$):

$$\frac{\partial P}{\partial t} + \frac{1}{2}\sigma^2 \frac{\partial^2 P}{\partial r^2} + \mu(r, t)\frac{\partial P}{\partial r} = rP \tag{10.20}$$

subject to:

$$P(r, T, T) = 1$$

The solution to this bond pricing equation is given by the Feynman-Kac formula:

$$P(t, T) = E_t^Q \left[\exp\left(-\int_t^T r(u)du \right) \right]$$

which is exactly (10.1). The expectation is calculated under the risk-neutral measure Q:

$$dr = \mu(r, u)du + \sigma(r, u)dz, \qquad u \in [t, T] \tag{10.21}$$

subject to some initial condition:

$$r(t) = r$$

This is the risk-neutral process for the short rate—the short rate process under the risk neutral measure Q (in the risk-neutral world).

The relationship between the real-world and risk-neutral drifts of the short rate process is:

$$\mu(r,\ t) = m(r,\ t) - \sigma(r,\ t)\lambda(r,\ t) \qquad (10.22)$$

where $\lambda(r,\ t)$ is the market price of interest rate risk:

$$\lambda = \frac{m - \mu}{\sigma} \qquad (10.23)$$

Note that we do not need to know $m(r,\ t)$ and $\lambda(r,\ t)$ separately in order to price bonds—we just need to know the risk-neutral drift $\mu(r,\ t)$.

10.3   RISK-NEUTRAL DRIFT OF THE SHORT RATE

There are two approaches to calculating the drift $\mu(r,\ t)$:

1. In an equilibrium approach, we assume a functional form for $\mu(r,\ t)$. Then bonds of different maturities and all other interest rate contingent claims (bonds options, etc.) are priced using this assumed drift. The problem is that the prices of zero-coupon bonds $P(t,\ T)$ we get by pricing with a specified $\mu(r,\ t)$ are generally inconsistent with observable market prices of discount bonds $P_{market}(t,\ T)$.
2. In an arbitrage-free approach, we fit the risk-neutral drift to the observable market prices of zero-coupon bonds $P_{market}(t,\ T)$. This process of fitting the drift is called *model calibration* (drift calibration).

Suppose now that we have $\mu(r,\ t)$ (we either assumed a functional form or fitted the drift to current observable bond prices). The prices $P(t,\ T)$ are then given by the Feynman-Kac solution to the bond pricing PDE:

$$P(t,\ T) = E_t^Q \left[\exp\left(-\int_t^T r(u) du \right) \right]$$

where the expectation is computed under Q in (10.1). The expectation can be calculated either analytically (if possible), by Monte Carlo simulation, by binomial or trinomial trees, or by finite difference schemes. If the model is arbitrage-free, the bond prices are calculated in such as way that they will match the actual observable market prices of zero-coupon bonds.

All other interest rate derivatives f paying $F(r(T))$ at some time T in the future (note that P pays \$1 at time T—the simplest possible payoff) also satisfy the same pricing PDE:

$$\frac{\partial f}{\partial t} + \frac{1}{2}\sigma^2 \frac{\partial^2 f}{\partial r^2} + \mu(r,\ t)\frac{\partial f}{\partial r} = rf \tag{10.24}$$

subject to the terminal condition:

$$f(r(T),\ T) = F(r(T))$$

The solution is given by the Feynman-Kac formula:

$$f(t,\ T) = E_t^Q \left[\exp\left(-\int_t^T r(u)du \right) F(r(T)) \right] \tag{10.25}$$

where the expectation is calculated under Q:

$$dr = \mu(r,\ u)du + \sigma(r,\ u)dz, \qquad u \in [t,\ T] \tag{10.26}$$

subject to some initial condition:

$$r(t) = r$$

The expectation can be calculated either analytically (if possible); by Monte Carlo simulation; or by binomial, trinomial, or finite difference schemes.

10.4   SINGLE-FACTOR MODELS

Many single-factor short rate models follow Markov diffusion processes and are special cases of the following diffusion process:

$$dr = (\alpha_1 + \alpha_2 r + \alpha_3 r \ln r)dt + (\beta_1 + \beta_2 r)^\gamma dz \tag{10.27}$$

where $\alpha_i = \alpha_i(t)$, $\beta_i = \beta_i(t)$, $\gamma \geq 0$.

Many single-factor models were originally specified as equilibrium models with constant drift and diffusion coefficients (i.e., constant (time-independent) parameters α and β) or as a function of the short rate. They were later extended to allow for time-dependent parameters to better fit observable market data (fit to the current yield curve and the term structure of volatilities). In one-factor models, rates move in the same direction over any short time interval, but not by the same amount. Moreover, while the models are more restrictive than a two-factor model, the term structures can have different shapes and they do not always have the same slope.

One important feature that a good short rate model should have is mean reversion. Empirical observation shows that interest rates revert back to their long-run levels: When r is high, mean reversion tends to cause it to have a negative drift, whereas when r is low, mean reversion tends to cause it to have a positive drift. Single-factor models price discount bonds of the following form:

$$P(t, T) = A(t, T)e^{-B(t,T)r(t)} \qquad (10.28)$$

If $A(t, T)$ is an exponential function, (10.28) can be expressed as:

$$P(t, T) = e^{A(t,T) - B(t,T)r(t)}$$

Each model determines the parameters $A(t, T)$ and $B(t, T)$ differently depending on the specified diffusion process of the short rate. One single-factor model that is widely used in practice that exhibits mean reversion is the Vasicek model. The specified form (10.28) for discount bonds ensures that the continuously compounded spot rate $R(t, T)$ is an affine function of the short rate $r(t)$, that is,

$$R(t, T) = \alpha(t, T) + \beta(t, T)r(t) \qquad (10.29)$$

where α and β are deterministic functions of time, and can be chosen as

$$\alpha(t, T) = -(\ln A(t, T))/(T - t), \qquad \beta(t, T) = B(t, T)/(T - t)$$

from (10.28).

There is a relationship between the coefficients in the risk-neutral process of the short rate and affinity in the term structure. Suppose the short rate follows a general time-homogenous process as in (10.21); that is,

$$dr(t) = \mu(t, r(t))dt + \sigma(t, r(t))dz(t)$$

If the coefficients μ and σ are affine (linear) functions themselves, then the resulting short rate model will exhibit an affine term structure. Thus, if the coefficients μ and σ have the form

$$\mu(t, x) = \lambda(t)x + \eta(t), \qquad \sigma^2(t, x) = \gamma(t)x + \kappa(t)$$

for suitable deterministic time functions λ, η, γ, and κ, then the model has an affine term structure.[1] Consequently, A and B in (10.28), and thus α and β in (10.29), de-

---

[1] Brigo and Mercurio (2001c), 61.

pend on the chosen functions λ, η, γ, and κ. While affinity in the coefficients leads to affinity in the term structure, the converse is also true: If a model has an affine term structure and has time-homogenous coefficients $\mu(t, x) = \mu(x)$ and $\sigma(t, x) = \sigma(x)$, then the coefficients are necessarily affine (linear) functions of x.[2] In the Vasicek model, $\lambda(t) = -a$, $\eta(t) = a\bar{r}$, $\gamma(t) = 0$, $\kappa(t) = \sigma^2$, and in the Cox-Ingersoll-Ross model, $\lambda(t) = -a$, $\eta(t) = a\bar{r}$, $\gamma(t) = \sigma^2$, and $\kappa(t) = 0$. Both models have explicit bond prices that can be written in the form (10.28) since A and B can be found from solving (Riccati) differential equations, as we see in the following sections.

10.5   VASICEK MODEL

In Vasicek's (1977) model, the risk-neutral process for r is

$$dr = a(\bar{r} - r)dt + \sigma dz \qquad (10.30)$$

where a, $\bar{r}$, and σ are constants, a is the rate of mean reversion to $\bar{r}$, $\bar{r}$ is the long-run average (steady-state) of the short rate, and σ is the diffusion coefficient. The parameters can also be deterministic functions of time only with no state parameters (in such case, the model becomes the Hull-White extension of the original Vasicek model).

In addition to mean reversion, the model is analytically tractable, as we will show. However, in the model interest rates can get negative, a major disadvantage that can be managed if the short rate is far above zero since the probability of rates becoming negative is very small due to mean reversion—though it is not zero.

We will show that the price at time t of a zero-coupon bond that pays \$1 at time T is:

$$P(t, T) = A(t, T)e^{-B(t,T)r(t)}$$

where

$$B(t, T) = \frac{1 - e^{-a(T-t)}}{a} \qquad (10.31)$$

and

$$A(t, T) = \exp\left[\frac{(B(t, T) - (T-t))(a^2\bar{r} - \sigma^2/2)}{a^2} - \frac{\sigma^2 B(t, T)^2}{4a}\right] \qquad (10.32)$$

---

[2]Ibid.

When $a = 0$, $B(t, T) = T - t$ and $A(t, T) = \exp(\sigma^2(T - t)^3/6)$.

Consider a deterministic case of zero volatility. Then (10.30) becomes:

$$dr = a(\bar{r} - r)dt$$

This ordinary differential equation (ODE) can be integrated to yield:

$$\int \frac{dr}{\bar{r} - r} = at + C \Rightarrow \ln(\bar{r} - r) = -(at + C) \Rightarrow r(t) = \bar{r} - e^{-at-C}$$

where C is a constant of integration. The initial condition at $t = t_0$ is

$$r(t_0) = r_0$$

so that

$$r(t_0) = \bar{r} - e^{-at_0 - C} = r_0$$

Thus, the constant of integration is

$$C = -at_0 - \ln(\bar{r} - r_0)$$

yielding the solution

$$r(t) = \bar{r} + (r_0 - \bar{r})e^{-a(t - t_0)}$$

We can see that the trajectory starts at the initial point $r(t_0) = r_0$ and in the limit $t \to \infty$ reverts to its long-run limiting value (steady state) $\bar{r}$.

When $\sigma > 0$, we need to solve an Ornstein-Uhlenbeck SDE. It can be integrated in closed form to yield for each $s \leq t$.

$$r(t) = \bar{r} + (r(s) - \bar{r})e^{-a(t-s)} + \sigma \int_{t_0}^{t} e^{-a(t-u)}dz(u) \qquad (10.33)$$

In particular at time t_0, we have

$$r(t) = \bar{r} + (r_0 - \bar{r})e^{-a(t - t_0)} + \sigma \int_{t_0}^{t} e^{-a(t-u)}dz(u)$$

The first two terms are the mean of $r(t)$:

$$E_s[r(t)] = \bar{r} + (r(s) - \bar{r})e^{-a(t-s)} \qquad (10.34)$$

where E is the expectation conditional on the filtration up to time s, and the third term is a martingale (Ito's integral with respect to the Brownian motion). The short rate $r(t)$ is normally distributed with mean given by (10.33) and variance given by

$$\mathrm{Var}_s[r(t)] = \frac{\sigma^2}{2a}(1 - e^{-2a(t-s)}) \qquad (10.35)$$

Sample paths of the Vasicek short rate process can be simulated for Monte Carlo by discretizing (10.30):

$$r_{i+1} = r_i + a(\bar{r} - r_i)\Delta t + \sigma\sqrt{\Delta t}\varepsilon_{i+1}$$

A key property of the Vasicek model is expressed by the following theorem:

THEOREM 1. The Vasicek (Ornstein-Uhlenbeck) process is a time-changed (subordinated) Brownian motion:

$$r(t) = \bar{r} + (r(s) - \bar{r})e^{-a(t-s)} + e^{-a(t-s)}z(\tau) \qquad (10.36)$$

where the new time clock is:

$$\tau = \beta(t) = \frac{\sigma^2}{2a}\left[e^{2a(t-s)} - 1\right]$$

$z(\tau)$ is a standard Brownian motion with respect to the new time clock τ with the standard properties of Brownian motion:

$$z(0) = 0, \qquad E[z(\tau)] = 0, \quad E[z^2(\tau)] = \tau$$

and $r(t_0) = r_0$ is the initial condition.

PROOF. Consider the process

$$r(t) = \alpha(t)z(\beta(t)) + C(t) \qquad (10.37)$$

where α, β, and C are some deterministic functions of time, and z is a standard Brownian motion started at time 0. We compute dr:

$$dr = \frac{d\alpha}{dt}z(\beta(t))dt + \alpha(t)dz(\beta(t)) + \frac{dC}{dt}dt \qquad (10.38)$$

Now, since

$$z(\beta(t)) = \frac{r(t) - C(t)}{\alpha(t)}$$

we can rewrite (10.38) as:

$$dr = \left[\dot{C} + \frac{\dot{\alpha}}{\alpha}(r - C) \right] dt + \alpha(t) dz(\beta(t))$$

We now compute the mean and variance of dr:

$$E[dr] = \left[\dot{C} + \frac{\dot{\alpha}}{\alpha}(r - C) \right] dt$$

and

$$V[dr] = E[\alpha^2 (dz(\beta(t)))^2] = \alpha^2 \, E[(dz(\beta(t)))^2]$$

We now need to calculate the variance of the time-changed Brownian motion.

$$E[(dz(\beta(t)))^2] = E[(dz(\tau))^2 = d\tau = d\beta(t) = \dot{\beta}(t) dt \qquad (10.39)$$

and

$$V(dr) = \alpha^2 \dot{\beta}(t) dt \qquad (10.40)$$

Thus, we can rewrite

$$\alpha dz(\beta(t)) = \alpha \sqrt{\left| \dot{\beta} \right|} d\hat{z}(t)$$

where $\hat{z}(t)$ is a standard Brownian motion (Wiener process). Combining our results, we get

$$dr = \left[\dot{C} + \frac{\dot{\alpha}}{\alpha}(r - C) \right] dt + \alpha(t) \sqrt{\left| \dot{\beta}(t) \right|} dz(t) \qquad (10.41)$$

If we compare (10.41) to the Vasicek process in (10.30),

$$dr = a(\bar{r} - r) dt + \sigma dz$$

we get three differential equations for three unknowns that need to be satisfied for the processes to be equal:

$$\frac{\dot{\alpha}}{\alpha} = -a, \quad \alpha(t_0) = 1$$

$$\dot{C} + aC = a\bar{r}, \; C(t_0) = r_0$$

$$\alpha\sqrt{|\dot{\beta}|} = \sigma, \quad \beta(t_0) = 0$$

Solving the first equation by integration yields,

$$\alpha = e^{-a(t-t_0)} \tag{10.42}$$

Substituting this into $\alpha^2\dot{\beta} = \sigma^2$ yields $\dot{\beta} = \sigma^2 e^{2a(t-t_0)}$, which when integrated gives

$$\beta(t) = \frac{\sigma^2}{2a}e^{2a(t-t_0)} + \beta_0$$

Taking into account the initial condition, we can find the constant of integration and solve to get

$$\beta(t) = \frac{\sigma^2}{2a}(e^{2a(t-t_0)} - 1) \tag{10.43}$$

Finally, integrating $\dot{C} + aC = a\bar{r}$, $C(t_0) = r_0$, yields,

$$C(t) = \bar{r} + e^{-a(t-t_0)}(r_0 - \bar{r}) \tag{10.44}$$

Substituting (10.41), (10.42), and (10.43) into the original process (10.37) proves that (10.36) holds, namely,

$$r(t) = \bar{r} + (r_0 - \bar{r})e^{-a(t-t_0)} + e^{-a(t-t_0)}z(\tau)$$

with the new time clock

$$\tau = \beta(t) = \frac{\sigma^2}{2a}\left[e^{2a(t-t_0)} - 1\right]$$

is indeed a solution to the Vasicek SDE $dr = a(\bar{r} - r)dt + \sigma dz$ subject to the initial condition $r(t_0) = r_0$.

We can now solve all problems for the Vasicek process by using this representation as a time-changed Brownian motion. In particular, the mean and the variance of the short rate over a finite time horizon are:

$$\eta = \eta(t_0, t) - E_{t_0}[r(t)] = \bar{r} + (r_0 - \bar{r})e^{-a(t-t_0)}$$

and

$$v^2 = v^2(t_0, t) = V_{t_0}[r(t)] = E_{t_0}[e^{-2a(t-t_0)}z^2(\beta(t))] = e^{-2a(t-t_0)}\beta(t)$$

$$= e^{-2a(t-t_0)}\frac{\sigma^2}{2a}(e^{2a(t-t_0)} - 1)$$

$$= \frac{\sigma^2}{2a}(1 - e^{-2a(t-t_0)})$$

The transition probability density $p(r(t), t \mid r_0, t_0)$ for the short rate process is a normal density with the mean η and the variance v^2:

$$p(r(t), t \mid r_0, t_0) = \frac{1}{\sqrt{2\pi v^2(t_0, t)}} \exp\left\{ -\frac{(r(t) - \bar{r} - (r_0 - \bar{r})e^{-a(t-t_0)})^2}{2v^2(t_0, t)} \right\}$$

This is also a Green's function for the backward PDE for the Vasicek process:

$$\frac{\partial p}{\partial t} + \frac{1}{2}\sigma^2 \frac{\partial^2 p}{\partial r^2} + a(\bar{r} - r)\frac{\partial p}{\partial r} = 0$$

subject to the delta-function terminal condition:

$$p(r, t_0 \mid r_0, t_0) = \delta(r - r_0)$$

To fit the observable market data (the current yield curve and observable implied cap volatilities), the Vasicek model was extended by Hull and White to allow for time dependence of the parameters:

$$dr = a(t)(\bar{r}(t) - r)dt + \sigma(t)dz \tag{10.45}$$

THEOREM 2. The Vasicek process with time-varying coefficients can also be represented as a time-changed Brownian motion (subordinated Wiener process) with parameters:

$$r(t) = \alpha(t)z(\beta(t)) + C(t)$$

where

$$\alpha(t) = \exp\left(-\int_{t_0}^{t} a(u)du\right)$$

$$\beta(t) = \int_{t_0}^{t}\left(\frac{\sigma(u)}{\alpha(u)}\right)^2 du$$

$$C(t) = \alpha(t)\left[r_0 + \int_{t_0}^{t}\frac{a(u)\bar{r}(u)}{\alpha(u)}du\right]$$

The proof is similar to the case with constant coefficients.

In particular, to fit the yield curve only (not the cap implied volatilities), it is enough to assume that only $\bar{r}(t)$ depends on time and that a and σ are constant. In this particular case, we get:

$$r(t) = e^{-a(t-t_0)}\left[r_0 + a\int_{t_0}^{t}e^{a(u-t_0)}\bar{r}(u)du\right] + e^{-a(t-t_0)}z(\beta(t))$$

where

$$\beta(t) = \frac{\sigma^2}{2a}[e^{2a(t-t_0)} - 1]$$

This is the solution to the SDE:

$$dr = a(\bar{r}(t) - r)dt + \sigma dz, \quad r(t_0) = r_0$$

In this case, the mean and the variance of the short rate over some finite horizon are

$$\eta = \eta(t_0, t) = E_{t_0}[r(t)] = e^{-a(t-t_0)}\left[r_0 + a\int_{t_0}^{t}e^{a(u-t_0)}\bar{r}(u)du\right]$$

and

$$v^2 = v^2(t_0, t) = \frac{\sigma^2}{2a}(1 - e^{-2a(t-t_0)})$$

10.6 PRICING ZERO-COUPON BONDS IN THE VASICEK MODEL

We can compute the expectation to price zero-coupon bonds:

$$P(t,\ T) = E_t^Q \left[\exp \left(-\int_t^T r(u) du \right) \right]$$

where r follows the Vasicek process. We could solve the bond pricing PDE in (10.20) but we can take advantage of the Gaussian nature of the underlying process and compute the expectation directly. Consider a random variable (average interest rate over the lifetime of the bond):

$$I(t,\ T) = \int_t^T r(u) du$$

For each t and T, $I(t,\ T)$ is normally distributed (it follows from the fact that $r(u)$ is normally distributed). We can compute the mean and variance of this random variable:

$$m = E_t^Q \left[\int_t^T r(u) du \right] = \int_t^T E_t^Q [r(u)] du = \int_t^T (\bar{r} + (r_0 - \bar{r}) e^{-a(u-t_0)}) du$$

$$= \bar{r}\tau + \frac{1}{a}(r - \bar{r})(1 - e^{-a\tau})$$

and

$$s^2 = \mathrm{Var}_t^Q \left[\int_t^T r(u) du \right] = E_t^Q \left[\left(\int_t^T r(u) du \right)^2 \right] - m^2$$

$$= E_t^Q \left[\left(\int_t^T ((\bar{r} + (r_0 - \bar{r}) e^{-a(t-t_0)}) + e^{-a(u-t)} z(\beta(u))) du \right)^2 \right] - m^2$$

$$= E_t^Q \left[\left(\int_t^T e^{-a(u-t)} z(\beta(u)) du \right)^2 \right]$$

$$= \int_t^T \int_t^T e^{-a(u+s-2t)} E_t^Q [z(\beta(u)) z(\beta(s))] du ds$$

$$(10.46)$$

We need to calculate the covariance of two values of Wiener processes at two different times. This is called the *correlation function* of the process.

We will make use of the fact that for a standard Brownian motion:

$$E[z(u)z(s)] = \min(u, s) \Rightarrow E[z(\beta(u))z(\beta(s))] = \min(z(\beta(u)), z(\beta(s))) \qquad (10.47)$$

Substituting (10.47) into (10.46), the integral for the variance, yields:

$$s^2 = \int_t^T \int_t^T e^{-a(u+s-2t)} \min(z(\beta(u))z(\beta(s)))duds$$

$$= 2\int_t^T \int_t^u e^{-a(u+s-2t)} \frac{\sigma^2}{2a}(e^{2a(s-t)} - 1)dsdu$$

Now we need to calculate this double integral. The integration result is

$$s^2 = \frac{\sigma^2}{2a^3}[4e^{-a\tau} + 2a\tau - e^{-2a\tau} - 3], \quad \tau = T - t \qquad (10.48)$$

Now it is easy to find the expectation for the bond price:

$$P(r, t, T) = E_t^Q[e^{-I(t,T)}]$$

Since $I(t, T)$ is a normally distributed random variable with mean m and variance s^2, the exponential $e^{-I(t,T)}$ is lognormally distributed with mean $e^{-(m-s^2/2)}$ (mean of the lognormal distribution). Thus, the bond pricing formula in the Vasicek model is:

$$P(r, t, T) = \exp\left(-(m - \frac{s^2}{2})\right)$$

$$= \exp\left(-\left(\bar{r}\tau + \frac{1}{a}(r - \bar{r})(1 - e^{-a\tau}) - \frac{\sigma^2}{4a^3}[4e^{-a\tau} + 2a\tau - e^{-2a\tau} - 3]\right)\right)$$

The bond pricing formula can also be written as follows:

$$P(r, t, T) = \exp(A(\tau) - B(\tau)r)$$

where

$$B(\tau) = \frac{1}{a}(1 - e^{-a\tau}) \quad \text{and} \quad A(\tau) = \bar{r}(B(\tau) - \tau) + \frac{s^2}{2}$$

The same answer could be derived by solving the bond pricing PDE in (10.20). Thus, given the short rate r at time t, we can determine the entire term structure $P(r, t, T)$. The yield curve is determined by:

$$R(r, t, T) = -\frac{1}{\tau}\ln P(r, t, T) = \frac{B(\tau)}{\tau}r - \frac{A(\tau)}{\tau} \qquad (10.49)$$

The yield curve is linear in the short rate. The forward curve is determined by:

$$f(r, t, T) = -\frac{\partial}{\partial T}\ln P(r, t, T) = \frac{\partial B(\tau)}{\partial \tau}r - \frac{\partial A(\tau)}{\partial \tau} \qquad (10.50)$$

Since

$$\frac{\partial B(\tau)}{\partial \tau} = e^{-a\tau} \text{ and } \frac{\partial A(\tau)}{\partial \tau} = \bar{r}(e^{-a\tau} - 1) + \frac{\sigma^2}{2a^2}(1 - e^{-a\tau})^2$$

we can write the forward curve as:

$$f(r, t, T) = \bar{r} + e^{-a\tau}(r - \bar{r}) - \frac{\sigma^2}{2a^2}(1 - e^{-a\tau})^2 = E_t^Q[r(t)] - \frac{\sigma^2}{2a^2}(1 - e^{-a\tau})^2 \qquad (10.51)$$

We can simulate the stochastic evolution of $P(r, t, T)$, $R(r, t, T)$, and $f(r, t, T)$ as r evolves in time according to the Vasicek process:

$$r_{i+1} = r_i + a(\bar{r} - r_i)\Delta t + \sigma\sqrt{\Delta t}\varepsilon_{i+1}$$

by just recalculating $P(r_i, T - t_i)$, $R(r_i, T - t_i)$, and $f(r_i, T - t_i)$ as r_i evolves. Note that the functions $P(r, t, T)$, $R(r, t, T)$, and $f(r, t, T)$ depend only on $\tau = T - t$; that is, they are time homogenous.

Example: Suppose we generate an initial yield curve using the Vasicek process,

$$r_{i+1} = r_i + 0.2(0.08 - r_i)\Delta t + 0.02\sqrt{\Delta t}\varepsilon_{i+1}$$

where $a = 0.2$, $\bar{r} = 0.08$, and $\sigma = 0.02$. We assume the time step is one month (i.e., $\Delta t = 1/12 = 0.0833$) and that the initial rate at time 0 is $r_0 = 0.06$. Suppose we simulate the initial yield curve out 5 years (60 months). At each time step, we need to generate a random normal deviate ε_i. (See Chapter 2 for a discussion of generating random normal deviates.) Suppose $\varepsilon_i = 0.6291$. Then,

$$r_1 = 0.06 + 0.2(0.08 - 0.06)(0.0833) + 0.02\sqrt{0.0833}(0.6291) = 0.064$$

At the second time step, $2\Delta t$, we generate $\varepsilon_2 = -2.0553$. Then,

$$r_2 = 0.064 + 0.2(0.08 - 0.064)(0.083) + 0.02\sqrt{0.0833}(-2.055) = 0.0524$$

At the third time step, $3\Delta t$, we generate $\varepsilon_3 = 0.8602$. Then,

$$r_3 = 0.0524 + 0.2(0.08 - 0.0524)(0.0833) + 0.02\sqrt{0.0833}(0.8602) = 0.0568$$

We continue on up to r_{60}. Suppose we generate the initial yield curve (spot rates) as shown in Figure 10.1 and we want to evolve the yield curve out to bond maturities of $T = 15$ years for each spot rate for each of the 60 months on the initial curve. From (10.49), we can compute the future spot rate for each r_i, $0 \le i \le 60$, by computing

$$R(r_i,\ t,\ T) = \frac{B(\tau)}{\tau} r_i - \frac{A(\tau)}{\tau}$$

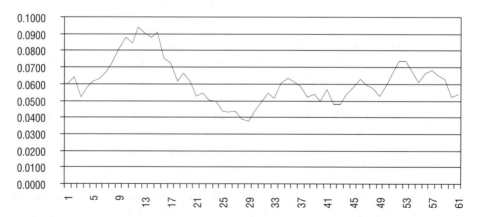

FIGURE 10.1   Simulated Initial Yield Curve (Spot Rates)

where

$$B(\tau) = \frac{1}{a}(1 - e^{-a\tau}) \text{ and } A(\tau) = \bar{r}(B(\tau) - \tau) + \frac{s^2}{2}$$

Thus, suppose we want to compute yield curves today at time $t = 0$ for bond maturities at $T = 8$ ($\tau = T$ since we assume $t = 0$). We first compute the bond rate variance:

$$s^2 = \frac{\sigma^2}{2a^3}[4e^{-a\tau} + 2a\tau - e^{-2a\tau} - 3]$$

$$= \frac{(0.02)^2}{2(0.2)^3}[4e^{-0.2(8)} + 2(0.2)(8) - e^{-2(0.2)(8)} - 3]$$

$$= 0.0242$$

We compute

$$B(8) = \frac{1}{0.2}(1 - e^{-0.2(8)}) = 3.991 \text{ and } A(8) = 0.08(3.991 - 8) + \frac{0.0242}{2} = -0.31$$

Now, we can compute the future spot rate for each r_i:

$$R(r_i, \ 0, \ 8) = \frac{3.991}{8}r_i - \frac{(-0.31)}{8}$$

So after one month, $r_i = 0.064$, and so

$$R(r_i, \ 0, \ 8) = \frac{3.991}{8}(0.064) + \frac{0.31}{8} = 0.071$$

After two months, $r_2 = 0.0524$, and

$$R(r_2, \ 0, \ 8) = \frac{3.991}{8}(0.0524) + \frac{0.31}{8} = 0.0649$$

If we continue the computation for all 60 months, we get the future yield curve at $T = 8$ shown in Figure 10.2.

We can generate a zero-coupon bond yield surface $\{R(t, T), 0 \le T \le 15\}$ where (current) time t is in months and T is the bond maturity in years. Using an Excel

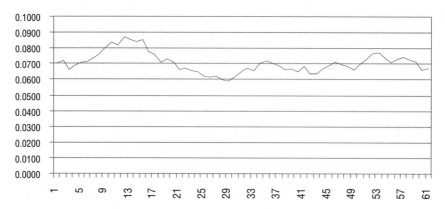

FIGURE 10.2   Future Spot Yield Curve ($T = 8$)

spreadsheet, we can easily compute all future spot rates and thus generate a bond yield surface as shown in Figure 10.3 or viewed from another angle in Figure 10.4.

Using (10.50), we can also generate forward rate curves by computing:

$$f(r_i, \ t, \ T) = -\frac{\partial}{\partial T} \ln P(r_i, \ t, \ T) = \frac{\partial B(\tau)}{\partial \tau} r_i - \frac{\partial A(\tau)}{\partial \tau}$$

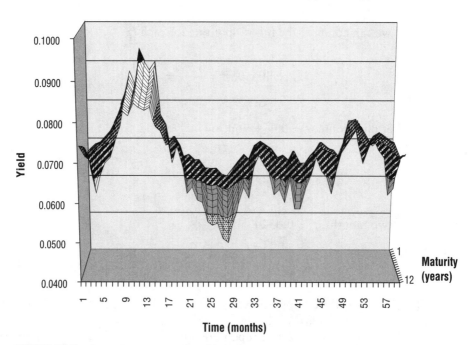

FIGURE 10.3   Zero-Coupon Bond Yield Surface

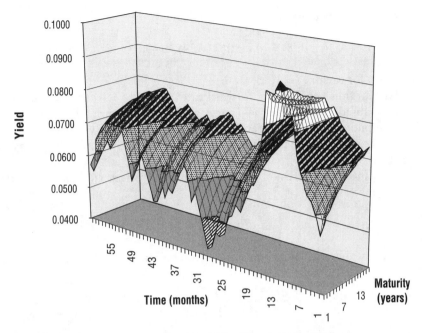

FIGURE 10.4   Zero-Coupon Bond Yield Surface—a Different Angle

Suppose we want to generate the forward curve today at $t = 0$ for bond maturities of $T = 8$ years. We compute:

$$\frac{\partial B(\tau)}{\partial \tau} = e^{-a\tau} = e^{-0.2(8)} = 0.202$$

and

$$\frac{\partial A(\tau)}{\partial \tau} = \bar{r}(e^{-a\tau} - 1) + \frac{\sigma^2}{2a^2}(1 - e^{-a\tau})^2 = 0.08(e^{-0.2(8)} - 1) + \frac{(0.02)^2}{2(0.2)^2}(1 - e^{-0.2(8)})^2 = -0.05986$$

So that after one month, the first time step, we have the forward rate spanning $(0, 8]$.

$$f(r_1, 0, 8) = (0.202)(0.064) - (-0.05986) = 0.0728$$

After two months (two time steps), we have

$$f(r_2, 0, 8) = (0.202)(0.0524) - (-0.05986) = 0.0704$$

and so on for each r_i, $i = 1, \ldots, 60$.

We can thus generate the forward rate curve at $t = 0$ for $T = 8$ using the spot rates generated in the initial yield curve as shown in Figure 10.5.

Computing the forward rate curves for all maturities, we generate the forward rate surface (each curve is a slice of the surface for a given maturity T) as shown in Figure 10.6.

We can derive diffusion processes for bond prices and forward rates. Using Ito's lemma,

$$dP(r, t, T) = d(e^{A(\tau) - B(\tau)r})$$

we find that the price of a T-maturity zero-coupon bond follows the process

$$\frac{dP(r(t), t, T)}{P(r(t), t, T)} = r(t)dt - \sigma_P(t, T)dz(t) \tag{10.52}$$

where the instantaneous volatility of the T-maturity bond price is:

$$\sigma_P(t, T) = \sigma B(t, T) = \frac{\sigma}{a}(1 - e^{-a\tau}) \tag{10.53}$$

As $t \to T$ (closer to maturity), $\tau \to 0$ and $\sigma_p \to 0$, which intuitively should happen since at maturity the bond is worth exactly \$1, so as maturity nears, the volatility

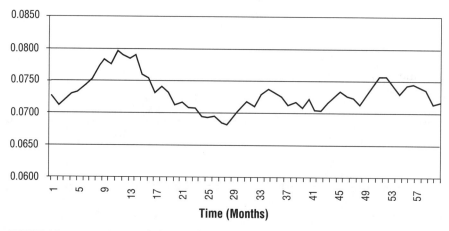

FIGURE 10.5 Forward Curve ($T = 8$)

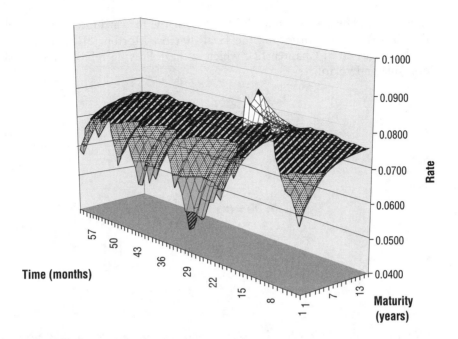

FIGURE 10.6   Forward Rate Surface

of the bond decreases. Also, the risk-neutral drift rate of the bond is equal to the short rate $r(t)$ since the bond is a traded asset.

In the Vasicek model, the bond price process is lognormal. We can also derive the process for the T-maturity instantaneous forward rate using Ito's lemma:

$$df(r,\ t,\ T) = d(\bar{r} + e^{-a\tau}(r - \bar{r}) - \frac{\sigma^2}{2a^2}(1 - e^{-a\tau})^2)$$

and the result is:

$$df(r, t, T) = \mu_f(t, T)dt + \sigma_f(t, T)dz(t) \qquad (10.54)$$

where the instantaneous volatility and drift rate of the forward rate are:

$$\sigma_f(t, T) = \sigma e^{-a(T-t)} \qquad (10.55)$$

and

$$\mu_f(t, T) = \frac{\sigma^2}{a} e^{-a(T-t)}(1 - e^{-a(T-t)}) \qquad (10.56)$$

respectively. Thus, we see that the process for the forward rate is also Gaussian in the Vasicek model. Moreover, the Heath-Jarrow-Morton (HJM) condition holds (to be discussed in Chapter 12), which is the following relationship between the drift rate and volatility:

$$\mu_f(t, T) = \sigma_f(t, T)\int_t^T \sigma_f(t, u)du \tag{10.57}$$

Indeed,

$$\mu_f(t, T) = \sigma^2 e^{-a(T-t)}\int_t^T e^{-a(u-t)}du$$

$$= -\frac{\sigma^2}{a}e^{-a(T-t)}\left(e^{-a(u-t)}\Big|_t^T\right)$$

$$= \frac{\sigma^2}{a}e^{-a(T-t)}(1-e^{-a(T-t)})$$

Moreover, the relationship between the instantaneous bond and forward rate volatilities is given by:

$$\sigma_P(t, T) = \int_t^T \sigma_f(t, u)du$$

$$= \frac{\sigma}{a}(1-e^{-a(T-t)})$$

10.7   PRICING EUROPEAN OPTIONS ON ZERO-COUPON BONDS WITH VASICEK

Now that we know how to compute the price of a discount bond as shown in the previous section, we can price bond options and other interest rate derivatives using the Vasicek model. Suppose we want to price a bond option on a zero-coupon bond today at time t. The option expires at time T and pays off $\max(P(T, T^*) - X, 0)$ where T^*, $T^* \geq T$ is the maturity date of the bond such that $P(T^*, T^*) = 1$, and X is the strike price of the bond option. From (10.25) we know the price of the (European call) bond option is:

$$C(T) = E_t^Q\left[\exp\left(\int_t^T r(u)du\right)\max(P(T, T^*) - X, 0)\right] \tag{10.58}$$

To calculate this expectation, we will use a *change of numeraire*. Instead of choosing dollars as the numeraire, we will choose a zero-coupon bond $P(t, T)$ as the new numeraire. Thus, we denominate all other assets in the units of the bond rather than in dollars. We call the corresponding probability measure the T-maturity forward risk-neutral measure and denote it by Q_T. We denote the expectation with respect to Q_T by $E_t^T[.]$, that is, the expectation at time T conditional on time t.

We will show how to compute the domestic T-maturity forward risk-neutral measure. Suppose at time t we want to value some domestic cash flow $C(T)$ that will occur at time T in the domestic economy. Suppose further that this cash flow is contingent on the state of the economy at time T only (and is independent of the path of the economy from t to T). The domestic risk-neutral pricing formula gives the value of this cash flow at time t as:

$$C(t) = E_t^Q \left[\exp\left(-\int_t^T r(u)du \right) C(T) \right]$$

(10.59)

Note that the discount factor is stochastic. The expectation can be calculated by changing to the domestic T-maturity forward risk-neutral measure. We choose the domestic zero-coupon bond $P(t, T)$ as the new numeraire, and consider prices of all other securities in this numeraire. Consider the forward bond price:

$$F(t; T, S) = \frac{P(t, S)}{P(t, T)}$$

(10.60)

From Ito's lemma applied to the ratio of two Ito processes $X(t) > 0$ and $Y(t) > 0$, Ito's division rule (see Appendix B), the forward price follows the process

$$\frac{dF(t; T, S)}{F(t; T, S)} = -(\sigma_S(t, S) - \sigma_P(t, T))\sigma_P(t, T)dt + (\sigma_P(t, S) - \sigma_P(t, T))dz(t)$$

where σ_p is the Vasicek volatility of the bond option (10.52). By Girsanov's theorem, there exists an equivalent measure such that the process

$$dz^T(t) = dz(t) - \sigma_p(t, T)dt$$

or

$$z^T(t) = z(t) - \int_0^t \sigma_P(u, t)du$$

(10.61)

is a Brownian motion under this measure. Note that $\lambda(t) = \sigma_p(t, T)$ is the market price of risk. This measure is called the domestic T-maturity risk-neutral measure.

Under this measure, the forward bond price is a martingale; that is, the drift is zero:

$$\frac{dF(t;\,T,\,S)}{F(t;\,T,\,S)} = (\sigma_P(t,\,S) - \sigma_P(t,\,T))dz^T(t) \tag{10.62}$$

The expectation under this measure (with respect to the $P(t,\,T)$ numeraire) will be denoted by $E_t^T[.]$. By Girsanov's theorem, for all Ito processes $X(t)$ the expectations under the two measures are related by the formula:

$$E_t^T[X(T)] = E_t^Q[\xi(T)X(T)], \text{ for all } t \le T \tag{10.63}$$

where the Radon-Nikodym derivative

$$\xi(T) = \exp\left(\int_t^T \sigma_P(u,\,t)dz(u) - \frac{1}{2}\int_t^T |\sigma_P(u,\,T)|^2 du\right) \tag{10.64}$$

solves the SDE

$$\frac{d\xi(u)}{\xi(u)} = \sigma_P(u,\,T)dz(u) \text{ and } \xi(t) = 1$$

and noting that

$$1 = P(T,\,T) = P(t,\,T)\exp\left(\int_t^T \left(r(u) - \frac{1}{2}|\sigma_P(u,\,T)|^2\right)du + \int_t^T \sigma_P(u,\,T)dz(u)\right) \tag{10.65}$$

so that

$$P(t,\,T) = \frac{1}{\exp\left(\int_t^T \left(r(u) - \frac{1}{2}|\sigma_P(u,\,T)^2|du\right) + \int_t^T \sigma_P(u,\,T)dz(u)\right)}$$

which is an integrated version of the SDE for $P(t,\,T)$. Substituting (10.64) into (10.63) yields the change of numeraire formula:

$$E_t^T[X(T)] = \frac{E_t^Q\left[\exp\left(-\int_t^T r(u)du\right)X(T)\right]}{P(t,\,T)} \tag{10.66}$$

We can now rewrite the domestic risk-neutral pricing formula in (10.59) in terms of the T-maturity forward risk-neutral expectation:

$$C(t) = P(t, T)E_t^T[C(T)] \qquad (10.67)$$

Thus, under the forward measure the stochastic discount factor and the future cash flow are decoupled (separable). Since the cash flow depends only on the state of the economy at time T, the preceding expectation can be calculated if one knows the joint distribution of the state variables in the economy at time T conditional on time t. In particular, if the model is Gaussian, the state variables at time T will have a joint normal distribution and the expectation can be calculated in closed form.

The relationship between the two domestic forward measures of different maturities T and S, $T \leq S$ on the interval $[0, S]$ is

$$dz^T(t) = dz^S(t) - (\sigma_p(t, T) - \sigma_p(t, S))dt \qquad (10.68)$$

Returning to our bond pricing formula, we have

$$C(t) = P(t, T)E_t^T[\max(F(t; T, S) - X, 0)] \qquad (10.69)$$

where the expectation is with respect to the forward bond price process:

$$\frac{dF(t; T, S)}{F(t; T, S)} = (\sigma_P(t, S) - \sigma_P(t, T))dz^T(t)$$

The forward bond price is a martingale and its instantaneous volatility is deterministic. Thus, the expectation is given by the Black-Scholes formula:

$$C(t) = P(t, T)[F(t; T, S)N(d_+) - XN(d_-)] \qquad (10.70)$$

where $F(t; T, S)$ is the forward bond price given in (10.60),

$$d_\pm = \frac{1}{\sigma_P(t; T, S)}\ln\left(\frac{F(t; T, S)}{X}\right) \pm \frac{\sigma_P(t; T; S)}{2}$$

and $\sigma_p(t; T, S)$ is the standard deviation of the normal distribution of the logarithm of the forward bond price $F(T; T, S)$ at time T, given the information at time t:

$$\sigma_P^2(t; T, S) = \int_t^T (\sigma_P(u, S) - \sigma_P(u, T))^2 du = \frac{\sigma^2}{a^2}\int_t^T (e^{-a(T-u)} - e^{-a(S-u)})^2 du$$

$$= \frac{\sigma^2}{2a^3}(1 - e^{-a(S-T)})^2(1 - e^{-2a(T-t)}) \qquad (10.71)$$

Finally, substituting the expression for the forward bond price (10.60) into the bond pricing formula (10.70), gives the final result for a European call bond option:

$$c(t, T, S) = P(t, S)N(d_+) - XP(t, T)N(d_-)$$ (10.72)

where

$$d_\pm = \frac{1}{\sigma_P(t; T; S)} \ln\left(\frac{P(t, S)}{XP(t, T)}\right) \pm \frac{\sigma_P(t; T, S)}{2}$$ (10.73)

and

$$\sigma_P(t; T, S) = \frac{\sigma}{a}(1 - e^{-a(S-T)})\sqrt{\frac{1}{2a}(1 - e^{-2a(T-t)})}$$ (10.74)

For a European put bond option, we get:

$$p(t, T, S) = XP(t, T)N(-d_-) - P(t, S)N(-d_+)$$ (10.75)

In the case of no mean reversion ($a = 0$), the formula for volatility (10.74) reduces to that of a Merton-Ho-Lee model:[3]

$$\sigma_P(t; T, S) = \sigma(S - T)\sqrt{T - t}$$

The instantaneous bond price volatility in the Merton-Ho-Lee model is

$$\sigma_p(t, T) = \sigma(T - t)$$

It turns out that the bond option pricing formula in (10.72) is actually Black's 1976 formula where the volatility of the bond price is given by (10.74), namely,

$$\sigma_P(t; T, S) = \frac{\sigma}{a}(1 - e^{-a(S-T)})\sqrt{\frac{1}{2a}(1 - e^{-2a(T-t)})}$$

---

[3]The Merton-Ho-Lee model has the short rate follow the process $dr = \mu(t)dt + \sigma(t)dz$. The model does not incorporate mean reversion. Short rates can go to plus/minus infinity. Moreover, interest rates in this model can get negative, creating arbitrage opportunities. Because of these two drawbacks, the models are not used in practice.

where σ and a are the volatility and the mean reversion rate of the Vasicek short rate process. Black's 1976 formula can be used to price bond options, caps, floors, swaps, captions, floortions, and some exotic interest rate derivatives. We will price these fixed-income instruments in Chapter 11 with various models and with Black's model in section 10.7.

10.8 HULL-WHITE EXTENDED VASICEK MODEL

We can extend the previous Vasicek results for $P(r, t, T)$ and $f(r, t, T)$ to the case of a time-dependent long-run rate $\bar{r}(t)$ (the Hull-White model). In the Hull-White extended Vasicek model, short rates evolve according to the following process:

$$dr(t) = a(\bar{r}(t) - r(t))dt + \sigma dz(t) \qquad (10.76)$$

To price bonds, we can take advantage of the Gaussian distribution of $r(T)$ by considering

$$I(t, T) = \int_t^T r(u)du$$

the average rate over the period $[t, T]$, where the short rate is, by integrating (10.76),

$$
\begin{aligned}
r(t) &= r(s)e^{-a(t-s)} + a\int_s^t e^{-a(t-u)}\bar{r}(u)du + \sigma\int_s^t e^{-a(t-u)}dW(u) \\
&= r(s)e^{-a(t-s)} + \alpha(t) - \alpha(s)e^{-a(t-s)} + \sigma\int_s^t e^{-a(t-u)}dW(u)
\end{aligned}
\qquad (10.77)
$$

where

$$\alpha(t) = f(t_0, t) + \frac{\sigma^2}{2a^2}(1 - e^{-at})^2 \qquad (10.78)$$

This is due to the fact that (as we will show later in the section)

$$\bar{r}(t) = f(t_0, t) + \frac{1}{a}\frac{\partial f(t_0, t)}{\partial t} + \frac{\sigma^2}{2a^2}(1 - e^{-2at})$$

We can also write the short rate in terms of the subordinated time-changed Wiener process, for $t \le u$.

$$r(u) = e^{-a(u-t)}\left[r(t) + a\int_t^u e^{a(s-t)}\bar{r}(s)ds\right] + e^{-a(u-t)}z(\beta(u)) \qquad (10.79)$$

The mean m at time t is now:

$$m = E_t^Q\left[\int_t^T r(u)du\right] = \int_t^T\left(e^{-a(u-t)}\left[r(t) + a\int_t^u e^{a(s-t)}\bar{r}(s)ds\right]\right)du$$

$$= \frac{1}{a}(1-e^{-a(T-t)})r(t) + a\int_t^T\int_t^u e^{-a(u-s)}\bar{r}(s)dsdu \qquad (10.80)$$

and the variance s^2 remains the same as (10.48), namely:

$$s^2 = \frac{\sigma^2}{2a^3}[4e^{-a\tau} + 2a\tau - e^{-2a\tau} - 3], \ \tau = T - t$$

Thus, the bond price is

$$P(r, t, T) = \exp(-(m - \frac{s^2}{2})) = \exp(A(t, T) - B(\tau)r)$$

where

$$B(T - t) = \frac{1}{a}(1 - e^{-a(T-t)}) \text{ and } A(t, T) = \frac{s^2}{2} - a\int_t^T\int_t^u e^{-a(u-s)}\bar{r}(s)dsdu$$

Now, the forward curve is given by

$$f(r, t, T) = -\frac{\partial P(r, t, T)}{\partial T} = \frac{\partial B(\tau)}{\partial \tau}r - \frac{\partial A(t, T)}{\partial T}$$

which is linear in r since

$$\frac{\partial B(\tau)}{\partial \tau} = e^{-a\tau} \text{ and } \frac{\partial A(t, T)}{\partial T} = -a\int_t^T e^{-a(T-s)}\bar{r}(s)ds + \frac{\sigma^2}{2a^2}(1-e^{-a\tau})^2$$

Now suppose $t = t_0$ is today's date. At this time (today), we know the current forward curve $f(t_0, T)$ since it is observable in the market. Thus, we have a relationship between the long-run rate function $\bar{r}(u)$ and today's forward curve:

$$f(t_0, T) = e^{-a(T-t_0)}r_0 + a\int_t^T e^{-a(T-s)}\bar{r}(s)ds - \frac{\sigma^2}{2a^2}(1 - e^{-a(T-t_0)})^2 \qquad (10.81)$$

This equation can be solved with respect to the function $\bar{r}(u)$:

$$\bar{r}(t) = f(t_0, t) + \frac{1}{a}\frac{\partial f(t_0, t)}{\partial t} + \frac{\sigma^2}{2a^2}(1 - e^{-2a(t-t_0)}) \qquad (10.82)$$

where $f(t_0, t) = \dfrac{-\partial}{\partial T}\ln P_{\text{market}}(t, T)$

is the initial forward curve known from market data. Indeed, if we substitute this solution for $\bar{r}$ into the equation for the forward curve (10.78), we get:

$$f(t_0, T) = e^{-a(T-t_0)}r_0 + a\int_{t_0}^T e^{-a(T-s)}(f(t_0, s) + \frac{1}{a}\frac{\partial f(t_0, s)}{\partial s} + \frac{\sigma^2}{2a^2}(1 - e^{-2a(s-t_0)}))ds$$

$$- \frac{\sigma^2}{2a^2}(1 - e^{-a(T-t_0)})^2$$

$$= e^{-a(T-t_0)}r_0 + a\int_{t_0}^T \frac{\partial}{\partial s}(e^{-a(T-s)}f(t_0, s))ds + \frac{\sigma^2}{2a^2}\int_t^T (e^{-a(T-s)} - e^{-a(T+s-2t_0)})ds$$

$$- \frac{\sigma^2}{2a^2}(1 - e^{-a(T-t_0)})^2$$

$$= e^{-a(T-t_0)}r_0 + f(t_0, T) - e^{-a(T-t_0)}f(t_0, t_0)$$

Recall from (10.11) that $f(t_0, t_0) = r_0$, so that we get $f(t_0, T) = f(t_0, T)$. Thus the Hull-White extended Vasicek process

$$dr = a(\bar{r}(t) - r)dt + \sigma dz$$

is consistent with the initial forward curve (calibrated to the forward curve) if the function $\bar{r}(t)$ is selected as follows:

$$\bar{r}(t) = f(t_0, t) + \frac{1}{a}\frac{\partial f(t_0, t)}{\partial t} + \frac{\sigma^2}{2a^2}(1 - e^{-2a(t-t_0)})$$

where $f(t_0, t)$ is the known (observable in the market) forward curve at time t_0.

Finally, for the bond prices in the Hull-White extended Vasicek model we have:

$$P(r, t, T) = \frac{P(t_0, T)}{P(t_0, t)} \exp\left(-B(T-t)(r(t) - f(t_0, t)) - \alpha(t_0; t, T)\right) \qquad (10.83)$$

where

$$f(t_0, t) = -\frac{\partial}{\partial t} \ln P(t_0, t)$$

$$B(T-t) = \frac{1}{a}(1 - e^{-a(T-t)}) \qquad (10.84)$$

$$\alpha(t_0; t, T) = \frac{\sigma^2}{4a^3}(e^{-a(T-t_0)} - e^{-a(t-t_0)})(e^{2a(t-t_0)} - 1)$$

and $P(t_0, T)$ and $P(t_0, t_0)$ are initial zero-coupon bond prices at time t_0, the time when the model was calibrated to fit the initial term structure.

We could have written the Hull-White extended Vasicek model as:

$$dr(t) = a(t)(\bar{r}(t) - r(t))dt + \sigma(t)dz \qquad (10.85)$$

where a, $\bar{r}$ and σ are time-dependent. Such a model can be calibrated to the term structure of interest rates and to the term structure of spot- or forward-rate volatilities. However, if an exact calibration to the current yield curve is a desired feature of the model, then also making an exact fitting to a volatility term structure can lead to problems, and caution must be exercised. There are two reasons for this. As Brigo and Mercurio state, "First, not all the volatilities that are quoted in the market are significant: some market sectors are less liquid, with the associated quotes that may be neither informative nor reliable. Second, the future volatility structures implied by [equation (10.83)] are likely to be unrealistic in that they do not conform to typical market shapes, as was remarked by Hull and White (1995) themselves."[4] Consequently, many practitioners use the version of the model analyzed by Hull and White (1994) where a and σ are constant as in (10.76).

Notice that if we define the Ornstein-Uhlenbeck process x by

$$dx(t) = -ax(t)dt + \sigma dW(t), \ x(0) = 0 \qquad (10.86)$$

we get for each $s < t$,

$$x(t) = x(s)e^{-a(t-s)} + \sigma\int_s^t e^{-a(t-u)}dW(u) \qquad (10.87)$$

---

[4]Brigo and Mercurio (2001c), 64.

so that we can write $r(t) = x(t) + \alpha(t)$; to see this, just compare (10.77) with (10.87) for each t where $\alpha(t)$ is in (10.78). We will make use of (10.86) in the Hull-White and lognormal Hull-White tree building procedures in the next chapter.

Finally, it is important to note that while the Gaussian nature of the short rate gives analytical solutions to bond prices, bond options, and long-term rates, there is still the drawback that rates can become negative in the model. However, the probability that this occurs is very small.

10.9   EUROPEAN OPTIONS ON COUPON-BEARING BONDS

Jamshidian developed a technique to value derivatives on coupon-bearing bonds. Jamshidian showed that options on coupon-bearing bonds can be decomposed into a portfolio of options on individual discount bonds decomposed from the coupon-bearing bond.

A coupon-bearing bond

$$B(T) = \sum_{i=1}^{N} c_i P(T, T_i)$$

pays N coupons c_i on each coupon-payment date T_i, $i = 1, 2, \ldots, N$. On the last coupon-payment date T_N (i.e., the maturity date of the bond), the bondholder receives c_N as well as the principal amount of the bond. A European call option on a coupon-bearing bond pays off:

$$C(T) = \max(B(T) - X, 0)$$
$$= \max\left(\sum_{i=1}^{N} c_i P(T, T_i) - X, 0\right)$$

at the option maturity T. This payoff can be viewed as a call option on a portfolio of zero-coupon bonds that can be decomposed into a sum of payoffs from calls on the individual bonds. Jamshidian formulated the following strike decomposition to value the option. First, determine r^* such that the coupon-bearing bond price is equal to the strike (see Appendix D for implementation from QuantLib):

$$\sum_{i=1}^{N} c_i P(r^*, T, T_i) = X$$

This equation can be solved numerically by the Newton-Raphson method when bond prices are known functions of the short rate as in the Vasicek model. Second, calculate individual strikes X_i:

$$P(r^*, T, T_i) = X_i$$

Clearly, the following relation must hold:

$$\sum_{i=1}^{N} c_i X_i = X$$

Third, note that all zero-coupon bond prices are strictly decreasing functions of the short rate (see 10.28). Therefore,

$$\max\left(\sum_{i=1}^{N} c_i P(r(T), T, T_i) - X, \ 0\right) = \begin{cases} \sum_{i=1}^{N} c_i P(r(T), T, T_i) - X, & r(T) < r^* \\ 0, & r(T) \leq r^* \end{cases}$$

and for each individual zero bond,

$$\max\left(\sum_{i=1}^{N} P(r(T), T, T_i) - X_i, \ 0\right) = \begin{cases} \sum_{i=1}^{N} P(r(T), T, T_i) - X_i, & r(T) < r^* \\ 0, & r(T) \leq r^* \end{cases}$$

Since

$$\sum_{i=1}^{N} c_i X_i = X$$

the payoffs from an option on the coupon-bearing bond and a portfolio of options on the zero-coupon bonds are equivalent:

$$\max\left(\sum_{i=1}^{N} c_i P(T, T_i) - X, \ 0\right) = \sum_{i=1}^{N} c_i \max(P(T, T_i) - X_i, \ 0)$$

and we can value options on coupon-bearing bonds as portfolios of options on zeros:

$$C = \sum_{i=1}^{N} c_i [P(t, T_i)N(d_{i,+}) - X_i P(t, T)N(d_{i,-})]$$

where

$$d_{i,\pm} = \frac{1}{\sigma_P(t; T, T_i)} \ln\left(\frac{P(t, T_i)}{X_i P(t, T)}\right) \pm \frac{\sigma_P(t; T, T_i)}{2}$$

It should be noted that swaptions can be regarded as options on coupon-bearing bonds. Thus, the Jamshidian strike decomposition allows us to price swaptions in the Vasicek model analytically.

10.10 COX-INGERSOLL-ROSS MODEL

The Cox-Ingersoll-Ross (CIR) model (1985) is a general equilibrium model with a "square-root" term in the diffusion coefficient of a Vasicek short-rate process modeled under the risk-neutral measure Q:

$$dr(t) = a(\bar{r} - r(t))dt + \sigma\sqrt{r(t)}dW(t), \quad r(0) = r_0 \qquad (10.88)$$

The model is analytically tractable and because of the square-root diffusion term, the instantaneous short rate is always positive (unlike the Vasicek model) if the Feller condition

$$2a\bar{r} > \sigma^2 \qquad (10.89)$$

holds (this ensures the origin cannot be reached).

The process can also be measured under an equivalent martingale measure—the objective measure $\tilde{Q}$, that is, for historical estimation purposes, by formulating the model as:

$$dr(t) = (a\bar{r} - (a + \lambda\sigma)r(t))dt + \sigma\sqrt{r(t)}d\tilde{W}(t), \quad r(0) = r_0$$

where

$$\lambda(t) = \lambda\sqrt{r(t)}$$

is the market price of risk under Girsanov's change of measure where the Radon-Nikodym derivative is:

$$\frac{dQ}{d\tilde{Q}} = \exp\left(\int_0^t \lambda\sqrt{r(s)}d\tilde{W}(s) - \frac{1}{2}\int_0^t \lambda^2 r(s)ds\right)$$

The short-rate process in (10.88) follows a noncentral chi-squared distribution. Denote $p_x(x)$ as the density function of the random variable X so that

$$p_{r(t)}(x) = P_{\chi^2(v,\lambda(t))}(x) = c(t)p_{\chi^2(v,\lambda(t))}(c(t)x)$$

where

$$c(t) = \frac{4a}{\sigma^2(1 - e^{-at})}$$

$$v = \frac{4a\bar{r}}{\sigma^2}$$

$$\lambda(t) = c(t)r_0 e^{-at}$$

where the noncentral chi-squared distribution function $\chi^2(\cdot,\, v,\, \lambda)$ with v degrees of freedom and noncentrality parameter λ has the density[5]

$$p_{\chi^2(v,\lambda)}(z) = \sum_{i=0}^{\infty} \frac{e^{-\lambda/2}(\lambda/2)^i}{i!}p_{\Gamma(i+v/2,1/2)}(z)$$

$$p_{\Gamma(i+v/2,1/2)}(z) = \frac{(1/2)^{i+v/2}}{\Gamma(i+v/2)}z^{i-1+v/2}e^{-z/2} = p_{\chi^2(v+2i)}(z)$$

where $p_{\chi^2(v+2i)}(z)$ denotes the density of a (central) chi-squared distribution function with $v + 2i$ degrees of freedom.[6]

The mean and variance of $r(t)$ (conditioned) at time s are

$$E_s[r(t)] = \bar{r} + e^{-a(t-s)}(r(s) - \bar{r})$$

and

$$\text{Var}_s[r(t)] = r(s)\left(\frac{\sigma^2}{a}\right)(e^{-a(t-s)} - e^{-2a(t-s)}) + \bar{r}\frac{\sigma^2}{2a}(1 - e^{-a(t-s)})^2$$

---

[5]Ibid., 57.
[6]Ibid., 57.

The CIR bond-pricing PDE is:

$$\frac{1}{2}\sigma^2 r \frac{\partial^2 P}{\partial r^2} + a(\bar{r} - r)\frac{\partial P}{\partial r} + \frac{\partial P}{\partial t} = rP \tag{10.90}$$

which admits a solution by separation of variables if $P(t, T) = e^{-(B(t,T)r(t)+A(t,T))}$ is substituted into (10.90) We find ODEs for A and B:

$$\frac{\partial A(t, T)}{\partial t} = -a\bar{r}B(t, T), \text{ subject to } A(T, T) = 0$$

or, equivalently,

$$A(t, T) = \int_t^T a\bar{r}B(u, T)du$$

and

$$\frac{\partial B(t, T)}{\partial t} + 1 - aB(t, T) - \frac{1}{2}\sigma^2 B^2(t, T) = 0$$

subject to $B(T, T) = 0$, to ensure that $P(T, T) = 1$.

The solution is:[7]

$$A(t, T) = -\frac{2a\bar{r}}{\sigma^2}\ln\left[\frac{2\gamma\exp\left(\frac{(a+\gamma)(T-t)}{2}\right)}{2\gamma + (a+\gamma)(e^{\gamma t} - 1)}\right]$$

and $$\tag{10.91}$$

$$B(t, T) = \frac{2(e^{\gamma(T-t)} - 1)}{2\gamma + (a+\gamma)(e^{\gamma(T-t)} - 1)}$$

$$\gamma = \sqrt{a^2 + 2\sigma^2}$$

---

[7] Ibid., 58.

We can also rewrite the solution (the price at time t of a zero-coupon bond maturing at time T) as:

$$P(t, T) = A(t, T)e^{-B(t,T)r(t)}$$

where

$$A(t, T) = \left[\frac{2\gamma \exp\left(\frac{(a+\gamma)\tau}{2}\right)}{2\gamma + (a+\gamma)(e^{\gamma(T-t)} - 1)} \right]^{\frac{2a\bar{r}}{\sigma^2}}$$

and $B(t, T)$ and γ are the same.

We can derive forward rates from the bond price:

$$f(r, t, T) = \frac{\partial A(t, T)}{\partial T} + r\frac{\partial B(t, T)}{\partial T}$$

where

$$\frac{\partial B(t, T)}{\partial T} = \frac{4\gamma^2 e^{\gamma(T-t)}}{((a+\gamma)(e^{\gamma(T-t)} - 1) + 2\gamma)^2}$$

Thus, the forward rate volatility structure for the CIR model is:

$$\sigma_f(r, t, T) = \frac{\partial B(t, T)}{\partial t}\sigma\sqrt{r}$$

so that the bond price volatility is

$$\sigma_P(t, T) = \int_t^T \sigma_f(r, u, T)du = B(t, T)\sigma\sqrt{r}$$

Using Ito's formula, we can derive the bond price dynamics using the CIR model under the risk-neutral measure Q:

$$dP(t, T) = r(t)P(t, T)dt - B(t, T)P(t, T)\sigma\sqrt{r(t)}dW(t)$$

which can be written as:

$$dP(t,\ T) = \frac{1}{B(t,\ T)} \ln\left(\frac{A(t,\ T)}{P(t,\ T)}\right) P(t,\ T)dt - \sigma P(t,\ T)\sqrt{B(t,\ T)\ln\left(\frac{A(t,\ T)}{P(t,\ T)}\right)}dW(t)$$

by inverting the bond-pricing formula. This can be rewritten as:

$$d\ln P(t,\ T) = \left(\frac{1}{B(t,\ T)} - \frac{1}{2}\sigma^2 B(t,\ T)\right)(\ln A(t,\ T) - \ln P(t,\ T))dt$$
$$- \sigma\sqrt{B(t,\ T)}(\ln A(t,\ T) - \ln P(t,\ T))dW(t)$$

Cox, Ingersoll, and Ross (1985a) show that the price at time t of a European call option that matures at time T, $T > t$, on a zero-coupon bond maturing at time s, $s > T$, is given by:

$$C(t) = P(t,\ s)\chi^2\left(2\bar{r}(\rho + \psi + B(T,\ s));\ \frac{4a\bar{r}}{\sigma^2},\ \frac{2\rho^2 r(t)e^{\gamma(T-t)}}{\rho + \psi + B(T,\ s)}\right)$$
$$- XP(t,\ T)\chi^2\left(2\tilde{r}(\rho + \psi);\ \frac{4a\bar{r}}{\sigma^2},\ \frac{2\rho^2 r(t)e^{\gamma(T-t)}}{\rho + \psi}\right) \tag{10.92}$$

where

$$\rho = \rho(T - t) = \frac{2\gamma}{\sigma^2(\exp(\gamma(T - t)) - 1)}$$

$$\psi = \frac{a + \gamma}{\sigma^2}$$

$$\tilde{r} = \tilde{r}(s - T) = \frac{\ln(A(T,\ s)/X)}{B(T,\ s)}$$

The short-rate dynamics under the T-forward measure Q^T are:

$$dr(t) = (a\bar{r} - (a + B(t,\ T)\sigma^2)r(t))dt + \sigma\sqrt{r(t)}dW^T(t) \tag{10.93}$$

where the Q^T-Brownian motion W^T is defined by:

$$dW^T(t) = dW(t) + \sigma B(t,\ T)\sqrt{r(t)}dt$$

From the CIR short-rate dynamics in (10.93), we can derive the implied forward-rate dynamics:

$$F(t;\ T,\ S) = \frac{1}{\tau(T,\ S)}\left[\frac{P(t,\ T)}{P(t,\ S)} - 1\right]$$

where $\tau(T,\ S)$ is the fraction of time between T and S. By Ito's formula, it can be shown that under the forward measure Q^S, the dynamics of the forward rate are:

$$dF(t;\ T,\ S) = \sigma\frac{A(t,\ T)}{A(t,\ S)}(B(t,\ S) - B(t,\ T))e^{(-(B(t,T)-B(t,S))r(t))}\sqrt{r(t)}dW^S(t)$$

which can be rewritten as:

$$dF(t;\ T,\ S) = \sigma\left(F(t;\ T,\ S) + \frac{1}{\tau(T,\ S)}\right)$$

$$\cdot\sqrt{(B(t,\ S) - B(t,\ T))\ln\left((\tau(T,\ S)F(t;\ T,\ S) + 1)\frac{A(t,\ S)}{A(t,\ T)}\right)}dW^S(t)$$

10.11   EXTENDED (TIME-HOMOGENOUS) CIR MODEL

Consider now the CIR model with time-dependent parameters:

$$dr = a(t)(\bar{r}(t) - r)dt + \sigma(t)\sqrt{r}dz \qquad (10.94)$$

To make the origin inaccessible so that rates are always positive, the parameters must satisfy the Feller condition:

$$2a(t)\bar{r}(t) \geq \sigma^2(t)$$

which must hold for all times t. Consider again a solution for bond prices in the separated form:

$$P(r, t, T) = \exp(-rB(t, T) - A(t, T))$$

Substituting this into the extended (time-homogenous) CIR PDE:

$$\frac{1}{2}\sigma^2(t)r\frac{\partial^2 P}{\partial r^2} + a(t)(\bar{r}(t) - r)\frac{\partial P}{\partial r} + \frac{\partial P}{\partial t} = rP$$

we find ODEs for A and B:

$$\frac{\partial A(t,\ T)}{\partial t} = -a(t)\bar{r}(t)B(t,\ T), \quad \text{subject to } A(T,\ T) = 0 \qquad (10.95)$$

and

$$\frac{\partial B(t,\ T)}{\partial t} - a(t)B(t,\ T) - \frac{1}{2}\sigma^2(t)B^2(t,\ T) + 1 = 0 \qquad (10.96)$$

subject to $B(T,\ T) = 0$ (to ensure that $P(T,\ T) = 1$). The equation for B (10.95) is a Riccati differential equation. There is no closed-form solution for time-dependent coefficients, so it needs to be integrated numerically. If $B(t,\ T)$ is solved numerically, then $A(t,\ T)$ is given by the integral

$$A(t,\ T) = \int_t^T a(u)\bar{r}(u)B(u,\ T)du$$

The drift parameter $\bar{r}(t)$ can be calibrated to the initial term structure as follows. We know that the bond price is:

$$P(t,\ T) = \exp\left(-r(t)B(t,\ T) - \int_t^T a(u)\bar{r}(u)B(u,\ T)du\right)$$

For $t = 0$, we have:

$$\int_0^T f(0,\ u)du = f(0,\ 0)B(0,\ T) + \int_t^T a(u)\bar{r}(u)B(u,\ T)du$$

Differentiating with respect to T,

$$\int_0^T a(u)\bar{r}(u)\beta(u,\ T)du = f(0,\ T) - \beta(0,\ T)f(0,\ 0) \qquad (10.97)$$

where

$$\beta(t,\ T) = \frac{\partial B(t,\ T)}{\partial T}$$

In the derivation, we use the facts that $B(T, T) = 0$ and $f(0, 0) = r(0)$. Equation (10.97) is an integral Voltera equation for the unknown drift parameter $\bar{r}(t)$. It can be solved numerically.

We can calibrate the extended CIR model to the initial volatility curve. The forward rate volatility in the extended CIR model is:

$$\sigma_f(t, T) = \beta(t, T)\sigma(t)\sqrt{r}$$

Suppose at time 0 we want to match a given implied initial forward volatility curve,

$$\sigma_f(0, T) = \beta(0, T)\sigma(0)\sqrt{r(0)}$$

We wish to calibrate our model parameters $\sigma(t)$ and $a(t)$ to produce the desired $\beta(0, T)$.

Jamshidian (1995) showed that the following condition must be satisfied to properly calibrate the model parameters:

$$\sigma^2(t) = -\frac{\partial^2}{\partial t^2}\ln\beta(0, t) + \frac{1}{2}\left(\frac{\partial\ln\beta(0, t)}{\partial t}\right)^2 - \frac{1}{2}a^2(t) - \frac{da(t)}{dt} \qquad (10.98)$$

If we assume that a is known (i.e., constant), then this formula provides the expression for $\sigma(t)$. If we assume that σ is known (i.e., constant), then $a(t)$ can be found by solving the ODE. Thus, the CIR model can be calibrated to the initial yield curve and the initial volatility curve fairly straightforwardly (at least in theory).

10.12   BLACK-DERMAN-TOY SHORT RATE MODEL

The Black-Derman-Toy (BDT) model (1990) is a single-factor Markovian short rate model that can be calibrated to match the observed term structure of spot interest rates as well as the term structure of spot rate volatilities. The model is a particular case of the Black-Karasinski model (discussed in the next chapter). The model is developed algorithmically using a discrete-time binomial tree structure. A binomial tree for the short rate is constructed so that the observed yield curve and term structure of spot volatilities, inputs to the model, are calibrated to the model at each node. In the continuous time limit, the BDT model becomes the following SDE:

$$d\ln r(t) = \left[\theta(t) + \frac{\sigma'(t)}{\sigma(t)}\ln r(t)\right]dt + \sigma(t)dz$$

The BDT model utilizes two independent parameters that are functions of time, $\theta(t)$ and $\sigma(t)$, that are chosen so that the model is calibrated to the initial term structure of spot rates and the term structure of spot rate volatilities. Changes in the short rate are lognormally distributed so that rates can never become negative. Once $\theta(t)$ and $\sigma(t)$ are chosen, the future short rate volatility is completely deterministic. However, for certain specifications of the volatility function $\sigma(t)$, rates can become mean-fleeing instead of mean-reverting. Due to the lognormality of the short rates, the model is not analytically tractable; that is, neither analytic solutions for the prices of bonds nor the prices of bond options are available, and pricing can be computed only with numerical procedures such as trees and simulations.

10.13 BLACK'S MODEL TO PRICE CAPS

In this section, we discuss pricing the important interest rate derivatives of caps and swaptions with Black's (1976) model and then discuss how to price them with the single-factor models.

Consider a floating-rate loan with a principal loan amount N that has the floating interest rate $R(t_i, t_{i+1})$—that is, three-month London Interbank Offered Rate (LIBOR)—at n payment dates, $t_i, i = 1, \ldots, n$, where $0 = t_0 < t_1 < \ldots < t_n$ and $R(t_i, t_{i+1})$ is determined at time t_i for the next time period $\tau_i = t_{i+1} - t_i$ (i.e., three months). At time t_{i+1}, the payment made is $\tau N R(t_i, t_{i+1})$. A borrower who pays the floating rate to the lender is said to be short a floater, and a lender who receives the floating rate from the borrower is said to be a long floater. A borrower is exposed to the risk of, say a rising three-month LIBOR rate in the future. A cap guarantees that the rate charged on the loan will not be more than the cap rate $\bar{R}$. A long position in a cap protects a short position in LIBOR against rising rates in the future—the cap holder receives the difference between LIBOR rate and the cap rate, $\bar{R}$, if the LIBOR rate goes above $\bar{R}$. The payoff from a cap at time t_i:

$$\tau N \max(R(t_{i-1}, t_i) - \bar{R}, 0) \tag{10.99}$$

The payoff is similar to that of a call option where $\bar{R}$ is the strike price. The option is written on $R(t_{i-1}, t_i)$, the simple interest rate for the period $[t_{i-1}, t_i]$ set time t_{i-1}.

Each individual cash flow in the cap is called a caplet. Thus, a cap is a portfolio of caplets. Each caplet is a call option on the interest rate $R(t_{i-1}, t_i)$ at time t_{i-1}, but paid in arrears at time t_i. Caps are normally structured so that there is no payoff at time t_1 since the rate $R(t_0, t_1)$ is already known at time t_0 and there is no uncertainty to hedge against.

A cap can be viewed as a portfolio of puts on zero-coupon bonds. The payoff at time t_i in the amount of $\tau N \max(R(t_{i-1}, t_i) - \bar{R}, 0)$ is equivalent to the payoff at time t_{i-1}:

$$\frac{\tau N}{1 + \tau R(t_{i-1}, t_i)} \max(R(t_{t-1}, t_i) - \bar{R}, 0)$$

where

$$\frac{1}{1 + \tau R(t_{i-1},\, t_i)}$$

is the discount factor for the time interval $[t_{i-1},\, t_i]$, that is, a zero-coupon bond $P(t_{i-1},\, t_i)$ paying \$1 at time t_{i+1} (one-period discount bond):

$$P(t_{i-1},\, t_i) = \frac{1}{1 + \tau R(t_{i-1},\, t_i)}$$

We can rewrite the caplet payoff as follows:

$$
\begin{aligned}
\frac{\tau N}{1 + \tau R(t_{i-1},\, t_i)} \max(R(t_{i-1},\, t_i) - \overline{R},\, 0) &= N \max\left(1 - \frac{1 + \tau \overline{R}}{1 + \tau R(t_{i-1},\, t_i)},\, 0\right) \\
&= N \max(1 - (1 + \tau \overline{R})P(t_{i-1},\, t_i),\, 0) \\
&= N(1 + \tau \overline{R}) \max\left(\frac{1}{1 + \tau \overline{R}} - P(t_{i-1},\, t_i),\, 0\right) \qquad (10.100) \\
&= \frac{N}{\overline{P}} \max(\overline{P} - P(t_{i-1},\, t_i),\, 0)
\end{aligned}
$$

A caplet can be viewed as a quantity N/P of put options on a one-period zero-coupon bond $P(t_{i-1},\, t_i)$ with a strike of

$$\overline{P} = \frac{1}{1 + \tau \overline{R}}$$

Thus, as mentioned, a cap can be regarded as a portfolio of put options.

Interest rate floors, in contrast to caps, protect holders from drops in floating rates by placing a lower limit on the interest rate charged on a loan. Thus, the payoff in a floor is:

$$\tau N \max(\overline{R} - R(t_{i-1},\, t_i),\, 0)$$

To purchase a cap, a borrower needs to pay the premium for the cap. To reduce the premium, the borrower can sell a floor. This is analogous to selling an out-of-the-money (OTM) put to pay for an OTM protective call that protects a short position in the underlying asset. The individual payments between $[t_{i-1},\, t_i]$ are called floorlets. A cap (floor) with strike $\bar{R}$ with payment times $t_1, \ldots, t_n$ is said to be ATM if and only if:

$$\bar{R} = \bar{R}_{ATM} = \frac{P(0, t_1) - P(0, t_n)}{\sum_{i=1}^{n} \tau_i P(0, t_i)} \tag{10.101}$$

The cap is said to be ITM if $\bar{R} < \bar{R}_{ATM}$ and OTM if $\bar{R} > \bar{R}_{ATM}$, with the converse holding for a floor.

Caps can be valued with Black's 1976 model. If we assume the rate $R(t_{i-1}, t_i)$ is lognormally distributed with some known (estimated) standard deviation of $\ln R(t_{i-1}, t_i)$ equal to

$$\sigma(t_i) = \sigma(t_i; t_{i-1}, t_i) = \sigma\sqrt{t_{i-1}}$$

where σ is the common volatility parameter that is retrieved from market quotes at time t, then we can use Black's formula for a caplet C_i that pays at time t_i:

$$C_i = \tau_i NP(t, t_i)(f(t; t_{i-1}, t_i)\Phi(d_+) - \bar{R}\Phi(d_-)) \tag{10.102}$$

where $P(t, t_i) = e^{-R(t,t_i)(t-t_i)}$ is the one-period discount bond, $f(t; t_{i-1}, t_i)$ is the forward LIBOR rate for the period, $\Phi(\cdot)$ is the cumulative normal distribution, and

$$d_\pm = \frac{1}{\sigma(t; t_{i-1}, t_i)}\left(\ln\left(\frac{f(t; t_{i-1}, t_i)}{\bar{R}}\right) \pm \frac{\sigma^2(t; t_{i-1}, t_i)}{2}\right)$$

Note that in (10.102), both $\bar{R}$ and $f(t; t_{i-1}, t_i)$ are expressed with a compounding frequency of τ_i. The forward rate can be expressed through bond prices:

$$P(t, t_i) = P(t, t_{i-1})\frac{1}{1+\tau f(t; t_{i-1}, t_i)}$$

so that

$$f(t; t_{i-1}, t_i) = \frac{1}{\tau}\left(\frac{P(t, t_{i-1})}{P(t, t_i)} - 1\right) \tag{10.103}$$

Floorlets are valued similarly:

$$P_i = \tau_i NP(t, t_i)(\bar{R}\Phi(-d_-) - f(t; t_{i-1}, t_i)\Phi(-d_+)) \tag{10.104}$$

The volatilities used are forward rate volatilities, the volatility of the future spot LIBOR rate at time t_{i-1} covering the period $[t_{i-1}, t_i]$ conditional on the information at time t. This volatility is time-dependent and exhibits a pronounced hump effect, especially in the cap markets.

Note that we assumed that the forward LIBOR rate was lognormally distributed. This assumption is consistent with the lognormal LIBOR Brace, Gatarek, and Musiela (BGM) (market) model of the term structure of interest rates. However, it is possible to value caplets and floorlets as options on zero-coupon bonds and assume that the bond price is lognormal. This assumption is consistent with the Gaussian Heath-Jarrow-Morton (HJM) (Hull-White extended Vasicek) model of the term structure of interest rates.

An alternative way to price caplets and caps is to use no-arbitrage arguments following the results of Harrison and Kreps (1979). In any market where there is no arbitrage, for any given numeraire security whose price is $g(t)$ there exists a measure for which $S(t)/g(t)$ is a martingale for all security prices $S(t)$. Denote this measure $M\{g(t)\}$. If we let the discount bond with maturity t_i be the numeraire—that is, $g(t) = P(t, t_i)$—then:

$$\frac{S(t)}{P(t, t_i)}$$

is a martingale for all security prices $S(t)$. Thus,

$$\frac{S(0)}{P(0, t_i)} = E^i\left[\frac{S(t)}{P(t, t_i)}\right] \tag{10.105}$$

where E^i denotes the expectation with respect to the measure $M\{P(t, t_{i+1})\}$. Set $S(t) = P(t, t_{i-1}) - P(t, t_i)$ in (10.101). We then get

$$f_i(0; t_{i-1}, t_i) = E^i[R(t_{i-1}, t_i)] \tag{10.106}$$

where $f_i(t; t_i, t_{i+1})$ is the forward rate for the period (t_i, t_{i+1}) at time t, and $R(t_{i-1}, t_i)$ is the future spot rate for (t_i, t_{i+1}). Thus, equation (10.106) shows that, under the assumed measure, the forward rate at time 0 is equal to the expected future spot rate for (t_i, t_{i+1}). If we set $S(t)$ equal to the price of the $(i-1)$th caplet and note that $P(t_i, t_i) = 1$, then we see from (10.105) that:

$$S(0) = P(0, t_i)E^i[S(t_i)] \tag{10.107}$$

or

$$S(0) = P(0, t_i)\tau N E^i[\max(R(t_{i-1}, t_i) - \bar{R}, 0)]$$

Assuming $R(t_{i-1}, t_i)$ is lognormal, with a standard deviation of $\ln(R(t_{i-1}, t_i))$ equal to

$$\sigma_{i-1}\sqrt{t_{i-1}}$$

this becomes:

$$S(0) = \tau N P(0, t_i)(E^i(R(t_{i-1}, t_i)\Phi(d_1) - \bar{R}\Phi(d_2)) \qquad (10.108)$$

where

$$d_i = \frac{\ln(E^i(R(t_{i-1}, t_i))/\bar{R}) + \sigma_{i-1}^2 t_{i-1}/2}{\sigma_{i-1}\sqrt{t_{i-1}}}$$

$$d_2 = d_1 - \sigma_{i-1}\sqrt{t_{i-1}}$$

and $\Phi(\cdot)$ is the cumulative normal distribution. Substituting (10.106) into (10.108) gives the standard market price for a caplet:

$$S(0) = \tau N P(0, t_i)(f(0; t_{i-1}, t_i)\Phi(d_1) - \bar{R}\Phi(d_2))$$

In general for any $t > 0$, we get the price of the $(i-1)$th caplet at time t:

$$S(t) = \tau N P(t, t_i)(f(t; t_{i-1}, t_i)\Phi(d_1) - \bar{R}\Phi(d_2))$$

which is consistent with (10.102). Similarly, for the price of the $(i-1)$th floorlet:

$$S(t) = \tau N P(t, t_i)(\bar{R}\Phi(-d_2) - f(t; t_{i-1}, t_i)\Phi(-d_1))$$

which is consistent with (10.104).

10.14   BLACK'S MODEL TO PRICE SWAPTIONS

Swaptions give the holder the right to enter a swap at a certain time in the future. An interest rate swap is an agreement to exchange a fixed-rate bond (fixed-rate interest payment) for a floating-rate bond (floating payments, i.e., LIBOR). If a swaption gives the holder the right to pay fixed and receiving floating, it is a put option on the fixed-rate bond and is known as a *payer swaption*. If a swaption gives the holder the right to pay floating and receive fixed, then it is a call option on the fixed-rate bond and is known as a *receiver swaption*. We can value European swaptions with Black's 1976 model. Consider a swaption with an inception at a swaption expiration (the time to enter into the swap if exercised), swap reset dates

$T_0, T_1, \ldots, T_{n-1}$, and corresponding payment dates $T_1, T_2, \ldots, T_n$, where T_n is the swap maturity date.

Swaptions give holders the right to enter into a swap at the fixed swap rate $\bar{R}$, given in (10.102) at time t_0, allowing the holder to lock in the future swap rate today. The swap rate is the fixed rate, which when exchanged for floating in a forward start swap causes the value of the swap to equal zero. At the swaption maturity, the current swap rate is $R(T_0)$. This swap rate may be less advantageous than today's swap rate so the swaption protects the holder from rising rates. The cost for this protection is the premium paid for the swaption. At time t_0, the value of the swap with swap rate $\bar{R}$, assuming a payer swap, is:

$$V(T_0) = B_{floater} - B_{fixed}$$

where B_{fixed} is a fixed-rate bond that can be expressed as:

$$B_{fixed} = \tau N \bar{R} \sum_{i=1}^{n} P(T_0, T_i) + NP(T_0, T_n)$$

This is simply the sum of the discounted interest payments plus the discounted principal repaid at maturity. Denote

$$A(t) = \sum_{i=1}^{n} \tau_{i-1} P(t, T_i)$$

This is the present value at time t of an annuity paying \$1 at time T_i and $\tau_{i-1} = t_i - t_{i-1}$. Then the fixed bond price can be written:

$$B_{fixed} = \tau N \bar{R} A(T_0) + NP(T_0, T_n)$$

The floating-rate bond is worth par at time T_0:

$$B_{floater}(T_0) = N(1 + \tau R(T_0, T_1))P(T_0, T_1) = L$$

The present value of the swap at time T_0 is given by:

$$V(T_0) = N(1 - \tau \bar{R} A(T_0) - P(T_0, T_n)) = L(1 - B(T_0))$$

where $B(T_0)$ is a coupon-bearing bond:

$$B(T_0) = N(\tau \bar{R} A(T_0) + P(T_0, T_n))$$

Payoff from a payer's swaption at time T_0, $S_{payer}(T_0)$, is:

$$S_{payer}(T_0) = \max(V(T_0), 0) = N \max(1 - B(T_0), 0)$$

Thus, a payer's swaption is a put option on the coupon-bearing bond. The payoff from the receiver's swaption, $S_{receiver}(T_0)$, at time T_0 is:

$$S_{receiver}(T_0) = \max(-V(T_0), 0) = N\max(B(T_0) - 1, 0)$$

Thus, a receiver's swaption is a call option on the coupon-bearing bond. There is a fundamental relationship between a receiver and payer swaption known as *forward start swap parity*:

$$\text{Forward start swap parity} = S_{receiver}(T_0) - S_{payer}(T_0)$$

If we are long a receiver's swaption and short a payer's swaption (both with the same swap rates $\bar{R}$), we have:

$$N\max(B(T_0) - 1, 0) - N\max(1 - B(T_0), 0) = N(B(T_0) - 1)$$

The expression on the right-hand side is nothing but the present value of the swap starting at T_0. Discounting back to t_0, we see that the payer's and receiver's swaptions are just two halves of the forward start swap.

We can value a swaption using Black's 1976 model. The current swap rate at T_0, $R(T_0)$, is a coupon rate that makes the fixed bond worth par (par yield bond):

$$R(T_0) = \frac{1 - P(T_0, T_n)}{\tau A(T_0)}$$

We substitute the following identity:

$$\tau R(T_0)A(T_0) + P(T_0, T_n) = 1$$

into the payer's swaption payoff:

$$S_{payer}(T_0) = N\max(1 - \tau\bar{R}A(T_0) - P(T_0, T_n), 0)$$
$$= \tau N A(T_0)\max(R(T_0) - \bar{R}, 0)$$

Thus, a payer's swaption is a call option on the swap rate at time T_0.

Let $S(t_0; T_0, T_n) = S_{0,n}(t_0)$ be a forward swap rate for a forward-start swap (t_0 is the inception of the forward-start swap, T_0 is the inception of the underlying swap, and T_n is the termination date of the swap). We have:

$$S_{0,n}(t_0) = \frac{P(t_0, T_0) - P(t_0, T_n)}{\tau A(T_0)} \tag{10.109}$$

the forward swap rate for a swap starting at T_0 and lasting through T_n as seen at time t_0. Moreover, $S_{0,n}(t_0) = f(T_0; T_0, T_n)$. In Black's model, we assume the swap rate $R(T_0)$ is lognormally distributed with the mean equal to the current forward swap rate $S_{0,n}(t_0)$, and the volatility of the log future spot swap rate, $\ln R(T_0)$, conditional on information at time t_0 is equal to $\sigma(t_0; T_0, T_n)$. We set

$$\sigma(t_0; T_0, T_n) = \sigma_{0,n}\sqrt{T_0}$$

where $\sigma_{0,n}$ is the implied volatility parameter that is retrieved from market quotes at time T_0 for a swap that matures at T_n. By Black's formula (a Black-Scholes-like formula), we get the formula for a payer's swaption:

$$S_{payer}(t_0) = \tau N A(t_0)(S_{0,n}(t_0)\Phi(d_+) - \overline{R}\Phi(d_-))$$

$$= \tau N \sum_{i=1}^{n} P(t, T_i)(S_{0,n}(t_0)\Phi(d_+) - \overline{R}\Phi(d_-)) \qquad (10.110)$$

and the formula for a receiver's swaption:

$$S_{receiver}(t_0) = \tau N A(t_0)(\overline{R}\Phi(-d_+) - S_{0,n}(t_0)\Phi(-d_-))$$

$$= \tau N \sum_{i=1}^{n} P(t, T_i)(\overline{R}\Phi(-d_+) - S_{0,n}(t_0)\Phi(-d_-)) \qquad (10.111)$$

where

$$d_\pm = \frac{1}{\sigma(t_0; T_0, T_n)}\left(\ln\left(\frac{S_{0,n}(t_0)}{\overline{R}}\right) \pm \frac{\sigma^2(t_0; T_0, T_n)}{2}\right)$$

and $\Phi(\cdot)$ is the standard cumulative normal distribution.[8]

We can also derive the price of European swaptions using a no-arbitrage argument similar to the one used to price caps. Let

$$A(t) = \sum_{i=1}^{n} \tau_{i-1} P(t, T_i)$$

---

[8]We are using $\Phi(\cdot)$ instead of $N(\cdot)$ to denote the cumulative distribution function so as not to cause confusion with N, the principal swap amount.

be the numeraire. Under the measure $M\{A(t)\}$,

$$\frac{f(t)}{A(t)}$$

is a martingale for all security prices $f(t)$. Hence:

$$\frac{f(0)}{A(0)} = E^A\left[\frac{f(T_n)}{A(T_n)}\right] \qquad (10.112)$$

where E^A denotes the expectation under the measure $M\{A(t)\}$. Let $f(t) = P(t, T_0) - P(t, T_n)$ in (10.112). The we get:

$$S_{0,n}(0) = E^A\,[S_{0,n}(T_n)] = E^A\,[R(T_n)] \qquad (10.113)$$

Thus, the forward swap rate equals the expected future swap rate under the measure. We set $f(t)$ equal to the price of the swaption. From (10.112), we get:

$$f(0) = A(0)E^A\left[\frac{f(T_n)}{A(T_n)}\right]$$

Substituting the payoff of a swaption for $f(T_n)$ we get:

$$f(0) = NA(0)E^A\,[\max(R(T_n) - \bar{R}, 0)]$$

Since we assume that $R(T_n)$ is lognormally distributed with a standard deviation of $\ln(R(T_n))$ equal to

$$\sigma(t_0;\, T_0;\, T_n) = \sigma_i(t_0;\, T_0;\, T_n) = \sigma_{0,n}\sqrt{T_{i-1}}$$

this becomes:

$$f(0) = NA(0)[E^A(R(T_n))\Phi(d_+) - \bar{R}\Phi(d_-)] \qquad (10.114)$$

Substituting (10.113) into (10.114) gives the standard Black's market model price for pricing the swaption:

$$f(0) = NA(0)[S_{0,n}(0)\Phi(d_+) - \bar{R}\Phi(d_-)]$$

where

$$d_+ = \frac{\ln(S_{0,n}(0)/\overline{R}) + \sigma_{0,n}^2 T_0/2}{\sigma_{0,n}\sqrt{T_0}}$$

$$d_- = d_+ - \sigma_{0,n}\sqrt{T_0}$$

It should be noted that in pricing formulas for caps, floors, and swaptions, the fraction of time between each payment can vary by letting $\tau = \tau_i$, $i = 1, \ldots, n$, though in most cases, τ_i is three months.[9] Moreover, the volatility can be made to vary with payment time by letting

$$\sigma(t_0; T_0; T_n) = \sigma_i(t_0; T_0; T_n) = \sigma_{0,n}\sqrt{T_{i-1}}$$

10.15   PRICING CAPS, CAPLETS, AND SWAPTIONS WITH SHORT RATE MODELS

All the single short rate models discussed in this chapter can be used to price bond options, caps, floors, caplets, floorlets, swaptions, and other interest rate products. The main unknown in all of the models is what volatility to use. This issue is dealt with by calibrating the models to market option prices so that we can determine the implied volatility to use in the model. Suppose that we have a set of M pure discount bond put options, the market price of which we denote $market_i = 1, \ldots, M$. One way to determine the volatility via calibration is to minimize the following function with respect to the parameter σ:

$$\min_\sigma \sqrt{\sum_{i=1}^M \left(\frac{model_i(\sigma) - market_i}{market_i}\right)^2} \qquad (10.115)$$

where $model_i(\sigma)$ is the model price of the ith option, obtained by using the Black-Scholes formulas for pricing T-maturity European put options on S-maturity pure discount bonds given in equation (10.75) since we know from section 10.11 that

---

[9]Usually in practice, T_0 is equal to three months with all other T_i's equally three-month-spaced or T_0 is equal to three months, the next T_i's up to one year are equally three-month-spaced, and all other T_i's are equally six-month-spaced.

interest rate caps can be expressed as European put options on pure discount bonds. Thus, if we know the price of caps, we can find the implied volatility parameter by using equation (10.75).

The optimization, which can be done using a Newton-Raphson type procedure, involves searching over all possible values of the parameter σ. The value of σ that minimizes the function is the volatility that best calibrates the model to the market for the choice of function to be minimized. We could use (10.115) to calibrate a Ho and Lee model since only the volatility needs to be determined—the volatility is not a function of any other parameters. In contrast to the Ho and Lee model, the Vasicek (and Hull-White extended Vasicek) spot rate volatility equation contains two parameters, a and σ, so that in order to calibrate the model to market prices we need to find the best fit for both a and σ simultaneously to market data. If we have M individual European pure discount bond put prices, we can minimize

$$\min_{a,\sigma} \sqrt{\sum_{i=1}^{M} \left(\frac{model_i(a,\sigma) - market_i}{market_i} \right)^2} \qquad (10.116)$$

where $model_i(a, \sigma)$ is the option value derived from the price of a European put option from equation (10.75) with the volatility given in (10.71).

As an example, suppose we want to calibrate the Hull-White model to a single caplet. Assume that the short parameters are $a = 0.10$ and $\sigma = 0.012$, and that the term structures (with continuous compounding), cap volatilities, and spot rates are given in Table 10.1. Furthermore, suppose that the cap rate is $\bar{R} = 7.00$ percent, the principal is normalized to $N = \$1$, and the face value (FV) of the bond is $N(1 + \bar{R}\tau) = 1(1 + 0.07\,(0.25)) = 1.0175$. Suppose we want to calibrate the Hull-White model to a caplet covering the period between the first and second payment dates

TABLE 10.1 Hull-White Model to a Single Caplet

Maturity in Years	Spot Rate	Cap Volatility
0.25	0.0625	0.1625
0.50	0.0654	0.1725
0.75	0.0690	0.1725
1.00	0.0710	0.1750
1.25	0.0731	0.1795
1.50	0.0749	0.1795
1.75	0.0757	0.1800
2.00	0.0768	0.1800
2.25	0.0771	0.1750
2.50	0.0774	0.1725

(i.e., $0.50 - 0.25 = 0.25$). Since the market quotes are cap volatilities and not cash prices, it is necessary to compute the cash prices from the quotes' volatilities:

$$P(t, T) = P(0, 0.25) = e^{-0.0625(0.25)} = 0.9845$$

$$P(t, S) = FV^* \ P(0, 0.50) = 1.0175 e^{-0.0654(0.50)} = 0.9848$$

$$p(t, T, S) = 1(0.9845)N(-d_2) - (0.9848)N(-d_1)$$

where

$$d_1 = \frac{\ln((0.9848)/(1 \times 0.9845))}{\sigma_P} + \frac{\sigma_P}{2}$$

$$d_2 = d_1 - \sigma_P$$

$$\sigma_P^2 = \frac{\sigma^2}{2a^3}(1 - e^{-2(0.25)a})(1 - e^{-a(0.50-0.25)})^2$$

so that with $a = 0.10$, and $\sigma = 0.012$, $\sigma_p = 0.0015$, which implies a caplet value of 0.00045. The other caplets are valued similarly. Using (10.116), we find the a and σ best fit is $a = -0.4823$ and $\sigma = 0.0076$. The following is the code that calibrates the Hull-White model to market quotes:

```
/********************************************************************************
priceCapHW: computes the price of caplets using the Hull-White model by calibrating
            to market cash prices
[in]  : vector<double> mats       : vector of caplet maturities
        vector<double> vols       : vector of market quote caplet volatilities
        vector<double> rates      : vector of short rates
        vector<double> Rcap       : cap rate
        double FV                 : face value of loan
        double volatility         : length between payment time
        double tenor              : length of time between payment dates
        double L                  : principal amount of loan
[out] : vector<double>            : stores volatility and alpha parameters
********************************************************************************/
vector<double> HullWhiteModel::priceCapHW(vector<double> mats, vector<double> vols,
    vector<double> rates, double a, double FV, double volatility, double Rcap,
    double tenor, double L)
{
    int i;
    int cnt = 0;                        // count number of Newton-Raphson iterations
    double d1, d2;                      // evaluation arguments of normal
                                        // distribution
    double K = L;                       // store principal
    double volP = 0.0;                  // bond volatility
    double a1 = 0.0;                    // initial alpha value
```

```
double tmp = 0.0;                      // temp variable
double totalsum = 0.0;                 // total sum
double sum, sum1, sum2 = 0.0;          // stores sums used in Newton-Raphson
                                       // optimization
double tau, tau1, tau2, tau3 = 0.0;    // stores tenors between caplet maturity
                                       // (reset) dates
double error = 0.0;                    // calibration error of volatility parameter
double error1 = 0.0;                   // calibration error of alpha parameter
double volSum2 = 0.0;                  // sum of volatility squared
double vol1, vol2 = 0.0;               // volatility parameters to be calibrated
double d1prime, d2prime = 0.0;         // derivatives storage variables
double d3prime, d4prime = 0.0;         // more derivatives storage variables
double volPrime = 0.0,                 // derivative with respect to volatility
double aprime = 0.0;                   // stores part of aPrime calculation
double aPrime = 0.0;                   // derivative with respect to alpha
const double epsilon = 0.001;          // error tolerance level
const int maxIterations = 20;          // maximum number of iterations allowed
vector<double> P;                      // vector of discount bond prices
vector<double> caplet;                 // vector of caplets
vector<double> model;                  // vector of Hull White model prices
vector<double> market;                 // vector of cash market prices
vector<double> params;                 // stores volatility and alpha parameters
int len = vols.size();                 // size of volatility vector


// compute pure discount bond prices
for (i = 0; i < len; i++)
{
  tmp = exp(-mats[i]*rates[i]);
  P.push_back(tmp);
}
// compute cash prices from market quotes (cap volatilities)
BlackModel bm;
market = bm.priceBlackCap(vols,P,mats,Rcap,L,tenor);
for (i = 0; i < len-1; i++)
{
  volP = sqrt(((volatility*volatility)/(2*a*a*a))*(1 - exp(-2*mats[i]*a))*(1 -
    exp(-a*(mats[i+1]-mats[i])))*(1- exp(-a*(mats[i+1]-mats[i])))));
  d1 = log((FV*P[i+1])/(K*P[i]))/volP + volP/2;
  d2 = d1 - volP;
  tmp = K*P[i]*util.normalCalc(-d2) - FV*P[i+1]*util.normalCalc(-d1);
  model.push_back(tmp);
}


// compute sum of squared errors between model and market prices
sum = 0;
for (i = 0; i < len-1; i++)
{
  sum = sum + ((model[i] - market[i])/market[i])*((model[i] -
    market[i])/market[i]);
}

// initialize numerical values
```

```
totalsum = sum;          // assign sum of squared errors
vol1 = volatility;       // assign initial volatility
a1 = a;                  // assign initial alpha


// two dimensional Newton-Raphson minimization routine
do
{
  // initialize sums for each iteration
  sum1 = 0;
  sum2 = 0;
  volSum2 = 0;

  for (i = 0; i < len-2; i++)
  {
    tau = mats[i+1] - mats[i];
    tau1 = mats[i];
    tau2 = mats[i+1];
    tau3 = mats[i+1] + mats[i];
    volP = sqrt(((vol1*vol1)/(2*a1*a1*a1))*(1 - exp(-2*tau1*a1))*(1 - exp(-
      a1*(tau)))*(1 - exp(-a1*(tau))));

    // compute d1 and d2
    d1 = log((FV*P[i+1])/(K*P[i]))/volP + volP/2;
    d2 = d1 - volP;
    aprime = -3*pow(a1,-4);

    // compute volatility derivative
    volPrime = 0.5*(pow(volP,-0.5))*(2*vol1/(2*a1*a1*a1))*((1 - exp(-
      2*tau1*a1))*(1 - exp(-a1*(tau)))*(1 - exp(-a1*(tau))));

    // compute alpha derivative
    aPrime = 0.5*pow(volP,-0.5)*((0.5*vol1*vol1*pow(a1,-3)*(2*tau*exp(-a1*tau) -
      2*tau*exp(-2*a1*tau) + 2*tau1*exp(-2*tau1*a1) - 2*tau3*exp(-a1*tau3) +
        2*tau2*exp(-2*a*tau2)) + (0.5*aprime*vol1*vol1)*(1 - 2*exp(-a1*tau) +
        exp(-2*a1*tau) - exp(-2*a1*tau1) + 2*exp(-a1*tau3) - exp(-2*a1*tau2))));

    d1prime = -((log(FV*P[i+1]/K*P[i]))/(volP*volP))*volPrime + 0.5*volPrime;
    d2prime = d1prime - volPrime;
    d3prime = -((log(FV*P[i+1]/K*P[i]))/(volP*volP))*aPrime + 0.5*aPrime;
    d4prime = d3prime - aPrime;
    sum1 = sum1 + (K*P[i]*util.normalCalc(-d2) - FV*P[i+1]*util.normalCalc(-d1) -
      market[i])/market[i];
    volSum2 = volSum2 + (K*P[i]*util.normalCalcPrime(-d2)*(-d2prime) -
      FV*P[i+1]*util.normalCalcPrime(-d1)*(-d1prime))/market[i];
    sum2 = sum2 + (K*P[i]*util.normalCalcPrime(-d2)*(-d4prime) -
      FV*P[i+1]*util.normalCalcPrime(-d1)*(-d3prime))/market[i];
  }
  vol2 = vol1 - sum1/volSum2;
  error = abs(vol2 - vol1);
  vol1 = vol2;
```

```
      a2 = a1 - sum1/-sum2;
      error1 = abs(a2 - a1);
      a1 = a2;

      cnt++;                    // increment number of iterations in loop
      if (cnt > maxIterations)
        break;
    }
    while ((error > epsilon) || (error1 > epsilon));


    params.push_back(alpha);
    params.push_back(vol);
    if (cnt < 20)
    {
      std::cout << "Calibrated alpha = " << a1 << endl;
      std::cout << "Calibrated vol = " << vol1 << endl;
    }
    else
    {
      std::cout << "No Convergence for Calibration. Try different values." << endl;
    }


    return params;
}


/*********************************************************************************
priceBlackCap : computes the price of caplets using BlacksFormula
[in]: vector<double> capVol    : vector of cap volatilities
      vector<double> PDB       : price of pure discount bonds
      vector<double> maturity  : vector of caplet maturities (payment times)
      vector<double> Rcap      : cap rate
      double L                 : principal amount of loan
      double tenor             : length of time between payment times (reset dates)
[out]: vector<double>          : caplets
*********************************************************************************/
vector<double> RateModel::priceBlackCap(vector<double> capVol, vector<double> PDB,
  vector<double> maturity, double Rcap, double L, double tenor)
{
  int i;
  vector<double> f;                  // forward rates
  vector<double> R;                  // yield price
  vector<double> capV;               // stores caplet volatilities
  vector<double> P;                  // stores pure bond prices
  vector<double> t;                  // payment dates
  vector<double>::iterator iter;     // vector iterator
  vector<double> caplet;             // stores caplets
  double faceValue = 0.0;            // bond face value
  double tmp = 0.0;                  // temp variable

  // compute face value
  faceValue = L*(1 + Rcap*tenor);
```

```
    // store cap volatilities
    for (iter = capVol.begin(); iter != capVol.end(); iter++)
    {
      tmp = *iter;
      capV.push_back(tmp);
    }

    // compute pure discount bond prices
    for (iter = PDB.begin(); iter != PDB.end(); iter++)
    {
      tmp = *iter;
      P.push_back(tmp);
    }

    // store payment dates
    for (iter = maturity.begin(); iter != maturity.end(); iter++)
    {
      tmp = *iter;
      t.push_back(tmp);
    }

    // compute forward rates
    for (i = 0; i < capVol.size(); i++)
    {
      tmp = -(1/t[i])*(log(P[i]));
      R.push_back(tmp);

      tmp = -(1/tenor)*log(P[i+1]/P[i]);
      f.push_back(tmp);
    }

    // compute caplets with Blacks Formula
    for (i = 0; i < capVol.size()-1; i++)
    {
      tmp = BlacksFormula(f[i],P[i],faceValue,Rcap,capV[i],t[i],tenor);
      caplet.push_back(tmp);
    }
    return caplet;
}


/************************************************************************
BlacksFormula       : computes the price of cap using Black's 1976 model
[in]:   double f    : forward rate
        double P    : price of pure discount bond
        double L    : principal amount of bond
        double Rcap : cap rate
        double vol  : market volatility
        double tau  : length between payment times
        double dtau : fixed tenor between reset times
[out] : double      : price of cap
*************************************************************************/
double BlackModel::BlacksFormula(double f, double P, double L, double Rcap, double
  vol, double tau, double dtau)
```

```
{
  double d1 = (log(f) / Rcap) + ((vol*vol)/2)*tau)/(vol*sqrt(tau));
  double d2 = d1 - vol*sqrt(tau);

  return P*dtau*L*(f*util.normalCalc(d1) - Rcap*util.normalCalc(d2));
}
```

10.16   VALUATION OF SWAPS

Swaps are interest rate derivatives contracts that obligate the holder to receive fixed-rate loan payments and pay floating-rate loan payments (or vice versa) at specified payment dates until the maturity date of the swap. Swaps enable financial institutions to synthetically alter the composition of their liabilities by transforming fixed-rate liabilities into floating-rate liabilities (or vice versa). A financial institution may do this to hedge a loan (or bond) exposure or to use a comparative advantage it has in borrowing in, say, the fixed-rate market when it in fact wants to borrow at floating-rate LIBOR. Consider a financial institution that has made a $10 million three-year loan to a company at a 5.58 percent fixed rate paid semiannually. The financial institution thinks that LIBOR rates will rise over the term of the loan and decides it would rather have floating-rate exposure than fixed-rate exposure. It decides to enter a three-year swap with a swap dealer (i.e., another financial institution) to pay 6.51 percent fixed and receive LIBOR + 1.5 percent on a semiannual basis. Effectively, by entering such a swap as shown in Figure 10.7, it is loaning at LIBOR + 0.87 percent (LIBOR + 1.5 percent + 5.58 percent – 6.51 percent = LIBOR + 0.87 percent) instead of at 5.5 percent. The financial institution will earn LIBOR + 0.87 percent if the company and swap dealer do not default on their payments.

The fixed rate that is paid in the swap is called the swap rate. Day count conventions do affect payments in the swap. Since six-month LIBOR is a money-market rate, it is quoted on an actual/360 basis with semiannual compounding. Swap rates are often quoted from the U.S. dollar swap curve, though Treasury note rates can be used. However, Treasury note rates are quoted on an actual/actual (in period) basis with semiannual compounding, so to make a six-month LIBOR rate comparable to a Treasury rate in a 365-day year, the Treasury note must be multiplied by 360/365. The swap payments are netted at each payment date before ex-

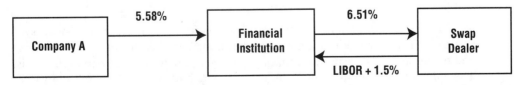

FIGURE 10.7   Swap

change of payment occurs and the principals cancel and are never exchanged. The LIBOR rate used in the payment calculation is based on the quote on the last payment date.

Let N denote the notional value of the swap, $C(t_i)$ the payment amount at time t_i, $L(t_i, t_{i+1})$ the LIBOR rate between t_i and t_{i+1} quoted at t_i with compounding frequency $\delta = n/360$ where n is the actual number of days, R the fixed swap rate with compounding frequency $\delta = n/365$, and $S(t)$ the swap value. The fixed-rate payment at time t_i is $C_{fix}(t_i) = \delta NR$, and the floating payment at time t_i (swap payments are made in arrears) is $C_{float}(t_i) = \delta NL(t_i, t_{i+1})$. We can view a fixed-for-floating swap as a long position in a fixed-rate bond and a short position in a floating-rate bond. The present value of the fixed-rate bond (fixed-rate leg) is:

$$V_{fixed}(t) = \delta RN \sum_{i=1}^{n} P(t, t_i) + NP(t, T)$$

and the present value of the floating-rate bond (floating-rate leg) payments is:

$$V_{float}(t) = N$$

since immediately after a payment date, the floating-rate bond is always equal to the notional principal N, the par value of the bond. To determine the fair swap rate, we note that at time 0, the par swap has zero present value:

$$S(0) = V_{fixed}(0) - V_{float}(0) = 0$$

or

$$N(\delta R \sum_{i=1}^{n} P(0, t_i) + P(0, T)) - N = 0$$

so that the swap rate is:

$$R = \frac{1 - P(0, T)}{\delta \sum_{i=1}^{n} P(0, t_i)} \tag{10.117}$$

As Jarrow (2002) states, there are three basic ways of creating a swap synthetically. The first method is to short the money market account (pay floating) and to synthetically create the coupon bond as a portfolio of zero-coupon bonds. The value of the combined position at each date and state will match the values of the swap and its cash flows. This method is independent of any particular model for the evolution of the term structure of rates, but is not practical since all zero-coupon bonds may not trade and the initial transaction costs will be high. The second method to synthetically replicate a swap is to use a portfolio of forward contracts written on the spot rate of futures dates. This method is also independent of any term structure of rates. The third method is to use a dynamic portfolio consisting of a single zero-coupon bond (for a one-factor model) and the money market account. This method requires a specification of the term structure of rates and can be synthetically replicated using single-factor models such as those discussed in this chapter. At each node, the amount of shares held in the money market account and those in the zero-coupon bond are determined as well as the net cash flows and swap value. At the first node, the swap has a zero value and zero cash flow. We value synthetic swaps in section 12.12 using the Heath-Jarrow-Morton (HJM) single-factor model.

There are many other types of swaps, including currency swaps, fixed-for-floating dual currency swaps, commodity swaps, equity swaps, forward start (deferred) swaps, capped swaps, callable and putable swaps, constant maturity swaps, and index amortizing swaps. Index amortizing swaps are valued in section 14.7 using the HJM model.

10.17 CALIBRATION IN PRACTICE

When calibrating trees, in practice, for valuation of swaptions, bond options, synthetic swaps, and caps to the term structure of rates, it is helpful to employ a generic calibration engine that can be used to calibrate multiple types of models and instruments. Moreover, it is helpful to create separate optimization routines such as a simplex, Brent's method, and so on that can be used by the calibration engine to calibrate models and instruments to market data. Consider a generic (abstract) *Model* class that contains a *CalibrationFunction* class and a *calibrate* method for calibrating models:

```
class CalibrationSet;

/******************************************************************************
Abstract short-rate model class
******************************************************************************/
class Model : public Patterns::Observer,
  public Patterns::Observable
{
  public:
    Model(Size nArguments);
    void update()
    {
      generateArguments();
      notifyObservers();
```

```
    }

    virtual Handle<Lattices::Lattice> tree(const TimeGrid& grid) const = 0;

    // Calibrate to a set of market instruments (caps/swaptions)
    void calibrate(CalibrationSet& instruments,
      const Handle<Optimization::Method>& method);

    const Handle<Optimization::Constraint>& constraint() const;

    // Returns array of arguments on which calibration is done
    Array params();
    void setParams(const Array& params);
  protected:
    virtual void generateArguments() {}
    std::vector<Parameter> arguments_;
    Handle<Optimization::Constraint> constraint_;

  private:
    class PrivateConstraint;   // constraint imposed on arguments
    class CalibrationFunction;       // calibration cost function class
    friend class CalibrationFunction;
};
```

The *calibrate* method computes the optimizations required for calibration.
The instruments to be calibrated are passed in as well as the optimization method
to use.

```
/****************************************************************************
calibrate                                  : calibrates model to market
                                             instrument prices
[in]   CalibrationSet& instruments         : instruments to calibrate
       Handle<Optimization::Method> & method : method of optimization
[out]  void
****************************************************************************/
void Model::calibrate(CalibrationSet& instruments, const
  Handle<Optimization::Method>& method)
{
  CalibrationFunction f(this, instruments);

  method->setInitialValue(params());
  method->endCriteria().setPositiveOptimization();
  Optimization::Problem prob(f, *constraint_, *method);
  prob.minimize();

  Array result(prob.minimumValue());
  setParams(result);
}
```

The optimization problem—that is, minimization of (10.115), via a *Problem* class—is solved and the results are stored in the *setParams* method:

```
/*******************************************************************************
setParams       : stores array of parameters
[in] Array& params      : array of parameters
[out] void
*******************************************************************************/
void Model::setParams(const Array& params)
{
Array::const_iterator p = params.begin();
  for (Size i=0; i<arguments_.size(); i++)
  {
    for (Size j=0; j<arguments_[i].size(); j++, p++)
    {
      QL_REQUIRE(p!=params.end(),"Parameter array too small");
      arguments_[i].setParam(j, *p);
    }
  }
  QL_REQUIRE(p==params.end(),"Parameter array too big!");
  update();
}
```

where the *params* function is given by:

```
/*******************************************************************************
params : returns an array of arguments that are calibrated to model
[in] none
[out] Array of parameters
*******************************************************************************/
Array Model::params()
{
  Size size = 0, i;
  for (i=0; i<arguments_.size(); i++)
    size += arguments_[i].size();
  Array params(size);
  Size k = 0;
  for (i=0; i<arguments_.size(); i++)
  {
    for (Size j=0; j<arguments_[i].size(); j++, k++)
      params[k] = arguments_[i].params()[j];
  }
  return params;
}
```

The *CalibrationFunction* class is given by:

```
/**************************************************************************
CalibrationFunction helper class for calibrating model
**************************************************************************/
class Model::CalibrationFunction : public Optimization::CostFunction
{
  public:
    CalibrationFunction(Model* model, CalibrationSet& instruments)
      : model_(model, false), instruments_(instruments) {}
    virtual ~CalibrationFunction() {}

    virtual double value(const Array& params) const
    {
      model_->setParams(params);
      double value = 0.0;
      for (Size i=0; i<instruments_.size(); i++)
      {
        double diff = instruments_[i]->calibrationError();
        value += diff*diff;
      }
      return sqrt(value);
    }
    virtual double finiteDifferenceEpsilon() const { return 1e-6; }
  private:
    Handle<Model> model_;
    CalibrationSet& instruments_;
};
```

The *Problem* class, used for constrained optimization problems, is:

```
/**************************************************************************
Constrained optimization problem
**************************************************************************/
class Problem
{
  public:
    // default constructor
    Problem(CostFunction& f ,              // function and it gradient vector
      Constraint& c,                       // constraint
      Method& meth)                        // optimization method
      : costFunction_(f), constraint_(c), method_(meth) {}

    // call cost function computation and increment evaluation counter
    double value(const Array& x) const;

    // call cost function gradient computation and increment
```

```
    // evaluation counter
    void gradient(Array& grad_f, const Array& x) const;

    // call cost function computation and it gradient
    double valueAndGradient(Array& grad_f, const Array& x) const;

    // Constrained optimization method
    Method& method() const { return method_; }

    // Constraint
    Constraint& constraint() const { return constraint_; }

    // Cost function
    CostFunction& costFunction() const { return costFunction_; }

    // Minimization
    void minimize() const { method_.minimize(*this); }

    Array& minimumValue() const { return method_.x (); }

  protected:
    CostFunction& costFunction_;      // Unconstrained cost function
    Constraint& constraint_;          // Constraint
    Method& method_;                  // constrained optimization method
};


/******************************************************************************
value returns value of cost function at evaluated data points
[in]  Array& x : data points
[out] double    : value of cost function
******************************************************************************/
inline double Problem::value(const Array& x) const {
  method_.functionEvaluation()++;
  return costFunction_.value(x);
}


/******************************************************************************
gradient : computes cost function gradient (first derivative with respect to x)
[in]  Array& grad_f    : gradient function
      Array& x : data points
[out] void
/*****************************************************************************/
inline void Problem::gradient(Array& grad_f, const Array& x) const {
  method_.gradientEvaluation()++;
  costFunction_.gradient(grad_f, x);
}


/******************************************************************************
valueAndGradient : computes both the gradient and cost function with respect to x
[in]  Array& grad_f    : gradient function
      Array& x : data points
[out] double    : value at gradient
*****************************************************************************/
inline double Problem::valueAndGradient(Array& grad_f, const Array& x) const
```

```
{
  method_.functionEvaluation()++;
  method_.gradientEvaluation()++;
  return costFunction_.valueAndGradient(grad_f, x);
}
```

The abstract *CostFunction* class for computing first derivatives is:

```
/***************************************************************************
Cost function abstract class for optimization problem
***************************************************************************/
class CostFunction
{
  public:
    virtual ~CostFunction() {}
    // method to overload to compute the cost functon value in x
    virtual double value(const Array& x) const = 0;

    // method to overload to compute grad_f, the first derivative of
    // the cost function with respect to x
    virtual void gradient(Array& grad, const Array& x) const
    {
      double eps = finiteDifferenceEpsilon(), fp, fm;
      Array xx(x);

      for (int i=0; I <x.size(); i++)
      {
        xx[i] += eps;
        fp = value(xx);
        xx[i] -= 2.0*eps;
        fm = value(xx);
        grad[i] = 0.5*(fp - fm)/eps;
        xx[i] = x[i];
      }
    }

    // method to overload to compute grad_f, the first derivative of
    // the cost function with respect to x and also the cost function
    virtual double valueAndGradient(Array& grad, const Array& x) const
    {
      gradient(grad, x);
      return value(x);
    }

    // Default epsilon for finite difference method :
    virtual double finiteDifferenceEpsilon() const { return 1e-8; }
};
```

Use of a *CalibrationHelper* class has also aided in some of the intermediary calculations used in calibration:

```
/********************************************************************************
Class representing liquid market instruments used during calibration
********************************************************************************/
class CalibrationHelper : public Patterns::Observer, public Patterns::Observable
{
  public:
    CalibrationHelper(const RelinkableHandle<MarketElement>& volatility)
      : volatility_(volatility), blackModel_(volatility_) {
    registerWith(volatility_);
    }

    void update() {
      marketValue_ = blackPrice(volatility_->value());
      notifyObservers();
    }

    // returns the actual price of the instrument (from volatility)
    double marketValue() { return marketValue_; }

    // returns the price of the instrument according to the model
    virtual double modelValue() = 0;

    // returns the error resulting from the model valuation
    virtual double calibrationError() {
      return fabs(marketValue() - modelValue())/marketValue();
    }

    virtual void addTimes(std::list<Time>& times) const = 0;

    // Black volatility implied by the model
    double impliedVolatility(double targetValue,
      double accuracy,
      Size maxEvaluations,
      double minVol,
      double maxVol) const;

    // Black price given a volatility
    virtual double blackPrice(double volatility) const = 0;

    // set pricing engine
    void setPricingEngine(const Handle<PricingEngine>& engine) {
      engine_ = engine;
    }
  protected:
    double marketValue_;
    RelinkableHandle<MarketElement> volatility_;
    Handle<BlackModel> blackModel_;
    Handle<PricingEngine> engine_;
```

```
    private:
      class ImpliedVolatilityHelper;
};
```

```
/****************************************************************************
Set of calibration instruments. For the moment, this is just here to facilitate the
assignment of pricing engine to a set of calibration helpers
****************************************************************************/
class CalibrationSet : public std::vector<Handle<CalibrationHelper> >
{
  public:
    void setPricingEngine(const Handle<PricingEngine>& engine)
    {
      for (Size i=0; i<size(); i++)
        (*this)[i]->setPricingEngine(engine);
    }
};
```

The *CalibrationHelper* contains an *ImpliedVolatilityHelper* class that aids in computing implied volatilities:

```
/****************************************************************************
ImpliedVolatilityHelper nested class used by CalibrationHelper for calibrating
Black volatilities to implied market volatilities
****************************************************************************/
class CalibrationHelper::ImpliedVolatilityHelper : public ObjectiveFunction
{
  public:
    ImpliedVolatilityHelper(const CalibrationHelper& helper, double value)
      : helper_(helper), value_(value) {}

    double operator()(double x) const
    {
      return value_ - helper_.blackPrice(x);
    }
  private:
    const CalibrationHelper& helper_;
    double value_;
};
```

```
/****************************************************************************
impliedVolatility             : computes implied volatility using Brent's 1-dim solver
[in]    double targetValue    : target value
        double accuracy       : degree of accuracy
        Size maxEvaluations   : maximum number of iterations allowed
        double minVol         : minimum volatility constraint
        double maxVol         : maximum volatility constraint
[out] : double                : solution to minimization problem
```

```
****************************************************************************/
double CalibrationHelper::impliedVolatility(double targetValue,
  double accuracy, Size maxEvaluations, double minVol, double maxVol) const
{

  ImpliedVolatilityHelper f(*this,targetValue);
  Solvers1D::Brent solver;
  solver.setMaxEvaluations(maxEvaluations);
  return solver.solve(f,accuracy,volatility_->value(),minVol,maxVol);
}
```

Finally, we use a *calibrateModel* function that accepts the model to be calibrated, sets the optimization routine to be used (i.e., simplex optimization procedure), and acts as a wrapper to other calibration methods that need to be called.
The Black volatilities from the calibrated model are then displayed:

```
/****************************************************************************
calibrateModel: calibrates a model to market data
[in]    Handle<Model>& model    : model used
        CalibrationSet& calibs   : set of instruments to calibrate
        double lambda            : parameter for simplex optimization routine
[out] : void
****************************************************************************/
void calibrateModel(const Handle<Model>& model,
  CalibrationSet& calibs,
  double lambda)
{
  // use simplex method
  Handle<Optimization::Method> om(new Optimization::Simplex(lambda, 1e-9));
  om->setEndCriteria(Optimization::EndCriteria(10000, 1e-7));

  // calibrate model to calibration set
  model->calibrate(calibs, om);
  // output the implied Black volatilities
  int i;
  for (i=0; i<numRows; i++)
  {
    for (int j=0; j<numCols; j++)
    {
      int k = i*numCols + j;
      double npv = calibs[k]->modelValue();
      double implied = calibs[k]->impliedVolatility(npv, 1e-4,1000, 0.05,
        0.50)*100.0;
      cout << implied << " (";
      k = i*10 + j;
      double diff = implied - swaptionVols[k];
      cout << diff << ")";
```

```
    }
    cout << endl;
  }
}
```

An example using these methods is given in Chapter 14 when valuing Bermudan swaptions.

CHAPTER 11

Tree-Building Procedures

In the preceding chapter, we discussed the properties and analytics of various single-factor models. In some cases, such as in the Vasicek, CIR, and Hull-White (HW) models, analytical formulas exist for bond prices and European options on bonds. In some cases, however, when closed-form solutions do not exist such as in the BDT model, it is necessary to build an interest rate tree calibrated to observed market data (i.e., current yield curve and term structure of volatility) to price interest rate derivatives. In this chapter, we discuss the details for building trees for the BDT, Hull-White, and lognormal Hull-White (a particular case of the Black-Karasinski) models. In the BDT, we build a binomial tree that is calibrated first to the initial yield curve and then to both the yield curve and term structure of yield volatilities. Likewise, we build trinomial trees with the Hull-White extended Vasicek and lognormal models calibrated to both the yield curve and the term structure of volatilities. We discuss how to price various interest rate derivatives with these trees including bond options, swaptions, swaps, and caps.

In section 11.1, we discuss building binomial short trees for the BDT short-rate model. In section 11.2, we discuss building the BDT tree calibrated to the yield curve, providing an implementation, while in section 11.3 we build the BDT calibrated to both the initial yield and volatility curves and also provide an implementation. In section 11.4, we discuss how to construct a binomial tree that approximates the Hull-White (extended Vasicek) short rate process consistent with the initial yield curve and provide an implementation. In section 11.5, we discuss constructing a lognormal Hull-White (restricted Black-Karasinski) tree while in section 11.6, we discuss building Hull-White trees calibrated to both the initial yield and volatility curves. Implementions are also given. In section 11.7, we give generic object-oriented implementations for the Vasicek and Black-Karasinski models. In section 11.8, we provide an implementation for the CIR model. In section 11.9, we discuss a general deterministic-shift extension approach to better fit short rate models. In section 11.10, we discuss the shift-extended Vasicek model, and in section 11.11 we discuss the shift-extended CIR model and provide an implementation. Finally, in section 11.12, we use the models to price bond options, swaps, and caps.

11.1   BUILDING BINOMIAL SHORT RATE TREES FOR BLACK, DERMAN, AND TOY

Unlike normal single-factor models like the Vasicek, Hull-White, and CIR, the BDT model does not have analytical tractability to generate explicit closed-form formulas for bond prices and bond option prices. This is due to the lognormal structure of the BDT model. To price interest rate derivatives, a short rate tree has to be built out until the end of the life of the instrument underlying the derivative. In the BDT model, we assume that the initial yield and volatility curves are specified and known (i.e., observable in the market), so that the prices for the discount bonds and their associate yield volatilities for each time step can be calculated. We will build a binomial tree with risk-neutral probabilities that are equal to $\frac{1}{2}$ for up and down branches. The binomial tree works well for models that are described by Jamshidian (1991a) as "Brownian path-independent."

The tree has i time steps, $i = 0, \ldots, N$, and j states at each step, $j = -i, -i + 2, \ldots, i - 2, i$. Thus, there are $i + 1$ states at each time step. Node (i, j) represents state j at time step i. At time step N, j has a centralized binomial distribution with mean 0 and variance N. The tree is constructed so that at each node, the short rate r is determined so that it matches the initial specified market curves. The initial rate $r = r_{0,0}$ is just the yield on the bond that matures at the end of the first period Δt. The initial rate can either go up with probability $\frac{1}{2}$ or down with probability $\frac{1}{2}$. The next step is to choose the short rates, r_u and r_d, from an up movement to node u and a down movement to node d, to match the initial yield curve. To match the initial yield curve, it is necessary to price a bond that matures in two periods, $2\Delta t$, so that the bond has a value of \$1 in the three states at $i = 2$, uu, ud, and dd.

Denote y_k, $k = 1, \ldots, N$, as the yield on a discount bond P_k with maturity $k\Delta t$; that is,

$$P_k = e^{-y_k (k\Delta t)} \tag{11.1}$$

and denote σ_k as the volatility of y_k. In the model, it is assumed that the yields can increase or decrease with equal probability according to the binomial process as shown in Figure 11.1. Consequently, to match the initial volatility curve the following relationship must hold at time step k:

$$y_k^u = y_k^d e^{2\sigma_k \sqrt{\Delta t}}$$

so that

$$\sigma_k = \frac{1}{2\sqrt{\Delta t}} \ln\left(\frac{y_k^u}{y_k^d}\right) \tag{11.2}$$

where y_k^u and y_k^d are determined from the tree as the yields on bonds maturing at time step $k + 1$. Notice that the volatility is dependent on time only.

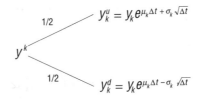

FIGURE 11.1   Model BDT Time Step

To satisfy these two requirements, a numerical procedure such as the Newton-Raphson method can be used. Once r_u and r_d are determined, the next step is to determine the rates r_{uu}, r_{ud}, and r_{dd} by matching the price and yield volatility of a three-period bond and so on for the remaining time steps. Since we are constructing a binomial tree, we can take advantage of the fact that an up movement followed by a down movement is the same as a down movement followed by an up movement to limit the search for two short rates instead of three:[1]

$$r_{ud}^2 = r_{uu} r_{dd}$$

Moreover, at time step k, the following relationships hold:

$$\log\left(\frac{r_{u^k}}{r_{u^{k-1}d}}\right) = \log\left(\frac{r_{u^{k-1}d}}{r_{u^{k-2}d^2}}\right) = \ldots = \log\left(\frac{r_{ud^{k-1}}}{r_{d^k}}\right) \tag{11.3}$$

The BDT tree construction was developed by Jamshidian (1991a) using a technique of forward induction. Jamshidian (1991a) shows that the level of the short rate at time t in the BDT model is given by:

$$r(t) = U(t)e^{(\sigma(t)z(t))} \tag{11.4}$$

where $U(t)$ is the median of the (lognormal) distribution for r at time t, $\sigma(t)$ is the level of the short-rate volatility, and $z(t)$ is the level of standard Brownian motion. $U(t)$ and $\sigma(t)$ are determined at each time step so that the model fits the observable yield and volatility curves. If we assume $\sigma(t)$ is constant so that the model is build to fit only the yield curve, then it is only necessary to determine the median $U(t)$. The level of the short rate is then given by:

$$r(t) = U(t)e^{(\sigma z(t))} \tag{11.5}$$

If j follows a centralized binomial distribution, the process

$$j\sqrt{\Delta t}$$

---

[1]Clewlow and Strickland (1998a), 234.

is distributed with mean 0 and variance t, so that as $\Delta t \to 0$ the process converges to the Wiener process $z(t)$. We can then discretize (11.2) and thus determine the short (Δt-period) rate at the (i, j) node by:

$$r_{i,j} = U(i)e^{(\sigma(i)j\sqrt{\Delta t})} \tag{11.6}$$

so that the time step i replaces t and

$$j\sqrt{\Delta t}$$

replaces $z(t)$. We assume $U(0) = r_{0,0} = y_1$.

Determining $U(i)$ and $\sigma(i)$

We will use Arrow-Debreu state prices to help determine these functions. These are the most fundamental securities and the building blocks of all other securities. Define $Q_{i,j}$ as the value of a security, at time 0, that pays off \$1 if node (i, j) is reached and \$0 otherwise. By definition, $Q_{0,0} = 1$. The $Q_{i,j}$'s can be viewed as discounted probabilities. We can use these discounted probabilities to price a pure discount bond that matures at time $(i + 1)\Delta t$:

$$P_{i+1} = \sum_{j=-i}^{i} Q_{i,j} d_{i,j} \tag{11.7}$$

where $d_{i,j}$ denotes the price at time $i\Delta t$ and state j of the zero-coupon bond maturing at time $(i + 1)\Delta t$. Thus, $d_{i,j}$ is the one-period discount factor (with simple compounding) at node (i, j):

$$d_{i,j} = \frac{1}{1 + r_{i,j}\Delta t} \tag{11.8}$$

If continuous compounding is used, then

$$d_{i,j} = e^{-r_{i,j}\Delta t} \tag{11.9}$$

As we move forward through the tree, we need to update the pure security prices $Q_{i,j}$ at time step i and node j from the known values from the previous time step $i - 1$ based on the following relationship (assuming simple compounding):

$$\begin{aligned}
Q_{i,j} &= \frac{1}{2}Q_{i-1,j-1}d_{i-1,j-1} + \frac{1}{2}Q_{i-1,j+1}d_{i-1,j+1} \quad j = -i+1, \ldots, i-1 \\
&= \frac{1}{2}Q_{i-1,j-1}\frac{1}{1 + r_{i-1,j-1}\Delta t} + \frac{1}{2}Q_{i-1,j+1}\frac{1}{1 + r_{i-1,j+1}\Delta t}
\end{aligned} \tag{11.10}$$

Equation (11.8) states that pure security price at node (i, j) is the sum of the product of the state prices, one-period discount factors, and transitional probabilities for the two nodes that branch into (i, j) at time step $i - 1$. The equation is valid for all nodes at time step i except the upper and lower nodes, (i, i) and $(i, -i)$, which have the values

$$Q_{i,i} = \frac{1}{2}Q_{i-1,j-1}d_{i-1,i-1} \tag{11.11}$$

$$Q_{i,-i} = \frac{1}{2}Q_{i-1,-i+1}d_{i-1,-i+1}$$

11.2   BUILDING THE BDT TREE CALIBRATED TO THE YIELD CURVE

We want to build the following short rate tree as shown in Figure 11.2, so that at each node we need to find the rates that are fitted to the observed yield curve.

In the BDT tree, we will set the mean reversion parameter (the ratio of the slope of the volatility to its level) to zero so that the BDT short rate process becomes:

$$d\ln r = a\bar{r}(t)dt + \sigma dz \tag{11.12}$$

$$r_{i,j} = U(i)e^{(\sigma j\sqrt{\Delta t})}$$

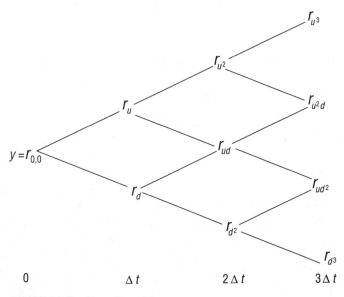

FIGURE 11.2   Short Rate Tree

so that only $\bar{r}(t)$ needs to be calibrated to the yield curve. From equation (11.6), we can rewrite the price of a pure discount bound at time step $i+1$ as

$$P_{i+1} = \sum_{\substack{j=-i \\ step\,2}}^{i} Q_{i,j} \frac{1}{1+U(i)e^{(\sigma j\sqrt{\Delta t})}\Delta t} = \frac{1}{(1+y_{i+1}\Delta t)^{(i+1)\Delta t}} \tag{11.13}$$

If we use continuous compounding, then we solve for $U(i)$ from

$$P_{i+1} = \sum_{\substack{j=-i \\ step\,2}}^{i} Q_{i,j} \exp\left(-U(i)e^{(\sigma j\sqrt{\Delta t})}\Delta t\right) = e^{-y_{i+1}(i+1)\Delta t} \tag{11.14}$$

This equates the market price of pure discount bond on the right-hand side to the BDT model price on the left-hand side. The y_i's are all known from the observable yield curve so that the market price of pure discount bonds P_i is known at each time i. $U(i)$ in equation (11.13) (on the left-hand side) cannot be solved explicitly, so a numerical procedure such as the Newton-Raphson method must be used. Once $U(i)$ is known, we can use equation (11.13) to determine the rates in the tree at time step i.

In the Newton-Raphson method, we make an initial guess for $U(i)$. We keep iterating,

$$U_{i+1} = U_i - \frac{\displaystyle\sum_{\substack{j=-i \\ step\,2}}^{i} Q_{i,j} \frac{1}{1+U_i e^{(\sigma j\sqrt{\Delta t})}\Delta t} - P_{i+1}}{\phi(U_i)} \tag{11.15}$$

updating $U_i = U_{i+1}$ after each iteration until $|U_{i+1} - U_i| < \varepsilon$ where ε is arbitrarily small (i.e., 0.0001) and

$$\phi(U_i) = \frac{\partial P_{i+1}}{\partial U_i} = \sum_{\substack{j=-i \\ step\,2}}^{i} Q_{i,j} \frac{1}{(1+U_i e^{(\sigma j\sqrt{\Delta t})}\Delta t)^2} e^{\sigma j\sqrt{\Delta t}}\Delta t \tag{11.16}$$

The following are the steps to build the tree. We assume that $i > 0$; that we are using simple compounding; and that $U(i-1)$, $Q_{i-1,j}$, $r_{i-1,j}$, and $d_{i-1,j}$ have been found for all j at time step $i-1$. We can start construction of the tree from the initial values: $U(0) = r_{0,0}$, $Q_{0,0} = 1$, $d_{0,0} = 1/(1+r_{0,0}\Delta t)$. At each time step i, we compute the $Q_{i,j}$ from (11.10) and (11.11). We then solve for $U(i)$ from P_{i+1} in (11.13) by fitting the observable yield (and thus bond price) to the model price. Once we determine $U(i)$, we can calculate the short rate and compute the discount factors for all nodes at time i from (11.6) and (11.8).

TABLE 11.1   Yield Curve
Term Structure

Maturity	Yield
1	0.0500
2	0.0575
3	0.0625
4	0.0675
5	0.0700

As an example, suppose that the initial yield curve has the structure shown in Table 11.1, with a constant short rate volatility of 10 percent and time steps of $\Delta t = 1$. $U(0) = r_{0,0} = 0.05$; $d_{0,0} = P_1 = 1/(1 + 0.05(1)) = 0.9524$; $Q_{1,1} = Q_{1,-1} = Q_{0,0}(0.5)(0.9524) = 0.4762$; $P_2 = 1/(1 + (0.0575)(1))^2 = 0.8942$. We need to solve for $U(1)$ as the solution to:

$$P_2 = \sum_{\substack{j=-1 \\ step2}}^{1} Q_{1,j} \frac{1}{1 + U(1)e^{(\sigma j \sqrt{\Delta t})}}$$

$$= (0.4762)\frac{1}{1 + U(1)e^{(0.1*(1)*\sqrt{1})}(1)} + (0.4762)\frac{1}{1 + U(1)e^{(0.1*(-1)*\sqrt{1})}(1)}$$

$$= 0.8942$$

Solving this equation by the Newton-Raphson method using equations (11.15) and (11.16) yields $U(1) = 0.0498$ so that at node (1, 1):

$$r_{1,1} = (0.0498)e^{(0.10*(1)*\sqrt{1})} = 5.5\%, \quad d_{1,1} = 1/(1 + (0.055)(1)) = 0.9479$$

and at node (1, –1):

$$r_{1,-1} = (0.0498)e^{(0.10*(-1)*\sqrt{1})} = 4.51\%, \quad d_{1,-1} = 1/(1 + (0.0451)(1)) = 0.9569$$

At time step $i = 2$, we compute $Q_{2,2} = 0.5Q_{1,1}d_{1,1} = 0.5(0.4762)(0.9479) = 0.2257$, $Q_{2,-2} = 0.5Q_{1,-1}d_{1,-1} = 0.5(0.4762)(0.9569) = 0.2257$, and $Q_{2,0} = 0.5Q_{1,1}d_{1,1} + 0.5Q_{1,-1}d_{1,-1} = 0.2257 + 0.2278 = 0.4535$. Now, we solve for $U(2)$,

$$P_3 = \sum_{\substack{j=-2 \\ step2}}^{2} Q_{2,j} \frac{1}{(1 + U(2)e^{(0.1 j \sqrt{\Delta t})})}$$

$$= (0.2257)\frac{1}{(1 + U(2)e^{(0.1*2*\sqrt{1})})} + (0.4535)\frac{1}{(1 + U(2)e^{(0.1*0*\sqrt{1})})} + (0.2278)\frac{1}{(1 + U(2)e^{(0.1*(-2)*\sqrt{1})})}$$

$$= 0.8824$$

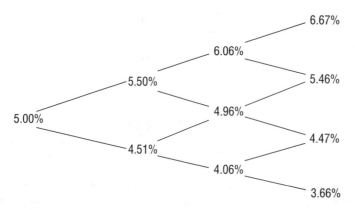

FIGURE 11.3 $N = 3$ Short Rate Tree

Solving for $U(2)$ using Newton-Raphson, we get $U(2) = 0.0496$. We can now determine the short rates and discount factors at $i = 2$.

$$r_{2,2} = (0.0496)e^{(0.1*2*\sqrt{1})} = 6.06\%, \quad d_{2,2} = 1/(1+(0.0606)(1)) = 0.9428$$

$$r_{2,0} = (0.0496)e^{(0.1*0*\sqrt{1})} = 4.96\%, \quad d_{2,0} = 1/(1+(0.0496)(1)) = 0.9527$$

$$r_{2,-2} = (0.0496)e^{(0.1*-2*\sqrt{1})} = 4.06\%, \quad d_{2,-2} = 1/(1+(0.0406)(1)) = 0.9610$$

The short rate tree for $N = 3$ is given in Figure 11.3.
The following is code to build the BDT tree:

```
/**************************************************************************
buildBDT                              : constructs a BDT tree calibrated to the yield
[in]   vector<double> yield_curve     : vector of yield curve
       int N                          : number of time steps
       int T                          : time to maturity
       double inityield               : initial guess for Newton-Raphson method
[out] void
**************************************************************************/
void BlackDermanToy::buildBDT(vector<double> yield_curve, double vol, int N, double
  T, double inityield)
{
  double U[20] = {0.0};                // median of the (lognormal) distribution for
                                       // r at time t
  double dt = 0.0;                     // time step
  double P[20] = {0.0};                // bond prices
  double R[20] = {0.0};                // discount factors
  const double epsilon = 0.001;        // error tolerance in numerical search
  double error = 0.0;                  // error between model and target values
```

```
double sum1 = 0.0;                  // sum of first derivatives
double sum2 = 0.0;                  // sum of second derivatives
double alpha1 = 0.05;               // parameter to calibrate U(i)
double alpha2 = 0.0;                // updates alpha1 in numerical search
int i,j;

// precompute constants - assume 1 year time steps
dt = 1;

// initialize yield curve
for (i = 1; i <= N; i++)
{
  R[i] = yield_curve[i-1];
  P[i] = 1/(pow((1 + R[i]*dt),i*dt));
}

// initialize first node
Q[0][0] = 1;
P[0] = 1;
U[0] = yield_curve[0];
r[0][0] = yield_curve[0];
d[0][0] = 1/(1 + r[0][0]*dt)

// evolve the tree for the short rate
for (i = 1; i <= N; i++)
{
// update pure security prices at time i
  Q[i][-i] = 0.5*Q[i-1][-i+1]*d[i-1][-i+1];
  Q[i][i] = 0.5*Q[i-1][i-1]*d[i-1][i-1];
  for (j = -i+2; j <= i-2; j += 2)
    {
  Q[i][j] = 0.5*Q[i-1][j-1]*d[i-1][j-1] + 0.5*Q[i-1][j+1]*d[i-1][j+1];
    }
  // use numerical search to solve for U[i]
  // Newton-Raphson method
  alpha1 = inityield;
  do
  {
    sum1 = 0;
    sum2 = 0;
    for (j = -i; j <= i; j += 2)
    {
      sum1 += Q[i][j]*(1/(1 + alpha1*exp(vol*j*sqrt(dt))*dt));
      sum2 += Q[i][j]*(pow((1+ alpha1*exp(vol*j*sqrt(dt))*dt),-
        2)*exp(vol*j*sqrt(dt))*dt);
    }
    alpha2 = alpha1 - (sum1 - P[i+1])/(-sum2);
    error = alpha2 - alpha1;
    alpha1 = alpha2;
  }
  while (error > epsilon);
  U[i] = alpha1;
  // set r[.] and d[.]
```

```
for (j = -i; j <= i; j+= 2)
{
   r[i][j] = U[i]*exp(vol*j*sqrt(dt));
   d[i][j] = 1/(1 + r[i][j]*dt);
}
}
}
```

11.3   BUILDING THE BDT TREE CALIBRATED TO THE YIELD AND VOLATILITY CURVE

We will now extend the BDT model to fit both the rate and volatility struc-tures. In order to fit the term structure of volatilities, the volatility is now time-dependent so that the level of the short rate at node (i, j) is

$$r_{i,j} = U(i)e^{(\sigma(i)j\sqrt{\Delta t})} \tag{11.17}$$

In order to calibrate to both the spot rate yield and volatility curves, we need to now solve for two discount functions, P_{i+1}^u and P_{i+1}^d, for all $i \geq 2$ (we have two un-knowns, $U(i)$ and σ_i, so we need two equations) where P_{i+1}^u and P_{i+1}^d are related to the known market discount bond prices at time i, P_i, by:

$$\frac{1}{(1+r_{0,0}\Delta t)}(0.5P_i^u + 0.5P_i^d) = P_i \quad i = 2, \ldots, N \tag{11.18}$$

where u denotes the up node and d denotes the down node. The initial volatilities can be recovered from equation (11.2) by expressing the volatility in terms of P_i^u and P_i^d:

$$\sigma(i) = \frac{1}{2\sqrt{\Delta t}}\ln\left(\frac{\ln P_i^u}{\ln P_i^d}\right) \quad i = 2, \ldots, N \tag{11.19}$$

Solving equations (11.18) and (11.19) simultaneously yields:

$$P_i^d = P_i^{u^{\exp(-2\sigma(i)\sqrt{\Delta t})}} \tag{11.20}$$

where P_i^u is found as the solution to:

$$P_i^u = P_i^{u^{\exp(-2\sigma(i)\sqrt{\Delta t})}} = 2P_i(1+r_{0,0}\Delta t) \tag{11.21}$$

Equation (11.21) cannot be solved explicitly for P_i^u so a numerical search procedure like the Newton-Raphson method must be used. Forward induction from the initial starting values is used to determine the time-dependent functions that ensure consistency with the initial yield curve data.[2] The state prices are determined from the state prices at both the up and down nodes, u and d, respectively, where

$$Q_{i,j}^u = \frac{1}{2}Q_{i-1,j-1}^u d_{i-1,j-1} + \frac{1}{2}Q_{i-1,j+1}^u d_{i-1,j+1} \tag{11.22}$$

$$Q_{i,j}^d = \frac{1}{2}Q_{i-1,j-1}^d d_{i-1,j-1} + \frac{1}{2}Q_{i-1,j+1}^d d_{i-1,j+1} \tag{11.23}$$

$Q_{i,j}^u$ is the value of a security that pays off \$1 if node (i, j) is reached and zero otherwise as seen from node u. Similarly, $Q_{i,j}^d$ is the value of a security that pays off \$1 if node (i, j) is reached and zero otherwise as seen from node d. By definition, $Q_{1,1}^u$ = 1 and $Q_{1,-1}^d$ = 1. The tree is constructed similarly to the procedure outlined in the previous section except there are now two equations to compute, similar to (11.7):

$$P_{i+1}^u = \sum_{\substack{j=-1 \\ step2}}^{i} Q_{i,j}^u d_{i,j} \tag{11.24}$$

$$P_{i+1}^d = \sum_{\substack{j=-i \\ step2}}^{i} Q_{i,j}^d d_{i,j} \tag{11.25}$$

and where now the discount factor is:

$$d_{i,j} = \frac{1}{1 + r_{i,j}\Delta t} = \frac{1}{1 + U(i)e^{(\sigma(i)j\sqrt{\Delta t})}\Delta t} \tag{11.26}$$

Equations (11.24) and (11.25) define two equations with two unknowns, $U(i)$ and $\sigma(i)$, which can be solved by a two-dimensional Newton-Raphson method.[3] We fit the BDT model to both the yield and volatility curves by equating the model prices P_{i+1}^u and P_{i+1}^d to the observed market prices P_i:

$$P_{i+1}^u = \sum_{\substack{j=-i \\ step2}}^{i} Q_{i,j}^u \frac{1}{1 + U(i)e^{(\sigma(i)j\sqrt{\Delta t})}\Delta t} = \frac{1}{(1 + y_{i+1}\Delta t)^{(i+1)\Delta t}} \tag{11.27}$$

---

[2]Ibid., 241.
[3]Ibid., 241.

$$P_{i+1}^d = \sum_{\substack{j=-i \\ step\,2}}^{i} Q_{i,j}^d \frac{1}{1 + U(i)e^{(\sigma(i)j\sqrt{\Delta t})}\Delta t} = \frac{1}{(1 + y_{i+1}\Delta t)^{(i+1)\Delta t}} \tag{11.28}$$

Note that adding (11.28) to (11.27) gives equation (11.18). It is necessary to start with initial values (guesses) for $U(i)$ and $\sigma(i)$. The two-dimensional Newton-Raphson method computes the following equations simultaneously:

$$U_{i+1}^u = U_i - \frac{\displaystyle\sum_{\substack{j=-i \\ step\,2}}^{i} Q_{i,j}^u \frac{1}{1 + U_i e^{(\sigma_i j\sqrt{\Delta t})}\Delta t} - P_{i+1}^u}{-\phi^u(U_i,\,\sigma_i)} \tag{11.29}$$

$$U_{i+1}^d = U_i - \frac{\displaystyle\sum_{\substack{j=-i \\ step\,2}}^{i} Q_{i,j}^d \frac{1}{1 + U_i e^{(\sigma_i j\sqrt{\Delta t})}\Delta t} - P_{i+1}^d}{-\phi^d(U_i,\,\sigma_i)} \tag{11.30}$$

$$\sigma_{i+1}^u = \sigma_i - \frac{\displaystyle\sum_{\substack{j=-i \\ step\,2}}^{i} Q_{i,j}^u \frac{1}{1 + U_i e^{(\sigma_i j\sqrt{\Delta t})}\Delta t} - P_{i+1}^u}{-\gamma^u(U_i,\,\sigma_i)} \tag{11.31}$$

$$\sigma_{i+1}^d = \sigma_i - \frac{\displaystyle\sum_{\substack{j=-i \\ step\,2}}^{i} Q_{i,j}^d \frac{1}{1 + U_i e^{(\sigma_i j\sqrt{\Delta t})}\Delta t} - P_{i+1}^d}{-\gamma^d(U_i,\,\sigma_i)} \tag{11.32}$$

where

$$\phi^u(U_i,\,\sigma_i) = \frac{\partial P_{i+1}^u}{\partial U_i} = \sum_{\substack{j=-i \\ step\,2}}^{i} Q_{i,j}^u \frac{1}{(1 + U_i e^{(\sigma_i j\sqrt{\Delta t})}\Delta t)^2} e^{(\sigma_i j\sqrt{\Delta t})}\Delta t \tag{11.33}$$

$$\phi^d(U_i,\,\sigma_i) = \frac{\partial P_{i+1}^d}{\partial U_i} = \sum_{\substack{j=-i \\ step\,2}}^{i} Q_{i,j}^d \frac{1}{(1 + U_i e^{(\sigma_i j\sqrt{\Delta t})}\Delta t)^2} e^{(\sigma_i j\sqrt{\Delta t})}\Delta t \tag{11.34}$$

$$\gamma^u(U_i,\,\sigma_i)=\frac{\partial P^u_{i+1}}{\partial\sigma_i}=\sum_{\substack{j=-i\\ step\,2}}^{i}Q^u_{i,j}\frac{1}{(1+U_ie^{(\sigma_i j\sqrt{\Delta t})}\Delta t)^2}(U_ij\sqrt{\Delta t})e^{(\sigma_i j\sqrt{\Delta t})}\Delta t \qquad (11.35)$$

$$\gamma^d(U_i,\,\sigma_i)=\frac{\partial P^d_{i+1}}{\partial\sigma_i}=\sum_{\substack{j=-i\\ step\,2}}^{i}Q^d_{i,j}\frac{1}{(1+U_ie^{(\sigma_i j\sqrt{\Delta t})}\Delta t)^2}(U_ij\sqrt{\Delta t})e^{(\sigma_i j\sqrt{\Delta t})}\Delta t \qquad (11.36)$$

updating $U_i = U^u_{i+1}$ and $\sigma_i = \sigma^u_{i+1}$ at each iteration until $|\,U^u_{i+1} - U_i\,| < \varepsilon$, $|\,U^d_{i+1} - U_i\,| < \varepsilon$, $|\,\sigma^u_{i+1} - \sigma_i\,| < \varepsilon$, and $|\,\sigma^d_{i+1} - \sigma_i\,| < \varepsilon$, for arbitrarily small $\varepsilon > 0$ (i.e., 0.0001).

The following are the steps to build the tree. We assume that $i > 0$, that we are using simple compounding, $\Delta t = 1$, and that $U(i-1)$, $\sigma(i-1)$, $Q^u_{i-1,j}$, $Q^d_{i-1,j}$, $r_{i-1,j}$ and $d_{i-1,j}$ have been determined for all j at time step $i-1$. We can start construction of the tree from the initial values:

$$U(0) = r_{0,0},\ \sigma(0) = \sigma_0,\ Q^u_{1,1} = 1,\ Q^d_{1,-1} = 1,\ d_{0,0} = 1/(1 + r_{0,0}\,\Delta t)$$

At each time step i, we compute the $Q^u_{i,j}$ and $Q^d_{i,j}$ from equations (11.22) and (11.23). We then solve for $U(i)$ from P_{i+1} in (11.13) by fitting the observable yield (and thus bond price) to the model price. Once we determine $U(i)$, we can calculate the short rate and compute the discount factors for all nodes at time i from (11.26).

Using the values of the previous example, we can construct a BDT tree calibrated to the yield and volatility curves. Suppose that the yield curve is as before and the volatility curve is as shown in Table 11.2.

The initial values of tree for $i = 1$ are:

$$U(0) = r_{0,0} = 0.05,\ Q^u_{1,1} = 1.0,\ Q^d_{1,-1} = 1.0,\ \text{and } \sigma(0) = \sigma_0 = 0.10$$

Using the yield curve, we compute P_i, $i = 2, \ldots, N$. For example, $P_2 = 1/(1 + 0.0575(1))^2 = 0.8942$ and $P_3 = 1/(1 + 0.0625(1))^3 = 0.8337$. Next, for $i = 2$,

TABLE 11.2 Short Rate Volatility Term Structure

Maturity	Volatility
1	0.1000
2	0.0950
3	0.0900
4	0.0850
5	0.0800

we need to solve for P_2^u by solving the equation using the Newton-Raphson method:

$$P_2^u + P_2^{u^{\exp(-\sigma_2 2\sqrt{\Delta t})}} = 2P_2(1 + r_{0,0}\Delta t)$$

Plugging in the values,

$$P_2^u + P_2^{u^{\exp(-(0.09)2\sqrt{1})}} = 2(0.8942)(1 + 0.05(1))$$

The solution is $P_2^u = 0.9336$ so that

$$P_2^d = (0.9336)^{\exp(-2(0.09)\sqrt{1})} = 0.9442$$

For $i = 3$, we solve for

$$P_3^u + P_3^{u^{\exp(-(0.08)2\sqrt{1})}} = 2(0.8337)(1 + 0.05(1))$$

Solving, we find $P_3^u = 0.8659$ and

$$P_3^d = (0.8659)^{\exp(-2(0.08)\sqrt{1})} = 0.8845$$

We can now find the values of $U(1)$ and $\sigma(1)$ as the solutions to

$$P_2^u = Q_{1,1}^u \frac{1}{1 + U(1)e^{(\sigma(1)(1\sqrt{1}))}(1)} = \frac{1}{1 + U(1)e^{(\sigma(1))}}$$

and

$$P_2^d = Q_{1,-1}^d \frac{1}{1 + U(1)e^{(\sigma(1)(-1\sqrt{1}))}(1)} = \frac{1}{1 + U(1)e^{(-\sigma(1))}}$$

with the two-dimensional Newton-Raphson method given by equations (11.29) to (11.36). The solution yields $U(1) = 0.0648$ and $\sigma(1) = 0.0923$.

It is important to note that the solution is *highly sensitive* to the initial values used and may give different values for different initial values and may not even converge at all if poor initial values are chosen.[4]

We can now determine the short rates and discount factors:

$$r_{1,1} = U(1)e^{(\sigma(1)(1)\sqrt{1})}(1) = (0.0648)e^{0.0923} = 0.0711$$

$$r_{1,-1} = U(1)e^{(\sigma(1)(-1)\sqrt{1})}(1) = (0.0648)e^{-0.0923} = 0.0591$$

$$d_{1,1} = \frac{1}{1+r_{1,1}\Delta t} = \frac{1}{1+(0.0711)(1)} = 0.9336$$

$$d_{1,-1} = \frac{1}{1+r_{1,1}\Delta t} = \frac{1}{1+(0.0591)(1)} = 0.9442$$

We can now solve for the pure security prices $Q^u_{2,2}, Q^u_{2,0}$, $Q^d_{2,-2}$, and $Q^d_{2,0}$ using the discount factors at time step 1 and then find $U(2)$ and $\sigma(2)$ as solutions to:

$$P^u_3 = 0.8660 = \sum_{\substack{j=0 \\ step\,2}}^{2} Q^u_{2,j} \frac{1}{1+U(2)e^{(\sigma(2)j\sqrt{1})}(1)}$$

$$= (0.4668)\frac{1}{1+U(2)e^{(\sigma(2)(0)\sqrt{1})}(1)} + (0.4668)\frac{1}{1+U(2)e^{(\sigma(2)(2)\sqrt{1})}(1)}$$

and

$$P^d_3 = 0.8846 = \sum_{\substack{j=-2 \\ step\,2}}^{0} Q^d_{2,j} \frac{1}{1+U(2)e^{(\sigma(2)j\sqrt{1})}(1)}$$

$$= (0.4721)\frac{1}{1+U(2)e^{(\sigma(2)(-2)\sqrt{1})}(1)} + (0.4721)\frac{1}{1+U(2)e^{(\sigma(2)(0)\sqrt{1})}(1)}$$

The solution yields $U(2) = 0.0724$ and $\sigma(2) = 0.0739$. The short rates and discount factors at $i = 2$ can then be computed and successively used in forward induction.

---

[4]It is always a good idea to test the model with different starting values to see if the values change and how stable they are. In the current example, initial guesses of $U_0 = 0.05$ and $\sigma_0 = 0.092$ were used.

The following is the code to build a BDT tree calibrated to the yield curve and volatility curve:

```
/*********************************************************************************
buildBDT : constructs a BDT tree calibrated to the yield curve and volatility curve
[in]    vector<double> yield_curve        : vector of yield curve
        vector<double> volatility_curve   : vector of volatility curves
        int N                             : number of time steps
        double T                          : time to maturity
[out] : void
*********************************************************************************/
void BlackDermanToy::buildBDT(vector<double> yield_curve,vector<double>
  volatility_curve, int N, double T)
{
  double r[20][20] = {0.0};              // short rate at node i, j
  double U[20] = {0.0};                  // median of the (lognormal)
                                         // distribution for r at time t
  double dt = 0.0;                       // time step
  double volR[20] = {0.0};               // short rate volatiliy
  double vol[20] = {0.0};                // stores calibrated volatility
                                         // parameter
  double P[20] = {0.0};                  // discount bond prices
  double Pu[20] = {0.0};                 // price of bond in up movement
  double Pd[20] = {0.0};                 // price of bond in down movement
  double Qu[20][20] = {0.0};             // state securities (Arrow-Debreu)
                                         // prices for an up movement
  double Qd[20][20] = {0.0};             // state securities (Arrow-Debreu)
                                         // prices for a down movement
  double R[20] = {0.0};                  // discount curve rates
  const double epsilon = 0.0001;         // error tolerance level
  double error, error1, error2 = 0.0;    // errors computed in numerical search
  double error3, error4 = 0.0;           // errors computed in numerical search
  double sum1, sum2 = 0.0;               // sums of first derivatives
  double sum3, sum4 = 0.0;               // sums of second derivatives
  double volSum1, volSum2 = 0.0;         // sum of volatilities
  double sigVal1 = 0.0;                  // calibrated volatility parameter
  double sigVal2, sigVal3 = 0.0;         // computed volatilities in numerical
                                         // search
  double alpha1 = 0.05;                  // calibrated U(i) parameter
  double alpha2 = 0.0;                   // updated alpha1 (U(i)) parameter
  double alpha3 = 0.10;                  // computed U(i) parameter in numerical
                                         // search
  int i,j;

  // precompute constants - assume one year time step
  dt = 1;

  // initialize yield and volatility curves

  for (i = 1; i <= N; i++)

  {
```

```
    R[i] = yield_curve[i-1];
    P[i] = 1/(pow((1 + R[i]*dt),i*dt)));
    volR[i] = volatility_curve[i-1];
}

// initialize nodes
U[0] = R[1];
r[0][0] = R[1];
d[0][0] = 1/(1 + r[0][0]*dt);
vol[0] = volR[1];
Qu[1][1] = 1;
Qd[1][-1] = 1;

// compute Pu[.] and Pd[.]
for (i = 2; i <= N; i++)
{
    // solve the following for Pu[i]
    sum1 = 0;
    sum2 = 0;
    error = 0;
    alpha1 = 0.92;

    do
    {
        sum1 = (alpha1 + pow(alpha1,exp(-2*volR[i]*sqrt(dt))))/(2*(1 + r[0][0]*dt));
        sum2 = (1/(2*(1 + r[0][0]*dt)))*(1 + exp(-2*volR[i]*sqrt(dt))*
            (pow(alpha1,exp(-2*volR[i]*sqrt(dt)) - 1)));
        alpha2 = alpha1 - (sum1 - P[i])/(sum2);
        error = abs(alpha2 - alpha);
        alpha1 = alpha2;
    }
    while (error > epsilon);

    Pu[i] = alpha1;
    Pd[i] = pow(Pu[i],exp(-2*volR[i]*sqrt(dt)));
}

// evolve tree for the short rate
for (i = 1; i < N; i++)
{
    // update pure security prices at time step i
    if (i > 1)
    {
        for (j = -i+2; j <= i; j += 2)
        {
            Qu[i][j]= 0.5*Qu[i-1][j-1]*d[i-1][j-1] + 0.5*Qu[i-1][j+1]*d[i-1][j+1];
        }

        for (j = i-2; j >= -i; j -= 2)
        {
            Qd[i][j] =0.5*Qd[i-1][j-1]*d[i-1][j-1] + 0.5*Qd[i-1][j+1]*d[i-1][j+1];
        }
    }
```

```
// solve simultaneously for U[i] and sig[i]
// using 2 dimensional Newton-Raphson
// initial guess
alpha1 = 0.05;
sigVal1 = 0.092;

do
{
  sum1 = 0;
  sum2 = 0;
  sum3 = 0;
  sum4 = 0;
  volSum1 = 0;
  volSum2 = 0;
  for (j = -i; j <= i; j += 2)
  {
    sum1 += Qu[i][j]*(1/(1 + alpha1*exp(sigVal1*j*sqrt(dt))*dt));
    sum2 += Qu[i][j]*(pow((1+alpha1*exp(sigVal1*j*sqrt(dt))*dt),-
      2)*(exp(sigVal1*j*sqrt(dt))*dt));
    volSum1 += Qu[i][j]*(pow((1+ alpha1*exp(sigVal1*j*sqrt(dt))*dt),-
      2)*(alpha1*(j*sqrt(dt))*
      dt*exp(sigVal1*j*sqrt(dt))));

    sum3 += Qd[i][j]*(1/(1 + alpha1*exp(sigVal1*j*sqrt(dt))*dt));
    sum4 += Qd[i][j]*(pow((1+ alpha1*exp(sigVal1*j*sqrt(dt))*dt),-
      2)*(exp(sigVal1*j*sqrt(dt))*dt));
    volSum2 += Qd[i][j]*(pow((1+ alpha1*exp(sigVal1*j*sqrt(dt))*dt),-2)*
      (alpha1*(j*sqrt(dt))*dt*exp(sigVal1*j*sqrt(dt))));
  }
  alpha2 = alpha1 - (sum1 - Pu[i+1])/(-sum2);
  error = abs(alpha2 - alpha1);
  alpha1 = alpha2;

  sigVal2 = sigVal1 - (sum1 - Pu[i+1])/(-volSum1);
  error1 = abs(sigVal2 - sigVal1);
  sigVal1 = sigVal2;

  alpha3 = alpha1 - (sum3 - Pd[i+1])/(-sum4);
  error3 = abs(alpha3 - alpha1);

  sigVal3 = sigVal1 - (sum3 - Pd[i+1])/(-volSum2);
  error4 = abs(sigVal3 - sigVal1);
  sigVal1 = sigVal3;
}
while ((error > epsilon) || (error1 > epsilon) || (error3 > epsilon) ||
  (error4 > epsilon));

U[i] = alpha;
vol[i] = sigVal1;

// set r[.] and d[.]
for (j = -i; j <= i; j += 2)
{
```

```
        r[i][j] = U[i]*exp(vol[i]*j*sqrt(dt));
        d[i][j] = 1/(1 + r[i][j]*dt);
    }
  }
}
```

11.4   BUILDING A HULL-WHITE TREE CONSISTENT WITH THE YIELD CURVE

Hull and White (1994) developed a general tree-building procedure (of a trinomial tree) to calibrate the HW extended Vasicek model:[5]

$$dr = a(\bar{r}(t) - r)dt + \sigma dz$$

or in its more common form,

$$dr = (\theta(t) - ar)dt + \sigma dz \tag{11.37}$$

to the yield curve. The approach can be used in constructing a BDT tree. In the BDT model, we built a binomial process with fixed probabilities (equal to $1/2$) and time steps, leaving only the freedom of adjusting the space step. For Hull-White trinomial trees, both the time and space steps are fixed (though they can be varied), allowing us the freedom to adjust the probabilities so that the changes in the short rate have the correct mean and standard deviation over each time interval Δt for the short rate process we are approximating.

In the first stage, Hull and White build a trinomial tree for the short rate $x = x(t)$ that follows the process in (10.86),

$$dx = axdt + \sigma dz, \qquad x(0) = 0$$

The process is symmetrical around $x = 0$ and $dx(t) = x(t + \Delta t) - x(t) \sim N(-ax(t)\Delta t, \sigma^2 \Delta t)$ for small time changes (assuming terms of higher order than Δt are ignored) so that both mean and variance of changes in x at each step are finite and normally distributed. The state space (i.e., the spacing between interest rates on the tree, Δr) is set to:

$$\Delta r = \sigma\sqrt{3\Delta t}$$

---

[5]In many books and papers, the model is written in a more general form: $dr = (\theta(t) - r)dt + \sigma dz$, where $\theta(t) = a\bar{r}(t)$.

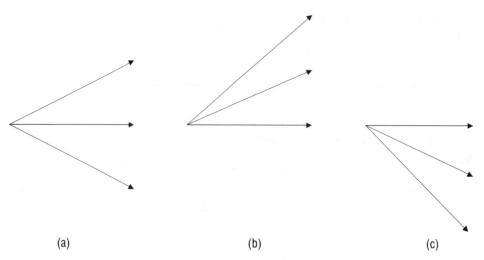

(a)   (b)   (c)

FIGURE 11.4   Three Alternative Branching Processes

where Δt is the length of each time step.[6]

The tree is built with N time steps denoted by $i = 1, \ldots, N$ with j nodes, $j = -i, -i + 1 \ldots, i - 1, i$ at each time step. The nodes are assumed to be evenly spaced in x and t, though this assumption can be relaxed and the tree can be built by letting changes in x and t vary (with the time step) (i.e., Δx_i and Δt_i).[7] Denote (i, j) as the node for which $t = i\Delta t$ and $x = j\Delta r$. At the (i, j) node, $x = r_{0,0} + j\Delta r$ and x can move up to the upper node $(i + 1, k + 1)$ with probability $p_{i,j}^u$, move to the center node $(i + 1, k)$ with probability $p_{i,j}^m$, and move down to the lower node $(i + 1, k - 1)$ with probability $p_{i,j}^d$. The integer n is chosen so that $r_{i,k}$ is as close to the mean of r. Thus, $p_{i,j}^u$, $p_{i,j}^m$, and $p_{i,j}^d$ are the probabilities of the highest, middle, and lowest branches leading from node (i, j) that sum to unity. The probabilities are constrained to all be positive. There are three possible alternative branching processes shown in Figure 11.4.

In terms of a mean-reverting short rate, the branching process in (a) is a normal branching process where the short rate can move up by Δr, stay the same, or move down by Δr. The branching process in (b) is the case where the short rate is currently low and can move up by $2\Delta r$, move up by Δr, or stay the same. The branching process in (c) is the case where the short rate is currently high and can stay the same, move down by Δr, or move down by $2\Delta r$. The branching process

---

[6]This relationship between Δr and Δt is considered a good choice since it satisfies stability convergence conditions of the trinomial method, which is the same as an explicit finite-difference scheme.
[7]Hull (1996), 69–72.

in (b) and (c) represent the mean-reversion movement of the short rate to its long-run average, from below and above, respectively. Because of the incorporation of mean reversion into the model, we cannot determine the upper and lower nodes of the state index j, where the branching process changes, until the tree is constructed. Note, however, that the expected value of the short rate at the next time step is at the central node. For the normal branching process in (a), $k = j$, and for the branching processes in (b) and (c), $k = j + 1$ and $k = j - 1$, respectively.

Most of the time, the normal branching process in (a) is appropriate, especially if there is little or no mean reversion ($a = 0$). However, when the mean reversion rate is positive (i.e., $a > 0$), it is necessary to switch to the branching process (c) for a sufficiently large j. Similarly, if $a > 0$, it is necessary to switch from the branching in (a) to the branching process in (b) when j is sufficiently negative. The converse of these cases holds if $a < 0$.

Define $\bar{j}$ as the value of j where we switch from branching in (a) to the branching in (c) and $\underline{j}$ as the value of j where we switch from the branching in (a) to the branching in (b). Hull and White show that if

$$\bar{j} = \left\lceil \frac{0.1835}{(a\Delta t)} \right\rceil \text{ and } \underline{j} = -\left\lceil \frac{0.1835}{(a\Delta t)} \right\rceil$$

(i.e., $\bar{j}$ is set to the smallest integer greater than $0.1835/(a\Delta t)$ and $\underline{j} = -\bar{j}$), then the probabilities are always positive. At $\bar{j}$ and $\underline{j}$, the tree gets "truncated" so that no states higher than $\bar{j}$ or lower than $\underline{j}$ are computed. This is accomplished by changing the branching process from (a) to (c) if state $\bar{j}$ is reached and changing the branching process from (a) to (b) if $\underline{j}$ is reached. Following Hull and White, if the branching process from node (i, j) is as in (a), then we can compute the probabilities from the following three equations (the first equation matches short rate changes to the mean, the second matches it to the variance, and the third sums the probabilities to unity):

$$p_{i,j}^u \Delta r - p_{i,j}^d \Delta r = -aj\Delta r\Delta t$$

$$p_{i,j}^u \Delta r^2 + p_{i,j}^d \Delta r^2 = \sigma^2\Delta t + a^2 j^2\Delta r^2\Delta t^2$$

$$p_{i,j}^u + p_{i,j}^m + p_{i,j}^d = 1$$

Solving these three equations for the probabilities, we find (using $\Delta r^2 = 3\sigma^2\Delta t$):

$$p_{i,j}^u = \frac{1}{6} + \frac{a^2 j^2\Delta t^2 - aj\Delta t}{2}$$

$$p_{i,j}^m = \frac{2}{3} - a^2 j^2\Delta t^2 \qquad (11.38)$$

$$p_{i,j}^d = \frac{1}{6} + \frac{a^2 j^2\Delta t^2 + aj\Delta t}{2}$$

If the branching process is as in (b) as when state j is reached, the probabilities are:

$$p_{i,j}^u = \frac{1}{6} + \frac{a^2 j^2 \Delta t^2 + aj\Delta t}{2}$$

$$p_{i,j}^m = -\frac{1}{3} - a^2 j^2 \Delta t^2 - 2aj\Delta t \qquad (11.39)$$

$$p_{i,j}^d = \frac{7}{6} + \frac{a^2 j^2 \Delta t^2 + 3aj\Delta t}{2}$$

and if the branching process is as in (c) as when state $\bar{j}$ is reached, the probabilities are:

$$p_{i,j}^u = \frac{7}{6} + \frac{a^2 j^2 \Delta t^2 - 3aj\Delta t}{2}$$

$$p_{i,j}^m = -\frac{1}{3} - a^2 j^2 \Delta t^2 + 2aj\Delta t \qquad (11.40)$$

$$p_{i,j}^d = \frac{1}{6} + \frac{a^2 j^2 \Delta t^2 - aj\Delta t}{2}$$

Notice that the probabilities at j are the reflection of those at $\bar{j}$.

The second stage of the tree building procedure involves converting the tree for x into a tree for r by displacing the nodes on the x tree by $\alpha(t)$ so that they fit the initial term structure. Thus, the new tree contains the short rate at each node where $r(t) = x(t) + \alpha(t)$ so that $\alpha(t) = r(t) - x(t)$. Recall that $dr = (\theta(t) - ar)dt + \sigma dz$ and that $dx = -axdt + \sigma dz$. Consequently,

$$d\alpha(t) = (\theta(t) - a\alpha(t))dt$$

Solving, we find:

$$\alpha(t) = e^{-at}\left[r_0 + \int_0^t e^{au}\theta(u)du \right]$$

$$= e^{-at}\left[r_0 + a\int_0^t e^{au}\bar{r}(u)du \right]$$

Substituting in the value for $\bar{r}(u)$ in (10.82) and $f(0, 0) = r_0$, we have:

$$\alpha(t) = e^{-at}\left[f(0, 0) + a\int_0^t e^{au}(f(0, u) + \frac{1}{a}\frac{\partial f(0, u)}{\partial t} + \frac{\sigma^2}{2a^2}(1 - e^{2au}))du \right]$$

$$= e^{-at}f(0, 0) + a\int_0^t e^{-a(t-u)}f(0, u)du + \int_0^t e^{-a(t-u)}\frac{\partial f(0, u)}{\partial t}du + \frac{\sigma^2}{2a}\int_0^t e^{-a(t-u)}(1 - e^{2au})du$$

which reduces to

$$\alpha(t) = f(0, t) + \frac{\sigma^2}{2a^2}(1 - e^{-at})^2 \tag{11.41}$$

Thus, in the r tree we displace each node by $x(i\Delta t) + \alpha(i\Delta t)$. While this model works well, it is not exactly consistent with the initial term structure. This is because it uses continuous-time displacements in a discrete-time model. An alternative approach that is exactly consistent with the initial term structure computes the $\alpha(t)$'s iteratively. Define $\alpha_i = r(i\Delta t) - x(i\Delta t)$ and $Q_{i,j}$ as pure securities (or discounted probabilities) that pay off \$1 if node (i, j) is reached and zero otherwise. We can compute α_i and $Q_{i,j}$ iteratively using forward induction so as to exactly match the initial term structure. By definition, $Q_{0,0} = 1$. α_0 is set equal to the initial Δt-period interest rate. From (11.37), we can compute the probabilities at time 0. From the initial term structure, we can also compute the discount factors $d_{i,j} = e^{-r_{i,j}\Delta t}$ at each time step, that is, at time 0, $d_{0,0} = e^{-r_0\Delta t}$. We can compute $Q_{1,1}, Q_{1,0}$, and $Q_{1,-1}$, by using these probabilities, discount factors, and $Q_{0,0}$:

$$Q_{1,1} = Q_{0,0} d_{0,0} p_{0,0}^u$$

$$Q_{1,0} = Q_{0,0} d_{0,0} p_{0,0'}^m \tag{11.42}$$

$$Q_{1,-1} = Q_{0,0} d_{0,0} p_{0,0}^d$$

We compute the value of discount bonds for each time step, $P_i = e^{-r_i i\Delta t}$, $i = 1, \ldots,$ N. α_1 is chosen to give the market price of a discount bond maturing at time $2\Delta t$. This can be done using the Newton-Raphson method by solving,

$$P_2 = \sum_{j=-1}^{1} Q_{1,j} e^{-(\alpha_1 + j\Delta r)}$$

for α_1. In general, suppose that the tree has been constructed up to time $m\Delta t$ and that the $Q_{i,j}$'s have been determined for $i \leq n$. The next step is to determine α_m so that the tree correctly prices a discount bond maturing at time $(m + 1)\Delta t$. By construction, the interest rate at node (m, j) is $\alpha_m + j\Delta r$. Thus, the price of a discount bond maturing at time $(m + 1)\Delta t$ is

$$P_{m+1} = \sum_{j=-n_m}^{n_m} Q_{m,j} \exp(-(\alpha_m + j\Delta r)\Delta t) \tag{11.43}$$

where n_k is the number of nodes on each side of the central node at time $m\Delta t$. Equation (11.41) can be explicitly solved for α_m:

$$\alpha_m = \frac{\ln \sum_{j=-n_m}^{n_m} Q_{m,j} e^{-j\Delta r \Delta t} - \ln P_{m+1}}{\Delta t} \tag{11.44}$$

After α_m is computed from (11.41), the $Q_{i,j}$ for $i = m + 1$ can be calculated using

$$Q_{m+1j} = \sum_k Q_{m,k} q_{k,j} \exp(-(\alpha_m + k\Delta r)\Delta r) \tag{11.45}$$

where $q_{k,j}$ is the probability of moving from node (m, k) to node $(m + 1, j)$ and the summation is taken over all values of l for which this is nonzero.[8] This approach is computationally efficient and can be extended to models where there are no analytical formulas such as the Black-Karasinski (lognormal Hull-White), shown in the next section. However, the approach is valid only for models where the short rate or functions of the short rate follow a mean-reverting, arithmetic process.

As an example of use of this methodology, we will continue to use the previous term structure values. We assume $\Delta t = 1$ and that the speed of mean reversion, a, is 0.10. At time 0, $x_{0,0} = 0$, $d_{0,0} = e^{-0.05(1)} = 0.9512$,

$$\Delta x = \Delta r = \sigma\sqrt{3\Delta t} = 0.01\sqrt{3(1)} = 0.0173$$

$$\bar{j} = \left\lceil \frac{0.1835}{(0.10(1))} \right\rceil = \lceil 1.835 \rceil = 2$$

and $j = -\bar{j} = -2$. At time $i = 1$, we can compute the pure securities $Q_{1,1}$, $Q_{1,0}$, and $Q_{1,-1}$ from (11.40). We also compute the discount bond prices for all time steps $i = 1, \ldots, N$; that is, $P_2 = e^{-(0.055)(2)(1)} = 0.8958$. Next, we compute the sum of the pure securities,

$$\sum_{j=-1}^1 Q_{1,j} d_{1,j} = \sum_{j=-1}^1 Q_{1,j} e^{-j\Delta r \Delta t}$$
$$= 0.1585 e^{-(-1)(0.0173)(1)} + 0.6343 e^{-(0)(0.0173)(1)} + 0.1585 e^{-(1)(0.0173)(1)}$$
$$= 0.9514$$

---

[8]Brigo and Mercurio (2001), 442–444.

From (11.43), we can compute α_1

$$\alpha_1 = \frac{\ln(0.9514) - \ln(0.8958)}{1} = 0.0602$$

Since the tree changes the branching process at $\bar{j} = 2$, we use a normal branching process at nodes (1, 1), (1, 0) and (1, –1). We compute the probabilities using (11.37) and find $p_{1,1}^u = 0.122$, $p_{1,1}^m = 0.657$, and $p_{1,-1}^d = 0.222$. At node (1, 0), $p_{1,0}^u = 0.167$, $p_{1,0}^m = 0.667$, and $p_{1,0}^d = 0.167$. At node (1, –1), the probabilities are those "reflected" at node (1, 1), that is, $p_{1,-1}^u = p_{1,1}^d = 0.222$, $p_{1,1}^m = p_{1,-1}^m = 0.657$, and $p_{1,-1}^d = p_{1,1}^u = 0.222$. We can compute the short rate and discount factors. At node (1, 1) we find:

$$r_{1,1} = x_{1,1} + \alpha_1$$
$$= x_{0,0} + 1(\Delta x) + \alpha_1$$
$$= 0.0 + 0.0173 + 0.0602 = 0.0775$$

$$d_{1,1} = e^{-r_{1,1}\Delta t} = e^{-(0.0775)(1)} = 0.9254$$

At node (1, 0),

$$r_{1,0} = x_{1,0} + \alpha_1$$
$$= x_{0,0} + 0(\Delta x) + \alpha_1$$
$$= 0.0 + 0.0 + 0.0602 = 0.0602$$

$$d_{1,0} = e^{-(0.0602(1))} = 0.9416$$

At node (1, –1), we get:

$$r_{1,-1} = x_{1,-1} + \alpha_1$$
$$= x_{0,0} - 1(\Delta x) + \alpha_1$$
$$= 0.0 - 0.0173 + 0.0602 = 0.0429$$

$$d_{1,0} = e^{-(0.0429(1))} = 0.9580$$

We repeat this process for all other time steps, $i > 1$, until the short rate is built up to time step N. However, we must change the branching processes (as discussed earlier), and thus transitional probabilities at states $\bar{j} = 2$ and $\underline{j} = -2$ where the tree gets truncated.

The following is the code to build a Hull-White tree calibrated to the initial short rate term structure:

```
/*******************************************************************************
buildHW: constructs a lognormal Hull-White tree calibrated to the yield curve
[in]:   vector<double> zero  : vector of zero rates
        double a             : speed of mean reversion
        double volatility    : volatility of short rate
        int N                : number of time steps
        double T             : time to maturity
[out]: void
*******************************************************************************/
void HullWhite::buildHW(vector<double> zero, double a, double volatility, int N,
    double T)
{
  int i, j, k;
  int jmax;                             // max upward branch
  int jmin;                             // min downward branch
  double pu[20] = {0.0};                // up probabilities
  double pm[20] = {0.0};                // middle probabilities
  double pd[20] = {0.0};                // down probabilities
  double sum = 0.0;                     // sum of shifted discount Arrow-Debreu
                                        // securities
  double sum1 = 0.0;                    // sums of discount Arrow-Debreu
                                        // securities
  double sum2[20] = {0.0};              // sum of weighted discount Arrow-Debreu
                                        // securities
  double alpha[20] = {0.0};             // the value of r(i*dt) - r*(i*dt)
  double alpha1[20][20];                // alpha value at node i, j
  double B[20] = {0.0};                 // discount bond price at time step i
  double dt = T/N;                      // time step size
  double dr = volatility*sqrt(3*dt);    // state step size

  jmax = (int) ceil(0.1835/(a*dt));
  jmin = -jmax;
  B[0] = 1;                             // par value of discount bond at time 0

  // calculate bond prices based on initial term structure
  for (i = 0; i <= N; i++)
  {
    for (j = i; j >= -i; j--)
    {
      // normal branching a
      if ((j != jmax) && (j != jmin))
      {
        pu[j] = 0.167 + 0.5*(a*a*j*j*dt*dt - a*j*dt);
        pm[j] = 0.666 - a*a*j*j*dt*dt;
        pd[j] = 0.167 + 0.5*(a*a*j*j*dt*dt + a*j*dt);
      }
      else if (j == jmin)
      {
```

```
              // up branching if a == 0
              pu[j] = 0.167 + 0.5*(a*a*j*j*dt*dt + a*j*dt);
              pm[j] = -0.333 - a*a*j*j*dt*dt - 2*a*j*dt;
              pd[j] = 1.167 + 0.5*(a*a*j*j*dt*dt + 3*a*j*dt);
            }
            else
            {
              pu[j] = 1.167 + 0.5*(a*a*j*j*dt*dt - 3*a*j*dt);
              pm[j] = -0.333 - a*a*j*j*dt*dt + 2*a*j*dt;
              pd[j] = 0.167 + 0.5*(a*a*j*j*dt*dt - a*j*dt);
            }
          }
        }
      }

// generate short rate tree
for (i = 0; i <= N; i++)
{
  for (j = i; j >= -i; j--)
  {
    r[i][j] = j*dr;
  }
}

// initialize values at node 0, 0
alpha[0] = zero[0];
r[0][0] = alpha[0];
Q[0][0] = 1.0;

// compute discount bond prices
for (i = 0; i <= N+1; i++)
{
  B[i+1] = exp(-zero[i]*(i+1)*dt);
}

for (jmax = 0; jmax <= N+1; jmax++)
{
  // reinitialize values for next iteration
  sum = 0;
  sum1 = 0;

  for (j = jmax+1; j >= -(jmax+1); j--)
  {
    sum2[j] = 0;
  }
  for (j=jmax; j >= -jmax; j--)
  {
    sum1 += (Q[jmax][j]*exp(-j*dr*dt));
  }
  alpha[jmax] = (1/dt)*(log(sum1/B[jmax+1]));

  for (j = jmax; j >= -jmax; j--)
  {
    sum += Q[jmax][j]*exp(-(alpha[jmax] + j*dr)*dt);
```

```
    }
    P[jmax] = sum;                    // assign bond price equal to sum of shifted Arrow-
                                      // Debreu price

    // determine Q[i][j] for i = m+1
    if (jmax == 0)
    {
      Q[1][1] = 0.167*exp(-(alpha[jmax] + dr));
      Q[1][0] = 0.666*exp(-alpha[jmax]);
      Q[1][-1] = 0.167*exp(-(alpha[jmax] - dr));
    }
    else        // if (jmax > 1)
    {
      for (k = jmax; k >= -jmax; k--)
      {
        for (j = k+1; j >= k-1; j--)
        {
          if (j == jmax + 1)
          {
            Q[jmax+1][jmax+1] = Q[jmax][jmax]*pu[jmax]*(-(alpha[jmax] +
              jmax*dr)*dt);
          }
          if (j == -(jmax + 1))
          {
            Q[jmax+1][-jmax-1] = Q[jmax][-jmax]*pd[-jmax]*(-(alpha[jmax] +
              (- jmax)*dr)*dt);
          }
    if ((pu[k] > 0) && (j - k == 1))
          {
            sum2[j] += Q[jmax][k]*pu[k]*exp(-(alpha[jmax] + k*dr)*dt);
          }
          if ((pm[k] > 0) && (j - k == 0))
          {
            sum2[j] += Q[jmax][k]*pm[k]*exp(-(alpha[jmax] + k*dr)*dt);
          }
          if ((pd[k] > 0) && (j - k == -1))
          {
            sum2[j] += Q[jmax][k]*pd[k]*exp(-(alpha[jmax] + k*dr)*dt);
          }
          Q[jmax+1][j] = sum2[j];
        }
      }
    }
}

r[0][0] = 0;
P[0] = 1;
for (i = 0; i <= N; i++)
{
  for (j = i; j >= -i; j--)
  {
    alpha1[i][j] = alpha[i];
    rate[i][j] = alpha1[i][j] + r[i][j];
```

```
        d[i][j] = exp(-rate[i][j]*dt);
    }
  }
}
```

We have assumed that the length of the time step is constant. But it is possible to build the tree with time steps of varying lengths. When the x^* tree is constructed, the spacing between the nodes at time t_{i+1} is set equal to

$$\sigma\sqrt{3(t_{i+1}-t_i)}$$

The branching probabilities are chosen so that the mean and standard deviation of the change in x^* are matched. The central node that branches from t_{i+1} is chosen to be the node closest to $E[x^*]$; that is, $x_i^* - a(t_{i+1} - t_i)x_i^*$. The final tree for x is constructed from the tree for x^* in a similar manner to the constant time step case.[9]

11.5 BUILDING A LOGNORMAL HULL-WHITE (BLACK-KARASINSKI) TREE

The procedure outlined in the preceding section can be extended to functions of the short rate and models with no analytical results, that is, $f(r) = \log r$. In particular, it is quite applicable to lognormal processes for the short rate. The lognormal HW model or restricted Black-Karasinski (1991) model can be represented as:

$$d\ln r(t) = a(\ln \bar{r} - \ln r(t))dt + \sigma dz \qquad (11.46)$$

or written in its more general Black-Karasinski form

$$d\ln r(t) = (\theta(t) - a\ln r(t))dt + \sigma dz \qquad (11.47)$$

This lognormal process does not allow negative rates. It is often used by practitioners for this reason. The time-dependent term in the drift is used to calibrate the model to the initial yield curve. The time-homogenous (constant) parameters a and σ determine the volatility term structure. From (11.47), by Ito's lemma, we find:

$$dr(t) = r(t)\left[\theta(t) + \frac{\sigma^2}{2} - a\ln r(t)\right]dt + \sigma r(t)dz(t)$$

---

[9]Hull (1996), 447.

which has the explicit solution for $s \leq t$.

$$r(t) = \exp\left(\ln r(s)e^{-a(t-s)} + \int_s^t e^{-a(t-u)}\theta(u)du + \sigma\int_s^t e^{-a(t-u)}dz(u)\right)$$

Therefore, $r(t)$ conditional on $\mathfrak{I}_s$ is lognormally distributed and has first and second moments given by:

$$E_s\left[r(t)\right] = \exp\left(\ln r(s)e^{-a(t-s)} + \int_s^t e^{-a(t-u)}\theta(u)du + \frac{\sigma^2}{4a}\left(1 - e^{-2a(t-s)}\right)\right)$$

and

$$E_s\left[r^2(t)\right] = \exp\left(2\ln r(s)e^{-a(t-s)} + 2\int_s^t e^{-a(t-u)}\theta(u)du + \frac{\sigma^2}{a}\left(1 - e^{-2a(t-s)}\right)\right)$$

We can adapt the Black-Karasinski model to the methodology outlined in the preceding section to construct a short rate tree (for computing discount bond and bond options that do not have closed-form analytical solutions). First, we set $x = \ln r$, yielding the process:

$$dx = (\theta(t) - ax)dt + \sigma dz$$

We then set $\theta(t) = 0$, so that the process becomes:

$$dx = -axdt + \sigma dz$$

as before. At time 0, $x = 0$. We assume that

$$\Delta r = \Delta x = \sigma\sqrt{3\Delta t}$$

the same as before. The tree is symmetrical with equally spaced state and time steps. The model, however, can be modified to have time-dependent changes in Δr and Δt; that is, $\Delta_i = t_{i+1} - t_i$ and

$$\Delta r_i = \sigma\sqrt{3\Delta t_i}$$

for each i. At node (i, j), we compute $x_{i,j} = j\Delta x$. We then need to compute the pure security prices $Q_{i,j}$ at each node (i, j) and the displacement (shift) parameters α_i at each time step $i = 1, \ldots, N$. The α_i's are chosen to correctly price a $(i + 1)\Delta t$-maturity discount bond. The Δt-period interest rate at the jth node at time $i\Delta t$ becomes:

$$r_{i,j} = \exp(\alpha_i + x_{i,j})$$
$$= \exp(\alpha_i + j\Delta x) \tag{11.48}$$

Writing bond prices as the sum of discounted pure securities in (11.7) using the short in (11.47) yields:

$$P_{i+1} = \sum_{j=-n_i}^{n_i} Q_{i,j} \exp(-\exp(\alpha_i + j\Delta r)\Delta t) \tag{11.49}$$

where n_i denotes the uppermost node at time step i (recall that we don't know what n_i is until the tree is built—if $j < \bar{j}$ then $n_i = i$, otherwise $n_i = \bar{j}$). If $i = 0$, $\alpha_0 = \ln(r_{0,0})$. We can solve for the α_i by using the Newton-Raphson method. We iterate:

$$\alpha_{k+1} = \alpha_k - \frac{\displaystyle\sum_{j=-n_i}^{n_i} Q_{i,j} \exp(-\exp(\alpha_k + j\Delta r)\Delta t) - P_{i+1}}{\phi(\alpha_k)} \tag{11.50}$$

where

$$\phi(\alpha_k) = \frac{\partial P_{i+1}}{\partial \alpha_k} = \sum_{j=-n_i}^{n_i} Q_{i,j} \exp(-\exp(\alpha_k + j\Delta r)\Delta t) \exp(\alpha_k + j\Delta r)\Delta t \tag{11.51}$$

updating $\alpha_k = \alpha_{k+1}$ at each time step until $|\alpha_{k+1} - \alpha_k| < \varepsilon$, for arbitrarily small ε (i.e., 0.0001). Once the tree for x is built and we determine the α_i, we can build the tree for r by applying (11.48) at each node.

The following is the code to build a lognormal Hull-White tree:

```
/******************************************************************************
buildHWLog: constructs and builds a lognormal Hull-White tree calibrated to the
            yield curve
[in]: vector<double> zero   : vector of zero rates (typically, bootstrapped from
                              yield curve)
      double a              : level of mean reversion
      int N                 : number of time steps
      double T              : time to maturity
```

```
           double volatility  : volatility of short rate
           double inityield   : initial yield guess for Newton-Raphson method
[out]:  void
********************************************************************************/
void HullWhiteLog::buildHWLog(vector<double> zero, double a, int N, double T,
  double volatility, double inityield)
{
  int i, j, k;
  int jmax = 0;                      // max upward branching level
  int jmin = 0;                      // min downward branching level
  double P[20] = {0.0};              // sum of Arrow-Debreu securities at time
                                     // step i

  double pu1[20][20] = {0.0};        // up probability at node i,j
  double pm1[20][20] = {0.0};        // middle probability at node i,j
  double pd1[20][20] = {0.0};        // down probability at node i,j
  double sum = 0.0;                  // sum of discounted Arrow-Debreu securities
                                     // at branch jmax

  double sum1= 0.0;                  // sum of discounted Arrow-Debreu securities
  double sum2 = 0.0;                 // sum of first derivatives of Arrow-Debreu
                                     // securities
  double alpha[20] = {0.0};          // the value of r(i*dt) - r*(i*dt)
  double alpha1[20][20] = {0.0};     // calibrated shift parameter at node i,j
  double alpha2 = 0.0;               // computed Newton-Raphson shift param value
  double alpha3 = 0.0;               // updates alpha2
  double r[20][20] = {0.0};          // short rate at node i, j
  double error = 0.0;                // computed error in Newton-Raphson method
  double B[20] = {0.0};              // zero bond price at time step i
  double Q[20][20] = {0.0};          // the present value of a security that pays
                                     // off $1 if node (i,j) is reached, else 0.
  const double tolerance = 0.00001;  // error tolerance level
  double dt = T/N;                   // time step size (typically, 0.5 or 1 year)
  double dr = volatility*sqrt(3*dt); // state size step


  jmax = (int) ceil(0.1835/(a*dt));
  jmin = -jmax;


  // first stage of HW procedure
  for (i = 0; i < N; i++)
  {
    for (j = i; j >= -i; j--)
    {
      // normal branching a
      if ((j != jmax) && (j != jmin))
      {
        pu[j] = 0.167 + 0.5*(a*a*j*j*dt*dt - a*j*dt);
        pm[j] = 0.666 - a*a*j*j*dt*dt;
        pd[j] = 0.167 + 0.5*(a*a*j*j*dt*dt + a*j*dt);
      }
      else if (j == jmin)
      {
        // up branching if a == 0
        pu[j] = 0.167 + 0.5*(a*a*j*j*dt*dt + a*j*dt);
```

```
        pm[j] = -0.333 - a*a*j*j*dt*dt - 2*a*j*dt;
        pd[j] = 1.167 + 0.5*(a*a*j*j*dt*dt + 3*a*j*dt);
      }
      else
      {
        pu[j] = 1.167 + 0.5*(a*a*j*j*dt*dt - 3*a*j*dt);
        pm[j] = -0.333 - a*a*j*j*dt*dt + 2*a*j*dt;
        pd[j] = 0.167 + 0.5*(a*a*j*j*dt*dt - a*j*dt);
      }
      pu1[i][j] = pu[j];
      pm1[i][j] = pm[j];
      pd1[i][j] = pd[j];
    }
}

// generate r-tree
for (i = 0; i <= jmax+1; i++)
{
  for (j = i; j >= -i; j--)
  {
    r[i][j] = j*dr;
  }
}

// initialize
Q[0][0] = 1.0;
B[0] = 1.0;
alpha[0] = inityield; // log(r1[0]);

// calculate bond prices based on initial term structure
for (i = 0; i <= N; i++)
{
  B[i+1] = exp(-zero[i]*(i+1)*dt);
}

// second stage of HW procedure
for (jmax = 0; jmax < N; jmax++)
{
  // reinitialize values for next iteration
  i = jmax;
  sum = 0;
  error = 0.10;
  Q[0][0] = 1.0;

  // determine Q[i][j] for i = m+1
  if (i == 1)
  {
    Q[1][1]  = Q[0][0]*pu1[0][0]*d[0][0];
    Q[1][0]  = Q[0][0]*pm1[0][0]*d[0][0];
    Q[1][-1] = Q[0][0]*pd1[0][0]*d[0][0];
  }
  else if (i == 2)
  {
```

```
      Q[2][2]  = Q[1][1]*pu1[1][1]*d[1][1];
      Q[2][1]  = Q[1][1]*pm1[1][1]*d[1][1]  + Q[1][0]*pu1[1][0]*d[1][0];
      Q[2][0]  = Q[1][1]*pd1[1][1]*d[1][1]  + Q[1][0]*pm1[1][0]*d[1][0]
                  + Q[1][-1]*pu1[1][-1]*d[1][-1];
      Q[2][-1] = Q[1][0]*pd1[1][0]*d[1][0]  + Q[1][-1]*pm1[1][-1]*d[1][-1];
      Q[2][-2] = Q[1][-1]*pd1[1][-1]*d[1][-1];
   }
   else
   {
      for (j = -i+1; j <= i-1; j++)
      {
         if (j == i-1)
         {
            // top node values
            Q[i][j]  = Q[i-1][j-1]*pu1[i-1][j-1]*d[i-1][j-1];
         }
         else if (j == -i+1)
         {
            // bottom node values
            Q[i][j]  = Q[i-1][j+1]*pd1[i-1][j+1]*d[i-1][j+1];
         }
         else if (j == -i+2)
         {
            Q[i][j]  = Q[i-1][j]*pm1[i-1][j]*d[i-1][j]  + Q[i-1][j+1]*pd1[i-
               1][j+1]*d[i-1][j+1];
         }
         else if (j == i-2)
         {
            Q[i][j]  = Q[i-1][j]*pm1[i-1][j]*d[i-1][j]  + Q[i-1][j-1]*pu1[i-1][j-
               1]*d[i-1][j-1];
         }
         else
         {
            Q[i][j]  = Q[i-1][j]*pm1[i-1][j]*d[i-1][j]  + Q[i-1][j+1]*pd1[i-
               1][j+1]*d[i-1][j+1]  + Q[i-1][j-1]*pu1[i-1][j-1]*d[i-1][j-1];
         }
      }
   }
}


if (jmax > 0)
{
   alpha2 = inityield; // for example, -2.741;

   do
   {
      sum1 = 0;
      sum2 = 0;
      for (j = jmax; j >= -jmax; j--)
      {
         sum1 += Q[i][j]*exp(-dt*exp(alpha2 + j*(dr)));
         sum2 += Q[i][j]*exp(-dt*(alpha2 + j*(dr)))*(exp(-dt*(exp(alpha2 +
            j*(dr)))));
```

```
      }
      alpha3 = alpha2 - (sum1 - B[jmax+1])/(-(dt)*sum2);
      error = abs(alpha3 - alpha2);
      alpha2 = alpha3;
   }
   while (error > tolerance);

   alpha[jmax] = alpha2;
}

for (k = i; k >= -i; k--)
{
   alpha1[i][k] = alpha[i];
   rate[i][k] = exp(alpha1[i][k] + r[i][k]);
   d[i][k] = exp(-rate[i][k]*dt);
}
for (j = jmax; j >= -jmax; j--)
{
   sum += Q[jmax][j]*exp(-dt*exp(alpha[jmax] + j*(dr)));
}
P[jmax+1] = sum;
}
rate[0][0] = zero[0];
d[0][0] = exp(-rate[0][0]*dt);
}
```

11.6 BUILDING TREES FITTED TO YIELD AND VOLATILITY CURVES

The Hull-White methodology to building trinomial trees can be extended to be consistent with both yield and volatility data. Since we are now calibrating the model to both market yield and volatility data, the Hull-White model in (11.37) needs be extended to have two time-dependent drift parameters, $\theta(t)$ and $a(t)$:

$$dr = (\theta(t) - a(t)r)dt + \sigma dz \qquad (11.52)$$

Making the mean-reversion rate, a, time-dependent allows the model to fit market volatility data. Increasing the parameterization of the model allows a fitting to more data and thus a model more consistent with the market. However, overparameterization (i.e., using too many time-varying parameters) can be a problem since it can cause a less regular evolution in time of market volatility structures—in fact, future implied volatility structures are likely to be unrealistic. Moreover, analytical tractability can be lost.

It is analogous to the binomial case of the BDT tree, but requires a change in the geometry of the tree after the first step. It is binomial in the first time step, with equal probabilities of up and down movements, converting to a trinomial tree afterward. We first compute the discount bond prices $P_i = e^{-r_i i\Delta t}$, $i = 1, \ldots, N$, and then solve for P_i^u and P_i^d. We will use continuously compounded rates. We must solve

$$\frac{1}{2}e^{-r_{0,0}\Delta t}(P_i^u + P_i^d) = P_i$$

and

$$\sigma_i = \frac{1}{2\sqrt{\Delta t}}\ln\left(\frac{\ln P_i^u}{\ln P_i^d}\right)$$

simultaneously for $i \geq 2$. As in the BDT tree, we get:

$$P_i^d = P_i^{u^{\exp(-2\sigma_i\sqrt{\Delta t})}}$$

where P_i^u is the solution to:

$$P_i^u + P_i^{u^{\exp(-2\sigma_i\sqrt{\Delta t})}} = 2P_i e^{r_{0,0}\Delta t}$$

Once we determine P_i^u and P_i^d, we can compute the short rates at the first time step:

$$r_{1,1} = -\frac{1}{\Delta t}\ln P_2^u \quad \text{and} \quad r_{1,-1} = -\frac{1}{\Delta t}\ln P_2^d$$

At time $i \geq 2$, the short rate at node (i, j) can be computed as:

$$r_{i,j} = r_{0,0} + j\Delta r$$

where

$$\Delta r = \sigma\sqrt{3\Delta t}$$

The tree is constructed for time steps $i > 1$ using the procedure similar to the BDT methodology for calibrating to the yield and volatility curves in section 11.1. The time-dependent parameters $\theta(t)$ and $a(t)$ are chosen to be consistent with P_i^u and P_i^d. The pure security prices, $Q_{i,j}^u$ and $Q_{i,j}^d$, at node (i, j) are found by computing:

$$Q_{i,j}^u = \sum_{j'} Q_{i-1,j'}^u p_{j',j} d_{i-1,j'}$$

$$Q_{i,j}^d = \sum_{j'} Q_{i-1,j'}^d p_{j',j} d_{i-1,j'}$$

where $p_{j',j}$ is the transitional probability of moving from node $(i-1, j')$ to node (i, j), $d_{i-1,j'}$'s are the one-period discount factors at time step $i-1$, $Q_{1,1}^u = 1$, and $Q_{1,-1}^d = 1$. Suppose the tree has been constructed up to time $i\Delta t$ for $i > 1$. As before, we need to determine the branching process at each node for the next time step. This is done by computing the expected change in the short rate process, $(\theta(t) - a(t)r)\Delta t$, so that $\theta(i\Delta t)$ and $a(i\Delta t)$ are consistent with P_i^u and P_i^d. Hull and White (1994) show that:

$$\theta(i\Delta t) = \frac{de - bf}{ad - bc} \qquad a(i\Delta t) = \frac{af - ce}{ad - bc}$$

where

$$a = \sum_j Q_{i,j}^u e^{-2r_{i,j}\Delta t} \Delta t^2 \qquad b = -\sum_j Q_{i,j}^u e^{-2r_{i,j}\Delta t} r_{i,j}\Delta t^2$$

$$c = \sum_j Q_{i,j}^d e^{-2r_{i,j}\Delta t} \Delta t^2 \qquad d = -\sum_j Q_{i,j}^d e^{-2r_{i,j}\Delta t} r_{i,j}\Delta t^2$$

$$e = \sum_j Q_{i,j}^d e^{-2r_{i,j}\Delta t} - P_{i+2}^u \qquad f = \sum_j Q_{i,j}^d e^{-2r_{i,j}\Delta t} - P_{i+2}^d$$

The drift rate of the short rate at node (i, j), $\mu_{i,j}$, at time $i\Delta t$ can then be computed as

$$\mu_{i,j} = (\theta(i\Delta t) - a(i\Delta t)r_{i,j})\Delta t$$

once the drift parameters, $\theta(i\Delta t)$ and $a(i\Delta t)$, are determined. The transitional probabilities from nodes at time i to nodes at time $(i + 1)\Delta t$ are shown to be

$$p_{i,j}^u = \frac{\sigma^2 \Delta t + \eta^2}{2\Delta r^2} + \frac{\eta}{2\Delta r}$$

$$p_{i,j}^m = 1 - \frac{\sigma^2 \Delta t + \eta^2}{\Delta r^2}$$

$$p_{i,j}^d = 1 - p_{i,j}^u - p_{i,j}^m$$

where $\eta = \mu_{i,j} + (j - k)\Delta r$. The expected change of r at node (i, j) is $r_{i,j} + \mu_{i,j}$. At $i = 1$, $\eta = r_{1,j} + \mu_{1,j} - (r_{0,0} + k\Delta r)$. At time step $i > 1$, for a normal expected change in the short rate, $k = j$ with drift $\eta = \mu_{i,j}$; for an upward expected change, $k = j - 1$ with drift $\eta = \mu_{i,j} + \Delta r$; and for a downward expected change, $k = j + 1$ with drift $\eta = \mu_{i,j} - \Delta r$.

The following is the code to build a Hull-White model calibrated to both the yield and volatility curves:

```
/*********************************************************************
buildHWLog: constructs a lognormal Hull-White tree calibrated to the yield curve
[in]:   vector<double> yield_curve      : vector of yield curve
        double a1                        : level of mean reversion
        int N                            : number of time steps
        double T                         : time to maturity
        vector<double> yield             : yield to maturity rates
        vector<double> volatility_curve  : vector of yield volatilities
        int abs_flag                     : flag to indicate whether volatilities are
                                           annualized
[out] : void
*********************************************************************/
void HullWhiteLog::buildHWLog(int N, double T, double a1, vector<double> yield,
  vector<double> volatility_curve, int abs_flag)
{
  double R[20] = {0.0};              // zero yield rates
  double P[20] = {0.0};              // discount bond prices
  double Pu[20] = {0.0};             // discount bond price in up nodes
  double Pd[20] = {0.0};             // discount bond price in down nodes
  double r[20][20] = {0.0};          // short rate at node i, j
  double volR[20] = {0.0};           // volatility of short rate
  double vol, a, b, c, d1, e, f;     // log HW parameters
  double pu[20][20] = {0.0};         // up probability at node i,j
  double pm[20][20] = {0.0};         // middle probability at node i,j
  double pd[20][20] = {0.0};         // down probability at node i,j
  double Qu[20][20] = {0.0};         // prices of Arrow-Debreu in up state
  double Qd[20][20] = {0.0};         // prices of Arrow-Debreu in down state
  double d[20][20] = {0.0};          // discount rate
  double theta[20] = {0.0};          // theta parameter
  double mu[20][20] = {0.0};         // mu parameter
  double tolerance = 0.0001;         // error tolerance level
  double error = 0.0;                // numerical search error
  double diff = 0.0;                 // drift difference r[i][j] - mu[i][j];
  double val = 0.0;                  // f(alpha)
  double val1 = 0.0;                 // first derivative of f(alpha)
  double alpha[20] = {0.0};          // alpha (a) parameter
  double eta = 0.0;                  // eta parameter
  double topNode[20] = {0.0};        // stores top branch level
  double lowNode[20] = {0.0};        // stores low branch level
  int jmax = 0;                      // max upper branch level
  int jmin = 0;                      // min lower branch level
  int i, j, k;

  // pre-compute constants
  double dt = T/N;                   // time step size (typically, 0.5 or 1 year)
  double dr = vol*sqrt(3*dt);        // state step size
  double sdt = sqrt(dt);             // square root of time step
```

```
// initialize yield curve
vol = volatility_curve[0];
for (i = 1; i <= N+1; i++)
{
  R[i] = yield[i-1];
  P[i] = exp(-R[i]*i*dt);

  // compute volatility depending on whether volatilities are annualized
  if (abs_flag == 1)
    volR[i] = volatility_curve[i-1]/R[i];
  else
    volR[i] = volatility_curve[i-1];
}

r[0][0] = R[1];
jmax = (int) ceil(0.1835/(a1*dt));
jmin = -jmax;

for (i = 0; i < N; i++)
{
  if (i < jmax)
    topNode[i] = i;
  else
    topNode[i] = jmax;

  if (i > jmin)
    lowNode[i] = -i;
  else
    lowNode[i] = jmin;
}

// compute Pu[.] and Pd[.]
double alpha2 = 0.0;
for (i = 2; i <= N; i++)
{
  // initial guess - change value if convergence does not occur
  double alpha1 = 0.94;
  // use Newton-Raphson numerical search to solve for Pu[i]
  do
  {
    // compute f(x) = 0
    val = alpha1 + pow(alpha1,exp(-2*volR[i]*sdt)) - 2*P[i]*exp(r[0][0]*dt);
    // compute derivative
    val1 = 1 + exp(-2*volR[i]*sdt)*pow(alpha1,exp(-2*volR[i]*sdt) - 1);
    alpha2 = alpha1 - val/val1;
    error = abs(alpha2 - alpha1);
    alpha1 = alpha2;
  }
  while (error > tolerance);

  Pu[i] = alpha1;
  Pd[i] = pow(Pu[i],exp(-2*volR[i]*sdt));
}
```

```
// initialize first node
pu[0][0] = 0.5;
pd[0][0] = 0.5;
d[0][0] = exp(-r[0][0]*dt);

// initialize up (U) and down (D) nodes
r[1][1] = -log(Pu[2])/dt;
r[1][-1] = -log(Pd[2])/dt;
d[1][1] = exp(-r[1][1]*dt);
d[1][-1] = exp(-r[1][-1]*dt);
Qu[1][1] = 1.0;
Qd[1][1] = 0.0;
Qd[1][-1] = 1.0;
Qu[1][-1] = 0.0;

// find theta and alpha for first time step
a = exp(-2*r[1][1]*dt)*pow(dt,2);
b = -exp(-2*r[1][1]*dt)*r[1][1]*dt*dt;
c = exp(-2*r[1][-1]*dt)*dt*dt;
d1= -exp(-2*r[1][-1]*dt)*r[1][-1]*dt*dt;
e = exp(-2*r[1][1]*dt)-Pu[3];
f = exp(-2*r[1][-1]*dt)-Pd[3];

theta[1] = ((d1*e) - (b*f))/((a*d1) - (b*c));
alpha[1] = ((a*f) - (c*e))/((a*d1) - (b*c));

for (j = -1; j <= 1; j += 2)
{
  mu[1][j] = (theta[1] - alpha[1]*r[1][j])*dt;
  // decide branch process [determines k]
  diff = r[1][j] - mu[1][j];
  if (abs(diff) < 0.01)
    k = 0; // normal branching
  else if (diff > r[1][j])
    k = -1; // upward branching
  else if (diff < r[1][j])
    k = 1; // downward branching

  eta = r[1][j] + mu[1][j] - (r[0][0] + k*dr);

  // calculate probabilities
  pu[1][j] = (vol*vol*dt + eta*eta)/(2*dr*dr) + eta/(2*dr);
  pm[1][j] = 1 - (vol*vol*dt + eta*eta)/(dr*dr);
  pd[1][j] = 1 - pu[1][j] - pm[1][j];
}

// grow tree for the short rate
for (i = 2; i <= N-1; i++)
{
  // using m[i-1][j] create nodes at time step i
  for (j = -i+1; j <= i-1; j++)
  {
    r[i][j] = r[0][0] + j*dr;
```

```
      d[i][j] = exp(-r[i][j]*dt);
}

// update pure security prices at time step i
if (i == 2)
{
  Qu[2][1] = Qu[1][1]*pu[1][1]*d[1][1];
  Qd[2][1] = Qd[1][-1]*pu[1][-1]*d[1][-1];

  Qu[2][0] = Qu[1][1]*pm[1][1]*d[1][1];
  Qd[2][0] = Qd[1][-1]*pm[1][-1]*d[1][-1];

  Qu[2][-1] = Qu[1][1]*pd[1][1]*d[1][1];
  Qd[2][-1] = Qd[1][-1]*pd[1][-1]*d[1][-1];
}
else if (i == 3)
{
  Qu[3][2] = Qu[2][1]*pu[2][1]*d[2][1];
  Qd[3][-2] = Qd[2][-1]*pd[2][-1]*d[2][-1];

  Qu[3][1] = Qu[2][1]*pm[2][1]*d[2][1] + Qd[2][0]*pu[2][0]*d[2][0];
  Qd[3][1] = Qd[2][1]*pm[2][1]*d[2][1] + Qd[2][0]*pu[2][0]*d[2][0];

  Qu[3][-1] = Qu[2][-1]*pm[2][-1]*d[2][-1] + Qu[2][0]*pd[2][0]*d[2][0];
  Qd[3][-1] = Qd[2][-1]*pm[2][-1]*d[2][-1] + Qd[2][0]*pd[2][0]*d[2][0];

  Qu[3][0] = Qu[2][1]*pd[2][1]*d[2][1] + Qu[2][0]*pm[2][0]*d[2][0] +
    Qu[2][-1]*pu[2][-1]*d[2][-1];
  Qd[3][0] = Qd[2][1]*pd[2][1]*d[2][1] + Qd[2][0]*pm[2][0]*d[2][0]
    + Qd[2][-1]*pu[2][-1]*d[2][-1];
}
else
{
  for (j = -i+1; j <= i-1; j++)
  {
    if (j == i-1)
    {
      // top node values
      Qu[i][j] = Qu[i-1][j-1]*pu[i-1][j-1]*d[i-1][j-1];
      Qd[i][j] = Qd[i-1][j-1]*pu[i-1][j-1]*d[i-1][j-1];
    }
    else if (j == -i+1)
    {
      // bottom node values
      Qu[i][j] = Qu[i-1][j+1]*pd[i-1][j+1]*d[i-1][j+1];
      Qd[i][j] = Qd[i-1][j+1]*pd[i-1][j+1]*d[i-1][j+1];
    }
    else if (j == -i+2)
    {
      Qu[i][j] = Qu[i-1][j]*pm[i-1][j]*d[i-1][j] + Qu[i-1][j+1]*
        pd[i-1][j+1]*d[i-1][j+1];
      Qd[i][j] = Qd[i-1][j]*pm[i-1][j]*d[i-1][j] + Qd[i-1][j+1]*
        pd[i-1][j+1]*d[i-1][j+1];
```

```
      }
      else if (j == i-2)
      {
        Qu[i][j] = Qu[i-1][j]*pm[i-1][j]*d[i-1][j] + Qu[i-1][j-1]*pu[i-1][j-
          1]*d[i-1][j-1];
        Qd[i][j] = Qd[i-1][j]*pm[i-1][j]*d[i-1][j] + Qd[i-1][j-1]*pu[i-1][j-
          1]*d[i-1][j-1];
      }
      else
      {
        Qu[i][j] = Qu[i-1][j]*pm[i-1][j]*d[i-1][j] + Qu[i-1][j+1]*pd[i-
          1][j+1]*d[i-1][j+1] + Qu[i-1][j-1]*pu[i-1][j-1]*d[i-1][j-1];
        Qd[i][j] = Qd[i-1][j]*pm[i-1][j]*d[i-1][j] + Qd[i-1][j+1]*pd[i-
          1][j+1]*d[i-1][j+1]+ Qd[i-1][j-1]*pu[i-1][j-1]*d[i-1][j-1];
      }
    }
  }
}


// find theta and alpha
a = b = c = d1 = e = f = 0;
for (j = -i+1; j <= i-1; j++)
{
  a = a + Qu[i][j]*exp(-2*r[i][j]*dt)*dt*dt;
  b = b - Qu[i][j]*exp(-2*r[i][j]*dt)*r[i][j]*dt*dt;
  c = c + Qd[i][j]*exp(-2*r[i][j]*dt)*dt*dt;
  d1 = d1 - Qd[i][j]*exp(-2*r[i][j]*dt)*r[i][j]*dt*dt;
  e = e + Qu[i][j]*exp(-2*r[i][j]*dt);
  f = f + Qd[i][j]*exp(-2*r[i][j]*dt);
}
e = e - Pu[i+2];
f = f - Pd[i+2];


theta[i] = ((d1*e) - (b*f))/((a*d1) - (b*c));
alpha[i] = ((a*f) - (c*e))/((a*d1) - (b*c));


// compute drift and decide branch process
for (j = -i+1; j <= i-1; j++)
{
  mu[i][j] = (theta[i] - alpha[i]*r[i][j])*dt;
  // decide branch process [determines k]
  diff = r[i][j] - mu[i][j];
  if (abs(diff) < 0.02)
    k = j; // normal branching
  else if (diff > r[i][j])
    k = j-1;        // upward branching
  else if (diff < r[i][j])
    k = j+1;        // downward branching


  eta = mu[i][j] + (j - k)*dr;


  // calculate probabilities
```

```
    pu[i][j] = (vol*vol*dt + eta*eta)/(2*dr*dr) + eta/(2*dr);
    pm[i][j] = 1 - (vol*vol*dt + eta*eta)/(dr*dr);
    pd[i][j] = 1 - pu[i][j] - pm[i][j];
  }
 }
}
```

11.7   VASICEK AND BLACK-KARASINSKI MODELS

In this section, we provide general object-oriented and robust implementations for the Vasicek and Black-Karasinski models (which are extended by Hull-White and Black-Derman-Toy models, respectively). See Appendix D on the CD-ROM for a discussion on robust pricing implementations in practice.

Consider the *Vasicek* class:

```
#include "OneFactorModel.h"

namespace QuantLib
{
  namespace ShortRateModels
  {
    /********************************************************************
    Vasicek model class
    This class implements the Vasicek model defined by
    dr_t = a(b - r_t)dt + \sigma dW_t , where a , b and sigma are constants.
    ********************************************************************/
    class Vasicek : public OneFactorAffineModel
    {
      public:
        Vasicek(Rate r0 = 0.05, double a = 0.1, double b = 0.05, double sigma =
          0.01);
        virtual double discountBondOption(Option::Type type, double strike, Time
          maturity, Time bondMaturity) const;
        virtual Handle<ShortRateDynamics> dynamics() const;
      protected:
        virtual double A(Time t, Time T) const;
        virtual double B(Time t, Time T) const;
        double a() const { return a_(0.0); }
        double b() const { return b_(0.0); }
        double sigma() const { return sigma_(0.0); }
      private:
        class Dynamics;
        double r0_;
        Parameter& a_;
        Parameter& b_;
        Parameter& sigma_;
    };
```

```
/*************************************************************************
Short-rate dynamics in the Vasicek model
The short-rate follows an Ornstein-Uhlenbeck process with mean b.
*************************************************************************/
class Vasicek::Dynamics : public ShortRateDynamics
{
  public:
    Dynamics(double a, double b, double sigma, double r0)
      : ShortRateDynamics(Handle<DiffusionProcess>(
        new OrnsteinUhlenbeckProcess(a, sigma, r0 - b))), a_(a), b_(b),
          r0_(r0) {}

    virtual double variable(Time t, Rate r) const {
      return r - b_;
    }
    virtual double shortRate(Time t, double x) const {
      return x + b_;
    }
  private:
    double a_, b_, r0_;
};

// inline definitions

inline Handle<OneFactorModel::ShortRateDynamics>
Vasicek::dynamics() const {
  return Handle<ShortRateDynamics>(new Dynamics(a(), b() , sigma(), r0_));
}
```

The class has the following method definitions:

```
#include "Vasicek.h"
#include "BlackModel.h"

namespace QuantLib
{
  namespace ShortRateModels
  {
    using Optimization::NoConstraint;
    using Optimization::PositiveConstraint;

    Vasicek::Vasicek(Rate r0, double a, double b, double sigma) :
      OneFactorAffineModel(3), r0_(r0), a_(arguments_[0]), b_(arguments_[1]),
      sigma_(arguments_[2])
    {
      a_ = ConstantParameter(a, PositiveConstraint());
      b_ = ConstantParameter(b, NoConstraint());
      sigma_ = ConstantParameter(sigma, PositiveConstraint());
    }
```

```
double Vasicek::A(Time t, Time T) const
{
  double sigma2 = sigma()*sigma();
  double bt = B(t, T);
  return exp((b() - 0.5*sigma2/(a()*a())))*(bt - (T - t)) -
    0.25*sigma2*bt*bt/a());
}

double Vasicek::B(Time t, Time T) const
{
  return (1.0 - exp(-a()*(T - t)))/a();
}

/*************************************************************************
discountBondOption: fits shift parameter to term structure and mean reversion
                   parameter a and volatility
[in]  Option::Type type   : option type (C)all or (P)ut
      double strike        : strike price
      Time maturity        : maturity of bond option
      Time bondMaturity    : maturity of bond
[out] double               : bond option price
*************************************************************************/
double Vasicek::discountBondOption(Option::Type type, double strike, Time
  maturity, Time bondMaturity) const
{
  double v;
  if (fabs(maturity) < QL_EPSILON)
  {
    v = 0.0;
  }
  else
  {
    v = sigma()*B(maturity, bondMaturity)*sqrt(0.5*(1.0 - exp
      (-2.0*a()*maturity))/a());
  }
  double f = discountBond(0.0, bondMaturity, r0_);
  double k = discountBond(0.0, maturity, r0_)*strike;
  double w = (type==Option::Call)? 1.0 : -1.0;

  return BlackModel::formula(f, k, v, w);
  }
 }
}
```

We now define the *BlackKarasinski* class:

```
#include "ShortRateModels/onefactormodel.h"

namespace QuantLib
```

```
{
  namespace ShortRateModels
  {
    /*************************************************************************
    Standard Black-Karasinski model class.
    This class implements the standard Black-Karasinski model defined by
    d\ln r_t = (\theta(t) - \alpha \ln r_t)dt + \sigma dW_t, where alpha and sigma
    are constants.
    *************************************************************************/
    class BlackKarasinski : public OneFactorModel, public
      TermStructureConsistentModel
    {
      public:
        BlackKarasinski(const RelinkableHandle<TermStructure>& termStructure,
          double a = 0.1, double sigma = 0.1);
        Handle<ShortRateDynamics> dynamics() const {
          throw Error("No defined process for Black-Karasinski");
        }
        Handle<Lattices::Lattice> tree(const TimeGrid& grid) const;
      private:
        class Dynamics;
        class Helper;
        double a() const { return a_(0.0); }
        double sigma() const { return sigma_(0.0); }
        Parameter& a_;
        Parameter& sigma_;
    };


    /*************************************************************************
    Short-rate dynamics in the Black-Karasinski model
    The short-rate is here r_t = exp{\varphi(t) + x_t} where varphi(t) is the
      deterministic time-dependent parameter (which can not be determined
      analytically) used for term-structure fitting and x_t is the state variable
      following an Ornstein-Uhlenbeck process.
    *************************************************************************/
    class BlackKarasinski::Dynamics : public BlackKarasinski::ShortRateDynamics
    {
      public:
        Dynamics(const Parameter& fitting, double alpha, double sigma)
          : ShortRateDynamics(Handle<DiffusionProcess>(new
            OrnsteinUhlenbeckProcess(alpha, sigma))), fitting_(fitting) {}


        double variable(Time t, Rate r) const {
          return log(r) - fitting_(t);
        }
        double shortRate(Time t, double x) const {
          return exp(x + fitting_(t));
        }
      private:
        Parameter fitting_;
```

```
        };
    }
}
```

The class has the following method definitions:

```cpp
#include "BlackKarasinski.h"
#include "Trinomialtree.h"
#include "Brent.h"

namespace QuantLib
{
  namespace ShortRateModels
  {
    using namespace Lattices;

    /*************************************************************************
    Private function used by solver to determine time-dependent parameter
    *************************************************************************/
    class BlackKarasinski::Helper : public ObjectiveFunction
    {
      public:
        Helper(Size i, double xMin, double dx, double discountBondPrice,
          const Handle<ShortRateTree>& tree) : size_(tree->size(i)),
            dt_(tree->timeGrid().dt(i)), xMin_(xMin), dx_(dx), statePrices_
              (tree->statePrices(i)), discountBondPrice_(discountBondPrice) {}

        double operator()(double theta) const
        {
          double value = discountBondPrice_;
          double x = xMin_;
          for (Size j=0; j<size_; j++)
          {
            double discount = exp(-exp(theta+x)*dt_);
            value -= statePrices_[j]*discount;
            x += dx_;
          }
          return value;
        }
      private:
        Size size_;
        Time dt_;
        double xMin_, dx_;
        const Array& statePrices_;
        double discountBondPrice_;
```

```
};

using Optimization::PositiveConstraint;

/****************************************************************************
BlackKarasinski : Constructor
[in] RelinkableHandle<TermStructure>& termStructure : term structure
      double a          : mean reversion parameter
      double sigma      : volatility parameter
****************************************************************************/
BlackKarasinski::BlackKarasinski(const RelinkableHandle<TermStructure>&
  termStructure, double a, double sigma)
    : OneFactorModel(2), TermStructureConsistentModel(termStructure),
    a_(arguments_[0]), sigma_(arguments_[1])
{
  a_ = ConstantParameter(a, PositiveConstraint());
  sigma_ = ConstantParameter(sigma, PositiveConstraint());
}


/****************************************************************************
tree: builds trinomial tree that approximates Black-Karasinski
[in]  TimeGrid& grid               : time grid
[out] Handle<Lattices::Lattice>    : Hull-White tree
****************************************************************************/
Handle<Lattice> BlackKarasinski::tree(const TimeGrid& grid) const
{
  TermStructureFittingParameter phi(termStructure());

  Handle<ShortRateDynamics> numericDynamics(new Dynamics(phi, a(), sigma()));

  Handle<TrinomialTree> trinomial(
    new TrinomialTree(numericDynamics->process(), grid));

  Handle<ShortRateTree> numericTree(
    new ShortRateTree(trinomial, numericDynamics, grid));

  Handle<TermStructureFittingParameter::NumericalImpl> impl =
    phi.implementation();
  impl->reset();
  double value = 1.0;
  double vMin = -50.0;
  double vMax = 50.0;
  for (Size i=0; i<(grid.size() - 1); i++)
  {
    double discountBond = termStructure()->discount(grid[i+1]);
    double xMin = trinomial->underlying(i, 0);
    double dx = trinomial->dx(i);
    Helper finder(i, xMin, dx, discountBond, numericTree);
    Solvers1D::Brent s1d = Solvers1D::Brent();
    s1d.setMaxEvaluations(1000);
    value = s1d.solve(finder, 1e-7, value, vMin, vMax);
    impl->set(grid[i], value);
```

```
            // vMin = value - 10.0;
            // vMax = value + 10.0;
        }
        return numericTree;
    }
  }
}
```

11.8   COX-INGERSOLL-ROSS IMPLEMENTATION

The following is an implementation of the Cox-Ingersoll-Ross (1985a) model:

```
#include "OneFactorModel.h"

namespace QuantLib
{
  namespace ShortRateModels
  {
    /***********************************************************************
    Cox-Ingersoll-Ross model class.
    This class implements the Cox-Ingersoll-Ross model defined by
    dr_t = k(theta - r_t)dt + sqrt{r_t}\sigma dW_t .
    ***********************************************************************/
    class CoxIngersollRoss : public OneFactorAffineModel
    {
      public:
        CoxIngersollRoss(Rate r0 = 0.05, double theta = 0.1, double k = 0.1,
          double sigma = 0.1);
        virtual double discountBondOption(Option::Type type, double strike, Time
          maturity, Time bondMaturity) const;
        virtual Handle<ShortRateDynamics> dynamics() const;
        virtual Handle<Lattices::Lattice> tree(const TimeGrid& grid) const;
        class Dynamics;
      protected:
        double A(Time t, Time T) const;
        double B(Time t, Time T) const;
        double theta() const { return theta_(0.0); }
        double k() const { return k_(0.0); }
        double sigma() const { return sigma_(0.0); }
        double x0() const { return r0_(0.0); }
      private:
        class VolatilityConstraint;
        class HelperProcess;
        Parameter& theta_;
        Parameter& k_;
        Parameter& sigma_;
```

```
      Parameter& r0_;
  };


  class CoxIngersollRoss::HelperProcess : public DiffusionProcess
  {
    public:
      HelperProcess(double theta, double k, double sigma, double y0)
        : DiffusionProcess(y0), theta_(theta), k_(k), sigma_(sigma) {}
      double drift(Time t, double y) const {
        return (0.5*theta_*k_ - 0.125*sigma_*sigma_)/y - 0.5*k_*y;
      }
      double diffusion(Time t, double y) const {
        return 0.5*sigma_;
      }
    private:
      double theta_, k_, sigma_;
  };


  /******************************************************************************
  Dynamics of the short-rate under the Cox-Ingersoll-Ross model
  The state variable y_t will here be the square-root of the short-rate. It
    satisfies the following stochastic differential equation
  dy(t)= (2k)/theta+ (sigma ^2)/8){1}y(t)- {k}{2}y(t)dt+ (sigma/2)dW(t).
  ******************************************************************************/
  class CoxIngersollRoss::Dynamics : public ShortRateDynamics
  {
    public:
      Dynamics(double theta, double k, double sigma, double x0)
        : ShortRateDynamics(Handle<DiffusionProcess>(new HelperProcess(theta, k,
          sigma, sqrt(x0)))) {}

      virtual double variable(Time t, Rate r) const {
        return sqrt(r);
      }
      virtual double shortRate(Time t, double y) const {
        return y*y;
      }
  };
  }
}
```

The class has the following method definitions:

```
#include "Coxingersollross.h"
#include "Trinomialtree.h"
#include "Chisquaredistribution.h"
```

```
namespace QuantLib
{
  namespace ShortRateModels
  {
    using namespace Lattices;
    using Optimization::Constraint;
    using Optimization::PositiveConstraint;


    /**************************************************************************
    Volatility Constraint class
    Constraints volatility to satisfy the Feller condition.
    **************************************************************************/
    class CoxIngersollRoss::VolatilityConstraint : public Constraint
    {
      private:
        class Impl : public Constraint::Impl
        {
          public:
            Impl(const Parameter& theta, const Parameter& k)
              : theta_(theta), k_(k) {}
            bool test(const Array& params) const
            {
              if (params[0] <= 0.0)
                return false;
              if (params[0] >= sqrt(2.0*k_(0.0)*theta_(0.0)))
                return false;

                return true;
            }
          private:
            const Parameter& theta_;
            const Parameter& k_;      // mean reversion
        };
      public:
        VolatilityConstraint(const Parameter& theta, const Parameter& k)
         : Constraint(Handle<Constraint::Impl>(new
           VolatilityConstraint::Impl(theta, k))) {}
    };


    /**************************************************************************
    CoxIngersollRoss           : Constructor
    [in]  Rate r0              : initial risk-free rate
          double theta         : theta paramater
          double k             : k parameter for Feller condition
          double volatility    : volatility of short rate
    **************************************************************************/
    CoxIngersollRoss::CoxIngersollRoss(Rate r0, double theta, double k, double
      sigma) : OneFactorAffineModel(4), theta_(arguments_[0]), k_(arguments_[1]),
      sigma_(arguments_[2]), r0_(arguments_[3])
    {
      theta_ = ConstantParameter(theta, PositiveConstraint());
```

```
    k_ = ConstantParameter(k, PositiveConstraint());
    sigma_ = ConstantParameter(sigma, VolatilityConstraint(theta_, k_));
    r0_ = ConstantParameter(r0, PositiveConstraint());
}
/************************************************************************
dynamics: generates and returns CIR dynamics
[in]   [none]
[out] Handle<OneFactor::ShortRateDynamics> : CIR dynamics
*************************************************************************/
Handle<OneFactorModel::ShortRateDynamics> CoxIngersollRoss::dynamics() const
{
    return Handle<ShortRateDynamics>( new Dynamics(theta(), k() , sigma(),
      x0()));
}


/************************************************************************
A: computes A term of discount bond price for CIR
[in]    Time t : current time
        Time T: end time (option maturity)
[out]   double A
*************************************************************************/
double CoxIngersollRoss::A(Time t, Time T) const
{
    double sigma2 = sigma()*sigma();
    double h = sqrt(k()*k() + 2.0*sigma2);
    double numerator = 2.0*h*exp(0.5*(k()+h)*(T-t));
    double denominator = 2.0*h + (k()+h)*(exp((T-t)*h) - 1.0);
    double value = log(numerator/denominator)*2.0*k()*theta()/sigma2;
    return exp(value);
}


/************************************************************************
B: computes B term of discount bond price for CIR
[in]   Time t : current time
       Time T : end time (option maturity)
[out] double B
*************************************************************************/
double CoxIngersollRoss::B(Time t, Time T) const
{
    double h = sqrt(k()*k() + 2.0*sigma()*sigma());
    double temp = exp((T-t)*h) - 1.0;
    double numerator = 2.0*temp;
    double denominator = 2.0*h + (k()+h)*temp;
    double value = numerator/denominator;
    return value;
}


/************************************************************************
discountBondOption: prices discount bond option using CIR model
[in]   Option::Type type : option type
       Time t             : current (initial) time
       Time s             : end time
[out] double             : price of discount bond
```

```
**********************************************************************/
double CoxIngersollRoss::discountBondOption(Option::Type type, double strike,
  Time t, Time s) const
{
  double discountT = discountBond(0.0, t, x0());
  double discountS = discountBond(0.0, s, x0());

  if (t < QL_EPSILON)
  {
    switch(type)
    {
      case Option::Call: return max(discountS - strike, 0.0);
      case Option::Put: return max(strike - discountS, 0.0);
      default: throw Error("unsupported option type");
    }
  }

  double sigma2 = sigma()*sigma();
  double h = sqrt(k()*k() + 2.0*sigma2);
  double b = B(t,s);

  double rho = 2.0*h/(sigma2*(exp(h*t) - 1.0));
  double psi = (k() + h)/sigma2;

  std::cout << "exp: " << (exp(h*t) - 1.0) << std::endl;
  std::cout << "rho: " << rho << std::endl;
  std::cout << "psi: " << psi << std::endl;

  double df = 4.0*k()*theta()/sigma2;
  double ncps = 2.0*rho*rho*x0()*exp(h*t)/(rho+psi+b);
  double ncpt = 2.0*rho*rho*x0()*exp(h*t)/(rho+psi);

  std::cout << "df: " << df << std::endl;
  std::cout << "ncps: " << ncps << std::endl;
  std::cout << "ncpt: " << ncpt << std::endl;

  Math::NonCentralChiSquareDistribution chis(df, ncps);
  Math::NonCentralChiSquareDistribution chit(df, ncpt);

  double z = log(A(t,s)/strike)/b;
  double call = discountS*chis(2.0*z*(rho+psi+b)) -
    strike*discountT*chit(2.0*z*(rho+psi));

  std::cout << "chis: " << chis(2.0*z*(rho+psi+b)) << std::endl;
  std::cout << "chit: " << chit(2.0*z*(rho+psi)) << std::endl;

  if (type == Option::Call)
    return call;
  else
    return call - discountS + strike*discountT;
}
```

```
/*******************************************************************
tree: builds trinomial tree that approximates Cox-Ingersoll-Ross process
[in] TimeGrid& grid              : time grid
[out] Handle<Lattices::Lattice> : Hull-White tree
*******************************************************************/
Handle<Lattice> CoxIngersollRoss::tree(const TimeGrid& grid) const
{
    Handle<Tree> trinomial(new TrinomialTree(dynamics()->process(), grid, true));
    return Handle<Lattice>(new ShortRateTree(trinomial, dynamics(), grid));
}
  }
}
```

11.9   A GENERAL DETERMINISTIC-SHIFT EXTENSION

In the Hull-White methodology, we build the short rate tree by displacing or shifting the nodes of the tree for x by $\alpha(t)$. This displacement is developed more formally in this section by describing a general deterministic-shift extension methodology. A procedure to extend any time-homogenous short rate model so as to exactly fit the observed term structure of interest rates while preserving the possible analytical tractability of the original model has been developed from the works of Brigo and Mercurio (1998, 2001a), Dybvig (1997), Scott (1995), and Avellaneda and Newman (1998).

The shift-extension approach can make some models more analytically tractable such as the Cox-Ingersoll-Ross (1985a). The extended model exhibits the following properties: (1) exact fitting of the model to any observed term structure; (2) analytical formulas for bond prices, bond option prices, swaptions, and cap prices; (3) the distribution of the instantaneous spot rate has fatter tails than in the Gaussian case—a more realistic distributional property; (4) the term structure is affine in the short rate; and (5) through certain restrictions on the parameters, it is always possible to guarantee positive rates without worsening the volatility calibration in most situations.[10]

We now discuss the basic assumptions and properties of the deterministic-shift extension approach. Consider a time-homogeneous stochastic process x^α, whose dynamics under a risk-adjusted martingale measure Q^x evolve according to:

$$dx^\alpha(t) = \mu(x^\alpha(t); \alpha)dt + \sigma(x^\alpha(t); \alpha)d^x z(t)$$

where W^x is a standard Brownian motion; $\alpha = \{\alpha_1, \ldots, \alpha_n\} \in \Re^n$, $n \geq 1$, is a vector of parameters; $x^\alpha(0)$ is a given initial value; and μ and σ are sufficiently well be-

---

[10]Brigo and Mercurio (2001c), 86–87.

haved real functions.[11] Denote by $P^x(t, T)$ the price at time t of a zero-coupon bond maturing at time T and with a unit face value, so that:

$$P^x(t, T) = E_t^x \left\{ \exp\left(-\int_t^T x^\alpha(s)ds \right) \right\} \qquad (11.53)$$

where E_t^x denotes the expectation under the risk-adjusted measure Q^x at time t conditional on all information (i.e., the sigma field) generated by x^α up to time t. Following Brigo and Mercurio, we also assume that there exists an explicit real function Π^x defined on a suitable subset of $\Re^{n+3}$ such that:

$$P^x(t, T) = \Pi^x(t, T, x^\alpha(t); \alpha) \qquad (11.54)$$

The Vasicek (1977) model, the Dothan (1977), and the Cox-Ingersoll-Ross (1985a) model satisfy these assumptions.

Define the instantaneous short rate by:

$$r(t) = x(t) + \varphi(t; \alpha), \, t \geq 0 \qquad (11.55)$$

where x is a stochastic process that has the same dynamics under the risk-neutral measure Q as x^α has under Q^x. φ is a deterministic function, chosen to fit the initial term structure of interest rates, that depends on the parameters' vector $(\alpha, x(0))$ and is integrable on closed intervals.[12] $x(0)$ can be chosen to be any real value as long as:

$$\varphi(0; \alpha) = r(0) - x(0)$$

The short rate r depends on $\alpha_1, \ldots, \alpha_n, x(0)$, both through the process x and the shift function φ. We can determine these parameters by calibrating the model to the current term structure of volatilities, by fitting, for example, cap, floor, or swaption prices.[13] If φ is differentiable, then the SDE for the short process is:

$$dr(t) = \left(\frac{d\varphi(t; \alpha)}{dt} + \mu(r(t) - \varphi(t; \alpha); \alpha) \right) dt + \sigma(r(t) - \varphi(t; \alpha); \alpha)dz(t) \qquad (11.56)$$

If the coefficients in (11.56) are time-homogenous, then from section 10.4, we

---

[11]Ibid., 87.
[12]Ibid., 88.
[13]Ibid., 88.

know that an affine short-rate term structure is equivalent to affine drift and squared diffusion coefficients.[14]

From (11.55), we find that the price at time t of a zero-coupon bond maturing at time T is:

$$P(t, T) = \exp\left(-\int_t^T \varphi(s; \alpha)ds\right)\Pi^x(t, T, r(t) - \varphi(t; \alpha); \alpha) \qquad (11.57)$$

This can be seen as follows. Notice that:

$$P(t, T) = E_t\left[\exp\left(-\int_t^T (x(s) + \varphi(s; \alpha))ds\right)\right]$$

$$= \exp\left(-\int_t^T \varphi(s; \alpha)ds\right)E_t\left[-\int_t^T x(s)ds\right]$$

$$= \exp\left(-\int_t^T \varphi(s; \alpha)ds\right)\Pi^x(t, T, x(t); \alpha)$$

where the expectation is taken under the risk-neutral measure Q at time t conditional on the sigma algebra generated by x up to time t. In the last step, equivalence of the dynamics of x under Q and x^α and Q^α is made.

Moreover, model (11.55) fits the currently observed term structure of discount factors if and only if:

$$\varphi(t; \alpha) = \varphi^*(t; \alpha) = f(0, t) - f^x(0, t; \alpha) \qquad (11.58)$$

where

$$f^x(0, t; \alpha) = -\frac{\partial \ln P^x(0, t)}{\partial t} = -\frac{\partial \ln \Pi^x(0, t, x_0; \alpha)}{\partial t}$$

is the instantaneous forward rate at time 0 for a maturity t. Equivalently, calibration to the term structure occurs if and only if:

$$\exp\left(-\int_t^T \varphi(s; \alpha)ds\right) = \Phi^*(t, T, x_0; \alpha) = \frac{P(0, T)}{\Pi^x(0, T, x_0; \alpha)}\frac{\Pi^x(0, t, x_0; \alpha)}{P(0, t)} \qquad (11.59)$$

---

[14]Ibid., 88.

Furthermore, the corresponding zero-coupon bond prices at time t are given by $P(t, T) = \Pi(t, T, r(t); \alpha)$, where

$$\Pi(t, T, r(t); \alpha) = \Phi^*(t, T, x_0; \alpha)\Pi^x(t, T, r(t) - \varphi^*(t; \alpha); \alpha) \qquad (11.60)$$

This can be proven as follows. From (11.57), we have

$$P(0, t) = \exp\left(-\int_0^t \varphi(s; \alpha)ds\right)\Pi^x(0, t, x(0); \alpha) \qquad (11.61)$$

We get (11.58) by taking the natural logarithm of both sides of (11.61) and then differentiating. From (11.61), we also can obtain (11.59) by noting that:

$$\exp\left(-\int_t^T \varphi(s; \alpha)ds\right) = \exp\left(-\int_0^T \varphi(s; \alpha)ds\right)\exp\left(\int_0^t \varphi(s; \alpha)ds\right)$$

$$= \frac{P(0, T)}{\Pi^x(0, T, x(0); \alpha)} \frac{\Pi^x(0, T, x(0); \alpha)}{P(0, t)} \qquad (11.62)$$

which when combined with (11.57) yields (11.60).[15]

If the deterministic-shift extension $\varphi(t; \alpha)$ is chosen as in (11.58), then the short rate model with (11.55) will exactly fit the observed term structure of interest rates regardless of the chosen values of α and $x(0)$.[16] Since the extension preserves analytical tractability for option prices via analytical correction factors defined in terms of φ, we can compute prices at time t of European options with maturity T on zero-coupon bonds that mature at time S with a strike price of X. This is given by

$$V^x(t, T, S, X) = E_t^x\left[\exp\left(-\int_t^T x^\alpha(s)ds\right)(P^x(T, S) - X)^+\right]$$

Following Brigo and Mercurio, we assume there exists a closed-form real function ψ^x defined on a suitable subset of $\Re^{n+5}$, such that:

$$V^x(t, T, S, X) = \psi^x(t, T, S, X, x^\alpha(t); \alpha)$$

---

[15]Ibid., 88–89.
[16]Ibid., 89.

Under model (11.55), the price of a European call option on a zero-coupon bond is:

$$C(t,\ T,\ S,\ X) = \exp\left(-\int_t^S \varphi(s;\ \alpha)ds\right)\psi^x\left(t,\ T,\ S,\ X\exp\left(-\int_T^S \varphi(s;\ \alpha)ds\right),\ r(t) - \varphi(t;\ \alpha);\ \alpha\right)$$

This formula holds for any chosen φ. In particular, when calibrating to the initial term structure of interest rates, (11.55) must be used to yield:

$$C(t,\ T,\ S,\ X) = \psi(t,\ T,\ S,\ X,\ r(t);\ \alpha)$$

where

$$\psi(t,\ T,\ S,\ X,\ r(t);\ \alpha) = \Phi^*(t,\ S,\ x(0);\ \alpha)\psi^x(t,\ T,\ S,\ X\Phi^*(S,\ T,\ x(0);\ \alpha),\ r(t) - \varphi^*(t;\ \alpha);\ \alpha)$$

The price of European put can be computed from the put-call parity for bond options. If Jamshidian's (1989) decomposition for coupon-bearing bonds holds under the dynamics for x^α, given by $dx^\alpha(t) = \mu(x^\alpha(t);\ \alpha)dt + \sigma(x^\alpha(t);\ \alpha)d^xz(t)$, then it can be applied under the extended model so that analytical prices exist for coupon-bearing bonds and swaptions.

11.10   SHIFT-EXTENDED VASICEK MODEL

If we assume that the time-homogenous model x^α evolves according to the Vasicek model given in equation (10.30), with parameter vector $\alpha = (a,\ \bar{r},\ \sigma)$, then it can be extended by (10.55). In the extended case, the short rate dynamics become:

$$dr(t) = \left[a\bar{r} + a\varphi(t;\ \alpha) + \frac{d\varphi(t;\ \alpha)}{dt} - ar(t)\right]dt + \sigma dz(t) \tag{11.63}$$

We can compute the Vasicek shift function $\varphi(t;\ \alpha) = \varphi^{\text{Vasicek}}(t;\ \alpha)$ from (11.58) as follows:

$$\varphi^{\text{Vasicek}}(t;\ \alpha) = f(0,\ t) - f^x(0,\ t)$$

where

$$f^x(0,\ t) = -\frac{\partial \ln P^x(0,\ t)}{\partial t} = -\frac{\partial \ln A(0,\ t)}{\partial t} + \frac{\partial B(0,\ t)x(0)}{\partial t}$$

$$= -\frac{\partial\left(\dfrac{(B(0,\ t)-t)(a^2\bar{r}-\sigma^2/2)}{a^2} - \dfrac{\sigma^2 B(0,\ t)^2}{4a}\right)}{\partial t} + x(0)\frac{\partial B(0,\ t)}{\partial t}$$

$$= -\frac{a^2\bar{r}-\sigma^2/2}{a^2}\left(\frac{\partial B(0,\ t)}{\partial t} - 1\right) + \frac{\sigma^2}{2a}B(0,\ t)\frac{\partial B(0,\ t)}{\partial t} + x(0)\frac{\partial B(0,\ t)}{\partial t}$$

$$= -\frac{a^2\bar{r}-\sigma^2/2}{a^2}\left(e^{-at}-1\right) + \frac{\sigma^2}{2a^2}\left(1-e^{-at}\right)e^{-at} + x(0)e^{-at}$$

so that:

$$\varphi^{Vasicek}(t;\ \alpha) = f(0,\ t) + \frac{a^2\bar{r}-\sigma^2/2}{a^2}(e^{-at}-1) - \frac{\sigma^2}{2a^2}(1-e^{-at})e^{-at} - x(0)e^{-at} \quad (11.64)$$

The price at time t of a zero-coupon bond maturing at time T can be computed from (11.60):

$$P(t,\ T) = \left(\frac{P(0,\ T)A(0,\ t)e^{-B(0,t)x(0)}}{P(0,\ t)A(0,\ T)e^{-B(0,T)x(0)}}\right)A(t,\ T)e^{-B(t,T)(r(t)-\varphi^{Vasicek}(t;\alpha))} \quad (11.65)$$

The price at time t of European call option with maturity T and strike X, written on a zero-coupon bond maturing at time S, is:

$$C(t,\ T) = \left(\frac{P(0,\ S)A(0,\ t)e^{-B(0,t)x(0)}}{P(0,\ t)A(0,\ S)e^{-B(0,S)x(0)}}\right)$$

$$\cdot\left(\Psi^{Vasicek}\left(t,\ T,\ S,\ X\left(\frac{P(0,\ T)A(0,\ S)e^{-B(0,S)x(0)}}{P(0,\ S)A(0,\ T)e^{-B(0,T)x(0)}}\right),\ r(t)-\varphi^{Vasicek}(t;\ \alpha);\ \alpha\right)\right)$$

where

$$\psi^{Vasicek}(t,\ T,\ S,\ X,\ x;\ \alpha) = A(t,\ T)e^{-B(t,S)x}\Phi(h) - XA(t,\ T)e^{-B(t,T)x}\Phi(h-\bar{\sigma})$$

$\Phi(\cdot)$ is the cumulative normal distribution function,

$$h = \frac{1}{\sigma}\ln\left[\frac{A(t,\ S)e^{-B(t,S)x}}{XA(t,\ T)e^{-B(t,T)x}} + \frac{\bar{\sigma}}{2}\right]$$

$$\bar{\sigma} = \sigma B(T,\ S)\sqrt{\frac{1-e^{-2a(T-t)}}{2a}}$$

$$A(t,\ T) = \exp\left[\frac{(B(t,\ T)-(T-t))(a^2\bar{r}-\sigma^2/2)}{a^2} - \frac{\sigma^2 B(t,\ T)^2}{4a}\right]$$

$$B(t,\ T) = \frac{1-e^{-a(T-t)}}{a}$$

From (11.63), define the shift-extended drift as:

$$\theta(t) = \bar{r} + \varphi(t;\ \alpha) + \frac{1}{a}\frac{d\varphi(t;\ \alpha)}{dt}$$

The Vasicek model can be written as:

$$dr(t) = a(\theta(t) - r(t))dt + \sigma dz(t) \qquad (11.66)$$

which coincides with the Hull-White (1994) extended Vasicek model (10.76).[17] Moreover, from (11.66), we can obtain (11.64) by setting

$$\varphi(t;\ \alpha) = e^{-at}\varphi(0;\ \alpha) + a\int_0^t e^{-a(t-s)}\theta(s)ds - \bar{r}(1-e^{-at})$$

If we set $\bar{r} = 0$, then:

$$\varphi^{Vasicek}(t;\ \alpha) = f(0,\ t) - \frac{\sigma^2}{2a^2}(e^{-at}-1) - \frac{\sigma^2}{2a^2}(1-e^{-at})e^{-at} - x(0)e^{-at}$$

$$= f(0,\ t) + \frac{\sigma^2}{2a^2}(1-e^{-at})^2 - x(0)e^{-at}$$

[17]Ibid., 92.

If we compare the similarity of this to

$$\alpha(t) = f(0,\ t) + \frac{\sigma^2}{2a^2}(1 - e^{-at})^2$$

from (10.78), we notice that the initial rate $r(0)$ is completely absorbed by α whereas in the shift function $\varphi^{Vasicek}$, $r(0)$ is partly absorbed by $x(0)$ and partly by $\varphi^{Vasicek}(0;\alpha)$. Due to the linearity of the short rate model, $x(0)$ does not add further flexibility to the extended model and so we can set $x(0) = r(0)$ and $\varphi^{Vasicek}(0;\alpha) = 0$ without affecting the model-fitting quality.[18]

The following is a more robust and object-oriented implementation of the Hull-White model.[19] It breaks up the construction of the tree into multiple task-specific methods and avoids the inefficient use of double arrays as in the previous implementation.

```
#ifndef _HULLTREE_H
#define _HULLTREE_H

#include <vector>
#include "math.h"
using namespace std;

struct myRateNode
{
  public:
      int nodeNumber;                // node id
      int depth;                     // equals depth of the tree
      int relativePosition;          // equals j (-2,-1,-0, 1, 2) for the node
      double rate;                   // equals R for the node
      double presentValue;           // equals Q for the node
      double alpha;                  // equals value of center node= term struct
      double pu;                     // probability of going up
      double pm;                     // probability of going in the middle
      double pd;                     // probability of going down
      myRateNode * up;               // pointer to up node
      myRateNode * middle;           // pointer to middle node
      myRateNode * down;             // pointer to down node
      myRateNode(int & i, int & a, int & b, double & c, double & d, double & e,
         double & z, double & y, double & x, myRateNode * f = NULL, myRateNode * g =
            NULL, myRateNode* h = NULL) : nodeNumber(i), depth(a),
         relativePosition(b), rate(c), presentValue(d), alpha(e), pu(z), pm(y),
         pd(x), up(f), middle(g), down(h)
```

---

[18]Ibid., 93.
[19]See Li (2002).

```
      { }
};


class HullTree
{
  public:
    HullTree();  // constructor
    ~HullTree(); // destructor
    void udm(myRateNode * node);
    void addBondPrices(vector<double> structure);
    vector<myRateNode *> findConnectors(myRateNode * node);
    double addPresentValue(myRateNode * node, vector<myRateNode *> depthVector,
      vector<double> structure);
    void addRemainingRates(myRateNode * tempNode, vector<myRateNode *>
      depthVector);
    void addRates(vector<double> structure);
    int expand(int lastNodeNumber, int nodesInDepth, int tempDepth);
    int maintain(int lastNodeNumber, int nodesInDepth, int tempDepth);
    void connectNodes(vector<double> structure);
    void outputTree();
    void buildTree(vector<double> structure, double a, double dT, double dR, double
      min, double max);
    vector<myRateNode *> myTree;
  private:
    vector<double> alphaStructure;       // same size as structure, saves alpha
                                         // values per term
    vector<double> bondPrices;           // same size as structure, saves bond
                                         // prices per term
    vector<int> width;                   // same size as structure, saves width
                                         // per term
    myRateNode * rootNode;
    double meanReversion;
    double deltaT;
    double deltaR;
    double jMin;
    double jMax;
};
#endif
```

The method definitions are:

```
#include "hullwhite.h"
#include "math.h"
#include <string>
#include <iostream>
#include <fstream>

// default constructor
```

```
HullTree::HullTree() { }
// destructor
HullTree::~HullTree() { }


/*****************************************************************************
udm: figures out the Pu, Pm, and Pd for each node
[in]: myRateNode* node: pointer to current node
[out]: none
*****************************************************************************/
void HullTree::udm(myRateNode * node)
{
  if (node->relativePosition * deltaR * 100 > jMax)
  {
    node->pu = (7.00000/6.00000) + (((meanReversion * meanReversion *
    node->relativePosition * node->relativePosition * deltaT *
      deltaT)- (3 * meanReversion * node->relativePosition*deltaT))/2);
    node->pm = (0.00000-(1.00000/3.00000)) - (meanReversion *
      meanReversion * node->relativePosition * node->relativePosition * deltaT
        *deltaT) + (2 * meanReversion * node->relativePosition*deltaT);
    node->pd = (1.00000/6.00000) + (((meanReversion * meanReversion *
      node->relativePosition * node->relativePosition * deltaT * deltaT)-
        (meanReversion * node->relativePosition*deltaT))/2);
  }
  else if (node->relativePosition * deltaR * 100 < jMin)
  {
    node->pu = (1.00000/6.00000) + (((meanReversion * meanReversion *
      node->relativePosition * node->relativePosition * deltaT *
      deltaT)+(meanReversion * node->relativePosition*deltaT))/2);
    node->pm = (0.00000-(1.00000/3.00000)) - (meanReversion *
      meanReversion * node->relativePosition * node->relativePosition * deltaT *
      deltaT) - (2 * meanReversion * node->relativePosition*deltaT);
    node->pd = (7.00000/6.00000) + (((meanReversion * meanReversion *
      node->relativePosition * node->relativePosition * deltaT *deltaT)+(3 *
        meanReversion * node->relativePosition*deltaT))/2);
  }
  else
  {
    node->pu = (1.00000/6.00000) + (((meanReversion * meanReversion *
      node->relativePosition * node->relativePosition * deltaT *
      deltaT)-(meanReversion * node->relativePosition*deltaT))/2);
    node->pm = (2.00000/3.00000) - (meanReversion * meanReversion *
      node->relativePosition * node->relativePosition * deltaT * deltaT);
    node->pd = (1.00000/6.00000) + (((meanReversion * meanReversion *
      node->relativePosition * node->relativePosition * deltaT *
      deltaT)+(meanReversion * node->relativePosition*deltaT))/2);
  }
}


/*****************************************************************************
addBondPrices: calculates bond prices based on the term structure
```

```
[in]: vector<double> structure : yield term structure
[out]: void
********************************************************************************/
void HullTree::addBondPrices(vector<double> structure)
{
  for (int a = 0; a < structure.size(); a++)
  {
    double temp = exp(0.00000 - (structure[a] * (a+1)*deltaT));
    bondPrices.push_back(temp);
  }
}


/*******************************************************************************
findConnectors: finds and returns connecting nodes for the calculation of Q
[in]: myRateNode* node : pointer to node
[out]: vector<myRateNode*> : vector of connected nodes to current node
********************************************************************************/
vector<myRateNode*> HullTree::findConnectors(myRateNode * node)
{
  vector<myRateNode *> tempVector;
  for (int count = 0; count < myTree.size(); count++)
  {
    if (myTree[count]->up == node || myTree[count]->middle == node
      ||myTree[count]->down == node)
    {
      myRateNode * tempNode = myTree[count];
      tempVector.push_back(tempNode);
    }
  }
  return tempVector;
}


/*******************************************************************************
addPresentValue: adds Q-- given depthVector, the Arrow-Debreu prices for the
                 current node[a] in depthVector is calculated.
[in]:  myRateNode* node : pointer to current node
       vector<myRateNode *> depthVector: vector of nodes at current depth
[out]: double : sum of present value of Arrow-Debreu securities
********************************************************************************/
double HullTree::addPresentValue(myRateNode * node, vector<myRateNode *>
  depthVector, vector<double> structure)
{
  double alpha= 0.00000;
  for (int a = 0; a > depthVector.size(); a++)
  {
    depthVector[a]->presentValue = 0;
    // find connecting nodes to each node of the same depth
    vector<myRateNode *> tempVector = findConnectors(depthVector[a]);
    // going through those connecting nodes, finding Q for depthVector[a]
    for (int b = 0; b < tempVector.size(); b++)
    {
      if (tempVector[b]->up == depthVector[a])
```

```
      {
        depthVector[a]->presentValue = tempVector[b]->pu * exp(0.00000 -
          ((tempVector[b]->rate)*deltaT)) * tempVector[b]->presentValue +
          depthVector[a]->presentValue;
      }
      else if (tempVector[b]->middle == depthVector[a])
      {
        depthVector[a]->presentValue = tempVector[b]->pm * exp(0.00000 -
          ((tempVector[b]->rate)*deltaT)) * tempVector[b]->presentValue +
          depthVector[a]->presentValue;
      }
      else if (tempVector[b]->down == depthVector[a])
      {
        depthVector[a]->presentValue = tempVector[b]->pd * exp(0.00000 -
          ((tempVector[b]->rate)*deltaT)) * tempVector[b]->presentValue +
          depthVector[a]->presentValue;
      }
    }
  }

  for (int c = 0; c < depthVector.size(); c++)
  {
    alpha = alpha + (depthVector[c]->presentValue * exp(0.00000 - (deltaR* deltaT *
      depthVector[c]->relativePosition)));
  }
  alpha = log(alpha);
  alpha = alpha - log(bondPrices[depthVector[0]->depth]);
  alpha = alpha / deltaT;

  return alpha;
}

/*************************************************************************************
addRemainingRates: adds the remaining rates
[in]: myRateNode* tempNode : pointer to node
      vector<myRateNode *> depthVector :
*************************************************************************************/
void HullTree::addRemainingRates(myRateNode * tempNode, vector<myRateNode *>
  depthVector)
{
  for (int a = 0; a < depthVector.size(); a++)
  {
    depthVector[a]->rate = depthVector[a]->relativePosition * deltaR +
      tempNode->rate;
  }
}

/*************************************************************************************
addRates: adds the term structure onto the center nodes
[in]: vector<double> structure : term structure of rates
[out]: void
*************************************************************************************/
void HullTree::addRates(vector<double> structure)
```

```
{
  myTree[0]->rate = structure[0];
  myTree[0]->presentValue = 1;
  myRateNode * tempNode = myTree[0];
  vector<myRateNode *> depthVector;
  int tempDepth = 1;

  for (int a = 1; a < myTree.size(); a++)
  {
    // we're put all nodes of the same depth on a vector
    if (myTree[a]->depth == tempDepth)
    {
      depthVector.push_back(myTree[a]);
    }
    else
    {
      // getting the center node
      tempNode = tempNode->middle;
      // calling present value (sum of Arrow-Debreu securities)
      // with the center node and vector of nodes with the same depth
      tempNode->rate = addPresentValue(tempNode, depthVector, structure);
      // add remaining rates to the nodes in the same depth as tempNode
      addRemainingRates(tempNode, depthVector);
      tempDepth++;
      // clear and add the first node of the next depth
      depthVector.clear();
      a--;
    }
  }

  // getting the center node
  tempNode = tempNode->middle;
  // calling present value with the center node and vector of nodes with the same
  // depth
  tempNode->rate = addPresentValue(tempNode, depthVector, structure);
  addRemainingRates(tempNode, depthVector);
}

/**********************************************************************************
expand: expands node
[in]: int lastNodeNumber : position of last number
       int nodesInDepth : number of nodes deep
       int tempDepth    : current (temp) depth size
[out]: int nodesInDepth  : number of nodes in depth + 2
**********************************************************************************/
int HullTree::expand(int lastNodeNumber, int nodesInDepth, int tempDepth)
{
  int beginningNode = lastNodeNumber-nodesInDepth+1;
  int t = 0;
  // temp variables, then adding on new blank nodes
  int aa = 0;
  double bb = 0;
  for (int c = 0; c < nodesInDepth + 2; c++)
```

```
  {
    myRateNode * tempNode = new
      myRateNode(aa,tempDepth,aa,bb,bb,bb,bb,bb,bb,NULL,NULL,NULL);
    myTree.push_back(tempNode);
  }

  while (t < nodesInDepth)
  {
    myTree[beginningNode+t]->up = myTree[beginningNode + t + nodesInDepth];
    myTree[beginningNode+t]->middle = myTree[beginningNode + t + nodesInDepth + 1];
    myTree[beginningNode+t]->down = myTree[beginningNode + t + nodesInDepth + 2];
    t++;
  }

  // adding relativePosition
  int divider = (nodesInDepth + 1) / 2;
  for (int a = 0; a < nodesInDepth+2; a++)
  {
    myTree[beginningNode + nodesInDepth + a]->relativePosition = divider - a;
  }
  return nodesInDepth + 2;
}

/********************************************************************************
maintain:
[in]:   int lastNodeNumber : position of last number
        int nodesInDepth   : number of nodes deep
        int tempDepth      : current (temp) depth size
[out]:  int nodesInDepth   : depth size of nodes
********************************************************************************/
int HullTree::maintain(int lastNodeNumber, int nodesInDepth, int tempDepth)
{
  int beginningNode = lastNodeNumber-nodesInDepth+1;
  // temp variables, then adding on new blank nodes
  int aa = 0;
  double bb = 0;
  for (int c = 0; c < nodesInDepth; c++)
  {
    myRateNode * tempNode = new
    myRateNode(aa,tempDepth,aa,bb,bb,bb,bb,bb,bb,NULL,NULL,NULL);
    myTree.push_back(tempNode);
  }
  // prevent the top node from expanding
  myTree[beginningNode]->up = myTree[beginningNode + nodesInDepth];
  myTree[beginningNode]->middle = myTree[beginningNode + nodesInDepth + 1];
  myTree[beginningNode]->down = myTree[beginningNode + nodesInDepth + 2];
  // expand the middle nodes accordingly
  for (int i = 1; i <= nodesInDepth - 2; i++)
  {
    myTree[beginningNode + i]->up = myTree[beginningNode + i + nodesInDepth - 1];
    myTree[beginningNode + i]->middle = myTree[beginningNode + i + nodesInDepth];
    myTree[beginningNode + i]->down = myTree[beginningNode + i + nodesInDepth + 1];
  }
```

```
myTree[lastNodeNumber]->up = myTree[lastNodeNumber + nodesInDepth - 2];
myTree[lastNodeNumber]->middle = myTree[lastNodeNumber + nodesInDepth - 1];
myTree[lastNodeNumber]->down = myTree[lastNodeNumber + nodesInDepth];

// adding relativePosition
int divider = (nodesInDepth - 1) / 2;
for (int a = 0; a < nodesInDepth; a++)
{
  myTree[beginningNode + nodesInDepth + a]->relativePosition = divider - a;
}
return nodesInDepth;
}


/******************************************************************************
connectNodes: goes down the vector of myRateNodes and connects the nodes to each
  other
[in]: vector<double> structure : term structure of rates
[out]: void
******************************************************************************/
void HullTree::connectNodes(vector<double> structure)
{
  // temporary variables
  myRateNode * tempNode;
  // temp variables, originally making a max of 9 nodes
  int aa = 0;
  double bb = 0;
  for (int c = 0; c < 9; c++)
  {
    myRateNode * tempNode = new
      myRateNode(aa,aa,aa,bb,bb,bb,bb,bb,bb,NULL,NULL,NULL);
    myTree.push_back(tempNode);
  }
  // initializing the root node
  myTree[0]->depth = 0;
  myTree[0]->relativePosition = 0;
  myTree[0]->presentValue = 1.00000;

  width.push_back(1);
  if (structure.size() > 1)
  {
    myTree[0]->up = myTree[1];
    myTree[0]->middle = myTree[2];
    myTree[0]->down = myTree[3];
    myTree[1]->depth = 1;
    myTree[2]->depth = 1;
    myTree[3]->depth = 1;
    myTree[1]->relativePosition = 1;
    myTree[2]->relativePosition = 0;
    myTree[3]->relativePosition = -1;
    width.push_back(3);
  }
  if (structure.size() > 2)
```

```
  {
    myTree[1]->up = myTree[4];
    myTree[1]->middle = myTree[5];
    myTree[1]->down = myTree[6];
    myTree[2]->up = myTree[5];
    myTree[2]->middle = myTree[6];
    myTree[2]->down = myTree[7];
    myTree[3]->up = myTree[6];
    myTree[3]->middle = myTree[7];
    myTree[3]->down = myTree[8];
    myTree[4]->depth = 2;
    myTree[5]->depth = 2;
    myTree[6]->depth = 2;
    myTree[7]->depth = 2;
    myTree[8]->depth = 2;
    myTree[4]->relativePosition = 2;
    myTree[5]->relativePosition = 1;
    myTree[6]->relativePosition = 0;
    myTree[7]->relativePosition = -1;
    myTree[8]->relativePosition = -2;
    width.push_back(5);
  }
  if (structure.size() > 3)
  {
    for (int count = 3; count < structure.size(); count++)
    {
      tempNode=myTree[myTree.size()-1];
      // see if tempNode->relativePosition * deltaR is greater than jMax or less
        than jMin
      if (100 * tempNode->relativePosition * deltaR > jMax || 100 *
        tempNode->relativePosition * deltaR < jMin)
      {
        width.push_back(maintain(myTree.size()-1, width[count-1], count));
      }
      // if not, then make it even bigger
      else
        width.push_back(expand(myTree.size()-1, width[count-1], count));
    }
  }
}


/******************************************************************************
outputTree: used for debugging purposes
[in]: none
[out]: void
******************************************************************************/
void HullTree::outputTree()
{
  string filename = "OUTPUT.txt";
  ofstream output(filename.c_str());
  for (int count = 0; count < myTree.size(); count++)
  {
```

```
      myTree[count]->nodeNumber = count;
   }
   cout <<"count " <<"depth " <<"RP " <<" rate " <<"pu " <<"pm " <<"pd " <<endl;
   for (count = 0; count < myTree.size(); count++)
   {
      output <<count <<" ";
      cout <<count <<" ";
      output <<myTree[count]->depth <<" ";
      cout <<myTree[count]->depth <<" ";
      output <<myTree[count]->relativePosition <<" ";
      cout <<myTree[count]->relativePosition <<" ";
      output <<myTree[count]->rate <<" ";
      cout <<myTree[count]->rate <<" ";
      output <<myTree[count]->pu <<" ";
      cout <<" " <<myTree[count]->pu <<" ";
      output <<myTree[count]->pm <<" ";
      cout <<" " <<myTree[count]->pm <<" ";
      output <<myTree[count]->pd <<endl;
      cout <<" " <<myTree[count]->pd <<endl;
   }
}


/**********************************************************************************
buildTree: builds the tree
[in]: vector<double> structure : term structure of rates
        double a : mean reversion parameter
        double dT: time step
        double dR: state step size
        double min : min downward branching level
        double max: max upward branching level
[out] : void
**********************************************************************************/
void HullTree::buildTree(vector<double> structure, double a, double dT, double dR,
   double min, double max)
{

   // variables which equal referenced values
   meanReversion = a;
   deltaT = dT;
   deltaR = dR;
   jMin = min;
   jMax = max;
   connectNodes(structure); // connect the nodes
   for (int count = 0; count < myTree.size(); count++)
   {
      udm(myTree[count]);
   }
   addBondPrices(structure);
   addRates(structure);
   outputTree();
}
```

Another alternative and more robust object-oriented implementation of the Hull-White model is adapted from the QuantLib library.

```cpp
#include "Vasicek.h"

namespace QuantLib
{
  namespace ShortRateModels
  {

    /**************************************************************************
    Single-factor Hull-White (extended Vasicek) model class.
    This class implements the standard single-factor Hull-White model defined by
    dr_t = (theta(t) - alpha r_t)dt + \sigma dW_t where alpha and sigma are
    constants.
    **************************************************************************/
    class HullWhite : public Vasicek, public TermStructureConsistentModel
    {
      public:
        HullWhite(const RelinkableHandle<TermStructure>& termStructure,
          double a = 0.1, double sigma = 0.01);

        Handle<Lattices::Lattice> tree(const TimeGrid& grid) const;
        Handle<ShortRateDynamics> dynamics() const;
        // previous method to build tree
        void buildHW(vector<double> zero, double a, double volatility, int N,
          double T);
        double discountBondOption(Option::Type type, double strike, Time maturity,
          Time bondMaturity) const;
      protected:
        void generateArguments();
        double A(Time t, Time T) const;
      private:
        class Dynamics;
        class FittingParameter;
        Parameter phi_;
    };


    /**************************************************************************
    Short-rate dynamics in the Hull-White model
    The short-rate is here r_t = varphi(t) + x_t where varphi(t) \is the
      deterministic time-dependent parameter used for term-structure fitting and x_t
      is the state variable following an Ornstein-Uhlenbeck process.
    **************************************************************************/
    class HullWhite::Dynamics : public ShortRateDynamics
    {
      public:
        Dynamics(const Parameter& fitting, double a, double sigma)
```

```
          : ShortRateDynamics(Handle<DiffusionProcess>(new
            OrnsteinUhlenbeckProcess(a, sigma))),
            fitting_(fitting) {}
            double variable(Time t, Rate r) const {
              return r - fitting_(t);
            }
            double shortRate(Time t, double x) const {
              return x + fitting_(t);
            }
    private:
      Parameter fitting_;
};


/******************************************************************************
Analytical term-structure fitting parameter varphi(t).
varphi(t) is analytically defined by varphi(t) = f(t) + 1/2/(sigma(1-exp{-
   at})}{a}]^2), where f(t) is the instantaneous forward rate at t.
******************************************************************************/
class HullWhite::FittingParameter : public TermStructureFittingParameter
{
  private:
    class Impl : public Parameter::Impl
      {
        public:
          Impl(const RelinkableHandle<TermStructure>& termStructure,
            double a, double sigma)
            : termStructure_(termStructure), a_(a), sigma_(sigma) {}
          double value(const Array& params, Time t) const {
            double forwardRate = termStructure_->instantaneousForward(t);
            double temp = sigma_*(1.0 - exp(-a_*t))/a_;
            return (forwardRate + 0.5*temp*temp);
          }
        private:
          RelinkableHandle<TermStructure> termStructure_;
          double a_, sigma_;
      };
  public:
      FittingParameter(const RelinkableHandle<TermStructure>& termStructure,
        double a, double sigma)
        : TermStructureFittingParameter(Handle<Parameter::Impl>(
          new FittingParameter::Impl(termStructure, a, sigma))) {}
};


/******************************************************************************
dynamics: generates and returns extended HW dynamics
[in]: none
[out]: Handle<OneFactor::ShortRateDynamics> : HW dynamics
******************************************************************************/
inline Handle<OneFactorModel::ShortRateDynamics> HullWhite::dynamics() const {
  return Handle<ShortRateDynamics>(new Dynamics(phi_, a(), sigma()));
```

```
      }
    }
}
```

The class has the follwing method definitions:

```
#include "HullWhite.h"
#include "Trinomialtree.h"
#include "Blackmodel.h"

namespace QuantLib
{
  namespace ShortRateModels
  {
    using namespace Lattices;

    /***************************************************************************
    HullWhite : Constructor
    [in] RelinkableHandle<TermStructure>& termStructure : term structure
         double a: mean reversion parameter
         double sigma: volatility
    ***************************************************************************/
    HullWhite::HullWhite(const RelinkableHandle<TermStructure>& termStructure,
      double a, double sigma) : Vasicek(termStructure->instantaneousForward(0.0),
        a, 0.0, sigma), TermStructureConsistentModel(termStructure)
    {
      arguments_[1] = NullParameter();
      generateArguments();
    }


    /***************************************************************************
    tree: builds Hull-White tree
    [in] TimeGrid& grid            : time grid
    [out] Handle<Lattices::Lattice>  : Hull-White tree
    ***************************************************************************/
    Handle<Lattices::Lattice> HullWhite::tree(const TimeGrid& grid) const
    {
      TermStructureFittingParameter phi(termStructure());

      // create Hull-White short rate dynamics
      Handle<ShortRateDynamics> numericDynamics(new Dynamics(phi, a(), sigma()));

      // generate trinomial tree approximated by Hull-White process
      Handle<TrinomialTree> trinomial(new TrinomialTree(numericDynamics->process(),
        grid));

      // build Hull-White short rate (trinomial tree) using Hull-White dynamics
```

```
Handle<ShortRateTree> numericTree(new ShortRateTree(trinomial,
  numericDynamics, grid));

Handle<TermStructureFittingParameter::NumericalImpl> impl =
  phi.implementation();
impl->reset();

// evolve forward computing state prices (short rates)
for (Size i=0; i<(grid.size() - 1); i++)
{
  double discountBond = termStructure()->discount(grid[i+1]);
  const Array& statePrices = numericTree->statePrices(i);
  Size size = numericTree->size(i);
  double dt = numericTree->timeGrid().dt(i);
  double dx = trinomial->dx(i);
  double x = trinomial->underlying(i,0);
  double value = 0.0;
  for (Size j=0; j<size; j++)
  {
    value += statePrices[j]*exp(-x*dt);
    x += dx;
  }
  value = log(value/discountBond)/dt;
  impl->set(grid[i], value);
}
return numericTree;
}


/*****************************************************************************
A: computes A term of discount bond price
[in]  Time t : current time
      Time T : end time (option maturity)
[out] double A
*****************************************************************************/
double HullWhite::A(Time t, Time T) const
{
  double discount1 = termStructure()->discount(t);
  double discount2 = termStructure()->discount(T);
  double forward = termStructure()->instantaneousForward(t);
  double temp = sigma()*B(t,T);
  double value = B(t,T)*forward - 0.25*temp*temp*B(0.0,2.0*t);
  return exp(value)*discount2/discount1;
}


/*****************************************************************************
generateArguments: fits shift parameter to term structure and mean reversion
                   parameter a and volatility
[in] none
[out] void
*****************************************************************************/
```

```
   void HullWhite::generateArguments() {
     phi_ = FittingParameter(termStructure(), a(), sigma());
   }


/***********************************************************************
discountBondOption: fits shift parameter to term structure and mean reversion
                    parameter a and volatility
[in]   Option::Type type  : option type (C)all or (P)ut
       double strike       : strike price
       Time maturity       : maturity of bond option
       Time bondMaturity   : maturity of bond
[out]  double              : bond option price
***********************************************************************/
   double HullWhite::discountBondOption(Option::Type type, double strike, Time
     maturity, Time bondMaturity) const
   {
     double v = sigma()*B(maturity, bondMaturity)*sqrt(0.5*(1.0 - exp(-
       2.0*a()*maturity))/a());
     double f = termStructure()->discount(bondMaturity);
     double k = termStructure()->discount(maturity)*strike;

     double w = (type==Option::Call)? 1.0 : -1.0;

     return BlackModel::formula(f, k, v, w);
   }
  }
}
```

11.11 SHIFT-EXTENDED COX-INGERSOLL-ROSS MODEL

The shift-extension procedure can be extended to the CIR model; the result is often referred to as CIR++. As before, we have a process x^α that follows (11.53) with the parameter vector $\alpha = (a, \bar{r}, \sigma)$. The CIR++ short rate model is:

$$dx(t) = a(\bar{r} - x(t))dt + \sigma\sqrt{x(t)}dz(t)$$
$$r(t) = x(t) + \varphi(t)$$

(11.67)

where a, $\bar{r}$, and σ are positive values that satisfy $2a\bar{r} > \sigma^2$, so that the rates remain positive. We can compute the shift extension $\varphi(t; \alpha) = \varphi^{CIR}(t; \alpha)$ as:

$$\varphi^{CIR}(t; \alpha) = f(0, t) - f^{CIR}(0, t; \alpha)$$

where

$$
\begin{aligned}
f^{CIR}(0,\,t;\,x) &= -\frac{\partial \ln P^{x}(0,\,t)}{\partial t} = -\frac{\partial \ln A(0,\,t)}{\partial t} + x(0)\frac{\partial B(0,\,t)}{\partial t} \\[2mm]
&= \frac{\partial}{\partial t}\left[\frac{2a\bar{r}}{\sigma^{2}}\ln\left[\frac{2\gamma e^{\left(\frac{(a+\gamma)t}{2}\right)}}{2\gamma + (a+\gamma)(e^{\gamma t}-1)}\right]\right] + x(0)\frac{\partial}{\partial t}\left(\frac{2(e^{\gamma t}-1)}{2\gamma + (a+\gamma)(e^{\gamma t}-1)}\right) \\[2mm]
&= \frac{a\bar{r}(e^{\gamma t}-1)}{2\gamma + (a+\gamma)(e^{\gamma t}-1)} + x(0)\frac{4\gamma^{2}e^{\gamma t}}{(2\gamma + (a+\gamma)(e^{\gamma t}-1))^{2}}
\end{aligned}
$$

and

$$
\gamma = \sqrt{a^{2} + 2\sigma^{2}}
$$

The price at time t of a zero-coupon maturing at time T is

$$
P(t,\,T) = \bar{A}(t,\,T)e^{-B(t,T)r(t)}
$$

where

$$
P(t,\,T) = \left(\frac{P(0,\,T)A(0,\,t)e^{-B(0,t)x(0)}}{P(0,\,t)A(0,\,T)e^{-B(0,T)x(0)}}\right)A(t,\,T)e^{B(t,T)\varphi^{CIR}(t;\alpha)} \tag{11.68}
$$

and $A(t,\,T)$ and $B(t,\,T)$ are defined in (10.91). The price at time t of a European call option with maturity T and a strike of X on a zero-coupon bond maturing at $S > T$,

$$
\begin{aligned}
C(t,\,T,\,S,\,X) &= \left(\frac{P(0,\,S)A(0,\,t)e^{-B(0,T)x(0)}}{P(0,\,t)A(0,\,S)e^{-B(0,S)x(0)}}\right)\cdot \\[2mm]
&\quad \Psi^{CIR}\left(t,\,T,\,S,\,X\frac{P(0,\,T)A(0,\,S)e^{-B(0,S)x(0)}}{P(0,\,S)A(0,\,T)e^{-B(0,T)x(0)}},\,r(t)-\varphi^{CIR}(t;\,\alpha);\,\alpha\right)
\end{aligned} \tag{11.69}
$$

where $\psi^{CIR}(t,\,T,\,S,\,X,\,x;\,\alpha)$ is the CIR option price from (10.92) where $r(t) = x$. By simplifying (11.69) we get:

$$
\begin{aligned}
C(t,\,T,\,S,\,X) &= P(t,\,S)\chi^{2}\left(2\tilde{r}(\rho+\psi+B(t,\,S));\frac{4a\bar{r}}{\sigma^{2}},\,\frac{2\rho^{2}(r(t)-\varphi^{CIR}(t;\,\alpha))e^{\gamma(T-t)}}{\rho+\psi+B(T,\,S)}\right) \\[2mm]
&\quad - XP(t,\,T)\chi^{2}\left(2\tilde{r}(\rho+\psi);\frac{4a\bar{r}}{\sigma^{2}},\,\frac{2\rho^{2}(r(t)-\varphi^{CIR}(t;\,\alpha))e^{\gamma(T-t)}}{\rho+\psi}\right)
\end{aligned} \tag{11.70}
$$

where

$$\tilde{r} = \frac{1}{B(T,\,S)}\left[\ln\left(\frac{A(T,\,S)}{X}\right) - \ln\left(\frac{P(0,\,T)A(0,\,S)e^{-B(0,S)x(0)}}{P(0,\,S)A(0,\,T)e^{-B(0,T)x(0)}}\right)\right]$$

ρ and ψ come from (10.92) in section 10.10, and χ^2 is the noncentral chi-squared distribution.

The following is an implementation of the extended CIR model given in the QuantLib library:

```
/**************************************************************************
Extended Cox-Ingersoll-Ross model class.
This class implements the extended Cox-Ingersoll-Ross model defined by
dr(t) = (theta(t) - alpha*r(t))dt + sqrt(r(t))sigma*dW(t)
**************************************************************************/
class ExtendedCoxIngersollRoss : public CoxIngersollRoss, public TermStructure
  ConsistentModel
{
  public:
    ExtendedCoxIngersollRoss(const RelinkableHandle<TermStructure>& termStructure,
        double theta = 0.1, double k = 0.1, double sigma = 0.1, double x0 = 0.05);
    Handle<Lattices::Lattice> tree(const TimeGrid& grid) const;
    Handle<ShortRateDynamics> dynamics() const;
    double discountBondOption(Option::Type type,
        double strike,
        Time maturity,
        Time bondMaturity) const;
  protected:
    void generateArguments();
    double A(Time t, Time T) const;
  private:
    class Dynamics;
    class FittingParameter;
    Parameter phi_;
};


/**************************************************************************
Short-rate dynamics in the extended Cox-Ingersoll-Ross model
The short-rate is here r(t) = \varphi(t) + y(t)^2 where varphi(t) is the
deterministic time-dependent parameter used for term-structure fitting and y_t is
the state variable, the square-root of a standard CIR process.
**************************************************************************/
class ExtendedCoxIngersollRoss::Dynamics: public CoxIngersollRoss::Dynamics
{
  public:
    Dynamics(const Parameter& phi, double theta, double k, double sigma, double x0)
```

```
          : CoxIngersollRoss::Dynamics(theta, k, sigma, x0), phi_(phi) {}


      virtual double variable(Time t, Rate r) const {return sqrt(r - phi_(t));
      }
      virtual double shortRate(Time t, double y) const {return y*y + phi_(t);
      }
        private:
          Parameter phi_;
};




/****************************************************************************
Analytical term-structure fitting parameter varphi(t).
varphi(t) is analytically defined by
varphi(t) = f(t) - {2k\theta(e^{th}-1)}/{2h+(k+h)(e^{th}-1)} - {4 x_0 h^2
  e^{th}}/{(2h+(k+h)(e^{th}-1))^1},
where f(t) is the instantaneous forward rate at t and h = sqrt{k^2 + 2\sigma^2}.
****************************************************************************/
class ExtendedCoxIngersollRoss::FittingParameter : public TermStructureFitting
  Parameter
{
  private:
    class Impl : public Parameter::Impl
    {
    public:
      Impl(const RelinkableHandle<TermStructure>& termStructure, double theta,
        double k, double sigma, double x0) : termStructure_(termStructure),
        theta_(theta), k_(k), sigma_(sigma), x0_(x0) {}


      double value(const Array& params, Time t) const {
        double forwardRate = termStructure_->instantaneousForward(t);
        double h = sqrt(k_*k_  + 2.0*sigma_*sigma_);
        double expth = exp(t*h);
        double temp = 2.0*h + (k_+h)*(expth-1.0);
        double phi = forwardRate - 2.0*k_*theta_*(expth - 1.0)/temp -
          x0_*4.0*h*h*expth/(temp*temp);


        return phi;
      }
    private:
      RelinkableHandle<TermStructure> termStructure_; double theta_, k_, sigma_,
        x0_;
    };
  public:
    FittingParameter(const RelinkableHandle<TermStructure>& termStructure,
    double theta, double k, double sigma, double x0)
    : TermStructureFittingParameter(Handle<Parameter::Impl>(
      new FittingParameter::Impl(termStructure, theta, k, sigma, x0))) {}
};
```

```
/*****************************************************************************
dynamics: generates and returns extended CIR dynamics
[in] none
[out] Handle<OneFactor::ShortRateDynamics> : extended CIR dynamics
*****************************************************************************/
inline Handle<OneFactorModel::ShortRateDynamics> ExtendedCoxIngersollRoss::dynamics
  () const
{
  return Handle<ShortRateDynamics>(new Dynamics(phi_, theta(), k() , sigma(),
    x0()));
}


/*****************************************************************************
generateArguments: fits shift parameter to term structure, mean reversion parmamter,
  and volatility
[in] none
[out] void
*****************************************************************************/
inline void ExtendedCoxIngersollRoss::generateArguments()
{
  phi_ = FittingParameter(termStructure(), theta(), k(), sigma(), x0());
}
```

The class has the following method definitions:

```
namespace QuantLib
{
  namespace ShortRateModels
  {
    using namespace Lattices;

    /*************************************************************************
    ExtendedCoxIngersollRoss : Constructor
    [in] RelinkableHandle<TermStructure>& termStructure : term structure
    double theta          : shift parameter
    double k              : mean reversion parameter
    double sigma          : volatility of short rate
    double x0             : initial short rate
    *************************************************************************/
    ExtendedCoxIngersollRoss::ExtendedCoxIngersollRoss(const
      RelinkableHandle<TermStructure>& termStructure, double theta, double k,
        double sigma, double x0)
        : CoxIngersollRoss(theta, k, sigma, x0), TermStructureConsistentModel
        (termStructure)
    {
      generateArguments();
    }
```

```
/***************************************************************************
tree: builds trinomial tree that approximates Black-Karasinski
[in] TimeGrid& grid              : time grid
[out] Handle<Lattices::Lattice>  : Hull-White tree
***************************************************************************/
Handle<Lattice> ExtendedCoxIngersollRoss::tree(const TimeGrid& grid) const
{
  TermStructureFittingParameter phi(termStructure());
  Handle<Dynamics> numericDynamics(new Dynamics(phi, theta(), k(), sigma(),
    x0()));

  Handle<Tree> trinomial(new TrinomialTree(numericDynamics->process(), grid,
    true));
  return Handle<Lattice>(new ShortRateTree(trinomial, numericDynamics,
    phi.implementation(), grid));
}


/***************************************************************************
A: computes A term of discount bond price for Extended CIR
[in]   Time t : current time
       Time T : end time (option maturity)
[out] double A
***************************************************************************/
double ExtendedCoxIngersollRoss::A(Time t, Time s) const
{
  double pt = termStructure()->discount(t);
  double ps = termStructure()->discount(s);
  double value = CoxIngersollRoss::A(t,s)*exp(B(t,s)*phi_(t))*
    (ps*CoxIngersollRoss::A(0.0,t)*exp(-B(0.0,t)*x0()))/
    (pt*CoxIngersollRoss::A(0.0,s)*exp(-B(0.0,s)*x0()));
  return value;
}


/***************************************************************************
discountBondOption: prices discount bond option using extended CIR model
[in]   Option::Type type : option type (C)all or (P)ut
       double strike      : strike price
       Time maturity      : maturity of bond option
       Time bondMaturity  : maturity of bond
[out] double             : bond option price
***************************************************************************/
double ExtendedCoxIngersollRoss::discountBondOption(Option::Type type, double
  strike, Time t, Time s) const
{
  double discountT = termStructure()->discount(t);
  double discountS = termStructure()->discount(s);
  if (t > QL_EPSILON)
  {
    switch(type)
    {
      case Option::Call: return max(discountS - strike, 0.0);
```

```
                  case Option::Put: return max(strike - discountS, 0.0);
                  default: throw Error("unsupported option type");
                }
            }

        double sigma2 = sigma()*sigma();
        double h = sqrt(k()*k() + 2.0*sigma2);
        double r0 = termStructure()->instantaneousForward(0.0);
        double b = B(t,s);

        double rho = 2.0*h/(sigma2*(exp(h*t) - 1.0));
        double psi = (k() + h)/sigma2;

        double df = 4.0*k()*theta()/sigma2;
        double ncps = 2.0*rho*rho*(r0-phi_(0.0))*exp(h*t)/(rho+psi+b);
        double ncpt = 2.0*rho*rho*(r0-phi_(0.0))*exp(h*t)/(rho+psi);

        Math::NonCentralChiSquareDistribution chis(df, ncps);
        Math::NonCentralChiSquareDistribution chit(df, ncpt);

        double z = log(CoxIngersollRoss::A(t,s)/strike)/b;

        double call = discountS*chis(2.0*z*(rho+psi+b)) -
          strike*discountT*chit(2.0*z*(rho+psi));

        if (type == Option::Call)
          return call;
        else
          return call - discountS + strike*discountT;
        }
      }
}
```

where

```
/*****************************************************************************
NonCentralChiSqureDistribution class evaluates the noncentral chi squared
  distribution using the noncentrality parameter lambda (ncp_) and dg degrees of
  freedom. The sum of the squares of n normally distributed random variables with
  variance 1 and nonzero means follows.
*****************************************************************************/
class NonCentralChiSquareDistribution : public std::unary_function<double,double>
{
  public:
    NonCentralChiSquareDistribution(double df, double ncp) : df_(df), ncp_(ncp) {}
    double operator()(double x) const;
  private:
    static const double pi_;
    double df_, ncp_;
};
```

```
/******************************************************************************
operator() : overloaded nonchi squared distribution evaluation operator
[in]: double x : evaluation argument
[out]: double  : nonchi squared distribution value evaluated at x
******************************************************************************/
double NonCentralChiSquareDistribution::operator()(double x) const
{
  if (x <= 0.0)
    return 0.0;

  const double errmax = 1e-12;
  const int itrmax = 10000;
  double lam = 0.5*ncp_;

  double u = exp(-lam);
  double v = u;
  double x2 = 0.5*x;
  double f2 = 0.5*df_;
  double f_x_2n = df_ - x;

  double t = 0.0;
  if (f2*QL_EPSILON > 0.125 && fabs(x2-f2) < sqrt(QL_EPSILON)*f2)
  {
    t = exp((1 - t)*(2 - t/(f2+1)))/sqrt(2.0*pi_*(f2 + 1.0));
  }
  else
  {
    t = exp(f2*log(x2) - x2 - GammaFunction().logValue(f2 + 1));
  }

  double ans = v*t;
  bool flag = false;
  int n = 1;
  double f_2n = df_ + 2.0;
  f_x_2n += 2.0;

  double bound;
  for (;;)
  {
    if (f_x_2n > 0)
    {
      flag = true;
      goto L10;
    }
    for (;;)
    {
      u *= lam / n;
      v += u;
      t *= x / f_2n;
      ans += v*t;
      n++;
      f_2n += 2.0;
```

```
      f_x_2n += 2.0;
      if (!flag && n <= itrmax)
        break;
    L10:
      bound = t * x / f_x_2n;
      if (bound <= errmax || n > itrmax)
        goto L_End;
    }
  }

  L_End:
    if (bound > errmax)
      throw Error("Didn't converge");

  return (ans);
}
```

11.12   PRICING FIXED INCOME DERIVATIVES WITH THE MODELS

Once a short rate tree has been constructed, calibrated to the initial term structure, it is straightforward to price various fixed income derivatives. Suppose we want to value a European bond option on a pure discount bond using a Hull-White tree. After building the tree, we determine if it is optimal to exercise at maturity by computing the payoffs. We then use backward induction to compute the price of the bond option at each time step by discounting the future payoffs at the next step until we get to the first node at time step 0. Pricing an American bond option also starts at maturity and involves the same backward induction procedure as in the European case except that at each node the payoff has to be determined by comparing the immediate exercise value with the risk-neutral price at the node. Here is the code implementation:

```
/*****************************************************************************
priceDiscountBondsHW        : prices discount bond options using the Hull-White tree
[in]: vector<double> zero   : vector of spot curve rates
      int Ns                : bond maturity
      int NT                : option maturity
      double volatility     : bond volatility
      double a              : Hull-White mean reversion parameter
      double T              : time to maturity
      double strike         : strike price
      char type             : 'C'all or 'P'ut
      char exercise         : 'E'uropean or 'A'merican
[out] bond option price
*****************************************************************************/
double HullWhite::priceDiscountBondsHW(vector<double> zero, int Ns, int NT, double
  volatility, double a, double T, double strike, char type, char exercise)
```

```
{
  int i,j, k;
  double Ps[20][20] = {0.0};

  // build Hull-White tree
  buildHW(zero,a,volatility,Ns,T);

  // initialize maturity condition for pure discount bond underlying the option
  for (j = -Ns+1; j <= Ns-1; j++)
    Ps[Ns][j] = 1;

  // backward induction for pure discount bond price
  for (i = Ns - 1; i >= 0; i--)
  {
    for (j = -i; j <= i; j++)
    {
      Ps[i][j] = d[i][j]*(pu[j]*Ps[i+1][j+1] + pm[j]*Ps[i+1][j] +
        pd[j]*Ps[i+1][j-1]);
    }
  }

  // initialize maturity condition for option
  for (j = -NT; j <= NT; j++)
  {
    if (type == `C')
      C[NT][j] = max(0,Ps[NT][j] - strike);
    else
      C[NT][j] = max(0,strike - Ps[NT][j]);
  }

  if (exercise == `E')
  {
    // European price determined via the state prices
    C[0][0] = 0;
    for (j = -NT; j <= NT; j++)
    {
      C[0][0] = C[0][0] + Q[NT][j]*C[NT][j];
    }
  }
  else // compute American price
  {
    // backward induction for American option price
    for (i = NT-1; i >= 0; i--)
    {
      for (j = -i; j <= i; j++)
      {
        C[i][j] = d[i][j]*(pu[j]*C[i+1][j+1] + pm[j]*C[i+1][j] +
          pd[j]*C[i+1][j-1]);
        if (type == `C')
          C[i][j] = max(C[i][j],Ps[i][j] - strike);
        else
          C[i][j] = max(C[i][j],strike - Ps[i][j]);
```

```
      }
    }
  }
  return C[0][0];
}
```

Pricing swaptions is a similar process. The short rate tree is constructed and then backward induction follows. Suppose we want to value an American payer swaption using a BDT tree. After we build the BDT short rate tree, we compute the bond prices at each node. Then we start at the last step, compute the payoff, and then work backward comparing the intrinsic exercise value at each node with the risk-neutral value—using the higher of the two values—until we reach the first node. We need to account for swap payments (the fixed rate leg payments) and the frequency of the payments and thus the swap payment dates.

The following is the implementation:

```
/**********************************************************************************
payerSwaptionBDT              : prices swaptions using the BDT tree
[in]:  vector<double> rates   : vector of spot curve rates
       int Ns                 : swap maturity
       int NT                 : swaption maturity
       double volatility      : volatility of short rate
       double swapRate        : fixed leg payment
       double inityield       : current short rate
       double principal       : notional amount of swap
       double frequency       : frequency of payments (annually, semiannually,
                                 quarterly)
[out] double                  : swaption price
**********************************************************************************/
double BlackDermanToy::payerSwaptionBDT(vector<double> rates, int Ns, int NT,
  double volatility, double swapRate, double inityield, double principal, double
  frequency)
{
  int i, j;
  double B[20][20] = {0.0};   // discount bond prices
  double C[20][20] = {0.0};   // swaption prices

  // build short rate tree
  buildBDT(rates,volatility,Ns,NT,inityield);

  // initialize coupon bond maturity condition for fixed side of swap
  for (j = -Ns; j <= Ns; j += 2)
  {
    B[Ns][j] = principal + swapRate/frequency;
  }
  / /derive the coupon bond price in the tree via the discounted expectations
  for (i = Ns - 1; i >= NT; i--)
```

```
{
   for (j = -i; j <= i; j += 2)
   {
     if (i % frequency == 0)
        B[i][j] = d[i][j]*0.5*(B[i+1][j+1] + B[i+1][j-1] + swapRate/frequency);
     else
        B[i][j] = d[i][j]*0.5*(B[i+1][j+1] + B[i+1][j-1]);
   }
}
// initialize maturity condition for option
for (j = -NT; j <= NT; j += 2)
{
   C[NT][j] = max(0,(principal-B[NT][j]));
}

// for European swaption value utilize the pure security prices
C[0][0] = 0;
for (j = -NT; j <= NT; j+=2)
{
   C[0][0] = C[0][0] + max(0,Q[NT][j]*(principal-B[NT][j]));
}

for (i = NT-1; i >= 0; i--)
{
   for (j = -i; j <= i; j += 2)
   {
     C[i][j] = d[i][j]*(0.5*(C[i+1][j+1] + C[i+1][j-1]));
   }
}
return C[0][0];
}
```

Consider a two-year payer swaption on a three-year swap. We assume the term structure is upward sloping and given by {0.055, 0.0575, 0.0600, 0.0625, 0.0650, 0.070} and the short-rate volatility is assumed to be 10 percent. The swap rate is 6.5 percent and we assume annual payments. We assume the notional face value or principal is $100. Figure 11.5 shows the BDT tree built.

The price of the payer swaption is $16.31. At each node, the top number is the short rate, the middle number is the bond price (swap value), and the bottom number is the swaption price. Swap prices are not given at the first time step because the swap cannot be exercised until the second time step, at maturity of the swaption. Similarly, since the swaption expires in the second year, no swaption values are given after the second time step.

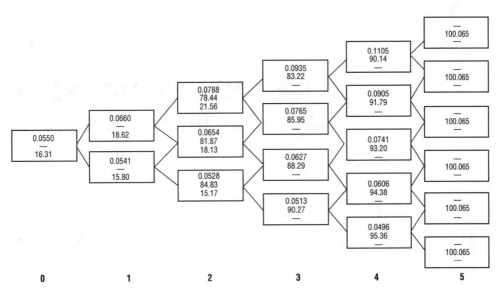

FIGURE 11.5   Valuing Two-Year Payer Swaption Using BDT Tree

CHAPTER 12

Two-Factor Models and the Heath-Jarrow-Morton Model

In the preceding chapter we focused on single-factor models. In each model, the short rate was the underlying factor with only one source of randomness, the Wiener process $z(t)$. From the short rate and its distributional properties, we can construct bond prices from the relationship

$$P(t,\ T) = E_t\left[\exp\left(-\int_t^T r(s)ds\right)\right]$$

and from all bond prices $P(t,\ T)$ at time t we can "reconstruct the whole zero-coupon interest-rate curve at the same time t, so that indeed the evolution of the whole curve is characterized by the evolution of the single quantity r."[1]

While many single-factor models work well in practice, such as the Black-Karasinski, Hull-White (HW), and exponential Vasicek models, they are not satisfactory for models that have payoffs dependent on two or more correlated underlying factors such as two continuously compounded spot rates for bonds of different maturities (i.e., T_1 and T_2). Thus, if the payoff depends on two underlying factors that are terminally correlated, then their joint distribution depends on their correlation—a consideration that a single-factor model cannot capture. In order to capture realistic correlation patterns, and thus covariance structures, multifactor models such as two-factor models are needed. Essentially, what this means is that the correlation in the model depends on, among other factors, instantaneously correlated sources of randomness between the factors (i.e., $dz_1 dz_2 = \rho$).

In practice, the optimal number of factors to use in a model is a trade-off between numerically efficient implementation and the ability of the model to represent realistic correlation patterns and to adequately fit to enough market data. For ex-

---

[1]Brigo and Mercurio (2001c) 127.

ample, a two-factor model has better tractability and implementability than a three-factor model, which in turn can explain more variation in the yield curve than the two-factor model. Empirical research and historical analysis of yield curves using principal component analysis or factor analysis indicate that two components can explain 85 percent to 90 percent of variations in the yield curve.[2]

In this chapter, we discuss principal component analysis as well as the properties and implementation issues of two-factor models. In such models, we consider additive models of the form

$$r(t) = x(t) + y(t) + \varphi(t)$$

where φ is a deterministic shift that is added in order to fit exactly the initial zero-coupon curve, as in the one-factor case discussed in the preceding chapter. We consider this in light of a deterministic-shift two-factor Vasicek model, known as G2++, and a two-factor Hull-White model. We can analyze these models in a risk-neutral world since a change of the objective probability measure to the risk-neutral probability measure does not change the instantaneous-covariance structure. In choosing a two-factor model, we need to consider how well the model can be calibrated to the term structure of volatilities and to swaption and cap prices. Can the model exhibit the hump-shaped curve often exhibited by the instantaneous standard deviation of the forward rate? How analytically tractable is the model—can it generate explicit formulas for discount bonds, European options on discount bonds, swaptions, and caps? Finally, we will discuss models that are based on forward rates using the Heath-Jarrow-Morton (HJM) approach as an alternative to building models based on the short rate.

The chapter is broken down as follows. In section 12.1, we discuss the two-factor Gaussian (G2++) model, and in section 12.2 we discuss building a G2++ quadrinomial tree. In section 12.3, we discuss the two-factor Hull-White model. In section 12.4, we discuss the Heath-Jarrow-Morton (HJM) model in a continuous-time framework. In section 12.5, we discuss pricing discount bond options with a Gaussian HJM model. In section 12.6, we discuss pricing discount bond options in a general HJM framework In section 12.7, we discuss the single-factor HJM discrete-state model. In section 12.8, arbitrage-free restrictions in a single factor model are given. In section 12.9, we discuss computation of arbitrage-free HJM term structure evolutions. In section 12.10, an implementation of a single-factor HJM model is given. In section 12.11, we implement an HJM single-factor tree to value a (synthetic) swap. In section 12.12, we introduce the two-factor HJM model, while in section 12.13 a two-factor HJM implementation is given. In section 12.14 we introduce the Ritchken-Sankarasubramanian (RS) model, and in section 12.15 the RS short rate process is discussed. In section 12.16, an improvement of the RS model—

---

[2]See Jamshidian and Zhu (1997) and Alexander (2001a).

the Li-Ritchken-Sankarasubramanian (LRS) model—is given and in section 12.17, we discuss how to implement an LRS tree.

12.1   THE TWO-FACTOR GAUSSIAN G2++ MODEL

In the G2++ model, a useful model in practice, rates have a Gaussian distribution. Rates can in become negative, though unlikely. The joint Gaussian distribution of the two factors makes pricing many interest rate derivatives, especially exotic products, simpler due to analytical tractability created by the additive nature of linear Gaussian variables (unlike the CIR++ model, which loses tractability due to the nonadditive nature of noncentral chi-squared variables). Thus, explicit formulas for discount bond prices, European options, and a number of non-plain-vanilla instruments exist, which in turn leads to efficient numerical procedures for pricing any payoff.[3] The nonperfect correlation between the two factors allows for better calibration to correlation-based products like European swaptions.

Consider the dynamics of instantaneous short rate process under the risk-neutral measure Q:

$$r(t) = x(t) + y(t) + \varphi(t), \ r(0) = r_0 \qquad (12.1)$$

where the processes $\{x(t) : t \geq 0\}$ and $\{y(t) : \geq 0\}$ follow

$$dx(t) = -ax(t)dt + \sigma dz_1(t), \ x(0) = 0$$
$$dy(t) = -by(t)dt + \eta dz_2(t), \ y(0) = 0 \qquad (12.2)$$

where the Brownian motions $z_1(t)$ and $z_2(t)$ have instantaneous correlation ρ, $0 \leq \rho \leq 1$,

$$dz_1(t)dz_2(t) = \rho dt$$

and r_0, a, b, σ, η are positive constants.

Integration of equations (12.2) yields

$$r(t) = x(s)e^{-a(t-s)} + y(s)e^{-b(t-s)} + \sigma \int_s^t e^{-a(t-u)} dz_1(u) + \eta \int_s^t e^{-b(t-u)} dz_2(u) + \varphi(t)$$

---

[3]Brigo and Mercurio (2001c), 132.

for each $s < t$. The short rate, conditional on the sigma field at time s, $\mathfrak{R}_s$, is normally distributed with mean and variance given respectively by

$$E_s[r(t)] = x(s)e^{-a(t-s)} + y(s)e^{-b(t-s)} + \varphi(t)$$

$$\text{Var}_s[r(t)] = \frac{\sigma^2}{2a}(1 - e^{-2a(t-s)}) + \frac{\eta^2}{2b}(1 - e^{-2b(t-s)}) + 2\rho\frac{\sigma\eta}{a+b}(1 - e^{-(a+b)(t-s)})$$

Through a Cholesky decomposition (see section 2.3) of the variance-covariance matrix of $(z_1(t), z_2(t))$, the dynamics of the processes x and y can also be written in terms of two independent Brownian motions $\tilde{z}_1$ and $\tilde{z}_2$:

$$dx(t) = -ax(t)dt + \sigma d\tilde{z}_1(t)$$

$$dy(t) = -by(t)dt + \eta\rho d\tilde{z}_1(t) + \eta\sqrt{1-\rho^2}\, d\tilde{z}_2$$

where

$$dz_1(t) = d\tilde{z}_1$$

$$dz_2(t) = \rho d\tilde{z}_2 + \sqrt{1-\rho^2}\, d\tilde{z}_2(t)$$

so that we can rewrite $r(t)$ as:

$$r(t) = x(s)e^{-a(t-s)} + y(s)e^{-b(t-s)} + \sigma\int_s^t e^{-a(t-u)}d\tilde{z}_1(u)$$

$$+ \eta\rho\int_s^t e^{-b(t-u)}d\tilde{z}_1(u) + \eta\sqrt{1-\rho^2}\int_s^t e^{-b(t-u)}d\tilde{z}_2(u) + \varphi(t)$$

(12.3)

We price a zero-coupon bond as follows. Define the random variable

$$I(t,\ T) = \int_t^T \big(x(u) + y(u)\big)du$$

It can be shown that the mean and variance of $I(t,\ T)$ are

$$\mu(t,\ T) = \frac{1 - e^{-a(T-t)}}{a}x(t) + \frac{1 - e^{-b(T-t)}}{b}y(t)$$

and

$$v(t,\ T) = \frac{\sigma^2}{a^2}\left[(T-t) + \frac{2}{a}e^{-a(T-t)} - \frac{1}{2a}e^{-2a(T-t)} - \frac{3}{2a}\right]$$

$$+ \frac{\eta^2}{b^2}\left[(T-t) + \frac{2}{b}e^{-b(T-t)} - \frac{1}{2b}e^{-2b(T-t)} - \frac{3}{2b}\right]$$

$$+ 2\rho\frac{\sigma\eta}{ab}\left[(T-t) + \frac{e^{-a(T-t)} - 1}{a} + \frac{e^{-b(T-t)} - 1}{b} - \frac{e^{-(a+b)(T-t)} - 1}{a+b}\right]$$

(12.4)

respectively.[4] Equivalently, note that by differentiating

$$v(t,\ T) = \frac{\sigma^2}{a^2} \int_t^T (1 - e^{-a(T-t)})^2\, du + \frac{\eta^2}{b^2} \int_t^T (1 - e^{-b(T-u)})^2\, du$$

$$+ 2\rho \frac{\sigma\eta}{ab} \int_t^T (1 - e^{-a(T-u)})(1 - e^{-b(T-u)})\, du \tag{12.5}$$

with respect to T, we obtain (12.4). Thus, the price at time t of a zero-coupon bond maturing at time T and with unit face value is:

$$P(t,\ T) = \exp\left\{ -\int_t^T \varphi(u)du - \mu(t,\ T) + \frac{1}{2}v(t,\ T) \right\} \tag{12.6}$$

Moreover, the model fits the currently observed term structure of discount factors if and only if for each T,

$$\varphi(T) = f(0,\ T) + \frac{\sigma^2}{2a^2}(1 - e^{-aT})^2 + \frac{\eta^2}{2b^2}(1 - e^{-bT})^2 + \rho \frac{\sigma\eta}{ab}(1 - e^{-aT})(1 - e^{-bT}) \tag{12.7}$$

where

$$f(0,\ T) = -\frac{\partial \ln P(0,\ T)}{\partial T}$$

is the instantaneous forward rate at time 0. This is equivalent to

$$\exp\left(-\int_t^T \varphi(u)du \right) = \frac{P(0,\ T)}{P(0,\ t)} \exp\left(-\frac{1}{2}(v(0,\ T) - v(0,\ t)) \right) \tag{12.8}$$

so that the zero-coupon bond prices at time t are

$$P(t,\ T) = \frac{P(0,\ T)}{P(0,\ t)} e^{A(t,T)} \tag{12.9}$$

where

$$A(t,\ T) = \frac{1}{2}(v(t,\ T) - v(0,\ T) + v(0,\ t)) - \mu(t,\ T)$$

[4]Ibid., 160–161.

This can be shown as follows: Note that at time 0,

$$P(0,\ T) = \exp\left(-\int_0^T \varphi(u)du + \frac{1}{2}v(0,\ T)\right)$$

If we take the logs of both sides and differentiate with respect to T, we get (12.6) by using (12.5). Since

$$\exp\left(-\int_t^T \varphi(u)du\right) = \exp\left(-\int_0^T \varphi(u)du\right)\exp\left(\int_0^t \varphi(u)du\right)$$

$$= \frac{P(0,\ T)}{P(0,\ t)} \frac{e^{\left(-\frac{1}{2}v(0,T)\right)}}{e^{\left(-\frac{1}{2}v(0,t)\right)}}$$

Equation (12.9) follows from (12.6) and (12.8).

In order to compute the price at time t of a European call option with maturity T and strike X, we need to evaluate the expectation

$$E_t\left[e^{-\int_t^T r(s)ds}\ \max(P(T,\ S)-X,\ 0)\right]$$

This can be accomplished via a change in probability measure using the Radon-Nikodym derivative:

$$\frac{dQ^T}{dQ} = \frac{B(0)}{B(T)}\frac{P(T,\ T)}{P(0,\ T)} = \frac{e^{-\int_0^T r(u)du}}{P(0,\ T)}$$

$$= \frac{\exp\left(-\int_0^T \varphi(u)du - \int_0^T (x(u)+y(u))du\right)}{P(0,\ T)}$$

$$= \exp\left(-\frac{1}{2}v(0,\ T)-\int_0^T (x(u)+y(u))du\right)$$

where B is the bank account numeraire, and Q^T is T-forward risk-adjusted measure.

The processes x and y under the forward measure Q^T have the dynamics:

$$dx(t) = \left[-ax(t) - \frac{\sigma^2}{a}(1 - e^{-a(T-t)}) - \rho \frac{\sigma\eta}{b}(1 - e^{-b(T-t)}) \right] dt + \sigma d\tilde{z}_1^T(t)$$

$$(12.10)$$

$$dy(t) = \left[-by(t) - \frac{\eta^2}{b}(1 - e^{-b(T-t)}) - \rho \frac{\sigma\eta}{a}(1 - e^{-a(T-t)}) \right] dt + \eta d\tilde{z}_2^T(t)$$

where Q_1^T and Q_2^T are two correlated Brownian motions under Q^T with $dQ_1^T dQ_2^T = \rho dt$.

The explicit solutions of (12.10) are, for $s \leq t \leq T$,

$$x(t) = x(s)e^{-a(t-s)} - \mu_x^T(s, t) + \sigma \int_s^t e^{-a(t-u)} dz_1^T(u)$$

$$y(t) = y(s)e^{-b(t-s)} - \mu_y^T(s, t) + \eta \int_s^t e^{-b(t-u)} dz_2^T(u)$$

where

$$\mu_x^T(s, t) = \left(\frac{\sigma^2}{a^2} + \rho \frac{\sigma\eta}{ab} \right)(1 - e^{-a(t-s)}) - \frac{\sigma^2}{2a^2}(e^{-a(T-t)} - e^{-a(T+t-2s)})$$

$$- \frac{\rho\sigma\eta}{b(a+b)}\left(e^{-b(T-t)} - e^{-bT-at+(a+b)s} \right)$$

$$\mu_y^T(s, t) = \left(\frac{\eta^2}{b^2} + \rho \frac{\sigma\eta}{ab} \right)(1 - e^{-b(t-s)}) - \frac{\eta^2}{2b^2}(e^{-b(T-t)} - e^{-b(T+t-2s)})$$

$$- \frac{\rho\sigma\eta}{a(a+b)}\left(e^{-a(T-t)} - e^{-aT-bt+(a+b)s} \right)$$

We can compute the mean and variance of the distribution of $r(t)$ under Q^T conditional on the sigma field at time s as[5]

$$E^{Q^T}[r(t)] = x(s)e^{-a(t-s)} - \mu_x^T(s, t) + y(s)e^{-b(t-s)} - \mu_y^T(s, t) + \varphi(t)$$

$$\text{Var}^{Q^T}[r(t)] = \frac{\sigma^2}{2a}(1 - e^{-2a(t-s)}) + \frac{\eta^2}{2b}(1 - e^{-2b(t-s)}) + 2\rho \frac{\sigma\eta}{a+b}(1 - e^{-(a+b)(t-s)})$$

---

[5]Ibid., 144–145.

It can be shown that the price time t of a European call option with maturity T and strike X, written on a zero-coupon bond with a face value of N and maturity S, is given by:

$$c(t, T, S, X) = NP(t, S)\Phi\left(\frac{\ln\left(\frac{NP(t, S)}{XP(t, T)}\right)}{v(t, T, S)} + \frac{v(t, T, S)}{2}\right) - P(t, T)X\Phi\left(\frac{\ln\left(\frac{NP(t, S)}{XP(t, T)}\right)}{v(t, T, S)} - \frac{v(t, T, S)}{2}\right) \quad (12.11)$$

where

$$v(t, T, S) = \frac{\sigma^2}{2a^3}(1 - e^{-a(S-T)})^2(1 - e^{-2a(T-t)}) + \frac{\eta^2}{2b^3}(1 - e^{-2b(S-T)})^2(1 - e^{-2b(T-t)})$$

$$+ \frac{2\rho\sigma\eta}{ab(a+b)}(1 - e^{-a(S-T)})(1 - e^{-b(S-T)})(1 - e^{-(a+b)(T-t)})$$

Similarly, the price at time t of a European put option with maturity T and strike X, written on a zero-coupon bond with a face value of N and maturity S, is given by

$$p(t, T, S, X) = P(t, T)X\Phi\left(\frac{\ln\left(\frac{XP(t, T)}{NP(t, S)}\right)}{v(t, T, S)} + \frac{v(t, T, S)}{2}\right) - NP(t, S)\Phi\left(\frac{\ln\left(\frac{XP(t, T)}{NP(t, S)}\right)}{v(t, T, S)} - \frac{v(t, T, S)}{2}\right) \quad (12.12)$$

We can also price caps, caplets, and swaptions. If $L(T_1, T_2)$ is the LIBOR rate at time T_1 for the maturity T_2 and τ is the fraction of time between T_1 and T_2, then

$$L(T_1, T_2) = \frac{1}{\tau}\left[\frac{1}{P(T_1, T_2)} - 1\right]$$

Since a caplet can be viewed as put option maturing at time T_1 on a discount bond maturing at T_2, we get the no-arbitrage value as:

$$caplet(t, T_1, T_2, N, X) = NP(t, T_1)\Phi\left(\frac{\ln\left(\frac{NP(t, T_1)}{N'P(t, T_2)}\right)}{v(t, T_1, T_2)} + \frac{1}{2}v(t, T_1, T_2)\right)$$

$$- N'P(t, T_2)\Phi\left(\frac{\ln\left(\frac{NP(t, T_1)}{N'P(t, T_2)}\right)}{v(t, T_1, T_2)} - \frac{1}{2}v(t, T_1, T_2)\right)$$

where $N' = N(1 + \tau X)$. Since the price of a cap is the sum of the prices of the underlying caplets, the price at time t of a cap with cap rate (strike) X, nominal value N, and year fractions τ between payment dates is:

$$
cap(t, \tau, N, X) = N \sum_{i=1}^{n} \left[P(t_i, T_{i-1}) \Phi \left(\frac{\ln\left(\frac{P(t, T_{i-1})}{(1 + X\tau_i)P(t, T_i)} \right)}{v(t, T_{i-1}, T_i)} + \frac{v(t, T_{i-1}, T_i)}{2} \right) \right.
$$

$$
\left. - (1 + \tau_i X)P(t, T_i) \Phi \left(\frac{\ln\left(\frac{P(t, T_{i-1})}{(1 + X\tau_i)P(t, T_i)} \right)}{v(t, T_{i-1}, T_i)} - \frac{v(t, T_{i-1}, T_i)}{2} \right) \right]
$$

We can price a European swaption with strike X, maturity T, and nominal value N, which gives the holder the right to enter at time $t_0 = T$ an interest-rate swap with payments at times $t_1, \ldots, t_n$, which allows the holder to pay (receive) at the fixed rate X and receive (pay) LIBOR. Denote the fixed payments $c_i = X\tau_i$, $i = 1, \ldots, n - 1$ and $\tau_i = t_i - t_{i-1}$, $i = 1, \ldots, n - 1$. At time t_n, assume unit face value, $c_n = 1 + X\tau_n$. A European swaption at time 0 can be valued numerically as

$$
S^{payer}(0, T, \tau, N, X) = NP(0, T)E^T \left(\max(1 - \sum_{i=1}^{n} c_i P(T, t_i), 0) \right)
$$

$$
= NP(0, T) \int_{-\infty}^{+\infty} \int_{-\infty}^{+\infty} \max((1 - \sum_{i=1}^{n} c_i A(T, t_i)e^{-B(a,T,t_i)x - B(b,T,t_i)y}), 0)p(x, y)dydx
$$

where p is the joint probability density function of $x(T)$ and $y(T)$; that is,

$$
p(x, y) = \frac{\exp\left(-\frac{1}{2(1 - \rho_{xy}^2)} \left(\left(\frac{x - \mu_x}{\sigma_x} \right)^2 - 2\rho_{xy} \frac{(x - \mu_x)(y - \mu_y)}{\sigma_x \sigma_y} + \left(\frac{y - \mu_y}{\sigma_y} \right)^2 \right) \right)}{2\pi\sigma_x \sigma_y \sqrt{1 - \rho_{xy}^2}}
$$

$$
= NP(0, T) \int_{-\infty}^{+\infty} \frac{e^{-\frac{1}{2}\left(\frac{x - \mu_x}{\sigma_x} \right)^2}}{\sigma_x \sqrt{2\pi}} \left(\Phi(-h_1(x)) - \sum_{i=1}^{n} \lambda_i(x)e^{\alpha_i(x)} \Phi(-h_2(x)) \right) dx
$$

where

$$
h_1(x) = \frac{\bar{y} - \mu_y}{\sigma_y \sqrt{1 - \rho_{xy}^2}} - \frac{\rho_{xy}(x - \mu_x)}{\sigma_x \sqrt{1 - \rho_{xy}^2}}
$$

$$h_2(x) = h_1(x) + B(b, T, t_i)\sigma_y \sqrt{1 - \rho_{xy}^2}$$

$$\lambda_i(x) = c_i A(T, t_i) e^{-B(a,T,t_i)x}$$

$$\alpha_i(x) = -B(b, T, t_i)\left(\mu_y - \frac{1}{2}(1 - \rho_{xy}^2)\sigma_y^2 B(b, T, t_i) + \rho_{xy}\sigma_y\left(\frac{x - \mu_x}{\sigma_x}\right)\right)$$

$\bar{y} = \bar{y}(x)$ is the unique solution of the following equation:

$$\sum_{i=1}^{n} c_i A(T, t_i) e^{-B(a,T,t_i)x - B(b,T,t_i)\bar{y}} = 1$$

where

$$\mu_x = -\mu_x^T$$

$$\mu_y = -\mu_y^T$$

$$\sigma_x = \sigma \sqrt{\frac{1 - e^{-2aT}}{2a}}$$

$$\sigma_y = \eta \sqrt{\frac{1 - e^{-2bT}}{2b}}$$

$$\rho_{xy} = \frac{\rho\sigma\eta}{(a+b)\sigma_x\sigma_y}(1 - e^{-(a+b)T})$$

For a receiver swaption,

$$S^{receiver}(0, T, \tau, N, X) = -NP(0, T)\int_{-\infty}^{+\infty} \frac{e^{-\frac{1}{2}\left(\frac{x - \mu_x}{\sigma_x}\right)^2}}{\sigma_x\sqrt{2\pi}}\left(\Phi(h_1(x)) - \sum_{i=1}^{n}\lambda_i(x)e^{\alpha_i(x)}\Phi(h_2(x))\right)dx$$

12.2 BUILDING A G2++ TREE

We can construct a trinomial tree that approximates the G2++ diffusion process. Essentially, we are constructing two individual binomial trees to approximate the dynamics in (12.2)—one for $x(t)$ and one for $y(t)$ and then combining them to create a quadrinomial tree. We know that from the previous section, we have

$$E_t[x(t + \Delta t)] = x(t)e^{-a\Delta t}$$

$$\text{Var}_t[x(t + \Delta t)] = \frac{\sigma^2}{2a}(1 - e^{-2a\Delta t})$$

$$E_t[y(t + \Delta t)] = y(t)e^{-b\Delta t}$$

$$\text{Var}_t[y(t + \Delta t)] = \frac{\eta^2}{2b}(1 - e^{-2b\Delta t})$$

and

$$\text{Cov}_t[x(t + \Delta t), y(t + \Delta t)] = E_t[(x(t + \Delta t) - E_t[x(t + \Delta t)])(y(t + \Delta t) - E_t[y(t + \Delta t)])]$$

$$= \sigma \eta E_t\left[\int_t^{t+\Delta t} e^{-a(t+\Delta t - u)}dz_1(u) \int_t^{t+\Delta t} e^{-b(t+\Delta t - u)}dz_2(u) \right]$$

$$= \sigma \eta \rho \int_t^{t+\Delta t} e^{-(a+b)(t+\Delta t - u)}du$$

$$= \frac{\sigma \eta \rho}{a+b}(1 - e^{-(a+b)\Delta t})$$

At time t, $x(t)$ $(y(t))$ can move up with probability p (q) to $x(t) + \Delta x$ $(y(t) + \Delta y)$ and down with probability $1 - p$ $(1 - q)$ to $x(t) - \Delta x$ $(y(t) - \Delta y)$, respectively. We chose the quantities Δx, Δy, p, and q to match (in first-order Δt) the conditional mean and variance of the (continuous-time) processes x and y:

$$p(x(t) + \Delta x) + (1 - p)(x(t) - \Delta x) = x(t)(1 - a\Delta t)$$

$$p(x(t) + \Delta x)^2 + (1 - p)(x(t) - \Delta x)^2 - (x(t)(1 - a\Delta t))^2 = \sigma^2\Delta t$$

and, equivalently,

$$q(x(t) + \Delta x) + (1 - q)(x(t) - \Delta x) = x(t)(1 - b\Delta t)$$

$$q(x(t) + \Delta x)^2 + (1 - q)(x(t) - \Delta x)^2 - (x(t)(1 - b\Delta t))^2 = \eta^2\Delta t$$

Solving the preceding equations, we get:

$$\Delta x = \sigma\sqrt{\Delta t}$$

$$p = \frac{1}{2} - \frac{x(t)a\Delta t}{2\Delta x} = \frac{1}{2} - \frac{x(t)a}{2\sigma}\sqrt{\Delta t}$$

$$\Delta y = \eta \sqrt{\Delta t}$$

$$q = \frac{1}{2} - \frac{y(t)b\Delta t}{2\Delta y} = \frac{1}{2} - \frac{y(t)b}{2\eta}\sqrt{\Delta t}$$

To build a tree for the short rate, $r(t)$, we can combine the individual trees for $x(t)$ and $y(t)$ into a quadrinomial tree so that

$$(x(t) + \Delta x, y(t) + \Delta y) \text{ with probability } \pi_1$$
$$(x(t) + \Delta x, y(t) - \Delta y) \text{ with probability } \pi_2$$
$$(x(t) - \Delta x, y(t) + \Delta y) \text{ with probability } \pi_3$$
$$(x(t) - \Delta x, y(t) - \Delta y) \text{ with probability } \pi_4$$

where $0 \le \pi_1, \pi_2, \pi_3, \pi_4 \le 1$ and $\pi_1 + \pi_2 + \pi_3 + \pi_4 = 1$. The probabilities are chosen to match the marginal distributions of the binomial trees and the conditional variance between the processes x and y. Consequently, we have the requirements

$$\pi_1 + \pi_2 + \pi_3 + \pi_4 = 1$$
$$\pi_1 + \pi_2 = p$$
$$\pi_3 + \pi_4 = 1 - p \qquad (12.13)$$
$$\pi_1 + \pi_3 = q$$
$$\pi_2 + \pi_4 = 1 - q$$

Matching the conditional covariance, we have the additional constraint:

$$(\Delta x + ax(t)\Delta t)(\Delta y + by(t)\Delta t)\pi_1 + (\Delta x + ax(t)\Delta t)(-\Delta y + by(t)\Delta t)\pi_2$$
$$+ (ax(t)\Delta t - \Delta x)(\Delta y + by(t)\Delta t)\,\pi_3 + (ax(t)\Delta t - \Delta x)(-\Delta y + by(t)\Delta t)\,\pi_4 = \rho\sigma\eta\Delta t \quad (12.14)$$

Solving (12.13) and (12.14), we get:

$$\pi_1 = \frac{1+\rho}{4} - \frac{b\sigma y(t) + a\eta x(t)}{4\sigma\eta}\sqrt{\Delta t}$$

$$\pi_2 = \frac{1-\rho}{4} + \frac{b\sigma y(t) - a\eta x(t)}{4\sigma\eta}\sqrt{\Delta t}$$

$$\pi_3 = \frac{1-\rho}{4} - \frac{b\sigma y(t) - a\eta x(t)}{4\sigma\eta}\sqrt{\Delta t}$$

$$\pi_4 = \frac{1+\rho}{4} + \frac{b\sigma y(t) - a\eta x(t)}{4\sigma\eta}\sqrt{\Delta t}$$

To build the G2++ tree, we define a *TwoFactorModel* as our abstract base class for a G2++ class:[6]

```
#include "DiffusionProcess.h"
#include "Model.h"
#include "Lattice2d.h"
typedef size_t Size;
typedef double Time;
```

```
/*************************************************************************
Abstract base-class for two-factor models
*************************************************************************/
class TwoFactorModel : public Model
{
  public:
    TwoFactorModel(Size nParams);
    class ShortRateDynamics;
    class ShortRateTree;
    // Returns the short-rate dynamics
    virtual Handle<ShortRateDynamics> dynamics() const = 0;
    // Returns a two-dimensional trinomial tree
    virtual Handle<Lattices::Lattice> tree(const TimeGrid& grid) const;
};

/*************************************************************************
Class describing the dynamics of the two state variables
We assume here that the short-rate is a function of two state variables x and y,
   r(t) = f(t, x(t), y(t)), a function of two state variables x(t) and y(t). These
   stochastic processes satisfy

x(t) = mu_x(t, x(t))dt + sigma_x(t, x(t)) dWx(t) and y(t) = mu_y(t, y(t))dt +
   sigma_y(t, y(t)) dWy(t)

where Wx and Wy are two Brownian motions satisfying dWx(t) dWy(t) = rho dt

*************************************************************************/

class TwoFactorModel::ShortRateDynamics
{
  public:
```

---

[6]These classes have been adapted from the QuantLib library.

```
    ShortRateDynamics(const Handle<DiffusionProcess>& xProcess, const
      Handle<DiffusionProcess>& yProcess, double correlation)
      : xProcess_(xProcess), yProcess_(yProcess),
    correlation_(correlation) {}
    virtual ~ShortRateDynamics() {}

    virtual Rate shortRate(Time t, double x, double y) const = 0;
    // Risk-neutral dynamics of the first state variable x
    const Handle<DiffusionProcess>& xProcess() const {
      return xProcess_;
    }
    // Risk-neutral dynamics of the second state variable y
    const Handle<DiffusionProcess>& yProcess() const {
      return yProcess_;
    }
    // Correlation rho between the two Brownian motions.
    double correlation() const {
      return correlation_;
    }
  private:
    Handle<DiffusionProcess> xProcess_, yProcess_;
    double correlation_;
};


/*****************************************************************************
Recombining two-dimensional tree discretizing the state variable
*****************************************************************************/
class TwoFactorModel::ShortRateTree : public Lattices::Lattice2D
{
  public:
    // Plain tree build-up from short-rate dynamics
    ShortRateTree(const Handle<Lattices::TrinomialTree>& tree1, const
      Handle<Lattices::TrinomialTree>& tree2, const Handle<ShortRateDynamics>&
      dynamics);

    DiscountFactor discount(Size i, Size index) const
    {
      Size modulo = tree1_->size(i);
      Size index1 = index % modulo;
      Size index2 = index / modulo;

      double x = tree1_->underlying(i, index1);
      double y = tree1_->underlying(i, index2);
      double r = dynamics_->shortRate(timeGrid()[i], x, y);
      return exp(-r*timeGrid().dt(i));
    }
  private:
    Handle<ShortRateDynamics> dynamics_;
};
```

with method definitions:

```
/******************************************************************************
TwoFactorModel: Constructor
[in] : Size nArguments : number of arguments
******************************************************************************/
TwoFactorModel::TwoFactorModel(Size nArguments) : Model(nArguments) {}
```

```
/******************************************************************************
tree : constructs and builds a two factor lattice
[in] : TimeGrid& grid : time grid
[out]: Handle<Lattice> : two factor short rate tree
******************************************************************************/
Handle<Lattice> TwoFactorModel::tree(const TimeGrid& grid) const
{
  Handle<ShortRateDynamics> dyn = dynamics();
  Handle<TrinomialTree> tree1(new TrinomialTree(dyn->xProcess(), grid));
  Handle<TrinomialTree> tree2(new TrinomialTree(dyn->yProcess(), grid));
  return Handle<Lattice>(new TwoFactorModel::ShortRateTree(tree1, tree2, dyn));
}

TwoFactorModel::ShortRateTree::ShortRateTree(
  const Handle<TrinomialTree>& tree1,
  const Handle<TrinomialTree>& tree2,
  const Handle<ShortRateDynamics>& dynamics)
  : Lattice2D(tree1, tree2, dynamics->correlation()), dynamics_(dynamics) {}
```

where

```
/******************************************************************************
Two-dimensional lattice.
This lattice is based on two trinomial trees and primarily used for the G2 short-
  rate model.
******************************************************************************/
class Lattice2D : public Lattice
{
  public:
    Lattice2D(const Handle<TrinomialTree>& tree1,
      const Handle<TrinomialTree>& tree2, double correlation);
    Size size(Size i) const { return tree1_->size(i)*tree2_->size(i); }
  protected:
    Size descendant(Size i, Size index, Size branch) const;
    double probability(Size i, Size index, Size branch) const;
    Handle<Tree> tree1_, tree2_;
```

```
  private:
    Math::Matrix m_;
    double rho_;
};
```

The class has the following method definitions:

```
using namespace Lattices;

/*******************************************************************************
descendant: compute branches that are descendants of the current node
[in] : Size i       : ith step
[in] : Size index : index (state position) of branch
[in] : Size branch : number of branch
*******************************************************************************/
Size Lattice2D::descendant(Size i, Size index, Size branch) const
{
    Size modulo = tree1_->size(i);

    Size index1 = index % modulo;
    Size index2 = index / modulo;
    Size branch1 = branch % 3;
    Size branch2 = branch / 3;

    modulo = tree1_->size(i+1);
    return tree1_->descendant(i, index1, branch1) + tree2_->descendant(i, index2,
      branch2)*modulo;
}

/*******************************************************************************
probability: compute the branching probabilities
[in] : Size i       : ith step
[in] : Size index : index (state position) of branch
[in] : Size branch : number of branch
*******************************************************************************/
double Lattice2D::probability(Size i, Size index, Size branch) const
{
    Size modulo = tree1_->size(i);

    Size index1 = index % modulo;
    Size index2 = index / modulo;
    Size branch1 = branch % 3;
    Size branch2 = branch / 3;

    double prob1 = tree1_->probability(i, index1, branch1);
    double prob2 = tree2_->probability(i, index2, branch2);

    return prob1*prob2 + rho_*(m_[branch1][branch2])/36.0;
```

```
}


/*******************************************************************************
Lattice2D : constructor - creates a 2-dimensional lattice
[in]: Handle<Trinomial>& tree1      : trinomial tree for first factor
      Handle<Trinomial>& tree2      : trinomial tree for second factor
      double correlation            : correlation between first and second factor
********************************************************************************/
Lattice2D::Lattice2D(const Handle<TrinomialTree>& tree1, const
  Handle<TrinomialTree>& tree2, double correlation) : Lattices::Lattice
  (tree1->timeGrid(), 9), tree1_(tree1), tree2_(tree2), rho_(fabs(correlation))
{
  if (correlation < 0.0)
  {
    m_[0][0]  = -1.0;
    m_[0][1]  = -4.0;
    m_[0][2]  = 5.0;
    m_[1][0]  = -4.0;
    m_[1][1]  = 8.0;
    m_[1][2]  = -4.0;
    m_[2][0]  = 5.0;
    m_[2][1]  = -4.0;
    m_[2][2]  = -1.0;
  }
  else
  {
    m_[0][0]  = 5.0;
    m_[0][1]  = -4.0;
    m_[0][2]  = -1.0;
    m_[1][0]  = -4.0;
    m_[1][1]  = 8.0;
    m_[1][2]  = -4.0;
    m_[2][0]  = -1.0;
    m_[2][1]  = -4.0;
    m_[2][2]  = 5.0;
  }
}
```

We now define the *G2++* class:

```
/*******************************************************************************
Two-additive-factor Gaussian model class.
This class implements a two-additive-factor model defined by

dr_t = varphi(t) + x_t + y_t

where x(t) and y(t) are defined by dx(t) = -a x(t) dt + sigma dW^1_t, x_0 = 0
dy(t) = -b y(t)dt + sigma dW^2_t, y_0 = 0 and dW^1(t) dW^2(t) = rho dt.
```

```
**********************************************************************************/
class G2 : public TwoFactorModel, public AffineModel, public TermStructureConsistent
  Model
{
  public:
    G2(const RelinkableHandle<TermStructure>& termStructure,
      double a = 0.1,
      double sigma = 0.01,
      double b = 0.1,
      double eta = 0.01,
      double rho = 0.9);
    Handle<ShortRateDynamics> dynamics() const;
    double discountBondOption(Option::Type type,
      double strike, Time maturity, Time bondMaturity) const;
    double swaption(const Instruments::SwaptionArguments& arguments) const;
    DiscountFactor discount(Time t) const
    {
      return termStructure()->discount(t);
    }
  protected:
    void generateArguments();
    double A(Time t, Time T) const;             // parameter of discount bond
    double B(double x, Time t) const;           // parameter of discount bond
  private:
    class Dynamics;                             // G2 dynamics
    class FittingParameter;                     // analytical term-structure fitting
                                                // parameter
    double sigmaP(Time t, Time s) const;        // bond volatility
    Parameter& a_;                              // drift of x process
    Parameter& sigma_;                          // volatility of x process
    Parameter& b_;                              // drift of y process
    Parameter& eta_;                            // volatility of y process
    Parameter& rho_;                            // correlation of Brownian motions
    Parameter phi_;                             // shift parameter
    double V(Time t) const;
    double a() const { return a_(0.0); }
    double sigma() const { return sigma_(0.0); }
    double b() const { return b_(0.0); }
    double eta() const { return eta_(0.0); }
    double rho() const { return rho_(0.0); }
    class SwaptionPricingFunction;
    friend class SwaptionPricingFunction;
};


/*********************************************************************************
Dynamics class of the G2 model
**********************************************************************************/


class G2::Dynamics : public TwoFactorModel::ShortRateDynamics
{
  public:
```

```
      Dynamics(const Parameter& fitting, double a, double sigma, double b, double eta,
        double rho)
        : ShortRateDynamics(Handle<DiffusionProcess>(new OrnsteinUhlenbeckProcess(a,
          sigma)), Handle<DiffusionProcess>(new OrnsteinUhlenbeckProcess(b, eta)),
          rho), fitting_(fitting) {}
      virtual Rate shortRate(Time t, double x, double y) const {
        return fitting_(t) + x + y;
      }
    private:
      Parameter fitting_;
};


/******************************************************************************
Analytical term-structure fitting parameter varphi(t).
varphi(t) is analytically defined by
varphi(t) = f(t) + 0.5((sigma(1-exp(-at)))/{a})^2 + 0.5({eta(1-exp(-bt))}(b))^2 +
rho(sigma(1-exp(-at)))(a)/(eta(1-exp(-bt)))(b),
where f(t) is the instantaneous forward rate at t.
******************************************************************************/
class G2::FittingParameter : public TermStructureFittingParameter
{
  private:
    class Impl : public Parameter::Impl
    {
      public:
        Impl(const RelinkableHandle<TermStructure>& termStructure,
        double a, double sigma, double b, double eta, double rho)
        : termStructure_(termStructure), a_(a), sigma_(sigma), b_(b), eta_(eta),
          rho_(rho) {}


        double value(const Array& params, Time t) const
        {
          double forward = termStructure_->instantaneousForward(t);
          double temp1 = sigma_*(1.0-exp(-a_*t))/a_;
          double temp2 = eta_*(1.0-exp(-b_*t))/b_;
          double value = 0.5*temp1*temp1 + 0.5*temp2*temp2 + rho_*temp1*temp2 +
            forward;
          return value;
        }
      private:
        RelinkableHandle<TermStructure> termStructure_;
        double a_, sigma_, b_, eta_, rho_;
    };
  public:
    FittingParameter(const RelinkableHandle<TermStructure>& termStructure,
      double a, double sigma, double b, double eta, double rho)
      : TermStructureFittingParameter(Handle<Parameter::Impl>(
        new FittingParameter::Impl(termStructure, a, sigma, b, eta, rho))) {}
};
```

The class has the following method definitions:

```
using Optimization::PositiveConstraint;
using Optimization::BoundaryConstraint;


/**************************************************************************
G2 : constructor
[in]: RelinkableHandle<TermStructure>& termStructure : term structure
      double a           : drift of x process
      double sigma       : volatility of x process
      double b           : drift of y process
      double eta         : volatility of y process
      double rho         : correlation between Brownian motions of x and y processes
**************************************************************************/
G2::G2(const RelinkableHandle<TermStructure>& termStructure,
  double a, double sigma, double b, double eta, double rho)
  : TwoFactorModel(5), TermStructureConsistentModel(termStructure),
    a_(arguments_[0]), sigma_(arguments_[1]), b_(arguments_[2]),
      eta_(arguments_[3]), rho_(arguments_[4])
{
  a_    = ConstantParameter(a, PositiveConstraint());
  sigma_ = ConstantParameter(sigma, PositiveConstraint());
  b_    = ConstantParameter(b, PositiveConstraint());
  eta_  = ConstantParameter(eta, PositiveConstraint());
  rho_  = ConstantParameter(rho, BoundaryConstraint(-1.0, 1.0));
  generateArguments();
}


/**************************************************************************
dynamics : returns short rate dynamnics of G2 model
[in]  : none
[out] : Handle<TwoFactorModel::ShortRateDynamics> : G2 short rate dynamcs
**************************************************************************/
Handle<TwoFactorModel::ShortRateDynamics> G2::dynamics() const
{
  return Handle<ShortRateDynamics>(new Dynamics(phi_, a(), sigma(), b(), eta(),
    rho()));
}


/**************************************************************************
generateArguments: assign fitting parameter to phi
[in]  : none
[out] : none
**************************************************************************/
void G2::generateArguments()
{
  phi_ = FittingParameter(termStructure(), a(), sigma(), b(), eta(), rho());
}


/**************************************************************************
```

```
sigmaP: computes the bond volatility of a zero-coupon bond
[in]   : Time t : initial time (option maturity)
         Time s : end time (bond maturity)
[out]  : bond volatility
***************************************************************************/
double G2::sigmaP(Time t, Time s) const
{
  double temp = 1.0 - exp(-(a()+b())*t);
  double temp1 = 1.0 - exp(-a()*(s-t));
  double temp2 = 1.0 - exp(-b()*(s-t));
  double a3 = a()*a()*a();
  double b3 = b()*b()*b();
  double sigma2 = sigma()*sigma();
  double eta2 = eta()*eta();
  double value = 0.5*sigma2*temp1*temp1*(1.0 - exp(-2.0*a()*t))/a3 +
    0.5*eta2*temp2*temp2*(1.0 - exp(-2.0*b()*t))/b3 +
    2.0*rho()*sigma()*eta()/(a()*b()*(a()+b()))*temp1*temp2*temp;
  return sqrt(value);
}


/****************************************************************************
discountBondOption: price discount bond option using G2++ model
[in]   : Option::Type type  : option type
         double strike       : strike price
         Time maturity       : maturity of bond option
         Time bondMaturity   : maturity of bond
[out]  : price of bond opiton
***************************************************************************/
double G2::discountBondOption(Option::Type type, double strike, Time maturity, Time
  bondMaturity) const
{

  double v = sigmaP(maturity, bondMaturity);
  double f = termStructure()->discount(bondMaturity);
  double k = termStructure()->discount(maturity)*strike;
  double w = (type==Option::Call)? 1.0 : -1.0;
  return BlackModel::formula(f, k, v, w);
}


/****************************************************************************
V: computes subterms in the "A" term of the discount bond price
[in]   : Time t : current time
[out]  : returns
***************************************************************************/
double G2::V(Time t) const
{
  double expat = exp(-a()*t);
  double expbt = exp(-b()*t);
  double cx = sigma()/a();
  double cy = eta()/b();
  double valuex = cx*cx*(t + (2.0*expat - 0.5*expat*expat - 1.5)/a());
  double valuey = cy*cy*(t + (2.0*expbt - 0.5*expbt*expbt - 1.5)/b());
```

```
    double value = 2.0*rho()*cx*cy* (t + (expat - 1.0)/a() + (expbt - 1.0)/b()
        - (expat*expbt - 1.0)/(a()+b())));

    return valuex + valuey + value;
}

/******************************************************************************
A: computes the "A" term of the discount bond price
[in] :    Time t : initial time
          Time T: end time
[out] :   returns A
******************************************************************************/
double G2::A(Time t, Time T) const
{
    return termStructure()->discount(T)/termStructure()->discount(t)* exp(0.5*(V(T-t)
        - V(T) + V(t)));
}


/******************************************************************************
B: computes the "B" term of the discount bond price
[in] :    double x :
          Time t: current time
[out] :   returns B = (1 - exp(-xt))/x;
******************************************************************************/
double G2::B(double x, Time t) const
{
    return (1.0 - exp(-x*t))/x;
}
```

12.3   TWO-FACTOR HULL-WHITE MODEL

Hull and White (1994) developed a two-factor model where the short rate evolves according to

$$
\begin{aligned}
dr(t) &= (\theta(t) + u(t) - \bar{a}r)dt + \sigma_1 dz_1(t),\ r(0) = r_0 \\
du(t) &= -\bar{b}u(t)dt + \sigma_2 dz_2(t),\ u(0) = 0
\end{aligned}
\tag{12.15}
$$

where $u(t)$ can be interpreted as a random (stochastic) mean reversion level and r_0, $\bar{a}$, $\bar{b}$, σ_1, and σ_2 are positive constants. As in the one-factor HW model, $\theta(t)$ is a time-dependent function, allowing the model to fit the initial term structure. The addition of $u(t)$ to the model allows the model to have more possibilities for term structure movements and volatility structures. In the one-factor model, forward rates are perfectly instantaneously correlated. In the two-factor model, correlations can vary so that more realistic volatility patterns such as the humped volatility curve often seen in the cap markets can be generated. As in the two-factor G2++

model, we have correlated Wiener processes, $dz_1 dz_2 = \rho$. The G2++ is a specific case of the model, as we will show.

If we integrate (12.15), we get

$$r(t) = r(s)e^{-a(t-s)} + \int_s^t \theta(v)e^{-a(t-v)}dv + \int_s^t u(v)e^{-a(t-v)}dv + \sigma_1 \int_s^t e^{-a(t-v)}dz_1(v)$$

$$u(t) = u(s)e^{-b(t-s)} + \sigma_2 \int_s^t e^{-b(t-v)}dz_2(v)$$

If we substitute $u(t)$ into

$$\int_s^t u(v)e^{-a(t-v)}dv$$

and if we assume $a \neq b$,

$$\int_s^t u(v)e^{-a(t-v)}dv = \int_s^t u(s)e^{-b(v-s)-a(t-v)}dv + \sigma_2 \int_s^t e^{-a(t-v)}\int_s^v e^{-b(v-x)}dz_2(x)dv$$

$$= u(s)\frac{e^{-b(t-s)} - e^{-a(t-s)}}{a-b} + \sigma_2 e^{-at}\int_s^t e^{(a-b)v}\int_s^v e^{bx}dz_2(x)dv$$

Following Brigo and Mercurio, we can evaluate the rightmost term by integration by parts:

$$\sigma_2 \int_s^t e^{-(a-b)v}\int_s^v e^{bx}dz_2(x)dv = \frac{\sigma_2}{a-b}\int_s^t \left(\int_s^v e^{bx}dz_2(x)\right)d(e^{(a-b)v})$$

$$= \frac{\sigma_2}{a-b}\left[e^{(a-b)t}\int_s^t e^{bx}dz_2(x) - \int_s^t e^{(a-b)v}d\left(\int_s^v e^{bx}dz_2(x)\right)\right]$$

$$= \frac{\sigma_2}{a-b}\int_s^t (e^{(a-b)t} - e^{(a-b)v})d\left(\int_s^v e^{bx}dz_2(x)\right)$$

$$= \frac{\sigma_2}{a-b}\int_s^t (e^{at-b(t-v)} - e^{av})dz_2(v)$$

so that we can write the short rate as:

$$r(t) = r(s)e^{-a(t-s)} + \int_s^t \theta(v)e^{-a(t-v)}dv + \sigma_1\int_s^t e^{-a(t-v)}dz_1(v) + u(s)\left(\frac{e^{-b(t-s)} - e^{-a(t-s)}}{a-b}\right)$$

$$+ \frac{\sigma_2}{a-b}\int_s^t (e^{-b(t-v)} - e^{-a(t-v)})dz_2(v)$$

If we let $a > b$ and define

$$\sigma_3 = \sqrt{\sigma_1^2 + \frac{\sigma_2^2}{(a-b)^2} + 2\bar{\rho}\frac{\sigma_1\sigma_2}{b-a}}$$

$$\sigma_4 = \frac{\sigma_2}{a-b}$$

$$dz_3(t) = \frac{\sigma_1 dz_1(t) - \frac{\sigma_2}{a-b}dz_2(t)}{\sigma_3}$$

at time 0 we have

$$r(t) = r_0 e^{-at} + \int_0^t \theta(v)e^{-a(t-v)}dv + \int_0^t e^{-a(t-v)}\left(\sigma_1 dz_1(v) + \frac{\sigma_2}{b-a}dz_2(v)\right) + \frac{\sigma_2}{a-b}\int_0^t e^{-b(t-v)}dz_2(v)$$

$$(12.16)$$

$$= r_0 e^{-at} + \int_0^t \theta(v)e^{-a(t-v)}dv + \sigma_3\int_0^t e^{-a(t-v)}dz_3(v) + \sigma_4\int_0^t e^{-b(t-v)}dz_2(v)$$

Comparing this with the G2++ short rate in (12.3) shows that we can recover the short rate in the G2++ model if in (12.16) we set:

$$\sigma = \sigma_3$$
$$\eta = \sigma_4$$
$$\rho = \frac{\sigma_1\bar{\rho} - \sigma_4}{\sigma_3}$$

$$(12.17)$$

and the shift factor

$$\varphi(t) = r_0 e^{-at} + \int_0^t \theta(v)e^{-a(t-v)}dv$$

However, given the G2++ model in (12.3), we can recover the two-factor HW model if we set:[7]

$$\sigma_1 = \sqrt{\sigma^2 + \eta^2 + 2\rho\sigma\eta}$$
$$\sigma_2 = \eta(a - b)$$
$$\bar{\rho} = \frac{\sigma\rho + \eta}{\sqrt{\sigma^2 + \eta^2 + 2\rho\sigma\eta}} \qquad (12.18)$$
$$\theta(t) = \frac{d\varphi(t)}{dt} + a\varphi(t)$$

The price of a pure discount bond at time t that matures at s can be calculated analytically by:

$$P(t, s) = A(t, s)e^{-r(t)B(t,s)-u(t)C(t,s)}$$

where

$$B(t, s) = \frac{1}{a}(1 - e^{-a(s-t)})$$

and

$$C(t, s) = \frac{1}{a(a - b)}e^{-a(s-t)} - \frac{1}{b(a - b)}e^{-b(s-t)} + \frac{1}{ab}$$

The spot rate volatility is given by

$$\sigma_R(t, s) = \frac{1}{(s-t)}\sqrt{(B(t, s)\sigma_1)^2 + (C(t, s)\sigma_2)^2 + 2\rho\sigma_1\sigma_2 B(t, s)C(t, s)}$$

or expanded out

$$
\begin{aligned}
\sigma_R^2 = &\frac{\sigma_1^2}{2a} B(t, s)^2 (1 - e^{-2a(T-t)}) \\
&+ \sigma_2^2 \left[\frac{U^2}{2a}(e^{2a(T-t)} - 1) + \frac{V^2}{2b}(e^{2b(T-t)} - 1) - \frac{2UV}{a+b}(e^{(a+b)(T-t)} - 1) \right] \\
&+ \frac{2\rho\sigma_1\sigma_2}{a}(e^{-a(T-t)} - e^{-a(s-t)}) \left[\frac{U}{2a}(e^{2a(T-t)} - 1) - \frac{V}{a+b}(e^{(a+b)(T-t)} - 1) \right]
\end{aligned} \qquad (12.19)
$$

---

[7]Brigo and Mercurio (2001c), 151.

where

$$U = \frac{1}{a(a-b)}(e^{-a(s-t)} - e^{-a(T-t)})$$

$$V = \frac{1}{b(b-a)}(e^{-b(s-t)} - e^{-b(T-t)})$$

We can price European pure discount bond call and put options using the Black-Scholes formulas in (10.72) and (10.75), respectively, using the two-factor HW spot rate volatility given (12.17). Caps, caplets, swaptions, and other interest rate derivatives can be priced using the formulas given in the previous section for the G2++ model, except the formulas in (12.17) are used. Similarly, one can build a two-factor Hull-White tree just like the G2++ binomial tree except the formulas in (12.17) are used.

12.4   HEATH-JARROW-MORTON MODEL

Heath, Jarrow, and Morton (HJM) (1992) developed a general framework for modeling interest rates in terms of forward rates instead of spot rates. The HJM framework allows the volatility function to be a function of the entire forward rate curve. They assume that the instantaneous forward rate $f(t, T)$ evolves, under an objective measure, according to:

$$df(t, T) = \alpha(t, T)dt + \sum_{i=1}^{N}\sigma_i(t, T, f(t, T))dz_i(t) \tag{12.20}$$

or in vector form:

$$df(t, T) = \alpha(t, T)dt + \sigma(t, T)dz(t)$$

where $\sigma(t, T) = (\sigma_1(t, T), \ldots, \sigma_N(t, T))$ is a $1 \times n$ vector of volatilities (which are each adapted processes), $z = (z_1, \ldots, z_N)$ is an n-dimensional Brownian motion, and $\alpha(t, T)$ is an adapted process.

Heath, Jarrow, and Morton showed in their paper that in order for an equivalent martingale measure to exist, the drift $\alpha(t, T)$ cannot be chosen arbitrarily, independent of the volatility structure. Rather, the no-arbitrage drift, under the risk-neutral measure, must be:

$$\alpha(t, T) = \sum_{i=1}^{N}\sigma_i(t, T, f(t, T))\int_t^T\sigma_i(t, u, f(t, u))du \tag{12.21}$$

or in vector form:

$$\alpha(t,\ T) = \sigma(t,\ T) \int_t^T \sigma(t,\ s) ds$$

so that (12.20) can be written as:

$$df(t,\ T) = \left(\sum_{i=1}^N \sigma_i(t,\ T,\ f(t,\ T)) \int_t^T \sigma_i(t,\ u,\ f(t,\ u)) du \right) dt + \sum_{i=1}^n \sigma_i(t,\ T,\ f(t,\ T)) dz_i(t)$$

The forward rate model is completely specified in terms of the volatility functions $\sigma_i(\cdot)$, which in turn depend on the entire forward rate curve. The volatility function determines the volatilities and correlations of the forward rates. In the single-factor spot rate model, we specify only a single volatility function $\sigma_R(t)$ for the spot rate, and then solve for the forward rate's volatility function $\sigma_f(t,\ T)$. In the HJM model, we specify the *entire* forward volatility function. The initial forward rate curve is given and then the forward rates of different maturities evolve dynamically through time by (12.20). Thus, to compute derivatives prices using the HJM, it is necessary to specify explicitly the volatility function to be used.

Integrating the dynamics (12.20), we get

$$f(t,\ T) = f(0,\ T) + \sum_{i=1}^N \int_0^t \sigma_i(s,\ T,\ f(s,\ T)) \int_s^T \sigma_i(s,\ u,\ f(s,\ u)) du ds + \sum_{i=1}^N \int_0^t \sigma_i(s,\ T,\ f(s,\ T)) dz_i(s)$$

From the relationship between forward rates and bond prices, that is,

$$f(t,\ T) = -\frac{\partial \ln P(t,\ T)}{\partial T} \quad \text{and} \quad P(t,\ T) = \exp\left(-\int_t^T f(t,\ u) du \right)$$

we can use Ito's lemma to generate the dynamics of the zero-coupon bond price $P(t,\ T)$. From Ito:

$$d \ln P(t,\ T) = d\left(-\int_t^T f(t,\ u) du \right)$$

which becomes:

$$dP(t,\ T) = P(t,\ T)\left[r(t) dt - \sum_{i=1}^N \left(\int_t^T \sigma_i(t,\ u) du \right) dz_i(t) \right] \qquad (12.22)$$

or

$$dP(t,\ T) = P(t,\ T)\left[r(t)dt - \left(\int_t^T \sigma(t,\ s)ds\right)dz(t)\right]$$

in vector form, where $r(t)$ is the instantaneous short-term interest rate at time t:

$$r(t) = f(t,\ t) = f(0,\ t) + \sum_{i=1}^N \int_0^t \sigma_i(s,\ t,\ f(s,\ t)) \int_s^t \sigma_i(s,\ u,\ f(s,\ u))du\,ds$$

$$+ \sum_{i=1}^N \int_0^t \sigma_i(s,\ t,\ f(s,\ t))dz_i(s) \qquad (12.23)$$

which satisfies the following SDE:

$$dr(t) = \left[\frac{\partial f(0,\ t)}{\partial t} + \sum_{i=1}^N \left\{\int_0^t \left(v_i(s,\ t)\frac{\partial^2 v_i(s,\ t)}{\partial t^2} + \frac{\partial v_i(s,\ t)^2}{\partial t}\right)ds + \int_0^t \frac{\partial^2 v_i(s,\ t)}{\partial t^2}dz_i(s)\right\}\right]dt$$

$$+ \sum_{i=1}^N \frac{\partial v_i(s,\ t)}{\partial t}\Big|_{s=t}dz_i(s) \qquad (12.24)$$

where

$$v_i(s,\ t) = -\int_s^t \sigma_i(s,\ u)du$$

which relates the volatilities of forward rates and bond prices (for the ith factor).

The short rate process is non-Markovian in general. This is due to the fact that time t appears in the stochastic integral as the upper limit and inside the integrand function. This implies that the evolution of the term structure could depend on the entire path taken by the term structure since it was initialized at time 0.[8] However, there are conditions that can be imposed on the forward rate volatility that leads to a Markov short rate process. As Carverhill (1994) has shown, if the forward rate volatility satisfies a separable conditions, the volatility specification can be written as:

$$\sigma_i(t,\ T) = \xi_i(t)\psi_i(T) \qquad (12.25)$$

for each $i = 1, \dots, N$ where ξ_i and ψ_i are strictly positive and deterministic

---

[8]Clewlow and Strickland (1998a), 231.

functions of time, then the short rate process is Markov. In this case, we can write (12.23) as:

$$r(t) = f(0, t) + \sum_{i=1}^{N} \int_{0}^{t} \xi_i(s)\psi_i(t) \int_{s}^{t} \xi_i(s)\psi_i(u)du\,ds + \sum_{i=1}^{N} \int_{0}^{t} \xi_i(s)\psi_i(t)dz_i(s)$$

$$= f(0, t) + \sum_{i=1}^{N} \psi_i(t) \int_{0}^{t} \xi_i^2(s) \int_{s}^{t} \psi_i(u)du\,ds + \sum_{i=1}^{N} \psi_i(t) \int_{0}^{t} \xi_i(s)dz_i(s)$$

In the one-factor case ($N = 1$), let A be a strictly positive deterministic function defined by:

$$A(t) = f(0, t) + \psi_1(t) \int_{0}^{t} \xi_1^2(s) \int_{s}^{t} \psi_1(u)du\,ds \qquad (12.26)$$

If we assume A is differentiable, then we can write the short rate process as:

$$dr(t) = A'(t)dt + \psi_1'(t) \int_{0}^{t} \xi_1(s)dz_1(s) + \psi_1(t)\xi_1(t)dz_1(t)$$

$$= \left[A'(t) + \psi_1'(t)\left(\frac{r(t) - A(t)}{\psi_1(t)} \right) \right]dt + \psi_1(t)\xi_1(t)dz_1(t) \qquad (12.27)$$

$$= (a(t) + b(t)r(t))dt + c(t)dz_1(t)$$

where

$$a(t) = A'(t) - \frac{\psi_1'(t)A(t)}{\psi_1(t)}, \quad b(t) = \frac{\psi_1'(t)}{\psi_1(t)}, \quad \text{and } c(t) = \psi_1(t)\xi_1(t)$$

We end up with the general short rate process developed by Hull and White (1990); see (10.76). Therefore, it has been established that when the short rate process is Markov, there is an equivalence between the HJM one-factor model for which (12.24) holds and the Gaussian one-factor Hull-White short rate model (1990b). In fact, we can derive the HJM forward rate dynamics that is equivalent to the Hull-White dynamics in (10.76). Let us set

$$\sigma_1(t, T) = \sigma e^{-a}(T - t)$$

where a and σ are now real constants, so that

$$\xi_1(t) = \sigma e^{at}$$

$$\psi_1(t) = e^{-aT}$$

$$A(t) = f(0,\ t) + \frac{\sigma^2}{2a^2}(1 - e^{-at})^2$$

The volatility function can be estimated by (cross-sectional) nonlinear regression across different maturities.[9]

The resulting short-rate dynamics is then given by

$$dr(t) = \left[\frac{\partial f(0,\ t)}{\partial T} + \frac{\sigma^2}{a}(e^{-at} - e^{-2at}) - a\left(r(t) - f(0,\ t) - \frac{\sigma^2}{2a^2}(1 - e^{-at})^2\right)\right]dt + \sigma dz_1(t)$$

$$= \left[\frac{\partial f(0,\ t)}{\partial T} + af(0,\ t) + \frac{\sigma^2}{2a}(1 - e^{-2at}) - ar(t)\right]dt + \sigma dz_1(t)$$

which is equivalent to (10.76) when combined with (10.82).[10]

---

[9]Jarrow (1996), page 319. In the continuous-time HJM model, it can be shown that the variance of zero-coupon bonds over the time interval $[t,\ t + \Delta]$ satisfies the identity

$$\text{Var}(\log P(t + \Delta,\ T) - \log P(t,\ T) - r(t)\Delta) = \frac{\sigma^2(e^{-\lambda(T-t)} - 1)^2\Delta}{\lambda^2}$$

To estimate the variance on the left side of the equation, one can use zero-coupon bond prices generated by stripping coupon bonds to compute sample variances, v_T, by choosing $\Delta = 1/12$, for various maturities such as 3 months, 6 months, 1 year, 3 years, 5 years, 7 years, 10 years, and 20 years. Then, one can run the following (cross-sectional) nonlinear regression across different maturities to estimate the parameters (λ, σ):

$$v_T = \frac{\sigma^2(e^{-\lambda T} - 1)^2\Delta}{\lambda^2} + \varepsilon_T \text{ for all } T$$

where the error terms ε_T are assumed to be independent and identically distributed with zero mean and constant variance.

[10]Brigo and Mercurio (2001), 177.

12.5   PRICING DISCOUNT BOND OPTIONS WITH GAUSSIAN HJM

In a Gaussian HJM framework, we can derive analytic solutions for European discount bond options assuming Gaussian volatility structures. We change to an equivalent martingale measure by changing to a bank account numeraire

$$B(T) = \exp\left(\int_t^T r(u)du\right)$$

thus, eliminating the drift in (12.22), making the bond price process a martingale:

$$dP(t,\,T) = -P(t,\,T)\sum_{i=1}^{N}\left(\int_t^T \sigma_i(t,\,u)du\right)d\tilde{z}_i(t) \tag{12.28}$$

where under the new measure

$$d\tilde{z}_i(t) = dz_i(t) + \frac{r(t)}{\displaystyle\sum_{i=1}^{N}\int_t^T \sigma_i(t,\,u)du}\,dt$$

where the tilde denotes the measure under the savings account numeraire.

Given the non-Markovian short rate process in (12.25), it is better to value derivatives in the HJM framework using (12.28) since the drift is eliminated and because of the fact that bonds are traded assets whereas short rates are not. We can implement (12.28) via Monte Carlo simulation to price pure discount bond options. The value of the T-maturity European call option on a s-maturity pure discount bond with strike price X is:

$$c(t,\,T,\,s) = \tilde{E}_t\left[\exp\left(-\int_t^T r(u)du\right)\max(0,\,P(T,\,s)-X)\right] \tag{12.29}$$

We can change the numeraire to $P(t,\,T)$ (the forward measure to the maturity date of the option):

$$c(t,\,T,\,s) = P(t,\,T)E_t^T[\max(0,\,P(T,\,s)-X)] \tag{12.30}$$

where $E_t^T[\,]$ indicates the expectation with respect to the $P(t, T)$ numeraire. The solution to this equation is analogous to the Black-Scholes equation:[11]

$$c(t, T, s) = P(t, s)N(h) - XP(t, T)N(h - w) \qquad (12.31)$$

where

$$h = \frac{\ln\left(\dfrac{P(t, s)}{P(t, T)X}\right) + \dfrac{1}{2}w}{\sqrt{w}}$$

$$w = \sum_{i=1}^{N}\left\{\int_t^T (v_i(u, s) - v_i(u, T)^2)du\right\}$$

and w is the variance of the log of relative discount bond prices.

12.6   PRICING DISCOUNT BOND OPTIONS IN GENERAL HJM

In a general HJM framework, we can price discount bond options via Monte Carlo simulations to deal with the analytic intractability of a non-Markovian short rate process. Carverhill and Pang (1995) show that the price of a European call option on a pure discount bond given by

$$c(t, T, s) = \tilde{E}_t\left[\exp\left(-\int_t^T r(u)du\right)\max(0, P(T, s) - X)\right]$$

which can be rewritten in the general HJM framework as

$$c(t, T, s) = \tilde{E}_t[\max(0, P(t, s)Z(t, T, s) - XP(t, T)Z(t, T, T))] \qquad (12.32)$$

where

$$Z(t, T, s) = \exp\left[\int_t^T v(u, s)dz(u) - \frac{1}{2}\int_t^T v(u, s)^2\, du\right]$$

---

[11]See Brace and Musiela (1994) or Clewlow, Strickland, and Pang (1997).

We can simulate (12.32) via Monte Carlo simulation with $j = 1, \ldots, M$ simulations:

$$c(t, T, s) = -\frac{1}{M} \sum_{j=1}^{M} \max(0, P(t, s)Z_j(t, T, s) - XP(t, T)Z_j(t, T, T)) \quad (12.33)$$

where

$$Z_j(t, T, s) = \exp\left[\sum_{i=1}^{N} v(u_i, s)\varepsilon_i \sqrt{\Delta t} - \frac{1}{2}\sum_{i=1}^{N} v(u_i, s)^2 \Delta t\right]$$

We can estimate

$$v(u_i, s) \approx -\sum_{i=1}^{\bar{N}} \sigma(u_i, t)\Delta t$$

where $\bar{N}$ is the number of (very small) time steps and $\Delta t = T/\bar{N}$. For example, if we assume a negative exponential volatility function, then

$$v(u_i, s) \approx -\sigma \sum_{i=1}^{\bar{N}} e^{a(t-u_i)} \Delta t$$

and for simplicity, if we assume only one factor so that $N = 1$, then:

$$Z_j(t, T, s) = \exp\left[-\sigma\left(\sum_{i=0}^{\bar{N}} e^{a((\bar{N}-i)\Delta t)}\Delta t\right)\varepsilon\sqrt{\Delta t} - \frac{1}{2}\sigma^2 \sum_{i=0}^{\bar{N}} \sum_{k=0}^{\bar{N}} e^{a((\bar{N}-i)\Delta t + (\bar{N}-k)\Delta s)}\Delta t \Delta s\right]$$

It is easy to see that as we increase the number of factors, the computation becomes more complex as we are approximating multidimensional integrals and thus more computation time is needed.

12.7   SINGLE-FACTOR HJM DISCRETE-STATE MODEL

In a discrete-time economy, we denote the forward rate $f_\Delta(t, T)$, which represents "one plus the percentage" forward rate at time t for the future time period $[T, T + \Delta]$.

The continuously compounded (continuous-time) forward rate $f(t, T)$ corresponds to the rate such that

$$f_\Delta(t, T) \approx e^{f(t, T)\Delta}$$

This expression states that the continuously compounded rate for Δ units of time (i.e., a percentage) equals the discrete rate. More formally,

$$f(t, T) = \lim_{\Delta \to 0} \frac{\log(f_\Delta(t, T))}{\Delta}$$

assuming the limit exists. Since we are concerned with changes in continuously compounded forward rates, then we can write

$$f(t + \Delta, T) - f(t, T) \approx \frac{\log f_\Delta(t + \Delta, T)}{\Delta} - \frac{\log f_\Delta(t, T)}{\Delta}$$

Under the actual (empirical or objective) probability measure, the evolution of observed zero-coupon bonds and forward rates is generated by a continuous-time real-world economy process with drift $\mu^*(t, T)$ that represents expected changes in continuously compounded forward rates per unit time, and diffusion coefficient $\sigma(t, T)$, the standard deviation of changes in the continuously compounded forward rates per unit time—the forward rate's volatility. We would like to construct an approximating discrete-time empirical economy such that as the step size tends to 0 (i.e., $\Delta \to 0$) the discrete time process approaches the continuous-time process. The term "empirical" is meant to distinguish between the real-world economy from the transformation using a change in probability measure to the risk-neutral world, or "pseudo" economy.

We can characterize a discrete-time empirical economy by (1) real-world probabilities, $q_\Delta(t; s_t)$, that can be a function of time and current state s_t (mathematically, the filtration generated by the adapted process) and (2) the (one plus) percentage changes in the forward rates across various states (i.e., movements to up or down states). Under the real-world probability measure at time t, the approximation between the discrete and continuous-time processes can be made by matching their means and variances, respectively. From probability theory with certain technical conditions (see He [1990]), we get:

$$\lim_{\Delta \to 0} \frac{E_t\left[\dfrac{\log f_\Delta(t + \Delta, T)}{\Delta} - \dfrac{\log f_\Delta(t, T)}{\Delta}\right]}{\Delta} \to \mu^*(t, T)$$

and

$$\lim_{\Delta \to 0} \frac{\text{Var}_t\left[\dfrac{\log f_\Delta(t+\Delta,\, T)}{\Delta} - \dfrac{\log f_\Delta(t,\, T)}{\Delta}\right]}{\Delta} \to \sigma^2(t,\, T)$$

where the expectations and variances are obtained using the actual probabilities $q_\Delta(t; s_t)$. For sufficient small Δ, the discrete process will be a good approximation to the continuous-time process.

We know from no-arbitrage arguments that there exists an equivalent martingale measure such that unique risk-neutral (pseudo) probabilities $\pi_\Delta(t; s_t)$ exist that can be used for valuation of contingent claims. The discrete-time risk-neutral economy is characterized by (1) the probability of movements of forward rates $\pi_\Delta(t; s_t)$ and (2) the (one plus) percentage changes in forward rates across various states (i.e., movements to up and down states). There exists an arbitrage-free link between both discrete risk-neutral and empirical economies. The percentage changes in forward rates are identical in both discrete-time economies; only the likelihoods (probabilities) of the movements differ.[12] Under equivalent probability measure, $q_\Delta(t; s_t) = 0$ if and only if $\pi_\Delta(t; s_t) = 0$.

Similar to the discrete-time case, the assumption of no-arbitrage in the continuous-time model gives the existence of unique risk-neutral (pseudo) probabilities, which are used for the valuation of contingent claims. The risk-neutral economy process is characterized by the (1) drift, $\mu(t, T)$, the expected change in the continuously compounded forward rates per unit time, and (2) $\sigma(t, T)$, the standard deviation of changes in the continuously compounded forward rates per unit time. The standard deviations of changes in forward rates are the same in both the risk-neutral and empirical continuous-time economies; only the likelihoods (and, thus, expected changes in forward rates) differ so that there is an arbitrage-free (equivalent probability measure) link between the two limit economies. From Girsanov's theorem, we know that under a change of measure,

$$\lim_{\Delta \to 0} \frac{\tilde{E}_t\left[\dfrac{\log f_\Delta(t+\Delta,\, T)}{\Delta} - \dfrac{\log f_\Delta(t,\, T)}{\Delta}\right]}{\Delta} \to \mu(t,\, T)$$

and

$$\lim_{\Delta \to 0} \frac{\tilde{\text{Var}}_t\left[\dfrac{\log f_\Delta(t+\Delta,\, T)}{\Delta} - \dfrac{\log f_\Delta(t,\, T)}{\Delta}\right]}{\Delta} \to \sigma^2(t,\, T)$$

[12]Jarrow (1996), 278.

where the tildes denote expectations and variances under the risk-neutral probability measure. We know from Girsanov's theorem that the relationship between the actual and risk-neutral drift is $\mu^*(t, T) = \mu(t, T) - \lambda(t)\sigma(t, T)$ where $\lambda(t)$ is the risk premium or market price of risk—a measure of the excess expected return (above the risk-free rate) per unit of standard deviation (risk) for zero-coupon bonds. If the risk-neutral probabilities $\pi_\Delta(t; s_t)$ are chosen such that $\pi_\Delta(t; s_t) = 1/2$, then the computation of matching discrete and continuous time processes is simplified.

Following Jarrow (1996), in the discrete-time empirical economy, we can characterize the forward rate process by

$$f_\Delta(t + \Delta, T; s_{t+\Delta}) = \begin{cases} \alpha_\Delta(t, T; s_t)f_\Delta(t, T; s_t) & \text{if } s_{t+\Delta} = s_t u \text{ with prob. } q_\Delta(t; s_t) \\ \beta_\Delta(t, T; s_t)f_\Delta(t, T; s_t) & \text{if } s_{t+\Delta} = s_t d \text{ with prob. } 1 - q_\Delta(t; s_t) \end{cases}$$

where

$$\alpha_\Delta(t, T; s_t) = e^{[\mu(t,T;s_t)\Delta - \sigma(t,T;s_t)\sqrt{\Delta}]\Delta} \tag{12.34}$$

and

$$\beta_\Delta(t, T; s_t) = e^{[\mu(t,T;s_t)\Delta + \sigma(t,T;s_t)\sqrt{\Delta}]\Delta} \tag{12.35}$$

and

$$q_\Delta(t; s_t) = \frac{1}{2} + \frac{1}{2}\lambda(t; s_t)\sqrt{\Delta}$$

$$1 - q_\Delta(t; s_t) = \frac{1}{2} - \frac{1}{2}\lambda(t; s_t)\sqrt{\Delta}$$

$$\lambda(t; s_t) = \frac{\mu^*(t, T) - \mu(t, T)}{\sigma(t, T)}$$

and u and d represent up and down states. Thus, we can write the forward rate process as:

$$f_\Delta(t + \Delta, T; s_{t+\Delta}) =$$
$$\begin{cases} f_\Delta(t, T; s_t)e^{[\mu(t,T;s_t)\Delta - \sigma(t,T;s_t)\sqrt{\Delta}]\Delta} & \text{if } s_{t+\Delta} = s_t u \text{ with prob. } q_\Delta(t; s_t) \\ f_\Delta(t, T; s_t)e^{[\mu(t,T;s_t)\Delta + \sigma(t,T;s_t)\sqrt{\Delta}]\Delta} & \text{if } s_{t+\Delta} = s_t d \text{ with prob. } 1 - q_\Delta(t; s_t) \end{cases} \tag{12.36}$$

Taking the natural logarithms of both sides of expression (12.36), we get

$$
\frac{\log f_\Delta(t+\Delta,\ T;\ s_{t+\Delta})}{\Delta} - \frac{\log f_\Delta(t,\ T;\ s_t)}{\Delta}
$$
$$
= \begin{cases} \mu(t,\ T;\ s_t)\Delta - \sigma(t,\ T;\ s_t)\sqrt{\Delta} & \text{if } s_{t+\Delta} = s_t u \text{ with prob. } q_\Delta(t;\ s_t) \\ \mu(t,\ T;\ s_t)\Delta + \sigma(t,\ T;\ s_t)\sqrt{\Delta} & \text{if } s_{t+\Delta} = s_t d \text{ with prob. } 1 - q_\Delta(t;\ s_t) \end{cases} \qquad (12.37)
$$

The mean and variance changes in the forward rates can be calculated to be

$$
E_t\left[\frac{\log f_\Delta(t+\Delta,\ T)}{\Delta} - \frac{\log f_\Delta(t,\ T)}{\Delta} \right] = (\mu(t,\ T) - \lambda(t)\sigma(t,\ T))\Delta
$$

and

$$
\mathrm{Var}_t\left[\frac{\log f_\Delta(t+\Delta,\ T)}{\Delta} - \frac{\log f_\Delta(t,\ T)}{\Delta} \right] = \sigma(t,\ T)^2 \Delta - \lambda(t)^2 \sigma^2(t,\ T)\Delta^2
$$

Taking the limit as $\Delta \to 0$ of the mean and variance changes in forward rates (using (12.37)) and then dividing by Δ we get:

$$
\lim_{\Delta \to 0} \frac{E_t\left[\dfrac{\log f_\Delta(t+\Delta,\ T)}{\Delta} - \dfrac{\log f_\Delta(t,\ T)}{\Delta} \right]}{\Delta} = \mu(t,\ T) - \lambda(t)\sigma(t,\ T) = \mu^*(t,\ T)
$$

and

$$
\lim_{\Delta \to 0} \frac{\mathrm{Var}_t\left[\dfrac{\log f_\Delta(t+\Delta,\ T)}{\Delta} - \dfrac{\log f_\Delta(t,\ T)}{\Delta} \right]}{\Delta} = \sigma^2(t,\ T)
$$

In principle, we can estimate $\mu^*(t,\ T)$ and $\sigma(t,\ T)$ from historical observations of forward rates. $\lambda(t)$ is a stochastic process that is in general not empirically observable, which is why it is easier to work with in the risk-neutral world.

12.8 ARBITRAGE-FREE RESTRICTIONS IN A SINGLE-FACTOR MODEL

We can define the return at time t on the T-maturity zero coupon bond as

$$u_\Delta(t,\ T;\ s_t) = \frac{P_\Delta(t+1,\ T;\ s_t u)}{P_\Delta(t,\ T;\ s_t)} \text{ for } t+1 \le T \qquad (12.38)$$

and

$$d_\Delta(t,\ T;\ s_t) = \frac{P_\Delta(t+1,\ T;\ s_t d)}{P_\Delta(t,\ T;\ s_t)} \text{ for } t+1 \le T \qquad (12.39)$$

in the up and down states, respectively, where $u(t,\ T;\ s_t) > d_\Delta(t,\ T;\ s_t)$ for all $t < T - 1$ and s_t. The same symbols u and d are used for both the states and returns on the bond to visually link the state with changes in the underlying bond price process.[13] We can characterize the evolution of the one-factor zero-coupon bond price process as

$$P_\Delta(t+1,\ T;\ s_{t+1}) = \begin{cases} u_\Delta(t,\ T;\ s_t)P_\Delta(t,\ T;\ s_t) & \text{if } s_{t+1} = s_t u \text{ with } q(t;\ s_t) > 0 \\ d_\Delta(t,\ T;\ s_t)P_\Delta(t,\ T;\ s_t) & \text{if } s_{t+1} = s_t d \text{ with } q(t;\ s_t) > 0 \end{cases} \qquad (12.40)$$

From no-arbitrage arguments, we know there exists risk-neutral probabilities $\pi_\Delta(t;\ s_t)$ such that $P_\Delta(t+1,\ T;\ s_t)/B_\Delta(t+1;\ s_{t-1})$ is a martingale; that is,

$$\frac{P_\Delta(t,\ T;\ s_t)}{B_\Delta(t;\ s_{t-1})} = \tilde{E}_t \left[\frac{P_\Delta(t+1,\ T;\ s_t u)}{B_\Delta(t+1;\ s_t)} \right]$$

$$= \pi_\Delta(t,\ T;\ s_t) \frac{P_\Delta(t+1,\ T;\ s_t u)}{B_\Delta(t+1;\ s_t)} + (1 - \pi_\Delta(t,\ T;\ s_t)) \frac{P_\Delta(t+1,\ T;\ s_t u)}{B_\Delta(t+1;\ s_t)}$$

Since the bank account return over one time period is $B_\Delta(t+1;\ s_t)/B_\Delta(t;\ s_t) = r_\Delta(t;\ s_t)$, the risk-free rate, then we can write (in discrete time):

$$P_\Delta(t,\ T;\ s_t)r_\Delta(t;\ s_t) = \pi_\Delta(t,\ T;\ s_t)P_\Delta(t+1,\ T;\ s_t u) + (1 - \pi_\Delta(t,\ T;\ s_t))P_\Delta(t+1,\ T;\ s_t d)$$

which is equal to

$$r_\Delta(t;\ s_t) = \pi_\Delta(t,\ T;\ s_t) \frac{P_\Delta(t+1,\ T;\ s_t u)}{P_\Delta(t,\ T;\ s_t)} + (1 - \pi_\Delta(t,\ T;\ s_t)) \frac{P_\Delta(t+1,\ T;\ s_t d)}{P_\Delta(t,\ T;\ s_t)}$$

$$= \pi_\Delta(t,\ T;\ s_t)u_\Delta(t,\ T;\ s_t) + (1 - \pi_\Delta(t,\ T;\ s_t))d_\Delta(t,\ T;\ s_t)$$

---

[13]Ibid., 67.

so that the risk-neutral probabilities are

$$\pi_\Delta(t,\ T;\ s_t) = \frac{r_\Delta(t;\ s_t) - d_\Delta(t,\ T;\ s_t)}{u_\Delta(t,\ T;\ s_t) - d_\Delta(t,\ T;\ s_t)} \tag{12.41}$$

and

$$1 - \pi_\Delta(t,\ T;\ s_t) = \frac{u_\Delta(t,\ T;\ s_t) - r_\Delta(t;\ s_t)}{u_\Delta(t,\ T;\ s_t) - d_\Delta(t,\ T;\ s_t)} \tag{12.42}$$

We can relate the forward rate's rate of change parameters to the zero-coupon bond price process's rate of return parameters in the up and down states, respectively, as follows:

$$\alpha_\Delta(t,\ T;\ s_t) = \frac{u_\Delta(t,\ T;\ s_t)}{u_\Delta(t,\ T+1;\ s_t)} = \frac{f_\Delta(t+1,\ T;\ s_t u)}{f_\Delta(t,\ T;\ s_t)} \text{ for } t+1 \le T$$

and

$$\beta_\Delta(t,\ T;\ s_t) = \frac{d_\Delta(t,\ T;\ s_t)}{d_\Delta(t,\ T+1;\ s_t)} = \frac{f_\Delta(t+1,\ T;\ s_t d)}{f_\Delta(t,\ T;\ s_t)} \text{ for } t+1 \le T$$

Consequently, we can deduce the zero-coupon bond price process's rate of return parameters in the up and down states from the forward rate process. It can be shown that in the up state

$$u_\Delta(t,\ T;\ s_t) = \frac{r_\Delta(t;\ s_t)}{\displaystyle\prod_{j=t+1}^{T-1} \alpha_\Delta(t,\ j;\ s_t)} \text{ for } t+2 \le T \tag{12.43}$$

and in the down state

$$d_\Delta(t,\ T;\ s_t) = \frac{r_\Delta(t;\ s_t)}{\displaystyle\prod_{j=t+1}^{T-1} \beta_\Delta(t,\ j;\ s_t)} \text{ for } t+2 \le T \tag{12.44}$$

so that substituting (12.38) into (12.41) and (12.39) into (12.42), respectively, yields

$$u_\Delta(t,\ T;\ s_t) = r_\Delta(t;\ s_t)e^{\left(-\sum_{j=t+\Delta}^{T-\Delta} \mu(t,j;s_t)\Delta + \sum_{j=t+\Delta}^{T-\Delta} \sigma(t,j;s_t)\sqrt{\Delta}\right)\Delta} \tag{12.45}$$

and

$$d_\Delta(t,\ T;\ s_t) = r_\Delta(t;\ s_t)e^{\left(-\sum_{j=t+\Delta}^{T-\Delta} \mu(t,j;s_t)\Delta - \sum_{j=t+\Delta}^{T-\Delta} \sigma(t,j;s_t)\sqrt{\Delta}\right)\Delta} \tag{12.46}$$

Substituting (12.45) and (12.46) into the risk-neutral probability in (12.41) yields

$$
\pi_\Delta(t;\,s_t) = \frac{1 - e^{\left(-\sum\limits_{j=t+\Delta}^{T-\Delta}\mu(t,j;s_t)\Delta - \sum\limits_{j=t+\Delta}^{T-\Delta}\sigma(t,j;s_t)\sqrt{\Delta}\,\right)\Delta}}{e^{\left(-\sum\limits_{j=t+\Delta}^{T-\Delta}\mu(t,j;s_t)\Delta + \sum\limits_{j=t+\Delta}^{T-\Delta}\sigma(t,j;s_t)\sqrt{\Delta}\,\right)\Delta} - e^{\left(-\sum\limits_{j=t+\Delta}^{T-\Delta}\mu(t,j;s_t)\Delta - \sum\limits_{j=t+\Delta}^{T-\Delta}\sigma(t,j;s_t)\sqrt{\Delta}\,\right)\Delta}}
\tag{12.47}
$$

for all $0 \le t < T - \Delta$ and s_t. Using these risk-neutral probabilities, the change in the logarithm of forward rates is given by

$$
\frac{\log f_\Delta(t+\Delta,\,T;\,s_{t+\Delta})}{\Delta} - \frac{\log f_\Delta(t,\,T;\,s_t)}{\Delta} =
\begin{cases}
\mu(t,\,T;\,s_t)\Delta - \sigma(t,\,T;\,s_t)\sqrt{\Delta} \;\text{ if } s_{t+\Delta} \\
= s_t u \text{ with probability } \pi(t;\,s_t) \\
\mu(t,\,T;\,s_t)\Delta + \sigma(t,\,T;\,s_t)\sqrt{\Delta} \;\text{ if } s_{t+\Delta} \\
= s_t d \text{ with probability } 1 - \pi(t;\,s_t)
\end{cases}
\tag{12.48}
$$

Thus, the mean and variance of the changes in forward rates can be computed under the risk-neutral probabilities.

$$
\tilde{E}_t\left[\frac{\log f_\Delta(t+\Delta,\,T)}{\Delta} - \frac{\log f_\Delta(t,\,T)}{\Delta}\right] = \mu(t,\,T)\Delta + (1 - 2\pi_\Delta(t))\sigma(t,\,T)\sqrt{\Delta}
$$

and

$$
\tilde{Var}_t\left[\frac{\log f_\Delta(t+\Delta,\,T)}{\Delta} - \frac{\log f_\Delta(t,\,T)}{\Delta}\right] = 4\sigma^2(t,\,T)\Delta\pi_\Delta(t)(1 - \pi_t(t))
$$

To ensure a discrete approximation in the risk-neutral process to the risk-neutral continuous-time process requires three conditions. First, (12.47) holds. Second, as $\Delta \to 0$,

$$
\lim_{\Delta \to 0} \frac{\tilde{E}_t\left[\dfrac{\log f_\Delta(t+\Delta,\,T)}{\Delta} - \dfrac{\log f_\Delta(t,\,T)}{\Delta}\right]}{\Delta} = \mu(t,\,T)
\tag{12.49}
$$

and third,

$$
\lim_{\Delta \to 0} \frac{\tilde{Var}_t\left[\dfrac{\log f_\Delta(t+\Delta,\,T)}{\Delta} - \dfrac{\log f_\Delta(t,\,T)}{\Delta}\right]}{\Delta} = \sigma^2(t,\,T)
\tag{12.50}
$$

These three conditions imply that

$$\pi_\Delta(t;\, s_t) = \frac{1}{2} + o(\sqrt{\Delta}) \tag{12.51}$$

For computational efficiency, we assume $\pi_\Delta(t;\, s_t) = 1/2$ for all s_t and t. Thus, we set the left-hand side of equation (12.47) to 1/2 and then rearrange terms to get

$$\frac{1}{2}\left[e^{\left(-\sum\limits_{j=t+\Delta}^{T-\Delta}\mu(t,j;s_t)\Delta + \sum\limits_{j=t+\Delta}^{T-\Delta}\sigma(t,j;s_t)\sqrt{\Delta}\right)\Delta} - e^{\left(-\sum\limits_{j=t+\Delta}^{T-\Delta}\mu(t,j;s_t)\Delta - \sum\limits_{j=t+\Delta}^{T-\Delta}\sigma(t,j;s_t)\sqrt{\Delta}\right)\Delta} \right]$$
$$= \left[1 - e^{\left(-\sum\limits_{j=t+\Delta}^{T-\Delta}\mu(t,j;s_t)\Delta - \sum\limits_{j=t+\Delta}^{T-\Delta}\sigma(t,j;s_t)\sqrt{\Delta}\right)\Delta} \right] \tag{12.52}$$

which is true if and only if

$$e^{\left(\sum\limits_{j=t+\Delta}^{T-\Delta}\mu(t,j;s_t)\Delta\right)\Delta} = \frac{1}{2}\left[e^{\left(+\sum\limits_{j=t+\Delta}^{T-\Delta}\sigma(t,j;s_t)\sqrt{\Delta}\right)\Delta} + e^{\left(-\sum\limits_{j=t+\Delta}^{T-\Delta}\sigma(t,j;s_t)\sqrt{\Delta}\right)\Delta} \right]$$
$$= \cosh\left(\left[\sum\limits_{j=t+\Delta}^{T-\Delta}\sigma(t,j;\, s_t)\sqrt{\Delta}\right]\Delta\right) \tag{12.53}$$

where

$$\cosh(x) = \frac{1}{2}(e^x + e^{-x})$$

With the restriction on the risk-neutral probability as well as the conditions imposed on the drifts and volatilities, the forward rate process will be arbitrage-free and converge to the appropriate risk-neutral continuous-time process.

12.9   COMPUTATION OF ARBITRAGE-FREE TERM STRUCTURE EVOLUTIONS

We can use the results in the previous section to compute an arbitrage-free term structure evolution. We can compute the evolution of zero-coupon bonds by substitution of (12.53) into (12.45) and (12.46), which gives

$$
u_\Delta(t, T; s_t) = r_\Delta(t; s_t) \left[\cosh\left(\left[\sum_{j=t+\Delta}^{T-\Delta} \sigma(t, j; s_t)\sqrt{\Delta}\,\right]\Delta \right) \right]^{-1} e^{\left(\sum\limits_{j=t+\Delta}^{T-\Delta} \sigma(t,j;s_t)\sqrt{\Delta}\,\right)\Delta} \tag{12.54}
$$

and

$$
d_\Delta(t, T; s_t) = r_\Delta(t; s_t) \left[\cosh\left(\left[\sum_{j=t+\Delta}^{T-\Delta} \sigma(t, j; s_t)\sqrt{\Delta}\,\right]\Delta \right) \right]^{-1} e^{\left(-\sum\limits_{j=t+\Delta}^{T-\Delta} \sigma(t,j;s_t)\sqrt{\Delta}\,\right)\Delta} \tag{12.55}
$$

Substituting (12.54) and (12.55) into the zero-coupon bond process in (12.40) gives

$$
P_\Delta(t+\Delta, T; s_{t+\Delta}) = \begin{cases} P_\Delta(t, T; s_t) r_\Delta(t; s_t) \left[\cosh\left(\left[\sum\limits_{j=t+\Delta}^{T-\Delta} \sigma(t, j; s_t)\sqrt{\Delta}\,\right]\Delta \right) \right]^{-1} \cdot \\[2em] \quad e^{\left[\sum\limits_{j=t+\Delta}^{T-\Delta} \sigma(t,j;s_t)\sqrt{\Delta}\,\right]\Delta} \quad \text{if } s_{t+1} = s_t u \\[2em] P_\Delta(t, T; s_t) r_\Delta(t; s_t) \left[\cosh\left(\left[\sum\limits_{j=t+\Delta}^{T-\Delta} \sigma(t, j; s_t)\sqrt{\Delta}\,\right]\Delta \right) \right]^{-1} \cdot \\[2em] \quad e^{\left[-\sum\limits_{j=t+\Delta}^{T-\Delta} \sigma(t,j;s_t)\sqrt{\Delta}\,\right]\Delta} \quad \text{if } s_{t+1} = s_t d \end{cases} \tag{12.56}
$$

for $t < T - \Delta$ where t and T are integer multiples of Δ.

The bond price process in (12.56) gives the realization of the discrete-time bond price process. Using actual probabilities, $(1/2) + (1/2)\lambda(t; s_t)$, this process will converge to the limiting continuous-time empirical process for the bond's prices. If risk-neutral probabilities $\pi_\Delta(t; s_t) = 1/2$ are used, then the bond price process converges to the limiting continuous-time risk-neutral process for the bond's price. Since valuation of contingent claims in the risk-neutral economy is all that is required for arbitrage-free pricing, then it is not necessary to ever estimate the stochastic process $\lambda(t; s_t)$.

We can generate the forward rate process. By using equation (12.53), we get

$$e^{[\mu(t,t+\Delta;s_t)\Delta]\Delta} = \cosh\left(\left[\sigma(t,\ t+\Delta;\ s_t)\sqrt{\Delta t}\right]\Delta\right)$$

and

$$e^{[\mu(t,T;s_t)\Delta]\Delta} = \frac{\cosh\left(\left[\sum_{j=t+\Delta}^{T}\sigma(t,\ j;\ s_t)\sqrt{\Delta}\right]\Delta\right)}{\cosh\left(\left[\sum_{j=t+\Delta}^{T-\Delta}\sigma(t,\ j;\ s_t)\sqrt{\Delta}\right]\Delta\right)} \tag{12.57}$$

for $T \geq t + 2\Delta$.

Substituting this expression into the forward rate process yields

$$f_\Delta(t+\Delta,\ T;\ s_{t+\Delta}) = \begin{cases} f_\Delta(t,\ T;\ s_t)\dfrac{\cosh\left(\left[\sum_{j=t+\Delta}^{T}\sigma(t,\ j;\ s_t)\sqrt{\Delta}\right]\Delta\right)}{\cosh\left(\left[\sum_{j=t+\Delta}^{T-\Delta}\sigma(t,\ j;\ s_t)\sqrt{\Delta}\right]\Delta\right)}e^{[-\sigma(t,T;s_t)\sqrt{\Delta}]\Delta} & \text{if } s_{t+\Delta} = s_t u \\[4ex] f_\Delta(t,\ T;\ s_t)\dfrac{\cosh\left(\left[\sum_{j=t+\Delta}^{T}\sigma(t,\ j;\ s_t)\sqrt{\Delta}\right]\Delta\right)}{\cosh\left(\left[\sum_{j=t+\Delta}^{T-\Delta}\sigma(t,\ j;\ s_t)\sqrt{\Delta}\right]\Delta\right)}e^{[+\sigma(t,T;s_t)\sqrt{\Delta}]\Delta} & \text{if } s_{t+\Delta} = s_t d \end{cases} \tag{12.58}$$

for $T - \Delta \geq t$, t and T are integer multiples of Δ where for notational convenience we define

$$\cosh\left(\left[\sum_{j=t+\Delta}^{t}\sigma(t,\ j;\ s_t)\sqrt{\Delta}\right]\Delta\right) \equiv 1$$

so that we do not have to write out two expressions: one when $T = t + \Delta$ and one when $T = t + 2\Delta$. Using empirical probabilities, $(1/2) + (1/2)\lambda(t; s_t)$, the forward rate process in (12.58), converges to the empirical continuous-time forward rate process. Similarly, using risk-neutral probabilities, $\pi_\Delta(t; s_t) = 1/2$, it converges to the risk-neutral continuous-time forward rate process. Moreover, in the risk-neutral economy, a specification of the volatility of forward rates,

$$[\sigma(t, t + \Delta; s_t), \sigma(t, t + 2\Delta; s_t), \ldots, \sigma(t, T - \Delta; s_t)]$$

for all $0 \leq t \leq T - \Delta$ and s_t is sufficient to determine the evolution of the forward rate curve.[14] Notice that the market price of risk process $\lambda(t)$ does not appear in (12.58), which simplifies the implementation.

Two functional forms of the forward rate volatility function $\sigma(t, T; s_t)$ are used widely for implementation: (1) a deterministic volatility function, independent of the state s_t, and (2) a nearly proportional volatility function. A deterministic function restriction implies that forward rates can become negative. This case includes as special cases Ho and Lee's (1986) model where the volatility is a constant and the discrete-time approximation in the HJM model to Vasicek's (1977) exponential volatility function.[15]

$$\sigma(t, T; s_t) = \eta e^{-\lambda(T-t)} \qquad \eta, \lambda > 0 \text{ constants}$$

In the nearly proportional volatility specification, the form is

$$\sigma(t, T; s_t) = \eta(t, T)\min(\log f(t, T), M)$$

where $\eta(t, T)$ is a deterministic function and $M > 0$ is a large positive constant. Thus, under this specification, the forward rate volatility is proportional, by a factor $\eta(t, T)$, to the current value of the continuously compounded forward rate log $f(t, T)$. This proportionality ensures that forward rates are always nonnegative, a condition usually imposed on models since negative rates are inconsistent with the existence of cash currency, which can be stored at no interest rate.[16] Moreover, the larger the forward rate, the larger the volatility. However, if the forward rate becomes too large, then the volatility becomes bounded by $\eta(t, T)M$, which ensures forward rates do not explode with positive probability.

In general, the tree is nonrecombining so that an up movement followed by a down movement does not result in the same discount bond price as a down movement followed by an up movement. The tree recombines only if the forward rate volatility is a deterministic function of time. The number of nodes increases exponentially as the number of time steps increases: after N time steps, there are 2^N nodes. For example, after 20 time steps, there are more than 1 million nodes. Consequently, the storage and computational costs for an HJM tree are very high. One approach is to build a binary search tree (BST) to handle this problem.

---

[14]Ibid., 288.
[15]Ibid.
[16]Ibid.

12.10 SINGLE-FACTOR HJM IMPLEMENTATION

The following is an implementation of a single-factor HJM binomial tree to price bonds using a Vasicek exponential deterministic volatility function. The HJM tree is implemented as a binary search tree (BST) since we want (at most) two children per parent node. It is constructed by successively adding nodes to the tree in a manner that maintains symmetry of the tree (i.e., two child nodes at each branch). It does not use recursion, which is another possible and efficient way to build the tree.[17] We define the following *HJMTree* class, which we assume to be a subclass of a general *Tree* class:

```
#ifndef _HJMTREE__
#define _HJMTREE__

#include <vector>
#include <math.h>
#include "Utility.h"
using namespace std;

class HJMTree
{
  private:
    typedef struct BSTREE_NODE {
      double bondPrice[20];           // bond prices
      int nodeKey;                    // a value that identifies node
      double shortRate;               // interest rate
      double forwardRate[20];         // forward rates
      double simpleRate;              // simple short rate
      double cashFlow;                // cash flow for range notes
      double numMoneyMarket;          // number of shares held of money
                                      // market
      double numZeroCoupon;           // number of shares held of zero
                                      // coupon bond
      double moneyMarketAccount;      // money market account
      BSTREE_NODE *up_childptr;       // pointer to up child node
```

---

[17]A recursive function is one that is self-referential. Recursion applied to tree construction is a process that builds the tree in terms of itself using smaller subtrees that in turn build subtrees in terms of themselves and so on until the tree is built. Since, in general, the HJM tree built does not recombine and grows exponentially in the number of nodes, recursion leads to computational time that is less than exponenential. It can be shown that recursion has a computational time of the order of $O(n\log n)$. Not only is recursion efficient, but the code is parsimonious. S. Das, in his 1998 paper "On the Recursive Implementation of Term-Structure Models," generates an HJM recombining tree recursively using Mathematica software by recursively solving for the stochastic process followed by the vector for forward rates as they involve into the future, ensuring that arbitrage conditions are not violated.

```
      BSTREE_NODE *middle_childptr;        // pointer to middle node (only used
                                           // for 2-factor HJM)
      BSTREE_NODE *down_childptr;          // pointer to down child node
   } *TREE_PTR;


   TREE_PTR root_ptr;                      // root of the BST
   double initRate;                        // initial short rate
   double T;                               // maturity
   long N;                                 // number of time steps
   double vol;                             // coefficient of volatility function
                                           // of 1st factor
   double vol1;                            // coefficient of volatility function
                                           // of 2nd factor
   double lambda;                          // coefficient of exponent in
                                           // volatility of 1st factor
   double lambda1;                         // coefficient of exponent in
                                           // volatility of 2nd factor
   double swapRate;                        // swap Rate
   double dt;                              // step size
   int* A;                                 // stores a sequence of randomly
                                           // generated keys
   bool flag;                              // flag for counting height of tree
   int cnt;                                // counts the kth node added
   int rateMaturity_;                      // simple rate maturity
   double** C;                             // double array
   int nodeCnt;                            // counts total nodes for upper part
                                           // of tree
   int nodeCnt2;                           // counts total nodes for lower part
                                           // of tree

   typedef struct
   {
      double numMoneyMarket;               // number of shares of money market
                                           // account
      double numZeroCoupon;                // number of zero coupon bonds
      double value;                        // value of security at node
      double cashFlow;                     // cash flow at node
      double shortRate;                    // short rate
      double zeroCouponBond;               // number of shares of zero coupon
                                           // bonds
      double moneyMarketAccount;           // value of money market account
   } Shares;                               // node structure
   Shares** C;                             // double array of Shares
public:
   HJMTree() { }
   HJMTree(double rate, double T, long N, double vol, double lam);
   HJMTree(double rate, double T, long N, double vol, double lambda, double
      lambda1);
   virtual ~HJMTree();
   StatUtility util;                       // statistical utility
   void init_BSTree()
      { root_ptr = NULL; }                 // initialize BST
   int* generateKeys();                    // generate keys for BST
```

```
      int* generateKeys1();                    // generate keys for TST
      void buildHJMTree();                      // build HJMTree
      void buildHJMSwapTree();                  // build HJM Swap Tree
      void build2FactorHJMTree();               // build 2 factor HJM tree
      void addNodeHJM(int key);                 // add node to HJM tree
      void addNodeHJM(int key, int num);        // add node to HJM tree
      void addNodeHJMRangeNote(int key,
        int num, int rateMaturity);             // add node to range note tree
      void addNode2FactorHJM(int key,
        int num);                               // add node to 2 factor tree
      void traverseInorder(TREE_PTR
        tree_ptr);                              // traverse tree in order
      TREE_PTR get_root() { return
        root_ptr; }                             // returns root of tree
      int getTreeHeight(TREE_PTR
        root_ptr, int cnt);                     // returns height of tree
      int getHeightUp(TREE_PTR
        root_ptr);                              // returns height of "up" tree
      int getHeightDown(TREE_PTR
        root_ptr);                              // returns height of "down" tree
      double calcRangeNote();                   // compute range note value
      vector<double> calcSyntheticSwap
        (double principalAmount);               // compute synthetic swap value
};

#endif _HJMTREE__
/*******************************************************************************
addNodeHJM The procedure builds an HJM single-factor binomial tree to price
  discount bonds based on the discrete-time bond process in Equation (12.56)
[in]:  int key: a numeric key value that orders the nodes into a BST
       int num: used for computing tree height (represents the kth node created)
[out]: void
*******************************************************************************/
void HJMTree::addNodeHJM(int key, int num)
{
  TREE_PTR new_ptr, node_ptr, curr_ptr;
  double r, sum, sum1;
  double volsum = 0.0;
  double volsum1 = 0.0;
  double coshval = 0.0;
  double expvalPlus = 0.0;
  double expvalPlus1 = 0.0;
  double expvalMinus = 0.0;
  double expvalMinus1 = 0.0;
  double coshRatio = 0.0;
  int i;

  new_ptr = new BSTREE_NODE;
  new_ptr->up_childptr = NULL;
  new_ptr->down_childptr = NULL;
  new_ptr->prev_ptr = NULL;

  // get tree height
```

```
cnt = getTreeHeight(get_root(), num);
// Add key in the new node's data field
new_ptr->nodeKey = key;
// If the BST is empty, insert the new rate in root

if (root_ptr == NULL)
{
  for (i = 0; i <= N; i++)
  {
    new_ptr->bondPrice[i] = 1/(pow(initRate,i));
    new_ptr->forwardRate[i] = initRate;
  }
  root_ptr = new_ptr;
}
else
{
  TREE_PTR tree_ptr = root_ptr;
  while (tree_ptr != NULL)
  {
    node_ptr = tree_ptr;
    if (key == tree_ptr->nodeKey)
      return;
    else if (key < tree_ptr->nodeKey)
      // search its up side for insertion location
      tree_ptr = tree_ptr->up_childptr;
    else
      // search its down side for insertion location
      tree_ptr = tree_ptr->down_childptr;
  }
  // Now 'node_ptr' is the pointer to the parent of the new
  // node. Now determine where it will be inserted compute volatilites
  // sum is used for computing both bond prices and forward rates

  sum = 0.0;
  for (int k = cnt; k <= N; k++)
  {
    sum = sum + vol*exp(-lambda*(k*dt));
  }

  // used for coshRatio for forward rate computation
  sum1 = 0.0;
  for (k = cnt; k < N; k++)
  {
    sum1 = sum1 + vol*exp(-lambda*(k*dt));
  }

  volsum = sum*sqrt(dt)*dt;
  volsum1 = sum1*sqrt(dt)*dt;
  coshRatio = cosh(volsum)/cosh(volsum1);
  coshval = 1/cosh(volsum);
  expvalPlus = exp(volsum);
  expvalMinus = exp(-volsum);
  expvalPlus1 = exp(vol*exp(-lambda*cnt*dt)*sqrt(dt)*dt);
```

```
      expvalMinus1 = exp(-vol*exp(-lambda*cnt*dt)*sqrt(dt)*dt);

   if (key < node_ptr->nodeKey)
   {
      node_ptr->up_childptr = new_ptr;
      curr_ptr = node_ptr->up_childptr;

      for (i = cnt; i <= N; i++)
      {
         curr_ptr->forwardRate[i]=node_ptr->forwardRate[i]*coshRatio*expvalMinus1;
         if (i == cnt)
         {
            curr_ptr->bondPrice[cnt] = 1; // bond price at maturity
         }
         else
         {
            // get short rate r(t) from forward rate f(t,t)
            r = curr_ptr->forwardRate[cnt];
            curr_ptr->shortRate = r;
            // calculate bond prices
            curr_ptr->bondPrice[i] = (node_ptr->bondPrice[i])*(r*coshval*expval
               Plus);
         }
      }
   }
   else
   {
      node_ptr->down_childptr = new_ptr;
      curr_ptr = node_ptr->down_childptr;

      for (i = cnt; i <= N; i++)
      {
         curr_ptr->forwardRate[i]=(node_ptr->forwardRate[i]*coshRatio*expvalPlus1);
         if (i == cnt)
         {
            curr_ptr->bondPrice[cnt] = 1;
         }
         else
         {
            // get short rate r(t) from forward rate f(t,t)
            r = curr_ptr->forwardRate[cnt];
            curr_ptr->shortRate = r;
            // compute bond price
            curr_ptr->bondPrice[i] = (node_ptr->bondPrice[i]*r*coshval*expvalMinus);
         }
      }
   }
}
}

/*****************************************************************************
getTreeHeight : calculates the tree height (depth of tree)
[in]:  TREE_PTR root_ptr  : pointer to root of tree structure
```

```
        int num             : counts the kth node added to tree
[out]: int height          : height of tree
******************************************************************************/
int HJMTree::getTreeHeight(TREE_PTR root_ptr, int num)
{
  int depth_up = 0;
  int depth_down = 0;

  if (root_ptr == NULL)
    return 0;
  else
  {
    depth_up = getHeightUp(root_ptr->up_childptr);
    depth_down = getHeightDown(root_ptr->down_childptr);

    if ((depth_up == 0) && (depth_down == 0))
      return 1;        // the root has been added so there is now 1 node
    else
    {
      if ((int)pow(2,cnt) % cnt == 0)
        return max(depth_up,depth_down) + 1;
      else
        return max(depth_up,depth_down);
    }
  }
}

/*****************************************************************************
getTreeHeightUp           : calculates the tree height for "up" tree
[in]: TREE_PTR root_ptr   : pointer to root of tree structure
[out]: int                : height of "up" tree
******************************************************************************/
int HJMTree::getHeightUp(TREE_PTR root_ptr)
{
  if (root_ptr == NULL)
    return 0;
  else
    return 1 + getHeightUp(root_ptr->up_childptr);
}
/*****************************************************************************
getTreeHeightDown : calculates the tree height for "down" tree
[in]: TREE_PTR root_ptr : pointer to root of tree structure
[out]: int height of "down" tree
******************************************************************************/
int HJMTree::getHeightDown(TREE_PTR root_ptr)
{
  if (root_ptr == NULL)
    return 0;
  else
    return 1 + getHeightDown(root_ptr->down_childptr);
}

/*****************************************************************************
```

```
HJMTree : constructor
[in]:   double rate     : initial short rate r(0)
        double T         : time to maturity
        long N           : number of time steps
        double vol       : coefficient of volatility function
        double lambda    : coefficient in exponent of volatility function
**********************************************************************************/
HJMTree::HJMTree(double rate, double T, long N, double vol, double lam)
  : initRate(rate), T(T), N(N), vol(vol), lambda(lamda)
{
  root_ptr = NULL;            // initialize root pointer
  dt = (double) T/N;          // time step
  int* A = new int[200];

  // dynamically allocate memory for double array
  C = (Shares **)malloc(N*sizeof(Shares));
  for(int i= 0;i < N;i++)
    C[i]=(Shares *) malloc((pow(2,N))* sizeof(Shares));

  nodeCnt = 1;                // used for range note valuation
  nodeCnt2 = 0;               // used for range note valuation
}


/*********************************************************************************
buildHJMTree: builds a single factor HJM balance binary search tree (BST) tree with
  N time steps
[in]: none
[out]: none
**********************************************************************************/
void HJMTree::buildHJMTree()
{
  int i;
  int q, k, p;
  int M = pow(2, N) - 1;

  int* key = new int[M];
  int* key2 = new int[M];
  int j = pow(2, N-1); // number of nodes on last time step

  // generate keys: these numbers are insertion "keys" for the node and become the
    value of nodeKey
  // the keys are ordered so that they will produce a balanced BST (equal number of
    branches and children nodes)
  for (i = 0; i < j; i++)
    key2[(int)pow(2,N-1)+i] = 2*i + 1;

  q = N-1;
  k = 0;
  for (i = M-j; i >= 1; i--)
    key2[i] = 0.5*(key2[(int)2*i] + key2[(int)2*i+1]); // each node is the average
                                                       // of its children

  // add node
```

```
    for (i = 0; i < M; i++)
      addNodeHJM(key2[i+1]);
}
```

Suppose we want to build a single-factor HJM lattice to price discount bonds with $T = 4$ years, with $N = 4$ time steps, with an initial short rate of 2 percent, and with a Vasicek volatility function,

$$\sigma(t, T) = \sigma e^{-\lambda(T-t)} = 0.0076 e^{-0.054(T-t)}$$

then we can build the tree shown in Figure 12.1.

At each node is the vector of zero-coupon bonds. Above each node is the short rate. The short rate was determined by extracting it from the forward rate curve since $r(t) = f(t, t)$. At the initial node ($t = 0$), for example, we have the initial discount bond curve (vector) $[P(0, 0), P(0, 1), P(0, 2), P(0, 3), P(0, 4)]' = [1.000, 0.9804, 0.9612, 0.9423, 0.9238]$. At the next time step, with probability $\frac{1}{2}$ it can

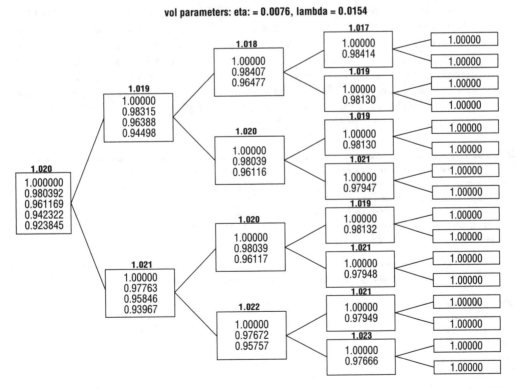

FIGURE 12.1   HJM Single-Factor Tree

go up to $[P(1, 1; u), P(1, 2; u), P(1, 3; u), P(1, 4; u)]' = [1.000, 0.9831, 0.9639,$ 0.94449]' or down with probability $\frac{1}{2}$ to $[P(1, 1; d), P(1, 2; d), P(1, 3; d), P(1, 4;$ $d)]' = 1.000, 0.9776, 0.9585, 0.9397]'$. The discount bond evolution is continued until out to the end of the maturity of the bond. Notice the tree does not recombine.

12.11 SYNTHETIC SWAP VALUATION

We can use the HJM single-factor model to price a fixed-for-floating T-maturity swap that can be synthetically created by dynamically trading shares in a T-maturity zero-coupon bond—long the fixed leg and short a (floating-rate) money market account (short the floating leg). Each node contains the swap value, cash value, and amount held in the money market account and amount held in the zero-coupon bond. Suppose we want to price a swap receiving fixed and paying floating with a three-year maturity and a notional amount of $100. The initial short rate is 2 percent. We assume the HJM volatility parameters are $\eta = 0.0076$ and $\lambda = 0.0154$. We can synthetically create a swap by trading (long) shares of a three-year zero and (short) shares of the money market account.

We first need to compute the swap rate, which can be computed from (10.114) where we assume that the time step is one year. The swap rate is computed as 2 percent. We then find the arbitrage-free evolution of bond prices and forward rates, by constructing the HJM tree starting at the root node, which are used to compute net cash flows between the long bond and short money market positions, as well as the swap value at each node. Finally, share amounts held in the three-year zero-coupon bond and the money market account are computed at each node. The following code implements this process:

```
/*********************************************************************************
addNodeHJMSwap : builds an HJM single-factor binomial tree to price swaps based on
                 the discrete-time bond process in Equation (12.56)
[in]:   int key : a numeric key value that orders the nodes into a BST
        int num : used for computing tree height (represents the kth node created)
        double principalAmount : notional amount of swap
[out]: void
*********************************************************************************/
void HJMTree::addNodeHJMSwap(int key, int num, double principalAmount)
{
  TREE_PTR new_ptr, node_ptr, curr_ptr = NULL;
  double r, sum, sum1, bondSum = 0;
  double volsum = 0.0;
  double volsum1 = 0.0;
  double coshval = 0.0;
  double expvalPlus = 0.0;
  double expvalPlus1 = 0.0;
  double expvalMinus = 0.0;
```

```
double expvalMinus1 = 0.0;
double coshRatio = 0.0;
double amortizingRate = 0;
int i;

new_ptr = new BSTREE_NODE;
new_ptr->up_childptr = NULL;
new_ptr->down_childptr = NULL;

// get tree height
cnt = getTreeHeight(get_root(),num);

// add key in the new node's data field
new_ptr->nodeKey = key;

// necessary initializations to make tree work
C[0][2].moneyMarketAccount = 1;
C[0][1].moneyMarketAccount = 1;
C[0][0].moneyMarketAccount = 1;
C[0][0].cashFlow = 0;
C[1][2].moneyMarketAccount = initRate;
C[0][2].shortRate = initRate;

// If the BST is empty, insert the new rate in root
if (root_ptr == NULL)
{
  C[cnt][nodeCnt].shortRate = initRate;
  C[cnt][nodeCnt].moneyMarketAccount = 1;
  C[cnt][nodeCnt].cashFlow = 0;
  C[cnt][nodeCnt].shortRate = initRate;

  for (i = 0; i <= N; i++)
  {
    new_ptr->bondPrice[i] = 1/(pow(initRate,i));
    if (i > 0)
      bondSum = bondSum + new_ptr->bondPrice[i];

    new_ptr->forwardRate[i] = initRate;
    new_ptr->moneyMarketAccount = initRate;
    new_ptr->shortRate = initRate;
    if (i == N)
      C[cnt][nodeCnt].zeroCouponBond = new_ptr->bondPrice[N];
  }
  // compute swapRate
  swapRate = (principalAmount - principalAmount*new_ptr->bondPrice[N])/bondSum;
  swapRate = swapRate/100;
  root_ptr = new_ptr;
  nodeCnt++;
}
else
{
  TREE_PTR tree_ptr = root_ptr;
  while (tree_ptr != NULL)
```

```
{
  node_ptr = tree_ptr;
  if (key == tree_ptr->nodeKey)
    return;
  else if (key < tree_ptr->nodeKey)
    tree_ptr = tree_ptr->up_childptr;    // search its up side for insertion
                                         // location
  else
    tree_ptr = tree_ptr->down_childptr;  // search its down side for insertion
                                         // location
}
// Now 'node_ptr' is the pointer to the parent of the new node. Now determine
// where it will be inserted
// compute volatilities

sum = 0.0; // sum is used for computing both bond prices and forward rates
for (int k = cnt; k <= N; k++)
  sum = sum + vol*exp(-lambda*(k*dt));


// used for coshRatio for forward rate computation
sum1 = 0.0;
for (k = cnt; k < N; k++)
  sum1 = sum1 + vol*exp(-lambda*(k*dt));

volsum = sum*sqrt(dt)*dt;
volsum1 = sum1*sqrt(dt)*dt;
coshRatio = cosh(volsum)/cosh(volsum1);
coshval = 1/cosh(volsum);
expvalPlus = exp(volsum);
expvalMinus = exp(-volsum);
expvalPlus1 = exp(vol*exp(-lambda*cnt*dt)*sqrt(dt)*dt);
expvalMinus1 = exp(-vol*exp(-lambda*cnt*dt)*sqrt(dt)*dt);

if (key < node_ptr->nodeKey)
{
  node_ptr->up_childptr = new_ptr;
  curr_ptr = node_ptr->up_childptr;

  for (i = cnt; i <= N; i++)
  {
    curr_ptr->forwardRate[i] = node_ptr->forwardRate[i]*coshRatio*expval
      Minus1;
    if (i == cnt)
    {
      curr_ptr->bondPrice[cnt] = 1; // bond price at maturity
    }
    else
    {
      // get short rate r(t) from forward rate f(t, t)
      r = curr_ptr->forwardRate[cnt];
      curr_ptr->shortRate = r;
```

```
         // calculate bond prices
         curr_ptr->bondPrice[i] = (node_ptr->bondPrice[i])*(r*coshval*expval
           Plus);
         C[cnt][nodeCnt].shortRate = r;
         r = node_ptr->shortRate;

         C[cnt][nodeCnt].cashFlow =
           swapRate*principalAmount - (C[cnt-1][nodeCnt/2].shortRate - 1)*
             principalAmount;

         C[cnt][nodeCnt].moneyMarketAccount =
           (C[cnt-1][nodeCnt/2].moneyMarketAccount)*(node_ptr->shortRate);

       if (i == N)
         C[cnt][nodeCnt].zeroCouponBond = new_ptr->bondPrice[N];
     }
   }
   // compute swap values
   if (cnt > 1)
     C[cnt][nodeCnt].swapValue = principalAmount*(1+swapRate)*(curr_ptr->bond
       Price[cnt+1]) - principalAmount;
   else if (cnt == 1)
     C[cnt][nodeCnt].swapValue = principalAmount*swapRate*(curr_ptr-
       >bondPrice[cnt+1])
       + principalAmount*(1 + swapRate)*(curr_ptr->bondPrice[cnt+2]) -
         principalAmount;
   else
     C[cnt][nodeCnt].swapValue = 0.0;
 }
 else
 {
   node_ptr->down_childptr = new_ptr;
   curr_ptr = node_ptr->down_childptr;

   for (i = cnt; i <= N; i++)
   {
     curr_ptr->forwardRate[i] = (node_ptr->forwardRate[i]*coshRatio*expval
       Plus1);
     if (i == cnt)
     {
       curr_ptr->bondPrice[cnt] = 1;
     }
     else
     {
       // get short rate r(t) from forward rate f(t, t)
       r = curr_ptr->forwardRate[cnt];
       curr_ptr->shortRate = r;

       // compute bond price
       curr_ptr->bondPrice[i] = (node_ptr->bondPrice[i]*r*coshval*expvalMinus);
```

```
                C[cnt][nodeCnt].shortRate = r;
                r = node_ptr->shortRate;

                C[cnt][nodeCnt].cashFlow = swapRate*principalAmount -
                   (C[cnt-1][nodeCnt-nodeCnt2].shortRate - 1)*principalAmount;

                C[cnt][nodeCnt].moneyMarketAccount =
                   (C[cnt-1][nodeCnt-nodeCnt2].moneyMarketAccount)*(node_ptr->shortRate);

                if (i == N)
                   C[cnt][nodeCnt].zeroCouponBond = new_ptr->bondPrice[N];
             }
          }
          // compute swap values
          if (cnt > 1)
             C[cnt][nodeCnt].swapValue =
                principalAmount*(1 + swapRate)*(curr_ptr->bondPrice[cnt+1]) - principal
                   Amount;
          else if (cnt == 1)
             C[cnt][nodeCnt].swapValue = principalAmount*swapRate*(curr_ptr->bond
                Price[cnt+1]) + principalAmount*(1 + swapRate)*(curr_ptr->bond
                Price[cnt+2]) - principalAmount;
          else
             C[cnt][nodeCnt].swapValue = 0.0;
       }
       if (nodeCnt != 1)
       {
          nodeCnt--;
          if (nodeCnt % 2 != 0)
             nodeCnt2--;
       }
       else
       {
          nodeCnt = pow(2, cnt+1);
          nodeCnt2 = pow(2, cnt);
       }
    }
 }
}

/****************************************************************************
calcSyntheticSwap: values a synthetic swap after building HJM tree
[in] double principalAmount : notional amount of swap
[out]: vector<double> deltaPos : initial positions in money market account and
       zero-coupon bond
****************************************************************************/
vector<double> HJMTree::calcSyntheticSwap(double principalAmount)
{
   int j = pow(2, N-2);
   double rate = 0.0;
   double floatRate = 0.0;
   double bondDiff = 0.0;
   double moneyAccount = 0.0;
```

```
    vector<double> deltaPos;      // store initial amount of money market and zero-
                                  // coupon bonds

  // initialize terminal swap value
  for (int i = pow(2, N-1); i >= 1; i--)
    C[N-1][i].swapValue = 0;


  C[0][1].swapValue = 0.0;
  for (i = N-2; i >= 0; i--)
  {
    for (j = pow(2, i); j >= 1; j--)
    {
      floatRate = C[i][j].shortRate;

      if (i <= 1)
      {
        bondDiff = C[i+1][2*j].zeroCouponBond - C[i+1][2*j-1].zeroCouponBond;
        C[i][j].numZeroCoupon = (1/bondDiff)*((C[i+1][2*j].swapValue
          + C[i+1][2*j].cashFlow) - (C[i+1][2*j-1].swapValue + C[i+1][2*j-
          1].cashFlow));

        moneyAccount = C[i][j].moneyMarketAccount;
        C[i][j].numMoneyMarket=(1/moneyAccount)*(C[i][j].swapValue -
          C[i][j].numZeroCoupon*(C[i][j].zeroCouponBond));
      }
      else //if (i == N-2)
      {
        C[i][j].numZeroCoupon = 0;
        C[i][j].numMoneyMarket = C[i][j].swapValue/
          (principalAmount*swapRate*C[i+1][2*j-1].zeroCouponBond +
            principalAmount*(1 + swapRate)*C[i+1][2*j].zeroCouponBond);
      }
    }
  }
  deltaPos.push_back(C[0][1].numMoneyMarket);
  deltaPos.push_back(C[0][1].numZeroCoupon);

  return deltaPos;
}


/****************************************************************************
buildHJMSwapTree: Builds a single factor HJM binary search tree
[in] : none
[out]: none
****************************************************************************/
void HJMTree::buildHJMSwapTree()
{
  int M = pow(2, N) - 1;      // number of nodes in tree
  int* key = new int[M];      // allocate memory for keys
  int j = pow(2, N-1);
  double principal = 100;
```

```
  // assign key values
  for (int i = 0; i < j; i++)
    key[(int)pow(2, N-1)+i] = 2*i + 1;

  // generate keys for each node
  for (i = M-j; i >= 1; i--)
    key[i] = 0.5*(key[(int)2*i] + key[(int)2*i+1]);

  // add nodes to HJM tree
  for (i = 0; i < M; i++)
    addNodeHJMSwap(key[i+1], i+1, principal);
}
```

The following HJM tree is built to value a synthetic swap by calling:

```
#include "HJMTree.h"
void main()
{
  double initrate = 1.02;
  int timeStep = 1;
  int numTimeSteps = 3;
  double eta = 0.0076;
  double lambda = 0.0154;

  HJMTree hm(1.02,1,4,0.0076,0.0154,0.017);
  hm.generateKeys1();
  hm.buildHJMTree();
  hm.calcSyntheticSwap(100);
}
```

Figure 12.2 shows the HJM tree built and the valuation of the synthetic swap at each node. For complete synthetic swap calculation details, see Jarrow (2002).

12.12 TWO-FACTOR HJM MODEL

Consider a two-factor HJM model where the forward rate process follows

$$f_\Delta(t+\Delta, T; s_{t+\Delta}) = \begin{cases} \alpha_\Delta(t, T; s_t)f_\Delta(t, T; s_t) & \text{if } s_{t+\Delta} = s_t u \text{ with prob. } 1/4 \\ \gamma_\Delta(t, T; s_t)f_\Delta(t, T; s_t) & \text{if } s_{t+\Delta} = s_t m \text{ with prob. } 1/4 \\ \beta_\Delta(t, T; s_t)f_\Delta(t, T; s_t) & \text{if } s_{t+\Delta} = s_t d \text{ with prob. } 1/2 \end{cases} \quad (12.59)$$

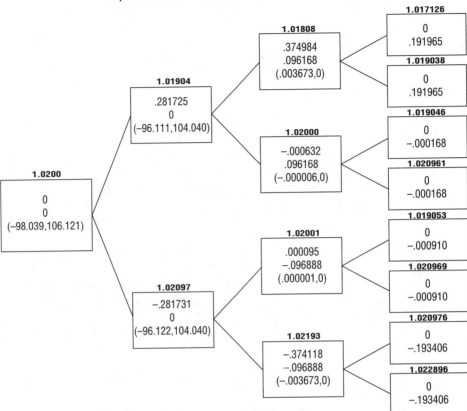

vol parameters: eta: = 0.0076, lambda = 0.0154, swap rate = 0.02

FIGURE 12.2 HJM Single-Factor Tree: Valuation of Synthetic Swap

where

$$\alpha_\Delta(t, T; s_t) = e^{[\mu(t,T;s_t)\Delta - \sigma_1(t,T;s_t)\sqrt{\Delta} - \sqrt{2}\sigma_2(t,T;s_t)\sqrt{\Delta}]\Delta}$$

$$\gamma_\Delta(t, T; s_t) = e^{[\mu(t,T;s_t)\Delta - \sigma_1(t,T;s_t)\sqrt{\Delta} + \sqrt{2}\sigma_2(t,T;s_t)\sqrt{\Delta}]\Delta} \qquad (12.60)$$

$$\beta_\Delta(t, T; s_t) = e^{[\mu(t,T;s_t)\Delta + \sigma_1(t,T;s_t)\sqrt{\Delta}]\Delta}$$

where the processes in (12.60) are parameterized in terms of three stochastic processes, $\mu(t, T; s_t)$, $\sigma_1(t, T; s_t)$, and $\sigma_2(t, T; s_t)$, which be interpreted as the drift and the volatilities, respectively, for the process $\log f_\Delta(t + \Delta, T; s_{t+\Delta}) - \log f_\Delta(t, T; s_t)$, with $(\sigma_1(t, T; s_t), \sigma_2(t, T; s_t))$ being the volatilities of the first and second factors. Thus, in the risk-neutral world, it can be shown that

$$\tilde{E}_t\left[\frac{\log f_\Delta(t+\Delta, T)}{\Delta} - \frac{\log f_\Delta(t, T)}{\Delta}\right] = \mu(t, T)\Delta$$

and

$$\tilde{Var}_t\left[\frac{\log f_\Delta(t+\Delta, T)}{\Delta} - \frac{\log f_\Delta(t, T)}{\Delta}\right] = \sigma_1^2(t, T)\Delta + \sigma_2^2(t, T)\Delta$$

Substituting (12.60) into (12.59) yields

$$f_\Delta(t+\Delta, T; s_{t+\Delta}) = \begin{cases} f_\Delta(t, T; s_t)e^{(\mu(t,T;s_t)\Delta - \sigma_1(t,T;s_t)\sqrt{\Delta} - \sqrt{2}\sigma_2(t,T;s_t)\sqrt{\Delta})\Delta} \\ \qquad \text{if } s_{t+\Delta} = s_t u \text{ with risk neutral prob. } 1/4 \\ f_\Delta(t, T; s_t)e^{(\mu(t,T;s_t)\Delta - \sigma_1(t,T;s_t)\sqrt{\Delta} + \sqrt{2}\sigma_2(t,T;s_t)\sqrt{\Delta})\Delta} \\ \qquad \text{if } s_{t+\Delta} = s_t m \text{ with risk neutral prob. } 1/4 \\ f_\Delta(t, T; s_t)e^{(\mu(t,T;s_t)\Delta + \sigma_1(t,T;s_t)\sqrt{\Delta})\Delta} \\ \qquad \text{if } s_{t+\Delta} = s_t d \text{ with risk neutral prob. } 1/2 \end{cases} \qquad (12.61)$$

For computational efficiency, the risk-neutral probabilities are set to $\pi_\Delta^u(t; s_t) = 1/4$, and $\pi_\Delta^m(t; s_t) = 1/4$, and $\pi_\Delta^d(t; s_t) = 1/2$. From (12.43) and (12.44), we compute

$$u_\Delta(t, T; s_t) = r_\Delta(t; s_t)e^{\left(-\sum_{j=t+\Delta}^{T-\Delta}\mu(t,j;s_t)\Delta + \sum_{j=t+\Delta}^{T-\Delta}\sigma_1(t,j;s_t)\sqrt{\Delta} + \sqrt{2}\sum_{j=t+\Delta}^{T-\Delta}\sigma_2(t,j;s_t)\sqrt{\Delta}\right)\Delta}$$

$$m_\Delta(t, T; s_t) = r_\Delta(t; s_t)e^{\left(-\sum_{j=t+\Delta}^{T-\Delta}\mu(t,j;s_t)\Delta + \sum_{j=t+\Delta}^{T-\Delta}\sigma_1(t,j;s_t)\sqrt{\Delta} - \sqrt{2}\sum_{j=t+\Delta}^{T-\Delta}\sigma_2(t,j;s_t)\sqrt{\Delta}\right)\Delta} \qquad (12.62)$$

$$d_\Delta(t, T; s_t) = r_\Delta(t; s_t)e^{\left(-\sum_{j=t+\Delta}^{T-\Delta}\mu(t,j;s_t)\Delta - \sum_{j=t+\Delta}^{T-\Delta}\sigma_1(t,j;s_t)\sqrt{\Delta}\right)\Delta}$$

From the martingale (no-arbitrage) property, we have

$$\frac{P_\Delta(t, T; s_t)}{B_\Delta(t; s_{t-1})} = \frac{P_\Delta(t, T; s_t)}{B_\Delta(t; s_{t-1})r_\Delta(t; s_t)}\left(\frac{1}{4}u_\Delta(t, T; s_t) + \frac{1}{4}m_\Delta(t, T; s_t) + \frac{1}{2}d_\Delta(t, T; s_t)\right) \qquad (12.63)$$

Substituting expression (12.62) into (12.63) yields, after some algebra, the no-arbitrage condition:

$$e^{\left(\sum\limits_{j=t+\Delta}^{T-\Delta}\mu(t,j;s_t)\Delta\right)\Delta} = \frac{1}{2}e^{\left(\sum\limits_{j=t+\Delta}^{T-\Delta}\sigma_1(t,j;s_t)\sqrt{\Delta}\right)\Delta}\left(\frac{1}{2}e^{\sqrt{2}\left(\sum\limits_{j=t+\Delta}^{T-\Delta}\sigma_2(t,j;s_t)\sqrt{\Delta}\right)\Delta} + \frac{1}{2}e^{-\sqrt{2}\left(\sum\limits_{j=t+\Delta}^{T-\Delta}\sigma_2(t,j;s_t)\sqrt{\Delta}\right)\Delta}\right)$$
$$+\frac{1}{2}e^{\left(-\sum\limits_{j=t+\Delta}^{T-\Delta}\sigma_1(t,j;s_t)\sqrt{\Delta}\right)\Delta} \qquad (12.64)$$

for $t \le T - 2\Delta$ and $T \le (N-1)\Delta$ where t and T are integer multiples of Δ.

Following Jarrow (2002), we can now compute the arbitrage-free term evolution of the forward rate curve in the two-factor economy. By taking the logs on both sides of (12.64), we get:

$$\left[\sum\limits_{j=t+\Delta}^{T-\Delta}\mu(t,j)\Delta\right]\Delta = \log\left(\frac{1}{2}e^{\left(\sum\limits_{j=t+\Delta}^{T-\Delta}\sigma_1(t,j;s_t)\sqrt{\Delta}\right)\Delta}\left(\frac{1}{2}e^{\sqrt{2}\left(\sum\limits_{j=t+\Delta}^{T-\Delta}\sigma_2(t,j;s_t)\sqrt{\Delta}\right)\Delta}\right.\right.$$
$$\left.\left.+\frac{1}{2}e^{-\sqrt{2}\left(\sum\limits_{j=t+\Delta}^{T-\Delta}\sigma_2(t,j;s_t)\sqrt{\Delta}\right)\Delta}\right)+\frac{1}{2}e^{\left(-\sum\limits_{j=t+\Delta}^{T-\Delta}\sigma_1(t,j;s_t)\sqrt{\Delta}\right)\Delta}\right) \qquad (12.65)$$

This system can be solved recursively, as

$$[\mu(t,t+\Delta)\Delta]\Delta$$
$$= \log\left(\frac{1}{2}e^{(\sigma_1(t,t+\Delta)\sqrt{\Delta})\Delta}\left(\frac{1}{2}e^{\sqrt{2}(\sigma_2(t,t+\Delta)\sqrt{\Delta})\Delta}+\frac{1}{2}e^{-\sqrt{2}(\sigma_2(t,t+\Delta)\sqrt{\Delta})\Delta}\right)+\frac{1}{2}e^{-(\sigma_1(t,t+\Delta)\sqrt{\Delta})\Delta}\right) \qquad (12.66)$$

and

$$[\mu(t,K)\Delta]\Delta = \log\left(\frac{1}{2}e^{\left(\sum\limits_{j=t+\Delta}^{T-\Delta}\sigma_1(t,j;s_t)\sqrt{\Delta}\right)\Delta}\left(\frac{1}{2}e^{\sqrt{2}\left(\sum\limits_{j=t+\Delta}^{T-\Delta}\sigma_2(t,j;s_t)\sqrt{\Delta}\right)\Delta}+\frac{1}{2}e^{-\sqrt{2}\left(\sum\limits_{j=t+\Delta}^{T-\Delta}\sigma_2(t,j;s_t)\sqrt{\Delta}\right)\Delta}\right)\right.$$
$$\left.+\frac{1}{2}e^{\left(-\sum\limits_{j=t+\Delta}^{T-\Delta}\sigma_1(t,j;s_t)\sqrt{\Delta}\right)\Delta}\right)-\sum\limits_{j=t+\Delta}^{K-\Delta}[\mu(t,j)\Delta]\Delta \qquad (12.67)$$

for $(N-1)\Delta \ge t + 2\Delta$.

Thus, given two vectors of volatilities,

$$\begin{bmatrix}\sigma_1(t,t+\Delta;s_t)\\\sigma_1(t,t+2\Delta;s_t)\\\dots\\\sigma_1(t,(N-1)\Delta)\end{bmatrix} \text{ and } \begin{bmatrix}\sigma_2(t,t+\Delta;s_t)\\\sigma_2(t,t+2\Delta;s_t)\\\dots\\\sigma_2(t,(N-1)\Delta)\end{bmatrix}$$

we can compute expressions (12.66) and (12.67), and in conjunction with (12.58) generate the evolution of forward rates in the risk-neutral world.[18] The evolution of the zero-coupon bond price process can be deduced from the forward rate process given the relationship between bond prices and forward rates in (12.43) and (12.44).

12.13   TWO-FACTOR HJM MODEL IMPLEMENTATION

The following is an implementation of a two-factor HJM model to build a forward rate curve. We assume both factors have volatilities generated by the Vasicek exponential volatility function; that is, $\sigma_i e^{-\lambda_i(T-t)}$, $i = 1, 2$.

```
/***********************************************************************
addNode2FactorHJM : builds a two-factor HJM (trinomial) tree to build the forward
                    rate curve evolution based on equations (12.58), (12.66), and
                    (12.67).
[in]: int key: a numeric key value that orders the nodes into a trinary search tree
[out]: void
***********************************************************************/
void HJMTree::addNode2FactorHJM(int key)
{
  TREE_PTR new_ptr, node_ptr, curr_ptr;
  double sum, sum2;
  double volsum1 = 0.0;
  double volsum2 = 0.0;
  double driftsum = 0.0;
  double mu[20] = {0.0};
  int i, k, cnt;

  new_ptr = new HJMTREE_NODE;
  new_ptr->up_childptr = NULL;
  new_ptr->middle_childptr = NULL;
  new_ptr->down_childptr = NULL;

  // Add key in the new node's data field
  new_ptr->nodeKey = key;

  // get tree height = current time step
  cnt = getTreeHeight(get_root());

  if (cnt == 0)
  {
```

----

[18]Jarrow (2002), 296.

```
  // insert initial zero-bond prices and forward rates in root
  for (i = 0; i <= N; i++)
  {
    new_ptr->bondPrice[i] = 1/(pow(initRate,i));
    new_ptr->forwardRate[i] = initRate;
  }
}

// if the tree is empty, insert the new data in root
if (root_ptr == NULL)
{
  root_ptr = new_ptr;
}
else
{
  TREE_PTR tree_ptr = root_ptr;
  while (tree_ptr != NULL)
  {
    node_ptr = tree_ptr;
    if (key == tree_ptr->nodeKey)
      tree_ptr = tree_ptr->middle_childptr;   // search middle for insertion
                                              // location

    else if (key < tree_ptr->nodeKey)
      tree_ptr = tree_ptr->up_childptr;       // search its up side for insertion
                                              // location

    else
      tree_ptr = tree_ptr->down_childptr;     // search its down side for
                                              // insertion location
  }
  sum = 0.0;
  sum2 = 0.0;

  for (i = 1; i <= N; i++)
  {
    for (k = 1; k <= i; k++)
    {
      sum = sum + vol*exp(-lambda*(k*dt));
      sum2 = sum2 + vol*exp(-lambda1*(k*dt));
    }
    volsum1 = sum;
    volsum2 = sum2;

    mu[1] = log(0.5*exp(volsum1*sqrt(dt)*dt))*(0.5*exp(sqrt(2)*volsum2*sqrt(dt)
      *dt) + 0.5*exp(-sqrt(2)*volsum2*sqrt(dt)*dt)) + 0.5*exp(-volsum1*sqrt(dt)
      *dt);
    mu[1] = mu[1]*dt*dt;

    if (i > 1)
    {
      for (k = 1; k < i; k++)
      {
        driftsum = driftsum + mu[k];
      }
```

```
          mu[i] =
            log(0.5*exp(volsum1*sqrt(dt)*dt))*(0.5*exp(sqrt(2)*volsum2*sqrt(dt)*dt)
            + 0.5*exp(-sqrt(2)*volsum2*sqrt(dt)*dt)) + 0.5*exp(-volsum1*sqrt(dt)*dt)
            - driftsum;
        }
      }
      // Now 'node_ptr' is the pointer to the parent of the new node. Now determine
        where it will be inserted

      if (key < node_ptr->nodeKey)
      {
        node_ptr->up_childptr = new_ptr;
        curr_ptr = node_ptr->up_childptr;

        for (i = cnt; i <= N; i++)
        {
          curr_ptr->forwardRate[i] = node_ptr->forwardRate[i]*exp((mu[i]*dt
            - vol*exp(-lambda*i*dt)*sqrt(dt) - sqrt(2)*vol1*exp(-lambda1*i*dt)*sqrt
            (dt))*dt);
        }
      }
      else if (key--node_ptr->nodeKey)
      {
        node_ptr->middle_childptr = new_ptr;
        curr_ptr = node_ptr->middle_childptr;

        for (i = cnt; i <= N; i++)
        {
          curr_ptr->forwardRate[i] =
            node_ptr->forwardRate[i]*exp((mu[i]*dt - vol*exp(-lambda*i*dt)*sqrt(dt)
              +sqrt(2)*vol1*exp(-lambda1*i*dt)*sqrt(dt))*dt);
        }
      }
      else
      {
        node_ptr->down_childptr=new_ptr;
        curr_ptr=node_ptr->down_childptr;

        for(i=cnt;i<=N;i++)
        {
          curr_ptr->forwardRate[i]=
            node_ptr->forwardRate[i]*exp((mu[i]*dt-vol*exp
              (-lambda*i*dt)*sqrt(dt))*dt);
        }
      }
    }
  }
}

/*****************************************************************************
build2FactorHJMTree: builds a two factor HJM trinary search tree
[in]:  none
[out]: none
*****************************************************************************/
void HJMTree::build2FactorHJMTree()
{
```

```
// builds a balanced trinary search tree (TST) with N time steps
int k, q, i, M = 0;
int num;
int num1;

// calculate total number of nodes
for (i = 0; i - N; i++)
M = M + pow(3, i);

int j = pow(3, N-1); // number of node in last row

int* key = new int[M];
int* key1 = new int[M];
int* key2 = new int[M];

// generate keys
// these numbers are insertion "keys" for the node and become the value of
// nodeKey. The keys are ordered so that they will produce a balanced TST (equal
// number of branches with three children nodes at each node).
key = generateKeys();

for (i = 0; i - j; i++)
  key1[i+(j/2+1)] = key[i];

q = 1;
k = 0;
key2[0] = key[j/2];
for (i = 2; i <= M - j; i++)
{
  if ((((int)pow(3, q) % 3) == 0) && (i % 2 != 0) && (i % 3 == 0))
    key2[i-1] = key[j/2];   // central nodes down middle of tree have same value
  else
  {
    num1 = pow(3, N-q-1);   // each node always has a value equal to i*(3^N-q-1)
    num = i*num1;
    key2[i-1] = key1[num];
  }
  k++;
  if (k == (int)pow(3, q))
  {
    k = 0;
    q++;
  }
}

int p = 1;
for (i = M; i >= M-j+1; i--)
{
  key2[M-j+p-1] = key[M-i];
  p++;
}

// add node to HJM Tree
for (i = 0; i < M; i++)
  addNode2FactorHJM(key2[i]);
}
```

```
/*****************************************************************************
HJMTree : constructor -- initializes variables
[in]: double rate     : initial short rate = initial forward rate
      double T         : time to maturity
      long N           : number of time steps
      double vol       : coefficient of volatility function of 1st factor
      double vol1      : coefficient of volatility function of 2nd factor
      double lambda    : coefficient in exponent of volatility function of 1st factor
      double lambda1   : coefficient in exponent of volatility function of 2nd factor
*****************************************************************************/
HJMTree::HJMTree(double rate, double T, long N, double vol, double lambda, double
  lambda1) :
  initRate(rate), T(T), N(N), vol(vol), vol1(vol1), lambda(lambda),
    lambda1(lambda1)
{
  root_ptr = NULL;     // initialize root pointer
  dt = (double) T/N;   // time step
  int* A = new int[200];

  // dynamically allocate memory for double array
  C = (Shares **)malloc(N*sizeof(Shares));
  for(int i= 0;i < N;i++)
    C[i]=(Shares *) malloc((pow(2,N))*sizeof(Shares));

  flag = false;
  cnt = 0;
  nodeCnt = 1;
  nodeCnt2 = 0;
}
```

12.14   THE RITCHKEN AND SANKARASUBRAMANIAN MODEL

Given the general non-Markovian nature and problems for nonrecombining trees in the HJM model, Ritchken and Sankarasubramanian (1995) derived necessary and sufficient conditions to price any interest rate derivative using a two-state Markov process (r, ϕ) that captures the path dependence of the short rate through the single sufficient statistic ϕ, which represents the accumulated volatility of the spot rate over the interval $(0, T)$. In the their model, RS specify the following forward volatility structure:

$$\sigma_f(t, T) = \sigma_{RS}(t, T) = \eta(t)k(t, T) = \eta(t)e^{-\int_t^T \kappa(x)dx} \qquad (12.68)$$

where $\eta(t)$ is an adapted process that turns out to be the instantaneous short-rate volatility so we can set $\eta(t) = \sigma_f(t, t) = \sigma_r(t)$, κ is a deterministic function, and

$$k(t, T) = \exp(-\int_t^T \kappa(x)dx)$$

As in the HJM model, the bond and forward rates are assumed to follow

$$\frac{dP(t,\ T)}{P(t,\ T)} = \mu_P(t,\ T)dt + \sigma_P(t,\ T)dz(t)$$

and

$$df(t,\ T) = \mu_f(t,\ T)dt + \sigma_f(t,\ T)dz(t)$$

respectively, under the objective measure. Since, by definition,

$$P(t,\ T) = \exp\left(-\int_t^T f(t,\ u)du\right) \tag{12.69}$$

then we can relate the bond and forward rate drift and diffusion coefficients by

$$\mu_f(t,\ T) = \sigma_f(t,\ T)(\lambda(t) - \sigma_P(t,\ T)) \tag{12.70}$$

and

$$\sigma_f(t,\ T) = -\frac{\partial}{\partial T}\sigma_P(t,\ T) \tag{12.71}$$

where

$$\lambda(t) = \frac{\mu_P(t,\ T) - r(t)}{\sigma_P(t,\ T)}$$

which is the market price of risk. From (12.70) and (12.71), we derive a more specific process for the forward rate:

$$df(t,\ T) = \sigma_f(t,\ T)(\lambda(t) - \sigma_P(t,\ T))dt + \sigma_f(t,\ T)dz(t) \tag{12.72}$$

In order to derive the bond price under the RS volatility structure given in (12.68), we integrate (12.71):

$$f(t,\ T) = f(0,\ T) + \int_0^t \sigma_f(s,\ T)(\lambda(s) - \sigma_P(s,\ T))ds + \int_0^t \sigma_f(s,\ T)dz(s)$$

$$= f(0,\ T) + k(t,\ T)\left[\int_0^t \sigma_f(s,\ t)(\lambda(s) - \sigma_P(s,\ T))ds + \int_0^t \sigma_f(s,\ t)dz(s)\right]$$

Substituting the last term with

$$\int_0^t \sigma_f(s, t)dz(s) = r(t) - f(0, t) - \int_0^t \sigma_f(s, t)(\lambda(s) - \sigma_P(s, t))ds$$

and using

$$\sigma_P(s, t) = -\int_s^t \sigma_f(s, u)du$$

we get

$$f(t, T) = f(0, T) + k(t, T)\left(r(t) - f(0, t) - \int_0^t \sigma_f^2(s, t)ds \int_t^T k(t, u)du\right)$$

$$= f(0, T) + k(t, T)(r(t) - f(0, t) - \beta(t, T)\phi(t))$$

where

$$\phi(t) = \int_0^t \sigma_f^2(s, t)ds \tag{12.73}$$

$$\beta(t, T) = \int_t^T k(t, u)du = \int_t^T e^{-\int_t^u \kappa(x)dx} du \tag{12.74}$$

From the definition of the bond price in (12.69), we get

$$P(t, T) = e^{-\int_t^T f(0,s)ds} \exp\left(\beta(t, T)(f(0, t) - r(t)) - \phi(t)\int_t^T k(t, s)\beta(t, s)ds\right)$$

$$= \left(\frac{P(0, T)}{P(0, t)}\right)\exp\left(\beta(t, T)(f(0, t) - r(t)) - \frac{1}{2}\phi(t)\beta^2(t, T)\right)$$

12.15 RS SPOT RATE PROCESS

Starting with the forward process at $T = t$, we get the short rate

$$r(t) = f(0, t) + \int_0^t \sigma_f(s, t)(\lambda(s) - \sigma_P(s, t))ds + \int_0^t \sigma_f(s, t)dz(s)$$

We then take the derivative of this process:

$$dr(t) = \left(\frac{\partial f(0, t)}{\partial t} + \int_0^t \frac{\partial \sigma_f(s, t)}{\partial t}((\lambda(t) - \sigma_P(s, t))ds + dz(s)) \right)dt$$

$$+ \left(\int_0^t \sigma_f^2(s, t)ds + \sigma_f(t, t)\lambda(t) \right)dt + \sigma_f(t, t)dz(t)$$

$$= \left(\frac{\partial f(0, t)}{\partial t} + \kappa(t)(f(0, t) - r(t))\phi(t) + \sigma_r(t)\lambda(t) \right)dt + \sigma_r(t)dz(t)$$

using

$$\frac{\partial \sigma_f(s, t)}{\partial t} = \frac{\partial}{\partial t}\left[\sigma_r(s) \cdot e^{-\int_s^t \kappa(x)dx} \right] = -\kappa(t)\sigma_f(s, t)$$

and

$$\phi(t) = \int_0^t \sigma_f^2(s, t)ds, \quad \sigma_f(t, t) = \sigma_r(t)$$

Finally, from the definition $\phi(t)$, we get the deterministic process of $\phi(t)$,

$$d\phi(t) = (\sigma_r^2(t) - 2\kappa(t)\phi(t))dt$$

We also have the process for the short rate

$$dr(t) = \mu(r, t)dt + \sigma_r(t)z(t)$$

with drift

$$\mu(r,\ t) = \kappa(t)[f(0,\ t) - r(t)] + \phi(t) + \frac{\partial f(0,\ t)}{\partial t}$$

This is a two-state Markov process with respect to the two state variables, $r(t)$ and $\phi(t)$.

12.16   LI-RITCHKEN-SANKARASUBRAMANIAN MODEL

The Li-Ritchken-Sankarasubramanian (LRS) model is an extension of the RS model with two more specifications. First, the zero bond return is assumed to be the risk-free interest rate so that $\lambda(t) = 0$. Second, the volatility of the spot rate process is assumed to have a constant elasticity γ. Consequently, the forward rate volatility (the RS volatility) has the form

$$\sigma_f(t,\ T) = \sigma_r(t)\exp\left(-\int_t^T \kappa(x)dx\right) = \sigma[r(t)]^\gamma e^{-\kappa(T-t)} \tag{12.75}$$

This specification leads to a model of the term structure specified by the parameters σ, κ, and γ. The formulation in (12.75) covers a lot of models. For example, with $\gamma = 0$, the volatility structure becomes that assumed by the generalized Vasicek (1977) and Hull-White (1993b). The process in this case is Markov with respect to the one state variable, the short rate. With $\gamma = 0.5$, we get the square root volatility structure used by Cox, Ingersoll, and Ross (1985a).

With the volatility structure in (12.75), the RS model becomes

$$dr(t) = \mu(r,\ s)dt + \sigma[r(t)]^\gamma dz(t) \tag{12.76}$$

$$d\phi(t) = [\sigma_r^2(t) - 2\kappa(t)\phi(t)]dt \tag{12.77}$$

where

$$\mu(r,\ t) = \kappa(t)[f(0,\ t) - r(t)] + \phi(t) + \frac{\partial f(0,\ t)}{\partial t}$$

In order to get a unit diffusion coefficient and state independent volatility (which eases building lattices for the short rate), (12.76) needs to be transformed as follows:

$$Y(r(t),\ t) = \int \frac{1}{\sigma \cdot [r(t)]^\gamma} dr(t) \tag{12.78}$$

Applying Ito's lemma with $\partial Y/\partial r = \sigma_r$, the process for $Y(r(t), t)$ becomes

$$dY(r(t),\ t) = \frac{\partial Y}{dt}dt + \frac{\partial Y}{\partial r}dr + \frac{1}{2}\frac{\partial^2 Y}{\partial r^2}dr^2$$

$$= \left[\frac{\partial Y}{\partial t} + \mu(r,\ t)\frac{\partial Y}{\partial r} + \frac{1}{2}\sigma_r^2(t)\frac{\partial^2 Y}{\partial r^2}\right]dt + dz(t)$$

As a result of the transformation, we get a constant volatility process:

$$dY(t) = m_Y(Y, \phi, t)dt + dz(t) \qquad (12.79)$$

where

$$m_Y(Y, \phi, t) = \frac{\partial Y}{\partial t} + \mu(r,\ t)\frac{\partial Y}{\partial r} + \frac{1}{2}\sigma_r^2(t)\frac{\partial^2 Y}{\partial r^2} \qquad (12.80)$$

Special Case γ = 1

LRS implemented this special case with a binomial tree. We assume $\kappa(t)$ is a constant κ and $r(t) > 0$. Since $\gamma = 1$, equation (12.78) becomes

$$Y(r(t),\ t) = \int \frac{1}{\sigma \cdot r(t)}dr(t) = \frac{\ln(r(t))}{\sigma} \qquad (12.81)$$

or equivalently, $r(t) = e^{\sigma Y(t)}$. Now using

$$\frac{\partial Y(r(t),\ t)}{\partial r} = \frac{1}{\sigma_r} \qquad \frac{\partial^2 Y(r(t),\ t)}{\partial r^2} = -\frac{\sigma}{\sigma_r^2}$$

the drift becomes

$$m(Y, \phi, t) = \frac{1}{\sigma_r}\left[\kappa[f(0,\ t) - r(t)] + \phi(t) + \frac{\partial f(0,\ t)}{\partial t}\right] - \frac{\sigma_r^2}{2}\frac{\sigma}{\sigma_r^2}$$

$$= \frac{e^{-\sigma Y}}{\sigma}\left[\kappa[f(0,\ t) - e^{\sigma Y(t)}] + \phi(t) + \frac{\partial f(0,\ t)}{\partial t}\right] - \frac{\sigma}{2} \qquad (12.82)$$

and the process for ϕ becomes

$$d\phi(t) = [\sigma^2 e^{2\sigma Y} - 2\kappa\phi(t)]dt \qquad (12.83)$$

A recombining tree can be built in terms of the transformed state variable $Y(t)$—and equivalently, for $r(t)$. However, the second state variable $\phi(t)$ that follows the deterministic process in (12.83) cannot be built in a recombining tree. Thus, for computational efficiency it is necessary to control the number of $\phi(t)$ at each node, which will be increasing exponentially through time. This is resolved in the next section, which discusses numerical implementation.

12.17   IMPLEMENTING AN LRS TRINOMIAL TREE

The process of building an LRS trinomial lattice can be split into two steps. The first step is to build the tree by marching forward from time 0 to the option maturity. In this step, three important variables are identified at each node, the two state variables r and ϕ, and the transition probabilities from a parent node to its three children nodes. The second step is the pricing of derivatives using the variables found in the first step.

In the trinomial scheme, each node $Y(t)$ is assumed to have three children nodes, $Y_+(t + \Delta t)$, $Y(t + \Delta t)$, and $Y_-(t + \Delta t)$, at up, middle, and down movements. We choose the number of time steps, fixing the tree size, and allow N multiple jumps in the tree. We also assume $E[Y(t + \Delta t)] = Y(t)$. We, thus, define the evolutionary jump size between the nodes

$$\Delta_+ = Y_+(t + \Delta t) - Y(t) = +N\sqrt{\Delta t} \tag{12.84}$$

$$\Delta_- = Y_-(t + \Delta t) - Y(t) = -N\sqrt{\Delta t} \tag{12.85}$$

At each time step and each node, $Y(t)$ is updated based on (12.84) and (12.85). The $r(t)$ is determined by converting the $Y(t)$ using $r(t) = e^{\sigma Y(t)}$; see (12.44). Consequently, we have a recombining tree of $r(t)$ in terms of $Y(t)$.

We can now update the second state variable $\phi(t)$ by using the updated first state variable $Y(t)$ via the deterministic process (12.83).

$$\phi_t = \phi_{t-\Delta t} + (\sigma^2 e^{2\sigma Y(t)} - 2\kappa\phi_{t-\Delta t})\Delta t \tag{12.86}$$

Unlike the $Y(t)$, the $\phi(t)$ keeps the path dependence and the number ϕ at each node is increasing exponentially as time increases except at the boundary nodes. As a result, for computational efficiency purposes, when a node in the tree has more than three ϕ, we can choose three representative $\phi(t)$, the maximum, the minimum, and the average. These three representative values are reference values for the interpolation of the payoff in the next step. Alternatively, for five ϕ, one can add ±1 standard deviations, for seven ϕ, one can add ±2 standard deviations, and so on.

Finally, based on the updated state variables $Y(t)$ and $\phi(t)$ at each node, we compute the drift term m_t, which is used for computing the probabilities.

$$m_t(Y_t, \phi_t) = \frac{e^{-\sigma Y_t}}{\sigma}\left(\kappa(f(0, t) - e^{\sigma Y_t}) + \phi_t + \Delta f(0, t)\right) - \frac{\sigma}{2} \qquad (12.87)$$

where

$$\Delta f(0, t) = \frac{f(0, t + \Delta t) - f(0, t)}{\Delta t}$$

The transitional probabilities, p_u, p_m, and p_d, of each path are computed by matching the first and second moments of the process, the mean and variance. Using the mean and variance of the transformed process dY, we get

$$\Delta_+ p_u + \Delta_- p_d = m_t \Delta t$$
$$(\Delta_+)^2 p_u + (\Delta_-)^2 p_d = \Delta t + (m_t \Delta t)^2$$
$$p_u + p_m + p_d = 1$$

Solving the system of equations, we solve for the probabilities

$$p_u = \frac{\Delta t \cdot (m_t^2 \Delta t - m_t \Delta_- + 1)}{\Delta_+(\Delta_+ - \Delta_-)} = \frac{m_t^2 + N m_t \sqrt{\Delta t} + 1}{2N^2} \qquad (12.88)$$

$$p_d = \frac{\Delta t \cdot (m_t^2 \Delta t - m_t \Delta_+ + 1)}{\Delta_-(\Delta_- - \Delta_+)} = \frac{m_t^2 + N m_t \sqrt{\Delta t} + 1}{2N^2} \qquad (12.89)$$

and

$$p_m = 1 - p_u - p_d$$

From (12.88) and (12.89) we get the following conditions that must be satisfied at all times for the probabilities to remain between 0 and 1:

$$0 \le m_t^2 \Delta t + N m_t \sqrt{\Delta t} + 1 \le 2N^2 \qquad (12.90)$$

$$0 \le m_t^2 \Delta t + N m_t \sqrt{\Delta t} - 1 \le 2N^2 \qquad (12.91)$$

and the sum of p_u and p_d gives:

$$m_t^2 \Delta t + 1 \leq N^2 \tag{12.92}$$

From (12.92), we notice that the multiple jump size N should be strictly larger than 1 and for a selected jump size N, the drift term m_t should satisfy

$$m_t^2 \Delta t \leq N^2 - 1$$

Once the LRS tree is built using the methodology described in the previous section, derivatives pricing starts by working backward from the last (Nth) time step based on the final payoff of the derivative, based on the price of the underlying asset at maturity. A bond price in the LRS framework is a function of two state variables and forward rates. We can price a European bond option using an LRS tree as follows. Let T be the option maturity and let $S = T + \Delta t$ be the maturity of the bond. Based on the information at T, the bond price at each node is

$$P(t, T) = \left(\frac{e^{-f(0,T)T}}{e^{-f(0,t)t}} \right) \exp\left(\beta(t)(f(0, t) - r(t)) - \frac{1}{2}\phi(t)\beta^2(t, T) \right) \tag{12.93}$$

where

$$\begin{aligned}
\beta(t, T) &= \int_t^T e^{\left(-\int_t^u \kappa dx \right)} du \\
&= \int_t^T e^{\kappa(t-u)} du \\
&= e^{\kappa t}\left(\frac{e^{-\kappa T} - e^{-\kappa t}}{-\kappa} \right) \\
&= \frac{1 - e^{-\kappa(T-t)}}{\kappa}
\end{aligned}$$

and

$$\phi(t) = \int_0^t \sigma^2 [r(u)]^{2\gamma} e^{-2\kappa(t-u)} du$$

The payoff of the option is given by $\max(P(t, T) - X, 0)$ where X is the strike price. For a European bond option, (12.93) is only used at maturity.

It should be noted that while the RS (and LRS) trees avoid the non-Markov nature of the HJM tree, Chien (2003) has shown that the RS tree can give rise to exponential-sized trees that can explode if the number of time steps is sufficiently large.[19] Chien notes that while the RS algorithm is more efficient than the HJM in the sense that the tree can have linear computation time for some periods, the RS tree is still limited in how small the time step Δt can be. Thus, he concludes that the RS algorithm for the model does not solve the fundamental problem of the HJM model, namely, exponential explosion, which means the algorithm suffers in both time and memory resources.[20]

[19]Chien (2003), 25.
[20]Ibid.

CHAPTER 13

LIBOR Market Models

The standard interest rate models are versions of Black's 1976 market model. However, one of the major problems with models discussed so far is that they are incompatible with the pricing of Black's model for both caps and swaptions. This is due to the fact that Black's model is based on oversimplistic and inexact assumptions on interest rate distributions. When Black's formula is used to price a caplet/floorlet (one element of a cap/floor), the underlying rate is assumed to be lognormal. When it is used to price swaptions, the underlying swap rate is also assumed to be lognormal. Jamshidian (1997) showed that while the cap/floor market model and the European swaption market are each internally consistent in the sense that they do not permit arbitrage opportunities, they are not precisely consistent with each other.

Brace, Gatarek, and Musiela (BGM) (1997), Musiela and Rutkowski (1997), Jamshidian (1997), and Miltersen, Sandmann, and Sondermann (1997) have developed the arbitrage-free LIBOR market models (LMMs) in an attempt to overcome these problems.[1] The LIBOR market models are widely used by practitioners since they price and hedge interest rate derivatives consistently with Black's formulas. They are extensions of the HJM (1992) model and, as BGM have shown, overcome some of the technical existence problems associated with the lognormal version of the HJM. Whereas the HJM model describes the dynamics of interest rates in terms of the behavior of instantaneous forward rates with continuous compounding, the LIBOR market models describe the behavior of forward rates underlying caps or swap rates underlying swaptions with conventional market compounding (the compounding period equals the tenor of the rate). These models assume a deterministic volatility structure and a lognormal distribution (under the appropriate measure) for forward and swap rates.

There are several advantages of the LMM over traditional instantaneous spot rate models—Vasicek (1977), Hull-White (1990), and Cox-Ingersoll-Ross (1985)—and instantaneous forward rate models—Heath-Jarrow-Morton (1992) and Ritchken-Sankarasubramanian (1995). First, the LMM prices consistently

---

[1]The LIBOR market model is also referred to as the BGM/J model.

with the Black market formula for cap and swaption prices, which makes calibration to market data simple since the quoted Black (implied) volatilities can be directly inputted into the model, avoiding the numerical fitting procedures that are needed for spot or forward rate models. Second, market models are based on observable market rates such as LIBOR and swap rates. They do not depend on, and thus one does not require, (unobservable) instantaneous spot and forward rates. However, due to the complex dynamics of LMMs and the fact that the forward rates have a fully state-dependent drift, recombining lattices/trees cannot be used to evolve interest rate dynamics, and thus price interest rate derivatives, as they can for instantaneous spot and forward rate models. Instead, Monte Carlo and other numerical techniques must be used to price caps, swaptions, and other (exotic) interest rate derivatives.

The BGM model, known also as the lognormal forward-LIBOR model (LFM), prices caps consistently with Black's formula. Consequently, implied volatilities quoted in the market are consistent with specified volatility structures used in the model. The lognormal forward-swap model (LSM), developed by Jamishidian (1997), prices swaptions consistently with Black's swaptions formula. However, the LFM and LSM are not compatible with each other. If forward LIBOR rates are lognormal each under its measure, as assumed by the LFM, forward swap rates cannot be lognormal at the same time under their measure, as assumed by the LSM. Despite this drawback, the LFM allows for a deterministic calculation, and thus evolution, of the future term structure of volatilities. This calculation requires no simulation while for other models this is not the case.

This chapter is broken down as follows. In section 13.1, we discuss the LIBOR market models. In section 13.2, specifications of the instantaneous volatility of forward rates are given. In section 13.3, Hull and White's adaptation and implementation of the LMM is given. In section 13.4, calibration of the LFM to cap prices is discussed. In section 13.5, pricing swaptions with the lognormal LFS model is discussed, while in section 13.6, approximate swaptions pricing using Hull and White's approach is detailed. In section 13.7, an LFM formula that approximates swaption volatilities is given. In section 13.8, Monte Carlo pricing of swaptions using the LFM is discussed and an implementation is given. In section 13.9, an improved Monte Carlo pricing of swaptions is given using a predictor-corrector. An implementation of this approach is given. In section 13.10, incompatibilities between the LSM and LFM are analyzed. In section 13.11, instantaneous and terminal correlation structures are discussed in the context of the LFM. In section 13.12, calibration to swaption prices using the LFM is given, while in section 13.13, the connection between caplet volatilities and $S \times 1$-swaption volatilities is made so that one can calibrate to both the cap and swaption market. In section 13.14, we discuss incorporating the observed volatility smile seen in the cap market into the LFM. In section 13.15, we discuss Rebonato's (2002) stochastic extension of the LIBOR market model to deal with recent changing dynamics in the market that the LMM is not capturing. Finally, in section 13.16, we discuss computing Greek sensitivities in the forward LIBOR model.

13.1   LIBOR MARKET MODELS

Since market models are models of forward rates, a specification of the volatility structure of the forward rates uniquely determines their instantaneous drifts via the no-arbitrage (HJM) condition. We consider a LIBOR market model based on N forward LIBOR rates $F_i(t)$, $i = 0, \ldots, N-1$, where $F_i(t) = F_i(t; T_{i-1}, T_i)$. Under the Q^i probability measure, the measure associated with the T_i-forward measure and the $P(\cdot, T_i)$ numeraire (i.e., the price of a bond whose maturity coincides with a maturity of the forward rate) the forward rate is a martingale. Note that $F_i(t)P(t, T_i)$ is the price of a tradable asset, the difference between two discount bonds with notional principal amounts $1/\tau_i$.

$$F_i(t)P(t, T_i) = (P(t, T_{i-1}) - P(t, T_i))/\tau_i$$

Since the price of the tradable asset $F_i(t)P(t, T_i)$ divided by the zero-coupon bond numeraire $P(\cdot, T_i)$ is a martingale, the ith forward rate evolves by

$$dF_i(t) = \sigma_i(t)F_i(t)dz_i(t)$$

In general, we need to know the dynamics of the forward rate $F_i(t)$ under a measure Q^k different from Q^i, for $t \leq \min(T_k, T_{i-1})$. We can obtain the dynamics of F_i under the forward-adjusted measure Q_k. We assume that each forward rate is driven by a standard Brownian motion z_i with a time-dependent lognormal volatility and a time-dependent instantaneous correlation structure $E[dz_i dz_j] = \rho_{ij}dt$. Under this general framework, the forward dynamics are given by

$$dF_i(t) = \mu_i(t)F_i(t)dt + \sigma_i(t)F_i(t)dz_i(t)$$

where the drift μ_i is determined by the no-arbitrage condition and depends on the choice of the numeraire (chosen measure). If we take a zero-coupon bond expiring at one of the reset times T_k to be the numeraire, $P(\cdot, T_k)$, then the instantaneous drift is:

$$\mu_i(t) = \begin{cases} \displaystyle\sum_{j=k+1}^{i} \frac{\rho_{ij}\tau_j\sigma_i(t)\sigma_j(t)F_j(t)}{1+\tau_j F_j(t)} & \text{if } k < i \\[4mm] 0 & \text{if } i = k \\[2mm] -\displaystyle\sum_{j=i+1}^{k} \frac{\rho_{ij}\tau_j\sigma_i(t)\sigma_j(t)F_j(t)}{1+\tau_j F_j(t)} & \text{if } k > i \end{cases} \qquad (13.1)$$

The computation of the drift can be seen by recovering the dynamics under the T_k-forward measure Q^k. Notice, for $k < i$,

$$\ln(P(t,\,T_i)\,/\,P(t,\,T_k)) = \ln\left(\frac{1}{\displaystyle\prod_{j=k+1}^{i}(1+\tau_j F_j(t))}\right) = -\sum_{j=k+1}^{i}\ln(1+\tau_j F_j(t))$$

From this, we compute the percentage drift μ_i from the change in drift formula (and using quadratic covariation):

$$\mu_k(t) = 0dt - d\ln(F_i)d\ln(P(\cdot,\,T_i)\,/\,P(\cdot,\,T_k)) = \sum_{j=k+1}^{i} d\ln(F_i)d\ln(1+\tau_j F_j(t))$$

$$= \sum_{j=k+1}^{i}\frac{\tau_j}{1+\tau_j F_j(t)}d\ln(F_i)dF_j = \sum_{j=k+1}^{i}\frac{\rho_{j,k}\tau_j\sigma_i(t)\sigma_j(t)F_j(t)}{1+\tau_j F_j(t)}$$

If $k > i$, then the numeraire is a bond with a maturity longer than the maturity of the forward rate being modeled. In this case, the derivation is similar, but we get

$$\ln(P(t,\,T_i)\,/\,P(t,\,T_k)) = \ln\left(\prod_{j=i+1}^{k}(1+\tau_j F_j(t))\right) = \sum_{j=i+1}^{k}\ln(1+\tau_j F_j(t))$$

whereby

$$\mu_k(t) = -\sum_{j=i+1}^{k}\frac{\rho_{ij}\tau_j\sigma_i(t)\sigma_j(t)F_j(t)}{1+\tau_j F_j(t)}$$

follows. Moreover, in the case $i > k$, we can compute from Ito's formula

$$d\ln F_i(t) = \sum_{j=k+1}^{i}\frac{\rho_{ij}\tau_j\sigma_i(t)\sigma_j(t)F_j(t)}{1+\tau_j F_j(t)}dt - \frac{\sigma_i(t)^2}{2}dt + \sigma_i(t)dz_i(t) \qquad (13.2)$$

Note that under the Q^k-measure, the dynamics of equation (13.2) are driftless, and we can write the explicit solution as

$$\ln F_k(T) = \ln F_k(0) - \int_0^T\frac{\sigma_i(t)^2}{2}dt + \int_0^T\sigma_i(t)dz_i(t)$$

Both the drift and diffusion coefficient are bounded and deterministic, ensuring the existence and uniqueness of a strong solution for the SDE.

Hull and White (1999) derive the LIBOR market model through a more formal change of numeraire framework. We consider their approach for the sake of completeness especially since their approach leads to a computationally efficient implementation. Consider a cap with reset dates $T_1, T_2, \ldots, T_{n-1}$ with corresponding payment dates $T_2, T_3, \ldots, T_n$. Let $\tau_{i-1} = T_i - T_{i-1}$ be the tenor between reset and payment dates and define $T_0 = 0$. Define the following:

> $F_i(t)$: forward rate observed at time t for the period (T_{i-1}, T_i) expressed with a compounding period of τ_{i-1}.
>
> $P(t, T)$: price at time t of a zero-coupon bond that provides a payoff of \$1 at time T.
>
> $m(t)$: index for the next reset date at time t. $m(t)$ is the smallest integer such that $t \leq t_{m(t)}$.
>
> p: number of factors.
>
> $\varsigma_{t,q}$: qth component of the volatility of $F_i(t)$ $(1 \leq q \leq p)$.
>
> $v_{t,q}$: qth component of the volatility of $P(t, T)$ $(1 \leq q \leq p)$.

It is assumed that the volatility components are independent, though this is not required since they can be orthogonalized. The processes followed by the forward rate and bond price are:

$$dF_i(t) = (\ldots)dt + \sum_{q=1}^{p} \varsigma_{t,q}(t)F_i(t)dz_q \tag{13.3}$$

$$dP(t, T_i) = (\ldots)dt + \sum_{q=1}^{p} v_{t,q}(t)P(t, T_i)dz_q$$

respectively, where the dz_q are independent Wiener processes and the drifts depend on the chosen measure. It is assumed that $\varsigma_{t,q}(t)$ is a function of only time, whereas the bond price volatility $v_{t,q}(t)$ is in general stochastic in the model.

The chosen numeraire is the money market account that is invested at time T_0 for a period of τ_0, reinvested at time T_1 for a period τ_1, reinvested at time T_2 for a period τ_2, and so on. This is equivalent to the numeraire at time t of $P(t, T_{m(t)})$. Under the chosen measure

$$\frac{f(t)}{P(t, T_{m(t)})}$$

is a martingale for all security prices $f(t)$ when $t_{m(t)-1} \le t \le t_{m(t)}$ so that

$$\frac{f(t_{m(t)-1})}{P(T_{m(t)-1},\ T_{m(t)})} = E^{m(t)}\left[\frac{f(t_{m(t)})}{P(T_{m(t)},\ T_{m(t)})}\right] \tag{13.4}$$

or

$$f(t_{m(t)-1}) = P(T_{m(t)-1},\ T_{m(t)})E^{m(t)}[f(t_{m(t)})]$$

where $E^{m(t)}$ denotes the expectation under the measure $P(t, T_{m(t)})$. Equation (13.4) shows that under the chosen measure, we can discount expected values "one accrual period at a time" when pricing securities. As Hull and White point out, this is an attractive feature of the measure since cash flows and early exercise opportunities usually occur on reset dates.[2]

As Jamshidian (1997) has shown, the qth component of the market price of risk under the $P(t, T_j)$-measure is the bond price volatility $v_{j,q}$ for all j. Since the forward rate $F_i(t)$ is a martingale under the $P(t, T_i)$-measure, and thus driftless, then it follows that the drift of $F_i(t)$ under the $P(t, T_{t(m)})$-measure (using the change in drift formula) is

$$\sum_{q=1}^{p} \varsigma_{i,q}(t)\Big(v_{m(t),q}(t) - v_{i+1,q}(t)\Big)$$

so that

$$\frac{dF_i(t)}{F_i(t)} = \sum_{q=1}^{p} \varsigma_{i,q}(t)\Big(v_{m(t),q}(t) - v_{i+1,q}(t)\Big)dt + \sum_{q=1}^{p} \varsigma_{i,q}(t)dz_q \tag{13.5}$$

We recall the relationship between bond prices and forward rates

$$\frac{P(t,\ T_j)}{P(t,\ T_{j+1})} = 1 + \tau_j F_j(t)$$

In conjunction with Ito's formula, we get

$$v_{j,q}(t) - v_{j+1,q}(t) = \frac{\tau_j F_j(t)\varsigma_{j,q}(t)}{1 + \tau_j F_j(t)}$$

---

[2] Hull and White (1999), 10.

Repeated iteration of the result yields

$$v_{m(t),q}(t) - v_{i+1,q}(t) = \sum_{j=m(t)}^{i} \frac{\tau_j F_j(t) \varsigma_{j,q}(t)}{1 + \tau_j F_j(t)} \tag{13.6}$$

If we substitute (13.6) into (13.5), we see that the process followed by $F_i(t)$

$$\frac{dF_i(t)}{F_i(t)} = \sum_{j=m(t)}^{i} \frac{\tau_j F_j(t) \sum_{q=1}^{p} \varsigma_{j,q}(t)\varsigma_{i,q}(t)}{1 + \tau_j F_j(t)} dt + \sum_{q=1}^{p} \varsigma_{i,q}(t) dz_q \tag{13.7}$$

If we take the limit of (13.7), allowing the τ_j's to tend to zero, we get

$$dF(t, T) = \sum_{q=1}^{p} \varsigma_q(t, T)F(t, T) \int_{t}^{T} \varsigma_q(t, \tau)F(t, \tau)d\tau + \sum_{q=1}^{p} \varsigma_q(t, T)F(t, T)dz_q \tag{13.8}$$

where now, in continuous time, $F(t, T)$ is the instantaneous forward rate at time t for maturity at time T. $\varsigma_q(t, T)$ is the qth component of the volatility of $F(t, T)$. Equation (13.8) is the HJM model, which, as we see, is a limiting case of the LIBOR market model.

13.2   SPECIFICATIONS OF THE INSTANTANEOUS VOLATILITY OF FORWARD RATES

It is often assumed that the forward rate $F_k(t)$ has a piecewise-constant instantaneous volatility. Moreover, the instantaneous volatility of $F_k(t)$ is constant in each "expiry-maturity" time interval, $T_{j-2} < t \le T_{j-1}$, that is associated with any other forward rate. The forward rate is said to be "alive" if it exists within the expiry-maturity interval and "dead" if not.

A general formulation of the instantaneous volatility is the separable structure:

$$\sigma_k(t) = \Phi_k \psi_\alpha, a = 1, \ldots, k \tag{13.9}$$

We can view $\Phi_k = \Phi_k(t)$ as a time-homogenous component and $\psi_\alpha = \psi_\alpha(T - t)$ as a idiosyncratic (forward-rate-specific) component of total instantaneous volatility. A general parameteric form of this instantaneous volatility is

$$\sigma_k(t) = \psi(T_{k-1} - t; a, b, c, d) = (a(T_{k-1} - t) + d)e^{-b(T_{k-1}-t)} + c \tag{13.10}$$

where $\Phi_k = 1$. This form allows a humped shape in the graph on the instantaneous volatility of the forward rate. This formulation can be made more flexible (which in turn allows for richer volatility forms) by setting

$$\sigma_k(t) = \Phi_k \psi(T_{k-1} - t; a, b, c, d) = \Phi_k((a(T_{k-1} - t) + d)e^{-b(T_{k-1}-t)} + c) \quad (13.11)$$

The flexibility that (13.11) adds improves the joint calibration of the model to caps and swaption markets. Figure 13.1 shows a typical hump-shaped term structure exhibited by caplet (instantaneous) volatilities of semiannual forward rates.

A similar type of evolution could be generated with the volatility formulation in (13.10) with $a = 0.19085664$, $b = 0.97462314$, $c = 0.08089168$, and $d = 0.01344948$, as demonstrated by Brigo and Mercurio (2001c).

Table 13.1 organizes the expiry-maturity of forward rates and their corresponding instantaneous volatilities.

Denote v_i as the instantaneous volatility of the ith caplet and $v_{T_{i-1}-caplet}$ as the volatility of a caplet with an underlying forward rate spanning the interval $[0, T_{i-1}]$. Then we set

$$v_{T_{i-1}-caplet} = \sqrt{\frac{1}{T_{i-1}} \int_0^{T_{i-1}} \sigma_i(t)^2 \, dt} \quad (13.12)$$

and

$$v_i = \sqrt{T_{i-1} v_{T_{i-1}-caplet}} \quad (13.13)$$

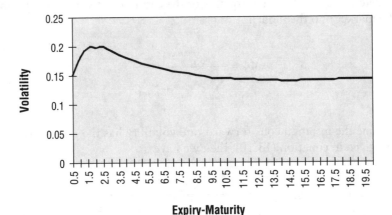

FIGURE 13.1   Caplet Volatilities of Semiannual Forward Rates

TABLE 13.1 Expiry-Maturity of Forward Rates

Instantaneous Volatility	$t \in (0,T_0]$	$(T_0,T_1]$	$(T_1,T_2]$	$\ldots$	$(T_{N-2},T_{N-1}]$
$f_1(t)$	$\Phi_1\psi_1$	Dead	Dead	$\ldots$	Dead
$f_2(t)$	$\Phi_2\psi_2$	$\Phi_2\psi_1$	Dead	$\ldots$	Dead
$\vdots$	$\vdots$	$\vdots$	$\vdots$	$\vdots$	$\vdots$
$f_N(t)$	$\Phi_N\psi_N$	$\Phi_N\psi_{N-1}$	$\Phi_N\psi_{N-2}$	$\ldots$	$\Phi_N\psi_1$

so that the v_i is the integrated instantaneous volatility while the T_{i-1}-caplet volatility, $v_{T_{i-1}}$-caplet is the square root of the average instantaneous (percentage) variance of the forward rate $F_i(t)$ for $t \in [0, T_{i-1})$. Note that $v^2_{T_{i-1}\text{-caplet}}$ is standardized with respect to time while v_i^2 is not. We can approximate (13.12) by

$$v^2_{T_{i-1}\text{-caplet}} = \frac{1}{T_{i-1}} \sum_{j=1}^{i} \tau_{j-2,j-1}\sigma_{i,j}^2 \tag{13.14}$$

If we assume that the piecewise-constant instantaneous forward volatilities follow the separable form in equation (13.9), then we get

$$v_i^2 = \Phi_i^2 \sum_{j=1}^{i} \tau_{j-2,j-1}\psi_{i-j+1}^2 \tag{13.15}$$

We can determine the Φ_i's if the squares of the cap implied volatilities are inputted from the market into the model:

$$\Phi_i^2 = \frac{(v_i^{market})^2}{\displaystyle\sum_{j=1}^{i} \tau_{j-2,j-1}\psi_{i-j+1}^2} \tag{13.16}$$

If we assume the instantaneous forward rate volatility has the parametric volatility structure given in equation (13.10), then we have

$$\Phi_i^2 = \frac{(v_i^{market})^2}{\displaystyle\int_0^{T_{i-1}} \left((a(T_{i-1}-t)+d)e^{-b(T_{i-1}-t)}+c\right)^2 dt} \tag{13.17}$$

so that the model is calibrated to market caplet volatilities through the parameters Φ. The integral in the denominator of (13.17) can be evaluated using numerical integration. In order to reduce the number of volatility parameters, one can assume the forward rate $F_k(t)$ rate has piecewise constant (time-independent) instantaneous volatility s_k:

$$v_i^2 = T_{i-1}s_i^2, \qquad v_{T_{i-1}\text{-caplet}} = s_i \qquad (13.18)$$

This leads to a less flexible model for calibration to the market quotes than the $\Phi_i\psi_a$ volatility formulation, but the s_i's can be completely determined (as discussed in the next section).

Hull-White (1999), in their approach, determine the volatility of the forward rates using a two-step method proposed by Rebonato (1999c). Using the model in equation (13.9), Hull and White assume $\varsigma_{i,q}(t)$ is a function only of the number of the whole accrual periods between the next reset date and time T_i. Define $\lambda_{j,q}$ as the value of $\varsigma_{i,q}(t)$ where there are j such accrual periods; that is, $j = i - m(t)$. This means

$$\varsigma_{i,q} = \lambda_{i-m(t),q}$$

Define Λ_j as the total volatility of the forward rate when there are j whole accrual periods until maturity so that

$$\Lambda_j = \sqrt{\sum_{q=1}^{p} \lambda_{j,q}^2} \qquad (13.19)$$

The Λ_j's can be computed from the spot volatilities, σ_i's, used to calculate caplets in equation (10.102). If we equate variances between the caplet spot variances and the total variance of the forward rate, we have

$$\sigma_i^2 T_i = \sum_{j=1}^{i} \tau_{j-1}\Lambda_{i-j}^2 \qquad (13.20)$$

The Λ_j's are obtained inductively. To determine the $\lambda_{j,q}$'s, Rebonato's two-stage approach is used. First, one computes the Λ_j's from market data, and then secondly one uses historical data to compute the $\lambda_{j,q}$ from the Λ_j. Rebonato's approach determines the $\lambda_{j,q}$ from the Λ_j so as to provide a fit as close as possible to the correlation matrix for the $F_j(t)$, $1 \le j \le n$. Rebonato suggests that such results are similar to those of principal component analysis. Thus, if the output (i.e., factor loads via eigenvectors and eigenvalues) of the principal component analysis is available, it can be used to determine the $\lambda_{j,q}$. Rebonato supposes that $\alpha_{i,q}$ is the factor loading of the ith forward rate and the qth factor and s_q is the standard deviation of the qth factor score. If the number of factors used is p, were equal to N, the number of forward rates, then it is correct to set

$$\lambda_{j,q} = \alpha_{j,q} s_q \tag{13.21}$$

for $1 \leq j, q \leq N$. When $p < N$, the $\lambda_{j,q}$ can be normalized so that the relation in (13.17) still holds, namely,

$$\lambda_{j,q} = \frac{\Lambda_j s_q \alpha_{j,q}}{\sqrt{\displaystyle\sum_{q=1}^{p} s_q^2 \alpha_{j,q}^2}} \tag{13.22}$$

The first factor corresponds roughly to a parallel shift in the yield curve; the second factor corresponds to a "twist" in the yield curve where short rate moves opposite of long rates; and the third factor corresponds to a "bowing" of the yield curve where short and long maturities move in one direction and intermediate maturities move in the opposite direction.

13.3   IMPLEMENTATION OF HULL-WHITE LIBOR MARKET MODEL

From equation (13.13), the process for $F_i(t)$ under the measure $M\{P(t, T_{m(t)})\}$ is,

$$\frac{dF_i(t)}{F_i(t)} = \sum_{j=m(t)}^{i} \frac{\tau_j F_j(t) \displaystyle\sum_{q=1}^{p} \lambda_{j-m(t),q} \lambda_{i-m(t),q}}{1 + \tau_j F_j(t)} dt + \sum_{q=1}^{p} \lambda_{i-m(t),q} dz_q \tag{13.23}$$

or

$$d \ln F_i(t) = \sum_{j=m(t)}^{i} \left[\frac{\tau_j F_j(t) \displaystyle\sum_{q=1}^{p} \lambda_{j-m(t),q} \lambda_{i-m(t),q}}{1 + \tau_j F_j(t)} - \sum_{q=1}^{p} \frac{\lambda_{i-m(t),q}^2}{2} \right] dt + \sum_{q=1}^{p} \lambda_{i-m(t),q} dz_q \tag{13.24}$$

An approximation that simplifies the Monte Carlo implementation of the model is that the drift of $\ln F_i(t)$ is constant between t_{i-1} and t_i so that

$$F_i(t_{k+1}) = F_i(t_k) \exp \left[\left(\sum_{j=k+1}^{i} \frac{\tau_j F_j(t_k) \displaystyle\sum_{q=1}^{p} \lambda_{j-k-1,q} \lambda_{i-k-1,q}}{1 + \tau_j F_j(t)} - \sum_{q=1}^{p} \frac{\lambda_{i-k-1,q}^2}{2} \right) \tau_k + \sum_{q=1}^{p} \lambda_{i-k-1,q} \varepsilon_q \sqrt{\tau_k} \right] \tag{13.25}$$

where ε_q are independent random standard normal deviates. Each Monte Carlo simulation consists of using equation (13.25) to generate a path for each forward rate under the $P(t, T_{t(m)})$-measure. The value of $F_i(t_{i-1})$ is the realized rate for the time period between t_{i-1} and t_i and enables the caplet payoff at time t_i to be computed. This payoff is discounted to time 0 using $F_j(t_{j-1})$ as the discount rate for the interval (t_{j-1}, t_j). The estimated caplet value is the average of the discounted payoffs.

13.4   CALIBRATION OF LIBOR MARKET MODEL TO CAPS

Since the LIBOR market model, LFM, as discussed already, prices consistently with Black's formula, then to calibrate the LFM model to the market one needs to input into the model Blacklike implied market volatilities for cap prices. In the market, quoted implied volatilities of caps typically have an initial reset time equal to three months, and all the other reset times are equally three-month spaces, or they have an initial reset time equal to six months, and all the other reset times are equally six-month spaced. To price caps, we take the risk-neutral expectation of the discounted payoff of the sum of the caplets:

$$Cap^{market}(0, T_j, X) = E^Q\left[\sum_{i=1}^{j}\tau_i D(0, T)\max(0, F_i(T_{i-1}) - X)\right] \tag{13.26}$$

$$= \sum_{i=1}^{j}\tau_i P(0, T_i)E^i\left[\max(0, F_i(T_{i-1}) - X)\right]$$

under the Q^i-forward-adjusted measure. Since the price of a T_{i-1}-caplet coincides with that of Black's caplet formula, then the price of a cap is

$$Cap^{market}(0, T_j, X) = \sum_{i=1}^{j}\tau_i P(0, T_i)\left(F_i(0)N(d_1) - XN(d_2)\right) \tag{13.27}$$

where the last term is Black's formula for a caplet, and

$$d_1 = \frac{\ln\left(\frac{F_i(T_{i-1})}{X}\right) + \frac{v_i^2}{2}}{v_i} \qquad d_2 = \frac{\ln\left(\frac{F_i(T_{i-1})}{X}\right) - \frac{v_i^2}{2}}{v_i}$$

with

$$v_i = \sqrt{T_{i-1}v_{T_j\text{-}cap}}$$

where the *same* average volatility $v_{T_j\text{-}cap}$ is assumed for all caplets up to j. The cap volatilities $v_{T_j\text{-}cap}$ are called *forward volatilities*. The market solves equation

(13.27) for $v_{T_{j}\text{-}cap}$ and quotes them annualized and in percentages. It is often assumed that the same average cap volatility $v_{T_{j}\text{-}cap}$ is used for all caplets concurring with the T_j-maturity cap. However, if the same caplets concur to a different cap, such as a T_{j+1}-maturity cap, their average volatility is changed. This seems to create inconsistencies since the same caplets are linked to different volatilities when concurring to different caps. To correct this inconsistency and to correctly quote cap prices, it is necessary that the following relationship be satisfied:

$$\sum_{i=1}^{j} \tau_i P(0, T_i) \text{Bl}(X, F_i(0), \sqrt{T_{i-1}} v_{j\text{-}cap}) = \sum_{i=1}^{j} \tau_i P(0, T_i) \text{Bl}(X, F_i(0), \sqrt{T_{i-1}} v_{T_{i-1}\text{-}caplet})$$

where "Bl" denotes Black's formula as a function of strike price, the forward rate, and volatility. The volatilities $v_{T_{i-1}\text{-}caplet}$ are sometimes called *forward forward volatilities*. Note that *different* average volatilities $v_{T_{i-1}\text{-}caplet}$ are assumed for different caplets concurring with the same T_j-maturity cap. The cap volatilities used by the market to price caps can be used to price swaptions.

Note also that correlations do not have an impact on the price of caps since the joint dynamics of forward rates are not involved in the payoff in equation (13.27). Thus, the marginal (normal) distributions of the single forward rates are enough to compute the expectations and correlations are not needed. This is not the case with swaptions, however, where the terminal correlation is quite relevant thus complicates the pricing.

The caplet volatilities can be stripped from the cap volatilities using a stripping algorithm for $j = 1, 2, \ldots$. Once the $v_{T_{j}\text{-}caplet}$'s are determined, we can plug them into equation (13.14) or (13.15) to solve for the general σ's and the $\Phi\psi$'s, respectively, via a numerical nonlinear equation solving procedure. However, we cannot completely fill Table 13.1 since there are more unknowns than equations. Having more parameters is useful, however, when pricing and calibrating swaptions is considered. On the other hand, if one assumes constant volatility formulations as in equation (13.16), then Table 13.1 can be completely determined (substitute the s_i's for $\Phi_i\psi_a$'s) since all the s's can be determined from the market by an algebraic numerical procedure.

13.5 PRICING SWAPTIONS WITH LOGNORMAL FORWARD-SWAP MODEL

There are two legs of an interest-rate swap (IRS), the floating-leg, based on LIBOR, and the fixed leg, where payments are exchanged between the two sides on prespecified dates, $T_{n+1}, \ldots, T_N$. The fixed leg pays out an amount corresponding to a fixed interest rate K, $\tau_j K$, where τ_j is the year fraction from T_{j-1} to T_j, while the floating leg pays an amount corresponding to the LIBOR rate $F_j(T_{j-1})$, set at the previous instant T_{j-1} for the maturity given by the current payment instant T_j. Thus, the floating-leg rate is reset at dates $T_n, T_{n+1}, \ldots, T_{N-1}$ and paid at dates $T_{n+1}, \ldots T_N$. The payoff at time T_n for the payer of the IRS is

$$\sum_{i=n+1}^{N} D(T_n, T_i)\tau_i\Big(F_i(T_{i-1}) - K\Big)$$

We can compute the value of the payer IRS (payer forward-start swap), $PFS(\cdot, [T_n, \ldots, T_N], K)$, by taking the expectation at time t:[3]

$$PFS(t, [T_n, \ldots, T_N], K) = E_t\left[\sum_{i=n+1}^{N} D(T_n, T_i)\tau_i\Big(F_i(T_{i-1}) - K\Big)\right]$$

$$= \sum_{i=n+1}^{N} P(t, T_i)\tau_i E_t^i\Big[F_i(T_{i-1}) - K\Big]$$

$$= \sum_{i=n+1}^{N} P(t, T_i)\tau_i(F_i(t) - K)$$

$$= \sum_{i=n+1}^{N} \Big[P(t, T_{i-1}) - (1 + \tau_i K)P(t, T_i)\Big]$$

In particular, at time T_n, the value of the payoff is

$$= \sum_{i=n+1}^{N} P(T_n, T_i)\tau_i(F_i(T_n) - K)$$

The discounted payoff at time t

$$= D(t, T_n)\sum_{i=n+1}^{N} P(T_n, T_i)\tau_i(F_i(T_n) - K)$$

has the value of

$$= P(t, T_n)\sum_{i=n+1}^{N} P(T_n, T_i)\tau_i\Big[P(T_n, T_{i-1}) - (1 + \tau_i K)P(T_n, T_i)\Big]$$

---

[3]Brigo and Mercurio (2001c), 221.

under the risk-neutral expectation.[4] Notice that the neither volatility nor correlation of the forward rates affects the pricing. The forward swap rate corresponding the above payer IRS is the value of the fixed-leg rate K that makes the contract fair (i.e., that makes the present value equal to zero). The forward swap rate is

$$S_{n,N}(t) = \frac{P(t, T_n) - P(t, T_N)}{\displaystyle\sum_{i=n+1}^{N} \tau_i P(t, T_i)}$$

which can be shown to equal

$$S_{n,N}(t) = \frac{1 - \displaystyle\prod_{j=n+1}^{N} \frac{1}{1 + \tau_j F_j(t)}}{\displaystyle\sum_{i=n+1}^{N} \tau_i \prod_{j=n+1}^{i} \frac{1}{1 + \tau_j F_j(t)}} \tag{13.28}$$

where

$$\frac{1}{1 + \tau_j F_j(t)}$$

is the *forward discount factor*. The expression in equation (13.28) can be expressed in terms of an exponential function; that is,

$$S_{n,N}(t) = \exp(\psi(F_{n+1}(t), F_{n+2}(t), \ldots, F_N(t)))$$

of the underlying forward rates to indicate that the forward swap rate is actually a (nonlinear) function of the underlying forward LIBOR rates.[5]

We can now value a swaption. From Chapter 10, we know that a swaption is a contract that gives its holder the right (but not the obligation) to enter at a future time $T_n > 0$ an IRS, with reset times $T_n, \ldots, T_{N-1}$ (the first reset time usually coincides with T_n), and with payments occurring at times $T_{n+1}, T_{n+2}, \ldots, T_N$. If we assume a unit notional amount, a (payer) swaption payoff can be expressed as

$$D(0, T_n) \max(S_{n,N}(T_n) - K, 0) \sum_{i=n+1}^{N} \tau_i P(T_n, T_i) \tag{13.29}$$

[4]Ibid., 221.
[5]Ibid., 222.

If the current forward swap rate equals the fixed strike price, $S_{n,N}(0) = K$, then the swaption is at-the-money. If $S_{n,N}(0) > K$, then the swaption is in-the-money and if $S_{n,N}(0) < K$, the swaption is out-of-the-money. The moneyness of a receiver swaption is the opposite of that for a payer swaption.

The forward swap rate process, assuming lognormal dynamics, follows a martingale if the numeraire chosen is

$$C_{n,N}(t) = \sum_{i=n+1}^{N} \tau_i P(t, T_i) \tag{13.30}$$

since $C_{n,N}(t)S_{n,N}(t) = P(t, T_n) - P(t, T_N)$ gives the price of a tradable asset that, expressed in $C_{n,N}(t)$ units, coincides with the forward rate swap.[6] Thus, under the $Q^{n,N}$ (forward-swap) measure associated with $C_{n,N}(t)$, the (driftless) dynamics are

$$dS_{n,N}(t) = \sigma^{(n,N)}(t)S_{n,N}(t)dz^{(n,N)}(t) \tag{13.31}$$

where $\sigma^{(n,N)}(t)$ is the deterministic instantaneous percentage forward swap rate volatility, and $z^{(n,N)}$ is a standard Brownian motion under $Q^{n,N}$. We define $v_{n,N}^2(t)$ as the average percentage variance of the forward swap rate in the interval $[0, T_n]$ multiplied by the interval length T_n.

$$v_{n,N}^2(T_n) = \int_0^{T_n} (\sigma^{(n,N)}(t))^2 dt = \int_0^{T_n} (d \ln S_{n,N}(t))(d \ln S_{n,N}(t)) \tag{13.32}$$

This model—equation (13.31)—of forward rate dynamics is known as the lognormal forward-swap rate model (LSM) since each swap rate $S_{n,N}(t)$ has a lognormal distribution under its forward swap measure[7] $Q^{n,N}$. The LSM model is consistent with Black's formula for pricing swaptions. In fact, the LSM payer swaption price PS^{LSM} is

$$PS^{LSM}(0, T_n, [T_n, \ldots, T_N], K) = C_{n,N}(0)Bl(K, S_{n,N}(0), v_{n,N}(T_n)) \tag{13.33}$$

where $Bl(\cdot, \cdot, \cdot)$ is Black's formula defined in (10.110). This can be seen if we take the risk-neutral expectation of the discounted payoff in (13.29),

$$E^Q(D(0, T_n)\max(S_{n,N}(T_n) - K, 0)C_{n,N}(T_n)) = C_{n,N}(0)E^{n,N}[\max(S_{n,N}(T_n) - K, 0)]$$

---

[6]Ibid., 223.
[7]Ibid., 224.

which follows from the change of measure associated with a numeraire formula given in (1.66) with $Z_T = \max(S_{n,N}(T_n) - K, 0)C_{n,N}(T_n)$, $U = B = Q$, and $N = C_{n,N}$; that is

$$E^{n,N}\left[\frac{\max(S_{n,N}(T_n) - K, 0)C_{n,N}(T_n)}{C_{n,N}(T_n)}\right] = E^Q\left[\frac{B(0)\max(S_{n,N}(T_n) - K, 0)C_{n,N}(T_n)}{C_{n,N}(0)B(T_n)}\right]$$

where $T = T_n$, $B(0) = 1$, and $D(0, T_n) = B(T_n)^{-1}$.

13.6 APPROXIMATE SWAPTION PRICING WITH HULL-WHITE APPROACH

Pricing European swaptions with the LIBOR market model has been suggested by Brace, Gatarek, and Musiela (1997) and Andersen and Andreasen (2000). Hull and White (1999) also provide an approximate, but accurate, procedure for pricing swaptions using the model given in equation (13.9). Consider an option, expiring at T, on a swap lasting from $T_n, \ldots, T_N$ with reset dates $T_{n+1}, \ldots, T_{N-1}$ (in general, $T_n = T$). We will assume that the reset dates for the swap coincide with the reset dates for caplets underlying the LIBOR market model.

We know that the relationship between bond prices and forward rates is

$$\frac{P(t, T_k)}{P(t, T_n)} = \prod_{j=n}^{k-1}\frac{1}{1+\tau_j F_j(t)}$$

for $k \geq n + 1$. It follows that the forward swap rate in equation in (10.109) can be written as

$$S_{n,N}(t) = \frac{1 - \prod_{j=n}^{N}\frac{1}{1+\tau_j F_j(t)}}{\sum_{i=n}^{N}\tau_i\prod_{j=n}^{i}\frac{1}{1+\tau_j F_j(t)}}$$

Given that empty sums are zero and empty products are one, we get

$$S_{n,N}(t) = \frac{\prod_{j=n}^{N}\left[1+\tau_j F_j(t)\right] - 1}{\sum_{i=n}^{N}\tau_i\prod_{j=i+1}^{N}\left[1+\tau_j F_j(t)\right]} \tag{13.34}$$

or

$$\ln S_{n,N}(t) = \ln\left(\prod_{j=n}^{N}(1+\tau_j F_j(t)) - 1\right) - \ln\left(\sum_{i=n}^{N}\tau_i\prod_{j=i+1}^{N}(1+\tau_j F_j(t))\right)$$

so that

$$\frac{1}{S_{n,N}(t)}\frac{\partial S_{n,N}(t)}{\partial F_k(t)} = \frac{\tau_k \gamma_k(t)}{1+\tau_k \gamma_k(t)}$$

where

$$\gamma_k(t) = \frac{\prod\limits_{j=n}^{N}(1+\tau_j F_j(t))}{\prod\limits_{j=n}^{N}(1+\tau_j F_j(t)) - 1} - \frac{\sum\limits_{i=n}^{k-1}\tau_i\prod\limits_{j=i+1}^{N}(1+\tau_j F_j(t))}{\sum\limits_{i=n}^{n}\tau_i\prod\limits_{j=i+1}^{N}(1+\tau_j F_j(t))}$$

From Ito's lemma, the qth component of the volatility $S_{n,N}(t)$ is

$$\sum_{k=n}^{N}\frac{1}{S_{n,N}(t)}\frac{\partial S_{n,N}(t)}{\partial F_k(t)}\varsigma_{k,q}(t)F_k(t)$$

or

$$\sum_{k=n}^{N}\frac{\tau_k \gamma_k(t)\varsigma_{k,q}(t)F_k(t)}{1+\tau_k F_k(t)}$$

The variance of the forward swap rate S_n, $N(t)$ is thus

$$\sum_{q=1}^{p}\left[\sum_{k=n}^{N}\frac{\tau_k \gamma_k(t)\varsigma_{k,q}(t)F_k(t)}{1+\tau_k F_k(t)}\right]^2$$

Assuming, as discussed in the previous section that forward rate volatility $\varsigma_{k,q} = \lambda_{k-m(t),q}$, then the variance of $S_{n,N}(t)$ is

$$\sum_{q=1}^{p}\left[\sum_{k=n}^{N}\frac{\tau_k \gamma_k(t)\lambda_{k-m(t),q}F_k(t)}{1+\tau_k F_k(t)}\right]^2 \qquad (13.35)$$

Equation (13.35) is in general stochastic suggesting that when forward rates under-lying caplets are lognormal, swap rates are not lognormal.[8] Assume $F_k(t) = F_k(0)$ so that the volatility of $S_{n,N}(t)$ is constant within each accrual period and the swap rate is lognormal. The average variance of $S_{n,N}(t)$ between time 0 and T_n is

$$\frac{1}{T_n}\sum_{j=0}^{n-1}\left\{\tau_j\sum_{q=1}^{p}\left[\sum_{k=n}^{N}\frac{\tau_k\lambda_{k-j-1,q}F_k(0)\gamma_k(0)}{1+\tau_kF_k(0)}\right]^2\right\}$$

so that the spot swaption volatility is

$$\sqrt{\frac{1}{T_n}\sum_{j=0}^{n-1}\left\{\tau_j\sum_{q=1}^{p}\left[\sum_{k=n}^{N}\frac{\tau_k\lambda_{k-j-1,q}F_k(0)\gamma_k(0)}{1+\tau_kF_k(0)}\right]^2\right\}} \qquad (13.36)$$

The swaption price can be calculated by substituting this volatility into swaption formulas given in (10.102) or (10.104).

13.7   LFM FORMULA FOR SWAPTION VOLATILITIES

Brigo and Mercurio (2001) suggest an approximation method, based on a Rebon-ato's work, to compute swaption prices using the LFM without using Monte Carlo simulation. Rebonato (1998) showed that forward swap rates can be interpreted as a linear combination of (weighted) forward rates, according to

$$S_{n,N}(t) = \sum_{i=n+1}^{N} w_i(t)F_i(t)$$

where

$$w_i(t) = w_i(F_{n+1}(t),\ F_{n+2}(t),\ \ldots,\ F_N(t)) = \frac{\tau_i\prod_{j=n+1}^{N}\frac{1}{1+\tau_jF_j(t)}}{\sum_{k=n+1}^{N}\tau_j\prod_{j=n+1}^{k}\frac{1}{1+\tau_jF_j(t)}}$$

[8]Hull and White (1999), 17.

As a first approximation, one can freeze the w's at time 0, obtaining,

$$S_{n,N}(t) \approx \sum_{i=n+1}^{N} w_i(0)F_i(t) \qquad (13.37)$$

which is justified by the fact that the variability of the w's are much smaller than the variability of the F's. This can be verified historically and through Monte Carlo simulation of the F's (and therefore the w's).[9]

Differentiating both sides of equation (13.37), we get

$$dS_{n,N}(t) \approx \sum_{i=n+1}^{N} w_i(0)dF_i(t) = (\ldots)dt + \sum_{i=n+1}^{N} w_i(0)\sigma_i(t)F_i(t)dz_i(t)$$

under any of the forward-adjusted measures. We then compute the quadratic variation

$$dS_{n,N}(t)dS_{n,N}(t) \approx \sum_{i,j=n+1}^{N} w_i(0)w_j(0)F_i(t)F_j(t)\rho_{i,j}\sigma_i(t)\sigma_j(t)dt$$

The percentage quadratic variation is given by

$$\left(\frac{dS_{n,N}(t)}{S_{n,N}(t)}\right)\left(\frac{dS_{n,N}(t)}{S_{n,N}(t)}\right) = (d\ln S_{n,N}(t))(d\ln S_{n,N}(t))$$

$$\approx \frac{\sum_{i,j=n+1}^{N} w_i(0)w_j(0)F_i(t)F_j(t)\rho_{i,j}\sigma_i(t)\sigma_j(t)}{S_{n,N}(t)^2}dt$$

We can provide a further approximation by freezing all the F's in the formula (as was done to the w's) to their time-zero value:

$$(d\ln S_{n,N}(t))(d\ln S_{n,N}(t)) \approx \sum_{i,j=n+1}^{N} \frac{w_i(0)w_j(0)F_i(0)F_j(0)\rho_{i,j}\sigma_i(t)\sigma_j(t)}{S_{n,N}(0)^2}dt$$

---

[9]Brigo and Mercurio (2001c), 247.

With this last formula, we can compute an approximation of the LFM swap rate integrated percentage variance, $(v_{n,N}^{LFM})^2$, given by

$$\int_0^{T_n} (d\ln S_{n,N}(t))(d\ln S_{n,N}(t)) \approx \sum_{i,j=n+1}^{N} \frac{w_i(0)w_j(0)F_i(0)F_j(0)\rho_{i,j}}{S_{n,N}(0)^2} \int_0^{T_n} \sigma_i(t)\sigma_j(t)dt$$

Thus, we get the LFM Blacklike (squared) swaption volatility (multiplied by T_n) that can be approximated by what is known as Rebonato's formula,

$$(v_{n,N}^{LFM})^2 = \sum_{i,j=n+1}^{N} \frac{w_i(0)w_j(0)F_i(0)F_j(0)\rho_{i,j}}{S_{n,N}(0)^2} \int_0^{T_n} \sigma_i(t)\sigma_j(t)dt \qquad (13.38)$$

As a result, the quantity $v_{n,N}^{LFM}$ can be used as a proxy for the Black volatility $v_{n,N}(T_n)$ of the swap rate $S_{n,N}$ so that using this quantity in Black's formula for swaptions allows one to compute approximated swaption prices with the LFM.[10]

13.8   MONTE CARLO PRICING OF SWAPTIONS USING LFM

Consider the swaption price

$$E^Q \left(D(0,\ T_n)\max(S_{n,N} - K,\ 0) \sum_{i=n+1}^{N} \tau_i P(T_n,\ T_i) \right)$$

$$= P(0,\ T_n)E^{Q^{P(\cdot,T_n)}} \left(\max(S_{n,N} - K,\ 0) \sum_{i=n+1}^{N} \tau_i P(T_n,\ T_i) \right)$$

where the expectation is taken with respect to the LFM numeraire $P(\cdot,\ T_n)$ rather than the LSM numeraire $C_{n,N}$. Notice that since the swap rate, given in (13.34), can be expressed in terms of spanning forward rates at time T_n, then the above expectation depends on the joint distribution of the spanning forward rates $F_{n+1}(T_n)$, $F_{n+2}(T_n), \ldots, F_N(T_n)$ and thus the forward rate correlations impact the price unlike in cap/floor pricing.[11]

To price a swaption using Monte Carlo, we need to generate M realizations of

---

[10]Ibid., 248.
[11]Ibid., 234.

the forward LIBOR rates $F_{n+1}(T_n)$, $F_{n+2}(T_n)$, ..., $F_N(T_n)$ using the LFM forward rate dynamics under $Q^{P(\cdot,T_n)}$.

$$dF_k(t) = \sigma_k(t)F_k(t) \sum_{j=n+1}^{k} \frac{\rho_{k,j}\tau_j\sigma_j(t)F_j(t)}{1+\tau_jF_j(t)}dt + \sigma_k(t)F_k(t)dz_k(t)$$

for $k = n + 1, \ldots, N$. For each realization, we compute the payoff

$$\max(S_{n,N}(T_n) - K,\ 0) \sum_{i=n+1}^{N} \tau_i P(T_n,\ T_i)$$

and then average over all $M = N - n$ payoffs. The above LFM process needs to be discretized for sufficiently (but not too) small time steps Δt since the LFM dynamics do not lead to a distributionally known process. Small time steps reduce the affects of random inputs to the independent Gaussian (and thus distributionally known) Brownian shocks,[12] $z(t + \Delta t) - z(t)$.

In Monte Carlo, it is often convenient and computationally simpler to work with logarithms as in (12.46). Thus to evolve the system of forward rates from their initial values $F_i(0)$ at time 0 to some time t in the future, we can use the standard Euler scheme and obtain the system of discretized SDEs:

$$d\ln F_k^{\Delta t}(t+\Delta t) = \ln F_k^{\Delta t}(t) + \sigma_k(t) \sum_{j=n+1}^{k} \frac{\rho_{k,j}\tau_j\sigma_j(t)F_j^{\Delta t}(t)}{1+\tau_jF_j^{\Delta t}(t)}\Delta t - \frac{\sigma_k^2(t)}{2}\Delta t + \sigma_k(t)\Delta z_k \quad (13.39)$$

where $k = n + 1, \ldots, N$.

It is important to note that discretizing the continuous-time exact dynamics does not lead to discrete-time interest-rate dynamics that are consistent with discrete-time no-arbitrage. Thus, the discretized process leads to bond prices that are not martingales when expressed with respect to the relevant numeraire. Despite this problem, for sufficiently small discretization steps, the violation of no-arbitrage conditions due to the time-discretization of no-arbitrage continuous-time processes is negligible.[13] However, Glasserman and Zhao (2000) developed a discretization scheme that maintains the martingale property required by no-arbitrage in discrete time.

The following is a Monte Carlo implementation of the LIBOR forward rate model to price a European swaption.

---

[12]Ibid., 234.
[13]Ibid., 236.

```
/***************************************************************************
MonteCarloLFM: A Monte Carlo simulation of the LIBOR log-forward dynamics in
               (13.39) to value a European swaption.
[in] SymmetricMatrix& R   : correlation matrix of forward rate
     Matrix &V            : variance/covariance matrix of forward rates.
                            Alternatively, can specify volatility structure of rates
                            which is done inside method
        double initrate   : initial forward (spot) rate
        double strike     : strike rate of swaption
        double T          : time to maturity of swaption
        long M            : number of simulations
        long N            : number of time steps per simulation path
        long m            : number of forward rates to simulate
        long numeraire    : numeraire underlying forward rate dynamics (1, . . . ,N)
[out]Returns: double      : swaptionPrice
****************************************************************************/
void RateModel::MonteCarloLFM(SymmetricMatrix &R, Matrix &V, double initrate,
  double strike, double T, long M, long N, long m, long numeraire)
{
  int i, j, l, k, n, q, p;
  long seed = -2;
  long* idum = &seed;                // pointer to seed
  double drift = 0.0;                // drift
  double deviate = 0.0;              // standard normal deviate
  double dt = T/N;                   // time step 0.5
  double F0 = initrate;              // initial rate
  double F[100] = {0.0};             // forward rates
  double v[100] = {0.0};             // forward rate volatiliites
  double tau[100] = {0.0};           // forward rate tenors
  double lnF[100] = {0.0};           // log forward rates
  double logF = 0.0;                 // stores log of forward rate
  vector<double> forwardVec[20];     // array of vector of forward rates
  double swapRate = 0.0;             // swap rate
  double payoff = 0.0;               // payoff of swaption
  double bondPrice = 0.0;            // bond price
  double value = 0.0;                // value
  double prod = 1;                   // product of forward rates to compute swap rate
  double prod1 = 1;                  // product of forward rates to compute bond price
  double swaptionPrice;              // swaption price
  double SD, SE = 0.0;               // standard deviation and error
  double sum = 0.0;                  // sum of prod1
  double sum1 = 0.0;                 // sum of squared values
  double a = 0.19085664;             // volatility parameter
  double b = 0.97462314;             // volatility parameter
  double c = 0.08089168;             // volatility parameter
  double d = 0.0134498;              // volatility parameter
  double mu = 0.0;                   // drift if numeraire < j
  double mu1 = 0.0;                  // drift if numeraire >= j

  // compute volatilities and tenors
  for (i = 1; i <= N; i++)
```

```
{
  v[i] = (a*(i*dt) + d)*exp(-b*(i*dt)) + c;
  tau[i] = 0.5;
}

// initialize RNG
srand(time(0));
seed = (long) rand() % 100;
idum = &seed;

for (i = 1; i <= M; i++) // number of simulations
{
  // initialize for each simulation
  drift = 0;
  prod = 1;
  prod1 = 1;
  sum = 0;
  sum1 = 0;
  mu = 0;
  mu1 = 0;

  for (l = 0; l < N; l++) // number of time steps
  {
    for (k = 1; k <= m; k++) // generate m forward rates
    {
      deviate = util.gasdev(idum);
      F[0] = F0;

      // compute drift coefficient
      if (k < numeraire)
      {
        for (j = k+1; j < numeraire; j++)
        mu = mu + ((R(k,j)*tau[j]*v[k]*F[j-1])/(1 + tau[j]*F[j-1]))*dt;
      }
      else // j >= numeraire
      {
        for (j = numeraire; j <= k; j++)
          mu1 = mu1 + ((R(k,j)*tau[j]*v[k]*F[j-1])/(1 + tau[j]*F[j-1]))*dt;
      }
      // compute drift
      drift = -mu + mu1;
      // simulate log forward rate
      logF = log(F[k-1]) + v[k]*drift - 0.5*(v[k]*v[k])*dt +
        v[k]*deviate*sqrt(dt);
      F[k] = exp(logF);
      forwardVec[l+1].push_back(F[k]);
    }
    // compute current swap rate
    for (p = 0; p < m; p++)
    {
```

```
            prod = prod*(1/(1+ tau[p]*forwardVec[l+1][p]));
            for (n = 1; n <= m; n++)
            {
               for (q = 1; q <= n; q++)
                  prod1 = prod1*(1/(1 + tau[q]*forwardVec[l+1][q]));

               sum = sum + tau[n]*prod1;
            }
         }
         swapRate = (1 - prod)/(sum);
         bondPrice = 1/prod1;

         value = max(swapRate - strike,0)*sum;
         payoff = payoff + value;
         sum1 = sum1 + value*value;
      }
   }
   swaptionPrice = exp(-initrate*T)*(payoff/M);

   cout.precision(4);
   cout << "swaption Price = " << " " << swaptionPrice << endl;

   SD = sqrt((sum1 - sum1*sum1/M)*exp(-2*initrate*T)/(M-1));
   cout << "stddev " << " " << SD << endl;

   SE = SD/sqrt(M);
   cout << "stderr " << " " << SE << endl;

   return swaptionPrice;
}
```

Suppose we want to value a European payer swaption with a strike rate of 6.5 percent, one year to maturity, an initial forward rate of 5 percent, and a unit notional amount. Furthermore, suppose we have a 1×10 swaption (a swaption maturing in one year and giving the holder the right to enter a 10-year swap. Suppose we consider maturities of 1, 2, 3, 4, 5, 7, and 10 years with underlying swap lengths of 1, 2, 3, 4, 5, 6, 7, 8, 9, and 10 years. Suppose the swaption Black implied at-the-money swaption volatility matrix (quoted by brokers) is given by V and the correlation matrix is given by R (which we assume to be estimated from historical data). Typically, V is used to calibrate the model. However, we will actually compute the volatilities from the formulation in (13.10) (using given values for a, b, c, and d), which is computed inside the *MonteCarloLFM* method.[14] Calibration to V can be achieved by a numerical optimization routine.

---

[14]In practice, we would want to read the data from a file or a database (it usually is not good coding practice to hard code the data, but we do so here so the reader can see each element input into the matrices). It is not to hard to implement either of these approaches. In fact, some other methods in the book do read data from files.

```
*************************************************************************
void main()
{

  LMModel lm;
  SymmetricMatrix R(10);
  Matrix V(10,7);

  V << 0.164 << 0.158 << 0.146 << 0.138 << 0.133 << 0.129 << 0.126 << 0.123
     << 0.120 << 0.117
     << 0.177 << 0.156 << 0.141 << 0.131 << 0.127 << 0.124 << 0.122 << 0.119
     << 0.117 << 0.114
     << 0.176 << 0.155 << 0.139 << 0.127 << 0.123 << 0.121 << 0.119 << 0.117
     << 0.115 << 0.113
     << 0.169 << 0.146 << .129 << 0.119 << 0.116 << 0.114 << 0.113 << 0.111 << 0.110
     << 0.108
     << 0.158 << 0.139 << 0.124 << 0.115 << 0.111 << 0.109 << 0.108 << 0.107
     << 0.105 << 0.104
     << 0.145 << 0.129 << 0.116 << 0.108 << 0.104 << 0.103 << 0.101 << 0.099
     << 0.098 << 0.096
     << 0.135 << 0.115 << 0.104 << 0.098 << 0.094 << 0.093 << 0.091 << 0.088
     << 0.086 << 0.084;

  R << 1.00
    << 0.924 << 1.00
    << 0.707 << 0.924 << 1.00
    << 0.557 << 0.833 << 0.981 << 1.00
    << 0.454 << 0.760 << 0.951 << 0.997 << 1.00
    << 0.760 << 0.951 << 0.997 << 0.963 << 0.924 << 1.00
    << 0.843 << 0.985 << 0.976 << 0.916 << 0.862 << 0.990 << 1.00
    << 0.837 << 0.983 << 0.979 << 0.921 << 0.867 << 0.992 << 1.00 << 1.00
    << 0.837 << 0.983 << 0.979 << 0.920 << 0.867 << 0.992 << 1.00 << 1.00 << 1.00
    << 0.920 << 1.00 << 0.928 << 0.838 << 0.767 << 0.954 << 0.986 << 0.985 << 0.985
    << 1.00;

  // in practice, we would calibrate our model to V
  lm.MonteCarloLFM(R,V,0.05,0.065,1,10000,10,10,1);
}
```

Then, a Monte Carlo simulation with $M = 10,000$ simulations, $N = 10$ time steps, simulated under the Q^1 numeraire, yields a swaption price of \$3.722 with a standard deviation of 0.0134 and a standard error of 0.00013.

13.9   IMPROVED MONTE CARLO PRICING OF SWAPTIONS WITH A PREDICTOR-CORRECTOR

We can improve the accuracy of the Monte Carlo swaption price estimate. We can rewrite equation (13.39) as

$$d \ln F_k^{\Delta t} = \left[\mu_k (\ln F(t),\ t) - \frac{1}{2} \sigma_k^2(t) \right] \Delta t + \sigma_k(t) \Delta_k z \qquad (13.40)$$

where

$$\mu_k(\ln F_k^{\Delta t},\ t) = \sigma_k(t) \sum_{j=n+1}^{k} \frac{\rho_{k,j}\tau_j\sigma_j(t)F_j^{\Delta t}(t)}{1+\tau_j F_j^{\Delta t}(t)} \Delta t$$

Thus, a single Euler step to evolve each of the state variables $\ln F_k$ from time 0 to time t denoted by Δt is given by

$$\ln F_k^{\Delta t}(t) = \ln F_k^{\Delta t}(0) + \left[\mu_k(\ln F(0),\ 0) - \frac{1}{2}\sigma_k^2(0)\right]\Delta t + \sigma_k(0)\varepsilon_k\sqrt{\Delta t} \qquad (13.41)$$

where ε_k's are standard normal deviates that are correlated according to $E[\varepsilon_i\varepsilon_j] = \rho_{ij}(0)$. For time-dependent instantaneous volatility, the Euler scheme in (13.41) can be improved by use of the integrated covariance matrix elements

$$c_{ij} = \int_0^t \rho_{ij}(s)\sigma_i(s)\sigma_j(s)ds$$

which can be split into its pseudo-square root A ($C = AA'$) defined by

$$c_{ik} = \sum_{j=0}^{N-1} a_{ij}a_{jk}$$

A Cholesky, spectral, or angular decomposition can be used generate a valid matrix A with elements a_{ij}. Given this definition of the integrated covariance matrix C, we can express an improved constant drift approximation $\hat{\mu}_k(Y, C)$ as

$$\hat{\mu}_k(Y,\ C) = -\sum_{j=k+1}^{\eta-1} c_{ij}\frac{\tau_j e^{Y_j}}{1+\tau_j e^{Y_j}} + \sum_{j=\eta}^{i} c_{ij}\frac{\tau_j e^{Y_j}}{1+\tau_j e^{Y_j}} \qquad (13.42)$$

where $Y_k = \ln F_k^{\Delta t}$, which leads to the log-Euler scheme,

$$Y_k(t) = Y_k(0) + [\hat{\mu}_k(Y(0),\ C) - \frac{1}{2}c_{kk}] + \sum_{j=0}^{N-1} a_{kj}\varepsilon_j \qquad (13.43)$$

where the ε_j are now independent standard normal random deviates. If we assume a piecewise-constant drift, we can carry out the numerical integration analytically and use the scheme

$$F_k^{\Delta t}(t + \Delta t) = F_t^{\Delta t}(t) \cdot e^{\mu_i(f(t),t)\Delta t - \frac{1}{2}c_{kk} + \sum_{j=0}^{N-1} a_{kj}\varepsilon_j} \tag{13.44}$$

The Euler scheme does not attempt to account for state dependence in the drifts, but instead uses the initial values of the (logarithms of the) forward rates in equation (13.41).[15] There are a number of ways to improve the Euler method of the numerical integration of SDEs such as with implicit, explicit, and standard predictor-corrector methods; see Kloeden and Platen (1999). Hunter, Jackel and Joshi[16] suggest a hybrid approach. They directly integrate the diffusion term $\sigma_k dz_k(t)$ similar to the standard Euler method. To account for the indirect stochastics of the drift term, they employ a predictor-corrector method. First, they predict the forward rates using the initial data, and then they use these values to correct the approximation of the drift coefficient. An algorithm for constructing one draw from the terminal distribution of the forward rates over one time step is given:

1. Evolve the logarithms of the forward rates as if the drifts were constant and equal to their initial values according to the log-Euler scheme in equation (13.43).
2. Compute the drifts at the terminal time with the evolved forward rates from step 1.
3. Average the initially calculated drift coefficients with the newly computed ones.
4. Re-evolve using the same normal deviates as initially but using the new predictor-corrector drift terms.

In the event that the volatilities are constant, then one gets the simplest predictor-corrector equation—equation (15.5.4) with $\alpha = \frac{1}{2}$ in Kloeden and Platen (1999),

$$Y_k(t) = Y_k(0) + \frac{1}{2}[\hat{\mu}_k(Y(t), C) + \hat{\mu}_k(Y(0), C) - c_{kk}] + \sum_{j=0}^{N-1} a_{kj}\varepsilon_j \tag{13.45}$$

The following is an implementation of a Monte Carlo simulation using a predictor-corrector equation (13.42) to value a European swaption.

---

[15]Hunter, Jackel, and Joshi (2001), 2.
[16]Ibid., 3.

```
/*****************************************************************************
MonteCarloLFM_PredCorr: A Monte Carlo simulation using a predictor-corrector method
                        of the LIBOR log-forward dynamics in (13.39) to value an
                        European swaption.
[in]:   SymmetricMatrix& R : correlation matrix of forward rates
        Matrix &V          : variance/covariance matrix of forward rates.
                             Alternatively, can specify volatility structure of
                             rates which is done inside method
        double initrate    : initial forward (spot) rate
        double strike      : strike rate of swaption
        double T           : time to maturity of swaption
        long M             : number of simulations
        long N             : number of time steps per simulation path
        long m             : number of forward rates to simulate
        long numeraire     : numeraire under which to simulate dynamics
[out]: double             : swaptionPrice
*****************************************************************************/
double LMModel::MonteCarloLFM_PredCorr(const SymmetricMatrix &R, Matrix &V, double
    initrate, double strike, double T, long M, long N, long m, long numeraire)
{
    int i, j, l, k, n, q, p;
    long seed = 0;
    long* idum;                         // pointer to seed
    double mu10 = 0.0;                  // drift by freezing forward rate F(0) if j <
                                        // numeraire
    double mu20 = 0.0;                  // drift by freezing forward rate F(0) if j >=
                                        // numeraire
    double mu_hat = 0.0;                // -mu10 + mu20
    double mu_hat2 = 0.0;               // -mu1 + mu2
    double deviate = 0.0;               // standard normal deviate
    double dt = T/N;                    // time step
    double F0 = initrate;               // initial forward rate
    double F[2000] = {0.0};             // forward rates
    double v[100] = {0.0};              // array of forward volatilities
    double tau[100] = {0.0};            // array of forward tenors
    double logF = 0.0;                  // log of forward rate
    double logEuler = 0.0;              // log of Euler scheme
    vector<double> forwardVec[100];     // array of vector of forward rates
    double swapRate = 0.0;              // swaprate
    double value = 0.0;                 // swaption payoff value
    double payoff = 0.0;                // sum of value
    double bondPrice = 0.0;             // bond price
    double prod = 1;                    // product of forward rates to compute
                                        // swaption price
    double prod1 = 1;                   // product of forward rates to compute bond price
    double swaptionPrice = 0.0;         // swaption price
    double SD, SE = 0.0;                // standard deviation and error
    double sum = 0;                     // sum of prod1
    double sum1 = 0.0;                  // sum of squared value
    double azSum = 0.0;                 // sum of A(i,j)*deviate (A is square root of
                                        // corr matrix)
```

```
StatUtility util;                      // statistical utility class

// volatility parameters
double a = 0.19085664;
double b = 0.97462314;
double c = 0.08089168;
double d = 0.0134498;

DiagonalMatrix D(10);                  // matrix of eigenvalues on diagonal
Matrix Z(10,10);                       // matrix of eigenvectors
SymmetricMatrix C(10);                 // correlation matrix
Matrix A(10,10);                       // pseudo square root of C

// compute volatilities and tenors
for (i = 1; i <= N; i++)
{
  v[i] = (a*(i*dt) + d)*exp(-b*(i*dt)) + c;
  tau[i] = 0.5;
}

double temp = 0.0;
// compute integrated covariance elements
for (i = 1; i <= N; i++)
{
  for (j = 1; j <= i; j++)
  {
    // evaluate integral using Simpson's Rule int_01 rho*vol[i]*vol[j]*dt
    C(i,j) = R(i,j)*util.EvaluateSimpson(0,i*dt,1000,j*dt,T);
  }
}

// eigenvector - eigenvalue decompositon
EigenValues(C,D,Z);
for (i = 1; i <= N; i++)
{
  if (D(i) < 0)
    D(i) = -D(i);
  D(i) = sqrt(D(i));
}
// compute Cholesky decomposition
A = Z*D;

// initialize RNG
srand(time(0));
seed = (long) rand() % 100;
idum = &seed;

for (i = 1; i <= M; i++) // number of simulations
{
  // initialize for each simulation
  mu10 = 0;
  mu20 = 0;
  azSum = 0;
```

```
mu_hat = 0;
mu_hat2 = 0;
prod = 1;
prod1 = 1;
sum = 0;
sum1 = 0;

for (l = 0; l < N; l++) // number of time steps
{
  for (k = 1; k <= m; k++) // generate m forward rates
  {
    F[0] = F0;
    // compute drifts for error predictor method
    if (k < numeraire)
    {
      for (j = k+1; j < numeraire; j++)
      {
        mu1 = mu1 + ((C(k,j)*tau[j]*F[j])/(1 + tau[j]*F[j]));
        // compute drift by freezing F(0)
        mu10 = mu10 + ((C(k,j)*tau[j]*F[0])/(1 + tau[j]*F[0]));
      }
    }
    else // j >= numeraire
    {
      for (j = numeraire; j <= k; j++)
      {
        mu2 = mu2 + ((C(k,j)*tau[j]*F[j])/(1 + tau[j]*F[j]));
        // compute drift by freezing forward rate F(0)
        mu20 = mu20 + ((C(k,j)*tau[j]*F[0])/(1 + tau[j]*F[0]));
      }
    }
    mu_hat = -mu10 + mu20;
    mu_hat2 = -mu1 + mu2;

    for (j = 1; j < N; j++)
    {
      deviate = util.gasdev(idum);
      azSum = azSum + A(k,j)*deviate;
    }
    // logEuler scheme
    logEuler = log(F0) + 0.5*(mu_hat + mu_hat2 - C(k,k)) + azSum;

    F[k] = exp(logEuler);
    forwardVec[l+1].push_back(F[k]);
  }

  for (p = 0; p < m; p++)
  {
    prod = prod*(1/(1+tau[p]*forwardVec[l+1][p]));
    for (n = 1; n <= m; n++)
    {
      for (q = 1; q <= n; q++)
        prod1 = prod1*(1/(1 + tau[q]*forwardVec[l+1][q]));
```

```
          sum = sum + tau[n]*prod1;
      }
   }
   swapRate = (1 - prod)/(sum);
   bondPrice = 1/prod1;

   value = max(swapRate - strike,0)*sum;
   payoff = payoff + value;
   sum1 = sum1 + value*value;
   }
}
swaptionPrice = exp(-initrate*T)*(payoff/M);
cout << "swaption Price = " << swaptionPrice << endl;

SD = sqrt((sum1 - sum1*sum1/M)*exp(-2*initrate*T)/(M-1));
cout << "SD = " << SD << endl;

SE = SD/sqrt(M);
cout << "SE = " << SE << endl;

return swaptionPrice;
}
```

where the method definition of *EvaluateSimpson* is given in the *StatUtility* class by:

```
class StatUtility
{
  private:
    double *x,*g;        // arrays used in Simpson's rule
    double h;            // segment length
  public:
    /**********************************************************************
    EvaluateSimpson      : evaluates integral using Simpson's Rule
    [in]:  double a      : lower limit of integration
           double b      : upper limit of integration
           long n        : number of segments for approximation
           double t      : current time
           double T      : maturity
    [out]: double        : value of integral
    **********************************************************************/
    double EvaluateSimpson(double a, double b, long n, double t, double T)
    {
      double value = 0.0;

      h=(b-a)/n;
      x = new double[n];
      g = new double[n];

      x[0]= a;
```

```
      g[0]=F(x[0],t,T);

      for(int i=1; i < n; i++)
      {
        x[i]=h+(x[i-1]);
        g[i]=F(x[i],t,T);
      }
      value = calcIntegral(n);

      return value;
    }
    /************************************************************************
    calcintegral        : calculates integral approximation using Simpson's Rule
    [in]: long n        : number of integral segments
    [out]: double       : integral approximation
    ************************************************************************/
    double calcIntegral(long n)
    {
      double oddValues = 0;
      double evenValues = 0;

      for(int i=1;i<n ;i+=2)
        oddValues +=g[i];
      for(int j=2;j <n-1;j+=2)
        evenValues+=g[j];

      double value=((h/3)*(g[0]+4*oddValues+2*evenValues+g[n-1]));

      return value;
    }

/************************************************************************
F:    volatility function to evaluate for LFM simulation
[in]: double t : function evaluation point
      double s : current time
      double T : maturity
[out]:
************************************************************************/
    double F(double t,double s, double T)
    {
      const double a = 0.19085664;
      const double b = 0.97462314;
      const double c = 0.08089168;
      const double d = 0.0134498;

      return ((a*(T-t) + d)*exp(-b*(T-t) + c))*((a*(T-s) + d)*exp(-b*(T-s) + c));
    }
    // . . . other method definitions
};
```

Pricing the same swaption in the previous section (using the same parameters) with predictor-corrector, we get a value of \$3.268, a standard deviation of 0.01203, and a standard error of 0.00012.

13.10   INCOMPATIBILITY BETWEEN LSM AND LSF

While the LSM model is convenient for pricing swaptions since it is consistent with Black's formula, in general there are no analytical formulas for pricing interest rate derivatives involving swap rates. Consequently, forward LIBOR rates, rather than forward swap rates, are used to model the yield curve. However, we may be interested in computing the dynamics of forward swap rates under the numeraire used for forward rates, namely $P(t, T_n)$. Thus, we are interested in expressing the dynamics of forward swap rates under the measure $Q^{P(\cdot, T_n)}$.

Following Brigo and Mercurio, by applying the change-of-drift formula given in equation (1.68), we obtain the percentage drift $m^{n,N}(t)$ for $S_{n,N}$ under $Q^{P(\cdot, T_n)}$ as

$$m^n = 0dt - d\ln(S_{n,N}(t))d\ln\left(\frac{C_{n,N}(t)}{P(t,\ T_n)}\right) \tag{13.46}$$

The covariation term is computed as follows:

$$\ln\left(\frac{C_{n,N}(t)}{P(t,\ T_n)}\right) = \ln\left(\frac{\sum_{i=n+1}^{N}\tau_i P(t,\ T_i)}{P(t,\ T_n)}\right) = \ln\left(\sum_{i=n+1}^{N}\tau_i\prod_{j=n+1}^{i}\frac{1}{1+\tau_j F_j(t)}\right) = \chi(F_{n+1}(t),\ \ldots,\ F_N(t))$$

Recalling that $S_{n,N}(t) = \exp(\psi(F_{n+1}(t), \ldots, F_N(t))$ so that $\ln S_{n,N}(t) = \psi(F_{n+1}(t), \ldots, F_N(t))$, we find

$$m^n dt = \sum_{j=n+1}^{N}\sum_{i=n+1}^{N}\frac{\partial\psi}{\partial F_i}\frac{\partial\chi}{\partial F_j}dF_i(t)dF_j(t)$$

It can be shown after some lengthy computations that the forward swap rate $S_{n,N}(t)$ under the numeraire $P(\cdot, T_n)$ follows the dynamics

$$dS_{n,N}(t) = m^n(t)S_{n,N}(t)dt + \sigma^S(t)S_{n,N}(t)dz(t)$$

where

$$m^n(t) = \frac{\sum_{h,k=n+1}^{N}\mu_{h,k}\tau_h\tau_k FP_h(t)FP_k(t)\rho_{h,k}\sigma_h(t)\sigma_k(t)F_h(t)F_k(t)}{1 - FP(t;\ T_n,\ T_N)}$$

$$\mu_{h,k}(t) = \frac{\sum_{i=k}^{N}\tau_i FP(t;\ T_n,\ T_i)\left(FP(t;\ T_n,\ T_N)\sum_{i=n+1}^{h-1}\tau_i FP(t;\ T_n,\ T_i) + \sum_{i=h}^{N}\tau_i FP(t;\ T_n,\ T_i)\right)}{\left(\sum_{i=n+1}^{N}\tau_i FP(t;\ T_n,\ T_i)\right)^2}$$

$$FP(t; T_n, T_i) = \frac{P(t, T_i)}{P(t, T_n)} = \prod_{i=n+1}^{N} \frac{1}{1 + \tau_i F_i(t)}$$

and z is a $Q^{P(\cdot, T_n)}$ standard Brownian motion and where $FP_k(t) = FP(t; T_n, T_k)$ for all k for brevity.

We can also compute the forward-rate LIBOR dynamics under the forward-rate swap measure $Q^{n,N}$ by computing the new drift

$$m^{n,N} = 0dt - d\ln F_n(t)d\ln\left(\frac{P(t, T_n)}{C_{n,N}(t)}\right)$$

After some lengthy computation, we find

$$dF_k(t) = \sigma_k(t)F_k(t)\mu_k^{n,N}(t)dt + \sigma_k(t)F_k(t)dz_k(t) \tag{13.47}$$

where

$$\mu_k^{n,N}(t) = \sum_{j=n+1}^{N} (2 \cdot 1_{(j \le k)} - 1)\tau_j \frac{P(t, T_j)}{C_{n,N}(t)} \sum_{i=\min(k+1,j+1)}^{\max(k,j)} \frac{\tau_i \rho_{k,i} \sigma_i(t) F_i(t)}{1 + \tau_i F_i(t)}$$

the z's are Brownian motion under $Q^{n,N}$, and $1_{(j \le k)}$ is the indicator function equal to 1 if $j \le k$ and 0 otherwise.

As we can see, there are two different possibilities for pricing swaptions with market models—and thus for computing the price as

$$E^Q[D(0, T_n)\max(S_{n,N}(T_n) - K, 0)C_{n,N}(T_n)] = C_{n,N}(0)E^{n,N}[\max(S_{n,N}(T_n) - K, 0)]$$

One can price the swaption through the preceding expectation either with the LSM in (13.31) under the forward-swap measure $Q^{n,N}$ or with the LFM, also under the swap measure $Q^{n,N}$, so that the swap rate is expressed in terms of the LFM dynamics in equation (13.47). If swaptions are priced with the LSM based on the swap-rate dynamics in equation (13.31), then the swap-rate distribution is exactly lognormal and the LSM expectation reduces to Black's formula (13.33). However, if this expectation is taken with the LFM, then the computations are based on the dynamics of forward LIBOR rates. Consequently, since the forward LIBOR rates define the swap rate through the relationship in equation (13.34), then the distribution of the swap rate obtained does not have to be lognormal, which shows why, *in theory*, the LSM and LFM are not distributionally compatible. However, Brace, Dun, and Barton (1998) argue while the implied distribution of swap rates by the LFM is not lognormal, it is not far from being lognormal *in practice*.

13.11   INSTANTANEOUS AND TERMINAL CORRELATION STRUCTURES

Derivatives, such as swaptions, are priced based on expected values of quantities involving several forward rates simultaneously. Thus, their prices depend on the terminal correlation between these rates, which in turn depends on the instantaneous correlations of forward rates as well the instantaneous volatility specification. We will examine these structures in this section.

The instantaneous correlation ρ represents the degree of dependence (co-movement) between changes dF of different forward rates. For example,

$$\rho_{1,2} = \frac{dF_1(t)dF_2(t)}{\text{Std}(dF_1(t))\text{Std}(dF_2(t))}$$

where "Std" denotes standard deviation conditional on the information available at time t, shows that instantaneous correlation is related to changes in forward rates. Terminal correlation, denoted "Corr," however, represents the degree of dependence between two different forward rates at a given terminal time instant. The T_1 terminal correlation between F_2 and F_3 is the correlation at time T_1 of $F_2(T_1)$ and $F_3(T_1)$. It turns out that, in general, terminal correlation depends both on the instantaneous correlation between different rates as well as the way the total average volatility of each forward rate (caplet volatility) is distributed in instantaneous volatility. Thus, the correlation between $F_2(T_1)$ and $F_3(T_1)$ depends on the instantaneous percentage volatilities of forward rates, namely the functions, $\sigma_2(t)$ and $\sigma_3(t)$, respectively, that are used to recover the average volatilities from cap prices, $v_2(t)$ and $v_3(t)$ over $[0, T_1]$ through integration. As Rebonato (1998) has pointed out, the average volatilities can be decomposed in two different ways, "a" (σ_2^a, σ_3^a) and "b" (σ_2^b, σ_3^b), which will lead to different correlations between $F_2(T_1)$ and $F_3(T_1)$.

Moreover, the instantaneous correlation does not depend on the particular probability measure (or numeraire asset) used while the terminal correlation does. In fact, Girsanov's theorem states that the instantaneous covariance structure is invariant for all equivalent measures that can be used to express the process, so that the measure used is irrelevant. However, as we will see, it is possible to approximate terminal correlations based on "freezing part of the drift" so that the dynamics are not dependent on the particular measure chosen.

In general, the computation of terminal correlations of forward rates at a future time instant using the LFM has to be based on Monte Carlo. Suppose we are interested in computing the terminal correlation between forward rates $F_i = F(\cdot; T_{i-1}, T_i)$ and $F_j = F(\cdot; T_{j-1}, T_j)$ at time T_n, $n < i - 1 < j$, under the measure Q^η, $\eta \geq n$. We compute

$$Corr^\eta(F_i(T_n), F_j(T_n)) = \frac{E^\eta\left[(F_i(T_n) - E^\eta F_i(T_n))(F_j(T_n) - E^\eta F_j(T_n))\right]}{\sqrt{E^\eta[(F_i(T_n) - E^\eta F_i(T_n))^2]}\sqrt{E^\eta[(F_j(T_n) - E^\eta F_j(T_n))^2]}} \quad (13.48)$$

The expected values appearing in the formula can be obtained by simulating the LFM dynamics based on the Milstein dynamics given in equation (13.39), namely,

$$d \ln F_k^{\Delta t}(t + \Delta t) = \ln F_k^{\Delta t}(t) + \sigma_k(t) \sum_{j=n+1}^{k} \frac{\rho_{k,j}\tau_j\sigma_j(t)F_j^{\Delta t}(t)}{1 + \tau_j F_j^{\Delta t}(t)} \Delta t - \frac{\sigma_k^2(t)}{2}\Delta t + \sigma_k(t)\Delta_k z$$

for $k = i$ and $k = j$ so as to simulate F_i and F_j up to time T_n. It is also possible to compute terminal correlations through an approximated formula by "freezing the drift in the dynamics":

$$\bar{\mu}_k^\eta(t) = \begin{cases} \displaystyle\sum_{j=i+1}^{k} \frac{\rho_{ij}\tau_j\sigma_j(t)F_j(t)}{1 + \tau_j F_j(t)} \approx \sum_{j=i+1}^{k} \frac{\rho_{ij}\tau_j\sigma_j(t)F_j(0)}{1 + \tau_j F_j(0)} & \text{if } i < k \\[4mm] 0 & \text{if } i = k \\[4mm] \displaystyle -\sum_{j=k+1}^{i} \frac{\rho_{ij}\tau_j\sigma_j(t)F_j(t)}{1 + \tau_j F_j(t)} \approx -\sum_{j=k+1}^{i} \frac{\rho_{ij}\tau_j\sigma_j(t)F_j(0)}{1 + \tau_j F_j(0)} & \text{if } i > k \end{cases}$$

Under this approximation, the forward-rate dynamics under Q_η is

$$dF_k(t) = \bar{\mu}_k^\eta(t)\sigma_k(t)F_k(t)dt + \sigma_k(t)F_k(t)dz_k(t) \qquad (13.49)$$

which can be directly integrated. The dynamics of (13.49) under the Q^η measure for $k = i$ and $k = j$ leads to jointly normally distributed variables $\ln F_i(T_n)$ and $\ln F_j(T_n)$. Consequently, an exact evaluation of the expected value in the numerator of (13.48) can be obtained from the relationship

$$F_k(T_n) = F_k(0)\exp\left[\int_0^{T_n}\left(\bar{\mu}_k^\eta(t) - \frac{\sigma_k^2(t)}{2}\right)dt + \int_0^{T_n}\sigma_k(t)dz_k(t)\right]$$

for $k \in \{i, j\}$, and

$$F_i(T_n)F_j(T_n) = F_i(0)F_j(0)\exp\left[\int_0^{T_n}\left(\bar{\mu}_i^\eta(t) + \bar{\mu}_j^\eta(t) - \frac{\sigma_i^2(t) + \sigma_j^2(t)}{2}\right)dt + \int_0^{T_n}\sigma_i(t)dz_i(t) + \int_0^{T_n}\sigma_j(t)dz_j(t)\right]$$

Moreover, by Ito's isometry the two-dimensional random vector is jointly normally distributed as

$$
\begin{bmatrix} \int\limits_0^{T_n} \sigma_i(t)dz_i(t) \\ \int\limits_0^{T_n} \sigma_j(t)dz_j(t) \end{bmatrix} \sim N \left(\begin{bmatrix} 0 \\ 0 \end{bmatrix}, \begin{bmatrix} \int\limits_0^{T_n} \sigma_i^2(t)dt & \rho_{i,j}\int\limits_0^{T_n} \sigma_i(t)\sigma_j(t)dt \\ \rho_{i,j}\int\limits_0^{T_n} \sigma_i(t)\sigma_j(t)dt & \int\limits_0^{T_n} \sigma_j^2(t)dt \end{bmatrix} \right)
$$

Consequently, we can approximate the terminal correlation based on this distribution without having to resort to Monte Carlo simulation or without having to evaluate equation (13.48). An approximate formula for terminal correlation is given by Rebonato's terminal-correlation formula:

$$
\mathrm{Corr}(F_i(T_n),\ F_j(T_n)) \approx \frac{\rho_{i,j}\int\limits_0^{T_n} \sigma_i(t)\sigma_j(t)dt}{\sqrt{\int\limits_0^{T_1} \sigma_i^2(t)dt}\sqrt{\int\limits_0^{T_1} \sigma_j^2(t)dt}}
$$

Rebonato (1999a, 1999d) also proposes a useful structure to use for calculating instantaneous correlation. In general, an instantaneous-correlation matrix with full rank has $M(M-1)/2$ parameters where $M = N - n$ is the number of forward rates. Given that M can be a large number, Rebonato offers an approach for reducing the number of parameters and thereby offering a more parsimonious form for the correlation structure. Since ρ is a positive-definite symmetric matrix, we can express it in terms of its eigenvectors and eigenvalues:

$$
\rho = P\Lambda P'
$$

where P is a real orthogonal matrix (i.e., $P'P = PP' = I_M$) that is spanned by the eigenvectors ρ. Λ is the diagonal matrix whose entries are the (positive) eigenvalues of ρ. Since Λ is a diagonal matrix we can (using a simple Cholesky decomposition) write it as $\Lambda = A'A$ where A is a matrix whose entries are the square roots of the corresponding entries of Λ. We can set $V = PA$ so that

$$
\rho = PAA'P' = VV'
$$

Rebonato suggests that the decomposition of $\rho = VV'$ be mimicked through a suitable n-rank $M \times n$ matrix W, such that WW' is an n-rank correlation matrix, with

$n < M$ (typically $n \ll M$). As a result, we generate new n-dimensional Brownian motion w by replacing the original random shocks $dz(t)$ with $Wdw(t)$ so that we go from a noise correlation structure

$$dzdz' = \rho dt$$

to

$$Wdw(Wdw)' = Wdwdw'W' = WW'dt$$

so that the dimension of the random noise has decreased to n. Thus, we set

$$\rho^W = WW'$$

Rebonato then suggests a suitable parametric form for W, such that WW' is a possible correlation matrix. He suggests the following form for the matrix:

$$W = \begin{bmatrix} \cos\theta_{1,1} & \cos\theta_{1,2}\sin\theta_{1,1} & \sin\theta_{1,1} & \cdots & \cos\theta_{1,k}\sin\theta_{1,1} & \cdots & \sin\theta_{1,k-1} & \cdots & \sin\theta_{1,1} & \cdots & \sin\theta_{1,n-1} \\ \vdots & \vdots & \vdots & & \vdots & & \vdots & & \vdots & \\ \cos\theta_{M,1} & \cos\theta_{M,2}\sin\theta_{M,1} & \sin\theta_{M,1} & \cdots & \cos\theta_{M,k}\sin\theta_{M,1} & \cdots & \sin\theta_{M,k-1} & \cdots & \sin\theta_{M,1} & \cdots & \sin\theta_{M,n-1} \end{bmatrix}$$

With this parametric form, ρ^W is positive-semidefinite and its diagonal terms are 1's. Thus, ρ^W possible correlation matrix with $M \times (n-1)$ parameters.

As an example, consider the $n = 2$ case with M parameters. Denote w_i is the ith row of W. Then

$$w_{i,1} = \cos\theta_{i,1}, \ w_{i,2} = \sin\theta_{i,2}$$

so that

$$\rho^W_{i,j} = w_{i,1}w_{j,1} + w_{i,2}w_{j,2} = \cos(\theta_i - \theta_j)$$

The matrix consists of M parameters $\theta_1, \ldots, \theta_M$. If M is large (i.e., 20), then there can be calibration problems so that it may be necessary to subparameterize the θ's as functions of a small number, say four or five, of the parameters; that is $\theta_k = v(k)$. Such a function could be linear-exponential in form, similar to the one used for volatility in equation (13.10). However, Brigo and Mercurio note that as the number of swaption parameters becomes large, subparameterization should not be used as more free parameters are needed for calibration.[17] Moreover, to ensure positivity of adjacent rate correlations, $\rho_{i,i-1} > 0$, we can impose constraints on the correlation angles

$$\frac{\pi}{2} < \theta_i - \theta_{i-1} < -\frac{\pi}{2}$$

With a rank-two matrix, it is difficult to obtain decorrelation. Empirical evidence shows that a plot of correlation versus parameter indexes will be sigmoidal in shape since positive correlations remain high (close to 1) for adjacent forward rates and then jump to values close to 0 between short and longer maturity rates.[18] While decorrelation improves by using a higher-rank matrix, in general only when the number of factors (parameters) approaches the number of forward rates will decorrelation lead (graphically) to a straight line between correlations and indexes. Decorrelation is important for market calibration, especially for swaptions, since decorrelation among different forward rates is actually observed in the market. Consequently, to get the best fit to market data, what matters most is calibration of terminal correlation, which in turn requires fitting both instantaneous correlation *and* instantaneous volatilities. Typically, one estimates instantaneous correlation historically from time series of zero-coupon rates at a given set of maturities, and then approximates it by a lower-rank matrix. This allows the θ's to be determined.[19]

13.12   CALIBRATION TO SWAPTION PRICES

To calibrate the LFM model, we choose the instantaneous-volatility parameters—that is, a, b, c, and d in (13.10)—and the correlation parameters (i.e., θ's), that reflect the swaption prices quoted in the market. Since Black's formula is used by traders to translate prices into implied volatilities, the LFM is used to incorporate and thus calibrate to as many prices as possible. For chosen parameters, we can generate an LFM table of prices corresponding to the table of quoted at-the-money swaption volatilities. Recall that we are given the market volatilities v_{market} and that we are using the volatility form in (13.10), we can determine the Φ's from (13.35). We can subsequently try to change the parameters, a, b, c, d, θ, and related Φ's so as to match the LFM table with the market swaptions table as closely as possible. Thus, we can minimize the sum of the squares

---

[17]Brigo and Mercurio (2001c), 231.
[18]Ibid., 231.
[19]Ibid., 254.

of the differences of the corresponding swaption prices in the two tables, namely, the function

$$\min_{a,b,c,d,\theta} \sum_{i=1}^{n} \left(\frac{v_{market} - \sigma_i^2(t)}{v_{market}} \right)^2 = \min_{a,b,c,d,\theta} \sum_{i=1}^{n} \left(\frac{v_{market} - ((a(T_{i-1}-t)+d)e^{-b(T_{i-1}-t_i)})+c)^2}{v_{market}} \right)^2 \quad (13.50)$$

using a numerical iteration routine such as the Newton-Raphson method, gradient-descent method, or a minimization optimization algorithm such as Brent's method. The LFM is calibrated to the swaption market when the parameters that minimize the sum of the squared differences of the swaption prices are determined. Such a minimization is possible since the sum is a function of the parameters.

Note that while the Φ's can be determined by the cap market as functions of a, b, c, and d, parameters that are also used in the calibration to swaption prices. However, if the number of swaptions is large, four parameters are not sufficient for practical purposes.[20] In this case, a richer parametric form of the instantaneous volatility such as that in equation (13.9) should be used. Moreover, joint calibration to both the cap and swaption market is common practice for traders. Reconciling the difference in cap and swaption volatility structures is important so that joint calibration can be achieved.

For a detailed discussion of swaption calibration using actual data as well as numerical results, see Brigo and Mercurio (2001c).

13.13   CONNECTING CAPLET AND S × 1-SWAPTION VOLATILITIES

In the cap market, forward rates are mostly semiannual, whereas those used in forward-swap-rate formulas are usually annual rates. To jointly calibrate to both the cap and swaption markets, the volatilities of semiannual forward rates needs to be reconciled with the volatilities of annual forward rates. Suppose we have three time instants $0 < S < T < U$ that are each six months spaced. Furthermore, suppose we have an $S \times 1$ swaption and both S and T-expiry six-month caplets. For example, $S = 4$ years, $T = 4.5$ years, and $U = 5$ years. We will derive a relationship between the Black swaption volatility and the two Black caplet volatilities.

Consider three forward rates $F_1(t) = F(t; S, T)$, $F_2(t) = F(t; T, U)$, and $F(t) = F(t; S, U)$, where the first two forward rates are semiannual while the third rate is annual and composed of the two "inner rates." Thus, the tenor for F_1 and F_2 is 0.5 and it is 1 for F. Using the relationships between forward rates and zero-coupon bond prices, we get

$$F_1(t) = \frac{1}{0.5}\left[\frac{P(t,S)}{P(t,T)} - 1\right], \quad F_2(t) = \frac{1}{0.5}\left[\frac{P(t,T)}{P(t,U)} - 1\right]$$

---

[20]Ibid., 254.

and

$$F(t) = \frac{1}{1}\left[\frac{P(t,\ S)}{P(t,\ U)} - 1\right]$$

Note that

$$F(t) = \frac{P(t,\ S)}{P(t,\ T)}\frac{P(t,\ T)}{P(t,\ U)} - 1$$

which can be written as

$$F(t) = \frac{F_1(t) + F_2(t)}{2} + \frac{F_1(t) + F_2(t)}{4} \tag{13.51}$$

by substituting the two inner fractions of discount factors from the preceding expressions for F_1 and F_2. Subsequently, if F_1 and F_2 are lognormal, then F cannot be lognormal at the same time.

Following Brigo and Mercurio (2001c), consider the following dynamics:

$$dF_1(t) = (\ \dots\ )dt + \sigma_1(t)F_1(t)dz_1(t)$$
$$dF_2(t) = (\ \dots\ )dt + \sigma_2(t)F_2(t)dz_2(t)$$
$$dz_1dz_2 = \rho$$

for the two semiannual rates. ρ is the "infra-correlation" between the inner rates F_1 and F_2. Thus, by differentiation of equation (13.13), we get

$$dF(t) = (\ \dots\ )dt + \sigma_1(t)\left(\frac{F_1(t)}{2} + \frac{F_1(t)F_2(t)}{4}\right)dz_1(t) + \sigma_2(t)\left(\frac{F_2(t)}{2} + \frac{F_1(t)F_2(t)}{4}\right)dz_2(t)$$

Taking the variance on both sides, conditional on the information available at time t, yields

$$\sigma^2(t)F^2(t) = \sigma_1^2(t)\left(\frac{F_1(t)}{2} + \frac{F_1(t)F_2(t)}{4}\right)^2 + \sigma_2^2(t)\left(\frac{F_2(t)}{2} + \frac{F_1(t)F_2(t)}{4}\right)^2$$

$$+ 2\rho\sigma_1(t)\sigma_2(t)\left(\frac{F_1(t)}{2} + \frac{F_1(t)F_2(t)}{4}\right)\left(\frac{F_2(t)}{2} + \frac{F_1(t)F_2(t)}{4}\right)$$

where $\sigma(t)$ is the percentage volatility of F. Set

$$u_1(t) = \frac{1}{F(t)}\left(\frac{F_1(t)}{2} + \frac{F_1(t)F_2(t)}{4}\right) \text{ and } u_2(t) = \frac{1}{F(t)}\left(\frac{F_2(t)}{2} + \frac{F_1(t)F_2(t)}{4}\right)$$

so that

$$\sigma^2(t) = u_1^2(t)\sigma_1^2(t) + u_2^2(t)\sigma_2^2(t) + 2\rho\sigma_1(t)\sigma_2(t)u_1(t)u_2(t) \qquad (13.52)$$

We can achieve a deterministic approximation to (13.48) by freezing all F's (and thus u's) at their time-zero value:

$$\sigma_{approx}^2(t) \approx u_1^2(0)\sigma_1^2(t) + u_2^2(0)\sigma_2^2(t) + 2\rho\sigma_1(t)\sigma_2(t)u_1(0)u_2(0) \qquad (13.53)$$

Since F is the (one-period) swap rate underlying the $S \times 1$ swaption, then the (squared) Black's swaption volatility is

$$
\begin{aligned}
v_{\text{Black}}^2 &\approx \frac{1}{S}\int_0^S \sigma_{approx}^2(t)dt \\
&= \frac{1}{S}\left[u_1^2(0)\int_0^S \sigma_1^2(t)dt + u_2^2(0)\int_0^S \sigma_2^2(t)dt + 2\rho u_1(0)u_2(0)\int_0^S \sigma_1(t)\sigma_2(t)dt \right]
\end{aligned}
\qquad (13.54)
$$

Since S is exactly the expiry of the semiannual rate $F_1(t)$, then the first integral can be computed directly as a market caplet volatility,

$$\frac{1}{S}\int_0^S \sigma_1^2(t)dt = v_{S\text{-}caplet}^2$$

The second and third integrals cannot be directly computed since they require some parametric assumption on the instantaneous volatility structure rates. The simplest solution is to assume forward rates have constant volatilities. Thus, the second integral can be computed as

$$\frac{1}{S}\int_0^S \sigma_2^2(t)dt = \frac{1}{S}\int_0^S v_{T\text{-}caplet}^2\, dt = v_{T\text{-}caplet}^2$$

and third one can be computed as

$$\frac{1}{S}\int_0^S \sigma_1(t)\sigma_2(t)dt = \frac{1}{S}\int_0^S v_{S\text{-}caplet}v_{T\text{-}caplet}\, dt = v_{S\text{-}caplet}v_{T\text{-}caplet}$$

so that the approximate Black volatility assuming constant volatility is

$$v_{\text{Black}}^2 \approx u_1^2(0)v_{S\text{-}caplet}^2 + u_2^2(0)v_{T\text{-}caplet}^2 + 2\rho u_1(0)u_2(0)v_{S\text{-}caplet}v_{T\text{-}caplet} \qquad (13.55)$$

Certainly, many other volatility term structures are possible. However, equation (13.55) is simple and it is one of the few that can be computed directly from market quantities. De Jong, Driessen, and Pelsser (1999) examined empirical data on forward rate volatility term structures. They found that flat volatilities in forward rates tend to overprice swaptions. Thus, the approximated formula in (13.53) gives volatilities that are slightly larger than actual market volatilities. This can be seen by looking at the third integral. By the Schwartz inequality, we have

$$\int_0^S \sigma_1(t)\sigma_2(t)dt \le \sqrt{\int_0^S \sigma_1^2(t)dt}\sqrt{\int_0^S \sigma_2^2(t)dt} \approx S v_{S\text{-}caplet} v_{T\text{-}caplet}$$

so in the case of positive correlation, equation (13.53) overestimates volatility with respect to (13.52).[21]

13.14   INCLUDING CAPLET SMILE IN LFM

Black's formula, the standard in the cap market, is consistent with the LFM, in that the expected value is the discounted caplet payoff under the related forward measure when the forward-rate dynamics are given by the LFM. Consider the price at time 0 of a T_2-maturity caplet resetting at time T_1 $(0 < T_1 < T_2)$ with strike X and a notional amount of 1. Let τ be the tenor (year fraction) between T_1 and T_2. The caplet pays off

$$\tau\max(F(T_1; T_1, T_2) - X, 0)$$

at time T_2. Thus its value at time 0 is

$$P(0, T_2)\tau E_0^2[\max(F(T_1; T_1, T_2) - X, 0)]$$

where the expectation is to take at time 0 under the T_2-forward measure so that F is a martingale. Thus, the dynamics for F, taken under the T_2-forward measure, follow the lognormal LFM dynamics

$$dF(t; T_1, T_2) = \sigma_2(t)F(t; T_1, T_2)dz(t) \tag{13.56}$$

---

[21]Ibid., 257.

Given the lognormality of the T_1-marginal distribution of this dynamics, the expectation results in Black's formula:

$$Cpl^{Black}(0, T_1, T_2, X) = P(0, T_2)\tau Black(X, F_2(0), v_2(T_1))$$

$$v_2(T_1)^2 = \int_0^{T_1} \sigma_2^2(t)dt$$

The average volatility of the forward rate in $[0, T_1]$, namely,

$$v_2(T_1)/\sqrt{T_1}$$

does not depend on the strike X of the option. Therefore, the strike price should not affect the volatility of the forward rate and we would expect two caplets with the same expiry-maturity, $T_1 - T_2$, and same underlying forward rates, but different strikes, to have the same underlying volatility. However, this is not the case. Each caplet market price requires its own Black market volatility $v_2^{market}(T_1, X)$. Thus, two different volatilities, $v_2(T_1, X_1)$ and $v_2(T_1, X_2)$, are required to match the observed market prices if one is using Black's formula:

$$Cpl^{Black}(0, T_1, T_2, X_1) = P(0, T_2)\tau Black(X_1, F_2(0), v_2^{market}(T_1, X_1))$$
$$Cpl^{Black}(0, T_1, T_2, X_2) = P(0, T_2)\tau Black(X_2, F_2(0), v_2^{market}(T_1, X_2))$$

The curve

$$X \to v_2^{market}(T_1, X)/\sqrt{T_1}$$

is known as the volatility smile of the caplet. If Black's formula were consistent along different strikes, one would expect this curve to be flat. However, the curve often exhibits "smiley" or "skewed" shapes. By skew, it is meant that for a fixed maturity, low-strike implied volatilities are higher than high-strike implied volatilities. A smile shape is meant to characterize volatility structures where, for a fixed maturity, the volatility has a minimum value around the value of the underlying forward rate.

Since only a fixed number of strikes are quoted in the market, the remaining points of

$$X \to v_2^{market}(T_1, X)/\sqrt{T_1}$$

can be found through interpolation. Suppose a few market caplet prices for expiry

T_1 and for a set of strikes X_i is given. By interpolation, it is possible to construct a function

$$X \to Cpl^{market}(T_1, X)/\sqrt{T_1}$$

by obtaining a caplet price for every other possible strike X. If the price corresponds to an expectation, then we have

$$Cpl^{market}(0, T_1, T_2, X) = P(0, T_2)\tau E_0^{T_2}[\max(F(T_1; T_1, T_2) - X, 0)]$$

$$= P(0, T_2)\tau \int_0^\infty \max(y - X, 0)p_2(y)dy \qquad (13.57)$$

where p_2 is the probability density function of $F_2(T_1)$ under the T_2-forward measure. If Black's formula were consistent with the distribution observed in the market, the probability density would be lognormal, coming, for example, from the dynamics in (13.56). However, since this is not the case, we must recover the density from some other method. Breeden and Litzenberger (1978) suggest differentiating (13.57) twice with respect to the strike X, so that

$$\frac{\partial Cpl^{market}(0, T_1, T_2, X)}{\partial X^2} = P(0, T_2)\tau p_2(X) \qquad (13.58)$$

Thus, differentiating the interpolated-prices curve, it is possible to find the density p_2 of the forward rate at time T_1 that is compatible with the given interpolated prices. However, the method of interpolation may interfere with the density recovery since a second derivative of the interpolated curve is involved.[22]
Alternative dynamics can be used to recover p_2. Consider

$$dF(t; T_1, T_2) = v(t, F(t; T_1, T_2))dz(t) \qquad (13.59)$$

under the T_2-forward measure where v can either be deterministic—that is, $v(t, F) = \sigma_2(t)F^\gamma$ (CEV model) where $0 \leq \gamma \leq 1$ and $\sigma_2(t)$ is itself deterministic—or be a stochastic function of $F(t; T_1, T_2)$—that is, $v(t, F) = \xi(t)F$ where ξ follows a second SDE. In the former case, we would be using a local-volatility model whereas in the latter case we would be using a stochastic-volatility model. In general, $v(t, \cdot)$ must be flexible enough for the curve $X \to v(X)$ to resemble or fit the corresponding market volatility curve or so that the chosen alternative forward rate

---

[22]Ibid., 268.

dynamics to equation (13.56) are as compatible as possible with density p_2 associated with market prices. This can be accomplished by calibrating directly the prices implied by the alternative model in (13.59) to the market prices $Cpl^{market}(0, T_1, T_2, X_i)$ given the observed set of strikes X_i. Equivalently, one can fit the model implied volatilities to the quoted market implied volatilities $v_2^{market}(T_1, X_i)$ for the observed strikes.

Following Brigo and Mercurio (2001c), we list the steps necessary to generate a volatility smile to be fitted to the market smile using the alternative dynamics in (13.59).

Step 1. Set the strike X to a starting value.

Step 2. Compute the model caplet price:

$$Cpl(X, T_1, T_2) = \tau P(0, T_2) E_0^{T_2}[\max(F(T_1; T_1, T_2) - X, 0)]$$

Step 3. Invert Black's formula for the strike by solving:

$$Cpl(X, T_1, T_2) = \tau P(0, T_2) \text{Black}(X_1, F_2(0), v(X)\sqrt{T_1})$$

in $v(X)$, thus obtaining the (average) model implied volatility $v(X)$.

Step 4. Change X and restart from step 2.

By acting on the coefficient $v(t, \cdot)$ in the dynamics given in (13.55), the four steps will eventually lead to model implied volatilities $v(\hat{X}_i)$ corresponding to the observed strikes to be made as close as possible to the corresponding market volatilities

$$v_2^{market}(T_1, X_i)/\sqrt{T_1}$$

Thus, a smile or skew will be generated. However, the problem becomes one of finding an implied-volatility surface since we have a caplet volatility surface for each considered expiry. One approach is to assume (alternative) explicit dynamics for the forward-rate process that generate smiles and skews. The CEV model of Cox (1975) and Cox and Ross (1976) discussed in section 7.6, or the displaced diffusion model of Rubinstein (1983), follow this approach. However, these models do not provide sufficient flexibility to properly calibrate the entire volatility surface. A second approach, formulated by Breeden and Litzenberger (1978) and developed upon by Dupire (1994, 1997) and Derman and Kani (1994, 1998), is based on the assumption of a continuum of traded strikes. However, the approach has the problem that it is necessary to smoothly interpolate option prices

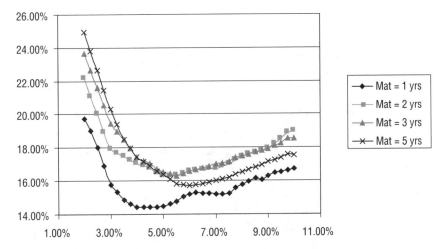

FIGURE 13.2   U.S. Market
Source: R. Rebonato and M. Joshi, 2002, "A Stochastic-Volatility, Displaced-Diffusion Extension of the LIBOR Market Model," see www.rebonato.com/StochasticVolatilityBGMFin.pdf; R. Rebonato, 2002, *Modern Pricing of Interest Rate Derivatives: The LIBOR Market Model and Beyond*, Princeton: Princeton Univ. Press. Used with permission from Ricardo Rebonato.

between successive strikes in order to differentiate them twice with respect to the strike.[23]

In general, since there are infinitely many curves connecting finitely many points, the problem of finding a distribution that consistently prices all quoted options is largely undetermined. One solution is to assume a particular parametric distribution depending on several time-dependent parameters and then find forward-rate dynamics consistent with the chosen parametric density. This solution is adopted by Brigo and Mercurio (2000a), who propose the lognormal-mixture approach, as discussed in section 7.7. The interested reader should see Brigo and Mercurio (2001c) for a discussion of its use in pricing caplets and recovering smile-shaped caplet volatility surfaces implied by option prices.

13.15   STOCHASTIC EXTENSION OF LIBOR MARKET MODEL

Figures 13.2, 13.3, and 13.4, taken from Rebonato and Joshi (2002), show how caplet smiles differ across markets in the U.S., U.K., and European markets, respectively, in August 2000.

---

[23]Ibid., 270.

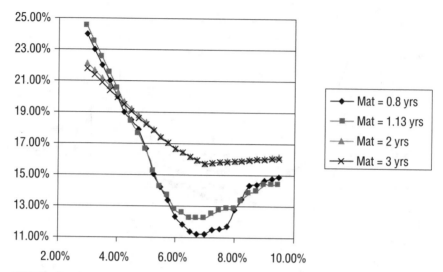

FIGURE 13.3 U.K. Market
Source: R. Rebonato and M. Joshi, 2002, "A Stochastic-Volatility, Displaced-Diffusion Extension of the LIBOR Market Model," see www.rebonato.com/StochasticVolatilityBGMFin.pdf; R. Rebonato, 2002, *Modern Pricing of Interest Rate Derivatives: The LIBOR Market Model and Beyond*, Princeton: Princeton Univ. Press. Used with permission from Ricardo Rebonato.

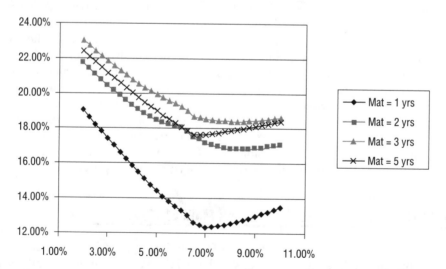

FIGURE 13.4 European Market
Source: R. Rebonato and M. Joshi, 2002, "A Stochastic-Volatility, Displaced-Diffusion Extension of the LIBOR Market Model," see www.rebonato.com/StochasticVolatilityBGMFin.pdf; R. Rebonato, 2002, *Modern Pricing of Interest Rate Derivatives: The LIBOR Market Model and Beyond*, Princeton: Princeton Univ. Press. Used with permission from Ricardo Rebonato.

As seen in these graphs, the smiles, especially in the U.K. and European markets, exhibit caplet implied volatility smiles that deviate from the typical near-symmetric smiles once seen in the markets. Over the past few years, to an increasing extent, the LIBOR market model has not priced consistently with the market in plain-vanilla interest rate options. Approximately around 1996, the implied volatility for caplets exhibited a monotonically decreasing shape and after the second half of 1998 assumed more of a hockey-stick shape, especially in the European markets. Consequently, nonflat but deterministic smile surfaces, as implied by the extended LMM, where CEV and displaced diffusion features are incorporated into the original LMM model, were no longer suitable to capture market dynamics. Thus, there has been a deviation away from lognormal behavior. Consequently, one can no longer determine implied volatilities by taking the root mean square of the instantaneous volatility as in equation (13.12) and plugging them into Black's formula since it is the wrong number to obtain the correct price.

Rebonato and Joshi (2002) have proposed a stochastic extension of the LMM that gives more flexibility to capture observed changes in the market structures of volatilities. The stochastic extended LMM model is given as

$$d(F_k(t) + \alpha) = \mu_k^\alpha(\{F\}, t)(F_k(t) + \alpha)dt + \sigma_k(t, T_k)(F_k(t) + \alpha)dz_k \qquad (13.60)$$

where the volatility structure is a stochastic version of equation (13.10),

$$\sigma_k(t) = \psi(T_{k-1} - t; a(t), b(t), c(t), d(t)) = (a(T_{k-1} - t) + b(t))e^{-c(T_{k-1}-t)} + d(t) \qquad (13.61)$$

where

$$da(t) = v_a(a - \eta_a)dt + \sigma_a dz_a$$

$$db(t) = v_b(b - \eta_b)dt + \sigma_b dz_b \qquad (13.62)$$

$$d\ln c(t) = v_c(\ln c - \eta_c)dt + \sigma_c dz_c$$

$$d\ln d(t) = v_d(\ln d - \eta_d)dt + \sigma_d dz_d$$

and the v_i's and η_i's, $i = a, b, c, d$, are the reversion speeds and reversion levels, respectively, of a, b, $\ln c$, and $\ln d$. Moreover, it is assumed that the Brownian motions are uncorrelated between the coefficients (i.e., $dz_i dz_j = 0$, $i, j = a, b, c, d, i \neq j$) and between the forward rates and the coefficients (i.e., $dz_i dz_j = 0$, $j = a, b, c, d$). σ_a, σ_b, σ_c, and σ_d are the coefficient volatilities. Figure 13.5, from Rebonato and Joshi (2002), shows instantaneous volatility curves when the volatility parameters are all stochastic and given by the values in Table 13.2.

The deterministic curve is given as a reference. The instantaneous volatility curves when only the parameter d is stochastic are shown in Figure 13.6.

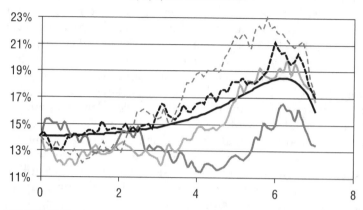

FIGURE 13.5   Instantaneous Volatility Curves
Source: R. Rebonato and M. Joshi, 2002, "A Stochastic-Volatility, Displaced-Diffusion Extension of the LIBOR Market Model," see www.rebonato.com/StochasticVolatilityBGMFin.pdf; R. Rebonato, 2002, *Modern Pricing of Interest Rate Derivatives: The LIBOR Market Model and Beyond*, Princeton: Princeton Univ. Press. Used with permission from Ricardo Rebonato.

The instantaneous terminal correlation of the forward rates is assumed to be of the form $\rho_{i,j} = e^{\beta(t_i - t_j)}$ and σ_k is the percentage volatility of $F_k(t) + \alpha$. The drift is assumed to be displaced diffusion so that the no-arbitrage percentage drift coefficients are

$$\mu_i^\alpha(t) = \begin{cases} \displaystyle\sum_{j=k+1}^{i} \frac{\rho_{ij}\tau_j\sigma_i^\alpha(t)\sigma_j^\alpha(F_j(t)+\alpha)}{1+\tau_j F_j(t)} & \text{if } k < i \\[4mm] 0 & \text{if } i = k \\[4mm] -\displaystyle\sum_{j=i+1}^{k} \frac{\rho_{ij}\tau_j\sigma_i^\alpha(t)\sigma_j^\alpha(t)(F_j(t)+\alpha)}{1+\tau_j F_j(t)} & \text{if } k > i \end{cases} \qquad (13.63)$$

TABLE 13.2   Stochastic Values

Parameter	Reversion Speed	Reversion Level	Volatility
$a = 0.02$	$v_a = 0.1$	$\eta_a = 0.02$	$\sigma_a = 0.008$
$b = 0.1$	$v_b = 0.1$	$\eta_b = 0.1$	$\sigma_b = 0.016$
$c = 1$	$v_c = 0.1$	$\eta_c = 0$	$\sigma_c = 0.12$
$d = 0.14$	$v_d = 0.1$	$\eta_d = -1.96611$	$\sigma_d = 0.1$

Source: R. Rebonato and M. Joshi, 2002, "A Stochastic-Volatility, Displaced-Diffusion Extension of the LIBOR Market Model," see www.rebonato.com/Stochastic VolatilityBGMFin.pdf; R. Rebonato, 2002, *Modern Pricing of Interest Rate Derivatives: The LIBOR Market Model and Beyond*, Princeton: Princeton Univ. Press. Used with permission from Ricardo Rebonato.

d stochastic

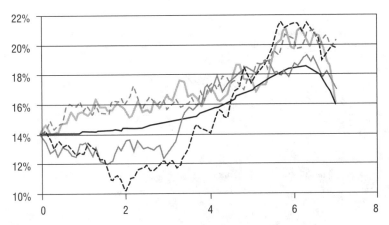

FIGURE 13.6 Instantaneous Volatility Curves
Source: R. Rebonato and M. Joshi, 2002, "A Stochastic-Volatility, Displaced-Diffusion Extension of the LIBOR Market Model," see www.rebonato.com/StochasticVolatilityBGMFin.pdf; R. Rebonato, 2002, *Modern Pricing of Interest Rate Derivatives: The LIBOR Market Model and Beyond*, Princeton: Princeton Univ. Press. Used with permission from Ricardo Rebonato.

so that equations (13.60), (13.61), (13.62), and (13.63) and the assumptions of uncorrelated Brownian motions given earlier completely characterize the no-arbitrage evolution of the spanning forward rates. It is important to note, however, that the choices for the drifts of the volatility parameters are not no-arbitrage conditions as any drift will result in a nonarbitragable price provided that the volatility of the parameter is nonzero.[24] The drifts are chosen to provide a realistic evolution of the term structure of volatilities. The extended LIBOR framework fits the stochastic volatility coefficients so that evolution of the term structure of volatilities fits the observed behavior in the market. Rebonato and Joshi show that their proposed method can exactly price ATM caplets, provides a good fit to the observed volatility smile surface, and produces a desirable and well-behaved time-homogenous evolution of the term structure of volatilities.

As an example, Rebonato and Joshi (2002) generate the implied volatility surface of (Great) British Pound (GBP) forward rates over a period of three months in 1996 as shown in Figure 13.7.

They then calibrate their stochastic, jump-diffusion model to fit across strikes to the market implied volatilities ("market" curve), obtained with the volatility parameters *a*, *b*, *c*, and *d* stochastic ("all stochastic" curve), and with just *d* stochastic ("fit" curve), for different maturities ranging from one to eight years. The one-year, three-year, five-year, and eight-year maturity calibrated curves are shown

---

[24]Rebonato and Joshi (2002).

Historical Implied Volatility (GBP)

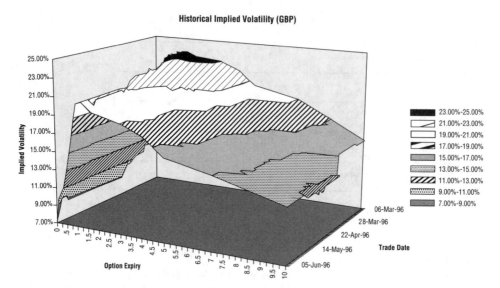

FIGURE 13.7   Historical Implied Volatility of (Great) British Pound
Source: R. Rebonato and M. Joshi, 2002, "A Stochastic-Volatility, Displaced-Diffusion Extension of
the LIBOR Market Model," see www.rebonato.com/StochasticVolatilityBGMFin.pdf; R. Rebonato,
2002, *Modern Pricing of Interest Rate Derivatives: The LIBOR Market Model and Beyond*, Princeton:
Princeton Univ. Press. Used with permission from Ricardo Rebonato.

in Figures 13.8, 13.9, 13.10, and 13.11. As the graphs show, the "all stochastic"
model gives a fit closer to the market implied volatilities curve than the "fit" model
and the convergence is better the longer the maturity.

To calibrate the model to caplets for instance, Rebonato and Joshi modify
equation (13.50) to deal with stochastic instantaneous volatilities as follows.
They note that the minimization in (13.50) does not exactly produce the market
caplet prices so that the instantaneous volatility is computed by imposing equation (13.17) so that the multiplicative correction factor Φ_i's can be determined.
Then they subdivide the interval from today to the expiry of the ith caplet $[0, T_i]$,
$i = 0, \ldots, N$ using sufficiently small step sizes Δs_r, $r = 1, \ldots, N$, to obtain accurate sampling of the volatility path. The stochastic volatility coefficients a, b, c,
and d are evolved over each of these steps. For each step, an element of the marginal variance matrix is computed $v_{r,i}$:

$$v_{r,i} = ((a(s_r) + b(s_r))\exp(-c(s_r)(T_i - s_r)) + d(s_r))^2 \, \Delta s_r \qquad (13.64)$$

Then a forward-rate specific variance vector $\mathbf{v_i}$ is formed by summing the elements
$v_{r,i}$, $r = 1, \ldots, N$:

$$\mathbf{v_i} = \sum_{r=1}^{N} v_{r,i} \qquad (13.65)$$

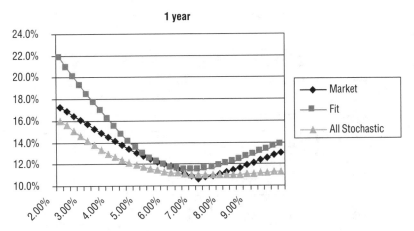

FIGURE 13.8 One-Year Caplet Volatility Calibration
Source: R. Rebonato and M. Joshi, 2002, "A Stochastic-Volatility, Displaced-Diffusion Extension of the LIBOR Market Model," see www.rebonato.com/StochasticVolatilityBGMFin.pdf; R. Rebonato, 2002, *Modern Pricing of Interest Rate Derivatives: The LIBOR Market Model and Beyond*, Princeton: Princeton Univ. Press. Used with permission from Ricardo Rebonato.

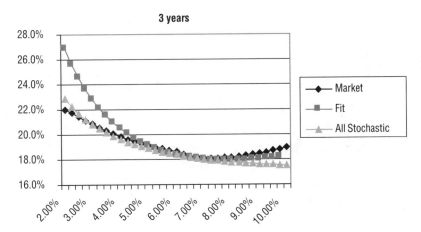

FIGURE 13.9 Three-Year Caplet Volatility Calibration
Source: R. Rebonato and M. Joshi, 2002, "A Stochastic-Volatility, Displaced-Diffusion Extension of the LIBOR Market Model," see www.rebonato.com/StochasticVolatility BGMFin.pdf; R. Rebonato, 2002, *Modern Pricing of Interest Rate Derivatives: The LIBOR Market Model and Beyond*, Princeton: Princeton Univ. Press. Used with permission from Ricardo Rebonato.

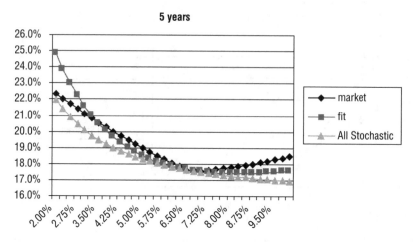

FIGURE 13.10 Five-Year Caplet Volatility Calibration
Source: R. Rebonato and M. Joshi, 2002, "A Stochastic-Volatility, Displaced-Diffusion Extension of the LIBOR Market Model," see www.rebonato.com/StochasticVolatility BGMFin.pdf; R. Rebonato, 2002, *Modern Pricing of Interest Rate Derivatives: The LIBOR Market Model and Beyond*, Princeton: Princeton Univ. Press. Used with permission from Ricardo Rebonato.

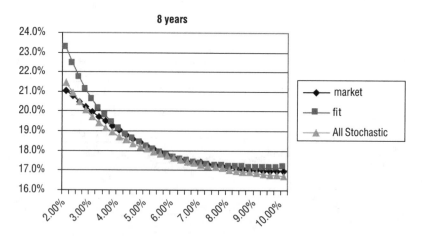

FIGURE 13.11 Eight-Year Caplet Volatility Calibration
Source: R. Rebonato and M. Joshi, 2002, "A Stochastic-Volatility, Displaced-Diffusion Extension of the LIBOR Market Model," see www.rebonato.com/StochasticVolatility BGMFin.pdf; R. Rebonato, 2002, *Modern Pricing of Interest Rate Derivatives: The LIBOR Market Model and Beyond*, Princeton: Princeton Univ. Press. Used with permission from Ricardo Rebonato.

Similarly, for a given step, we can generate a forward-rate marginal covariance matrix C_l^f. More formally, the (j, k)th entry of C_l^f is given by

$$C_l^f(j, k) = ((a_{s(l)} + b_{s(l)}(t_j - s_l))\exp(-c_{s(l)}(t_j - s_l) + d_{s(l)}) \cdot$$
$$(a_{s(l)} + b_{s(l)}(t_k - s_l))\exp(-c_{s(l)}(t_k - s_l) + d_{s(l)})\rho_{jk}\Delta s_l$$

After forming a covariance matrix C^f by summing C_l^f for $l = 1, \ldots, N$, we can then compute the pseudo-square root, A^f, of C^f by a Cholesky decomposition; that is, we determine the lower triangular matrix A^f such that $C^f = A^f (A^f)'$. Consequently, we can then evolve the forward rates across the interval $[T_r, T_{r+1}]$ according to

$$\log F_j(T_{r+1} + \alpha) = \log F_j(T_r + \alpha) + \mu_j(T_r)(T_{r+1} - T_r) + \sum_{i,j} a_{i,j} z_j \qquad (13.66)$$

where z_j are i.i.d. standard normal deviates. We can then improve our computations by use the predictor-corrector approximation in equation (13.45) on a path-by-path basis. The advantage of the technique is that only the volatility process needs to be small stepped, and the only loss of accuracy exists in the approximation to the drifts, which already exists in the nonstochastic volatility case.[25]

The ith caplet is priced by computing the root-mean squared volatility out to its expiry and using it in the displaced diffusion Black formula, $\text{Black}(T_i, v_i)$. Given the independence between the Brownian increments of the volatility coefficients and the forward rates, the price, c_i of the ith caplet can be computed by

$$c_i(T_i) = \int \text{Black}(T_i, v_i)\phi(v_i)dv_i \qquad (13.67)$$

which is an adaptation of a result by Hull and White (1987). However, the density $\phi(v_i)$ is not known analytically (given it is not lognormal), though it can be sampled efficiently using low-discrepancy sequences.[26] Finally, Rebonato and Joshi replicate the minimization procedure over all parameters used in the deterministic volatility case, but with quoted market caplet prices, c_i^{market}, for all available maturities and strikes:

$$\min_\theta \sum_{i=1}^N (c_i(T_i) - c_i^{market}(T_i))^2$$

As with in the deterministic case, the agreement between the market and the model will not be exact. In order to exactly match the model to market at-the-money

---

[25]Ibid., 18.
[26]Ibid., 18.

prices, the result that the Black function is almost exactly linear in volatility for the at-the-money strike (Wilmott (1998)) is used, which holds in a displaced-diffusion framework. Let $\Phi(T_i)$ be the ratio between the market and the model price (i.e., c_i^{market}/c_i). Given the linearity property for ATM strikes, we can use an alternative instantaneous volatility process $\bar{\sigma}_{inst}$ for the ith forward rate given by

$$\bar{\sigma}_{inst}(t,\, T_i) = \Phi(T_i)\sigma_{inst}(t) = \frac{c_i^{market}}{c_i}\left(\left(a(T_{i-1}-t)+b(t)\right)e^{-c(T_{i-1}-t)}+d(t)\right) \quad (13.68)$$

Thus, for any given path, the root-mean squared volatility for $\bar{\sigma}_{inst}$ will simply be equal to $\Phi(T_i)$ times the root-mean squared volatility for σ_{inst}. Given the approximate, but highly accurate, linearity, the price implied by the Monte Carlo simulation will also be multiplied by the same scaling factor, thus ensuring correct pricing for each at-the-money caplet.[27] The numerical implementation is quite efficient as only one simulation is used to price all the caplets. For a given volatility path, all strikes are calculated, and different stopping times along a path are used for different maturities.

European swaptions can also be quickly numerically priced in a similar manner to caplets using the displaced diffusion LIBOR model. Denote the instantaneous volatility of the kth swaption when the displacement of the diffusion has a value of α by $\sigma_{S(k)}(t)$. Let $n(k)$ denote the number of forward rates underlying the kth swap and let S_k be the kth swap rate. Then using a version of Rebonato's swap volatility approximation in equation (13.40),

$$\begin{aligned}
\sigma_{S(k)}^2(T)T &\cong \sum_{j=1}^{n(k)}\sum_{i=1}^{n(k)}(F_i(0)+\alpha)(F_j(0)+\alpha)\frac{\partial S_k}{\partial F_i}\frac{\partial S_k}{\partial F_j}\frac{1}{(S_k+\alpha)^2}\int_0^T\sigma_i(s)\sigma_j(s)\rho_{ij}ds \\
&= \sum_{j=1}^{n(k)}\sum_{i=1}^{n(k)}z_{ik}z_{jk}\int_0^T\sigma_i(s)\sigma_j(s)\rho_{ij}ds
\end{aligned} \quad (13.69)$$

where z_{ik} is given by

$$z_{ik} = \frac{\partial S_k}{\partial F_i}\frac{(F_i(0)+\alpha)}{(S_k+\alpha)}$$

which will be zero when $k < i$.

Pricing the swaption is done as follows. Like calibrating caplets with the model, we divide the time interval $[0,T]$ into N small steps Δs_r, $r = 1, \ldots, N$, gen-

---

[27]Rebonato and Jackel (2000), 19.

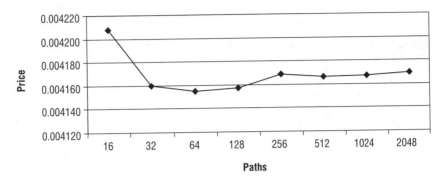

FIGURE 13.12 1×1 Swaption

Source: R. Rebonato and M. Joshi, 2002, "A Stochastic-Volatility, Displaced-Diffusion Extension of the LIBOR Market Model," see www.rebonato.com/StochasticVolatility BGMFin.pdf; R. Rebonato, 2002, *Modern Pricing of Interest Rate Derivatives: The LIBOR Market Model and Beyond*, Princeton: Princeton Univ. Press. Used with permission from Ricardo Rebonato.

erate a single path, evolving the volatility coefficients a, b, c, and d over each step. We can then generate the forward-rate covariance matrix of elements

$$C_l^f(j, k) = ((a_{s(l)} + b_{s(l)}(t_j - s_l))\exp(-c_{s(l)}(t_j - s_l) + d_{s(l)}) \cdot$$
$$(a_{s(l)} + b_{s(l)}(t_k - s_l))\exp(-c_{s(l)}(t_k - s_l) + d_{s(l)})\rho_{jk}\Delta s_l$$

which can then be used to price the swaption using the Black formula for swaptions using the input volatility given by equation (13.68). As a result, the swaption price is associated with a particular generated volatility path and the price under the influence of stochastic volatility is simply obtained by Monte Carlo averaging, as in the case of caplets.[28] This approach produces highly accurate swaption prices. Figures 13.12 and 13.13, from Rebonato and Joshi (2002), show the convergence of 1×1 swaption and 10×10 swaption as a function of the number of simulation paths.

Rebonato and Joshi (2002) also provide details for calibrating to co-terminal swaptions using the displaced-diffusion LIBOR model as well as give numerical results from using the calibration procedure.

---

[28]Rebonato and Joshi (2002), 20.

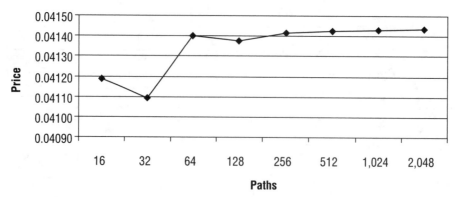

FIGURE 13.13 10×10 Swaption
Source: R. Rebonato and M. Joshi, 2002, "A Stochastic-Volatility, Displaced-Diffusion Extension of the LIBOR Market Model," see www.rebonato.com/StochasticVolatility BGMFin.pdf; R. Rebonato, 2002, *Modern Pricing of Interest Rate Derivatives: The LIBOR Market Model and Beyond*, Princeton: Princeton Univ. Press. Used with permission from Ricardo Rebonato.

13.16   COMPUTING GREEKS IN FORWARD LIBOR MODELS

Price sensitivities are important in any model for pricing derivatives because the sensitivities determine the trading strategy for hedging the derivative. The sensitivities are more commonly known as Greeks and in the LIBOR market model can be computed using Monte Carlo methods or likelihood ratio methods (LRMs). The difference between the two methods is in the dependence of the parameter under consideration (i.e., the initial value of a price or interest rate), for sensitivity estimation. In Monte Carlo methods, the dependence of the parameter is made in the underlying stochastic process via sample paths, which lead to estimators that differentiate the paths of the process, known as *pathwise* derivatives.[29] The LRM puts the dependence in the probability measure and leads to estimators based on differentiating probability densities. The following discussion is based on the work of Glasserman and Zhao (1999).

Assume a given tenor structure that is a finite set of dates $0 = T_0 < T_1 < \ldots < T_N < T_{N+1}$, representing maturities spaced three months for six months apart. We also assume that the day-count fractions $\delta_i = T_{i+1} - T_i$, $i = 0, \ldots, N$, are all equal to a fixed δ (i.e., $\delta = 0.25$ years). However, in practice, day-count conventions lead to intervals of different sizes. We assume the index of the next tenor date at time t satis-

---

[29]Glasserman and Zhao (1999).

fies $T_{\eta(t)-1} < t \leq T_{\eta(t)}$ where $\eta: (0, T_{n+1}] \to [1, \ldots, N + 1]$ is left-continuous. The forward LIBOR rate at time t over the accrual period $[T_i, T_{i+1}], t \leq T_i$ is

$$F_i(t) = \frac{1}{\delta}\left(\frac{B_i(t)}{B_{i+1}(t)} - 1 \right), \quad i = 1, \ldots, N \tag{13.70}$$

Consider a caplet with strike K paying $\delta\max((F_n(T_n) - K), 0)$ at time T_{n+1}. Using a change of measure, and thus a change of numeraire, using discount bond prices $P_n(T_i)$, where at a tenor date T_i the price of any bond P_n, $n > i$, that has not matured is given by

$$P_n(T_i) = \prod_{j=1}^{n-1} \frac{1}{1 + \delta F_j(T_i)}$$

we know that the time 0 price is

$$C_n(0) = P_1(0)\delta E\left[\max((F_n(T_n) - K), 0)\prod_{i=1}^{n} \frac{1}{1 + \delta F_i(T_n)} \right] \tag{13.71}$$

The expectation can be evaluated using Black's formula. To compute the delta sensitivity measure $\partial C_n(0)/\partial F_k(0)$, we compute the sensitivity of the expectation in equation (13.71) with respect to $F_k(0)$. Provided derivative and expectation can be interchanged, we have

$$\frac{\partial}{\partial F_k(0)} E\left[\max((F_n(T_n) - K), 0)\prod_{i=1}^{n} \frac{1}{1 + \delta F_i(T_n)} \right]$$

$$= E\left[\frac{\partial}{\partial F_n(0)} \left(\max((F_n(T_n) - K), 0)\prod_{i=1}^{n} \frac{1}{1 + \delta F_i(T_n)} \right) \right] \tag{13.72}$$

From the chain rule we have

$$\frac{\partial}{\partial F_n(0)} \left(\max((F_n(T_n) - K), 0)\prod_{i=1}^{n} \frac{1}{1 + \delta F_i(T_n)} \right)$$

$$= \sum_{i=1}^{n} \frac{\partial}{\partial F_i(T_n)} \left(\max((F_n(T_n) - K), 0)\prod_{i=1}^{n} \frac{1}{1 + \delta F_i(T_n)} \right) \frac{\partial F_i(T_n)}{\partial F_k(0)}$$

With probability 1, we have

$$\frac{\partial}{\partial F_k(0)} \max(F_n(T_n) - K, 0) = \mathbf{1}\{F_n(T_n) > K\} \frac{\partial F_n(T_n)}{\partial F_k(0)}$$

where $\mathbf{1}$ is the indicator function equal to 1 when the event in braces is true and 0 otherwise.

The delta sensitivity measure can be generalized for estimating any payoff g that is a Lipschitz continuous function of the forward LIBOR rates and arbitrary dates t_i

$$\frac{\partial}{\partial F_k(0)} E\big[g(F_1(t_1), \ldots, F_N(t_N))\big] \tag{13.73}$$

By bringing in the derive inside the expectation, we generate a (continuous) pathwise delta estimator:

$$\sum_{n=1}^{N}\left\{\frac{\partial}{\partial F_n(t_n)} g(F_1(t_1), \ldots, F_N(t_N))\right\}\Delta_{nk}(t_n)$$

where

$$\Delta_{nk}(t) = \frac{\partial F_n(t)}{\partial F_k(0)}, \; n, \; k = 1, \ldots, N$$

In practice, we can at best approximate continuous delta estimators with discrete-time approximations $\hat{F}_n$ and $\hat{\Delta}_j$ with a discretized pathwise delta estimator:

$$\sum_{n=1}^{N}\left\{\frac{\partial}{\partial F_n(t_n)} g(\hat{F}_1(t_1), \ldots, \hat{F}_N(t_N))\right\}\hat{\Delta}_{nk}(t_n) \tag{13.74}$$

Recall the forward dynamics given in equation (13.1). One can use an Euler scheme for $\log F_n$ to approximate (13.1) by

$$\hat{F}_n((i+1)h) = \hat{F}_n(ih)\exp\left[\left(\hat{\mu}_n(ih) - \frac{1}{2}\sigma_n(ih)\sigma_n(ih)'h + \sigma_n(ih)\sqrt{h}Z_{i+1}\right)\right] \tag{13.75}$$

where h is the time increment, $Z_1, Z_2, \ldots$ are independent d-dimensional standard normal vectors,

$$\hat{\mu}_n(ih) = \sum_{j=\eta(ih)}^{n} \frac{\delta\sigma_n(ih)\sigma_j(ih)'\hat{F}_j(ih)}{1+\delta\hat{F}_j(ih)} \tag{13.76}$$

and $\hat{F}_n(0) = F_n(0)$. Differentiating equation (13.75) with respect to F_k yields the exact pathwise delta algorithm:

$$\hat{\Delta}_{nk}((i+1)h) = \hat{\Delta}_{nk}(ih)\frac{\hat{F}_n((i+1)h)}{F_n(ih)} + \hat{F}((i+1)h)\sum_{j=1}^{N}\frac{\partial\hat{\mu}_n(ih)}{\partial F_j(ih)}\hat{\Delta}_{jk}(ih)h \qquad (13.77)$$

with the initial condition $\hat{\Delta}_j(0) = 1\{n = k\}$. The algorithm is exact in the sense that for every realization of $Z_1, \ldots, Z_i$,

$$\hat{\Delta}_{nk}(ih) = \frac{\partial\hat{F}_n(ih)}{\partial F_k(0)} \qquad (13.78)$$

The pathwise method makes it possible to estimate deltas from a single simulation path without actually having to change any initial values in the model. However, the method requires simulating both equations (13.75) and (13.77), which is computationally expensive. As Glasserman and Zhao state, "the computational effort required by [equation (13.74)] (for all $k = 1, \ldots, N$ and all $n = k, \ldots, N$) is comparable to the effort involved in resimulating all $\{\hat{F}_1, \ldots, \hat{F}_N\}$ an additional N times, slightly changing the value $F_k(0)$ on the kth of these."[30] Moreover, the recomputation of $\partial\hat{\mu}_n/\partial\hat{F}_j$ at every time step is one of the most computationally expensive steps in (13.77). For typical parameter values, $\hat{\mu}_n$ will be quite small (differing from 0 just enough to keep the forward rate dynamics arbitrage-free), so Glasserman and Zhao make a first approximation by setting $\partial\hat{\mu}_n/\partial\hat{F}_j = 0$ in the derivative recursion in (13.77) though continue to use the original $\hat{\mu}_n$ for the simulation of $\hat{F}_n$ in (13.75).[31] Under the zero drift assumption, equation (13.77) reduces to the zero drift pathwise approximation,

$$\hat{\Delta}_{nk}((i+1)h) = \hat{\Delta}_{nk}(ih)\frac{\hat{F}_n((i+1)h)}{F_n(ih)}$$

which requires just simulating the forward LIBOR rates themselves. Such an approximation is rather crude, so Glasserman and Zhao make an approximation that lies between the exact and zero-drift methods both in terms of computing time and the accuracy with which it estimates $\partial\hat{F}_n/\partial\hat{F}_k$. They differentiate $\hat{F}_n$ as though $\hat{\mu}_n$ in equation (13.77) were

$$\hat{\mu}_n(ih) = \sum_{j=\eta(ih)}^{n}\frac{\delta\sigma_n(ih)\sigma_j(ih)'\hat{F}_j(0)}{1+\delta\hat{F}_j(0)} \qquad (13.79)$$

---

[30]Ibid., 9.
[31]Ibid., 9.

thus, replacing the $\hat{F}_j(ih)$ with their time 0 forward values $\hat{F}_j(0)$ in a similar manner to the approximations of Brace, Gatarek, and Musiela (1997). The sensitivity of the approximate drift to F_k reduces to

$$\frac{\partial \hat{\mu}_n^0(ih)}{\partial F_k(0)} = \frac{\delta \sigma_n(ih) \sigma_k(ih)'}{(1 + \delta F_k(0))^2} \mathbf{1}\{\eta(ih) \leq k \leq n\} \tag{13.80}$$

which yields the forward drift approximation:

$$\hat{\Delta}_{nk}(ih) = \frac{\hat{F}_n((i+1)h)}{F_n(ih)} \mathbf{1}\{n = k\} + \hat{F}(ih) \sum_{j=0}^{i-1} \frac{\partial \hat{\mu}_n^0(jh)}{\partial F_k(ih)} \tag{13.81}$$

Note that the derivatives of $\hat{\mu}^0$ can be precomputed and, unlike the exact pathwise algorithm, do not require simulation of an additional recursion. However, the approximation method has the significant limitation that it is restricted to payoffs that are at least continuous.[32] Consequently, the method cannot be used to estimate deltas of derivatives with discontinuous payoffs such as a caplet with a digital payoff,

$$\mathbf{1}\{F_N(T_N) > K\}$$

or a knockout caplet with payoff

$$\max(F_N(T_N) - K, 0)\mathbf{1}\{\min_{i=1,\dots,N} F_i(T_i) > B\}$$

These derivatives do not allow the interchange of derivative and expectation so that (13.72) does not hold. The problem is that the indicator function has a discontinuity even though the pathwise derivative with respect to some $F_k(0)$ actually exists with probability 1.[33] To overcome this problem, the LRM can be used for estimating deltas by moving the dependence on $F_k(0)$ from the sample paths to the probability measure, thus removing the need for smoothness in the payoff. As Glasserman and Zhao note, this is analogous to two ways of adding a drift to Brownian motion (i.e., adding the drift μt at time t to each Brownian path), or leaving the paths unchanged and using Girsanov's theorem to add a drift through a change of probability measure.[34]

In the likelihood ratio method, in a Gaussian framework, one estimates sensi-

---

[32]Ibid., 12.
[33]Ibid., 12. For the digital caplet, the pathwise derivative is identically zero wherever it exists.
[34]Ibid., 12.

tivities with respect to a parameter of the mean of a Gaussian vector, which can be extended with some modification to LIBOR market models. Suppose one is given the random n-dimensional vector $\mathbf{X}$, which is multivariate normal with mean vector $\boldsymbol{\mu}(\theta)$ and covariance $\boldsymbol{\Sigma}$, where θ is a scalar parameter. One then can compute sensitivities with respect to θ. Suppose $\boldsymbol{\Sigma}$ has full rank and let the multivariate normal density of $\mathbf{X}$ given by

$$\Phi(x;\ \boldsymbol{\mu}(\theta),\ \boldsymbol{\Sigma}) = \frac{\exp\left(-\dfrac{1}{2}(x - \boldsymbol{\mu}(\theta))'\boldsymbol{\Sigma}^{-1}(x - \boldsymbol{\mu}(\theta))\right)}{(2\pi)^{n/2}\ |\ \boldsymbol{\Sigma}\ |^{1/2}}$$

so that the expectation of any payoff $\mathbf{g} : \mathfrak{R}^n \to \mathfrak{R}$ is given by

$$E^\theta[g(\mathbf{X})] = \int_{\mathfrak{R}^n} g(x)\Phi(x;\ \boldsymbol{\mu}(\theta),\ \boldsymbol{\Sigma})dx \tag{13.82}$$

where the superscript on the expectation denotes the dependence of the measure on θ. Following Glasserman and Zhao, differentiating and then interchanging the derivative and integral yields

$$\frac{d}{d\theta}E^\theta[g(\mathbf{X})] = \int g(x)\dot{\Phi}(x;\ \boldsymbol{\mu}(\theta),\ \boldsymbol{\Sigma})dx$$

$$= \int g(x)\frac{\dot{\Phi}(x;\ \boldsymbol{\mu}(\theta),\ \boldsymbol{\Sigma})}{\Phi(x;\ \boldsymbol{\mu}(\theta),\ \boldsymbol{\Sigma})}\Phi(x;\ \boldsymbol{\mu}(\theta),\ \boldsymbol{\Sigma})dx$$

where the dot on Φ indicates differentiation with respect to θ. Some algebra yields,

$$\frac{\dot{\Phi}(x;\ \boldsymbol{\mu}(\theta),\ \boldsymbol{\Sigma})}{\Phi(x;\ \boldsymbol{\mu}(\theta),\ \boldsymbol{\Sigma})} = (x - \boldsymbol{\mu}(\theta))'\boldsymbol{\Sigma}^{-1}\dot{\boldsymbol{\mu}}(\theta)) \tag{13.83}$$

Substituting this quantity into (13.82) and interpreting the integral there as an expectation, we get

$$\frac{d}{d\theta}E^\theta[g(\mathbf{X})] = E^\theta[g(\mathbf{X})(\mathbf{X} - \boldsymbol{\mu}(\theta))'\boldsymbol{\Sigma}^{-1}\dot{\boldsymbol{\mu}}(\theta)] \tag{13.84}$$

The expression inside the expectation provides an unbiased estimator of the derivative on the left side. The derivation requires only smoothness in the dependence of Φ on θ, but not smoothness in g. The key quantity in (13.83), $\dot{\Phi}/\Phi$, is the derivative with respect to ε of the likelihood ratio $\Phi(x; \mu(\theta + \varepsilon), \Sigma)/\Phi(x; \mu(\theta), \Sigma)$, hence the name "likelihood ratio method."[35]

In a simulation, one would typically sample $\mathbf{X}$ by letting $\mathbf{X} = \mu(\theta) + \mathbf{AZ}$ where $\mathbf{A}$ is an $n \times n$ matrix satisfying the Cholesky decomposition, $\mathbf{AA'} = \Sigma$, and $\mathbf{Z}$ is a vector of independent standard normal random variables. Substituting this expression in equation (13.84) yields

$$\frac{d}{d\theta} E^{\theta}[g(\mathbf{X})] = E[g(\mu(\theta) + \mathbf{AZ})\mathbf{Z'A}^{-1}\dot{\mu}(\theta)] \tag{13.85}$$

where the expectation of the right is respect to the n-dimensional standard normal distribution and thus is not superscripted in θ.

To apply the LRM to the LIBOR model, we take the logarithms of both sides of (13.75),

$$\log \hat{F}_n((i+1)h) = \log \hat{F}_n(ih) + \left(\hat{\mu}_n(ih) - \frac{1}{2}\|\sigma_n(ih)\|^2\right)h + \sigma_n(ih)\sqrt{h}Z_{i+1}, \quad n = 1, \ldots, N \tag{13.86}$$

Since the drift $\hat{\mu}_n$ is a function of the forward rate LIBOR rates themselves, and thus the $F_k(0)$'s, we differentiate as though the drift were deterministic (while simulating the forward LIBOR rates with the original drift) in order to remove the dependence of the $F_k(0)$'s out of the sample paths and into the probability measure.[36] Under the forward-drift approximation, equation (13.86) represents the evolution of a Gaussian process so the previous discussion of the LRM applies. However, equation (13.86) describes the evolution of a vector of N rates driven by (say) d-dimensional vectors of normal random variables, where d is the number of factors. The covariance matrix of the increments in (13.86), over a single time step, has rank d. If $d < N$ (and usually $d \ll N$), the matrix is singular and the matrix cannot be inverted, and so we cannot apply equation (13.85). However, by assumption, Σ is nonsingular, and this does not stop its use. Moreover, to overcome this problem, we consider the distribution of the increments over multiple time steps, in which case equation (13.86) becomes,

$$\log \hat{F}_n((i+1)h) = \log \hat{F}_n(ih) + h\sum_{j=0}^{i-1}\left(\hat{\mu}_n(ih) - \frac{1}{2}\|\sigma_n(ih)\|^2\right)$$
$$+ \sqrt{h}\Big(\sigma_n(0)\,\Big|\,\sigma_n(h)\,\Big|\ldots\Big|\,\sigma_n((i-1)h)\Big)\mathbf{Z}$$

[35]Ibid., 13.
[36]Ibid., 15.

where the row vectors $\sigma_n(jh)$ have been concatenated into a single vector of length $i \cdot d$ and the column vectors Z_j have been stacked into a column vector $\mathbf{Z}$ of the same length; that is,

$$\mathbf{Z} = \begin{bmatrix} Z_1 \\ Z_2 \\ \vdots \\ Z_i \end{bmatrix}$$

For sufficiently large i^*, the $N \times i^* d$ matrix,

$$\mathbf{L}_h(i^*) = \begin{pmatrix} \sigma_1(0) & \sigma_1(h) & \cdots & \sigma_1((i^*-1)h) \\ \sigma_2(0) & \sigma_2(h) & \cdots & \sigma_2((i^*-1)h) \\ \vdots & \vdots & \vdots & \vdots \\ \sigma_N(0) & \sigma_N(h) & \cdots & \sigma_N((i^*-1)h) \end{pmatrix}$$

may have rank N, even if $d < N$.[37] Consequently, the covariance matrix $\Lambda_h(i^*)\Lambda_h(i^*)'$ of the $\log F_n(i^*h)$, $n = 1, \ldots, N$ is invertible and we can apply the determinstic forward rate approximation in equation (13.76).

Suppose that $\Lambda_h(i^*)$ has full rank. To apply the LRM method in the form given in equation (13.84), Glasserman and Zhao make the following correspondences: $\theta \leftarrow \hat{F}_k(0)$,

$$\mathbf{X} \leftarrow (\log \hat{F}_1(i^*h), \ldots, \log \hat{F}_N(i^*h))' \tag{13.87}$$

$$\boldsymbol{\mu}_n(\theta) \leftarrow \log F_n(0) + h \sum_{r=0}^{i^*-1} \left(\hat{\mu}_n^0(rh) - \frac{1}{2} \|\sigma_n(rh)\|^2 \right), \quad n = 1, \ldots, N \tag{13.88}$$

$$\Sigma \leftarrow \sqrt{h}\Sigma_h(i^*) \equiv \sqrt{h}\Lambda_h(i^*)\Lambda_h(i^*)', \quad \mathbf{A} \leftarrow \sqrt{h}A_h(i^*)$$

for any $i^*d \times i^*d$ matrix $A_h(i^*)(A_h(i^*)' = \Lambda_h(i^*)\Lambda_h(i^*)'$, $\hat{\mu}^0$ is the forward drift approximation, and

$$\dot{\boldsymbol{\mu}}_n \leftarrow \frac{\mathbf{1}\{n = k\}}{F_k(0)} + h \sum_{r=0}^{i^*-1} \frac{\partial \hat{\mu}_n^0(rh)}{\partial F_k(0)}, \quad n = 1, \ldots, N \tag{13.89}$$

---

[37]Ibid., 16.

With these substitutions, we can determine the following LRM delta estimator for an arbitrary discounted payoff $g(\hat{F}_1(t_1), \ldots, \hat{F}_N(t_N))$:

$$g(\hat{F}_1(t_1), \ldots, \hat{F}_N(t_N))(\mathbf{X} - \boldsymbol{\mu})'\boldsymbol{\Sigma}^{-1}\boldsymbol{\mu} \tag{13.90}$$

Precomputing the vector $\boldsymbol{\Sigma}^{-1}\boldsymbol{\mu}$ reduces the computational time per simulated path to evaluate the quadratic form in (13.90) from $O(N^2)$ to linear time $O(N)$.[38] Setting $i^* = N/d$ so that $\boldsymbol{\Lambda}_h(i^*)$ is square, we can write

$$g(F_1(t_1), \ldots, F_N(t_N))h^{-1/2}\mathbf{Z}'\boldsymbol{\Lambda}_h(i^*)^{-1}\boldsymbol{\mu} \tag{13.91}$$

where $\mathbf{Z}$ is the column vector obtained by stacking the i^* d-vectors of independent normals used to simulate the d-factor model for i^* steps.

It can also be shown that the LRM gamma estimator of

$$\frac{\partial^2}{\partial F_k(0)^2} E\Big[g(\hat{F}_1(t_1), \ldots, \hat{F}_N(t_n)\Big]$$

is given by

$$g(\hat{F}_1(t_1), \ldots, \hat{F}_N(t_n))([(\mathbf{X} - \boldsymbol{\mu})'\boldsymbol{\Sigma}^{-1}\dot{\boldsymbol{\mu}}]^2 - \dot{\boldsymbol{\mu}}'\boldsymbol{\Sigma}^{-1}\dot{\boldsymbol{\mu}} + (\mathbf{X} - \boldsymbol{\mu})'\boldsymbol{\Sigma}^{-1}\ddot{\boldsymbol{\mu}})$$

with $\mathbf{X}, \boldsymbol{\mu}, \boldsymbol{\Sigma}, \dot{\boldsymbol{\mu}}$ given in (13.87) to (13.89), and $\ddot{\boldsymbol{\mu}}$ given by

$$\ddot{\boldsymbol{\mu}}_n = -\frac{\mathbf{1}_{\{n=k\}}}{F_k^2(0)} + h\sum_{r=0}^{i^*-1} \frac{\partial^2 \mu_n^0(rh)}{\partial F_k^2(0)}, \quad n = 1, \ldots, N \tag{13.92}$$

where

$$\frac{\partial^2 \mu_n^0(rh)}{\partial F_k^2(0)} = \frac{-2\delta^2 \sigma_n(ih)\sigma_k'(ih)}{(1 + \delta F_k(0))^3}\mathbf{1}\{\eta(ih) \le k \le n\}$$

It can also be shown that the exact pathwise algorithm for estimating vega is

$$\hat{\Delta}_n((i+1)h) = \hat{\Delta}_n(ih)\frac{\hat{F}_n((i+1)h)}{\hat{F}_n(ih)} + F_n((i+1)h)\left(\left\{\frac{\partial\hat{\mu}_n(ih)}{\partial\theta} - \frac{\partial\sigma_n(ih)}{\partial\theta}\sigma_n'(ih)\right\}h + \frac{\partial\sigma_n}{\partial\theta}Z_{n+1}\sqrt{h}\right) \tag{13.93}$$

---

[38]Ibid., 17.

with the initial condition

$$\hat{\Delta}_n(0) \equiv \frac{\partial \hat{F}_n(0)}{\partial \theta} \equiv 0$$

where $\partial \sigma_n / \partial \theta$ and σ_n are row vectors, Z_{i+1} and σ_n' are column vectors, and the differentiated drift is given by

$$\frac{\partial \hat{\mu}_n}{\partial \theta} = \sum_{j=\eta(ih)}^{n} \left(\frac{\partial \hat{\mu}_n}{\partial \hat{F}_j} \hat{\Delta}_j + \sum_{k=1}^{d} \frac{\partial \hat{\mu}_n}{\partial \sigma_{jk}} \frac{\partial \sigma_{jk}}{\partial \theta} \right) \tag{13.94}$$

with σ_{jk} denoting the kth component of σ_j. The existence of $\hat{\Delta}_j = \partial \hat{F}_j(t)/\partial \theta$ in this expression makes the simulation of equation (13.93) computationally expensive, requiring "effort comparable to simulating another copy of the LIBOR rates with a perturbed value of θ."[39]

Glasserman and Zhao then use the forward-drift approximation, which does not have these computational problems. Differentiating $\hat{\mu}_n^0$ with respect to θ yields

$$\frac{\partial \hat{\mu}_n^0(ih)}{\partial \theta} = \sum_{j=\eta(ih)}^{n} \frac{\delta F_j(0)}{1+\delta F_j(0)} \left(\frac{\partial \sigma_n(ih)}{\partial \theta} \sigma_j'(ih) + \frac{\partial \sigma_j(ih)}{\partial \theta} \sigma_n'(ih) \right) \tag{13.95}$$

which is independent of the simulated path and can be precomputed.[40] Substituting $\hat{\mu}$ with $\hat{\mu}^0$ in equation (13.75), differentiating, and then simplifying the resulting expression yields the forward drift approximation of vega:

$$\hat{\Delta}_n(ih) = \hat{F}_n(ih) \left(\sum_{j=1}^{i} \left\{ \frac{\partial \hat{\mu}_n^0(jh)}{\partial \theta} - \frac{\partial \sigma_n(jh)}{\partial \theta} \sigma_n(jh)' \right\} h + \sum_{j=1}^{i} \frac{\partial \sigma_n(jh)}{\partial \theta} Z_j \sqrt{h} \right) \tag{13.96}$$

Other than $\hat{F}_n$, the only term on the right-hand side of equation (13.96) that cannot be precomputed is

$$\sum_{j=1}^{i} \frac{\partial \sigma_n(jh)}{\partial \theta} Z_j \sqrt{h}$$

---

[39]Ibid., 25.
[40]Ibid., 25.

However, as Glasserman and Zhao note, "evaluating this expression along each simulated path requires very little effort, making [equation (13.96)] much faster than the exact pathwise method or simulation of a second copy of the LIBOR rates."[41] The interested reader can get the derivation details of the gamma and vega formulas as well as obtain numerical results in Glasserman and Zhao's paper.

The following code, developed by Glasserman and Zhao, simulates these Greek sensitivities. The following code computes the delta of a caplet using the forward drift approximation in equation (13.78).

```
define N 20
define m 1
#include "forwardDrift.h"
#include "random.h"

/*******************************************************************************
calcDeltaCaplet: computed delta of a caplet
[in]: long M : number of simulations
[out]: none
*******************************************************************************/
void ForwardDrift::calcDeltaCaplet(long M)
{
  /* The program for Forward Drift method to compute Delta of Caplet */

  double nyear=5, delta=.25, epsilon=.25,B=1;        /* time structure */
  float F0[N],sigma[N];
  FILE *file_ptr;
  int i,j,k,run,n,t;

  double F[N],res[N][N+1],z[m],B0[N],K[N],Del[N][N],Dell[N][N];
  double v,discount,lam,sen;

  // Input initial term structure of Libor rates: F0[n];
  // and volatility structure sigma[n].

  file_ptr=fopen("F0","rt");
  if(file_ptr==NULL)
    cout << "File not found" << endl;

  for(i=0;i<N;i++)
    fscanf(file_ptr,"%f", &(F0[i]));

  fclose(file_ptr);
  file_ptr=fopen("sigma","rt");
  if(file_ptr==NULL)
    cout << "File not found" << endl;
```

---

[41]Ibid., 25.

```
for(i=0;i<(N*m);i++)
   fscanf(file_ptr,"%f", &(sigma[i]));

fclose(file_ptr);

/* Recover bond price at time 0, B0[n], from inputted Libor rates */
for ( j=0; j<N; j++)
{
  B0[j]=B/(1+delta*F0[j]);
  B=B0[j];
  K[j]=F0[j];
  for(k=0; k < N+1;k++)
     res[j][k]=0;
}
B=1/(1+delta*F0[0]);

for (i=1;i<N;i++)
{
  for(j=1;j<=i;j++)
  {
     Dell[i][j]=delta*sigma[i-1]*sigma[j-1]/(1+delta*F0[j])/(1+delta*F0[j]);
  }
}

/* Starting simulation */
for (run=1; run <= M; run++)
{
  for(j=1; j < N; j++)
  {
     F[j]=F0[j];
  }
  discount=1.;
  for(t=1;t < N; t++)
  {
     random.nrandv(m,z);
     for ( i=1; i<=m; i++)
     {
       v=0;
       for(n=t; n<N;n++)
       {
         lam=sigma[(n-t)*m+i-1];
         v=v+(delta*F[n]*lam)/(1+delta*F[n]);
         F[n]=F[n]*exp((-lam/2+v)*lam*epsilon + lam*sqrt(epsilon)*z[i-1]);
       }
     }

     // computing Delta of Caplet
     discount=discount*(1+delta*F[t]);
     for(k=1; k < t;k++)
     {
       Del[t][k]=F[t]*Dell[t][k]*t*m*epsilon;
       v=0;
       for(n=k;n<t+1;n++)
```

```
        v+=delta*Del[n][k]/(1+delta*F[n]);

      sen=B*delta*ind(F[t],K[t])/discount*Del[t][k] - B*delta*max(F[t]-
        K[t],0)/discount*v;
      res[t][k]+=sen;
      res[N-t][N+1-k]+=sen*sen;
    }
    Del[t][t]=F[t]/F0[t]+F[t]*Dell[t][t]*t*m*epsilon;
    v=delta*Del[t][t]/(1+delta*F[t]);
    sen=B*delta*ind(F[t],K[t])/discount*Del[t][k] - B*delta*max(F[t]-
      K[t],0)/discount*v;
    res[t][t]+=sen;
    res[N-t][N+1-t]+=sen*sen;
    }
  }

  for(i=1; i < N; i++)
  {
    cout << i << "        ",
    for(j=1;j< 2;j++)
    {
      sen=res[i][j]/M;
      res[N-i][N+1-j]=sqrt(res[N-i][N+1-j]-sen*sen*M)/M;
      cout << sen << " ";
    }
    cout << "\n        ";
    for(j=1;j< 2;j++)
    cout << res[N-i][N+1-j]) << " ";
    cout << "\n " << endl;
  }
}
```

The following code computes the delta of a digital option using the likelihood ratio method:

```
#include "lrm_dlg.h"
#include <stdio.h>
#include <iostream.h>
#define N 20
#define m 1
#define max(a,b)  ((a > b) ? a : b)
#define indicator(a,b)  (((a)>(b)) ? (1) : (0) )

/*****************************************************************************
digitalDelta: computes the delta of a digital option
[in]: M : number of simulations
[out]: none
*****************************************************************************/
```

```
void LRM::digitalDelta(long M)
{

  double nyear=5, delta=.25, epsilon=.25, B=1;        /* time structure */
  int ind = 0;
  float F0[N],sigma[N*m];
  FILE *file_ptr;
  int i,j,k,t,run,n,a=0;
  double F[N],
  res[N+1][N+2],z[m],B0[N],K[N];
  double v,discount,sen,lam,zz[N],b[N],Dd[N][N],am1[N][N];

  // Input initial term structure of Libor rates: F0[n];
  // and volatility structure sigma[n].

  try
  {

    file_ptr=fopen("F0","rt");
    if(file_ptr==NULL)
      cout << "File not found" << endl;

    for(i=0;i<N;i++)
      fscanf(file_ptr,"%f", &(F0[i])); // read in forward LIBOR rates

    fclose(file_ptr);
    file_ptr=fopen("sigma","rt");

    if (file_ptr==NULL)
      cout << "File not found" << endl;

    for(i=0;i<(N*m);i++)
      fscanf(file_ptr,"%f", &(sigma[i])); // read in volatilities

    fclose(file_ptr);

    // Recover bond price, B0[n], at time 0 from inputted Libor rates;
    // and compute the inverse of the matrix sigma.
    j=0;
    B0[j]=B/(1+delta*F0[j]);
    B=B0[j];
    K[j]=F0[j];
    for( k=0;k<N+1;k++){ res[j][k]=0;}
      b[0]=1/sigma[0];

    for ( j=1; j<N; j++)
    {
      B0[j]=B/(1+delta*F0[j]);
      B=B0[j];
      K[j]=F0[j];

      for( k=0;k<N+2;k++)
        res[j][k]=0;
```

```
    v=0;
    for (k=0; k<j; k++)
      v+=b[k]*sigma[j-k];

    b[k]=-v/sigma[0];
}
B=1/(1+delta*F0[0]);

for (i=1;i<N;i++)
{
    for( j=0; j<N;j++)
    {
      Dd[i][j]=0;
    }
    Dd[i][i-1]=1/delta/B0[i]/F0[i];
    Dd[i][i]=-B0[i-1]/delta/B0[i]/B0[i]/F0[i];
}

    for(t=1;t<N;t++)
    {
    for (i=t;i<N;i++)
    {
      for( j=t; j<i+1;j++)
      {
        sen=epsilon*delta*sigma[(i-t)]*sigma[(j-
          t)]/(1+delta*F0[j])/(1+delta*F0[j]);
        Dd[i][j-1]+=sen/delta/B0[j];
        Dd[i][j]+=-sen*B0[j-1]/delta/B0[j]/B0[j];
      }
    }
    for (k=0;k<t+1;k++)
    {
      am1[t][k]=0;
      for(j=1;j<t+1;j++)
        am1[t][k]+=b[j-1]*Dd[t+1-j][k];
    }
}

// Starting simulation
for (run = 1; run <= M;run++)
{
    ind=0;
for( j=1;j<N;j++)
  F[j]=F0[j];

discount=1.;
for( t=1;t<N;t++)
{
  random.nrandv(m,z);
  for ( i=1; i<=m; i++)
  {
    if (ind<N) { zz[ind]=z[i-1];
      ind+=1;
```

```
          }
        v=0;
        for(n=t; n<N;n++)
        {
           lam=sigma[(n-t)*m+i-1];
           v = v+(delta*F[n]*lam)/(1+delta*F[n]);
           F[n]=F[n]*exp((-lam/2+v)*lam*epsilon +lam*sqrt(epsilon)*z[i-1]);
        }
      }
    discount=discount*(1+delta*F[t]);
    for(i=0;i<t+1;i++)
    {
       v=0;
       for(j=1;j<t+1;j++)
       {
          v += zz[j-1]*am1[j][i];
       }
       sen=B*delta*indicator(F[t]-K[t],0)/discount*v/sqrt(epsilon)-0.2*v;
       res[t][i]+=sen;
       res[N-t][N+1-i]+=sen*sen;
    }
  }

  for (i=1; i < N; i++)
  {
    cout << " " << i;
    for(j=0;j < 2;j++)
    {
      sen=res[i][j]/M;
      res[N-i][N+1-j]=sqrt(res[N-i][N+1-j]-sen*sen*M)/M;
      cout <<\> " " << sen;
    }
    cout << "\n       ";
    for(j=0; j < 2; j++)
      cout << " " << res[N-i][N+1-j];
    cout << "\n\n";
  }
}
catch (const char* s)
{
  cout << "Exception : " << s << endl;
}
}
```

which uses the *Random* class:

```
#ifndef _RANDOM__
#define _RANDOM__
#include <stdlib.h>
```

```
#include <math.h>
#include <time.h>
#define initialize srand(time(0))
#define PI 3.1415926535897932385
#define urand() ((float) rand() / (2147483647 + 1.0)) //define a function of
  generating uniform random variables

class Random
{
  public:
    Random() {};
    ~Random() {};
    /**************************************************************************
    nrand : generates two random numbers
    [in]: vec : double array
    [out]: void
    **************************************************************************/
    inline void nrand(double* vec) {
      double R, theta;
      initialize;
      R = sqrt(-2.*log((float) urand()));
      theta = 2.*PI*urand();
      vec[0] = R*cos(theta);
      vec[1] = R*sin(theta);
    }
    /**************************************************************************
    nrandv : using Box Muller method, generates a vector of i.i.d.
    Gaussian random variables of given length. Each random variable has mean zero
    and variance 1.
    [in]:   int i       : length of the vector
            double* vec : double array
    [out]: double       : vector of random variables
    **************************************************************************/
    inline void nrandv(const int i, double* vec) {
      int j;
      double R, theta;
      for ( j = 0 ; j < i-1 ; j += 2)
      {
        R = sqrt(-2.*log(urand()));
        theta = 2.*PI*urand();
        vec[j] = R*cos(theta);
        vec[j+1] = R*sin(theta);
      }
      if (j == i-2)
        return;
      R = sqrt(-2.*log(urand()));
      theta = 2.*PI*urand();
      vec[i-1] = R*cos(theta);
      vec[i-2] = R*sin(theta);
    }
};
```

The following code computes the gamma approximation of a caplet using the finite difference method:

```
/*****************************************************************************
capletGamma : finite different method to compute gamma of caplet.
[in] : long M : number of simulations
[out]: void
*****************************************************************************/
void FiniteDiffMethod::capletGamma(long M)
{
  float nyear=5, delta=.25, epsilon=.25,B=1,delb=0.003;

  float F0[N],sigma[N];
  FILE *file_ptr;
  int i,j,run,n,t,k,kd=10,mean;

  double F[N],Fu[N],Fu0[N],Fd[N],Fd0[N],res[N][2],z[m],B0[N],K[N],Bu[N],Bd[N];
  double v,vu,vd,discount,disu,disd,sig,sen,c,cu,cd,B1,B2,rr[N],cor[N];

  try
  {
    file_ptr=fopen("L0","rt");
    if(file_ptr==NULL)
      cout << "File not found" << endl;

    for(i=0;i<N;i++)
      fscanf(file_ptr,"%f", &(F0[i]));

    fclose(file_ptr);
      file_ptr=fopen("lambda","rt");

    if (file_ptr==NULL)
      cout << "File not found" << endl;

    for(i=0;i<(N*m);i++)
      fscanf(file_ptr,"%f", &(sigma[i]));

    fclose(file_ptr);

    for ( j=0; j<N; j++)
    {
      B0[j]=B/(1+delta*F0[j]);
      Bu[j]=B0[j];
      Bd[j]=B0[j];
      B=B0[j];
      K[j]=F0[j];
      res[j][0]=0;
      res[j][1]=0;
      Fu0[j]=F0[j];
      Fd0[j]=F0[j];
```

```
    }
  B=1/(1+delta*F0[0]);
  Bu[kd-1]=Bu[kd-1]+delb;
  Bd[kd-1]=Bd[kd-1]-delb;
  B1=Bu[0];
  B2=Bd[0];

  Fu0[kd-1]=(Bu[kd-2]/Bu[kd-1]-1)/delta;
  Fd0[kd-1]=(Bd[kd-2]/Bd[kd-1]-1)/delta;
  Fu0[kd]=(Bu[kd-1]/Bu[kd]-1)/delta;
  Fd0[kd]=(Bd[kd-1]/Bd[kd]-1)/delta;

  for (run=1;run<=M;run++)
  {
    for( j=1;j<N;j++)
    {
      F[j]=F0[j];
      Fu[j]=Fu0[j];
      Fd[j]=Fd0[j];
    }
    discount=1.;
    disu=1;
    disd=1;
    for( t=1;t<N;t++)
    {
      nrandv(m,z);
      for ( i=1; i<=m; i++)
      {
        v=0;
        vu=0;
        vd=0;
        for(n=t; n<N;n++)
        {
          sig= sigma[(n-t)*m+i-1];
          v+=(delta*F[n]*sig)/(1+delta*F[n]);
          vu+=(delta*Fu[n]*sig)/(1+delta*Fu[n]);
          vd+=(delta*Fd[n]*sig)/(1+delta*Fd[n]);
          F[n]=F[n]*exp((-sig/2+v)*sig*epsilon + sig*sqrt(epsilon)*z[i-1]);
          Fu[n]=Fu[n]*exp((-sig/2+vu)*sig*epsilon + sig*sqrt(epsilon)*z[i-1]);
          Fd[n]=Fd[n]*exp((-sig/2+vd)*sig*epsilon + sig*sqrt(epsilon)*z[i-1]);
        }
      }
      discount=discount*(1+delta*F[t]);
      disu=disu*(1+delta*Fu[t]);
      disd=disd*(1+delta*Fd[t]);
      c=B*delta*max(F[t]-K[t],0)/discount;
      cu=B1*delta*max(Fu[t]-K[t],0)/disu;
      cd=B2*delta*max(Fd[t]-K[t],0)/disd;
      sen=(cu+cd-2*c)/(delb*delb);
      res[t][0]+=sen;
      res[t][1]+=sen*sen;
    }
  }
```

```
      cout << " Gamma    Std Err\n";
      for(i= 1; i < N; i++)
      {
        cout << i << "    ";
        sen=res[i][0]/M;
        res[i][1]=sqrt(res[i][1]-sen*sen*M)/M;
        cout << sen << " " << res[i][1] << endl;
      }
    }
    catch (const char* s)
    {
      cout << "Exception : " << s << endl;
    }
}
```

Finally, the following code implements a vega approximation:

```
/*******************************************************************************
calcVega: computes the pathwise approximation of vega assuming del_lambda?del_theta
          = 1
[in]: M : number of simulations
[out]: none
*******************************************************************************/
void VegaApprox::calcVega(long M)
{
  float nyear=5, delta=.25, epsilon=.25,B=1;
  int m=1, N=20;
  float F0[20],sigma[20];
  FILE *file_ptr;
  int i,j,run,n,t;

  double F[20],res[20][2],z[1],B0[20],K[20],sumz,dd;
  double v,w,discount,lam,sen,Del_dft[20],Del[20];
  cout.precision(9);

  try
  {
    file_ptr=fopen("F0","rt");
    if(file_ptr==NULL)
      cout << "File not found" << endl;

    for(i=0;i<N;i++)
    fscanf(file_ptr,"%f", &(F0[i]));

    fclose(file_ptr);
    file_ptr=fopen("sigma","rt");
    if (file_ptr==NULL)
      cout << "File not found" << endl;
```

```
for(i=0;i<(N*m);i++)
  fscanf(file_ptr,"%f", &(sigma[i]));

fclose(file_ptr);

for ( j=0; j<N; j++)
{
  B0[j]=B/(1+delta*F0[j]);
  B=B0[j];
  K[j]=F0[j];
  res[j][0]=0;
  res[j][1]=0;
  Del_dft[j]=0;
  Del[j]=0;
}
B=1/(1+delta*F0[0]);

for( t=1;t<N;t++)
{
  for ( i=1; i<=m; i++)
  {
    w=0;
    v=0;
    for (n=t; n<N; n++)
    {
      lam=sigma[(n-t)*m+i-1];
      v+=(delta*F0[n]*lam)/(1+delta*F0[n]);
      w+=delta*F0[n]/(1+delta*F0[n]);
      Del_dft[n]+=(v+w*lam)*epsilon-epsilon*lam;
    }
  }
}

for (run=1;run<=M;run++)
{
  sumz=0;
  dd=0;
  for( j=1;j<N;j++)
  {
    F[j]=F0[j];
  }
  discount=1.;
  for(t=1; t<N; t++)
  {
    random.nrandv(m,z);
    for ( i=1; i<=m; i++)
    {
      v=0;
      for(n=t; n<N;n++)
      {
        lam=sigma[(n-t)*m+i-1];
        v+=(delta*F[n]*lam)/(1+delta*F[n]);
        F[n]=F[n]*exp((-lam/2+v)*lam*epsilon + lam*sqrt(epsilon)*z[i-1]);
      }
```

```
          }
          sumz+=z[i-1];
      }
      discount=discount*(1+delta*F[t]);
      Del[t]=F[t]*(Del_dft[t]+sqrt(epsilon)*sumz);
      dd+=delta*Del[t]/(1+delta*F[t]);
      sen=B*delta*ind(F[t],K[t])/discount*Del[t]- B*delta*max(F[t]-
        K[t],0)/discount*dd;
      res[t][0]+=sen;
      res[t][1]+=sen*sen;
    }
  }
  cout << " Vega" << endl;
  for(i=1;i<N;i++)
  {
    cout << i << "    ";
    sen=res[i][0]/M;
    res[i][1]=sqrt(res[i][1]-sen*sen*M)/M;
    cout << sen << " " << res[i][1] << endl;
  }
}
catch (const char* s)
{
  cout << "Exception " << s << endl;
}
}
```

CHAPTER 14

Bermudan and Exotic
Interest Rate Derivatives

This chapter focuses on the pricing of various exotic interest rate derivatives including Bermudan swaptions, constant maturity swaps, trigger swaps, index amortizing swaps, and quantos. These interest rate derivatives are heavily traded by many financial institutions and an understanding of them is essential for any quant working with traders on a fixed income trading desk.

In section 14.1, we discuss the characteristics and method to price Bermudan swaptions. In section 14.2, we give a practical implementation for pricing Bermudan swaptions. In section 14.3, we discuss Andersen's (1999) method for pricing Bermudan swaptions. In section 14.4, we discuss the least-squares Monte Carlo (LSMC) technique, developed by Longstaff and Schwartz. In section 14.5, we discuss the stochastic mesh method as a technique for building lattices to value interest rate derivatives. In section 14.6, we discuss the valuation of range notes and provide an implementation using the HJM model. In section 14.7, we discuss the valuation of index amortizing swaps and provide an implementation using the HJM model. In section 14.8, we discuss the pricing of trigger swaps. In section 14.9, we discuss pricing quanto (multicurrency) derivatives including quanto caps, floors, and swaptions. Finally, in section 14.10, we discuss the Gaussian quadrature procedure for numerically evaluating integrals for valuation of derivatives.

14.1   BERMUDAN SWAPTIONS

A Bermudan swaption is an option that at each date, in a schedule of exercise dates, $0 = T_0 < T_1 < T_2 < \ldots < T_k = T$, gives the holder the right, but not the obligation, to enter into an interest rate swap, provided the right was not exercised at any previous date in the schedule. Bermudan swaptions are quoted as "X-noncall-Y," meaning that a swaption, which is noncallable, has Y years until maturity for the holder to exercise the option and enter into an interest rate swap lasting X years.

Since Bermudan swaptions are useful hedges for callable bonds, they are actively traded and one of the most liquid fixed income derivatives with built-in early exercise features. To price Bermudan options, many banks use one- or two-factor short rate models such as the BDT (1990), Black and Karasinski (1991), Hull and White (1990), and Ritchken and Sanksarasubramanian (1995). A characteristic common to each of these models is that they can be implemented numerically in low-dimension lattices (such as finite differences or binomial trees), which are well suited for handling the free boundary problem that arises for options with early exercise features.[1]

The ease of implementation that these models provide comes at the expense of realism. For instance, these models usually have only one driving Brownian motion, implying perfect correlation of all forward rates. Since the models are based on the short rate as the underlying quantity, there usually are not enough degrees of freedom to precisely calibrate these models to quoted market instruments such as caps and swaptions. Trying to improve the fit by using time-dependent parameters in these short rate models can lead to a nonstationary and largely unpredictable term structure evolution.[2] LIBOR market models (LMM) provide a more realistic framework since they can incorporate volatility skews, price liquid instruments in closed form, and have enough degrees of freedom to allow for a good fit while maintaining a largely stationary term structure.[3] But, due to the high number of state variables in the LMM, recombining lattices are not computationally feasible and valuation of all contingent claims is almost always done by Monte Carlo simulation. Although flexible and easy to implement, Monte Carlo has slow convergence and difficulties dealing with early-exercise features of American- and Bermudan-style options. The first problem is overcome with variance reduction techniques such as antithetics and control variates. The second problem was long thought to be a problem that Monte Carlo could not overcome. However, the work of Longstaff and Schwartz (2001), Tilley (1993), and Broadie and Glasserman (1997a) has proven this belief to be incorrect although practical implementation obstacles still exist.

There are several methods for pricing American-style derivatives in the LMM or closely related HJM (1992) model that have been proposed in the literature. The first is the use of nonrecombining trees, known as "bushy" trees, which is set up to approximate the continuous-time dynamics of interest rates (see Heath et al. (1992) and Brace, Gatarek, and Musiela (1997)). Backward induction algorithms can be applied and early exercise features easily incorporated. Unfortunately, as the number of time steps increases, the number of nodes (states) increases exponentially making its use computationally expensive.[4] Bushy trees are far too slow for general pricing, especially for long-dated derivatives that require more than 15 steps to achieve convergence (the total number of tree nodes is 1.4 billion in a three-factor

---

[1]Andersen (1999), 1.
[2]Ibid. See Carverhill (1995a) and Hull and White (1995) for discussions of this issue.
[3]Andersen (1999), 1.
[4]For m stochastic factors and n time steps, the total number of nodes is $((m + 1)^{n+1} - 1)/m$.

model). However, a nonexploding bushy tree construction technique was developed by Tang and Lange in 1999 to overcome this problem.[5]

Carr and Yang (1997) developed a method based on the stratification technique of Barraquand and Martineau (1995). Carr and Yang use buckets or "cells" for the money market account (numeraire) in the LMM and use Markov chain dynamics for the transition between buckets. The Markov chain transitional probabilities are computed via Monte Carlo simulation. During each simulation, each particular bucket of the money market numeraire is associated with a state on the yield curve. The curve is found by averaging all simulated yield curves that passed through the bucket. Once the Markov chain of numeraires and yield curves has been constructed, a backward induction algorithm similar to the one applied to lattices allows American and Bermudan-style options to be valued.[6] While the algorithm yields good results, it is subject to several potential problems and biases. First, the stratification variable, the money market account, is a weak indicator of the state of the yield curve. As Andersen (1999) points out, some of the biases include (1) a bias from forcing Markovian dynamics on a non-Markovian variable; (2) a bias from averaging yield curves at each bucket; (3) a bias from basing the exercise decision solely on the state of the numeraire; and (4) a bias from, in effect, using the same random paths to determine both the exercise strategy and the option price.[7]

A third method for pricing Bermudan swaptions was postulated by Clewlow and Strickland. The method, as with Carr and Yang (1997), is based on reducing the exercise decision to the state of single variable, which is chosen to be the fixed side of a swap. Clewlow and Strickland use a two-factor Gaussian HJM, but determine the early exercise boundary by using the information extracted from a calibrated one-factor Gaussian model implemented as a lattice. The calculated boundary from the one-factor model is then used in a Monte Carlo simulation of the two-factor model. The approach generates only lower bounds on the price, and bias potentially exists since information obtained from a one-factor model may be of limited use in a two-factor model. However, since the bias has a predictable sign, better control of model risk exists over that of Carr and Yang's model.[8]

Andersen (1999) developed a direct search approach for an early exercise boundary parameterized in intrinsic value and the values of still-alive swaptions. His approach is done in an extended LMM framework—see Andersen and Andraesen (1998)—using Monte Carlo simulation. In the extended LMM, the forward-rate dynamics define a system of up to $k = 1, \ldots, N$ Markov variables and are given by

$$dF_k(t) = \varphi(F_k(t))\lambda_k(t)\mu_k(t)dt + \varphi(F_k(t))\lambda_k(t)dz(t) \tag{14.1}$$

[5]Tang and Lange (2001).
[6]Andersen (1999), 3.
[7]Ibid., 3.
[8]Ibid., 3.

where

$$\mu_k(t) = \sum_{j=n(t)}^{k} \frac{\tau_j \varphi(F_k(t))\lambda_k(t)}{1 + \tau_j F_j(t)}$$

$n(t)$, which is 1 plus the number of payments as of date t; that is, $n(t) = \{m : T_{m-1} < t \le T_m, \}$, $\varphi : \Re^+ \to \Re^+$, is a one-dimensional function satisfying certain regularity conditions, $\lambda_k(t)$ is a bounded m-dimensional deterministic function, and $z(t)$ is a m-dimensional Brownian motion under the measure Q.

For a sufficiently regular choice of φ, Andersen and Andraesen (1998) show how caps and European swaptions can be priced efficiently in a small set of finite difference grids, enabling fast calibration of the $\lambda_k(t)$ functions to market data.[9] In particular, in the constant elasticity of variance (CEV) case, φ is set to a power function, $\varphi(x) = x^\alpha$, $\alpha > 0$, and prices for caps and European swaptions are analytically tractable. Moreover, unlike Clewlow and Strickland, the early exercise boundary is not determined by a one-factor lattice, but rather is found by optimization on the results of a separate simulation of the full multifactor model. The method can be decomposed into a recursive series of simple one-dimensional optimization problems. The method is quite robust and produces accurate results with a very low bias that is in line with quoted bid-offer spreads. Moreover, both upper and lower bounds can be established.

Finally, a very promising method, least-squares Monte Carlo, developed by Longstaff and Schwartz, which is presented in section 14.4, allows very accurate pricing of Bermudan swaptions.

14.2   IMPLEMENTATION FOR BERMUDAN SWAPTIONS

We will price an ATM Bermudan swaption with the Hull-White model using a robust implementation.[10] First, we need to calibrate the model to the quoted swaption matrix. We input the following swaption lengths, swaption vol matrix, swap rates, and term structure:

```
using namespace QuantLib;
using namespace QuantLib::Instruments;
using namespace QuantLib::ShortRateModels;
using namespace QuantLib::Pricers;
```

---

[9]Ibid., 5.
[10]Implementation from the QuantLib library. See Appendix D on the CD-ROM for definitions of classes used in the implementation.

```cpp
using CalibrationHelpers::CapHelper;
using CalibrationHelpers::SwaptionHelper;

using DayCounters::ActualActual;
using DayCounters::Actual360;
using DayCounters::Thirty360;
using Indexes::Xibor;
using Indexes::Euribor;

using TermStructures::PiecewiseFlatForward;
using TermStructures::RateHelper;
using TermStructures::DepositRateHelper;
using TermStructures::SwapRateHelper;

int numRows = 5;
int numCols = 10;

try
{

    Date todaysDate(15, February, 2002);
    Calendar calendar = Calendars::TARGET();

    Date settlementDate(19, February, 2003);

    // Instruments used to bootstrap the yield curve:
    std::vector<Handle<RateHelper> > instruments;

    unsigned int swaptionLengths[] = {1, 2, 3, 4, 5, 7, 10, 15, 20, 25, 30};
                                            // length of swaptions
    int swapYears[13] = {1, 2, 3, 4, 5, 6, 7, 8, 9, 10, 15, 20, 30}; // length of
                                                                     // swaps

    double swaptionVols[] = {
    23.92, 22.80, 19.8, 18.1, 16.0, 14.26, 13.56, 12.79, 12.3, 11.09,
    21.85, 21.50, 19.5, 17.2, 14.7, 13.23, 12.59, 12.29, 11.1, 10.30,
    19.46, 19.40, 17.9, 15.9, 13.9, 12.69, 12.15, 11.83, 10.8, 10.00,
    17.97, 17.80, 16.7, 14.9, 13.4, 12.28, 11.89, 11.48, 10.5, 9.80,
    16.29, 16.40, 15.1, 14.0, 12.9, 12.01, 11.46, 11.08, 10.4, 9.77,
    14.71, 14.90, 14.3, 13.2, 12.3, 11.49, 11.12, 10.70, 10.1, 9.57,
    12.93, 13.30, 12.8, 12.2, 11.6, 10.82, 10.47, 10.21, 9.8, 9.51,
    12.70, 12.10, 11.9, 11.2, 10.8, 10.40, 10.20, 10.00, 9.5, 9.00,
    12.30, 11.60, 11.6, 10.9, 10.5, 10.30, 10.00, 9.80, 9.3, 8.80,
    12.00, 11.40, 11.5, 10.8, 10.3, 10.00, 9.80, 9.60, 9.5, 9.10,
    11.50, 11.20, 11.3, 10.6, 10.2, 10.10, 9.70, 9.50, 9.4, 8.60};

    //Swap rates
    Rate swapRates[13] = {
      3.6425, 4.0875, 4.38, 4.5815, 4.74325, 4.87375, 4.9775, 5.07, 5.13, 5.1825,
        5.36, 5.45125, 5.43875
    };

    int swFixedLegFrequency = 1; // one year
```

```
bool swFixedLegIsAdjusted = false;
DayCounter swFixedLegDayCounter = Thirty360(Thirty360::European); // assume 360
                                                                 // days per year
int swFloatingLegFrequency = 2; // six months (semiannual payments)

for (i=0; i<13; i++)
{
  Handle<MarketElement> swapRate(new SimpleMarketElement(swapRates[i]*0.01));
  Handle<RateHelper> swapHelper(new SwapRateHelper(
    RelinkableHandle<MarketElement>(swapRate),
    swapYears[i], Years, settlementDays,
    calendar, ModifiedFollowing,
    swFixedLegFrequency,
    swFixedLegIsAdjusted, swFixedLegDayCounter,
    swFloatingLegFrequency));

  instruments.push_back(swapHelper);
}

// bootstrap the yield curve
Handle<PiecewiseFlatForward> myTermStructure(new
  PiecewiseFlatForward(todaysDate, settlementDate, instruments,
    depositDayCounter));

RelinkableHandle<TermStructure > rhTermStructure;
rhTermStructure.linkTo(myTermStructure);

//Define the ATM swaps
int fixedLegFrequency = 1; // paid once a year
bool fixedLegIsAdjusted = false;
RollingConvention roll = ModifiedFollowing;
DayCounter fixedLegDayCounter = Thirty360(Thirty360::European); // 360 day year
int floatingLegFrequency = 2; // paid every six months (twice a year)
bool payFixedRate = true;
int fixingDays = 2;
Rate dummyFixedRate = 0.03;
Handle<Xibor> indexSixMonths(new Euribor(6, Months, rhTermStructure));

// price an ATM swap
Handle<SimpleSwap> atmSwap(new SimpleSwap(
  payFixedRate, settlementDate.plusYears(1), 5, Years,
  calendar, roll, 1000.0, fixedLegFrequency, fixedATMRate,
  fixedLegIsAdjusted, fixedLegDayCounter, floatingLegFrequency,
  indexSixMonths, fixingDays, 0.0, rhTermStructure));

// set swaption maturities
std::vector<Period> swaptionMaturities;
swaptionMaturities.push_back(Period(1, Months));
swaptionMaturities.push_back(Period(3, Months));
swaptionMaturities.push_back(Period(6, Months));
swaptionMaturities.push_back(Period(1, Years));
swaptionMaturities.push_back(Period(2, Years));
swaptionMaturities.push_back(Period(3, Years));
```

```cpp
swaptionMaturities.push_back(Period(4, Years));
swaptionMaturities.push_back(Period(5, Years));
swaptionMaturities.push_back(Period(7, Years));
swaptionMaturities.push_back(Period(10, Years));

// calibrate to set of swaptions
CalibrationSet swaptions;

//List of times that have to be included in the timegrid
std::list<Time> times;
for (i=0; i<numRows; i++)
{
  for (unsigned int j=0; j<numCols; j++)
  {
    unsigned int k = i*10 + j;
    Handle<MarketElement> vol(
      new SimpleMarketElement(swaptionVols[k]*0.01));
      swaptions.push_back(Handle<CalibrationHelper>(
        new SwaptionHelper(swaptionMaturities[j],
          Period(swaptionLengths[i], Years),
          RelinkableHandle<MarketElement>(vol),
          indexSixMonths,
          rhTermStructure)));
    swaptions.back()->addTimes(times);
  }
}
const std::vector<Time> termTimes = myTermStructure->times();
for (i=0; i<termTimes.size(); i++)
  times.push_back(termTimes[i]);
times.sort();
times.unique();
//Building time-grid
TimeGrid grid(times, 30);

Handle<Model> modelHW(new HullWhite(rhTermStructure));

std::cout << "Calibrating to swaptions" << std::endl;

std::cout << "Hull-White (analytic formulae):" << std::endl;
swaptions.setPricingEngine(
  Handle<PricingEngine>(new JamshidianSwaption(modelHW)));

calibrateModel(modelHW, swaptions, 0.25);
std::cout << "calibrated to "
  << ArrayFormatter::toString(modelHW->params(), 6)
  << std::endl
  << std::endl;

std::cout << "Hull-White (numerical calibration):" << std::endl;
swaptions.setPricingEngine(
  Handle<PricingEngine>(new TreeSwaption(modelHW2, grid)));

calibrateModel(modelHW2, swaptions, 0.25);
```

```
std::cout << "calibrated to "
<< ArrayFormatter::toString(modelHW2->params(), 6)
<< std::endl
<< std::endl;

// Define the Bermudan swaption
std::vector<Date> bermudanDates;
const std::vector<Handle<CashFlow> >& leg = swap->floatingLeg();
for (i=0; i<leg.size(); i++)
{
  Handle<CashFlows::Coupon> coupon = leg[i];
  bermudanDates.push_back(coupon->accrualStartDate());
}

Instruments::Swaption bermudanSwaption(atmSwap,
  BermudanExercise(bermudanDates), rhTermStructure,
  Handle<PricingEngine>(new TreeSwaption(modelHW, 100)));

// do the pricing
bermudanSwaption.setPricingEngine(
  Handle<PricingEngine>(new TreeSwaption(modelHW, 100)));

std::cout << "HW:   " << bermudanSwaption.NPV() << std::endl;

return 0;

}

catch (std::exception& e)
{
  std::cout << e.what() << std::endl;
  return 1;
}
catch ( . . . )
{
  std::cout << "unknown error" << std::endl;
  return 1;
}
```

The results are:

```
Calibrating to swaptions
Hull-White (analytic formulae):
1y|23.9 (-0.0)|22.1 (-0.7)|20.3 ( 0.5)|19.2 ( 1.1)|15.9 (-0.1)|15.0 ( 0.7)|13.9
( 0.3)|13.0 ( 0.3)|11.7 (-0.6)|10.7 (-0.4)|
2y|22.0 ( 0.1)|20.3 (-1.2)|18.9 (-0.6)|17.0 (-0.2)|15.1 ( 0.4)|14.1 ( 0.9)|13.2
( 0.6)|12.6 ( 0.3)|11.3 ( 0.2)|10.3 ( 0.0)|
3y|18.5 (-0.9)|18.3 (-1.1)|17.3 (-0.6)|15.9 ( 0.0)|14.3 ( 0.4)|13.5 ( 0.8)|12.7
( 0.5)|12.0 ( 0.1)|10.9 ( 0.1)| 9.9 (-0.1)|
```

```
4y|17.1 (-0.9)|16.5 (-1.3)|15.9 (-0.8)|15.0 ( 0.1)|13.6 ( 0.2)|12.8 ( 0.5)|12.0
( 0.1)|11.5 ( 0.0)|10.5 ( 0.0)| 9.6 (-0.2)|
5y|15.9 (-0.4)|15.5 (-0.9)|14.9 (-0.2)|14.2 ( 0.2)|13.1 ( 0.2)|12.2 ( 0.2)|11.6
( 0.1)|11.1 (-0.0)|10.2 (-0.2)| 9.2 (-0.5)|
calibrated to [ 0.078657 ; 0.008783 ]


Hull-White (numerical calibration):
1y|23.8 (-0.2)|21.5 (-1.3)|20.5 ( 0.7)|19.8 ( 1.7)|16.1 ( 0.1)|15.3 ( 1.0)|14.1
( 0.5)|13.3 ( 0.5)|11.9 (-0.4)|10.7 (-0.3)|
2y|22.1 ( 0.3)|19.9 (-1.6)|19.1 (-0.4)|17.4 ( 0.2)|15.2 ( 0.5)|14.3 ( 1.1)|13.3
( 0.7)|12.8 ( 0.5)|11.4 ( 0.3)|10.3 ( 0.0)|
3y|18.1 (-1.3)|17.7 (-1.7)|17.3 (-0.6)|16.2 ( 0.3)|14.3 ( 0.4)|13.6 ( 0.9)|12.8
( 0.6)|12.1 ( 0.3)|11.0 ( 0.2)| 9.9 (-0.1)|
4y|16.6 (-1.4)|15.7 (-2.1)|15.7 (-1.0)|15.1 ( 0.2)|13.5 ( 0.1)|12.8 ( 0.5)|12.0
( 0.2)|11.5 ( 0.1)|10.5 ( 0.0)| 9.5 (-0.3)|
5y|15.3 (-0.9)|14.6 (-1.8)|14.7 (-0.4)|14.2 ( 0.2)|12.9 (-0.0)|12.2 ( 0.2)|11.6
( 0.1)|11.1 ( 0.0)|10.1 (-0.3)| 9.1 (-0.7)|
calibrated to [ 0.095098 ; 0.009294 ]


Pricing an ATM Bermudan swaption
HW:      54.077
```

14.3   ANDERSEN'S METHOD

Consider an increasing maturity structure $0 = T_0 < T_1 < T_2 < \ldots < T_{K+1}$. Also consider an optimal stopping time τ^* and an early exercise indicator $I(t)$ that equals 1 if the exercise is optimal at time t and is zero otherwise. Thus we have

$$\tau^* = \inf[t \in \{T_s, T_{s+1, \ldots,} T_x\} : I(t) = 1]$$

To value an American or Bermudan swaption, we want to choose τ^* that maximizes its value V, under the risk-neutral measure, at time 0:

$$V(0) = \sup_{\tau \in \psi} B(0) E^Q \left[\frac{g(\tau)}{B(\tau)} \right]$$

where Ψ is the set of all exercise strategies, $g(\cdot)$ is the payoff, and $B(\cdot)$ is the money market account numeraire. Thus, the value of payer Bermudan swaption $S_{s,x,e}$ is

$$S_{s,x,e}(t) = \max_{k=s,\ldots,x} E^Q \left[\frac{\max(S_{k,e}(T_k), 0)}{B(T_k)} \right] \tag{14.2}$$

where $S_{k,e}(T_k)$ is given in equation (14.3).

Denote the price of a Bermudan swaption by $S_{s,x,e}$ that is characterized by three dates: the lockout date (the first exercise date), T_s; the last exercise date, T_x; and the final swap maturity date, T_e. We assume that $T_s < T_x < T_e$, and that all three dates coincide with the exercise schedule dates; that is, s, x, and e are all integers in $\{0, \ldots, K+1\}$. Moreover, to be consistent with market-traded swaptions, we assume $T_x = T_{e-1}$. Early exercise of the Bermudan swaption is restricted to dates in the discrete set $\{T_s, T_{s+1}, \ldots, T_x\}$. If exercise takes places at, say, $\tau^* = T_i$, then the swaption holder receives at time T_i,

$$S_{s,x,e}(T_i) = S_{i,e}(T_i)$$

where $S_{i,e}(T_i)$ which is the value of the remaining European swaption at T_i, with an underlying notional amount of \$1, given by

$$
\begin{aligned}
S_{s,e}(T_s) &= E^Q\left[\phi\sum_{k=s}^{e-1} P(T_s, T_{k+1})\tau_k \max(F_k(T_s) - X, 0)\right] \\
&= E^Q\left[\phi\max\left((1 - P(T_s, T_e) - X\sum_{k=s}^{e-1}\tau_k P(T_s, T_{k+1}), 0\right)\right]
\end{aligned}
\tag{14.3}
$$

where X is the strike price; $T_s > 0$, $s = 1, \ldots, K$, is the swaption maturity; and the flag ϕ is $+1$ if the option is a payer swaption (option holder pays fixed and receives floating) and is -1 if the option is a receiver swaption (option holder receives fixed and pays floating). We consider only swaps with cash-flow dates where fixed payments $\tau_{k-1}X$ are swapped against floating LIBOR (paid in arrears at time T_k) that coincide with the maturity schedule dates (i.e., $T_{s+1}, T_{s+2}, \ldots, T_e$) Thus, T_s and T_e are the start and end dates of the underlying swap, respectively, and we require $T_s < T_e \leq T_{k+1}$. There are many variations of Bermudan swaptions with different features, but all can be priced in the general pricing framework that follows.

Given the Markov dynamics in (14.1), the decision of whether to exercise a Bermudan swaption on one of the exercise dates $T_i \in \{T_s, T_{s+1}, \ldots, T_x\}$ in general depends on all of the state variables $F_k(T_i)$, $k = i, i+1, \ldots, e-1$. In order to reduce the dimensionality of the exercise decision, Andersen considers an indicator function $I(t)$ that is used to make exercise decisions, of the form

$$I(T_i) = f(S_{i,e}(T_i), S_{i+1,e}(T_i), \ldots, S_{x,e}(T_i); H(T_i))\tag{14.4}$$

where f is a Boolean function of only the European values of all still-alive "component" swaptions that compose the Bermudan swaption as well as a function of time, $H(t)$, that maximizes the value of the Bermudan swaption subject to the chosen exercise strategy in equation (14.4).

Any specification of f will satisfy

$$I(T_x) = \begin{cases} 1 \ if \ S_{x,e}(T_x) > 0 \\ 0, \ otherwise \end{cases} \tag{14.5}$$

which means that a Bermudan swaption will be exercised (if in-the-money) on the last exercise date if it has not been exercised earlier.

Andersen suggests two specifications of f. The first is

$$I(T_x) = \begin{cases} 1, \ if \ S_{i,e}(T_i) > H(T_i) \\ 0, \ otherwise \end{cases} \tag{14.6}$$

The second, and more restrictive, one is

$$I(T_x) = \begin{cases} 1, \ if \ S_{i,e}(T_i) > H(T_i) \ and \ S_{i,e}(T_i) \geq \max_{j=i+1,...,x} S_{j,e}(T_i) \\ 0, \ otherwise \end{cases} \tag{14.7}$$

That is, exercise only if the Bermudan swaption is worth more than some barrier level and also worth more than the remaining European swaptions contained in the Bermudan swaption.

Once a specific form for f is chosen, valuation of a Bermudan swaption amounts to determining the values $H(t)$ for $t = T_s, T_{s+1}, \ldots, T_x$.

Following Andersen, the steps to find the values of $H(t)$ and subsequently the value of the Bermudan option are:

Step 1. Decide on a function form for f for the exercise strategy in equation (14.5). The functional form is allowed to depend on the values of the European swaptions and one time-dependent function $H(t)$.

Step 2. Run an n-path Monte Carlo simulation where for each path and each time $T_s, T_{s+1}, \ldots, T_x$, the following is stored in memory:

1. The instrinsic value.

2. The numeraire B.

3. Other data necessary to compute f.

For the strategy in equation (14.7), item 3 would be the maximum value of the remaining European swaptions.

Step 3. Using equations (14.2) and (14.4) and the numbers stored in items 1 and 2 in step 2, compute the values $H(T_s), H(T_{s+1}), \ldots, H(T_x)$ such that the value of the Bermudan swaption is maximized. This optimization problem can be done using backward induction starting with $H(T_{x-1})$ and the boundary condition given in equation (14.5). In total, $x - s$ simple one-variable optimization problems need to be solved to determine the exercise strategy.[11]

Step 4. Change the random number generator seed to ensure independence to steps 2 and 3. Using the exercise strategy in step 3, price the option by an N-path ($N \gg n$) Monte Carlo simulation of equation (14.2).

Andersen suggests that to reduce the number of one-dimension optimizations done in step 3, the function $H(t)$ be specified as a linear (piecewise) spline with fewer spline points than exercise dates. This also reduces the number of simulations needed to get a smooth estimate of the exercise boundary.

14.4   LONGSTAFF AND SCHWARTZ METHOD

Longstaff and Schwartz developed a method to value American- and Bermudan-style options by computing both the intrinsic value and the expected value of holding the option, waiting for a later exercise date. As discussed earlier, due to complex dynamics, the LIBOR market model doesn't lend itself well to computational approximations with lattice methods, so Monte Carlo simulation must be used. However, a key problem is that the holding value is not immediately facilitated by simulation, in contrast to lattice methods. The Longstaff and Schwartz method (LSM) overcomes this problem by approximating the holding value by assuming that the holding value, considered as an expectation conditional on continuation, is a simple function of state variables observable at the exercise date in question. Using standard regression techniques, whereby *ex-post* realized payoffs are regressed against the specified *ex-ante* observed values, these functions can be estimated from cross-sectional information obtained in the simulation. This type of regression is referred to as least-squares Monte Carlo (LSMC). Estimation of such functions for each exercise date will provide an approximated functional expression for holding values at all exercise dates, which can be used to value American or Bermudan options directly by Monte Carlo.[12]

The method is based on the mathematical fact that any twice-differentiable function, such as the conditional expectation of the holding value, can be approximated by a countable set of linear independent basis functions. Except for linear independence, there are no restrictions on the choice of basis functions, except that the chosen basis functions influence the quality of the approximation, and so those

---

[11]Andersen suggests using the Golden Search Method or Brent's method for one-dimensional optimization algorithms; the Golden Search Method and Brent's method are given in Press et al. (1992).

[12]Pedersen (1999).

that give the best approximation should be used. Often, polynomial functions of the form $f(x) = \alpha_0 + \alpha_1 x + \alpha_2 x^2 + \ldots$ work well. In fact, Longstaff and Schwartz suggest using (weighted) Laguerre polynomials:[13]

$$L_0(x) = \exp(-x/2)$$
$$L_1(x) = \exp(-x/2)(1-x)$$
$$L_2(x) = \exp(-x/2)(1-2x+x^2/2) \tag{14.8}$$
$$L_n(x) = \exp(-x/2)\left(\frac{e^x}{n!}\frac{d^n}{dx^n}(x^n e^{-x})\right)$$

Following Longstaff and Schwartz, denote the functional form of the conditional expectation of the holding value at time t_{k-1} by $F(\omega; t_{k-1})$ where ω is a realized simulation path. Denote the path of random cash flows generated by the option, conditional on the option not being exercised at or prior to time t and on the option holder following the optimal stopping strategy for all $t < s \leq T$, by $C(\omega, s; t, T)$. Define $\mathfrak{I}_t$ as the filtration at time $t \in [0, T]$, generated by the asset process. It is assumed that the American option can be exercised only at K discrete times $0 \leq t_1 \leq t_2 \leq t_3 \leq \ldots \leq t_K = T$.

Note that at time t_k, the cash flow from immediate exercise is known to the option holder and the value of immediate exercise is simply the cash flow. However, the cash flows from continuation, thus choosing not exercising at t_k, are not known at t_k. However, from no-arbitrage considerations, the value of continuation is given by the expectation of the remaining discounted cash flows after t_k, taken under the risk-neutral measure Q. The expectation of the value of continuation at t_k is

$$F(\omega; t_k) = E^Q\left[\sum_{j=k+1}^{K} \exp\left(\int_{t_k}^{t_j} r(\omega, s)ds\right)C(\omega, t_j; t_k, T)\Big|\mathfrak{I}_{t_k}\right] \tag{14.9}$$

With basis functions, we can write $F(\omega; t_{K-1})$ as a linear function of the (orthonormal and independent) elements of the basis:

$$F(\omega; t_{K-1}) = \sum_{j=0}^{\infty} a_j L_j(x)$$

where the a_j's are constant coefficients that act as weights to the basis functions.

[13]Other basis types include Hermite, Legendre, Chebyshev, Jacobi, and Gegenbauer polynomials. Numerical tests also show Fourier or trigonometric series and even simple powers of the state variables yield accurate results.

The objective of the LSM algorithm is to provide a pathwise approximation to the optimal stopping rule that maximizes the value of the American option.[14] The LSM algorithm uses least-squares to approximate the conditional expectation function at times $t_{K-1}, t_{K-2}, \ldots, t_1$. The algorithm works backward starting at t_{K-1} since the (random) cash flows $C(\omega, s; t, T)$ generated by the option are defined recursively; $C(\omega, s; t_k, T)$ can differ from $C(\omega, s; t_{k+1}, T)$ since it may be optimal to stop at time t_{k+1}, thus changing all subsequent cash flows along a realized path ω.[15]

To implement the LSM, one approximates $F(\omega; t_{K-1})$ using the first $M < \infty$ basis functions and denotes the approximation $F_M(\omega; t_{K-1})$. After specifying the basis functions, $F_M(\omega; t_{K-1})$ is estimated by regressing the discounted values of $C(\omega, s; t_{K-1}, T)$ onto the basis functions for the paths where the option is in-the-money at time t_{K-1}.[16] As Longstaff and Schwartz point out, using only in-the-money paths limits the region over which the conditional expectation must be estimated and greatly reduces the number of basis functions needed to obtain an accurate approximation of the conditional expectation function. It can be shown that the estimated value of the regression $\hat{F}_M(\omega; t_{K-1})$ converges in mean square and in probability to $F_M(\omega; t_{K-1})$ (see Theorem 3.5 of White (1984)) and is the best linear unbiased estimator of $F_M(\omega; t_{K-1})$ based on a mean-squared metric (see Theorem 1.21 of Amemiya (1985)).

Once the conditional expectation function at time t_{K-1} is estimated by $\hat{F}_M(\omega; t_{K-1})$, one can determine whether early exercise at t_{K-1} is optimal for an in-the-money path ω by comparing the immediate exercise (intrinsic) value to $\hat{F}_M(\omega; t_{K-1})$, and repeating for each in-the-money path. Once the exercise decision is determined at t_{K-1}, the option cash flow paths $C(\omega, s; t_{K-2}, T)$ can then be approximated. The recursion proceeds by moving backward from t_{K-1} to time t_{K-2} and repeating the process back to t_1, so that exercise decisions at each exercise time along each path have been determined. An American option can then be valued by starting at time 0 and moving forward until the first stopping time occurs, discounting the resulting cash flow from exercise back to time 0, and then averaging over all paths ω.[17]

Convergence results of the LSM are provided by Proposition 1 and 2 by Longstaff and Schwartz (2001). Certainly, the number paths, N; the number of discrete exercise points along a path, K; and the number of basis functions, M; affect the convergence of the American price. However, it can be shown that as $N \to \infty$ and for a sufficiently large $M < \infty$, the LSM algorithm converges in probability to the actual American price, $V(x)$, for an arbitrary $\varepsilon > 0$; that is,

---

[14]Longstaff and Schwartz (2001), 121.
[15]Ibid., 122.
[16]Ibid., 122.
[17]Ibid., 123.

$$\lim_{N \to \infty} \left[\left| V(x) - \frac{1}{N} \sum_{i=1}^{N} LSM(\omega_i;\ M,\ K) \right| > \varepsilon \right] = 0 \qquad (14.10)$$

It is assumed that the holding function value W, evaluated at time t as a function of the underlying asset S_t, is given by the following function:

$$W_t = \alpha_0 + \alpha_1 S_t + \alpha_2 S_t^2$$

where the parameters $(\alpha_0, \alpha_1, \alpha_2)$ are estimated at each time t (except for the final exercise time) by regressing the holding function W_t on $X_t/\beta(t, t + 1)$ where $\beta(t, t + 1)$ is the one-period discount rate at time t. Denote W_t^* as the observed holding value, X_t the value of immediate exercise, and V_t the realized option value at time t when using W_t in the exercise decision. This leads to the following set of recursions for an American put:

$$X_t = \max(K - S_t,\ 0)$$
$$W_t = \alpha_0 + \alpha_1 S_t + \alpha_2 S_t^2$$
$$W_t^* = V_{t+1} / \beta(t,\ t+1)$$
$$V_t = \begin{cases} W_t^*, & W_t > X_t \text{ and } t < 3 \\ X_t, & W_t \le X_t \text{ or } t = 3 \end{cases}$$

The following is an implementation of the *LeastSquaresMC* class:

```
class LeastSquaresMC : public NumericalMethod
{
  public:
    LeastSquaresMC() { }
    LeastSquaresMC(long M, long N, double initPrice, double T, double strike,
      double rate, double vol);
    ~LSM() { }
    // runs LSM algorithm
    double computeLSM(int time, Matrix& Paths, Matrix& CashFlow, Matrix& Exercise);
    // computes American option value
    double computeValue(Matrix& CashFlow);
    // simulates Monte Carlo of asset diffusion process
    void calcLeastSquaresMC();
  private:
    long M_;                        // number of simulations
    long N_;                        // number of time steps
    double rate_;                   // interest rate
    double vol_;                    // volatilty
    double mu;_                     // drift
    double initPrice_;              // initial asset price
```

```
      double T_;                        // option maturity
      double dt_;                       // change in time size
      double strike_;                   // strike price
      vector<double> prices[500];       // stores asset price at each time step along each
                                        // path
      StatUtility util;                 // used for calling methods for generating
                                        // gaussian deviates
};
```

The following is the implementation.

```
/********************************************************************************
LSM: Constructor
[in]: long M           : number of simulations
      long N           : number of time steps
      double initPrice : initial asset price
      double T         : time to maturity
      double strike    : strike price
      double rate      : interest rate
      double vol       : asset volatiliy
*********************************************************************************/
LMC::LMC(long M, long N, double initPrice, double T, double strike, double rate,
   double vol)
   : M_(M), N_(N), initPrice_(initPrice), T_(T), strike_(strike), rate_(rate),
     vol_(vol)
{
   dt_ = T/N;
}

/********************************************************************************
calcLeastSquaresMC : runs a Monte Carlo simulation to generate prices at each time
   step along each path
[in]: none
[out]: none
*********************************************************************************/
void LSM::calcLeastSquaresMC()
{
   double lnS, S;
   double deviate;
   double voldt;
   int i, j;
   long seed = -2;            // seed for random number generator
   long* idum = &seed;

   Matrix Paths(M, 4);        // M x 4 matrix ; each row contains the prices for each
                              // time step
   Matrix Exercise(M, 4);     // M x 4 matrix; each row contains early exercise value
   Matrix CashFlow(M, 4);     // M x 4 matrix; each row contains optimal cash flow at
                              // the time step along path
```

```
  mu_ = (rate - vol*vol/2)*dt_;  // drift
  voldt = vol*sqrt(dt_);          // diffusion

  for (i = 1; i = M_; i++)
  {
    lnS = log(initPrice_);
    prices[i-1].push_back(initPrice_);
    for (j = 1; j < N_; j++)
    {
      // generate deviate
      deviate = util.gasdev(idum);
      lnS = lnS + mu_ + voldt*deviate;
      S = exp(lnS);
      prices[i-1].push_back(S);
    }
  }

  // create path matrix
  for (i = 1; i <= M_; i++)
  {
    Paths.Row(i) << prices[i-1][0] << prices[i-1][1] << prices[i-1][2] << prices[i-
      1][3];
    Exercise.Row(i) << max(strike_ - prices[i-1][1], 0) << max(strike_-prices[i-
      1][2], 0) <<
      max(strike_ - prices[i-1][3], 0);
  }

  // compute cash flows at maturity
  for (i = 1; i <= M_; i++)
    CashFlow(i, N_) = Exercise(i, N_);

  // recursion
  computeLSM(N_-1, Paths, CashFlow, Exercise);
}

/****************************************************************************
computeLSM : computes recursive Longstaff and Schwartz Least Squares simulation to
             value American simulation
[in]:   int time         : time step
        Matrix& Paths     : matrix of asset prices
        Matrix& CashFlow  : matrix of cash flows
        Matrix& Exercise  : matrix of exercise
[out]:  double            : American price
****************************************************************************/
double LSM::computeLSM(int time, Matrix& Paths, Matrix& CashFlow, Matrix& Exercise)
{
  double val = 0.0;            // value of American option
  double disc = 1/(1 + rate);  // discount factor
  double num[100] = {0.0};     // keeps track of in-the-money paths at each time
                               // step
  vector<double> cashFlow[100]; // cash flows
  int j;
  int i = 1;
```

```
int q = 1;
int k = 0;

try
{
  for (j = 1; j <= M_; j++)
  {
    val = prices[j-1].back();
    prices[j-1].pop_back();
    if (strike - val > 0)
    {
      num[j] = j;
      k++;   // count dimension for matrices
    }
  }

  ColumnVector Y(k);   // vector of payoffs (dependent variables)
  ColumnVector B(k);   // vector of regression coefficients
  ColumnVector C(k);   // continuation
  Matrix X(k, 3);      // 1 X X^2 (columns)

  for (j = 1; j <= M_; j++)
  {
    if (i <= k)
    {
      if (Exercise(j, time-1) > 0)
      {
        cashFlow[j].push_back(max(Exercise(j, time), 0)/disc);
        Y(i) = cashFlow[j].back();
        X.Row(i) << 1 << Paths(j, time-1) << Paths(j, time-1)*Paths(j, time-1);
        i++;
      }
    }
  }

  // calculate regression coefficients
  if (time > 2)
  {
    B = ((X.t()*X).i())*(X.t()*Y);
    C = X*B; // compute continuation (expected holding values)

    i = 1;
    for (j = 1; j <= M_; j++)
    {
      if (num[j] != 0)
      {
        if (Exercise(j, time-1) > C(i))
        {
          CashFlow(j, time-1) = Exercise(j, time-1);
          CashFlow(j, time) = 0.0;
          if (time-1 == 2)
            CashFlow(j, time+1) = 0.0;
        }
```

```
        else
        {
          CashFlow(j, time-1) = 0.0;
        }
      }
      else
      {
        CashFlow(j, time-1) = 0.0;
      }
    }
    computeLSM(time-1, Paths, CashFlow, Exercise);
  }
  return computeValue(CashFlow);
}
catch (const char* s)
{
  cout << s << endl;
  throw s;
}
return 0.0;
}
```

```
/*****************************************************************************
computeValue : computes the value of the American option based on the option
               exercise cash flows
[in]:   Matrix& CashFlow  : matrix of option exercise cash flows
[out]: double American    : price
*****************************************************************************/
double LSM::computeValue (Matrix& CashFlow)
{
  int i, j;
  double discValue = 0.0;      // discounted value

  for (i = 1; i <= M_; i++)
  {
    for (j = 2; j <= N_; j++)
    {
      if (CashFlow(i, j) > 0)
        discValue = discValue + CashFlow(i, j)/(pow(1+rate, j-1));
    }
  }
  return discValue/M_;
}
```

As an example, suppose we want to price an American put option on a nondividend stock with $M = 8$, $T = 4$, $N = 4$, $r = 0.06$, $K = 53$, $S_0 = 50$, $\beta(t, t + 1) = 1.062$, and $\sigma = 0.25$. Running the least-squares Monte Carlo, we generate the sample paths shown in Table 14.1. The regression pertaining to the exercise decision at

TABLE 14.1 Simulations

Path	Time 0	Time 1	Time 2	Time 3
1	50.00	48.44	46.01	47.36
2	50.00	50.06	48.91	49.53
3	50.00	49.23	50.59	48.00
4	50.00	46.96	47.42	48.12
5	50.00	50.07	50.80	50.64
6	50.00	49.95	52.74	52.85
7	50.00	50.09	49.28	47.99
8	50.00	50.93	54.23	54.67

time $t = 2$ is shown in Table 14.2. Note that at each time step only those paths in the regression that are in-the-money are included; that is, path 8 is excluded.

After discounting the cash flows (Table 14.3), the American price is \$3.39. For a more detailed example with all the intermediate regressions calculations, see Longstaff and Schwartz (2001). Longstaff and Schwartz also show that the LSM method can be applied to many types of exotic path-dependent derivatives including an American-Bermudan-Asian call option on the average of the price of a stock over some time horizon, where the call option can be exercised after some initial lockout period. As basis functions in the regression, they use a constant, the first two Laguerre polynomials evaluated at both the stock and average stock price, as well as the cross-product of these Laguerre polynomials up to third-order terms. Their results are compared with those using a finite-difference approximation using an alternating direction implicit (ADI) algorithm. The results of the LSM and finite-difference prices are quite similar and the differences in early exercise values are quite small, within bid-ask spread cost bounds.

TABLE 14.2 Estimated Regression at $t = 2$

Path	V_3	S_2	W_2^*	X_2	W_2	V_2
1	5.644	46.01	5.644 * 0.943 = 5.32	6.99	5.59	
2	3.470	48.91	3.470 * 0.943 = 3.27	4.09	4.96	3.272
3	4.995	50.59	4.995 * 0.943 = 4.71	2.41	3.51	4.710
4	4.879	47.42	4.879 * 0.943 = 4.602	5.58	5.58	
5	2.357	50.80	2.357 * 0.943 = 2.22	2.20	3.27	2.222
6	0.154	52.74	0.154 * 0.943 = 0.145	0.15	0.49	0.145
7	5.012	49.28	5.012 * 0.943 = 4.73	3.72	4.71	4.726
8	0.000					

$W_2 = -302.072 + 13.182S_2 - 0.142S_2^2$.

TABLE 14.3 Final Cash Flows

Path	Time 1	Time 2	Time 3
1	0.00	4.48	0.00
2	0.00	0.00	3.04
3	4.49	0.00	0.00
4	0.00	0.00	0.00
5	4.96	0.00	0.00
6	0.00	0.00	1.61
7	0.00	6.82	0.00
8	0.00	4.75	0.00

14.5   STOCHASTIC MESH METHOD

Broadie and Glasserman (1997b) developed an approach that combines the advantages of the lattice approach with the advantages of Monte Carlo simulation into a hybrid approach called the stochastic mesh. The method supports non-Markov processes and the valuation of path-dependent Bermudan options. Unlike nonrecombining trees, the stochastic mesh does not grow exponentially in size. Furthermore, a feature of many lattice methods is that the terminal nodes contribute very little to the computation of the present value of the contingent claim. To improve this, Broadie and Glasserman construct a hybrid lattice, or stochastic mesh, by letting a node at any time level have branches to all the nodes in the next branch level. Thus, a node at time $i + 1$ contributes to the valuation of all nodes at time i. The mesh width is defined as the number of nodes per time level, which remains constant over time levels. The branching probabilities are derived using the conditional marginal densities implied by the process definition.

Valuation of contingent claims using a stochastic mesh is done the same way for lattices. Consider a stochastic process with a state variable X_t with some dimension $| I |$. The initial state is denoted X_0 and node j at time t in the mesh is denoted by $X_{t,j}$. To generate the mesh, one generates as many sample paths of the state variables as the mesh width. For purposes of valuation, branching weights are required for all branches. To compute the branch weight $w(x, y, t)$ corresponding to the branch from state x at time t to state y at time $t + 1$, the marginal transition density of reaching state y at time $t + 1$ given state x at time t must be computed.[18] This is the central computational problem of the mesh method. Broadie and Glasserman (1997b) show that the way the weights are computed affects the convergence of the prices computed using the mesh.

---

[18]Pedersen (1999), 12.

Following Pedersen (1999), denote the conditional marginal density function at time $t + 1$ given state u at time t by $\varphi(u, t, \cdot)$. The weights $w(x, y, t)$ are computed as

$$w(x, y, t) = \frac{1}{m}\frac{\varphi(x, y, t)}{\varphi_{mesh}(y, t+1)} \tag{14.11}$$

where $\varphi_{mesh}(y, u)$ is the "mesh density" of being in state u at time $t + 1$ and m is the mesh width. With the following choice of mesh density, the convergence is controlled:

$$\varphi_{mesh}(t, u) = \begin{cases} \dfrac{1}{m}\displaystyle\sum_{j=1}^{m}\varphi(X_{t-1,j}, u, t-1) & t > 0 \\[2ex] \varphi(X_0, u, 0) & t = 0 \end{cases}$$

A sample mesh given by Pedersen (1999) is shown in Figure 14.1.[19]

Broadie and Glasserman (1997b) show that the price of a contingent claim using a mesh will be an upper bound to the true price.[20] A lower bound is found by

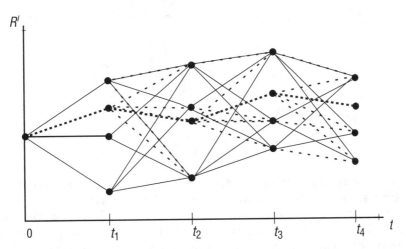

FIGURE 14.1   A Sample Mesh (Hard Lines). The mesh width b is 3 and the number of time discretization points n is 4. The dotted lines show a sample path connected at each time step to the mesh nodes at the next time level.
Source: Reproduced from M. Pedersen, July 1999, "Bermudan Swaptions in the LIBOR Market Model," preprint, see www.math.ku.dk/~brock/caroe2.pdf.

---

[19]Ibid., 13.
[20]Ibid., 13.

generating additional sample paths. Both bounds are shown to converge to the true price. For each generated sample path, the derivative is valued at each time step and linked to the corresponding time step in the mesh.

The estimates obtained from the mesh are high-biased (asymptotically unbiased) estimators. A low-biased (asymptotically unbiased) estimator can be obtained by using a single path using the mesh only for the estimating of the holding value. The low- and high-biased estimators are computed as follows. The high-biased estimator $\hat{Q} = \hat{Q}(t, X_{t,j})$ is given by the recursion:

$$\hat{Q}(t, X_{t,i}) = \begin{cases} \max\left(\pi(t, X_{t,i}), \sum_{j=1}^{m} w^*(X_{t,i}, X_{t+1,j}, t)\hat{Q}(t+1, X_{t+1,j})\right) & t < T \\ \pi(T, X_{T,i}), & t = T \end{cases}$$

where $X_{t,i}$ denotes the state vector at node i at time t, $\pi(t, x)$ is the payoff function from exercise in state x at time t, and $w^*(t, x, \cdot)$ is the normalized version of $w(t, x, \cdot)$, namely,

$$w^*(x, X_{t+1,j}, t) = \frac{w(x, X_{t+1,j}, t)}{\sum_{k=1}^{m} w(x, X_{t+1,k}, t)}$$

The low-biased estimator $\hat{q}$ is given by

$$\hat{q} = \pi(\hat{\tau}_S, S_{\hat{\tau}_S})$$

with $\hat{\tau}_S$ defined in terms of the entire path and the high-biased estimator:

$$\hat{\tau}_S = \arg\min_t \{\pi(t, S_t) \geq \hat{Q}(t, S_t)\}$$

Broadie and Glasserman (1997b) applied the stochastic mesh algorithm to a multivariate version of the Black-Scholes with five elements ($|I| = 5$) and around four time steps. When using stochastic meshes with the LIBOR market model, the state vector of forward rates becomes much larger and so computation time (and memory required) may become too high for the method to be practical. To compute branching weights, the conditional marginal densities need to be computed by numerical integration. However, approximations along the lines of the derivation of swaption price approximations can be used; (see Brace, Gatarek, and Musiela (1997)).[21] Moreover, transitional densities cannot be computed in the LMM model as the state vector of period forward rates has infinite dimension while the vector of

---

[21]Ibid., 14.

Brownian shocks has finite dimension. Despite the fact that the stochastic mesh method does not lend itself well to the LMM, Pedersen shows how the conditional marginal densities can be computed for a set of forward rates in a discretized model and shows how the stochastic mesh technique applied to the LMM model can be used to price Bermudan swaptions. The interested reader should see Pedersen (1999) for details.

14.6   VALUATION OF RANGE NOTES

Consider the simple interest rate, $R(t, T)$ with maturity $T - t$. We can define this rate in terms of a zero-coupon bond $P(t, T)$ as

$$R(t, T) = \frac{\dfrac{1}{P(t, T)} - 1}{T - 1} \tag{14.12}$$

so that

$$P(t, T) = \frac{1}{1 + R(t, T)(t - 1)} \tag{14.13}$$

We will make use of these relations to price exotic interest rates in a discrete-state HJM model. Consider a range note. A range note is a financial security with a principal of N dollars and a maturity date T that pays out spot rate of interest $r(t)$–1 times N—that is, $(r(t) - 1)N$—on any date t over the life of the contract when the simple interest rate with maturity T^*, $R(t, t + T^*)$, lies within lower and upper bounds, k_l and k_u, respectively, of the range (k_l, k_u). The cash flow is paid at time t + 1. Denote the index function

$$\mathbf{1}_{[k_l, R(j, j+T^*) < k_u]} = \begin{cases} 1 \ if \ k_l < R(j, \ j + T^*) < k_u \\ 0 \ \text{otherwise} \end{cases} \tag{14.14}$$

We can write the cash flows to a range note using this index function from time t + 1 to maturity as

$$CF(t + 1, T) = \sum_{j=t}^{T-1} (r(j) - 1)N\mathbf{1}_{\{k_l < R(j, j+T^*) < k_u\}} \tag{14.15}$$

Let $V(t)$ denote the value of the range note at time t. Then using risk-neutral valuation, we get

$$V(t) = \tilde{E}_t \left(\frac{\sum_{j=t}^{T-1} (r(j) - 1) N \mathbf{1}_{\{k_l < R(j, j+T^*) < k_u\}}}{B(j+1)} \right) B(t) \qquad (14.16)$$

A range note can be used as a partial hedge against a floating rate note with a cap and floor attached. If the floating rate note has principal N and pays based on the spot rate, then payments are $(r(t) - 1)N$. If the cap has a rate k_u and the floor has a rate k_l then these payments occur only in the range (k_l, k_u). These payments are given by equation (14.16). Outside this range, either $k_u N$ or $k_d N$ is received, but they are not included in (14.16).

Consider a range note with a maturity of $T = 3$ years with a principal of $N = 100$. Let the lower bound be $k_l = 0.016$ and the upper bound be $k_u = 0.023$ on a simple interest rate with maturity $T^* = 2$. To value this range note, we first compute the evolution of the simple interest rate $R(t, t + 2) = [1/(P(t, t, 2) - 1]/2$. We only need to find the evolution up to time 2 because the time 3 payment is based on the simple interest rate at time 2. We will use a single-factor HJM tree for valuation. We assume that the volatility structure is of the exponential Vasicek form, $\eta e^{-\lambda(T-t)}$, with $\eta = 0.0076$ and $\lambda = 0.0154$.

In order to value the range note, we construct a synthetic portfolio between the money market account and a four-year zero-coupon bond as shown in Figure 14.2.

Using the risk-neutral valuation procedure, we can compute the value of the range note at time t using the cash flows:

$$
\begin{aligned}
&V(t; s_t) \\
&= \frac{0.5[V(t+1; s_t u) + cashflow(t+1, s_t u)] + 0.5[V(t+1; s_t d) + cashflow(t+1; s_t d)]}{r(t; s_t)}
\end{aligned}
\qquad (14.17)
$$

and the number of shares held in the four-year zero-coupon bond, $n_4(t; s_t)$ is

$$n_4(t; s_t) = \frac{V(t+1; s_t u) + cashflow(t+1; s_t u) - [V(t+1; s_t d) + cashflow(t+1; s_t d)]}{[P(t+1, 4; s_t u) - P(t+1, 4; s_t d)]} \qquad (14.18)$$

and the number of shares held in the money market account, $n_0(t; s_t)$, is

$$n_0(t; s_t) = \frac{V(t; s_t) - n_4(t; s_t) P(t, 4; s_t)}{B(t; s_{t-1})} \qquad (14.19)$$

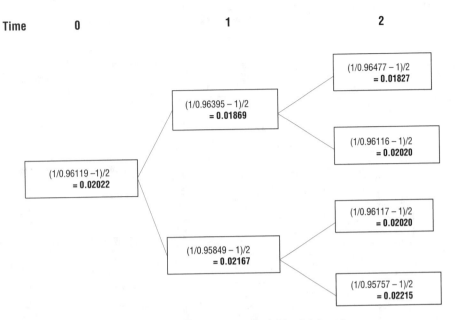

Time   **0**   **1**   **2**

(1/0.96477 − 1)/2
= **0.01827**

(1/0.96395 − 1)/2
= **0.01869**

(1/0.96116 − 1)/2
= **0.02020**

(1/0.96119 −1)/2
= **0.02022**

(1/0.96117 − 1)/2
= **0.02020**

(1/0.95849 − 1)/2
= **0.02167**

(1/0.95757 − 1)/2
= **0.02215**

FIGURE 14.2   Evolution of Simple Interest Rate with T = 2 Maturity

For example, at time 3, sample calculations for cash flows are

$$cashflow(2; uu) = 100[r(2; u) - 1]1_{\{0.019<R(1;4;u)<0.022\}} = 0$$

since $R(1, 4; u) = 0.18699$, which is below the lower bound $k_l = 0.019$. However,

$$cashflow(2; dd) = 100[r(2; d) - 1]1_{\{0.019<R(1;4;d)<0.022\}} = 2.097$$

since $R(1, 4; u) = 0.02167$ is below the upper bound $k_u = 0.022$. Figure 14.3 shows the constructed HJM tree to value the range note. At each node is the range note value, the cash flow, and the number of shares held in the money market and four-year zero-coupon bond. Note that if we used a three-year bond to hedge the portfolio instead of a four-year bond, then we could not hedge our position at time 2 since the number of shares in the money market account and in the three-year zero-coupon go to infinity; the denominator in equation (14.18), using three-year bonds, becomes 0 since the bonds in all states at time 3 are worth 1.

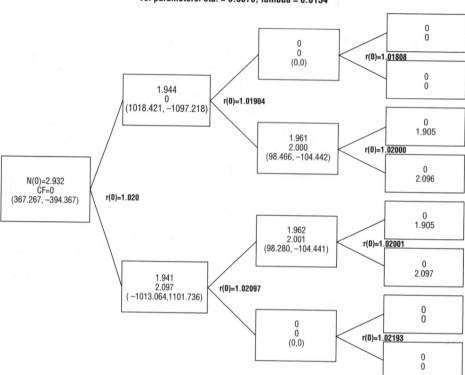

FIGURE 14.3   HJM Range Note

The following is the code:

```
#include "HJMTree.h"
#include <math.h>
#include <time.h>
#define max(a, b) ((a > b) ? a : b)
#define indicator(r, kl, ku) (((kl < r) ? r : ku) < ku ? 1 : 0)
#define indicator1(r, kl) ((r < kl) ? kl : 0)
#define indicator2(r, ku) ((r > ku) ? ku : 0)

/***************************************************************************
calcRangeNote : computes the value of a range note
[in] : none
[out]: double value of range note
***************************************************************************/
double HJMTree::calcRangeNote()
```

```
{
  int j = pow(2, N-2);         // number of nodes
  double rate = 0.0;           // simple short rate
  double bondDiff = 0.0;       // difference between zero coupon bonds
  double moneyAccount = 0.0;   // money market account

  for (int i = pow(2, N-1); i >= 1; i--)
  {
    C[N-1][i].simpleRate = C[N-2][j].simpleRate;
    C[N-1][i].value = 0;
    C[N-1][i].cashFlow = 100*((C[N-1][i].shortRate-1)*(indicator(C[N-
      1][i].simpleRate, 0.019, 0.022))));
    if (i % 2 != 0)
      j--;
  }

  for (i = N-2; i >= 0; i--)
  {
    for (j = pow(2, i); j >= 1; j--)
    {
      C[i][j].cashFlow = 100*((C[i][j].shortRate-1)*(indicator(C[i][j].simpleRate,
        0.019, 0.022))));
      rate = C[i][j].shortRate;

      C[i][j].value = 0.5*(1/rate)*((C[i+1][2*j].value + C[i+1][2*j].cashFlow)
        + (C[i+1][2*j-1].value + C[i+1][2*j-1].cashFlow));

      bondDiff = C[i+1][2*j].zeroCouponBond - C[i+1][2*j-1].zeroCouponBond;

      C[i][j].numZeroCoupon = (1/bondDiff)*((C[i+1][2*j].value +
        C[i+1][2*j].cashFlow)
        - (C[i+1][2*j-1].value + C[i+1][2*j-1].cashFlow));
      moneyAccount = C[i][j].moneyMarketAccount;

      C[i][j].numMoneyMarket =(1/moneyAccount)*(C[i][j].value
        - C[i][j].numZeroCoupon*(C[i][j].zeroCouponBond));
    }
  }
  return C[0][1].value;
}

/*****************************************************************************
addNodeHJMRangeNote       : adds nodes to an HJM tree to compute the value of a
                            range note
[in] : int key            : node key
[in] : int num            : node number added
[in] : int rateMaturity   : maturity of interest rate (number of years)
[out]: void               : value of range note
*****************************************************************************/
void HJMTree::addNodeHJMRangeNote(int key, int num, int rateMaturity)
{
  TREE_PTR new_ptr = NULL;    // pointer to BSTREE_NODE struct
  TREE_PTR node_ptr = NULL;   // node pointer
```

```
TREE_PTR curr_ptr = NULL;      // pointer to current node
double r = 0.0;                // forward rate at node
double sum, sum1 = 0.0;        // sum of volatilities
double volsum = 0.0;           // sum*sqrt(dt)*dt
double volsum1 = 0.0;          // sum1*sqrt(dt)*dt
double coshval = 0.0;          // 1/cosh(volsum);
double expvalPlus = 0.0;       // exp(volsum);
double expvalMinus = 0.0;      // exp(-volsum)
double expvalPlus1 = 0.0;      // exp(vol*exp(-lambda*cnt*dt)*sqrt(dt)*dt)
double expvalMinus1 = 0.0;     // exp(-vol*exp(-lambda*cnt*dt)*sqrt(dt)*dt);
double coshRatio = 0.0;        // cosh(volsum)/cosh(volsum1)
int i;

new_ptr = new BSTREE_NODE;
new_ptr->up_childptr = NULL;
new_ptr->down_childptr = NULL;

// get tree height
cnt = getTreeHeight(get_root(), num);
// Add key in the new node's data field
new_ptr->nodeKey = key;

// initialization for tree
C[0][2].moneyMarketAccount = 1;
C[0][1].moneyMarketAccount = 1;
C[0][0].moneyMarketAccount = 1;
C[1][2].moneyMarketAccount = initRate;
// If the BST is empty, insert the new rate in root
if (root_ptr == NULL)
{
  C[cnt][nodeCnt].shortRate = initRate;
  C[cnt][nodeCnt].moneyMarketAccount = 1;
  for (i = 0; i <= N; i++)
  {
    new_ptr->bondPrice[i] = 1/(pow(initRate, i));
    new_ptr->forwardRate[i] = initRate;
    new_ptr->moneyMarketAccount = initRate;
    new_ptr->shortRate = initRate;
    if (i == rateMaturity)
    {
      new_ptr->simpleRate = 0.5*(1/new_ptr->bondPrice[i] - 1);
    }
    if (i == N)
      C[cnt][nodeCnt].zeroCouponBond = new_ptr->bondPrice[N];
  }
  root_ptr = new_ptr;
  nodeCnt++;
}
else
{
  TREE_PTR tree_ptr = root_ptr;
  while (tree_ptr != NULL)
```

```
{
  node_ptr = tree_ptr;
  if (key == tree_ptr->nodeKey)
    return;
  else if (key < tree_ptr->nodeKey)
    tree_ptr = tree_ptr->up_childptr;      // search its up side for insertion
                                           // location

  else
     tree_ptr = tree_ptr->down_childptr;   // search its down side for insertion
                                           // location

}

// Now 'node_ptr' is the pointer to the parent of the new node. Now determine
// where it will be inserted.

// compute volatilities
// sum is used for computing both bond prices and forward rates
sum = 0.0;
for (int k = cnt; k <= N; k++)
{
  sum = sum + vol*exp(-lambda*(k*dt));
}
// used for coshRatio for forward rate computation
sum1 = 0.0;
for (k = cnt; k < N; k++)
{
  sum1 = sum1 + vol*exp(-lambda*(k*dt));
}
volsum = sum*sqrt(dt)*dt;
volsum1 = sum1*sqrt(dt)*dt;
coshRatio = cosh(volsum)/cosh(volsum1);
coshval = 1/cosh(volsum);
expvalPlus = exp(volsum);
expvalMinus = exp(-volsum);
expvalPlus1 = exp(vol*exp(-lambda*cnt*dt)*sqrt(dt)*dt);
expvalMinus1 = exp(-vol*exp(-lambda*cnt*dt)*sqrt(dt)*dt);

if (key < node_ptr->nodeKey)
{
  node_ptr->up_childptr = new_ptr;
  curr_ptr = node_ptr->up_childptr;

  for (i = cnt; i <= N; i++)
  {
    curr_ptr->forwardRate[i] = node_ptr->forwardRate[i]*coshRatio*expval
      Minus1;
    if (i == cnt)
    {
      curr_ptr->bondPrice[cnt] = 1; // bond price at maturity
      if (i == rateMaturity)
      {
        curr_ptr->simpleRate = 0.5*(1/curr_ptr->bondPrice[i + cnt] - 1);
      }
```

```
        }
        else
        {
          // get short rate r(t) from forward rate f(t, t)
          r = curr_ptr->forwardRate[cnt];
          curr_ptr->shortRate = r;

          // calculate bondprices
          curr_ptr->bondPrice[i] = (node_ptr->bondPrice[i])*(r*coshval*expval
            Plus);

          C[cnt][nodeCnt].shortRate = r;
          C[cnt][nodeCnt].moneyMarketAccount =
            (C[cnt-1][nodeCnt/2].moneyMarketAccount)*(node_ptr->shortRate);

          if (i == cnt + 2)
          {
            curr_ptr->simpleRate = 0.5*(1/curr_ptr->bondPrice[cnt + 2] - 1);
            node_ptr->simpleRate = curr_ptr->simpleRate;
            C[cnt][nodeCnt].simpleRate = node_ptr->simpleRate;
          }

          if (i == N)
            C[cnt][nodeCnt].zeroCouponBond = new_ptr->bondPrice[N];
        }
      }
    }
    else
    {
      node_ptr->down_childptr = new_ptr;
      curr_ptr = node_ptr->down_childptr;

      for (i = cnt; i <= N; i++)
      {
        curr_ptr->forwardRate[i] = (node_ptr->forwardRate[i]*coshRatio*expval
          Plus1);
        if (i == cnt)
        {
          curr_ptr->bondPrice[cnt] = 1;
        }
        else
        {
          // get short rate r(t) from forward rate f(t, t)
          r = curr_ptr->forwardRate[cnt];
          curr_ptr->shortRate = r;

          // compute bond price
          curr_ptr->bondPrice[i] = (node_ptr->bondPrice[i]*r*coshval*expvalMinus);

          C[cnt][nodeCnt].shortRate = r;

          C[cnt][nodeCnt].moneyMarketAccount =
            (C[cnt-1][nodeCnt-nodeCnt2].moneyMarketAccount)*(node_ptr->shortRate);
```

```
                    if (i == cnt + 2)
                    {
                       curr_ptr->simpleRate = 0.5*(1/curr_ptr->bondPrice[cnt+2] - 1);
                       node_ptr->simpleRate = curr_ptr->simpleRate;
                       C[cnt][nodeCnt].simpleRate = curr_ptr->simpleRate;
                    }
                    if (i == N)
                       C[cnt][nodeCnt].zeroCouponBond = new_ptr->bondPrice[N];
                 }
              }
           }
        if (nodeCnt != 1)
        {
          nodeCnt--;
          if (nodeCnt % 2 != 0)
          nodeCnt2--;
        }
        else
        {
          nodeCnt = pow(2, cnt+1);
          nodeCnt2 = pow(2, cnt);
        }
     }
}
```

We call the *addNodeHJMRangeNote* method in the *buildHJMTree* method:

```
/********************************************************************************
buildHJMTree : builds an HJM Tree to value a range note
[in]  : none
[out] : none
********************************************************************************/
void HJMTree::buildHJMTree()
{
  int M = pow(2, N) - 1;   // total number of nodes
  int* key = new int[M];   // array of keys
  int j = pow(2, N-1);     // compute number of nodes at last time step

  for (int i = 0; i < j; i++)
    key[(int)pow(2, N-1)+i] = 2*i + 1;

  for (i = M-j; i >= 1; i--)
    key[i] = 0.5*(key[(int)2*i] + key[(int)2*i+1]);

  for (i = 0; i < M; i++)
    addNodeHJMRangeNote(key[i+1], i+1, 2);
}
```

and can value a range note in the main method as follows:

```
void main()
{
  HJMTree hm(1.02, 1, 4, 0.0076, 0.0154, 0.017);
  hm.generateKeys1();
  std::cout << "Buiding HJM Tree" << endl;
  hm.buildHJMTree();
  std::cout << "Valuation of Range Note\n" << endl;
  hm.calcRangeNote();
}
```

14.7   VALUATION OF INDEX-AMORTIZING SWAPS

Index-amortizing swaps are interest rate swaps where the principal declines (amortizes) when interest rates decline. Unlike plain-vanilla swaps, these exotic swaps are path-dependent and thus difficult to value since their cash flows depend on the entire past (path) movements of the spot interest rate. However, they serve as useful (partial) hedges against prepayment risk (and thus declining principal) in mortgage-backed securities.

Formally, we define an index-amortizing swap as, say, a payer swap—receive fixed rate K, pay floating $r(t)$—with an initial principal N_0 that matures at time T in which the principal declines by an amortizing schedule based on the spot rate of interest. In general, the amortizing schedule does not apply until after a prespecified lockout $T^* > 0$ period has elapsed. For $t \leq T^*$, the principal is fixed at N_0. For $t > T^*$, the principal is reduced according to

$$N(t) = N(t-1)(1-a(t)) \qquad \text{for } t > T^* \tag{14.20}$$

where $N(T^*) = N_0$ and $a(t)$ is the amortizing amount that occurs at time t. Equation (14.20) states that the principal remaining at time t, $N(t)$, equals the principal at time $t-1$, $N(t-1)$, reduced by the time t amortizing schedule amount $a(t)$.

Following Jarrow (2002), a typical amortizing schedule might look like this:

$$a(t) = \begin{cases} 0 & \text{if } r(t) > k_4 \\ b_4 & \text{if } k_3 < r(t) \leq k_4 \\ b_3 & \text{if } k_2 < r(t) \leq k_3 \\ b_2 & \text{if } k_1 < r(t) \leq k_2 \\ b_1 & \text{if } k_0 < r(t) \leq k_1 \\ 1 & \text{if } r(t) \leq k_0 \end{cases} \tag{14.21}$$

where $k_4 > k_3 > k_2 > k_1 > k_0$ and $0 < b_4 < b_3 < b_2 < b_1 < b_0 < 1$ are positive constants determined at the initiation of the swap. The amortizing schedule depends on the spot rate at time t. If the spot rate is larger than k_4, no reduction in principal occurs so that $a(t) = 0$. If the spot rate falls between k_3 and k_4, a reduction of $a(t) = b_4$ percent of the principal occurs; if the spot rate falls between k_2 and k_3, a reduction of $a(t) = b_3$ percent of the principal occurs, and so on down the schedule. The schedule can be modified to handle an arbitrary number of amortization levels.

The time t cash flow to the payer index-amortizing swap can be written as

$$\text{Cash flow}(t) = (K - r(t-1))N(t-1) \qquad (14.22)$$

so that the cash flow at time t is determined at time $t - 1$. The cash flow can be viewed as the sum of receiving the fixed amount $(K-1)N(t-1)$ and paying floating $(r(t-1)-1)N(t-1)$, while the principal is determined by (14.20) and (14.21).

Let $IA(t)$ denote the time t value of the index-amortizing swap. Using risk-neutral valuation, we have

$$IA(t) = \tilde{E}_t \left(\sum_{j=t+1}^{T} \frac{(K - r(j-1))N(j-1)}{B(j)} \right) B(t) \qquad (14.23)$$

Expression (14.23) represents the present value of the cash flows to the index-amortizing swap from time $t + 1$ until its maturity T. It differs from the valuation of a plain-vanilla swap by the replacement of a constant principal N with the amortizing principal $N(j-1)$. Moreover, the principal $N(j-1)$ and the spot rate $r(j-1)$ are correlated, and in general the principal depends on the history of the interest rate process before time $j - 1$. This implies that the principal at time $T - 1$ is correlated with the spot interest rate occurring earlier at time t. These factors make the valuation complex.

As an example, consider a simple index-amortizing payer swap with the swap holder receiving fixed at rate $K = 1.021$ and paying the floating LIBOR rate. Let the swap's maturity be $T = 3$ years, let the initial principal be N_0, and let the lockout period be $T^* = 1$ year. Let the amortizing schedule be given by

$$a(t) = \begin{cases} 0 & \text{if } r(t) > 1.022 \\ .25 & \text{if } 1.021 < r(t) \le 1.022 \\ 0.50 & \text{if } 1.020 \le r(t) < 1.021 \\ 0.75 & \text{if } 1.019 \le r(t) < 1.020 \\ 1 & \text{if } r(t) < 1.019 \end{cases}$$

Unlike a plain-vanilla swap, which has a zero value at time 0, an index-amortizing swap *can* have negative value at time 0 since the principal decreases on the index-amortizing swap exactly when the payment stream is *potentially* the largest (i.e., when fixed minus floating is the largest).[22] We create a synthetic portfolio to replicate the index-amortizing swap by using the money market account and the three-year zero-coupon bond.

Using risk-neutral valuation, the value at time t is calculated by

$$IA(t; s_t)$$
$$= \frac{0.5(IA(t+1, s_t u) + cashflow(t+1, s_t u)) + 0.5(IA(t+1, s_t d) + cashflow(t+1, s_t d))}{r(t; s_t)} \quad (14.24)$$

The position held in the three-year period bond is given by

$$n_3(t; s_t) = \frac{(IA(t+1; s_t u) + cashflow(t+1, s_t u)) - (IA(t+1, s_t d) + cashflow(t+1; s_t d))}{P(t+1, 3; s_t u) - P(t+1, 3; s_t d)} \quad (14.25)$$

and the position held in the money market account is given by

$$n_0(t; s_t) = \frac{(IA(t; s_t) - n_3(t; s_t)P(t, 3; s_t)}{B(t)} \quad (14.26)$$

Figure 14.4 shows the index-amortizing swap cash flows at each node in the HJM tree and Figure 14.5 shows the index-amortizing values at each node. At each node, the index-amortizing swap value, the cash flow, and the positions held in the money market account and three-year bond are listed, respectively. The value today of the index-amortizing swap is –0.0288.

The following is the implementation:

```
/****************************************************************************
addNodeHJMIndexAmortizingSwap            : computes the value of an index
                                           amortizing swap
[in] int key                             : node key
     int num                             : current node number
     int lockOutPeriod                   : lock out time
     double fixedRate                    : fixed interest rate received in swap
     double principalAmount              : principal underlying swap
     vector<double> amortizingSchedule   : amortization schedule
[out] none
****************************************************************************/
void HJMTree::addNodeHJMIndexAmortizingSwap(int key, int num, int lockOutPeriod,
    double fixedRate, double principalAmount, vector<double> amortizingSchedule)
```

_____

[22]Jarrow (1996), 269.

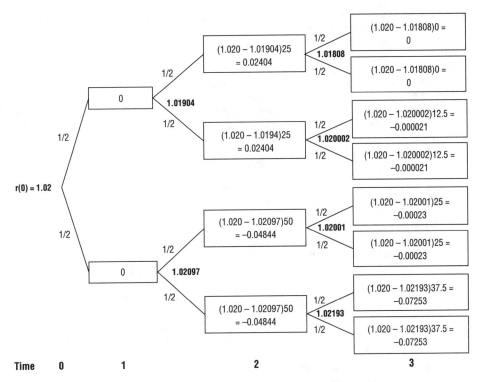

FIGURE 14.4 Index-Amortizing Swap Cash Flows with T = 3 Maturity

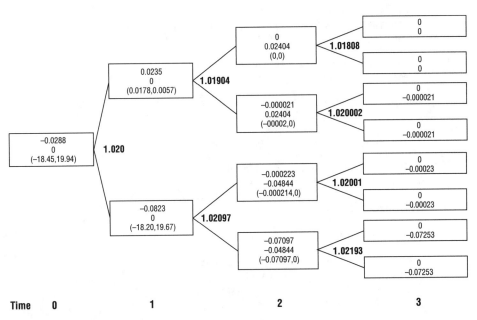

FIGURE 14.5 Index-Amortizing Swap Valuation with T = 3 Maturity

```
{
  TREE_PTR new_ptr = NULL;     // pointer to BSTREE_NODE struct
  TREE_PTR node_ptr = NULL;    // node pointer
  TREE_PTR curr_ptr = NULL;    // pointer to current node
  double r = 0.0;              // short rate
  double sum, sum1 = 0.0;      // sum of volatilities
  double volsum = 0.0;         // sum*sqrt(dt)*dt;
  double volsum1 = 0.0;        // sum1*sqrt(dt)*dt
  double coshval = 0.0;        // 1/cosh(volsum);

  double expvalPlus = 0.0;     // exp(volsum);
  double expvalMinus = 0.0;    // exp(-volsum);
  double expvalPlus1 = 0.0;    // exp(vol*exp(-lambda*cnt*dt)*sqrt(dt)*dt)
  double expvalMinus1 = 0.0;   // exp(-vol*exp(-lambda*cnt*dt)*sqrt(dt)*dt);
  double coshRatio = 0.0;      // cosh(volsum)/cosh(volsum1)
  double amortizingRate = 0;   // amortizing rate
  int i;

  new_ptr = new BSTREE_NODE;
  new_ptr->up_childptr = NULL;
  new_ptr->down_childptr = NULL;

  // get tree height
  cnt = getTreeHeight(get_root(), num);
  // add key in the new node's data field
  new_ptr->nodeKey = key;

  // initialization
  C[0][2].moneyMarketAccount = 1;
  C[0][1].moneyMarketAccount = 1;
  C[0][0].moneyMarketAccount = 1;
  C[1][2].moneyMarketAccount = initRate;
  C[0][2].shortRate = initRate;
  C[0][0].amortizedPrincipal = principalAmount;
  C[0][2].amortizedPrincipal = principalAmount;

  // if the BST is empty, insert the new rate in root
  if (root_ptr == NULL)
  {
    C[cnt][nodeCnt].shortRate = initRate;
    C[cnt][nodeCnt].moneyMarketAccount = 1;
    C[cnt][nodeCnt].indexAmortizingCashFlow = 0;
    C[cnt][nodeCnt].amortizingRate = 0;
    C[cnt][nodeCnt].amortizedPrincipal = principalAmount;
    C[cnt][nodeCnt].shortRate = initRate;

    for (i = 0; i <= N; i++)
    {
      new_ptr->bondPrice[i] = 1/(pow(initRate, i));
      new_ptr->forwardRate[i] = initRate;
      new_ptr->moneyMarketAccount = initRate;
      new_ptr->shortRate = initRate;
      if (i == N)
        C[cnt][nodeCnt].zeroCouponBond = new_ptr->bondPrice[N];
```

```
    }
    root_ptr = new_ptr;
    nodeCnt++;
}
else
{
    TREE_PTR tree_ptr = root_ptr;
    while (tree_ptr != NULL)
    {
        node_ptr = tree_ptr;
        if (key == tree_ptr->nodeKey)
            return;
        else if (key < tree_ptr->nodeKey)
            tree_ptr = tree_ptr->up_childptr;    // search its up side for insertion
                                                 // location

        else
            tree_ptr = tree_ptr->down_childptr;  // search its down side for insertion
                                                 // location

    }

    // Now 'node_ptr' is the pointer to the parent of the new node. Now determine
    // where it will be inserted
    // compute volatilities sum is used for computing both bond prices and forward
    // rates
    sum = 0.0;
    for (int k = cnt; k <= N; k++)
    sum = sum + vol*exp(-lambda*(k*dt));

    // used for coshRatio for forward rate computation
    sum1 = 0.0;
    for (k = cnt; k < N; k++)
        sum1 = sum1 + vol*exp(-lambda*(k*dt));

    volsum = sum*sqrt(dt)*dt;
    volsum1 = sum1*sqrt(dt)*dt;
    coshRatio = cosh(volsum)/cosh(volsum1);
    coshval = 1/cosh(volsum);
    expvalPlus = exp(volsum);
    expvalMinus = exp(-volsum);
    expvalPlus1 = exp(vol*exp(-lambda*cnt*dt)*sqrt(dt)*dt);
    expvalMinus1 = exp(-vol*exp(-lambda*cnt*dt)*sqrt(dt)*dt);

    if (key < node_ptr->nodeKey)
    {
        node_ptr->up_childptr = new_ptr;
        curr_ptr = node_ptr->up_childptr;

        for (i = cnt; i <= N; i++)
        {
            curr_ptr->forwardRate[i] = node_ptr->forwardRate[i]*coshRatio*expval
                Minus1;
            if (i == cnt)
            {
```

```
            curr_ptr->bondPrice[cnt] = 1; // bond price at maturity
         }
         else
         {
           // get short rate r(t) from forward rate f(t, t)
           r = curr_ptr->forwardRate[cnt];
           curr_ptr->shortRate = r;
           // calculate bondprices
           curr_ptr->bondPrice[i] = (node_ptr->bondPrice[i])*(r*coshval*expval
             Plus);
           C[cnt][nodeCnt].shortRate = r;

           r = node_ptr->shortRate;
           if (lockOutPeriod < cnt)
           {
             // compute amortization level
             if (r > amortizingSchedule[0])
               amortizingRate = 0;
             else if ((r <= amortizingSchedule[0]) && (r > amortizingSchedule[1]))
               amortizingRate = 0.25;
             else if ((r <= amortizingSchedule[1]) && (r > amortizingSchedule[2]))
               amortizingRate = 0.50;
             else if ((r <= amortizingSchedule[2]) && (r > amortizingSchedule[3]))
               amortizingRate = 0.75;
             else if (r <= amortizingSchedule[3])
               amortizingRate = 1;
           }

           C[cnt][nodeCnt].amortizingRate = amortizingRate;

           C[cnt][nodeCnt].amortizedPrincipal =
             C[cnt-1][nodeCnt/2].amortizedPrincipal*(1-amortizingRate);

           C[cnt][nodeCnt].indexAmortizingCashFlow =
             (fixedRate - C[cnt-1][nodeCnt/2].shortRate)
               *C[cnt][nodeCnt].amortizedPrincipal;

           C[cnt][nodeCnt].moneyMarketAccount =
             (C[cnt-1][nodeCnt/2].moneyMarketAccount)*(node_ptr->shortRate);

           // price bond if at maturity
           if (i == N)
             C[cnt][nodeCnt].zeroCouponBond = new_ptr->bondPrice[N];
         }
       }
    }
    else
    {
      node_ptr->down_childptr = new_ptr;
      curr_ptr = node_ptr->down_childptr;

      for (i = cnt; i <= N; i++)
      {
```

```
    curr_ptr->forwardRate[i] =
      (node_ptr->forwardRate[i]*coshRatio*expvalPlus1);

  if (i == cnt)
  {
    curr_ptr->bondPrice[cnt] = 1;
  }
  else
  {
    // get short rate r(t) from forward rate f(t, t)
    r = curr_ptr->forwardRate[cnt];
    curr_ptr->shortRate = r;

    // compute bond price
    curr_ptr->bondPrice[i] = (node_ptr->bondPrice[i]*r*coshval*expvalMinus);

    C[cnt][nodeCnt].shortRate = r;
    r = node_ptr->shortRate;
    if (lockOutPeriod < cnt) // check that we are past the lockout period
    {
      // compute amortization level
      if (r > amortizingSchedule[0])
        amortizingRate = 0;
      else if ((r <= amortizingSchedule[0]) && (r > amortizingSchedule[1]))
        amortizingRate = 0.25;
      else if ((r <= amortizingSchedule[1]) && (r > amortizingSchedule[2]))
        amortizingRate = 0.50;
      else if ((r <= amortizingSchedule[2]) && (r > amortizingSchedule[3]))
        amortizingRate = 0.75;
      else if (r <= amortizingSchedule[3])
        amortizingRate = 1;
    }

    C[cnt][nodeCnt].amortizingRate = amortizingRate;

    C[cnt][nodeCnt].amortizedPrincipal =
      C[cnt-1][nodeCnt/2].amortizedPrincipal*(1-amortizingRate);

    C[cnt][nodeCnt].indexAmortizingCashFlow =
      (fixedRate - C[cnt-1][nodeCnt/2].shortRate)*C[cnt][nodeCnt].amortized
        Principal;

    C[cnt][nodeCnt].moneyMarketAccount =
      (C[cnt-1][nodeCnt/2].moneyMarketAccount)*(node_ptr->shortRate);

    if (i == N)
      C[cnt][nodeCnt].zeroCouponBond = new_ptr->bondPrice[N];
    }
  }
}

if (nodeCnt != 1)
{
```

```
        nodeCnt--;
        if (nodeCnt % 2 != 0)
          nodeCnt2--;
      }
      else
      {
        nodeCnt = pow(2, cnt+1);
        nodeCnt2 = pow(2, cnt);
      }
    }
  }
}


/******************************************************************************
calcIndexAmortizingSwap  : computes the value of an index amortizing swap after HJM
                           tree is built
[in] : none
[out]: double            : value of index amortizing swap
******************************************************************************/
double HJMTree::calcIndexAmortizingSwap()
{
  int j = pow(2, N-2);           // stores number of nodes needed
  double floatRate = 0.0;        // floating short rate
  double bondDiff = 0.0;         // difference between zero coupon bonds
  double moneyAccount = 0.0;     // money market account
  cout.precision(4);             // set output precision

  for (int i = pow(2, N-1); i >= 1; i--)
    C[N-1][i].indexAmortizingValue = 0;

  for (i = N-2; i >= 0; i--)
  {
    for (j = pow(2, i); j >= 1; j--)
    {
      floatRate = C[i][j].shortRate;

      C[i][j].indexAmortizingValue =
        0.5*(1/floatRate)*((C[i+1][2*j].indexAmortizingValue
        + C[i+1][2*j].indexAmortizingCashFlow) + (C[i+1][2*j-
        1].indexAmortizingValue + C[i+1][2*j- 1].indexAmortizingCashFlow));

      bondDiff = C[i+1][2*j].zeroCouponBond - C[i+1][2*j-1].zeroCouponBond;

      C[i][j].numZeroCoupon = (1/bondDiff)*((C[i+1][2*j].indexAmortizingValue
        + C[i+1][2*j].indexAmortizingCashFlow)- (C[i+1][2*j-1].indexAmortizing
          Value + C[i+1][2*j-1].indexAmortizingCashFlow));
      moneyAccount = C[i][j].moneyMarketAccount;

      C[i][j].numMoneyMarket =(1/moneyAccount)*(C[i][j].indexAmortizingValue -
        C[i][j].numZeroCoupon*(C[i][j].zeroCouponBond));

      // output results at each node
```

```
         cout << "C[ " << i << "][" << j << "].shortRate = " << C[i][j].shortRate <<
            endl;
         cout << "C[ " << i << "][" << j << "].moneyAccount = " <<
            C[i][j].moneyAccount << endl;
         cout << "C[ " << i << "][" << j << "].moneyMarket = " <<
            C[i][j].numMoneyMarket << endl;
         cout << "C[ " << i << "][" << j << "].amortizedPrincipal = " <<
            C[i][j].amortizedPrincipal << endl;
         cout < "C[ " < i < "][" < j < "].numZeroCoupon = " << C[i][j].numZeroCoupon
            << endl;
         cout << "C[ " << i << "][" << j << "].indexCashFlow = " <<
            C[i][j].indexAmortizingCashFlow << endl;
         cout << "C[ " << i << "][" << j << "].indexValue = " <<
            C[i][j].indexAmortizingValue << endl;
         cout << "C[ " << i << "][" << j << "].amortizingRate = " <<
            C[i][j].amortizingRate << endl;
      }
   }
   return C[0][1].value;
}
```

We can build an HJM tree to value an index-amortizing swap with the following code:

```
/********************************************************************************
buildHJMTree1 : builds an HJM Tree to value an index-amortizing swap
[in]: none
[out]: none
********************************************************************************/
void HJMTree::buildHJMTree1()
{
   int M = pow(2, N) - 1;        // total number of nodes
   int* key = new int[M];        // array of node keys
   int j = pow(2, N-1);          // number of nodes at last time step
   vector<double> as;            // amortization schedule

   // build amortization schedule
   // could overload method and pass schedule in as a parameter
   as.push_back(1.022);
   as.push_back(1.021);
   as.push_back(1.020);
   as.push_back(1.019);

   // generate keys

   for (int i = 0; i < j; i++)
      key[(int)pow(2, N-1)+i] = 2*i + 1;

   for (i = M-j; i >= 1; i--)
```

```
    key[i] = 0.5*(key[(int)2*i] + key[(int)2*i+1]);

  for (i = 0; i < M; i++)
    addNodeHJMIndexAmortizingSwap(key[i+1], i+1, 1, 1.020, 100, as);
}
```

An index-amortizing swap can then be valued in the main method:

```
void main()
{
  HJMTree hm(1.02, 1, 4, 0.0076, 0.0154, 0.017);
  std::cout << "Buiding HJM Tree" << endl;
  hm.buildHJMTree();
  std::cout << "Valuation of Index Amortizing Swap" << endl;
  hm.calcIndexAmortizingSwap();
}
```

In addition to valuation by trees, Longstaff and Schwartz (2001) show how the Monte Carlo least-squares approach can be used to value index-amortizing swaps.

14.8   VALUATION OF TRIGGER SWAPS

A trigger swap is an interest rate swap where fixed payments are exchanged with a certain reference rate. The swap becomes "alive" or "terminates" when a certain index rate hits a prespecified level H. It is similar to barrier options in the equity markets. Usually the reference rate and the index rate are the same, but the index rate is observed at a higher frequency than the payment frequency of the reference rate. For example, the index rate and the reference rate can both be the six-month LIBOR rate, which can be observed daily for indexing and every six months for the payments. There are four standard basic types of trigger swaps: down and out (DO), up and out (UO), down and in (DI), and up and in (UI).

In a DO swap, the initial index rate is above H. The swap terminates its payments (goes out) as soon as the index rate hits the level H (from above, going down). In a UO swap, the initial index is below H. The swap terminates its payments (goes out) as soon as the index rate hits the level H (from below, going up). In a DI, the initial index rate is above H. The swap starts its payments (goes in) as soon as the index rate hits the level H (from above, going down). Finally, in a UI swap, the initial index rate is below H. The swap starts its payments (goes in) as soon as the index rate hits the level H (from below, going up).

Consider a DO trigger swap. Suppose the set of payment dates is $T_0, \ldots, T_n$ and suppose the dates are equally spaced by an amount δ (i.e., $\delta = 6$ months). Denote by $\Gamma = \{\tau_1, \ldots, \tau_m\}$ the set of future dates at which the reference rate (typically the six-month LIBOR rate) is quoted in the market up to time T_n. Denote by $L(t)$ the reference rate at the time instant t with maturity $t + \delta$.

Assume that the index rate and reference rate coincide and that the notional amount underlying the swap is N. We will consider forward rate dynamics considered under the forward-adjusted measure Q^n corresponding to the final payment date so that the forward rate is a martingale. Suppose the swap is still alive at time $t = T_{i-1}$; then at time T_i the following will occur:

Institution A (the fixed leg) pays to B (the floating leg) the fixed rate K at time T_{i-1} if at all previous instants in the interval $[T_{i-1}, T_i]$ the index rate L is above the triggering level H. If the swap is still alive at time T_{i-1}, then at time T_i institution A pays to B a cash flow CF^{fixed}.

$$CF^{fixed} = KN\tau_i \prod_{\tau \in \Gamma \cap (T_{i-1}, T_i)} \mathbf{1}(L(\tau) > H)$$

$$= KN\tau_i \mathbf{1}\{\min\{L(\tau), \tau \in \Gamma \cap (T_{i-1}, T_i)\} > H\}$$

where τ_i is the year fraction between the payment dates T_{i-1} and T_i, and $\mathbf{1}$ is the indicator function. Institution B pays to A (a percentage α of) the reference rate L at the last reset date T_{i-1} (plus a spread Q) if at all previous instants of the interval $[T_{i-1}, T_i]$ the index rate L is above the triggering level H. Formally, at time T_i, institution B pays to A the cash flow $CF^{floating}$:

$$CF^{floating} = (\alpha L(T_{i-1}) + Q)N\tau_i \mathbf{1}\{\min\{L(\tau), \tau \in \Gamma \cap (T_{i-1}, T_i)\} > H\}$$

The complete discounted payoff as seen from institution A can be expressed as

$$N \sum_{i=1}^{n} D(0, T_i)(\alpha L(T_{i-1}) + Q - K)\tau_i \mathbf{1}\{\min\{L(\tau), \tau \in \Gamma \cap (T_{i-1}, T_i)\} > H\}$$

and the contract value to institution A (under the Q^n) measure[23] is

$$E\left[N \sum_{i=1}^{n} D(0, T_i)(\alpha L(T_{i-1}) + Q - K)\tau_i \mathbf{1}\{\min\{L(\tau), \tau \in \Gamma \cap (T_{i-1}, T_i)\} > H\} \right]$$

$$= NP(0, T_n) \sum_{i=1}^{n} \tau_i E^n\left[\frac{(\alpha L(T_{i-1}) + Q)N\tau_i \mathbf{1}\{\min\{L(\tau), \tau \in \Gamma \cap (T_{i-1}, T_i)\} > H\}}{P(T_i, T_n)} \right]$$

---

[23]Brigo and Mercurio (2001c), 407–408.

We can numerically compute this value via Monte Carlo by recovering the spot rates $L(T_i) = F(T_i; T_i, T_{i+1}) = F_{i+1}(T_i)$ and discount factors $P(T_i, T_n)$ by generating for all i's spanning forward rates $F_{i+1}(T_i), F_{i+2}(T_i), \ldots, F_n(T_i)$ under Q^n according to discretized (Milstein) dynamics (see section 2.1). To recover spot rates in between rates $L(\tau)$, either a drift-interpolation or bridging technique can be used; see Brigo and Mercurio (2001c), Jackel (2002), and section 2.9.

14.9   QUANTO DERIVATIVES

Quantos are derivatives that have multicurrency features so that their value depends in general on both domestic and foreign interest rates and exchange rates.

Denote $P^f(t, T)$ as the foreign discount bond, r_f as the foreign risk-free rate, and $\chi(t)$ as the exchange rate at time t between the currencies in the domestic and foreign markets[24] so that 1 unit of the foreign currency equals $\chi(t)$ unit of the domestic currency. The reciprocal exchange rate $\bar{\chi}(t)$ is the number of units of foreign currency per unit of the domestic currency. We assume that the term structure of discount factor is observable in both the domestic and foreign markets at time t.

Let $F^f(t; T_1, T_2)$ be the forward rate in the foreign market at time t for the interval $[T_1, T_2]$ defined by

$$F^f(t; T_1, T_2) = \frac{P^f(t, T_1) - P^f(t, T_2)}{\tau_{1,2} P^f(t, T_2)} \qquad (14.27)$$

where $\tau_{1,2}$ is the year fraction between T_1 and T_2, and is assumed to be the same in both the domestic and foreign markets. Given the future times T_1 and T_2, we can compute the value of a quanto caplet that pays off at time T_2,

$$\tau_{1,2} N \max(F^f(T_1; T_1, T_2) - K, 0) \text{ in domestic currency} \qquad (14.28)$$

The no-arbitrage value at time t of the caplet payoff in (14.28) is given by taking the expectation of (14.28) under the domestic forward measure Q^2, denoted E^2, with numeraire $P(t, T)$:

$$QCpl(t, T_1, T_2, N, K) = \tau_{1,2} N P(t, T_2) E^2[\max(F^f(T_1; T_1, T_2) - K, 0 | \Im_t]$$

In order to compute this expectation, it is necessary to know the distribution of $F^f(T_1; T_1, T_2)$ under the measure Q^2. While the foreign forward measure, associated

---

[24]Note that from the perspective of a person not living in the domestic country, but in the foreign country, the foreign currency is their domestic currency and the domestic currency is their foreign currency.

with the numeraire $P^f(t, T_2)$, is a martingale, it is not so under the domestic forward measure $P(t, T_2)$. Since $P^f(t, T_1) - P^f(t, T_2)$ and $P(t, T_2)$ are tradable assets in the foreign market, then $\chi(t)[P^f(t, T_1) - P^f(t, T_2)$ and $\chi(t)P^f(t, T_2)$ are both tradable assets in the domestic market. The processes X and Y defined by

$$X(t) = \chi(t)\frac{P^f(t, T_1) - P^f(t, T_2)}{P^f(t, T_2)}$$

$$Y(t) = \chi(t)\frac{\tau_{1,2}P^f(t, T_2)}{P(t, T_2)} = \tau_{1,2}F_\chi(t, T_2)$$

are both martingales under Q^2, where $F_\chi(t, T_2)$ denotes the forward exchange rate at time t maturing at time T_2. Under Q^2, with lognormal assumptions, we have the SDEs

$$dX(t) = \sigma_X(t)X(t)dz_X(t)$$

$$dY(t) = \sigma_Y(t)Y(t)dz_Y(t)$$

where z_X and z_Y are two Brownian motions with $dz_X dz_Y = \rho_{XY}dt$. Then, under Q^2, using Leibnitz's rule (see Appendix B), we have

$$dF^f(t; T_1, T_2) = d\left(\frac{X(t)}{Y(t)}\right)$$

$$= X(t)\left[-\frac{1}{Y^2(t)}\sigma_Y Y(t)dz_Y(t) + \frac{1}{2}\frac{2}{Y^2(t)}\sigma_Y^2 Y^2(t)dt\right]$$

$$+ \frac{1}{Y(t)}\sigma_X X(t)dz_X(t) - \frac{X(t)}{Y(t)}\rho_{XY}\sigma_X\sigma_Y dt$$

so that rewritten,

$$dF^f(t; T_1, T_2) = F^f(t; T_1, T_2)(\sigma_Y^2 - \rho_{XY}\sigma_X\sigma_Y)dt + \sigma_X dz_X(t) - \sigma_Y dz_Y(t))$$

$$= F^f(t; T_1, T_2)(\mu dt + \sigma dz(t))$$

where

$$\mu = \sigma_Y^2 - \rho_{XY}\sigma_X\sigma_Y, \quad \sigma = \sqrt{\sigma_X^2 + \sigma_Y^2 - 2\rho_{XY}\sigma_X\sigma_Y}$$

and z is a Brownian motion under Q^2. Thus, under Q^2, $F^f(T_1; T_1, T_2)$ is lognormally distributed with

$$E^2\left[\ln\frac{F^f(T_1; T_1, T_2)}{F^f(t; T_1, T_2)}\mid\Im_t\right] = \left(\mu - \frac{1}{2}\sigma^2\right)(T_1 - t)$$

$$Var^2\left[\ln\frac{F^f(T_1; T_1, T_2)}{F^f(t; T_1, T_2)}\mid\Im_t\right] = \sigma^2(T_1 - t)$$

which implies that

$$QCpl(t, T_1, T_2, N, K) = \tau_{1,2}NP(t, T_2)[F^f(t; T_1, T_2)e^{\mu(T_1-t)}\Phi(d_1) - K\Phi(d_2)]$$

where

$$d_1 = \frac{\ln\dfrac{F^f(t; T_1, T_2)}{K} + \left(\mu + \dfrac{1}{2}\sigma^2\right)(T_1 - t)}{\sigma\sqrt{T_1 - t}}$$

$$d_2 = d_1 - \sigma\sqrt{T_1 - t}$$

In order to compute the price $QCpl(t, T_1, T_2, N, K)$ we need to determine the values of μ and σ in terms of observable quantities. The value σ can be implied from market data since it is the (proportional) volatility of the foreign forward rate $F^f(T_1; T_1, T_2)$.[25] We can determine the drift μ by the change of drift formula in (1.68) with $U = P(\cdot, T_2)$, $S = P^f(\cdot, T_2)$, and $m^S = 0$: where $X(t)$ in the foreign exchange rate:

$$\mu = m^U = 0 - d\ln F^f(\cdot; T_1, T_2)d\ln\left(\chi(t)\frac{P^f(\cdot, T_2)}{P(\cdot, T_2)}\right)$$

$$= -d\ln F^f(\cdot; T_1, T_2)d\ln F_\chi(t, T_2)$$ (14.29)

$$= -\rho_{F_\chi F^f}\sigma_{F_f}\sigma_{F_\chi}$$

where σ_{F_χ} is the level (proportional) volatility of the forward exchange rate and $\rho_{F_\chi F^f}$ is the instantaneous correlation between $F_\chi(t, T_2)$ and $F^f(t; T_1, T_2)$. Both σ_{F_χ} and $\rho_{F_\chi F^f}$ are observable in the market so that the drift in equation (14.29) can be determined.

---

[25]Brigo and Mercurio (2001c), 442.

Similarly, the arbitrage-free price of a quanto floorlet that pays off at time T_2,

$$\tau_{1,2} N \max(K - F^f(t; T_1, T_2), 0) \text{ in domestic currency}$$

is

$$QCpl(t, T_1, T_2, N, K) = \tau_{1,2} N P(t, T_2)(K\Phi(-d_2) - F^f(t; T_1, T_2)e^{\mu(T_1-t)}\Phi(-d_1))$$

It is easy to price quanto caps and floors. Let $\Gamma = \{t_0, t_1, \ldots, t_n\}$ denote the set of reset and payment times where t_0 is the first reset time and t_1 is the first payment time. Let τ_i denote the year fraction for the time interval $(t_{i-1}, t_i]$, $i = 0, \ldots, n$.

Since the price of a cap (floor) is the sum of prices of the underlying caplets (floorlets), the price at time t of a cap with cap rate (strike) K, nominal value N, and set of times Γ is then given by

$$
QCap(t, \Gamma, \tau, N, X) = N \sum_{i=1}^{n} \tau_i P(t, t_i) \left[F^f(t; t_{i-1}, t_i)e^{\mu_i(t_{i-1}-t)} \cdot \Phi\left(\frac{\ln\frac{F^f(t; t_{i-1}, t_i)}{K} + \left(\mu_i + \frac{1}{2}\sigma_i^2\right)(t_{i-1}-t)}{\sigma_i\sqrt{t_{i-1}-t}} \right) \right.
$$

$$
\left. - K\Phi\left(\frac{\ln\left(\frac{F^f(t; t_{i-1}, t_i)}{K}\right) - \left(\mu_i + \frac{1}{2}\sigma_i^2\right)(t_{i-1}-t)}{\sigma_i\sqrt{t_{i-1}-t}} \right) \right]
\tag{14.30}
$$

and the corresponding quanto floor price is

$$
QFloor(t, \Gamma, \tau, N, X) = N \sum_{i=1}^{n} \tau_i P(t, t_i) \left[K\Phi\left(\frac{\ln\left(\frac{K}{F^f(t; t_{i-1}, t_i)}\right) - \left(\mu_i - \frac{1}{2}\sigma_i^2\right)(t_{i-1}-t)}{\sigma_i\sqrt{t_{t-1}-t}} \right) \right.
$$

$$
\left. - F^f(t; t_{i-1}, t_i)e^{\mu_i(t_{i-1}-t)}\left(\frac{\ln\left(\frac{K}{F^f(t; t_{i-1}, t_i)}\right) - \left(\mu_i t \frac{1}{2}\sigma_i^2\right)(t_{i-1}-t)}{\sigma_i\sqrt{t_{t-1}-t}} \right) \right]
$$

A quanto swaption is an option on the difference between the foreign swap rate and the domestic swap rate, where the difference is denominated in domestic currency. Let the domestic swap rate at time t corresponding to the swap starting at T and with payments t_i, $i = 1, \ldots, n$, where $0 < T < t_1 < t_2 < \ldots < t_n$ be given by

$$S(t) = \frac{P(t, T) - P(t, t_n)}{C(t)}$$

where

$$C(t) = \sum_{i=1}^{n} \tau_i P(t, t_i)$$

and τ_i is the tenor (year fraction) from t_{i-1} to t_i. Let the foreign swap rate at time t corresponding to the swap starting at time T and with payment times t_i, $i = 1, \ldots, n$, be given by

$$S^f(t) = \frac{P^f(t, T) - P^f(t, t_n)}{C^f(t)}$$

where

$$C^f(t) = \sum_{i=1}^{n} \tau_i P^f(t, t_i)$$

and we assume that the year fraction τ_i is the same in both the domestic and foreign markets.

The quanto swaption payoff at time T, given a strike X, is

$$C(T)\max(\omega S^f(T) - \omega S(T) - \omega K, 0) \tag{14.31}$$

where $\omega = 1$ for a payer quanto swaption and $\omega = -1$ for a receiver quanto swaption. We can compute the value at time t, by choosing $C(t)$ as the numeraire and taking the expectation, denoted E^C under the domestic forward-swap Q^C measure:

$$QS(t, T, X) = C(t)E^C\{\max(\omega S^f(T) - \omega S(T) - \omega K, 0) \mid \Im_t\}$$

While the forward-swap process S^f is a martingale under the foreign forward-swap measure, it is not under Q^C and has a drift computed by Hunt and Pelsser (1998) by assuming that under Q^C the following martingales

$$M_1(t) = \frac{\chi(t)(P^f(t, T) - P^f(t, t_n))}{C(t)}$$

$$M_2(t) = \frac{\chi(t)C^f(t)}{C(t)}$$

are lognormally distributed, so that

$$S^f(t) = \frac{M_1(t)}{M_2(t)}$$

is lognormally distributed with the dynamics

$$dS^f(t) = \mu^f S^f(t)dt + \sigma^f S^f(t)dz^f(t)$$

where Z^f is a Brownian motion under Q^C and μ^f and σ^f are constants.[26] Hunt and Pelsser state that $M_2(t)$ can be approximated by the time T forward exchange rate

$$F_\chi(t,\,T) = \frac{\chi(t)P^f(t,\,T)}{P(t,\,T)}$$

and showed that the foreign drift rate (using the change of drift formula) is approximated by minus the instantaneous covariance of $\ln M_2(t)$ and $\ln S^f$ so that

$$\mu^f = -d\ln(S^f)d\ln\left(\frac{P^f(t,\,T)}{P(t,\,T)}\right)$$

$$= -\rho_{F,f}\sigma_f'\sigma_F$$

where σ_F is the (assumed constant) proportional volatility of the process F_χ, and $\rho_{F,f}$ is the instantaneous correlation between the foreign exchange rate F_χ and the foreign swap rate S^f.[27] (We have assumed the exchange rate $\chi(t)$ to be 1 for simplifying the drift computation.)

It can be shown—see Brigo and Mercurio (2001c) for details—using the fact that under Q^C, the joint distribution of

$$\left(\ln\frac{S^f(T)}{S^f(t)},\ \ln\frac{S(T)}{S(t)}\right)$$

conditional on $\Im_t$ is bivariate normal, that taking this expectation leads to the unique arbitrage-free price of the quanto swaption

$$QSwaption(t,\,T,\,X) = C(t)\int_{-\infty}^{+\infty}\frac{1}{\sqrt{2\pi}}e^{-\frac{1}{2}v^2}f(v)dv \tag{14.32}$$

[26]Ibid., 449.
[27]Ibid., 449.

where

$$f(v) = \omega S^f(t) \exp\left[(\mu^f - \frac{1}{2}\rho(\sigma^f)^2)\tau + \rho\sigma^f\sqrt{\tau}v\right] \cdot \Phi\left(\omega \frac{\ln\dfrac{S^f(t)}{q(v)} + (\mu^f + (\frac{1}{2} - \rho^2)(\sigma^f)^2)\tau + \rho\sigma^f\sqrt{\tau}v}{\sigma^f\sqrt{\tau(1-\rho^2)}}\right)$$

$$- \omega q(v)\Phi\left(\omega \frac{\ln\dfrac{S^f(t)}{q(v)} + (\mu^f - \frac{1}{2}(\sigma^f)^2)\tau + \rho\sigma^f\sqrt{\tau}v}{\sigma^f\sqrt{\tau(1-\rho^2)}}\right)$$

and

$$q(v) = K + S(t)e^{-\frac{1}{2}\sigma^2\tau + \sigma\sqrt{\tau}v}$$

and $dz(t)dz^f(t) = \rho dt$. The integral equation in (14.32), as well as many multidimensional problems, can be computed numerically using Gaussian quadrature (as discussed in section 14.10). The volatilities σ^f, σ, and σ_F can be obtained from market data of implied volatilities, and the correlations ρ and $\rho_{F,f}$ can be estimated from historical data.[28]

14.10   GAUSSIAN QUADRATURE

In many instances, computational speed and efficiency gains (while maintaining accuracy) can be made by using Gaussian quadrature for numerical evaluation of the integral equations in option pricing problems such as equation (14.32). Gaussian quadrature can be used to approximate option values via weighted functional values at discrete location points in the state space known as abscissas. Through a judicious choice of weighting coefficients and abscissas at which the function, typically a function like the lognormal density, is evaluated, a convergence order higher than that of the Newton-Cotes formula (such as Simpson's rule) can be achieved with the same number of points.

---

[28]Ibid., 451.

In a typical option valuation problem, the value V of an option on an asset S_i at time t_i is given by

$$V(S_i, t_i) = E^Q[e^{-r\Delta t_{i+1}}V(S_{i+1}, t_{i+1})]$$

where $\Delta t_{i+1} = t_{i+1} - t_i$ and Q is the risk-neutral measure, which is essentially computed using the numerical integration problem (a form of the Feynman-Kac pricing formula)

$$V(S_i, t_i) = e^{-r\Delta t_{i+1}} \int_0^\infty V(S_{i+1}, t_{i+1})f(S_{i+1})dS_{i+1}$$

We can solve this integral problem by noting that the integral of the function can be approximated with a linear combination of function values over a finite interval. A particular rule of this approximation specifies a set of abscissas x_i and associated weights w_i for estimating the value of the integral by a weighted sum:

$$\int_a^b f(x)dx \cong \sum_i w_i f(x_i) \tag{14.33}$$

In classic techniques to evaluate the integral in (14.32) such as the trapezoid rule or Simpson's rule, a fixed number of equally spaced abscissas are used and the weights are chosen to maximize the order. Typically, the interval of integration is divided into n subintervals of equal size, the rule is applied to each subinterval, and the sum of the results is used as an estimate of the integral. The classic rule converges to the actual integral as n increases when the integrand is a continuous function. However, convergence can be slow so that an accurate estimate may require a large n and many function evaluations.

It is possible to devise routines that give exact results when $f(x)$ is a polynomial function of a given degree. The highest-degree polynomial that can be computed exactly is called the order of the quadrature rule. Gaussian rules choose the n abscissas and n weights to produce a $2n - 1$ order rule, the highest possible with n points.

In quadrature, the choice of weights and abscissas can be made so that the integral is exact for a class of integrands "polynomials times some known function $W(x)$" rather than for just the usual class of integrand "polynomials."[29] Moreover, the function $W(x)$ can be chosen to remove singularities from the desired integral.

---

[29]Press et al. (1992), 147.

Given $W(x)$ and a chosen n, it is possible to find a set of weights w_i and abscissas x_i such that the approximation

$$\int_a^b W(x)f(x)dx \cong \sum_i w_i f(x_i) \tag{14.34}$$

is exact if $f(x)$ is a polynomial.[30] Define $g(x) = W(x)f(x)$ and $v_j = w_j/W(x_j)$. We can then rewrite (14.34) as

$$\int_a^b g(x)dx \cong \sum_{i=1}^N v_j g(x_j) \tag{14.35}$$

so that (14.34) can be written in the form of (14.33).

In general, weight functions $W(x)$ are chosen to be orthogonal polynomials such that the scalar product between two functions over the weight function is zero, that is,

$$<f\,|\,g>= \int_a^b W(x)f(x)g(x)dx = 0$$

We can find $W(x)$ as a set of polynomials that include exactly one polynomial of order j, and $p_j(x)$ for each $j = 1, 2, \ldots$, and which are mutually orthogonal over the specified weight function $W(x)$. To construct such orthogonal polynomials for the weight function, a recurrence relationship can be constructed:

$$p_{-1}(x) = 0$$
$$p_0(x) = 1 \tag{14.36}$$
$$p_{j+1}(x) = (x - a_j)p_j(x) - b_j p_{j-1}(x)$$

where

$$a_j = \frac{\langle xp_j\,|\,p_j\rangle}{\langle p_j\,|\,p_j\rangle} \qquad j = 0, 1, \ldots$$

$$b_j = \frac{\langle p_j\,|\,p_j\rangle}{\langle p_{j-1}\,|\,p_{j-1}\rangle} \qquad j = 1, 2, \ldots \tag{14.37}$$

[30]Ibid., 147.

The coefficient b_0 is arbitrary; we can take it to be zero.

The polynomial $p_j(x)$ can be shown to have exactly j roots in the interval (a, b). Moreover, it can be shown that the roots of $p_j(x)$ "interleave" the roots of $j - 1$ roots of $p_{j-1}(x)$; that is, there is exactly one root of the former in between each two adjacent roots of latter.[31] Based on this fact, one can find all the roots by starting with $p_1(x)$ and then, in turn, bracket the roots of each higher j, determining them at each stage more precisely via an iterative root-finding procedure like Newton-Raphson.

The fundamental theorem of Gaussian quadrature tells how to find all the abscissas. This states that the abscissas of the n-point Gaussian quadrature formulas (14.34) and (14.35) with the weighting function $W(x)$ in the interval (a, b) are exactly the roots of the orthogonal polynomial $p_n(x)$ for the same interval and weighting function. Thus, computing all the roots of $p_n(x)$ will yield the abscissas to use for the Gaussian quadrature formulas. Once the abscissas are calculated, $x_1, \ldots, x_n$, the weights need to be computed. They can be found by the following formula:

$$w_j = \frac{\langle p_{n-1} | p_{n-1} \rangle}{p_{n-1}(x_j) p_n'(x_j)} \qquad (14.38)$$

where $p_n'(x_j)$ is the derivative of the orthogonal polynomial evaluated as its zero x_j.

Following Press et al. (1992), the computation of Gaussian quadrature involves two distinct stages: (1) the generation of the orthogonal polynomials $p_0, \ldots, p_n$ for the computation of the coefficients a_j and b_j in (14.37); and (2) the determination of the zeros of $p_n(x)$, and the computation of the associated weights. For certain classical cases such as Gauss-Hermite and Gauss-Legendre quadrature, the coefficients are known and the first stage can be omitted.

In Gauss-Hermite quadrature, $W(x) = e^{-x^2}$, $-\infty < x < \infty$, and the recurrence relationship of the orthogonal polynomials is given by $p_{j+1} = 2x p_j - 2j p_{j-1}$. Given this fact, we can use Gauss-Hermite quadrature to evelute equation (14.32) as well as many multidimensional integral problems given the fact that the transitional probability density function of a multidimensional diffusion process is known to be a Green's function that can be reduced to the Gauss-Hermite weight. In general, given $\mathbf{x} \in \Re^d$, the analytical form of the multistep Green's function is not known. However, it is known over a short time step $\Delta t = t - t'$ so that the Green's function is given by

$$G(\mathbf{x}, t, \mathbf{x}', t') = (2\pi \Delta t)^{-d/2} (\det(A)\mathbf{x}, t)))^{-1/2} \exp(-\Delta t Q(\mathbf{x}, \mathbf{x}'; \Delta t)) \qquad (14.39)$$

---

[31]Ibid., 149.

where

$$\Delta t Q(\mathbf{x}, \mathbf{x}'; \varepsilon) = \frac{1}{2\Delta t} \sum_{n=1}^{d} \sum_{m=1}^{d} (x'_m - (x_m + \Delta t b_m(\mathbf{x}, t))) a_{mn}^{-1}(\mathbf{x}, t)(x'_n - (x_n + \Delta t b_n(\mathbf{x}, t)))$$

$b_n(\mathbf{x}, t)$ is the local drift of the multidimensional diffusion process, and $A(\mathbf{x}, t)$ the covariance matrix with elements $a_{mn}(\mathbf{x}, t)$. In statistics, Q is known as the infinitesimal generator for the corresponding Markov process. If the coefficients are constant, the transition function is just the standard multivariate normal density function. Equation (14.39), the Green's function, can be used to express the price of $f(\mathbf{x}, t)$ at time t by acting as the kernel or transitional probability density function in the Feynman-Kac formula:

$$f(\mathbf{x}, t) = \int_{\Re^n} G(\mathbf{x}, t; \mathbf{x}', t') f(\mathbf{x}', t') d\mathbf{x}' \tag{14.40}$$

Equation (14.40) reduces to a finite state d-dimensional Markov process:

$$f(x_{i_1}, \ldots, x_{i_d}, t - \Delta t) = \sum_{j_1 \ldots j_d = 1}^{M} p_{i_1 \ldots i_d; j_1 \ldots j_d}(\Delta t) f(x_{j_1}, \ldots, x_{j_d}, t) \tag{14.41}$$

where p is the multidimensional probability density function defined by

$$p_{i_1 \ldots i_d; j_1 \ldots j_d}(\Delta t) = G(x_{i_1}, \ldots, x_{i_d}, t - \Delta t; x_{j_1}, \ldots, x_{j_d}, t) \tag{14.42}$$

We can write the formula for the transition function in matrix notation as

$$G(\mathbf{x}^{(i)}, t - \Delta t, \mathbf{x}^{(j)}, t) = (2\pi\Delta t)^{-d/2} (\det(A(\mathbf{x}^{(j)})))^{-1/2} \exp(-\frac{1}{2\Delta t} \mathbf{x}^{(j)T} A^{-1}(\mathbf{x}^{(i)}) \mathbf{x}^{(j)})$$

where $\mathbf{x}^{(j)} = (x_{j_1}, \ldots, x_{j_d})$ is the vector of states over a discrete set of times $j = 1, \ldots, M$.[32] For simplicity the mean $\mathbf{x}^{(j)} = \mathbf{x}^{(j)} + \Delta t b(\mathbf{x}^{(j)})$ has been subtracted and the time arguments omitted on the right-hand side. Since the covariance matrix is symmetric, it can be diagonalized. Since we assume the covariance matrix is positive-definite, there exists a basis for which all diagonal coefficients are equal to +1. Making a change of variables,

$$\mathbf{z}^{(j)} = \sqrt{A(\mathbf{x}^{(i)})} \mathbf{x}^{(j)} \tag{14.43}$$

---

[32]Gustafsson and Merabet (2002), 32.

with Jacobian

$$(2\Delta t)^{-d/2} \sqrt{\det(A(\mathbf{x}^{(i)}))}$$

for each $\mathbf{x}^{(i)}$, the transition function can be written as an exponential sum of squares:

$$G(\mathbf{u}^{(i)}, t - \Delta t, \mathbf{u}^{(j)}, t) = \pi^{-d/2} \exp\left(-\frac{1}{2\Delta t} \sum_{m=1}^{d} (z_m^{(j)})^2\right) = \pi^{-d/2} \exp\left(-\sum_{m=1}^{d} (u_m^{(j)})^2\right) \qquad (14.44)$$

where

$$u_m^{(j)} = z_m^{(j)} / \sqrt{2\Delta t}$$

It turns out that the standardized $\mathbf{u}^{(j)}$ variables are the abscissas in a multidimensional Gauss-Hermite quadrature, one for each given $\mathbf{x}^{(i)}$. In just one dimension one can write the Feynman-Kac pricing formula at fixed time point $i = 0$, say, and M standardized abscissas $\mathbf{u}^{(j)}$ as

$$f(x^{(0)}, 0) = \int_{-\infty}^{+\infty} G((u^{(0)}), 0; u, \Delta t) f(u, \Delta t) du$$

$$= \frac{1}{\sqrt{\pi}} \int_{-\infty}^{+\infty} e^{-u^2} f(u, \Delta t) du = \frac{1}{\sqrt{\pi}} \sum_{j=1}^{M} w^{(j)} f(u^{(j)}, \Delta t) \qquad (14.45)$$

where $w^{(j)}$, $j = 1, \ldots, M$ are the Gauss-Hermite weights.[33] If this process is repeated, the weights for each point and dimension multiply just as they do in the analytical transition function. The weights are all that is left in the transition function aside from the constant $\pi^{-d/2}$; that is,

$$p_{i_1 \ldots i_d; j_1 \ldots j_d}(\Delta t) = G(u^{(i)}, t - \Delta t; u^{(j)}, , t) = \pi^{-d/2} w_{j_1} \ldots w_{j_d} \qquad (14.46)$$

Thus, the standardized weights are $p_m^{(j)} = w^{(j)}/\sqrt{\pi}$. This change of variable technique saves a lot of computational time and both weights and standardized abscissas can be computed using the methodology discussed and precomputed from values given in books; see Press et al. (1992).

Thus, we can now evaluate (14.33) using (14.45). However, before we compute the quadrature, we need to rescale back to the original prices $\mathbf{x}^{(i)}$ using an in-

---

[33]Ibid., 32.

verse transformation of (14.43) and then evaluate the original function at these corresponding rescaled prices.[34] Following Gustafsson and Merabet (2002), a general backward-induction multinomial algorithm for computing option values on a finite-space grid $(\mathbf{x}^{(i)}, t_k)$ can be found by: (1) using precomputing abscissas, weights, and transition probabilities; (2) calculating for each point and time step (and relevant boundary conditions) the rescaled original price and time grid $(\mathbf{x}^{(i)}, t_k)$; and (3) starting from the terminal payout, evaluating the payout $f(\mathbf{x}^{(i)}, t_k)$ for each price level, and using equation (14.41) recursively to find the option price for each time step.[35]

Gauss-Hermite quadrature is very useful in computing the value of spread options because, as it turns out, the unique arbitrage price of a spread option given by

$$\pi_t = e^{-r(T-t)} E^Q[\max(S_1(T) - S_2(T) - K, 0)]$$

can be computed from (14.33); see Brigo and Mercurio (2001c). Thus, we can compute the value of spread options (as well as quanto swaptions and many other derivatives) using Gauss-Hermite quadrature.

The following code computes the integral in (14.32) using Gauss-Hermite quadrature. It utilizes the algorithm given in Press et al. (1992) for computation of the weights and abscissas.

```
#include <iostream.h>
#include <stdlib.h>
#include <stdio.h>
#include <math.h>
#include "Utility.h"
#include "SpreadOption.h"
#define PI 3.141592653589793

/******************************************************************************
GaussianQuadrature class :
Approximates the integral in equation (14.31) using quadrature to value spread
  options
******************************************************************************/
class GaussianQuadrature
{
  public:
    GaussianQuadrature(const int order);
    GaussianQuadrature(const int order, double S1, double S2, double strike,
      double sig1, double sig2, double rho, double r, double q1, double q2, double
        T);
```

---

[34]Ibid., 33.
[35]Ibid., 33.

```
    double g(double x);                              // function to be evaluated
    double g(double v, double (*pf_g)(double));      // use a function pointer to
                                                     // evaluate g

    double h(const double x);                        // helper function of g
    void gaussHermite(double x[], double w[], int n); // computed Gauss-Hermite
                                                     // abscissas and weights
                                                     // utility for computing
    StatUtility util;                                // normal densities

  private:
    // variables used for spread option calculation - could also define friend class
    // SpreadOption
    // to separate SpreadOption objects from GaussianQuadrature class functionality
    double S1;       // asset price 1
    double S2;       // asset price 2
    double strike;   // strike price
    double mu1;      // drift for asset price 1
    double mu2;      // drift for asset price 2
    double r;        // risk-free rate
    double q1;       // dividend yield for asset 1
    double q2;       // dividend yield for asset 2
    double T;        // maturity
    double sig1;     // volatility for asset 1
    double sig2;     // volatility for asset 2
    double rho;      // correlation between asset 1 and 2
    int order;       // order of quadrature
    double sum;      // gaussian quadrature sum
};
```

The class has the following method definitions:

```
#include "GaussianQuadrature.h"
#define PIM4 0.7511255444649425  //(1/(P1)^(1/4))
#define MAXIT 10
#define EPS 3.0e-14      // relative precision

/*******************************************************************************
GaussianQuadrature constructor
*******************************************************************************/
GaussianQuadrature::GaussianQuadrature(const int order, double S1, double S2,
  double strike, double sig1, double sig2, double rho_, double r, double q1, double
  q2, double T)
  : order(order), S1(S1), S2(S2), strike(strike), mu1(r-q1), mu2(r-q2), sig1(sig1),
    sig2(sig2), rho(rho), r(r), q1(q1), q2(q2), T(T), sum(0.0);
{ }

/*******************************************************************************
g: the function to evaluate
[in]:  double v   : the abscissa
```

```
[out]: double     : the value of the computed function evaluated at the abscissa
****************************************************************************/
double GaussianQuadrature::g(double v)
{
  double x =(S1*exp(-q1*T - 0.5*rho*rho*sig1*sig1*T + rho*sig1*sqrt(T)*v))*
    util.normalCalc((log(S1/h(v)) + (mu1 + (0.5 - rho*rho)*sig1*sig1)*T
    + rho*sig1*sqrt(T)*v)/(sig1*sqrt(T)*sqrt(1-rho*rho))) - h(v)*exp(-
    r*T)*util.normalCalc((log(S1/h(v))
    + (mu1 - 0.5*sig1*sig1)*T + rho*sig1*sqrt(T)*v)/(sig1*sqrt(T)*sqrt(1-
    rho*rho)));

  return x;
}


/****************************************************************************
h: helper function of g
[in]: double v : the abscissa
[out]: double  : the value of the helper function evaluated at the abscissa
****************************************************************************/
double GaussianQuadrature::h(double v)
{
  return strike + S2*exp(((r - q2) - 0.5*sig2*sig2)*T + sig2*sqrt(T)*v);
}


/****************************************************************************
gaussHermite: computes the Gauss-Hermite quadrature -from Press, et al. (1992)
[in] double x[]   : array of abscissas to be computed and stored
     double w[]   : array of weights to be computed and stored
     int n        : order of quadrature
[out] : returns the filled in arrays of x and w
****************************************************************************/
void GaussianQuadrature::gaussHermite(double x[], double w[], int n)
{
  double p1, p2, p3, pp, z, z1;
  int i, its, j, m;
  m = (n + 1)/2;

  // the roots are symmetric about the origin so we have to find only half of them
  for (i = 1; i <= m; i++)               // loop over desired root
  {
    if (i == 1)                          // initial guess for the largest root
      z = sqrt((double)(2*n+1))-1.85575*pow((double)(2*n+1),-0.16667);
    else if (i == 2)                     // initial guess for the second largest
                                         // root
      z -= 1.14*pow((double)n,0.426)/z;
    else if (i == 3)                     // initial guess for the third largest
                                         // root
      z = 1.86*z - 0.86*x[1];
    else if (i == 4)                     // initial guess for the fourth largest
                                         // root
      z = 1.91*z - 0.91*x[2];
    else                                 // initial guess for the other roots
      z = 2.0*z - x[i-2];
```

```
    for (its = 1; its <= MAXIT; its++)      // refinement by Newton's method
    {
      p1 = PIM4;
      p2 = 0.0;
      for (j = 1; j <= n; j++)
      {
        p3 = p2;
        p2 = p1;
        p1 = z*sqrt(2.0/j)*p2-sqrt(((double)(j-1))/j)*p3;
      }

      // p1 is now the Hermite polynomial. We next compute pp, its derivative,
      // by the relation (4.5.21) using p2, the polynomial of one lower order
      pp = sqrt((double)2*n)*p2;
      z1 = z;
      z = z1 - p1/pp; // Newton's formula
      if (fabs(z-z1) <= EPS)
        break;
    }
    if (its > MAXIT)
      cout << "Too many iterations in GaussHermite" << endl;

    x[i] = z;           // store the root
    x[n+1-i] = -z;      // and its symmetric counterpart
    w[i] = 2.0/(pp*pp); // compute the weight
    w[n+1-i] = w[i];    // and its symmetric counterpart
  }
}
```

Suppose we want to compute the value of a spread option with $S_1 = 100$, $S_2 = 96$, $X = 4$, $\rho = 0.5$, $\sigma_1 = 0.1$, $\sigma_2 = 0.2$, $q_1 = 0.05$, $q_2 = 0.05$, $r = 0.1$, and $T = 1$. We can run the main function

```
void main()
{
  double sum = 0.0;
  int order = 12;                   // order of gaussian quadrature
  double *x = new double[200];      // store abscissas
  double *w = new double[200];      // store weights

  GaussianQuadrature gq(order,100, 96, 4, 0.10, 0.20, 0.5, 0.10, 0.05, 0.05, 1);
  gq.gaussHermite(x,w,order);
  for (int i = 1; i <= order i++)
  {
    // compute sum of weighted function g at rescaled original values
    sum += w[i]*gq.g(x[i]*sqrt(2)/(0.1*0.2*sqrt(1-0.5*0.5)));
  }
  cout << "value = " << sum*(1/(sqrt(PI))) << endl;
}
```

The value of the spread option using Gauss-Hermite quadrature with 12 abscissas is $7.138. Notice that it was necessary to rescale back to the original price from the standardized price by multiplying by

$$\sqrt{2}/(\sigma_1\sigma_2(1-\rho^2)) = \sqrt{2}/((0.1)(0.2)(1-0.25)) = \sqrt{2}/0.015$$

where the denominator is the square root of the determinant of the covariance matrix.

We can make the *GaussianQuadrature* class more generic and reusable for evaluating functions by using function pointers in the overloaded *g* method signature:

```
double GaussianQuadrature::g(double v, double (*pf_g)(double))
{
  return (*pf_g)(v);
}
```

Any function that has the prototype double *function_name*(double) can then be passed in as a second argument to *g* and evaluated at the *v* abscissas.

Probability Review

A.1 PROBABILITY SPACES

A probability space $(\Omega, \mathfrak{I}, P)$ is defined by a state space Ω, the event space (or the sigma algebra) $\mathfrak{I}$ (i.e., the set of measurable or observable events which are subsets of Ω), and a probability measure P. A state space Ω is the set of all possible states in the system. Typically, a probability space with an increasing sequence of sigma algebras is said to be equipped with a filtration that is augmented as time goes by since more information is obtained about the past. The defining properties of the probability measure P are:

(i) $P(\Omega) = 1$

(ii) $P(\bigcup\limits_{j=1}^{\infty} A_j) = \sum\limits_{j=1}^{\infty} P(A_j)$, for A_j pairwise disjoint

(iii) $0 \leq P(A_j) \leq 1$ for all j

Condition (i) states that it is certain that an event will occur in the state space. Condition (ii) states that P is countably additive, and condition (iii) states that the probability measure assigns a positive number between 0 and 1 to any measurable event $A \in \mathfrak{I}$.

DEFINITION. A collection $\mathfrak{I}$ of subsets of Ω is a sigma algebra if the following three conditions are satisfied:

(i) $\Omega \in \mathfrak{I}$

(ii) $A \in \mathfrak{I} \rightarrow A^c \in \mathfrak{I}$

(iii) $A_\alpha \in \mathfrak{I} \rightarrow \bigcup\limits_{\alpha} A^c \in \mathfrak{I}$

Condition (ii) states that if an event is measurable then its complement must also be measurable. Condition (iii) states that if a collection of sets A_α where α is an index is measurable, then the union must also be measurable.

As an example, consider a one-period binomial model where the underlying asset S can go up with probability $p = \frac{1}{2}$ to S_u or down with probability $1 - p = \frac{1}{2}$ to S_d as shown in Figure A.1.

The state space is $\Omega = \{S_u, S_d\}$. One possibility for the event space is $\Im = \{\Omega, \phi, \{S_u\}, \{S_d\}\}$ (i.e., the set of all subsets of Ω). An interpretation of $\Im$ is that it gives the amount of information available about the system. Since every subset of Ω is measurable, this case represents complete information.

Consider a basic two-period binomial model as shown in Figure A.2. In this model, there are four possible states: $\Omega = \{S_{uu}, S_{ud}, S_{du}, S_{dd}\}$. In a three-period model, there are eight possible states, and so forth. In general, in an n-period model there are 2^n states. We can define the event space for each time step:

$$\Im_2 = \{\phi, \Omega, \{S_{uu}\}, \{S_{ud}\}, \{S_{du}\}, \{S_{dd}\}\}$$
$$\Im_1 = \{\phi, \Omega, \{S_{uu}, S_{ud}\}, \{S_{du}, S_{dd}\}\}$$
$$\Im_0 = \{\phi, \Omega\}$$

where ϕ is the null set and $\Im_t$ is the filtration at time t. $\Im_1$ represents partial information in the two-period model since it is exactly the information that is available after just one period. The probability measure is $P(\{S_{uu}, S_{ud}\}) = P(\{S_{dd}, S_{du}\}) = \frac{1}{2}$.

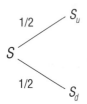

FIGURE A.1   One-Period Binomial Model

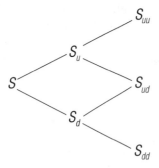

FIGURE A.2   Two-Period Binomial Model(s)

A.2 CONTINUOUS PROBABILITY SPACES

The state space Ω may be a continuous space. For example, $\Omega = (-\infty, +\infty)$. In this case, the sigma algebra of measurable events $\Im$ is the Borel sigma algebra. By definition, this is the smallest sigma algebra that contains all open intervals of the form (a, b). It can be shown that such a sigma algebra is quite rich as it contains all open and closed sets.

For the probability measure, one example is the normal distribution measure:

$$P(A) = \frac{1}{\sqrt{2\pi}} \int_A e^{-\frac{x^2}{2}} dx$$

where $P\{(-\infty, +\infty)\} = 1$ is a probability measure. Since stock prices always positive, Ω is not a realistic space. A more realistic situation is obtained by making a change of variables: $x = \ln(S)$. This changes Ω from $(-\infty, +\infty)$ to $(0, +\infty)$, or, if we allow $-\infty$ in the original space, to $(0, \infty)$. The new probability measure is

$$P(A) = \frac{1}{\sqrt{2\pi}} \int_A e^{-\frac{(\log(S))^2}{2}} dS$$

which is the standard lognormal distribution, commonly used to describe the behavior of stock prices.

A.3 SINGLE RANDOM VARIABLES

A random variable defined on a probability space $(\Omega, \Im, P)$ is a real valued function on Ω that is measurable with respect to $\Im$. Formally, X is a random variable if it is a function such that $X^{-1}(a, b) \in \Im$ for any interval (a, b) of the real line.

Let X be a real random variable with the probability density function $p(x)$. Let x be the real value of X. The probability of $X \in (-\infty, y]$ is

$$P\{X \in (-\infty, y]\} = \int_{-\infty}^{y} p(x)dx$$

where $p(x)dx$ is the probability measure of the infinitesimal interval dx. If $f(X)$ is a function of the random variable X, then its expected value is

$$E[f(X)] = \int_{-\infty}^{\infty} f(x)p(x)dx$$

In particular, moments about some value a are defined as

$$M_n(a) = E[(X - a)^n] = \int_{-\infty}^{\infty} (x - a)^n p(x)dx$$

The *mean* is defined as

$$\mu = \overline{X} = E[X] = \int_{-\infty}^{\infty} xp(x)dx$$

Moments are called central if $a = \overline{X}$:

$$M_n = E[(X - \overline{X})^n]$$

The variance is the second central moment:

$$\text{Var}[X] = M_2 = E[(X - \overline{X})^2] = E[X^2] - \overline{X}^2$$

A characteristic function is defined as a Fourier transform of the probability density:

$$\phi(\lambda) = E[e^{i\lambda x}] = \int_{-\infty}^{\infty} e^{i\lambda x} p(x)dx$$

The moments expansion of the characteristic function is:

$$\phi(\lambda) = \sum_{n=0}^{\infty} \frac{(i\lambda)^n}{n!} E[x^n] = \sum_{n=0}^{\infty} \frac{(i\lambda)^n}{n!} M_n(0)$$

where $M_n(0) = E[x^n]$ are moments about zero. The density of inverse Fourier transform:

$$p(x) = \frac{1}{2\pi} \int_{-\infty}^{\infty} e^{-i\lambda x} \phi(\lambda)d\lambda$$

A.4   BINOMIAL RANDOM VARIABLES

The binomial probability density (probability mass function) is given by

$$p_j = \binom{N}{j} p^j (1 - p)^{N-j} \quad j = 0, 1, \ldots, N$$

with mean:

$$E[j] = Np$$

and variance:

$$\text{Var}\,[j] = Np(1 - p)$$

A.5   NORMAL RANDOM VARIABLES

The normal density with mean μ and variance σ^2 is given by

$$p(x) = \frac{1}{\sqrt{2\pi\sigma^2}} e^{-\frac{(x-\mu)^2}{2\sigma^2}}$$

The characteristic function is obtained by calculating the Gaussian integral

$$\phi(\lambda) = \int_{-\infty}^{\infty} \frac{1}{\sqrt{2\pi\sigma^2}} e^{-\frac{(x-\mu)^2}{2\sigma^2} + i\lambda x} = e^{i\mu\lambda - \frac{\sigma^2\lambda^2}{2}}$$

The moments are:

$$E[X] = \mu$$
$$\text{Var}[X] = \sigma^2$$
$$E[(X - \mu)^{2n+1}] = 0,\ n = 0,\ 1,\ \ldots$$
$$E[(X - \mu)^{2n}] = (2n - 1)!!\sigma^{2n},\ n = 0,\ 1,\ \ldots$$

where the odd factorial is defined as $(2n - 1)!! = (2n - 1) \times (2n - 3) \ldots 3 \times 1$. These formulas for the moments can be checked by expanding the characteristic function in Taylor series. If $\mu = 0$ and $\sigma = 1$, we have

$$\phi(\lambda) = e^{-\frac{\lambda^2}{2}} = \sum_{n=0}^{\infty} \frac{(-1)^n}{2^n\,n!} \lambda^{2n}$$

Comparing the moments expansion,

$$\phi(\lambda) = \sum_{n=0}^{\infty} \frac{(i\lambda)^n}{n!} E[x^n] = \sum_{n=0}^{\infty} \frac{(i\lambda)^n}{n!} M_n(0)$$

we have

$$M_{2n+1}(0) = 0$$

and

$$M_{2n}(0) = \frac{(2n)!}{2^n \, n!} = (2n-1)!!$$

The case with mean μ and standard deviation σ is obtained by simply changing the variable $x \to (x - \mu)/\sigma$. The term x is called standard normal variable or standard normal deviate if $\mu = 0$ and $\sigma = 1$. Its probability density and probability distribution are

$$n(x) = \frac{1}{\sqrt{2\pi}} e^{-\frac{x^2}{2}} \text{ and } N(y) = \frac{1}{\sqrt{2\pi}} \int_{-\infty}^{y} e^{-\frac{x^2}{2}} dx$$

A.6   CONDITIONAL EXPECTATIONS

If X and Y are random variables that have a joint probability density $f(x, y)$ the conditional probability density of X, given $Y = y$, is defined for all y such that $f_Y(y) > 0$ by

$$p(x \mid y) = \frac{p(x, y)}{p_Y(y)}$$

and the conditional probability distribution of X, given $Y = y$, by

$$P(x \mid y) = P(X \le x \mid Y = y) = \int_{-\infty}^{x} p(x \mid y) dz$$

The conditional expectation of X, given $Y = y$, is defined, in this case, by

$$E[X \mid Y = y] = \int_{-\infty}^{+\infty} x p(x \mid y) dx$$

We can use this fact in the law of iterated expectations:

$$E[X] = E[E[X \mid Y = y]] = \int_{-\infty}^{\infty} E[X \mid Y = y] p(y) dy$$

We now want to define the conditional expectation of a random variable with respect to not just one event, but a sigma algebra of events. In this case the conditional expectation will be itself a random variable and not just a number. Intuitively, it will represent the best guess at X given the information given by the sigma algebra.

DEFINITION. The conditional expectation of random variable X with respect to a sigma algebra $\Im$ is the random variable $Y = E(X \mid \Im)$, which has the following properties:

(*i*) Y is $\Im$ measurable

(*ii*) $\int\limits_{A} YdP = \int\limits_{A} XdP$, for *any* $A \in \Im$

Condition (ii) is equivalent to the seemingly stronger

$$(ii')\int\limits_{\Omega} YZdP = \int\limits_{\Omega} XZdP$$

It can be shown that there exists a unique Y with these properties, though we do not show it here. We consider how to compute such expectation. When Ω is a discrete space, it turns out that the procedure is rather simple. We start by partitioning $\Im$ into pairwise disjoint sets B_i with the property that any $A \in \Im$ can be expressed as union of parts,

$$A = \bigcup B_k$$

The interpretation here is that the information contained in $\Im$ is equivalent to the fact that one knows which set B_k of the partition contains the true state of the world, but that is all that is known.

As an example, consider the two-period model and the sigma algebra containing the information at time $t = 1$, $\Im_1$. This can be decomposed into two disjoint sets: $B_1 = \{uu, dd\}$ and $B_2 = \{du, dd\}$. The information at time $t = 2$, $\Im_2$ is decomposed into the four parts that make up Ω (i.e., $B_1 = \{uu\}$, $B_2 = \{ud\}$, $B_3 = \{du\}$, and $B_4 = \{dd\}$).

PROPOSITION. Let B_i be the partition of $\Im$. Then the conditional expectation $Y = E(X \mid \Im)$ is given by

$$Y(w) = \frac{1}{P(B_i)} \int\limits_{B_i} XdP = E(X \mid B_i), \quad w \in B_i$$

PROOF. We need to show that the formula for Y given satisfies (i) and (ii) of the definition of conditional expectation with respect to a sigma algebra. Part (i) is triv-

778   PROBABILITY REVIEW

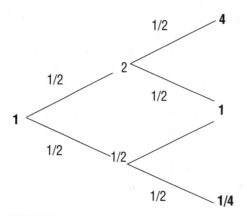

FIGURE A.3 Probabilities of Two-Period Binomial Model

ially satisfied, since Y is constant on each B_i and hence the event $Y \in (a, b)$ consists of the union of B_i's. As for part (ii), for any A $\mathfrak{J}$

$$\int_A X dP = \sum_k \int_{B_i} X dP = \sum_k \int_{B_i} Y dP = \int_A Y dP$$

Suppose we have a two-period binomial model as shown in Figure A.3. We wish to compute $Y = E(S(2) \mid \mathfrak{J}_1)$. The probabilities are written alongside each branch, and the payoff is given at the end of the branch. We can partition the σ algebra $\mathfrak{J}_1$ into two events, corresponding to the heads or tails flip on the first toss: $B_1 = \{uu, ud\}$ and $B_2 = \{du, dd\}$. Then,

$$Y = E(X \mid B_1) = \frac{1}{1/2}(4 \cdot 1/4 + 1 \cdot 1/4) = 5/2 \text{ on } B_1$$

$$Y = E(X \mid B_1) = \frac{1}{1/2}(1 \cdot 1/4 + 1/4 \cdot 1/4) = 5/8 \text{ on } B_2$$

A.7   PROBABILITY LIMIT THEOREMS

Let X_i be independent random variables with finite means μ_i and finite variances. Then

$$\frac{1}{n}\sum_{i=1}^{n} X_i \xrightarrow{n \to \infty} \frac{1}{n}\sum_{i=1}^{n} \mu_i$$

That is, all random fluctuations around the means cancel out in the limit when we add up a very large number of random variables with finite means and variances. This is known as the law of large numbers.

If, furthermore, the X_i's are independent and identically distributed (i.i.d.) with the common mean μ and variance σ^2, then the central limit theorem applies. This theorem states that the approach to the limit is asymptotically normal with mean μ and variance σ^2/n:

$$\lim_{n \to \infty} P\left\{ \frac{\sum\limits_{i=1}^{n} X_i - n\mu}{\sigma \sqrt{n}} \le a \right\} = \frac{1}{\sqrt{2\pi}} \int_{-\infty}^{a} e^{-\frac{x^2}{2}}\, dx$$

A.8   MULTIDIMENSIONAL CASE

We can extend all previous sections to the multidimensional case. Consider a D-dimensional random vector $\mathbf{X} = \{X_i, i = 1, 2, \ldots, D\}$ with means $E[X_i] = \mu_i$ and the covariance matrix $\text{Cov}(X_i, X_j) = E[(X_i - \mu_i)(X_j - \mu_j)] = \Sigma_{ij}$. The correlation matrix is defined by a covariance matrix normalized by the variances:

$$\rho_{ij} = \frac{\Sigma_{ij}}{\sigma_i \sigma_j}$$

where σ_i^2's are individual variances of X_i.

Consider the characteristic function:

$$\phi(\lambda_i) = \exp\left(i \sum_{k=1}^{D} \mu_k \lambda_k - \frac{1}{2} \sum_{i=1}^{D} \sum_{j=1}^{D} \lambda_i \lambda_j \Sigma_{ij} \right)$$

The D-dimensional normal density is obtained by taking the inverse Fourier transform (Gaussian integral):

$$p(x_1, x_2, \ldots, x_D) = \frac{1}{(2\pi)^D} \int_{\Re^D} \exp\left(i \sum_{k=1}^{D} (u_k - x_k)\lambda_k - \frac{1}{2} \sum_{i=1}^{D} \sum_{j=1}^{D} \lambda_i \lambda_j \Sigma_{ij} \right) d^D\lambda$$

$$= \frac{1}{\sqrt{(2\pi)^n \det(\Sigma_{ij})}} \exp\left\{ -\frac{1}{2} \sum_{i,j=1}^{D} (\Sigma^{-1})_{ij} (x_i - \mu_i)(x_j - \mu_j) \right\}$$

where Σ^{-1} is the inverse covariance matrix. The standard multivariate normal probability density is obtained by introducing new variables (standardizing)

$$y_i = \frac{x_i - \mu_i}{\sigma_i}$$

and the multivariate standard normal density is given by

$$n(y_1, y_2, \ldots, y_n) = \frac{1}{\sqrt{(2\pi)^n \det(\rho_{ij})}} \exp\left\{-\frac{1}{2}\sum_{i,j=1}^{D}(\rho^{-1})_{ij}y_iy_j\right\}$$

Moreover, we can introduce a new basis in $\mathfrak{R}^D$:

$$z_i = \sum_{j=1}^{D}b_{i,j}y_j$$

where $b_{i,j}$ are elements of the matrix B such that elements of the inverse matrix B^{-1}, $(b^{-1})_{i,j}$,

$$y_j = \sum_{i=1}^{D}(b^{-1})_{j,i}z_i$$

have the following orthogonal transformation property:

$$E[y_iy_j] = \sum_{k,l=1}^{D}(b^{-1})_{i,k}(b^{-1})_{j,l}\delta_{k,l} = \rho_{ij}$$

so that the z_i's are uncorrelated and have unit variances:

$$E[z_iz_j] = \delta_{ij}$$

where $\delta_{i,j}$ are elements of the identity matrix, that is, $\delta_{i,j} = 1\ (0)$ if $i = j\ (i \neq j)$, and

$$n(z_1, z_2, \ldots, z_D) = \prod_{i=1}^{D}\frac{1}{\sqrt{2\pi}}e^{-\frac{z_i^2}{2}}$$

A.9   DIRAC'S DELTA FUNCTION

Dirac's delta function, written $\delta(x)$, is a generalized function that can be interpreted as a probability density function of a deterministic random variable X that can take only one value with probability 1. It has the property that has a mean and variance of zero; that is,

$$E[X] = \int_{-\infty}^{+\infty} x\delta(x)dx = 0 \text{ and } \mathrm{Var}[X] = \int_{-\infty}^{+\infty} x^2\delta(x)dx = 0$$

and the total probability is 1,

$$\int_{-\infty}^{+\infty} \delta(x)dx = 1$$

More formally, the delta function is the limit of the (delta) sequence of one-parameter family of functions $\delta_\varepsilon(x)$ as $\varepsilon \to 0$ with the following properties:

    (*i*)   For each ε, $\delta_\varepsilon(x)$ is piecewise smooth.

    (*ii*) $\int_{-\infty}^{+\infty} \delta_\varepsilon(x)dx = 1.$

    (*iii*) For each $x \neq 0$, $\lim_{\varepsilon \to 0} \delta_\varepsilon(x) = 0.$

The delta function may be thought of as a limit of a sequence of normal distributions as the variance (the variance acts as ε) goes to zero:

$$\delta(x) = \lim_{\sigma \to 0} \frac{1}{\sqrt{2\pi\sigma^2}} e^{-\frac{x^2}{2\sigma^2}}$$

It is easy to show that the integral of this function is 1, and that for $x \neq 0$ its value tends to zero, while for $x = 0$ its value tends to infinity. The limiting function is not well behaved around $x = 0$. However, the integration smooths out the bad behavior. In fact, for any smooth test function $\phi(x)$

$$\int_{-\infty}^{+\infty} \delta(x)\phi(x)dx = \phi(0)$$

so that its integral action defines the delta function as the continuous linear map from smooth functions $\phi(x)$ to real numbers that have the value $\phi(0)$. Moreover,

$$\int_{-\infty}^{+\infty} \delta(x-a)\phi(x) = \phi(a)$$

for any test function $\phi(x)$. We also have that

$$\int_{-\infty}^{x} \delta(s)ds = H(x)$$

where $H(x)$ is the Heavyside function, defined by

$$H(x) = \begin{cases} 0 \text{ for } x < 0 \\ 1 \text{ for } x \geq 0 \end{cases}$$

so that $H'(x) = \delta(x)$. Delta functions are useful in analysis of differential equations with discontinuous functions or coefficients.

Stochastic Calculus Review

B.1 BROWNIAN MOTION

A Brownian motion is a continuous time process, $Z(t)$, with the following properties:

1. For any $t_1, t_2, \ldots, t_n$, the increments $Z(t_2) - Z(t_1)$, $Z(t_3) - Z(t_2)$, $\ldots$, $Z(t_n) - Z(t_{n-1})$ are independent random variables with a normal distribution of mean 0 and variance $t_2 - t_1$, $t_3 - t_2$, $\ldots$, $t_n - t_{n-1}$, respectively.

2. $Z(t)$ is continuous almost surely (a.s.), that is, with probability 1.

3. The Brownian motion process is uniquely described by the finite-dimensional distribution functions (f.d.d.), $F_{t_1, t_2, \ldots, t_n}(x_1, x_2, \ldots, x_n)$, which are joint distribution functions of $(W(t_1), W(t_2), \ldots, W(t_n))$. Specifically,

$$\int_A F_{t_1, t_2, \ldots, t_n}(x_1, x_2, \ldots, x_n) dx_1 dx_2 \ldots dx_n = P\{((Z(t_1), Z(t_2), \ldots Z(t_n)) \in A\}$$

for any $A \in \Re^n$. For example,

$$F_{t_1}(x_1) = P(W(t_1) \in A) = \int_A \frac{1}{\sqrt{2\pi t_1}} e^{-\frac{(x_1 - x_0)^2}{2t_1}} \, dx_1$$

In general,

$$F_{t_1, t_2, \ldots, t_n}(x_1, x_2, \ldots, x_n) = \prod_{i=1}^{n} \frac{1}{\sqrt{2\pi(t_i - t_{i-1})}} e^{-\frac{(x_i - x_{i-1})^2}{2(t_i - t_{i-1})}}$$

which is the multivariate normal distribution (we assume $t_0 = 0$).

If we define the transitional probability density function roughly as the probability to go from a point x at time s to a point y at time t,

$$p(s,\, x;\, t,\, y) = \frac{1}{\sqrt{2\pi(t-s)}}\, e^{-\frac{(x-y)^2}{2(t-s)}}$$

so that

$$P(Z(t) \in A \mid Z(s) = x) = \int_A p(s,\, x;\, t,\, y)\, dy$$

then

$$F_{t_1, t_2, \dots, t_n}(x_1,\, x_2,\, \dots,\, x_n) = p(0,\, x_0;\, t_1,\, x_1) p(t_1,\, x_1;\, t_2,\, x_2) \dots p(t_{n-1},\, x_{n-1};\, t_n,\, x_n)$$

B.2 BROWNIAN MOTION WITH DRIFT AND VOLATILITY

Consider the random walk

$$X_{k+1} = X_k + \xi_{k+1}$$

where

$$\xi_n = \begin{cases} \sigma\sqrt{\Delta t} & \text{with } p = 1/2 \\ -\sigma\sqrt{\Delta t} & \text{with } 1 - p = 1/2 \end{cases}$$

with a drift of zero. We can construct a continuous time process as follows. For $0 \le t \le T = n\Delta t$, let

$$S_{\Delta t}(t) = \begin{cases} X_k & t = k\Delta t \\ \text{linear interpolation} & \textit{otherwise} \end{cases}$$

It is proven by Donsker that as $\Delta t \to 0$, the asset price $S_{\Delta t}(t)$ converges in distribution to that of Brownian motion.

$$S_{\Delta t}(t) \xrightarrow{\ D\ } Z(t) \text{ for } 0 \le t \le T$$

Let $Z(t)$ be a Brownian motion. To make its volatility rate equal to σ we define:

$$X(t) = \sigma Z(t) \qquad (B2.1)$$

Then one can check that $X(t) - X(s) \sim N(0, \sigma^2 (t - s))$. To introduce a drift μ in addition to the volatility, set

$$X(t) = \mu t + \sigma Z(t) \qquad (B2.2)$$

Then, $X(t) - X(s) \sim N(\mu(t - s), \sigma^2 (t - s))$. Taking the differentials on both sides of (B2.2), we get

$$dX(t) = \mu dt + \sigma dZ(t) \qquad (B2.3)$$

where dW is the infinitesimal change in the Brownian motion W. The process X is called a Wiener process, and is the continuous limit of the random walk process with drift. Taking the integral of (B2.3) from 0 to t, we get

$$X(t) - X(0) = \mu t + \int_0^t \sigma dZ$$

The dW integral (i.e., the integral with respect to the Brownian motion) is well defined and is called a stochastic integral. We define this integral in detail in the next section. In this case, the integral is simply equal to $\sigma(Z(t) - Z(0)) = \sigma Z(t)$.

It is important to note that we cannot take the derivatives of (B2.2), that is,

$$\frac{dX}{dt} = \mu + \sigma \frac{dW}{dt}$$

since $W(t)$ is, with probability 1, nondifferentiable at every point.

B.3   STOCHASTIC INTEGRALS

The meaning of

$$dS = \mu S dt + \sigma S dZ$$

is given by the following integral equation:

$$S(t) - S(0) = \int_0^t \mu S(s) ds + \int_0^t \sigma S(s) dZ(s)$$

The first integral on the right is an ordinary integral with respect to the usual measure ds. The second integral is a stochastic integral with respect to Brownian motion. Both integrals are random variables, since integrands are random processes.

Let us now try to define what a stochastic integral is. We start with the following example:

$$\int_a^b Z(s)dZ(s)$$

If $Z(s)$ is deterministic—for example, a smooth function of s—then the integral is easily solved:

$$\int_a^b Z(s)dZ(s) = \int_a^b Z(s)Z'(s)ds = \frac{1}{2}\int_a^b (Z^2)'(s)ds = \frac{1}{2}(Z^2(b) - Z^2(a))$$

When $Z(s)$ is a random Brownian motion, the answer is more complicated. We consider the approximating Riemann sums of the form

$$I_{\Delta t}(\lambda) = \sum_{k=1}^n (\lambda Z(t_k) + (1 - \lambda)Z(t_{k-1}))(Z(t_k) - Z(t_{k-1}))$$

where λ is some parameter between 0 and 1 and $t_k = a + k\Delta t$, $n\Delta t = b - a$.

For a deterministic Z, the limit should be independent of λ. When Z is a Brownian motion, we have the following result:

$$I_{\Delta t}(\lambda) \rightarrow \frac{1}{2}(Z^2(b) - Z^2(a)) + (\lambda - \frac{1}{2})(b - a)$$

To prove this result, we first take $\lambda = 0$, (i.e., the left Riemann sum). Then

$$I_{\Delta t}(0) = \sum_{k=1}^n Z(t_{k-1})(Z(t_k) - Z(t_{k-1}))$$

$$= \sum_{k=1}^n (Z^2(t_k) - Z^2(t_{k-1})) - \sum_{k=1}^n Z(t_k)(Z(t_k) - Z(t_{k-1}))$$

$$= Z^2(t_n) - Z^2(t_0) - \sum_{k=1}^n Z(t_k)(Z(t_k) - Z(t_{k-1}))$$

At the same time,

$$I_{\Delta t}(0) = -\sum_{k=1}^{n}(Z(t_k) - Z(t_{k-1}))^2 + \sum_{k=1}^{n}Z(t_k)(Z(t_k) - Z(t_{k-1}))$$

Adding these two expressions, we get

$$2I_{\Delta t}(0) = (Z^2(t_n) - Z^2(t_0)) - \sum_{k=1}^{n}(Z(t_k) - Z(t_{k-1}))^2$$

$$= (Z^2(b) - Z^2(a)) - \sum_{k=1}^{n}(Z(t_k) - Z(t_{k-1}))^2$$

Since $(Z(t_k) - Z(t_{k-1}))^2$ are independent random variables with mean Δt, by the law of large numbers, the summation tends to $n\Delta t = (b - a)$. Therefore,

$$I_{\Delta t}(0) \to \frac{1}{2}(Z^2(b) - Z^2(a)) - \frac{1}{2}(b - a)$$

Similarly,

$$I_{\Delta t}(1) = I_{\Delta t}(0) + \sum_{k=1}^{n}(Z(t_k) - Z(t_{k-1}))^2 \to \frac{1}{2}(Z^2(b) - Z^2(a)) + \frac{1}{2}(b - a)$$

Finally,

$$I_{\Delta t}(\lambda) = \lambda I_{\Delta t}(1) + (1 - \lambda)I_{\Delta t}(0)$$

$$= \frac{1}{2}(Z^2(b) - Z^2(a)) + (\lambda - \frac{1}{2})(b - a)$$

This shows that the value of a stochastic integral depends on which Riemann sum is used. The definition that we shall use is the one in which $\lambda = 0$ (i.e., the one corresponding to the Riemann sums). This is called the *Ito integral*. Since for any t, $Z(t)$ is measurable with respect to $\mathfrak{I}_t$, the information at time t, $Z(t_{k-1})$ is independent of the increment $Z(t_k) - Z(t_{k-1})$. In this case, we say that the integrand Z is *nonanticipating*.

DEFINITION. Let $X(t)$ be a stochastic process. Suppose X is nonanticipating with respect to the Brownian motion Z (i.e., X is measurable with respect to $\mathfrak{I}_t$). The Ito integral of X with respect to the Brownian motion is defined as

$$I = \int_{a}^{b}X(s)dZ(s) = \lim_{\Delta t \to 0}I_{\Delta t} = \lim_{\Delta t \to 0}\sum_{k=1}^{n}X(t_{k-1})(Z(t_k) - Z(t_{k-1}))$$

The limit exists and defines the Ito integral as a random variable. Note that $E(I_{\Delta t}) = 0$ since X is nonanticipating and the increments in Z have mean zero. In addition,

$$\text{Var}(I_{\Delta t}) = E(I_{\Delta t}^2) = \sum_{k=1}^{n} E[X^2(t_{k-1})]E[(Z(t_k) - Z(t_{k-1}))^2]$$

$$= \sum_{k=1}^{n} E[X^2(t_{k-1})]\Delta t$$

Therefore,

$$E[I] = 0, \quad \text{Var}(I) = \int_a^b E(X^2(s))ds$$

Note: The integral

$$\int_0^t Z(2s)dZ(s)$$

is not well defined as an Ito integral since $Z(2s)$ is not a nonanticipating process.

B.4   ITO'S FORMULA

We provide the derivation for Ito's formula. Let $S(t)$ be the process

$$dS = \mu Sdt + \sigma SdZ$$

and consider the process $f(S(t), t)$ where f is a smooth function. Using a Taylor series expansion, we obtain

$$\begin{aligned} df &= \frac{\partial f}{\partial t}dt + \frac{\partial f}{\partial S}dS + \frac{1}{2}\frac{\partial^2 f}{\partial S^2}(dS)^2 \\ &= \frac{\partial f}{\partial t}dt + \frac{\partial f}{\partial S}(\mu Sdt + \sigma SdZ) + \frac{1}{2}\frac{\partial^2 f}{\partial S^2}\sigma^2 S^2 dt \\ &= \left(\frac{\partial f}{\partial t} + \frac{\partial f}{\partial S}\mu S + \frac{1}{2}\frac{\partial^2 f}{\partial S^2}\sigma^2 S^2\right)dt + \sigma S\frac{\partial f}{\partial S}dZ \end{aligned}$$

(B2.4)

where we have used the fact $(dZ)^2 = dt$, and ignored higher-order terms. Note that the drift term is the backward Black-Scholes partial differential diffusion equation. In a risk-neutral world, the drift must earn the risk-free rate so that

$$\frac{\partial f}{\partial t} + \frac{\partial f}{\partial S}\mu S + \frac{1}{2}\frac{\partial^2 f}{\partial S^2}\sigma^2 S^2 = rf$$

If we let $X = f(S) = \ln S$, in (B2.4), we obtain the following Wiener process:

$$dX = (\mu - \frac{1}{2}\sigma^2)dt + \sigma dZ$$

which is the continuous lognormal model for stock behavior.

B.5   GEOMETRIC BROWNIAN MOTION

If $\{X(t), t \geq 0\}$ is a Wiener process that follows $dX = \mu dt + \sigma dZ$, then the process $\{S(t), t \geq 0\}$, defined by

$$S(t) = e^{X(t)}$$

is called geometric Brownian motion. Let $f(X) = e^{X(t)}$. From Ito's lemma we have

$$df = \frac{\partial f}{\partial t} + \frac{\partial f}{\partial X}dX + \frac{\sigma^2}{2}\frac{\partial^2 f}{\partial X^2}dX^2$$

so that

$$dS = (1 + \mu S + \frac{1}{2}\sigma^2 S)dt + \sigma S dZ$$

which is the continuous geometric random walk.

B.6   STOCHASTIC LEIBNITZ RULE

Suppose X and U evolve under the measure Q^U according to

$$dX(t) = (\ldots)dt + \sigma^X(t)CdZ^U(t)$$
$$dU(t) = (\ldots)dt + \sigma^U(t)CdZ^U(t)$$

where both $\sigma^X(t)$ and $\sigma^U(t)$ are $1 \times n$ vectors, Z^U is an n-dimensional driftless (under Q^U) standard Brownian motion, and $CC' = \rho$. Then

$$d\,\frac{X(t)}{U(t)} = \frac{1}{U(t)}\,dS(t) + S(t)d\,\frac{1}{U(t)} + dS(t)d\,\frac{1}{U(t)} \qquad \text{(B2.5)}$$

where

$$d\,\frac{1}{U(t)} = -\frac{1}{U^2(t)}\,dU(t) + \frac{1}{U^3(t)}\,dU(t)dU(t)$$

from Ito's formula.

B.7   QUADRATIC VARIATION AND COVARIATION

The quadratic variation of a stochastic process $X(t)$ with continuous paths $t \to X(t, \omega)$ is defined as

$$<X,\ X>_T = \lim_{n \to \infty} \sum_{i=1}^{\infty} (X(T_i^n,\ \omega) - X(T_{i-1}^n,\ \omega))^2$$

We can write this as a second-order integral:

$$<X,\ X>_t = \int_0^T (dX(t,\ \omega))^2$$

or, in differential form,

$$d<X,\ X>_t = dX(t,\ \omega)dX(t,\ \omega)$$

If X is a Brownian motion, then

$$dZ(t,\ \omega)dZ(t,\ \omega) = dt$$

One can also define the quadratic covariation of two processes X and Y with continuous paths as

$$<X,\ Y>_T = \lim_{n \to \infty} \sum_{i=1}^{\infty} (X(T_i^n,\ \omega) - X(T_{i-1}^n,\ \omega))(Y(T_i^n,\ \omega) - Y(T_{i-1}^n,\ \omega))$$

We can write this as a second-order integral:

$$< X, \ Y >_T = \int_0^T dX(t, \ \omega) dY(t, \ \omega)$$

or, in differential form,

$$d < X, \ Y >_T = dX \ (t, \ \omega) dY(t, \ \omega)$$

We can write this as a second-order integral:

$$<X,\ Y>_T = \int_0^T dX(t,\ \omega)dY(t,\ \omega)$$

or, in differential form,

$$d<X,\ Y>_T = dX(t,\ \omega)dY(t,\ \omega)$$

Alexander, C. 2000. "Principle Component Analysis of Implied Volatility Smiles and Skews." ISMA Centre Discussion Papers in Finance 2000–10, University of Reading, UK, available from www.ismacentre.rdg.ac.uk.

Alexander, C. 2001a. *Market Models*. Chichester, UK: John Wiley & Sons.

Alexander, C. 2001b. "Principle of the Skew." *Risk* (January): S29–32.

Amemiya, T. 1985. *Advanced Econometrics*. London: Basil Blackwell.

Amin, K., and A. Morton. 1994. "Implied Volatility Functions in Arbitrage Free Term Structure Models." *Journal of Financial Economics* 35: 141–180.

Andersen, L. 1999. "A Simple Approach to the Pricing of Bermudan Swaptions in the Multi-Factor LIBOR Market Model." Preprint.

Andersen, L., and J. Andreasen. 2000. "Volatility Skews Extensions of the LIBOR Market Model." *Applied Mathematical Finance* 7: 1–32.

Andersen, L., and R. Brotherton-Ratcliffe. 1998. "The Equity Option Volatility Smile: An Implicit Difference Approach." *Journal of Computational Finance* 1(2): 5–37.

Avellaneda, M., C. Friedman, and D. Samperi. 1997. "Calibrating Volatility Surfaces via Relative-Entropy Minimization." *Applied Mathematical Finance* 4: 37–64.

Avellaneda, M., and J. Newman. 1998. "Positive Interest Rates and Nonlinear Term Structure Models." Preprint, Courant Institute of Mathematical Sciences, New York University.

Ayache, E., P. Forsyth, and K. Vetzal. 2003. "Valuation of Convertible Bonds with Credit Risk," *Journal of Derivatives*, 9–30.

Baillie, R., and T. Bollerslev. 1989. "The Message in Daily Exchange Rates: A Conditional Variance Tale." *Journal of Business and Economic Statistics* 7(3): 297–305.

Balduzzi, P., S. Das, S. Foresi, R. Sundaram. 1996. "A Simple Approach to Three-Factor Term Structure Models." *Journal of Fixed Income* 6: 43–53.

Barraquand, J., and D. Martineau. 1995. "Numerical Valuation of High Dimensional Multivariate American Securities." *Journal of Financial and Quantitative Analysis* 30: 383–405.

Benhamou, E. 2002. "Fast Fourier Transform for Discrete Asian Options." *Journal of Computational Finance* 6(1): 49–68.

Best, P. 1998. *Implementing Value at Risk*. Chichester, UK: John Wiley & Sons.

Bhupinder, B. 1999. "Implied Risk-Neutral Probability Density Functions from Options Prices: A Central Bank Perspective." In *Forecasting Volatility in Financial Markets*, Stephen Satchell (Ed.), Butterworth-Heinemann.

Bjerksund, P., and G. Stensland. 1996. "Implementation of the Black-Derman-Toy Interest Rate Model." *Journal of Fixed Income* (September): 67–75.

Black, F., E. Derman, and W. Toy. 1990. "A One-Factor Model of Interest Rates and Its Application to Treasury Bond Options." *Financial Analysts Journal* (January–February): 33–39.

Black, F., and P. Karasinski. 1991. "Bond and Option Pricing When Short Rates are Lognormal." *Financial Analysts Journal* (July–August): 52–59.

Bodurtha, J. Jr., and M. Jermakyan. 1999. "Nonparametric Estimation of an Implied Volatility Surface." *Journal of Computational Finance* 2(4): 29–59.

Bollerslev, T. 1986. "Generalized Autoregressive Conditional Heteroskedasticity." *Journal of Econometrics* 31: 307–327.

Bollerslev, T., R. Chou, and K. Kroner. 1992. "ARCH Modeling in Finance." *Journal of Econometrics* 52: 5–59.

Bollerslev, T., and H. Mikkelsen. 1996. "Modeling and Pricing Long Memory in Stock Market Volatility." *Journal of Econometrics* 73(1): 151–184.

Boyle, P. P. 1977. "Options: A Monte Carlo Approach." *Journal of Financial Economics* 4: 323–338.

Boyle, P. 1988. "A Lattice Framework for Option Pricing with Two State Variables." *Journal of Financial and Quantitative Analysis* 23: 1–26.

Boyle, P. 1991. "Multi-asset Path-Dependent Options." FORC Conference, UK: Warwick.

Boyle, P., and S. Lau. 1994. "Bumping Up Against the Barrier with the Binomial Method." *Journal of Derivatives*, 6–14.

Boyle, P., and Y. Tian. 1999. "Pricing Lookback and Barrier Options under the CEV Process." *Journal of Financial and Quantitative Analysis* 34. (Correction http://depts .washington.edu/jfqa/)

Brace, A., T. Dun, and G. Barton. 1998. "Towards a Central Interest Rate Model." *FMMA Notes*, Working Paper.

Brace, A., D. Gatarek, and M. Musiela. 1997. "The Market Model of Interest Rate Dynamics." *Mathematical Finance* 7: 127–155.

Brace, A., and M. Musiela. 1994. "A Multifactor Gauss Markov Implementation of Heath, Jarrow, and Morton." *Mathematical Finance* 4: 259–283.

Brace, A., and M. Musiela. 1997. "Swap Derivatives in a Gaussian HJM Framework." *Mathematics of Derivative Securities*, M.A.H. Dempster, Cambridge University Press, Cambridge, 336–368.

Breeden, D., and R. Litzenberger. 1978. "Prices of State-Contingent Claims Implicit in Option Prices." *Journal of Business* 51: 621–651.

Brennan, M., and E. Schwartz. 1978. "Finite Difference Methods and Jump Processes Arising in the Pricing of Contingent Claims: A Synthesis." *Journal of Financial and Quantitative Analysis* 13: 462–474.

Brennan, M., and E. Schwartz. 1979. "A Continuous Time Approach to the Pricing of Bonds." *Journal of Banking and Finance* 3: 133–155.

Brigo, D., and F. Mercurio. 1998. "On Deterministic Shift Extensions of Short Rate Models." Internal Paper, Banca IMI, Milan. Available at http://web.tiscalinet.it/Damianhome.

Brigo, D., and F. Mercurio. 2000a. "Fitting Volatility Smiles with Analytically-Tractable Asset Price Models." Internal Report, Banca IMI, Milan. Available at http://web.tiscalinet.it/damianhome.

Brigo, D., and F. Mercurio. 2000b. "A Mixed-up Smile." *Risk* (September)123–126.

Brigo, D., and F. Mercurio. 2001a. "A Deterministic-Shift Extension of Analytically-Tractable and Time-Homogenous Short Rate Models." *Finance and Stochastics*.

Brigo, D., and F. Mercurio. 2001b. "Displaced and Mixture Diffusions for Analytically-Tractable Smile Models." *Mathematical Finance*.

Brigo D., and F. Mercurio. 2001c. *Interest Rate Models: Theory and Practice*. New York: Springer-Verlag.

Broadie, M., and P. Glasserman. 1997a. "Pricing American Style Securities Using Simulation." *Journal of Economic Dynamics and Control* 21: 8–9, 1323–1352.

Broadie, M., and P. Glasserman. 1997b. "A Stochastic Mesh Method for Pricing High-Dimensional American Options." Working Paper, Columbia University.

Caflisch, R., and B. Moskowitz. 1995. "Modified Monte Carlo Methods Using Quasi-Random Sequences." In *Monte Carlo and Quasi–Monte Carlo Methods in Scientific Computing*, H. Niederreitter and P. Shiue (Eds.), New York: Springer-Verlag.

Cakici, N., and K. Topyan. 2000. "The GARCH Option Pricing Model: A Lattice Approach." *Journal of Computational Finance* 3(4): 71–85.

Carr, P., and G. Yang. 1997. "Simulating Bermudan Interest Rate Derivatives." Courant Institute at New York University, Preprint.

Carr, P., and G. Yang. 1998. "Simulating American Bond Options in an HJM Framework." Courant Institute at New York University, Preprint.

Carverhill, A. 1994. "When Is the Short Rate Markovian?" *Mathematical Finance* 4: 305–312.

Carverhill, A. 1995a. "A Note on the Models of Hull and White for Pricing Options on the Term Structure." *Journal of Fixed Income* 5: 89–96.

Carverhill, A. 1995b. "A Simplified Exposition of the Heath-Jarrow-Morton Model." *Stochastics and Stochastic Reports* 53: 227–240.

Carverhill, A., and K. Pang. 1995. "Efficient and Flexible Bond Option Valuation in the Heath, Jarrow, and Morton Framework." *Journal of Fixed Income* 5: 70–77.

Chien, H. 2003. "On the Complexity of the Ritchken-Sankarasubramanian Interest Rate Model." MBA Thesis. Department of Finance, National Taiwan University.

Clewlow, L., and A. Carverhill. 1994. "On the Simulation of Contingent Claims." *Journal of Derivatives* 2: 66–74.

Clewlow, L., and C. Strickland. 1998a. *Implementing Derivatives Models*. Chichester, UK: John Wiley & Sons.

Clewlow, L., and C. Strickland. 1998b. "Monte Carlo Valuation of Interest Rate Derivatives under Stochastic Volatility." *Journal of Fixed Income* 7: 35–45.

Clewlow, L., C. Strickland, and K. Pang. 1997. "Implementing Multi-Factor Gaussian HJM for Swap and Captions Pricing." Financial Options Research Centre, Preprint.

Cont, R., and J. da Fonseca. 2002. "Dynamics of Implied Volatility Surfaces." *Journal of Quantitative Finance* 2: 45–60.

Conze, A., and Viswanathan 1991. "Path-dependent Options—The Case of Lookback Options." 1991. *Journal of Finance* 46: 1893–1907.

Courtadon, G. 1982. "A More Accurate Finite Difference Approximation of the Valuation of Options." *Journal of Financial and Quantitative Analysis* 17: 697–703.

Cox, J. 1975. "Notes on Option Pricing I: Constant Elasticity of Variance Diffusions." Working Paper, Stanford University.

Cox, J., J. Ingersoll, and S. Ross. 1985a. "An Intertemporal General Equilibrium Model of Asset Prices." *Econometrica* 53: 363–384.

Cox, J., J. Ingersoll, and S. Ross. 1985b. "A Theory of the Term Structure of Interest Rates." *Econometrica* 385–407.

Cox, J., and M. Rubinstein. 1985. *Option Markets*. Englewood Cliffs, NJ: Prentice Hall.

Cox, J., and S. Ross. 1976. "The Valuation of Options for Alternative Stochastic Processes." *Journal of Financial Economics* 3: 145–166.

Cox, J., S. Ross, and M. Rubinstein. 1979. "Option Pricing: A Simplified Approach." *Journal of Financial Economics* 7: 229–263.

Das, Sanjiv R. 1998. "On the Recursive Implementation of Term-Structure Models." Working Paper, Harvard Business School.

De Jong, F., J. Driessen, and A. Pelsser. 1999. "LIBOR and Swap Market Models for the Pricing of Interest Rate Derivatives: An Empirical Analysis." Preprint.

Dempster, M., and S. Hong. 2002. "Spread Option Valuation and the Fast Fourier Transform." Center for Financial Research, Judge Institute of Management Studies at the University of Cambridge.

Derman, E. 1999. "Volatility Regimes." *Risk* 12(4): 55–59.

Derman, E., and I. Kani. 1994. "Riding on a Smile." *Risk* 7: 32–39.

Derman, E., and I. Kani. 1996. "The Ins and Outs of Barrier Options." *Derivatives Quarterly* (Winter): 55–67 (Part I) and (Spring): 73–80 (Part II).

Derman, E., and I. Kani. 1998. "Stochastic Implied Trees: Arbitrage Pricing with Stochastic Term and Strike Structure of Volatility." *International Journal of Theoretical and Applied Finance* 1: 61–110.

Derman, E., D. Ergener, and I. Kani. 1994. "Valuing Convertible Bonds as Derivatives." Quantitative Strategies Research Notes, Goldman Sachs.

Derman, E., I. Kani, D. Ergener, and I. Bardhan. 1995. "Enhanced Numerical Methods for Options with Barriers." Quantitative Strategies Research Notes, Goldman Sachs.

Derman, E., D. Ergener, and I. Kani. 1995. "Static Options Replication." *Journal of Derivatives* (Summer): 78–95.

Derman, E., I. Kani, and J. Zou. 1996. "The Local Volatility Surface: Unlocking the Information in Index Option Prices." *Financial Analysts Journal*, 25–36.

Dewynne, J., and P. Wilmott. 1993. "Lookback Options." OCIAM Working Paper, Mathematical Institute, Oxford University.

Dothan, L. U. 1977. "On the Term Structure of Interest Rates." *Journal of Financial Economics* 6: 385–407.

Douady, R. 1998. "Closed-Form Formulas for Exotic Options and Their Lifetime Distribution." *International Journal of Theoretical and Applied Finance* 2: 17–42.

Drost, F., and T. Nijman. 1993. "Temporal Aggregation of GARCH Processes," *Econometrica*, 61, 909–927.

Duan, J. 1995. "The GARCH Option Pricing Model." *Mathematical Finance* 5(1): 13–32.

Duan, J. 1996. "Cracking the Smile." *Risk* 9(12): 55–59.

Duan, J., G. Gauthier, and J. Simonato. 1999. "An Analytical Approximation for the GARCH Option Pricing Model." *Journal of Computational Finance* 2(4): 75–116.

Duffie, D. 1996. *Dynamic Asset Pricing Theory*, 2nd ed. Princeton: Princeton University Press.

Dumas, B., J. Fleming, and R. Whaley. 1998. "Implied Volatility Functions: Empirical Tests." *Journal of Finance* 53(6), 2059–2106.

Dupire, B. 1994. "Pricing with a Smile." *Risk* 7: 32–39.

Dupire, B. 1997. "Pricing and Hedging with Smiles." Pages 103–111 in *Mathematics of Derivative Securities*, M. Dempster and S. Pliska (Eds), Cambridge: Cambridge University Press.

Dybvig, P. 1997. "Bond and Bond Option Pricing Based on the Current Term Structure." Pages 271–293 in *Mathematics of Derivative Securities*, M. Dempster and S. Pliska (Eds.), Cambridge: Cambridge University Press.

Engle, R. 1982. "Autoregressive Conditional Heteroscedasticity with Estimates of the Variance of United Kingdom Inflation." *Econometrica* 50: 9871007.

Engle, R., and T. Bollerslev. 1986. "Modelling the Persistence of Conditional Variances." *Econometric Reviews* 5: 1–50, 81–87.

Engle, R., and G. Gonzalez-Riviera. 1991. "Semi-parametric GARCH Models." *Journal of Business and Economic Statistics* 11: 345–359.

Engle, R., and C. Mustaf. 1992. "Implied ARCH Models from Options Prices." *Journal of Econometrics* 52: 289–311.

Engle, R., and V. Ng. 1991. "Measuring and Testing the Impact of News on Volatility." *Journal of Finance* 48: 1749–1778.

Engle, R., and V. Ng. 1993. "Time Varying Volatility and the Dynamic Behavior of the Term Structure." *Journal of Money, Credit and Banking* 25: 336–349.

Faure, H. 1982. "Discrepance de suites associées à un systeme de numeration (en dimensions)." *Acta Arithmetica* 41: 337–351.

Flesaker, B. (1993). "Testing the Heath-Jarrow-Morton/Ho-Lee Model of Interest Rate Contingent Claims Pricing." *Journal of Financial and Quantitative Analysis* 28: 483–496.

Flesaker, B., and L. Hughston. 1997. "Dynamic Models for Yield Curve Evolution." *Mathematics of Derivative Securities*, Cambridge University Press, Cambridge, 294–314.

Fu, M., D. Madan, and T. Wang. 1999. "Pricing Continuous Asian Options: A Comparison of Monte Carlo and Leplace Transform Inverse Methods." *Journal of Computational Finance* 2: 49–74.

Geman, H., N. El Karoui, and J. Rochet. 1995. "Changes of Numeraire, Changes of Probability Measures, and Pricing of Options." *Journal of Applied Probability* 32: 443–458.

Geman, H., and M. Yor. 1992. "Bessel Processes, Asian Options, and Perpetuities." *Mathematical Finance* 6: 365–78.

Geman, H., and M. Yor. 1996. "Pricing and Hedging Double Barrier Options: A Probabilistic Approach." *Mathematical Finance* 6: 365–378.

Glasserman, P., and S. Kou. 2001b. "Cap and Swaption Approximations in LIBOR Market Models with Jumps." Preprint.

Glasserman, P., and S. Kou. 2001b. "Numerical Solution of Jump-Diffusion LIBOR Market Models." Preprint.

Glasserman, P., and S. Kou. 2002. "The Term Structure of Simple Forward Rates with Jump Risk." Preprint.

Glasserman, P., and Z. Zhao. 1999. "Fast Greeks in Forward LIBOR Models." Columbia University, Graduate School of Business, Preprint.

Glasserman, P., and Z. Zhao. 2000. "Arbitrage-Free Discretization of Lognormal Forward LIBOR and Swap Rate Models." *Finance and Stochastics* 4, Springer-Verlag, 35–68.

Goldman, Sosin, and Gatto. 1979. "Path Dependent Options: Buy at the Low, Sell at the High." *Journal of Finance* 34: 1111–1128.

Grant, D., and G. Vora. 1999. "Implementing No-Arbitrage Term Structure of Interest Rate Models in Discrete Time When Interest Rates Are Normally Distributed." *Journal of Fixed Income* 8: 85–98.

Gustafsson, T., and H. Merabet. 2002. "A Generalized Multinomial Method for Option Pricing in Several Dimensions." *Journal of Computational Finance* 5(3): 27–50.

Halton, J. 1960. "On the Efficiency of Certain Quasi-Random Sequences of Points in Evaluating Multi-dimensional Integrals." *Numerische Mathematik* 2: 84–90.

Hamilton, J. 1994. *Time Series Analysis*. Princeton: Princeton University Press.

Harrison, J., and D. Kreps. 1979. "Martingales and Arbitrage in Multiperiod Securities Markets." *Journal of Economic Theory* 20: 381–408.

Harrison, J., and S. Pliska. 1981. "Martingales and Stochastic Integrals in the Theory of Continuous Trading." *Stochastic Processes and Their Applications* 11: 215–260.

Harrison, J., and S. Pliska. 1983. "A Stochastic Calculus Model of Continuous Trading: Complete Markets." *Stochastic Processes and Their Applications* 15: 313–316.

He, H. 1990. "Convergence from Discrete-to-Continuous Time Contingent Claims Prices." *Review of Financial Studies* 3(4): 523–546.

He, H., W. Keirstead, and J. Rebholz. 1998. "Double Lookbacks." *Mathematical Finance* 8: 201–228.

Heath, D., R. Jarrow, and A. Morton. 1990a. "Bond Pricing and the Term Structure of Interest Rates: A Discrete Time Approximation." *Journal of Financial Quantitative Analysis* 25: 419–440.

Heath, D., R. Jarrow, and A. Morton, 1990b. "Contingent Claim Valuation with a Random Evolution of Interest Rates." *Review of Futures Markets* 9: 54–76.

Heath, D., R. Jarrow, and A. Morton. 1992. "Bond Pricing and the Term Structure of Interest Rates: A New Methodology for Contingent Claim Valuation." *Econometrica* 60: 77–105.

Ho, T. S. Y., and S.-B. Lee. 1986. "Term Structure Movements and Pricing Interest Rate Contingent Claims." *Journal of Finance* 41: 1011–1029.

Hui, H. 1997. "Time-Dependent Barrier Option Values." *Journal of Futures Markets* 17: 667–688.

Hull, J. 1997. *Options, Futures, and Other Derivatives*. Englewood Cliffs, NJ: Prentice Hall.

Hull, J., and A. White. 1987. "The Pricing of Options on Assets with Stochastic Volatilities." *Journal of Finance* 42: 2.

Hull, J., and A. White, A. 1990. "Valuing Derivative Securities Using the Explicit Finite Difference Method." *Journal of Financial and Quantitative Analysis* 25: 87–100.

Hull, J., and A. White. 1993a. "Bond Option Pricing Based on a Model for the Evolution of Bond Prices." *Advances in Futures and Options Research* 6: 1–13.

Hull J., and A. White. 1993b. "Efficient Procedures for Valuing European and American Path Dependent Options." *Journal of Derivatives* 1: 21–32.

Hull, J., and A. White. 1993c. "One-Factor Interest Rate Models and the Valuation of Interest Rate Derivative Securities." *Journal of Financial and Quantitative Analysis* 28: 235–254.

Hull J., and A. White. 1993d. "The Pricing of Options on Interest Rate Caps and Floors Using the Hull-White Model." *Journal of Financial Engineering* 2: 287–296.

Hull, J., and A. White. 1994a. "Numerical Procedures for Implementing Term Structure Models I: Single-factor Models." *Journal of Derivatives* 1, 21–32.

Hull, J., and A. White. 1994. "Numerical Procedures for Implementing Term Structure Models I: Single-factor Models." *Journal of Derivatives* 1: 21–32.

Hull, J., and A. White. 1995. "A Note on the Models of Hull and White for Pricing Options on the Term Structure: Response." *Journal of Fixed Income* 5 (September): 97–102.

Hull, J., and A. White. 1999. "Forward Rate Volatilities, Swap Rate Volatilities, and the Implementation of the LIBOR Market Model." Preprint.

Hunt, P., and A. Pelsser. 1998. "Arbitrage-Free Pricing of Quanto-Swaptions." *Journal of Financial Engineering* 7: 25–33.

Hunter, C., P. Jackel, and M. Joshi. 2001. "Drift Approximations in a Forward-Rate-Based LIBOR Market Model." Preprint. Available at www.rebonato.com.

Ioffe, G., and M. Ioffe. 2003. "Application of Finite Difference Method for Pricing Barrier Options." Paper available at www.egartech.com.

Jäckel, P. 2000. "Monte Carlo in the BGM/J Framework: Using a Non-Recombining Tree to Design a New Pricing Method for Bermudan Swaptions." Preprint.

Jäckel, P. 2002. *Monte Carlo Methods in Finance*. Chichester, UK: John Wiley & Sons.

Jackson, N., E. Süli, and S. Howison. 1999. "Computation of Deterministic Volatility Surfaces." *Journal of Computational Finance* 2(2): 5–32.

James, J., and N. Webber. 2000. *Interest Rate Modeling*. Chichester, UK: John Wiley & Sons.

James, P. 2002. *Option Theory*. Chichester, UK: John Wiley & Sons.

Jamshidian, F. 1989. "An Exact Bond Option Formula." *Journal of Finance* 44 (March): 205–209.

Jamshidian, F. 1991a. "Bond and Option Evaluation in the Gaussian Interest Rate Model." *Research in Finance* 9: 131–170.

Jamshidian, F. 1991b. "Forward Induction and Construction of Yield Curve Diffusion Models." *Journal of Fixed Income* 1: 62–74.

Jamshidian, F. 1995. "A Simple Class of Square-Root Interest Rate Models." *Applied Mathematical Finance* 2: 61–72.

Jamshidian, F. 1997. LIBOR and Swap Market Models and Measures." *Finance and Stochastics* 1: 43–67.

Jamshidian, F., and Y. Zhu. 1997. "Scenario Simulation: Theory and Methodology." *Finance and Stochastics* 1: 43–67.

Jarrow, R. 1997. "The HJM Model: Its Past, Present, and Future." *Journal of Financial Engineering* 6: 269–279.

Jarrow, R. 2002. *Modeling Fixed Income Securities and Interest Rate Options*. New York: McGraw-Hill.

Kamrad, B., and P. Ritchken. 1991. "Multinomial Approximating Models for Options with *k*-State Variables." *Management Science* 37(12): 1640–1652.

Kemma, A., and A. Vorst. 1990. "A Pricing Method for Options Based upon Average Asset Values." *Journal of Banking Finance* (March): 113–129.

Kennedy, D. 1997. "Characterizing Gaussian Models of the Term Structure of Interest Rates." *Mathematical Finance* 2: 107–118.

Kerman, J. 2002. "Numerical Methods for Option Pricing: Binomial and Finite Difference Approximations." Courant Institute of Mathematical Sciences, Preprint.

Kijima, M., and I. Nagayma. 1994. "Efficient Numerical Procedures for the Hull-White Extended Vasicek Model." *Journal of Financial Engineering* 3: 275–292.

Kijima, M., and I. Nagayma. 1996. "Numerical Procedure of the General One-Factor Interest Rate Model." *Journal of Financial Engineering* 5: 317–337.

Kloeden, P., and E. Platen. 1999. *Numerical Solution of Stochastic Differential Equations*. New York: Springer-Verlag.

Lamberton, D., and B. Lapeyre. 1997. *Introduction to Stochastic Calculus Applied to Finance*. London: Chapman and Hall.

Lapeyre, B., and E. Temam. 2001. "Competitive Monte Carlo Methods for the Pricing of Asian Options." *Journal of Computational Finance* 5(1): 39–57.

Levy, E. 1990. "Asian Arithmetic." *Risk* (May): 7–8.

Li, J. 2002. "A C++ Encoded Interest Rate Tree Builder." MBA Thesis, Duke University, Johnson Graduate School of Business.

Li, A., P. Ritchken, and L. Sankarasubramanian. 1995a. "Lattice Models for Pricing American Interest Rate Claims." *Journal of Finance* 50: 719–737.

Li, A., P. Ritchken, and L. Sankarasubramanian. 1995b. "Lattice Works." *Risk* 8: 65–69.

Linetsky, V. 1999. "Steps to the Barrier." *Risk* (April): 62–65.

Linetsky, V., and D. Davydov. 2002. "Structuring, Pricing, and Hedging Double-Barrier Step Options." *Journal of Computational Finance* 5,(2): 55–87.

Longstaff, F., and E. Schwartz. 1992a. "Interest Rate Volatility and the Term Structure: A Two-Factor General Equilibrium Model." *Journal of Finance* 47: 1259–1282.

Longstaff, F., and E. Schwartz. 1992b. "A Two-Factor Interest Rate Model and Contingent Claims Valuation." *Journal of Fixed Income* 3: 16–23.

Longstaff, F., and E. Schwartz. 1993. "Implementation of the Longstaff-Schwartz Interest Rate Model." *Journal of Fixed Income* 3: 7–14.

Longstaff, F., and E. Schwartz. 2001. "Valuing American Options by Simulation: A Simple Least Squares Approach." *Review of Financial Studies* 14(1): 113–147.

Madan, D., and P. Carr. 1999. "Option Valuation Using the Fast Fourier Transform." *Journal of Computational Finance* 2(4): 61–73.

Melick, W., and C. Thomas. (1997). "Recovering an Asset's Implied PDF from Option Prices: An Application to Crude Oil During the Gulf Crisis." *Journal of Financial and Quantitative Analysis* 32: 91–115.

Merabet, H., and T. Gustaffsson. 2002. "A Generalized Multinomial Method for Option Pricing in Several Dimensions." *Journal of Computational Finance* 5(3): 27–50.

Merton, R. 1973. "Theory of Rational Option Pricing." *Bell Journal of Economics and Management Science* 4: 141–183.

Miltersen, K., K. Sandmann, and D. Sondermann. (1997). "Closed Form Solutions for Term Structure Derivatives with Log-Normal Interest Rates." *Journal of Finance* 52: 409–430.

Moon, H., J. Sohn, and Y. Kwon. "Implementation of LRS Model Using Trinomial Lattice Method." Preprint. Available at www.math.nyu.edu/ms_students/ywk204.

Müller, U., et al. 1997. "Volatilities of Different Time Resolutions—Analyzing the Dynamics of Market Components." *Journal of Empirical Finance* 4: 213–239.

Musiela, M., and M. Rutkowski. (1997). "Continuous-Time Term Structure Models: Forward Measure Approach." *Finance and Stochastics* 4: 261–292.

Musiela, M., and M. Rutkowski. 1997. *Martingale Methods in Financial Modeling*, Berlin: Springer-Verlag.

Nelson, D. 1991. "Conditional Heteroskedasticity in Asset Returns: A New Approach." *Econometrica* 59: 347–370.

Nelson, D., and C. Cao. 1992. "Inequality Constraints in the Univariate GARCH Model." *Journal of Business and Economic Statistics* 10: 229–235.

Nelson, D., and K. Ramaswamy. 1990. "Simple Binomial Processes as Diffusion Approximations in Financial Models." *Review of Financial Studies* 3: 393–430.

Niederreiter, H. 1992. "Random Number Generation and Quasi Monte Carlo Methods." CBMS-NSF Conference Series in Applied Math, Vol. 63, SIAM.

Niederreiter, H., and P. Shiue (Eds.). 1995. "Monte Carlo and Quasi-Monte Carlo Methods in Scientific Computing." *Lecture Notes in Statistics* Vol. 106. New York: Springer-Verlag.

Oksendal, B. 1992. *Stochastic Differential Equations: An Introduction with Applications.* Berlin: Springer.

Pagan, A. 1996. "The Econometrics of Financial Markets." *Journal of Empirical Finance* Vol. 3(1), 15–102.

Pagan, A., and G. Schwert. 1990. "Alternative Models for Conditional Stock Volatility." *Journal of Econometrics* 45: 267–290.

Palm, F. 1996. "GARCH Models of Volatility." In G. S. Maddala and C. R. Rao (Eds.), *Handbook of Statistics* Vol. 14, Amsterdam:.

Papageorgiou, A. 2001. "The Brownian Bridge Does Not Offer a Consistent Advantage in Quasi-Monte Carlo Integration." *Journal of Complexity.* Available at www.idea library.com.

Pedersen, M. 1999. "Bermudan Swaptions in the LIBOR Market Model." Preprint.

Pelsser, A. 2000. *Efficient Methods for Valuing Interest Rate Derivatives.* Berlin: Springer-Verlag.

Press, W., S. Teukolsky, W. Vetterling, and B. P. Flannery. 1992. *Numerical Recipes in C: The Art of Scientific Computing*, 2nd ed. Cambridge: Cambridge University Press.

Rebonato, R. 1998. *Interest Rate Option Models*, 2nd ed., Chichester, UK: John Wiley & Sons.

Rebonato, R. 1999a. "Calibrating the BGM Model." *Risk* 12 (March): 74–79.

Rebonato, R. 1999b. "On the Pricing Implications of the Joint Lognormal Assumption for the Swaption and Cap Market." *Journal of Computational Finance* 2: 57–76.

Rebonato, R. 1999c. "On the Simultaneous Calibration of Multifactor Lognormal Interest Rate Models to Black Volatilities and to the Correlation Matrix." *Journal of Computational Finance* 2: 5–27.

Rebonato, R. 1999. *Volatility and Correlation*. Chichester, UK: John Wiley & Sons.

Rebonato, R. 2002. *Modern Pricing of Interest Rate Derivatives: The LIBOR Market Model and Beyond*. Princeton: Princeton University Press.

Rebonato, R. 2003. "Term Structure Models: A Review." Quantitative Research Center of the Royal Bank of Scotland, Preprint.

Rebonato R., and P. Jackel. 2000. "Linking Caplet and Swaption Volatilities in BGM/J Framework: Approximate Solutions." Quantitative Research Center of the Royal Bank of Scotland, Preprint.

Rebonato, R., and M. Joshi. 2002. "A Stochastic Volatility, Displaced-Diffusion Extension of the LIBOR Market Model." Quantitative Research Center of the Royal Bank of Scotland, Preprint. Available at www.rebonato.com.

Rebonato, R., and D. Kainth. 2002. "A Two-Regime, Stochastic Volatility Extension of the LIBOR Market Model: Theory and Empirical Evidence." QUARC-Royal Bank of Scotland, Preprint. Available at www.rebonato.com.

Rendleman, R., and B. Bartter. 1980. "The Pricing of Options on Debt Securities." *Journal of Financial and Quantitative Analysis* 15: 11–24.

Ritchey, R. 1990. "Call Option Valuation for Discrete Normal Mixtures." *Journal of Financial Research* 13: 285–296.

Ritchken, P. 1995. "On Pricing Barrier Options." *Journal of Derivatives* 3: 19–28.

Ritchken, P., and L. Sankarasubramanian. 1995. "The Importance of Forward-Rate Volatility Structures in Pricing Interest-Rate Sensitive Claims." *Journal of Derivatives*, 25–41.

Ritchken, P., and L. Sankarasubramanian. 1997. "Volatility Structures of Forward Rates and the Dynamics of the Term Structure." *Mathematical Finance* 5: 55–72.

Ritchken, P., and R. Trevor. 1999, "Pricing Options under Generalized GARCH and Stochastic Volatility Processes." *Journal of Finance* 54(1): 377–402.

Rogers, L., and O. Zane. 1997. "Valuing Moving Barrier Options." *Journal of Computational Finance* 1: 5–12.

Rubinstein, M. 1983. "Displaced Diffusion Option Pricing." *Journal of Finance* 38: 213–217.

Rubinstein, M. 1994. "Implied Binomial Trees." *Journal of Finance* 69: 771–818.

Rubinstein, M. 1997. "Edgeworth Binomial Trees." *Journal of Derivatives* 5(3): 20–27.

Rubinstein, M., and E. Reiner. 1991. "Breaking Down the Barriers." *Risk* (September): 28–35.

Rutkowski, M. 1999. "Models of Forward LIBOR and Swap Rates." Preprint.

Sandmann, K., and D. Sondermann. 1994. "On the Stability of Lognormal Interest Rate Models." University of Bonn, Discussion Paper No. B-263.

Santa Clara, P., and D. Sornette. 2001. "The Dynamics of the Forward Interest Rate Curve with Stochastic String Shocks." *Review of Financial Studies* 14: 149–185.

Schaefer, S., and E. Schwartz. 1984. "A Two Factor Model of Term Structure: An Approximate Analytical Solution." *Journal of Financial and Quantitative Analysis* 19: 413–424.

Schlogl, E., and D. Sommer. 1998. "Factor Models and the Shape of the Term Structure." *Journal of Financial Engineering* 7: 79–88.

Schmidt, W. 1997. "On a General Class of One-Factor Models for the Term Structure of Interest Rates." *Finance and Stochastics* 1: 3–24.

Schroder, M. 2000. "On the Valuation of Double-Barrier Options: Computational Aspects." *Computational Finance* 3: 4.

Scott, L. 1995. "The Valuation of Interest Rate Derivatives in a Multi-Factor Term Struct Model with Deterministic Components." Working Paper, University of Georgia.

Sidenius, J. 1998. "Double Barrier Options: Valuation by Path Counting." *Computational Finance* 1: 63–79.

Sobol, M. 1967. "On the Distribution of Points in a Cube and the Approximate Evaluation of Integrals." *U.S.S.R. Computational Math. and Math. Physics* 4: 86–112.

Taleb, N. 1997. *Dynamic Hedging*. New York: John Wiley & Sons.

Tang, Y., and J. Lange. 2001. "Nonexploding Bushy Tree Technique and Its Application to the Multifactor Interest Rate Market Model." *Journal of Computational Finance* 4(4).

Tavella, D. 1999. *Quantitative Methods in Derivatives Pricing: An Introduction to Computational Finance* Chichester, UK: John Wiley & Sons.

Thorsten, L. 2003. "Explaining Smiles: GARCH Option Pricing with Conditional Leptokurtosis and Skewness." Research Paper, Limburg Institute of Financial Economics, Masstricht University.

Thorsten, L., and C. de Jong. 2003. "Implied GARCH Volatility Forecasting." LIFE Working Paper, Limburg Institute of Financial Economics, Masstricht University.

Tikhonov, A., and V. Arsenin. 1977. *Solutions of Ill-Posed Problems*. Washington, DC: Winston-Wiley.

Tikhonov, A., and A. Samarskii. 1963. *Equations of Mathematical Physics*. New York: Macmillan.

Tilley, J. 1993. "Valuing American Options in a Path Simulation Model." *Transactions of the Society of Actuaries* 45: 83–104.

Trevor, R. 2000. "Modeling Volatility Surfaces with GARCH." Centre for Applied Finance, Maquarie University.

Trigeorgis, L. 1991. "A Log-transformed Binomial Numerical Analysis Method for Valuing Complex Multi-Option Investments." *Journal of Financial and Quantitative Analysis* 26: 309–326.

Tsiveriotis, K., and C. Fernandes. 1998. "Valuing Convertible Bonds with Credit Risk." *Journal of Fixed Income* 8: 5–102.

Vasicek, O. 1977. "An Equilibrium Characterization of the Term Structure." *Journal of Financial Economics* 5: 177–188.

Webber, J., and L. McCarthy. 2002. "Pricing in Three-Factor Models Using Icosahedral Lattices." *Journal of Computational Finance* 5: 1–36.

White, H. 1984. *Asymptotic Theory for Econometricians* New York: Academic Press.

Wilmott, P., S. Howison, and J. Dewynne. 1995. *The Mathematics of Financial Derivatives*. Cambridge: Cambridge University Press.

Wilmott, P. 1998. *Derivatives: The Theory and Practice of Financial Engineering*. Chichester, UK: John Wiley and Sons.

Wu, C. 2003. "An Accurate and Provably Efficient GARCH Option Pricing Tree." MBA Thesis, Department of Finance, National Taiwan University.

About the CD-ROM

INTRODUCTION

This CD-ROM contains the application, Excel spreadsheets, and code libraries for the information discussed in the text, as well as Appendixes C through F.

SYSTEM REQUIREMENTS

- A computer with a processor running at 120 Mhz or faster.
- At least 32 MB of total RAM installed on your computer; for best performance, we recommend at least 64 MB.
- A CD-ROM drive.

NOTE: Many popular word processing programs are capable of reading Microsoft Word files. However, users should be aware that a slight amount of formatting might be lost when using a program other than Microsoft Word.

WHAT'S ON THE CD

The following sections provide a summary of the software and other materials you'll find on the CD.

QuantPro

QuantPro is a Windows application for doing quantitative analysis of equity and fixed income derivatives. QuantPro computes Monte Carlo simulations, binomial trees, trinomial trees, implicit difference, and explicit difference methods for equity derivatives. It builds interest rate trees to price bonds, bond options, swaptions, caps, and floors using different interest rate models such as Hull-White, Black-Karasinski, and Black-Derman-Toy.

   Note: QuantPro does not include VC++/MFC source code—code for the application can be purchased separately. This application is an ongoing project that will include additional functionality in the next release, including database and charting support.

Quantitative Pricing Engine Library

Quantitative Pricing Engine Library includes many derivatives classes in C++ for pricing and valuation of most derivative securities, including most equity, fixed income, and exotic derivatives.

- Includes many of the author's own proprietary C++ classes such as HJM.
- Includes many complex pricing, statistical, and numerical algorithms and classes.
- Utilizes various numerical library classes such as QuantLib, Newmat matrix classes, and GNU scientific classes in C++.

Excel Spreadsheets and QuantLibXL

Excel spreadsheets and QuantLibXL add-ins are included for doing quantitative analysis such as modules for computing local volatility surfaces and option valuation.

Additional and Other Open Source C++ Libraries

Other libraries that can be installed and used separately on the user's machine include:

- QuantLib.
- Newmat matrix library.
- GNU Scientific Library.

Appendices

- *Appendix C*—Fast Fourier Transform Method
- *Appendix D*—Building Models, Pricing Engines, and Calibration in Practice
- *Appendix E*—Code Routines
- *Appendix F*—Solving the Black-Scholes PDE

APPLICATIONS

The following applications are on the CD-ROM:

Adobe Reader
Adobe Reader is a freeware application for viewing files in the Adobe Portable Document format.

Word Viewer
Microsoft Word Viewer is a freeware viewer that allows you to view, but not edit, most Microsoft Word files. Certain features of Microsoft Word documents may not display as expected from within Word Viewer.

Excel Viewer

Excel Viewer is a freeware viewer that allows you to view, but not edit, most
Microsoft Excel spreadsheets. Certain features of Microsoft Excel documents may not work as expected from within Excel Viewer.

Shareware programs are fully functional, trial versions of copyrighted programs. If you like particular programs, register with their authors for a nominal fee
and receive licenses, enhanced versions, and technical support.

Freeware programs are copyrighted games, applications, and utilities that are
free for personal use. Unlike shareware, these programs do not require a fee or provide technical support.

GNU software is governed by its own license, which is included inside the
folder of the GNU product. See the GNU license for more details.

Trial, demo, or evaluation versions are usually limited either by time or by
functionality (such as being unable to save projects). Some trial versions are very
sensitive to system date changes. If you alter your computer's date, the programs
will "time out" and no longer be functional.

CUSTOMER CARE

If you have trouble with the CD-ROM, please call the Wiley Product Technical
Support phone number at (800) 762-2974. Outside the United States, call 1(317)
572-3994. You can also contact Wiley Product Technical Support at **www
.wiley.com/techsupport**. John Wiley & Sons will provide technical support only
for installation and other general quality control items. For technical support on
the applications themselves, consult the program's vendor or author.

To place additional orders or to request information about other Wiley products,
please call (877) 762-2974.

GNU General Public License

Version 2, June 1991
Copyright © 1989, 1991 Free Software Foundation, Inc.
59 Temple Place - Suite 330, Boston, MA 02111-1307, USA

PREAMBLE

The licenses for most software are designed to take away your freedom to share and change it. By contrast, the GNU General Public License is intended to guarantee your freedom to share and change free software—to make sure the software is free for all its users. This General Public License applies to most of the Free Software Foundation's software and to any other program whose authors commit to using it. (Some other Free Software Foundation software is covered by the GNU Library General Public License instead.) You can apply it to your programs, too.

When we speak of free software, we are referring to freedom, not price. Our General Public Licenses are designed to make sure that you have the freedom to distribute copies of free software (and charge for this service if you wish), that you receive source code or can get it if you want it, that you can change the software or use pieces of it in new free programs; and that you know you can do these things.

To protect your rights, we need to make restrictions that forbid anyone to deny you these rights or to ask you to surrender the rights. These restrictions translate to certain responsibilities for you if you distribute copies of the software, or if you modify it.

For example, if you distribute copies of such a program, whether gratis or for a fee, you must give the recipients all the rights that you have. You must make sure that they, too, receive or can get the source code. And you must show them these terms so they know their rights.

We protect your rights with two steps: (1) copyright the software, and (2) offer you this license which gives you legal permission to copy, distribute and/or modify the software.

Also, for each author's protection and ours, we want to make certain that everyone understands that there is no warranty for this free software. If the software is modified by someone else and passed on, we want its recipients to know that what they have is not the original, so that any problems introduced by others will not reflect on the original authors' reputations.

Finally, any free program is threatened constantly by software patents. We wish to avoid the danger that redistributors of a free program will individually obtain patent licenses, in effect making the program proprietary. To prevent this, we have made it clear that any patent must be licensed for everyone's free use or not licensed at all. The precise terms and conditions for copying, distribution and modification follow.

TERMS AND CONDITIONS FOR COPYING, DISTRIBUTION AND MODIFICATION

0. This License applies to any program or other work which contains a notice placed by the copyright holder saying it may be distributed under the terms of this General Public License. The "Program", below, refers to any such program or work, and a "work based on the Program" means either the Program or any derivative work under copyright law: that is to say, a work containing the Program or a portion of it, either verbatim or with modifications and/or translated into another language. (Hereinafter, translation is included without limitation in the term "modification".) Each licensee is addressed as "you".

Activities other than copying, distribution and modification are not covered by this License; they are outside its scope. The act of running the Program is not restricted, and the output from the Program is covered only if its contents constitute a work based on the Program (independent of having been made by running the Program). Whether that is true depends on what the Program does.

1. You may copy and distribute verbatim copies of the Program's source code as you receive it, in any medium, provided that you conspicuously and appropriately publish on each copy an appropriate copyright notice and disclaimer of warranty; keep intact all the notices that refer to this License and to the absence of any warranty; and give any other recipients of the Program a copy of this License along with the Program.

You may charge a fee for the physical act of transferring a copy, and you may at your option offer warranty protection in exchange for a fee.

2. You may modify your copy or copies of the Program or any portion of it, thus forming a work based on the Program, and copy and distribute such modifications or work under the terms of Section 1 above, provided that you also meet all of these conditions:

- **a)** You must cause the modified files to carry prominent notices stating that you changed the files and the date of any change.
- **b)** You must cause any work that you distribute or publish, that in whole or in part contains or is derived from the Program or any part thereof, to be licensed as a whole at no charge to all third parties under the terms of this License.

■ c) If the modified program normally reads commands interactively when run, you must cause it, when started running for such interactive use in the most ordinary way, to print or display an announcement including an appropriate copyright notice and a notice that there is no warranty (or else, saying that you provide a warranty) and that users may redistribute the program under these conditions, and telling the user how to view a copy of this License. (Exception: if the Program itself is interactive but does not normally print such an announcement, your work based on the Program is not required to print an announcement.)

These requirements apply to the modified work as a whole. If identifiable sections of that work are not derived from the Program, and can be reasonably considered independent and separate works in themselves, then this License, and its terms, do not apply to those sections when you distribute them as separate works. But when you distribute the same sections as part of a whole which is a work based on the Program, the distribution of the whole must be on the terms of this License, whose permissions for other licensees extend to the entire whole, and thus to each and every part regardless of who wrote it.

Thus, it is not the intent of this section to claim rights or contest your rights to work written entirely by you; rather, the intent is to exercise the right to control the distribution of derivative or collective works based on the Program.

In addition, mere aggregation of another work not based on the Program with the Program (or with a work based on the Program) on a volume of a storage or distribution medium does not bring the other work under the scope of this License.

3. You may copy and distribute the Program (or a work based on it, under Section 2) in object code or executable form under the terms of Sections 1 and 2 above provided that you also do one of the following:

■ a) Accompany it with the complete corresponding machine-readable source code, which must be distributed under the terms of Sections 1 and 2 above on a medium customarily used for software interchange; or,

■ b) Accompany it with a written offer, valid for at least three years, to give any third party, for a charge no more than your cost of physically performing source distribution, a complete machine-readable copy of the corresponding source code, to be distributed under the terms of Sections 1 and 2 above on a medium customarily used for software interchange; or,

■ c) Accompany it with the information you received as to the offer to distribute corresponding source code. (This alternative is allowed only for noncommercial distribution and only if you received the program in object code or executable form with such an offer, in accord with Subsection b above.)

The source code for a work means the preferred form of the work for making modifications to it. For an executable work, complete source code means all the source code for all modules it contains, plus any associated interface definition files, plus the scripts used to control compilation and installation of the executable. However, as a special exception, the source code distributed need not include anything that is normally distributed (in either source or binary form) with the major components (compiler, kernel, and so on) of the operating system on which the executable runs, unless that component itself accompanies the executable.

   If distribution of executable or object code is made by offering access to copy from a designated place, then offering equivalent access to copy the source code from the same place counts as distribution of the source code, even though third parties are not compelled to copy the source along with the object code.

4. You may not copy, modify, sublicense, or distribute the Program except as expressly provided under this License. Any attempt otherwise to copy, modify, sublicense or distribute the Program is void, and will automatically terminate your rights under this License. However, parties who have received copies, or rights, from you under this License will not have their licenses terminated so long as such parties remain in full compliance.

5. You are not required to accept this License, since you have not signed it. However, nothing else grants you permission to modify or distribute the Program or its derivative works. These actions are prohibited by law if you do not accept this License. Therefore, by modifying or distributing the Program (or any work based on the Program), you indicate your acceptance of this License to do so, and all its terms and conditions for copying, distributing or modifying the Program or works based on it.

6. Each time you redistribute the Program (or any work based on the Program), the recipient automatically receives a license from the original licensor to copy, distribute or modify the Program subject to these terms and conditions. You may not impose any further restrictions on the recipients' exercise of the rights granted herein. You are not responsible for enforcing compliance by third parties to this License.

7. If, as a consequence of a court judgment or allegation of patent infringement or for any other reason (not limited to patent issues), conditions are imposed on you (whether by court order, agreement or otherwise) that contradict the conditions of this License, they do not excuse you from the conditions of this License. If you cannot distribute so as to satisfy simultaneously your obligations under this License and any other pertinent obligations, then as a consequence you may not distribute the Program at all. For example, if a patent license would not permit royalty-free redistribution of the Program by all those who receive copies directly or indirectly through you, then the only way you could satisfy both it and this License would be to refrain entirely from distribution of the Program.

   If any portion of this section is held invalid or unenforceable under any particular circumstance, the balance of the section is intended to apply and the section as a whole is intended to apply in other circumstances.

   It is not the purpose of this section to induce you to infringe any patents or other property right claims or to contest validity of any such claims; this section has the sole purpose of protecting the integrity of the free software distribution system, which is implemented by public license practices. Many people have made generous contributions to the wide range of software distributed through that system in reliance on consistent application of that system; it is up to the author/donor to decide if he or she is willing to distribute software through any other system and a licensee cannot impose that choice.

This section is intended to make thoroughly clear what is believed to be a consequence of the rest of this License.

8. If the distribution and/or use of the Program is restricted in certain countries either by patents or by copyrighted interfaces, the original copyright holder who places the Program under this License may add an explicit geographical distribution limitation excluding those countries, so that distribution is permitted only in or among countries not thus excluded. In such case, this License incorporates the limitation as if written in the body of this License.

9. The Free Software Foundation may publish revised and/or new versions of the General Public License from time to time. Such new versions will be similar in spirit to the present version, but may differ in detail to address new problems or concerns. Each version is given a distinguishing version number. If the Program specifies a version number of this License which applies to it and "any later version", you have the option of following the terms and conditions either of that version or of any later version published by the Free Software Foundation. If the Program does not specify a version number of this License, you may choose any version ever published by the Free Software Foundation.

10. If you wish to incorporate parts of the Program into other free programs whose distribution conditions are different, write to the author to ask for permission. For software which is copyrighted by the Free Software Foundation, write to the Free Software Foundation; we sometimes make exceptions for this. Our decision will be guided by the two goals of preserving the free status of all derivatives of our free software and of promoting the sharing and reuse of software generally.

NO WARRANTY

11. BECAUSE THE PROGRAM IS LICENSED FREE OF CHARGE, THERE IS NO WARRANTY FOR THE PROGRAM, TO THE EXTENT PERMITTED BY APPLICABLE LAW. EXCEPT WHEN OTHERWISE STATED IN WRITING THE COPYRIGHT HOLDERS AND/OR OTHER PARTIES PROVIDE THE PROGRAM "AS IS" WITHOUT WARRANTY OF ANY KIND, EITHER EXPRESSED OR IMPLIED, INCLUDING, BUT NOT LIMITED TO, THE IMPLIED WARRANTIES OF MERCHANTABILITY AND FITNESS FOR A PARTICULAR PURPOSE. THE ENTIRE RISK AS TO THE QUALITY AND PERFORMANCE OF THE PROGRAM IS WITH YOU. SHOULD THE PROGRAM PROVE DEFECTIVE, YOU ASSUME THE COST OF ALL NECESSARY SERVICING, REPAIR OR CORRECTION.

12. IN NO EVENT UNLESS REQUIRED BY APPLICABLE LAW OR AGREED TO IN WRITING WILL ANY COPYRIGHT HOLDER, OR ANY OTHER PARTY WHO MAY MODIFY AND/OR REDISTRIBUTE THE PROGRAM AS PERMITTED ABOVE, BE LIABLE TO YOU FOR DAMAGES, INCLUDING ANY GENERAL, SPECIAL, INCIDENTAL OR CONSEQUENTIAL DAMAGES

ARISING OUT OF THE USE OR INABILITY TO USE THE PROGRAM (IN-
CLUDING BUT NOT LIMITED TO LOSS OF DATA OR DATA BEING REN-
DERED INACCURATE OR LOSSES SUSTAINED BY YOU OR THIRD PARTIES
OR A FAILURE OF THE PROGRAM TO OPERATE WITH ANY OTHER PRO-
GRAMS), EVEN IF SUCH HOLDER OR OTHER PARTY HAS BEEN ADVISED
OF THE POSSIBILITY OF SUCH DAMAGES.

END OF TERMS AND CONDITIONS

Index

For more information about the CD-ROM
see the **About the CD-ROM** section on page 803.

WILEY